Student Study Guide

to accompany

Biology

Sixth Edition

Sylvia S. Mader

WCB
McGraw-Hill

Boston   Burr Ridge, IL   Dubuque, IA   Madison, WI   New York   San Francisco   St. Louis
Bangkok   Bogotá   Caracas   Lisbon   London   Madrid
Mexico City   Milan   New Delhi   Seoul   Singapore   Sydney   Taipei   Toronto

WCB/McGraw-Hill

A Division of The **McGraw·Hill** *Companies*

Student Study Guide to accompany
BIOLOGY, SIXTH EDITION

3 4 5 6 7 8 9 0 QPD/QPD 9 0 9

ISBN 0-697-34086-4

www.mhhe.com

CONTENTS

TO THE STUDENT

THE STUDY GUIDE

The *Study Guide* is designed to accompany your text, *Biology,* sixth edition, by Sylvia S. Mader. A number of different approaches are used to help you achieve mastery of the chapter concepts.

Chapter Review: Each chapter begins with a brief summary that is based on chapter concepts. If you read this summary before studying the textbook chapter, you will gain a quick overview of the content of the chapter before studying it in-depth.

Study Exercises: In this section, the exercises are tied to the chapter concepts, and one or two exercises are provided to help you understand each concept. The varied nature of the exercises—fill-ins, true-false, selecting the correct correlations, completion of tables, matching, and so forth—will sustain your interest. Each chapter also contains one or more labeling exercises.

KeyWord CrossWord: These crossword puzzles help you learn the boldface terms that appear in the chapter.

Chapter Test: This section helps you assess your mastery of chapter concepts. The test contains about 20 multiple-choice questions and 2 critical thinking questions, which require a written answer. The chapter test ends with directions for computing your score; if you are not satisfied with your score, more study is needed.

Games: Occasionally, a game is provided to help you learn the background information needed to understand a concept. Each type of game is different and provides a way for you to assess whether or not you are a winner.

THE TEXTBOOK

Biology also has many student aids that you should be sure to utilize. These will help you accentuate the benefit you receive from the *Study Guide.*

Part Introduction: An introduction for each part highlights the central ideas of that part and specifically tells you how the topics within each part contribute to biological knowledge.

Chapter Concepts: Each chapter begins with an integrated outline that identifies and numbers the major topics of the chapter and lists the concepts for each topic.

Chapter Introductions: Each chapter has an introduction on the chapter opening page that sparks interest in the themes for the chapter.

Internal Summary Statements: Internal summaries stress the chapter's key concepts. These appear at the ends of major sections and help you focus your study efforts on the basics.

Illustrations and Tables: The illustrations and tables in *Biology* are consistent with multicultural educational goals. Often, it is easier to understand a given process by studying a drawing, especially when it is carefully coordinated with the text. Every illustration appears on the same or facing page to its reference.

Connecting Concepts: These appear at the close of the text portion of the chapter, and they stimulate critical thinking by showing how chapter concepts are related to other concepts in the text.

End-of-Chapter Pedagogy: The numbered major topics are repeated in the *Summary,* which reviews the concepts for each topic. *Reviewing the Chapter* is a series of study questions whose sequence follows that of the chapter. *Testing Yourself* consists of objective questions that allow you to test your ability to answer recall-based questions. Answers to *Testing Yourself* questions are given in Appendix A. *Applying the Concepts* is a set of critical thinking questions based on biological concepts. *Using Technology* lists the available technology, including the Mader Home Page address, for the chapter. *Understanding the Terms* provides a page reference for boldfaced terms in the chapter. A matching exercise allows you to test your knowledge of the terms.

Further Readings: The list of readings at the end of each part suggests references for further study of the topics covered in the chapters of that part. The references were carefully chosen for readability and accessibility. New to this edition, references are followed by a short description and an indication of their level of rigor.

Appendices and Glossary: The appendices contain optional information. *Appendix A* is the answer key to the objective *Testing Yourself* and *Understanding the Terms* questions at the end of each chapter; *Appendix B* is an expanded periodic table of chemical elements; *Appendix C* explains the metric system; *Appendix D* is a classification of organisms; and *Appendix E* is a listing of acronyms used in the text, along with the complete term. The glossary defines the boldface terms in the text. These terms are the ones most necessary for the successful study of biology. Terms that are difficult to pronounce have a phonetic spelling.

Exploring the Internet: http://www.mhhe.com/sciencemath/biology/mader/

The Mader Home Page allows students and teachers from all over the world to communicate. *Biology* has a complete text-specific site developed exclusively for users of the sixth edition. By visiting this site, students can access additional study aids, explore links to other relevant biology sites, catch up on current information, and pursue other activities.

Several state-of-the-art technology products are available that are correlated to this textbook. These useful and enticing supplements can assist you in teaching and can improve student learning.

Exploring the Internet
http://www.mhhe.com/sciencemath/biology/mader/

The Mader Home Page allows students and teachers from all over the world to communicate. *Biology* has a complete text-specific site developed exclusively for users of the sixth edition. By visiting this site, students can access additional study aids, explore links to other relevant biology sites, catch up on current information, and pursue other activities.

The Internet Primer
by Fritz J. Erickson & John A. Vonk

This short, concise primer shows students and instructors how to access and use the Internet. The guide provides enough information to get started by describing the most critical elements of using the Internet.

The Dynamic Human CD-ROM

This guide to anatomy and physiology interactively illustrates the complex relationships between anatomical structures and their functions in the human body. Realistic, three-dimensional visuals are the premier feature of this exciting learning tool. The program covers each body system, demonstrating to the viewer the anatomy, physiology, histology, and clinical applications of each system. *The Dynamic Human* is listed in the Using Technology section at the end of each systems chapter.

Explorations in Human Biology CD-ROM; Explorations in Cell Biology and Genetics CD-ROM

These interactive CDs, by Dr. George B. Johnson, feature fascinating topics in biology. *Explorations in Human Biology* and *Explorations in Cell Biology and Genetics* have 33 different modules that allow students to study a high-interest biological topic in an interactive way. In this edition of *Biology*, the Explorations that correlate to the chapter are listed in the Using Technology section, which appears at the end of each chapter. The modules are briefly described in the Instructor's Manual.

Life Science Animations Videotapes

Fifty-three animations of key physiological processes are available on videotapes. The animations bring visual movement to biological processes that are difficult to understand on the text page. In this edition of *Biology*, the Explorations that correlate to the chapter are listed in the Using Technology section, which appears at the end of each chapter.

BioSource Videodisc

BioSource Videodisc, by WCB/McGraw-Hill and Sandpiper Multimedia, Inc., features 20 minutes of animations and nearly 10,000 full-color illustrations and photos, many from leading WCB/McGraw-Hill biology textbooks.

Bioethics Forums Videodisc

Bioethics Forums is an interactive program that explores societal dilemmas arising from recent breakthroughs in biology, genetics, and biomedical technology. The scenarios are fictional, but the underlying science and social issues are real. *Bioethics Forums* encourages students to explore the science behind decisions as well as the processes of ethical reasoning and decision-making.

Visual Resource Library

Our electronic art image bank is a CD-ROM that contains hundreds of biological images from *Biology,* Sixth Edition. The CD-ROM contains an easy-to-use program that enables you quickly to view images, and you may easily import the images into PowerPoint to create your own multimedia presentations or use the already prepared PowerPoint presentations. The CD-ROM also includes several video clips featuring key animated biological processes.

Virtual Biology Laboratory CD-ROM
by John T. Beneski and Jack Waber, West Chester University

This CD-ROM is designed primarily for nonscience major students. The exercises are designed to expose students to the types of tools used by biologists, allow students to perform experiments without the use of wet lab setups, and support and illustrate topics and concepts from a traditional biology course.

Virtual Physiology Laboratory CD-ROM

This CD-ROM features ten simulations of the most common and important animal-based experiments ordinarily performed in the physiology component of your laboratory. This revolutionary program allows students to repeat laboratory experiments until they adeptly master the principles involved. The program contains video, audio, and text to clarify complex physiological functions.

The Secret of Life Video Modules
WGBH, Boston and BBC-TV

WGBH has produced eight 15-minute video modules that illuminate the biological universe with unique stories and animation. Each module concludes with a series of stimulating questions for class discussion.

The Secret of Life Videodisc
WGBH, Boston

A two-sided videodisc is available as a companion to *Biology,* Sixth Edition. Topic coverage includes biotechnology, human reproduction, portraits of modern science and research, and human genetics.

Our CD-ROM products may be packaged with the text at a cost savings. Contact your WCB/McGraw-Hill sales representative for details.

Technology Correlations

The Sixth Edition of *Biology* has three technology learning tools that are correlated to the chapters. The Using Technology section at the end of the chapter lists those that are appropriate to that chapter.[1]

[1]Technology aids are described per chapter in the *Instructor's Manual.*

The Dynamic Human is an interactive CD-ROM with three-dimensional visuals demonstrating the anatomy, physiology, and histology, along with clinical applications, of each body system.

 Explorations in Human Biology and Explorations in Cell Biology and Genetics are interactive CD-ROMs consisting of 33 different modules that cover key topics in biology.

 *Life Science Animations* is a set of five videotapes containing 53 animations of processes integral to the study of biology.

Chapter 1 A View of Life
Life Science Animations 52 (Tape 5)

Chapter 2 Basic Chemistry
Life Science Animations 1 (Tape 1)

Chapter 4 Cell Structure and Function
Life Science Animations 2, 3, 4 (Tape 1)

Chapter 5 Membrane Structure and Function
Explorations in Cell Biology 2, 3
Life Science Animations 2, 3 (Tape 1)

Chapter 6 Metabolism: Energy and Enzymes
Explorations in Cell Biology 6, 8
Life Science Animations 7, 11 (Tape 2)

Chapter 7 Photosynthesis
Explorations in Cell Biology 9
Life Science Animations 8, 9, 10 (Tape 1)

Chapter 8 Cellular Respiration
Explorations in Cell Biology 8
Life Science Animations 5, 6, 7, 11 (Tape 1)

Chapter 9 Cell Division
Explorations in Cell Biology 5
Life Science Animations 12, 50 (Tapes 1 and 5)

Chapter 10 Meiosis and Sexual Reproduction
Explorations in Cell Biology 10
Life Science Animations 13, 14, 19, 20 (Tape 2)

Chapter 12 Chromosomes and Genes
Explorations in Cell Biology 11

Chapter 13 Human Genetics
Explorations in Cell Biology 1, 12, 13
Explorations in Human Biology 1

Chapter 14 DNA: The Genetic Material
Life Science Animations 15 (Tape 2)

Chapter 15 Gene Activity
Explorations in Cell Biology 1, 15
Life Science Animations 16, 17 (Tape 2)

Chapter 16 Regulation of Gene Activity
Explorations in Cell Biology 15, 16
Life Science Animations 18 (Tape 2)

Chapter 17 Recombinant DNA and Biotechnology
Explorations in Cell Biology 14, 17

Chapter 20 Origin and History of Life
Life Science Animations 53 (Tape 5)

Chapter 25 Ecosystems
Life Science Animations 51, 52 (Tape 5)

Chapter 27 Human Impact on the Global Environment
Explorations in Human Biology 16

Chapter 30 The Protists
Life Science Animations 45 (Tape 4)

Chapter 32 The Plants
Life Science Animations 46, 47

Chapter 36 Plant Structure
Life Science Animations 46 (Tape 5)

Chapter 37 Nutrition and Transport in Plants
Life Science Animations 47, 48 (Tape 5)

Chapter 38 Growth and Development in Plants
Life Science Animations 49 (Tape 5)

Chapter 40 Animal Organization and Homeostasis
Dynamic Human, Anatomical Orientation

Chapter 41 Circulation
Explorations in Human Biology 5
Life Science Animations 37, 38, 39, 40 (Tape 4)
Dynamic Human, Cardiovascular System

Chapter 42 Lymph Transport and Immunity
Explorations in Human Biology 12, 13
Life Science Animations 41, 42, 43, 44 (Tape 4)
Dynamic Human, Lymphatic System

Chapter 43 Digestion and Nutrition
Explorations in Human Biology 7
Life Science Animations 33 (Tape 4)
Dynamic Human, Digestive System

Chapter 44 Respiration
Explorations in Human Biology 3, 6
Dynamic Human, Respiratory System

Chapter 45 Osmotic Regulation and Excretion
Dynamic Human, Urinary System

Chapter 46 Neurons and Nervous Systems
Explorations in Cell Biology 8, 9
Explorations in Human Biology 10
Life Science Animations 22, 23, 24, 25 (Tape 3)
Dynamic Human, Nervous System

Chapter 47 Sense Organs
Life Science Animations 26, 27 (Tape 3)

Chapter 48 Support Systems and Locomotion
Explorations in Human Biology 4, 9
Life Science Animations 30, 31 (Tape 3)
Dynamic Human, Muscular System, Skeletal System

Chapter 49 Hormones and Endocrine Systems
Explorations in Cell Biology 4
Explorations in Human Biology 11
Life Science Animations 28 (Tape 3)
Dynamic Human, Endocrine System

Chapter 50 Reproduction
Explorations in Human Biology 13
Dynamic Human, Reproductive System

Chapter 51 Development
Life Science Animations 21, (Tape 2)

HELPFUL STUDY HINTS

Learning how to study efficiently is a prerequisite to being a successful student. The following suggestions will help you study more productively. Please realize that this list is not all-inclusive and that it may not apply to all individuals who come to this course with different backgrounds, interests, and abilities.

1. Be motivated. You cannot acquire this attitude from an instructor or a textbook; it must come from within yourself. Motivation requires commitment, discipline, and perseverance, even when you do not feel like studying. Maintain high expectations. Think positively.

2. Set aside several hours at a particular time of the day to go over old and new material. Preview and review your assigned material; repetition of the material and consistency in your study habits combine for successful learning. Review every chance you have. Try to stay one lecture ahead of the instructor. Study in a quiet, well-lit room away from distractions.

3. Try to grasp the big picture as well as the details in every chapter. Try to understand how this chapter is related to the rest of the textbook. Whenever possible, try to attach concepts to "sensible" images and build upon them for better recall. When necessary, make up rhymes by using the first letter of each word. Look for distinguishing characteristics when analyzing abstract concepts.

4. Continually ask yourself questions. Although it may be boring to remember some things, asking questions will keep you mentally alert. After each paragraph or main idea, you should ask: "What does this mean?" "How does this relate to what I've already learned?" "How can I put that idea into my own words?" or "How can I apply that concept?" Try to relate the information to your past experiences. Make sure you know the definitions of boldfaced or italicized words in the text. Change the statements in each paragraph into questions and answers. Draw a line on a paper, and write the question on one side and the answer on the other side.

5. Have a positive attitude. Even though all of us have personal problems that may interfere with learning, look at learning as a growing experience. A positive attitude means that you do not give up. Sometimes, you will have to dig the information out of the textbook by yourself. After all, that is what learning is ultimately all about: it is a lifelong process that we have to achieve basically by ourselves.

6. Have someone ask you questions. Asking and responding to questions from another person will improve your thinking and understanding of the material. Cover up definitions of terms and see if you can define the terms correctly. Ask the instructor if you can use a tape recorder in class and then listen to the lecture again at another time. Don't be embarrassed to ask the instructor during or after class about concepts you do not understand. Most instructors will be glad to help you. Use any other available study aids. Perhaps rewriting your notes into an outline format will be helpful as well.

7. Learn as much as possible while in class. You may want to avoid taking notes in class. Instead, listen very attentively, follow along with the instructor from the material in the textbook, and highlight key words that the instructor mentions. If you have previewed the lecture material, you will know where to find the information being discussed in class. If you do take lecture notes, be selective; do not try to take notes on everything mentioned. Abbreviate words and fill them in immediately after class. Review the same material from the textbook as soon as possible. Try to grasp the big picture given in class.

8. On the night prior to a test, make sure you get sufficient sleep. When taking the test, try to relax by taking several deep breaths or by tightening your muscles and then slowly relaxing them. When reading the questions, make sure you understand exactly what the teacher wants to know AND read carefully to understand any limitations placed upon the question. On essay questions that are very broad, limit your answers to what the teacher felt was relevant in the class. Make a quick outline of the salient, major points and then fill in the details as you write your essay. When exams are returned, review them so that you can learn from your mistakes. That information may be on the final comprehensive test.

1

A VIEW OF LIFE

Although living things are diverse, they share certain characteristics. The organization of living things is exhibited by the smallest unit of life, the cell. In multicellular organisms, similar cells compose a tissue, tissues form organs, and organs are part of organ systems. Each level of organization has emergent properties that cannot be accounted for by simply adding up the properties of the previous levels.

Living things acquire materials and energy from the environment that are used during **metabolism,** a process that maintains **homeostasis.** Living things respond to the environment. When they **reproduce** and develop, genetic changes are passed on that result in **adaptation** to the environment.

Evolution explains both the unity of life (similar characteristics) and the diversity of life (adaptation to different environments). Adaptations allow organisms to play diverse roles in **ecosystems** where they interact with each other and the physical environment. Biologists classify organisms into a particular kingdom (distantly related), phylum, class, order, family, genus, and **species.** Each organism is given a binomial name consisting of the genus and species. The five kingdom system recognizes these kingdoms: Monera (unicellular prokaryotes usually absorb food—e.g., bacteria); Protista (unicellular eukaryotes, various modes of nutrition—e.g., protozoa and algae); Fungi (usually multicellular, absorb food—e.g., mushrooms); Plantae (multicellular **photosynthesizers**); and Animalia (multicellular, ingest food).

Scientists gain information about the natural world through the use of the **scientific method.** This method utilizes accumulated scientific data to arrive at a **hypothesis** that is tested by observation and experimentation. **Inductive reasoning** is used to arrive at a hypothesis, and **deductive reasoning** is used to decide what types of observations and experiments are appropriate. New data are collected that result in a conclusion. Mathematical data are preferred because they are objective. The conclusion can prove the hypothesis wrong but can only support the hypothesis. No hypothesis can be proven "true."

Science often employs controlled experiments that involve two elements of interest: the **experimental variable** and the **dependent variable.** The experimenter deliberately alters the experimental variable. The group being tested in the experiment is compared with a **control group.** Significant differences in the results between the experimental group and the control group contribute to the investigation's conclusions. Descriptive research is based on observational data. Although a control group is not used, the steps of the scientific method are still employed.

The ultimate aim of all scientific investigations is to construct **theories.** Theories are conceptual ways of understanding the natural world. Scientists generally accept theories because they are so well supported by **data** and experimentation.

Study the text section by section as you answer the questions that follow.

1.1 HOW TO DEFINE LIFE (P. 2)

- Living things share certain common characteristics.
- At each level of biological organization, properties emerge that cannot be explained by the sum of the parts.
- All living things are related by descent from a common ancestor; various adaptations account for the diversity of life.

1. Match these characteristics of life with the situations that follow.
   Living things are organized.
   Living things take materials and energy from the environment.
   Living things respond to stimuli.
   Living things reproduce and develop.
   Living things adapt to the environment.

   Frogs have a life cycle that includes an egg, a larva (tadpole) that undergoes the process of metamorphosis, and an adult. a._____

   Humans immediately remove their hands from a hot object. b._____

   All living things are composed of cells. c._____

   A flounder is a flattened fish that lives on the bottom of bodies of water, while a tuna is a streamlined fish that swims in the open sea. d._____

   Most cells use the sugar glucose as an energy source. e._____

2. Homeostasis refers to keeping a._____ relatively stable, such as body
   b._____.

3. List the following levels of biological organization in order, from smallest to largest:

   cell   a._____ (smallest)

   community   _____

   ecosystem   _____

   molecule   _____

   organ   _____

   organism   _____

   organ system   _____

   population   _____

   tissue   _____ (largest)

   Living things have b._____ that cannot be accounted for by simply summing the parts. Among the levels of biological organization, the properties of life first emerge at the level of the c._____.

   Different groups of organisms interact with the environment at the level of the d._____.

4. Label each of the following statements as an example of either the unity of life (U) or the diversity of life (D):
   _____ a. Fungi absorb food; plants carry out photosynthesis.
   _____ b. Homeostasis, metabolism, and evolution are characteristics of living things.
   _____ c. Life began with single cells.
   _____ d. Living things consist of cells.
   _____ e. Maple trees have broad, flat leaves, and pine trees have needlelike leaves.

1.2 ECOSYSTEMS CONTAIN POPULATIONS (P. 6)

- Chemicals cycle and energy flows through the populations that interact within an ecosystem.
- Human activities are threatening the biodiversity of the biosphere.

5. Study the diagram that follows and then answer the questions.

   What part does the producer play in this food chain? a._____

   What part does the consumer play in this food chain? b._____

   What part does the decomposer play in this food chain? c._____

   How do producers interact with the abiotic environment? d._____

   How do producers interact with the biotic environment? e._____

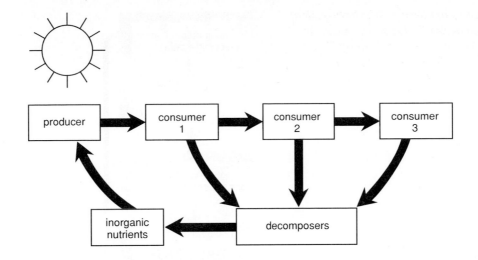

1.3 HOW LIVING THINGS ARE CLASSIFIED (P. 10)

- Living things are classified into categories according to their evolutionary relationships.

6. List the following levels of classification in order, from smallest (most exact) to largest (most general):

class   _____ (smallest)

family   _____

genus   _____

kingdom   _____

order   _____

phylum   _____

species   _____ (largest)

7. Name the kingdoms described in each of the following statements:

_____ a. ingest food
_____ b. absorb food; includes molds and mushrooms
_____ c. photosynthesizes food; includes ferns
_____ d. includes protozoa and algae
_____ e. absorbs food; includes bacteria

1.4 THE PROCESS OF SCIENCE (P. 11)

- Biologists often use the scientific method to gather information and to come to conclusions about the natural world.
- Various conclusions can sometimes be used to arrive at a theory, a general concept about the natural world.

8. Match the descriptions that follow with these theories: cell theory, theory of biogenesis, theory of evolution, gene theory.

Common descent with modification of form.   a._____

All organisms are composed of cells.   b._____

Organisms inherit coded information.   c._____

Life comes only from life.   d._____

9. Place the terms *conclusion, hypothesis,* and *theory* in the correct boxes of the adjacent diagram:

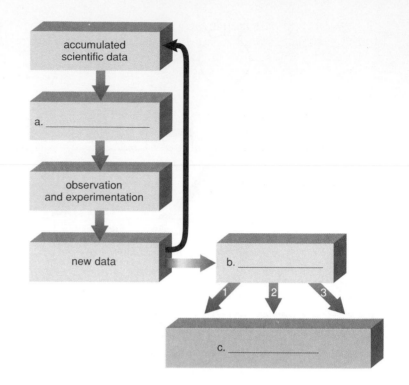

accumulated scientific data

a. _____

observation and experimentation

new data

b. _____

1 2 3

c. _____

10. Arrange the following steps of the scientific method in the normal order that scientists use them:

  accumulated scientific data
  conclusion
  formulation of hypothesis (requires inductive reasoning)
  new data
  observation and experimentation (requires deductive reasoning)

  _____ → _____ → _____ →

  _____ → _____

11. Each statement demonstrates a step of the scientific method used in a study. Match the steps from question 10 to these examples (one step is used twice).

  To spawn, striped bass migrate up a major river. In 1991 a dam was built on this river.

    a. _____

  Fishers reported catching fewer striped bass in the river in 1993. A study of the fish population in the river

    revealed decreased numbers of striped bass. b. _____

  A fish ladder is built along the dam. Scientists observe that ladder helps striped bass clear the dam and spawn

    upriver. c. _____

  Most likely, the dam is blocking the migration and spawning of striped bass. d. _____

  Survival of striped bass requires free migration of fish upriver to spawn. e. _____

  Construction of the fish ladder improves fishing. More fish are caught the following year, and studies indicate

    that the number of striped bass is increasing. f. _____

12. Biologists are doing a study on athletes' intake of steroids. Which of these would be the experimental variable (E) and which would be the dependent variable (D)?
  _____ a. average gain in body weight of a group of athletes
  _____ b. intake of anabolic steroids by an athlete

13. In the study in question 12, how would a control group of athletes differ from the experimental group? _____

  _____

14. Over a six-month period, the weight gain of the athletes in the experimental group in question 12 averaged 11%. Members of the control group experienced a gain of 4%.

What is the benefit of mathematical data like this? a. _____

_____

State the conclusion of this experiment b. _____

_____

15. Match the statements that follow with one of these three choices (some are used more than once):
descriptive research only (D)
experimental research only (E)
both experimental and descriptive research (E,D)

_____ a. Steps of the scientific method are used.
_____ b. A control group is employed.
_____ c. Much of the data required is purely observational.
_____ d. A hypothesis is disproven or supported.
_____ e. Observations are made.

KEYWORD CROSSWORD

Review the boldface key terms by completing this crossword puzzle, using the following alphabetized list of terms:
adaptation
biosphere
ecosystem
evolution
gene
homeostasis
metabolism
species
taxonomy

Across

Down

2 organism's modification in structure, function, or behavior suitable to the environment
4 taxonomic category that is the subdivision of a genus; its members can breed successfully with each other but not with members of another species
6 biological community together with the associated abiotic environment
8 unit of heredity passed on to offspring
9 all of the chemical reactions that occur in a cell during growth and repair

1 zone of air, land, and water at the surface of the earth in which living systems are found
3 branch of biology concerned with identifying and naming organisms
5 maintenance of internal conditions in a cell or in organisms; for example, relatively constant temperature, pH, and blood sugar
7 changes that occur in populations of organisms over time, often resulting in increased adaptation of organisms to the prevailing environment

OBJECTIVE QUESTIONS

Do not refer to the text when taking this test.

_____ 1. The binomial name *Notorcytes typhlops* refers to taxonomic levels of
   a. class and order.
   b. genus and species.
   c. kingdom and phylum.
   d. order and phylum.

_____ 2. Select the smallest, most exact taxonomic level among the following choices:
   a. class
   b. genus
   c. order
   d. phylum

_____ 3. Select the largest, broadest taxonomic level among the following choices:
   a. class
   b. order
   c. kingdom
   d. phylum

_____ 4. Each is a general characteristic of life EXCEPT
   a. the ability to respond.
   b. reproduction and development.
   c. organization.
   d. classification.

_____ 5. The smallest level of organization, where the characteristics of life emerge, is the _____ level.
   a. atomic
   b. cellular
   c. molecular
   d. population

_____ 6. The term *metabolism* refers best to
   a. chemical and energy transformations.
   b. maintenance of internal conditions.
   c. the ability to respond to stimuli.
   d. the lack of reproduction.

_____ 7. Plants are unique among living things in that they are
   a. multicellular and absorb food.
   b. unicellular and ingest food.
   c. multicellular and photosynthesize.
   d. All of these are correct.

_____ 8. Bacteria belong to the kingdom
   a. Animalia.
   b. Fungi.
   c. Monera.
   d. Protista.

_____ 9. Changes in _____ account for the ability of a species to evolve.
   a. abiotic factors
   b. ecosystems
   c. genes
   d. sunlight

_____10. Through evolution, populations can
   a. adapt to the environment.
   b. change their level of organization.
   c. fail to reproduce.
   d. eliminate cell structure.

_____11. Select the incorrect association.
   a. data—factual information
   b. deductive reasoning—general hypothesis to specific idea
   c. hypothesis—final conclusion
   d. inductive reasoning—specific data to general hypothesis

_____12. The _____ variable deals with the effects of an experiment.
   a. control
   b. dependent
   c. experimental
   d. independent

_____13. Valid scientific results should be repeatable by other scientific investigators.
   a. true
   b. false

_____14. The statement with the greatest acceptance and predictive value from scientists is the
   a. hypothesis.
   b. induction.
   c. observation.
   d. theory.

Answer in complete sentences.

15. Why is any level of organization not a mere sum of its parts?

16. Testing a hypothesis is the central core of the scientific method. Explain.

Test Results: _____ Number right ÷ 16 = _____ × 100 = _____ %

EXPLORING THE INTERNET

Use the Internet to further explore topics in this chapter, such as the scientific method, careers in biology, or phylogenetic relationships among organisms. Go to the Mader Home Page (http://www.mhhe.com/sciencemath/biology/mader/) and click on *Biology,* 6th edition. Go to Chapter 1 and select a Web site of interest.

ANSWER KEY

STUDY EXERCISES

1. **a.** reproduce and develop **b.** respond to stimuli **c.** are organized **d.** adapt to environment **e.** take materials and energy from the environment **2. a.** internal conditions **b.** temperature **3. a.** molecule, cell, tissue, organ, organ system, organism, population, community, ecosystem **b.** emergent properties **c.** cell **d.** ecosystem **4. a.** D **b.** U **c.** U **d.** U **e.** D **5. a.** makes food **b.** consumes food **c.** breaks down organic matter, making inorganic nutrients available to producers **d.** use solar energy and inorganic nutrients **e.** are eaten and supply energy to consumers **6.** species, genus, family, order, class, phylum, kingdom **7. a.** Animalia **b.** Fungi **c.** Plantae **d.** Protista **e.** Monera **8. a.** evolution **b.** cell **c.** gene **d.** biogenesis **9. a.** hypothesis **b.** conclusion **c.** theory **10.** accumulated scientific data → formulation of hypothesis → observation and experimentation → new data → conclusion **11. a.** accumulated scientific data **b.** accumulated scientific data **c.** experimentation **d.** formulation of hypothesis **e.** conclusion **f.** new data **12. a.** D **b.** E **13.** Control group would not take steroids. **14. a.** It is objective. **b.** Steroids cause weight gain. **15. a.** E, D **b.** E **c.** D **d.** E, D **e.** E, D

KEYWORD CROSSWORD

CHAPTER TEST

1. b **2.** b **3.** c **4.** d **5.** b **6.** a **7.** c **8.** c **9.** c **10.** a **11.** c **12.** b **13.** a **14.** d **15.** At each level, there are emergent properties not seen at lower levels of organization. For example, the cell, the basic living unit, is more than just a combination of chemicals. **16.** No matter the sequence of steps followed, scientists always test a hypothesis. The testing can take the form of making more observations rather than doing an experiment.

2

BASIC CHEMISTRY

CHAPTER REVIEW

Life has a chemical basis. All matter, living or nonliving, consists of elements composed of discrete units called **atoms.** The atom of each kind of element has its own arrangement of three subatomic particles: **protons, neutrons,** and **electrons.** The protons (positively charged) and neutrons (neutral) are located in the nucleus of the atom. The atoms of an element can differ by their number of neutrons. Atoms with the same atomic number but a different number of neutrons are called **isotopes.** The electrons (negatively charged) are located in energy shells at varying distances from the nucleus. In a neutral atom, the number of protons equals the number of electrons; this is the atomic number of the atom (element).

The arrangement and behavior of electrons—specifically the outermost electrons—determine the chemical properties of that element. The electrons are located in energy shells around the nucleus. These shells are designated by letters: the K shell is closest to the nucleus, the L shell is the next closest, and so forth. The potential energy of an electron increases with the increasing distance of these energy levels from the nucleus. **Orbitals** are the volumes of space where electrons are found within these energy shells. The first (K) shell holds a maximum of two electrons, the second (L) shell holds a maximum of eight electrons, and the third (M) shell holds eight electrons when it is the outer shell. This description applies to atoms of an atomic number less than 20.

The number of electrons in the outer shell determines the chemical reactivity of an atom. Atoms with two or more shells are most stable when the outer-shell has eight electrons. For atoms with only one shell (i.e., H, atomic number of 1), the stable electron configuration is two. Atoms fulfill their stable, outer-shell electron configuration by either sharing or transferring electrons with other atoms; that is, they form bonds. Two major kinds of bonds can form: ionic and covalent. **Ionic bonds** form by the transfer of electrons between an electron donor and an electron acceptor. Following an ionic reaction, the donor atoms are positively charged **ions,** and the acceptor atoms are negatively charged ions. An ionic bond is the attraction between oppositely charged ions. By contrast, **covalent bonds** develop from the sharing of electrons between atoms. A covalent bond is often represented by overlapping circular representations of the outer shells or by drawing a straight line between the atoms.

Chemical reactions are often represented by chemical equations. **Oxidation** and **reduction** are a part of these reactions. In reactions involving ionic bonding, oxidation is the loss of electrons, and reduction is the gain of electrons. In reactions involving covalent bonding, oxidation is the loss of a hydrogen atom (with its electron), and reduction is the gain of a hydrogen atom (with its electron).

Water is an important biological **compound,** making life possible on earth. Water **molecules** exhibit **polar covalent bonding.** The electrons between atoms (H and O) are shared, but not equally. The shared electrons spend more time near the oxygen atom. This establishes a positive end and a negative pole to the molecule and promotes **hydrogen bonding** between the water molecules. This weak bond between the molecules is the source of many remarkable properties of water: its role as a universal solvent, its ability to resist temperature changes and remain a liquid, and its formation of a maximum density at 4°C.

Acids (e.g., HCl) are compounds that release hydrogen ions in solution; **bases** (e.g., NaOH) are compounds that take up hydrogen ions in solution. The **pH scale** indicates the relative concentration of hydrogen and hydroxide ions in a solution. The scale ranges from 0 to 14, with 7 a neutral pH. Acids lower the pH of a solution from 7 by releasing hydrogen ions, and bases increase the pH above 7 by an opposite effect. **Buffers** are compounds in solution that resist these changes through chemical reaction, thus stabilizing the pH of a given solution.

Study the text section by section as you answer the questions that follow.

• Matter is composed of 92 naturally occurring elements, each having one type of atom.

1. Name the six elements commonly found in living things. _____

_____

Elements Contain Atoms (p. 20)

• Atoms have subatomic particles: electrons, protons, and neutrons.
• Atoms of the same type that differ by the number of neutrons are called isotopes.

2. The three most stable subatomic particles in an atom are _____, _____, and

_____.

3. An atom has nine protons and nine neutrons in each of its atoms. Its atomic number is a._____, its

atomic weight is b._____, and the number of electrons in this atom is c._____.

4. Isotopes have the same atomic a._____, but they differ in the number of b._____.

5. At least two forms of the oxygen atom exist in the environment: $^{16}_{8}O$ and $^{18}_{8}O$. Each atom has eight electrons.

$^{16}_{8}O$ and $^{18}_{8}O$ represent a._____ of the element oxygen.

The numbers 16 and 18 represent the b._____.

The atomic number of $^{16}_{8}O$ is c._____.

The atomic number of $^{18}_{8}O$ is d._____.

The number of protons in the atom of $^{16}_{8}O$ is e._____.

The number of neutrons in the atom of $^{18}_{8}O$ is f._____.

How do $^{16}_{8}O$ and $^{18}_{8}O$ differ in number of subatomic particles? g._____.

6. Complete the following table with the correct numbers:

Isotope	Protons	Neutrons	Atomic Number	Atomic Weight
$^{12}_{6}C$				
$^{14}_{6}C$				
$^{31}_{15}P$				
$^{33}_{15}P$				

Atoms Have Chemical Properties (p. 22)

> • Atoms can be diagrammed by showing the number of protons and neutrons in a nucleus and the number of electrons in shells about the nucleus.

7. Indicate whether the following statements are true (T) or false (F):
   _____ a. A neutral atom has the same number of protons and electrons.
   _____ b. The arrangement of protons and neutrons in an atom determines the atom's chemical properties.
   _____ c. The electrons of an atom are located in energy levels (electron shells) at varying distances from the nucleus.
   _____ d. Electrons in the K shell possess more energy than do electrons in the L shell.
   _____ e. When a chlorophyll molecule absorbs solar energy, electrons move to higher energy levels.

8. Electrons are most often found in volumes of space called a._____. The orbital at the first energy level is b._____ shaped. Of the four orbitals at the second energy level, one is c._____ shaped, and three are d._____ shaped.

9. An atom of an element with an atomic number of 9, has a._____ electrons in its K shell and b._____ electrons in its L shell.

10. An atom of the element neon (Ne) has eight electrons in its outer shell. An atom of the element sulfur (S) has six electrons in its outer shell.

    Which atom is reactive? a._____

    Which atom is inert? b._____

    Why is there a difference in the reactivity of these two elements? c._____

    _____

11. The magnesium atom has an atomic number of 12 and an atomic weight of 24. Draw its simplified atomic structure. Draw small circles to indicate the general distribution of electrons in concentric levels around the nucleus. In the nucleus, indicate the number of protons and neutrons.

2.2 ATOMS FORM COMPOUNDS AND MOLECULES (P. 24)

> • Atoms react with one another by giving up, gaining, or sharing electrons.

12. Which of the following are examples of compounds?
    _____ a. ^{14}C
    _____ b. H atom
    _____ c. O_2, oxygen molecule
    _____ d. NaCl, table salt
    _____ e. H_2O, water molecule

13. Calcium (Ca) has an atomic number of 12; chlorine (Cl) has an atomic number of 17.

 The number of electrons in the outer shell of calcium is ª·_____.

 The number of electrons in the outer shell of chlorine is ᵇ·_____.

 In a chemical reaction between these two atoms, ᶜ·_____ calcium atom(s) will react with

 _____ chlorine atom(s).

 Which element will gain electrons in this reaction? ᵈ·_____

 What will its charge be after the reaction? ᵉ·_____

 Which element will lose electrons in this reaction? ᶠ·_____

 What will its charge be after the reaction? ᵍ·_____

 What type of bond forms between these two atoms? ʰ·_____

 Write the formula for the compound produced through this chemical reaction. ⁱ·_____

14. Water is a polar molecule.
 a. Indicate on the following diagram which atoms are electronegative and which are electropositive in relation
    to the others. Put a δ⁺ charge and δ⁻ charges where appropriate.
 b. Label a hydrogen bond.

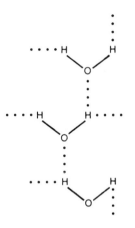

15. Label each of the following statements as describing covalent bonding (C), ionic bonding (I), or hydrogen
    bonding (H):
    _____ a. Electrons transfer between atoms.
    _____ b. Atoms share electrons.
    _____ c. This bond is present in sodium chloride.
    _____ d. This bond is present in the oxygen molecule.
    _____ e. A triple bond of this type is present in nitrogen gas.
    _____ f. This bond forms between water molecules.
    _____ g. The hydrogen atom in one molecule is attracted to the oxygen atom of another molecule.
    _____ h. This bond forms within a water molecule.

Oxidation Is the Opposite of Reduction (p. 25)

- Oxidation is the loss of electrons, and reduction is the gain of electrons.

16. Consider the following chemical reaction between a potassium (K) atom (atomic number 19) and a fluorine (F) atom (atomic number 9): $K + F \rightarrow KF$.

    Which atom is reduced in this reaction? a._____

    Which atom is oxidized in this reaction? b._____

    Write a short definition of oxidation. c._____

    Write a short definition of reduction. d._____

2.3 WATER IS ESSENTIAL TO LIFE (P. 27)

- The existence of living things depends on the chemical and physical characteristics of water.

17. In each of the pairs of statements that follow, check the one that correctly describes how hydrogen bonding affects the properties of water. Hydrogen bonding causes water

    Pair 1

    _____ a. to boil at a lower temperature than expected.

    _____ b. to boil at a higher temperature than expected.

    Pair 2

    _____ c. to be more dense as ice than as liquid water.

    _____ d. to be less dense as ice than as liquid water.

    Pair 3

    _____ e. to absorb heat with a minimal change in temperature.

    _____ f. to absorb heat with a maximum change in temperature.

    Pair 4

    _____ g. to be cohesive—the water molecules cling to each other.

    _____ h. molecules to shun one another.

18. Refer to the chemical properties of water when answering the following questions:

    What makes water a good solvent? a. _____

    _____

    How does water moderate temperatures? b. _____

    _____

    What allows ice to float on liquid water? c. _____

    _____

Water and Acids and Bases (p. 30)

- Living things are sensitive to the hydrogen ion (H^+) concentration, which can be indicated by utilizing the pH scale.

19. Label each of the following statements as describing an acid (A) or a base (B):
    _____ a. They take up hydrogen ions in solution.
    _____ b. HCl is an example.
    _____ c. NaOH is an example.
    _____ d. They release hydrogen ions in solution.
    _____ e. They lower the pH.
    _____ f. They raise the pH.

20. Complete the table for the following hydrogen ion concentrations [H^+]:

[H^+]	pH	Acid/Base/Neutral
1×10^{-7}		
1×10^{-3}		
1×10^{-8}		

21. Indicate whether the following statements are true (T) or false (F):
    _____ a. If the pH of blood changes from 7.4 to 7.6, it becomes more acidic.
    _____ b. When an acid is added to a solution, the pH decreases.
    _____ c. A basic pH indicates that OH^- ions outnumber H^+ ions.
    _____ d. An acidic pH indicates that H^+ ions outnumber OH^- ions.

22. The following questions relate to buffers:

    How do living things prevent drastic changes in pH?

    a. _____

    _____

    Complete the following reaction, showing how the carbonic acid buffer system deals with increasing hydrogen ions in the blood:
    $$H^+ + HCO_3^- \rightarrow \text{b.} \underline{\qquad\qquad}$$

    Complete the following reaction, showing how the carbonic acid buffer system deals with decreasing hydrogen ions in the blood:
    $$H_2CO_3 \rightarrow \text{c.} \underline{\qquad\qquad}$$

Review key terms by completing this crossword puzzle, using the following alphabetized list of terms:

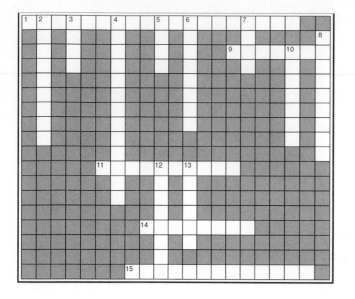

acid
atom
base
buffer
compound
covalent bond
electron
hydrogen bond
ionic bond
isotope
molecule
orbital
oxidation
polar covalent bond
reduction

Across

1 bond in which electron sharing between atoms is unequal (three words)

9 atoms having the same atomic number but a different atomic weight due to the number of neutrons

11 chemical bond in which ions attract one another by opposite charges (two words)

14 smallest part of a compound that retains the properties of the compound; formed by the union of two or more atoms by covalent or ionic bonding

15 weak bond that arises between a slightly positive hydrogen and a slightly negative oxygen, often on different molecules or separated by some distance (two words)

Down

2 loss of one or more electrons from an atom or molecule; in biological systems, generally the loss of hydrogen atoms

3 compound that tends to raise the hydrogen ion concentration in a solution and to lower its pH numerically

4 chemical bond in which the atoms share one pair of electrons (two words)

5 smallest particle of an element that displays its properties

6 negative subatomic particle, moving about in energy levels around the nucleus of the atom

7 compound that tends to lower the hydrogen ion concentration in a solution and to raise its pH numerically

8 gain of electrons by an atom or a molecule; in biological systems, generally the gain of hydrogen atoms

10 volume of space around a nucleus where electrons can be found most of the time

12 chemical substance having two or more different elements in fixed ratio

13 substance or group of substances that tend to resist pH changes in a solution, thus stabilizing the solution's relative acidity

OBJECTIVE QUESTIONS

Do not refer to the text when taking this test.

_____ 1. An element has an atomic number of 11 and an atomic weight of 23. The number of neutrons in each atom is
   a. 11.
   b. 12.
   c. 23.
   d. 24.

_____ 2. The atom of an element has one proton and two neutrons. Its atomic number is
   a. 1.
   b. 2.
   c. 3.
   d. 6

_____ 3. The atom of an element has six protons and eight neutrons. The number of electrons in this atom if neutral is
   a. 6.
   b. 8.
   c. 12.
   d. 14.

_____ 4. The relationship between $^{12}_{6}C$ and $^{14}_{6}C$ is that they are
   a. molecules.
   b. isomers.
   c. isotopes.
   d. polymers.

_____ 5. An atom has 11 electrons and 12 neutrons. Its atomic weight is
   a. 1.
   b. 11.
   c. 12.
   d. 23.

_____ 6. The energy possessed by electrons in the K shell is _____ than the energy possessed by electrons in the L shell.
   a. greater
   b. less

_____ 7. An element has an atomic number of 14. Its electron distribution over several energy shells is
   a. 1–4–8.
   b. 1–8–5.
   c. 2–8–2.
   d. 2–8–4.

_____ 8. An element has an atomic number of 13. The number of electrons in each atom's L energy shell is
   a. one.
   b. two.
   c. four.
   d. eight.

_____ 9. Select the reactive element by its atomic number.
   a. 2
   b. 10
   c. 12
   d. 18

_____10. Select the most stable element by its atomic number.
   a. 1
   b. 8
   c. 10
   d. 16

_____11. Select the compound.
   a. Ca
   b. H
   c. NaCl
   d. O_2

_____12. The atoms of which element tend to lose electrons in a chemical reaction?
   a. Cl
   b. Mg
   c. O
   d. S

_____13. In a chemical reaction between calcium and chlorine atoms, chlorine atoms tend to be
   a. oxidized.
   b. reduced.

_____14. Select the incorrect association.
   a. covalent bond—electrons transferred
   b. hydrogen bond—between water molecules
   c. ionic bond—charged particles formed
   d. polar covalent bond—present in the water molecule

_____15. The atoms of which element tend to be reduced in a chemical reaction?
   a. Ca
   b. Cl
   c. K
   d. Mg

_____16. Each is a property of water EXCEPT
   a. easily changed from liquid to gas.
   b. good solvent.
   c. maximum density at 4°C.
   d. molecules are cohesive.

_____17. Select the correct statement about acids.
   a. They cannot be buffered in a solution.
   b. They donate hydroxide ions in solution.
   c. HCl is an example.
   d. They tend to raise the pH.

_____18. Select the most basic pH of the given hydrogen ion concentrations.
   a. 1×10^{-3}
   b. 1×10^{-4}
   c. 1×10^{-9}
   d. 1×10^{-12}

_____19. Select the incorrect statement about bases.
   a. They can be buffered in solution.
   b. They furnish hydroxide ions in solution.
   c. NaOH is an example.
   d. They tend to lower the pH.

_____20. Which of the following is an example of a buffer?
   a. carbonic acid
   b. hydrogen ions
   c. hydroxide ion
   d. NaCl

CRITICAL THINKING QUESTIONS

Answer in complete sentences.

21. Element X has an atomic number of 4, whereas element Y has an atomic number of 18. Which element is more reactive, and why?

22. Chemical reactions in the human body produce many acid end products. Yet, the pH of the blood remains remarkably constant. Why?

Test Results: _____ Number right ÷ 22 = _____ × 100 = _____ %

EXPLORING THE INTERNET

Use the Internet to further explore topics in this chapter, such as the chemistry of salt or water and ice, or use a detailed periodic table of the elements. Go to the Mader Home Page (http://www.mhhe.com/sciencemath/biology/mader/) and click on *Biology,* 6th edition. Go to Chapter 2 and select a Web site of interest.

ANSWER KEY

STUDY EXERCISES

1. carbon, hydrogen, nitrogen, oxygen, phosphorus, sulfur **2.** protons, neutrons, electrons **3. a.** 9 **b.** 18 **c.** 9 **4. a.** number **b.** neutrons **5. a.** isotopes **b.** atomic weights **c.** 8 **d.** 8 **e.** 8 **f.** 10 **g.** $^{16}_{8}$O has eight neutrons in its nucleus; $^{18}_{8}$O has ten neutrons.
6.

Protons	Neutrons	Atomic Number	Atomic Weight
6	6	6	12
6	8	6	14
15	16	15	31
15	18	15	33

7. a. T **b.** F **c.** T **d.** F **e.** T **8. a.** orbitals **b.** spherical **c.** spherical **d.** dumbbell **9. a.** two **b.** seven **10. a.** S **b.** Ne **c.** S has six electrons in its outer shell, and if it reacts to gain two more it will have a stable outer configuration of eight; Ne already has a stable outer shell.

11.

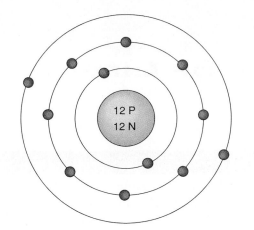

12. d, e **13. a.** two **b.** seven **c.** one, two **d.** Cl **e.** −1 **f.** Ca **g.** +2 **h.** ionic **i.** $CaCl_2$

14.

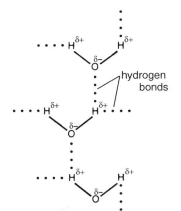

hydrogen bonds

15. a. I **b.** C **c.** I **d.** C **e.** C **f.** H **g.** H **h.** C **16. a.** F **b.** K **c.** loss of electrons **d.** gain of electrons **17.** b, d, e, g **18. a.** The partial charges of the water molecule attract and disperse charged particles in solution. **b.** It takes up and releases large amounts of heat without much change in temperature. **c.** Water is most dense at 4°C. It expands as the temperature drops from this point; it is less dense at 0°C, the temperature of ice. **19. a.** B **b.** A **c.** B **d.** A **e.** A **f.** B

20.

pH	Acid/Base/Neutral
7	neutral
3	acid
8	base

21. a. F **b.** T **c.** T **d.** T **22. a.** The pH is stabilized through the action of buffers, which are chemical systems that absorb either H^+ or OH^- to keep the pH steady. **b.** H_2CO_3 **c.** $HCO_3^- + H^+$

KEYWORD CROSSWORD

CHAPTER TEST

1. b **2.** a **3.** a **4.** c **5.** d **6.** b **7.** d **8.** d **9.** c **10.** c **11.** c **12.** b **13.** b **14.** a **15.** b **16.** a **17.** c **18.** d **19.** d **20.** a **21.** Element X is more reactive because its electron arrangement is 2–2. It has only two electrons in its outer shell. If it gives up these two electrons, its outer shell will be stable. The electron arrangement in Y is 2–8–8. It has eight electrons in its outer shell—a stable outer shell. **22.** Buffers in the body take up excess hydrogen ions and thereby act to keep the pH within normal limits.

3

THE CHEMISTRY OF LIFE

Carbon's unique properties permit the formation of many kinds of **organic molecules.** At the molecular level, this variety accounts for the diversity of living things. Many organic molecules have a carbon backbone plus functional groups. Some common functional groups are the hydroxyl, carboxyl, aldehyde, ketone, and amine groups.

Several kinds of small, organic molecules—sugars, fatty acids, amino acids, and nucleotides—serve as the monomers (building blocks) of **polymers** (larger organic molecules). These polymers (e.g., polysaccharides, lipids, proteins, nucleic acids) have important biological functions. Through a process called **condensation,** two monomers can bond chemically through the loss of a water molecule to produce a larger molecule. Repetition of this process produces even larger molecules—the polymers—in a cell. The reverse of this process, **hydrolysis,** breaks down polymers into their chemical subunits.

Several classes of organic molecules have biological importance. One of these, the **carbohydrates,** consists of several subclasses: the monosaccharides (e.g., glucose), the disaccharides (e.g., sucrose), and the polysaccharides (e.g., starch). The monosaccharides and disaccharides—the sugars—provide an immediate energy source for organisms. Some polysaccharides store energy (i.e., starch), whereas others contribute structurally (i.e., cellulose).

Fatty acids and glycerol are the building blocks of fats and oils. Fatty acids may be either saturated or un-saturated. Fats and oils store energy efficiently. Waxes and **phospholipids** differ in some of their components compared to fats. These structural differences endow these molecules with different biological abilities. Phospholipids, for example, are a major component of plasma membrane structure and help determine a membrane's properties.

Proteins have a variety of biological roles (transport, regularity, structural). The monomers of these polymers are **amino acids. Peptide bonds** join amino acids within the polypeptides of protein molecules. Proteins exhibit several levels of structure. The primary structure of a protein is the order of the amino acids bonded together. Several other structural levels (secondary, tertiary, quaternary) account for the molecule's three-dimensional shape and for the protein's biological properties.

DNA and **RNA** are **nucleic acids.** Nucleotides, which are the monomers of nucleic acids, contain a sugar, phosphate, and nitrogen-containing base. DNA makes up the genes in cells. The DNA molecule has the appearance of a twisted ladder; sugar and phosphate molecules make up the sides of the ladder and hydrogen-bonded bases named adenine, guanine, cytosine, and thymine make up the rungs of the ladder. The sequence of bases in DNA stores information regarding the order in which amino acids are to be joined within a protein. RNA conveys this information from the nucleus to the cytoplasm and, therefore, is an intermediary in the synthesis of proteins.

STUDY EXERCISES

Study the text section by section as you answer the questions that follow.

3.1 CELLS CONTAIN ORGANIC MOLECULES (P. 36)

- The characteristics of organic compounds depend on the chemistry of carbon.
- Macromolecules (large organic molecules) in cells are carbohydrates, lipids, proteins, and nucleic acids.

1. Indicate whether the following statements about a carbon atom are true (T) or false (F):
    _____ a. There are two electrons in its outer shell.
    _____ b. It can bond to other carbon atoms.
    _____ c. It can share two pairs of electrons with another atom.
    _____ d. Chains of 50 atoms are unusual in living systems.

2. Label this diagram with the following functional group names:
   amine
   carboxyl
   hydroxyl
   ketone

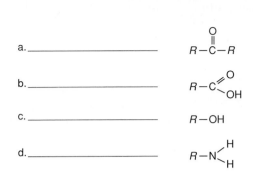

a. _____ $R-\overset{\overset{O}{\|}}{C}-R$

b. _____ $R-C\overset{O}{\underset{OH}{}}$

c. _____ $R-OH$

d. _____ $R-N\overset{H}{\underset{H}{}}$

3. Check the functional group(s) that can ionize (take on or give up a hydrogen ion).
   _____ a. amine (amino)
   _____ b. carboxyl
   _____ c. hydroxyl
   _____ d. ketone

Large Organic Molecules Have Monomers (p. 38)

- Macromolecules form when their specific monomers (unit molecules) join.

4. For each term on the left, write in the corresponding term; the first one is completed for you.

   polymer   monomer

   polysaccharide   a. _____

   fat   b. _____   and c. _____

   protein   d. _____

   nucleic acid   e. _____

5. Label this diagram with the following terms:
   condensation
   hydrolysis
   monomers
   polymer

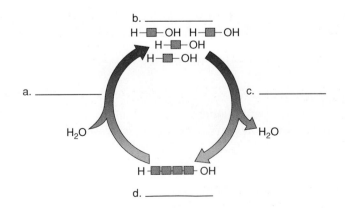

b. _____

a. _____   c. _____

d. _____

During hydrolysis, is water added to or taken away from the reactants? e. _____

During condensation, is water added to or taken away from the reactants? f. _____

3.2 CARBOHYDRATES (P. 39)

- Glucose is an immediate energy source for many organisms.
- Some carbohydrates (starch and glycogen) function as stored energy sources.
- Other carbohydrates (cellulose and chitin) function as structural compounds.

6. Write the molecular formula beneath each of these structural formulas by indicating the number of carbons, hydrogens, and oxygens in each.

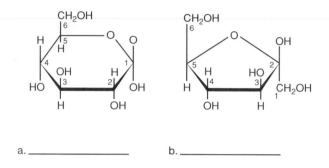

a. _____   b. _____

The term that refers to two structurally dissimilar molecules with the same molecular formula is

c. _____.

7. Complete the following table:

Carbohydrate	Monosaccharide Composition	Biological Function
sucrose		
lactose		
maltose		
starch		
glycogen		
cellulose		
chitin		

8. From the first column of the table in question 7, which are disaccharides? a. _____

Which are polysaccharides? b. _____

3.3 LIPIDS (P. 42)

- Lipids vary in structure and function.
- Fats function as long-term stored energy sources.
- Certain hormones are derived from cholesterol, a complex ring compound.

9. Complete the following table:

Lipid	Monomers	Biological Functions
fats and oils		
waxes		
phospholipids		

10. Write the word *saturated* or *unsaturated* beneath the appropriate structure.

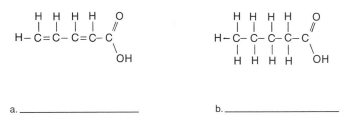

a. _____

b. _____

11. In this representation of a fat, draw a circle around the portion that is derived from glycerol. Draw lines under the portions that are derived from fatty acids.

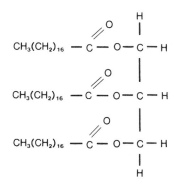

12. When phospholipids are placed in water, the ᵃ _____ face outward and the ᵇ _____ face each other. This property makes phospholipids suitable molecules to form the ᶜ _____ of cells.

13. Examples of steroids are ᵃ _____, ᵇ _____, and ᶜ _____.

14. Each steroid differs from other steroids by the _____ attached to the ring.

3.4 PROTEINS (P. 46)

- Some proteins (e.g., in muscle, hair, nails) function as structural compounds.
- Other proteins serve many and varied functions (e.g., enzymes, blood proteins, transport molecules).

15. Complete the following table:

Protein	Biological Function
enzymes	
actin, myosin	
insulin	
hemoglobin	

Peptide Bonds Join Amino Acids (p. 46)

16. Label this diagram with the following terms *carboxyl (acid) group, amino acid, amino group,* and *peptide bond* (one is used more than once).

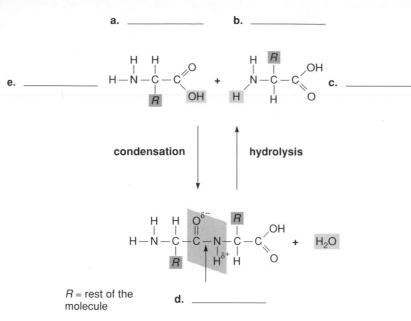

Proteins Have Levels of Structure (p. 48)

17. Study this representation of a polypeptide.

This is the ᵃ· _____ structure of a protein.

What are *R* groups? ᵇ· _____

_____

What shapes do the secondary structure of a protein normally assume? ᶜ· _____

What type of bond between amino acids is necessary to maintain secondary shape? ᵈ· _____

How does the tertiary shape of a globular protein come about? ᵉ· _____

_____

What would cause a protein to have a quaternary shape? ᶠ· _____

_____

_____

3.5 NUCLEIC ACIDS (P. 50)

• Genes are composed of DNA (deoxyribonucleic acid). DNA specifies the correct ordering of amino acids in proteins, with RNA as a needful intermediary.

18. Both DNA and RNA are polymers of _____.

19. On this diagram, label the following components of a nucleotide:
    base
    phosphate
    sugar

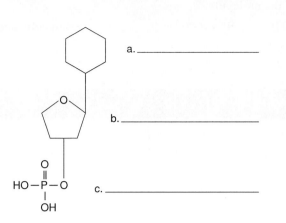

a. _____

b. _____

c. _____

20. Study this representation of a nucleic acid.

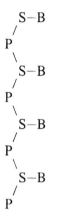

Which molecules make up the backbone of a nucleic acid? a. _____

Which molecules project to one side of the backbone? b. _____

21. a. Complete the following table to distinguish DNA from RNA:

	DNA	RNA
Sugar		
Bases		
Strands		
Helix		

What are the functions of DNA and RNA? b. _____

_____

ATP (Adenosine Triphosphate) (p. 51)

22. ATP is a(n) [a.]_____ ; its structure consists of three [b.]_____ groups attachaed to the five-carbon [c.]_____ of the molecule.

23. Complete this reaction: ATP → ADP + P + [a.]_____ . When cells need [b.]_____ , they break down the molecule [c.]_____ .

Organic Chemistry Las Vegas Style

Assume that organic molecules have the following worth:

amino acid	*25¢*
glucose	*20¢*
nucleotide	*15¢*
glycerol	*10¢*
fatty acid	*5¢*

1. How much should you bid in total for your first three cards?

a.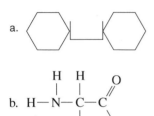

b.

$$H-N-C-C{\overset{O}{\underset{OH}{}}}$$

(structure: H—N—C—C with H, H on top, R below, O double-bonded, OH)

c. sugar-thymine
phosphate

How much should you raise in total for your next two cards?

d.

(peptide structure: H—N—C—C—N—C—C with H, H, O, H, H on top; R, R below; O and OH)

e.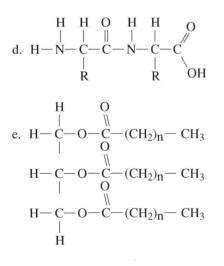

$$H-C-O-C-(CH_2)_n-CH_3$$
$$H-C-O-C-(CH_2)_n-CH_3$$
$$H-C-O-C-(CH_2)_n-CH_3$$
$$H$$

2. The next dealer opens a new deck of cards.

   How much should you bet in total for your first three cards?

   a. nucleic acid containing 100 units
   b. protein containing 150 units
   c. polysaccharide containing 50 units

   How much should you raise in total for your next two cards?

   d. tripeptide
   e. disaccharide

3. The next dealer has his own cards.

   How much should you bet, assuming that your first three cards are valued at their "unit" value?

   a. gene
   b. quick energy
   c. enzyme

   How much should you raise in total for your next two cards which are valued at their "unit" value.

   d. long-term stored energy
   e. plant structure

4. The next dealer opens her deck of cards.

   How much should you bet in total assuming that each of your first three cards is the value of its matched molecule?

   a. peptide bond
   b. unsaturated
   c. straight chain of ring compounds

   How much should you raise for your next two cards?

   d. contains nitrogen
   e. contains a free carboxyl (acid) grouping

5. This dealer deals again.

   How much should you bet, assuming that each of your first three cards is the value of its matched molecule?

   a. DNA
   b. hydrocarbon chain
   c. ribose

   How much should you raise in total for your next two cards?

   d. glycogen
   e. amino group

Review key terms by completing this crossword puzzle, using the following alphabetized list of terms:

amino acid
carbohydrate
condensation
DNA
enzyme
hydrolysis
hydrophilic
hydrophobic
isomer
lipid
nucleic acid
nucleotide
organic
peptide
phospholipid
polymer
protein
RNA
steroid

Across

1 organic molecule that has an amino group and an acid group, and that covalently bonds to produce protein molecules (two words)

6 monomer of DNA and RNA consisting of a five-carbon sugar bonded to a nitrogen-containing base and a phosphate group

7 nucleic acid polymer produced from covalent bonding of nucleotide monomers that contain the sugar ribose; carries information for protein synthesis from DNA

9 chemical change producing the covalent bonding of two monomers with the accompanying loss of a water molecule

12 splitting of a compound by the addition of water, with the H^+ being incorporated in one fragment and the OH^- in the other

13 type of lipid molecule having four interlocking rings; examples are cholesterol, progesterone, and testosterone

14 type of molecule that does not interact with water because it is nonpolar

15 molecule having the same structure as a fat except that a group that contains phosphate replaces one bonded fatty acid; an important component of plasma membranes

18 class of organic compounds that tend to be soluble in nonpolar solvents such as alcohol; includes fats and oils

Down

2 molecules with the same molecular formula but different structure and, therefore, shape

3 type of molecule that contains carbon and hydrogen; it usually also contains oxygen

4 class of organic compounds consisting of carbon, hydrogen, and oxygen atoms; includes monosaccharides, disaccharides, and polysaccharides

5 nucleic acid polymer produced from covalent bonding of nucleotide monomers that contain the sugar deoxyribose; the genetic material of nearly all organisms

8 polymer of nucleotides; includes both DNA and RNA (two words)

10 organic catalyst, usually a protein molecule, that speeds chemical reactions in living systems

11 type of molecule that interacts with water by dissolving in water or by forming hydrogen bonds with water molecules

15 macromolecule consisting of covalently bonded monomers

16 a polymer having, as its primary structure, a sequence of amino acids united through covalent bonding

17 a series of amino acids joined by covalent bonding

OBJECTIVE QUESTIONS

Do not refer to the text when taking this test. For questions 1–8 match each item to one of the following classes:

    a. carbohydrates
    b. fats and oils
    c. proteins
    d. nucleic acids

_____ 1. sucrose is a member

_____ 2. glycerol is a building block

_____ 3. specify the sequence of amino acids in a protein

_____ 4. contains the bases uracil and adenine

_____ 5. insulin is a member

_____ 6. triglycerides are members

_____ 7. exhibit a primary, secondary, and tertiary structure

_____ 8. some have enzymatic roles

_____ 9. Select the functional group that can ionize.
    a. amine (amino)
    b. carboxyl
    c. hydrogen
    d. hydroxyl

_____10. What is the relationship between glucose and fructose?
    a. disaccharides
    b. isomers
    c. isotopes
    d. polysaccharides

_____11. The products from the hydrolysis of sucrose are
    a. fructose and galactose.
    b. fructose and glucose.
    c. galactose and glucose.
    d. galactose and lactose.

_____12. Select the molecule with mainly a structural role.
    a. cellulose
    b. glycogen
    c. starch
    d. sucrose

_____13. Select the false statement.
    a. Fats provide short-term energy to organisms.
    b. Hydroxyl groups are polar.
    c. Saturated fatty acids do not have double bonds.
    d. Cellulose is a chain of glucose molecules.

_____14. Select the true statement about waxes.
    a. They are hydrophobic.
    b. They are liquids at room temperature.
    c. They are similar in structure to steroids.
    d. They consist of short-term fatty acids.

_____15. The alpha helix refers to a protein's _____ structure.
    a. primary
    b. secondary
    c. tertiary
    d. quaternary

_____16. Select the smallest structure.
    a. amino acid
    b. dipeptide
    c. polypeptide
    d. protein

_____17. Which of the following is NOT a common function of some proteins?
    a. energy storage
    b. hormonal regulation
    c. structural component
    d. transport

_____18. The opposing process to condensation is
    a. dehydration synthesis.
    b. hydrolysis.
    c. monomers.
    d. polymerization.

_____19. Select the base NOT present in DNA.
    a. C
    b. G
    c. T
    d. U

_____20. The monomers of proteins are
    a. amino acids.
    b. fatty acids.
    c. monosaccharides.
    d. nucleotides.

CRITICAL THINKING QUESTIONS

Answer in complete sentences.

21. What are the similarities and differences between glycogen and starch?

22. How does the primary structure of a polypeptide determine its secondary structure?

Test Results: _____ Number right ÷ 22 = _____ × 100 = _____ %

EXPLORING THE INTERNET

Use the Internet to further explore topics in this chapter, such as carbon chemistry, the structures and functions of proteins, or the structures and functions of nucleic acids in living things. Go to the Mader Home Page (http://www.mhhe.com/sciencemath/biology/mader/) and click on *Biology,* 6th edition. Go to Chapter 3 and select a Web site of interest.

ANSWER KEY

STUDY EXERCISES

1. a. F **b.** T **c.** T **d.** F **2. a.** ketone **b.** carboxyl **c.** hydroxyl **d.** amine **3. a.** (amine) **b.** (carboxyl group) **4. a.** monosaccharide **b.** fatty acid **c.** glycerol **d.** amino acid **e.** nucleotide **5. a.** hydrolysis **b.** monomers **c.** condensation **d.** polymer **e.** added to **f.** taken away from **6. a.** $C_6H_{12}O_6$ **b.** $C_6H_{12}O_6$ **c.** isomer

7.

Monosaccharide Composition	Biological Function
glucose, fructose	transport sugar in plants
glucose, galactose	in milk, energy source
glucose, glucose	digestive breakdown product of starch
glucose	energy storage in plants
glucose	energy storage in animals
glucose	plant structure
glucose	exoskeleton in crabs, lobsters, insects

8. a. maltose, lactose, sucrose **b.** starch, glycogen, cellulose, chitin

9.

Monomers	Biological Functions
three fatty acids, glycerol	long-term energy storage
long-chain fatty acid and long-chain alcohol	protective cuticle to prevent water loss in plants
glycerol, two fatty acids, phosphate group	plasma membrane structure and properties

10. **a.** unsaturated **b.** saturated
11.

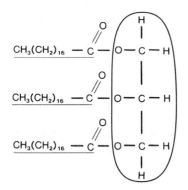

12. **a.** polar heads **b.** nonpolar tails **c.** plasma membrane 13. **a.** cholesterol **b.** aldosterone **c.** testosterone 14. functional groups
15.

Biological Function
catalysts that speed chemical reactions
contractile proteins in muscle
hormone involved in blood sugar regulation
oxygen pigment that transports in blood

16. **a.** amino acid **b.** amino acid **c.** carboxyl (acid) group **d.** peptide bond **e.** amino group   17. **a.** primary **b.** they represent the variable parts of the amino acids (i.e., H, CH_3, C chain, C ring) **c.** α (alpha) helix and β (beta) sheet **d.** hydrogen **e.** folding and twisting of polypeptide **f.** if it contained more than one polypeptide 18. nucleotides 19. **a.** base **b.** sugar **c.** phosphate 20. **a.** S—P (sugar-phosphate) **b.** B (bases)

21. **a.**

DNA	RNA
deoxyribose	ribose
A, T, C, G	A, U, C, G
double stranded	single stranded
yes	no

21. **b.** DNA stores information regarding the order of amino acids in a polypeptide (protein); RNA carries this information as a intermediary for the process of protein synthesis.
22. **a.** nucleotide **b.** phosphate **c.** sugar   23. **a.** energy **b.** energy **c.** ATP

ORGANIC CHEMISTRY LAS VEGAS STYLE

1. **a.** .40 **b.** .25 **c.** .15 = $ .80 **d.** .50 **e.** .25 = $ .75
2. **a.** $100 \times .15 = \$15.00$
b. $150 \times .25 =$ 37.50
c. $50 \times .20 =$ 10.00
           $62.50
d. $3 \times .25 =$ $ .75
e. $2 \times .20 =$ .40
          $ 1.15
3. **a.** .15 **b.** .20 **c.** .25 = $ .60
d. .15 **e.** .20 = $ .35
4. **a.** .25 **b.** .05 **c.** .20 = $ .50
d. .25 + .15 = $ .40
e. .25 + .05 =   .30
         $ .70
5. **a.** .15 **b.** .05 **c.** .15 = $ .35
d. .20 **e.** .25 = $ .45

KEYWORD CROSSWORD

```
 1A  M  I  N  O      4A  C  I  5D
     2S     3R          A   6N  U  C  L  E  O  T  I  D  E
     O     G      7R  N  A                              8N
     M     A          B                                  U
     E     N      9C  O  N  D 10E  N  S  A  T  I  O  N    C
     R     I          H        N                          L
     C              Y        Z      11H                   E
     D          12H  Y  D  R  O  L  Y  S  I  S            I
     R              M            D                         C
     A              E      13S  T  E  R  O  I  D
     T              O            A
     E          14H  Y  D  R  O  P  H  O  B  I  C
                    I            H
                    I            I                         D
               15P  H  O  S 16P  H  O  L  I 17P  I  D
                    O            R         I        E
                    L            O         C        P
                    Y            T                  T
                    M            E      18L  I  P  I  D
                    E            I                  D
                    R            N                  E
```

CHAPTER TEST

1. a   2. b   3. d   4. d   5. c   6. b   7. c   8. c   9. b
10. b   11. b   12. a   13. a   14. a   15. b   16. a
17. a   18. b   19. d   20. a   21. Both glycogen and starch are polysaccharides with glucose as the monomer. Both are energy-storing molecules, but starch fulfills this role in plants and glycogen does it in some animals. Glycogen exhibits more branching than starch.   22. The secondary structure of a polypeptide depends on hydrogen bonding between the *R* groups of the amino acids making up the polypeptide. Each particular polypeptide has its own sequence of amino acids and therefore *R* groups.

4

CELL STRUCTURE AND FUNCTION

Cells are the smallest units displaying the properties of life. Cells normally are measured in micrometers because they are so small. Their small size ensures a sufficient amount of plasma membrane to serve the **cytoplasm.**

All organisms are composed of cells. The two major kinds of cells are **prokaryotic** and **eukaryotic.** They differ by the organization of chromosomal DNA and the presence of **organelles** in the cytoplasm. Prokaryotic cells lack a nucleus and other membranous organelles.

The **nucleus** of eukaryotic cells (plant and animal) is defined by a nuclear envelope which separates the nucleoplasm from the cytoplasm. The chromosomal material exists as **chromatin** until the cell divides. The **nucleolus** in the nucleus contains ribosomal RNA and the proteins of ribosomal subunits.

The eukaryotic cell contains a variety of structures in the cytoplasm. Ribosomes are the site of protein synthesis. They may exist freely or be attached to the **endoplasmic reticulum.** Several structures are part of the endomembrane system in the cell. The endoplasmic reticulum provides channels that transport substances through the cell. Substances are processed and packaged by the **Golgi apparatus. Lysosomes** contain enzymes that promote the breakdown of cell substances.

Some organelles are specialized to handle energy in the cell. Chloroplasts are the site of photosynthesis, whereas the mitochondria are regions involved in cellular respiration. These organelles may be remnants of prokaryotes that inhabited eukaryotic cells over evolutionary time.

The cytoskeleton contains **microtubules,** intermediate filaments, and microfilaments. They maintain cell shape and assist movement of cell parts.

STUDY EXERCISES

Study the text section by section as you answer the questions that follow.

4.1 CELLS MAKE UP LIVING THINGS (P. 58)

- All organisms are composed of cells which arise from preexisting cells.
- A microscope is usually needed to see a cell because most cells are quite small.

1. Check the two statements that are tenets of the cell theory.
   _____ a. All organisms are made up of cells.
   _____ b. Cork cells are living.
   _____ c. Multicellular organisms are living.
   _____ d. Cells come only from preexisting cells.

2. Label each of the following statements as describing the bright-field light microscope (B) or the transmission electron microscope (T):
   _____ a. focusing by glass lenses
   _____ b. focusing by magnetic lenses
   _____ c. image viewed from photographic film or fluorescent screen
   _____ d. image viewed through the microscope

3. Name several other microscopes or microscopy techniques available to study cells today. _____
   _____

Cells Are Small (p. 59)

- Cell-volume-to-cell-surface relationships explain why cells are so very small.

4. As the volume of a cell ᵃ·_____, the proportionate amount of cell surface area ᵇ·_____.
5. A large cell requires more ᵃ·_____ and produces more ᵇ·_____ than a small cell. Materials are exchanged at the cell's ᶜ·_____. Because the surface area of a large cell actually ᵈ·_____, cell size stays ᵉ·_____.

4.2 PROKARYOTIC CELLS ARE LESS COMPLEX (P. 62)

- Prokaryotic cells have neither a membrane-bounded nucleus nor other organelles of eukaryotic cells.

6. Label this diagram of prokaryotic cells with the following terms (some are used more than once):

    capsule
    cell wall
    cytoplasm
    nucleoid region
    plasma membrane
    ribosome
    slime layer
    thylakoid

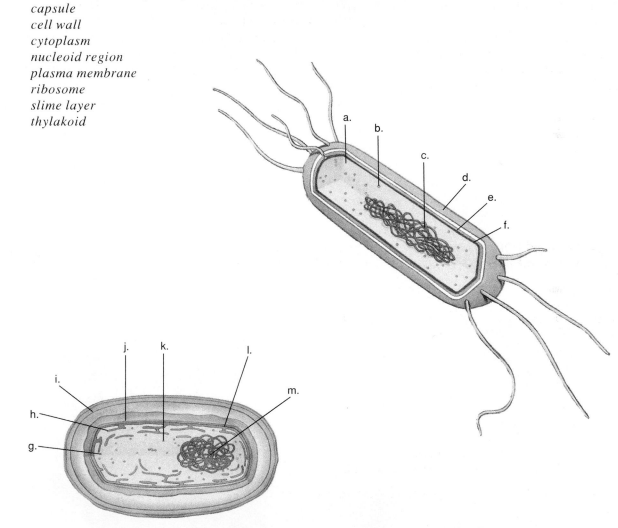

Which of these cells is a cyanobacterium? ⁿ·_____

For questions 7–12, match each of the following prokaryotic cell parts to its description:

_____ 7. capsule
_____ 8. cell wall
_____ 9. flagella
_____10. plasmid
_____11. ribosome
_____12. thylakoid

a. long, thin appendage from the cell
b. cytoplasmic granule
c. structure surrounding the cell wall
d. flattened membranous disks
e. external covering around plasma membrane
f. small accessory ring of DNA

13. Label this diagram of an animal cell
    with the following terms:

    centriole
    Golgi apparatus
    lysosome
    microtubule
    mitochondrion
    nucleolus
    nucleus
    ribosome
    rough ER
    smooth ER
    vacuole

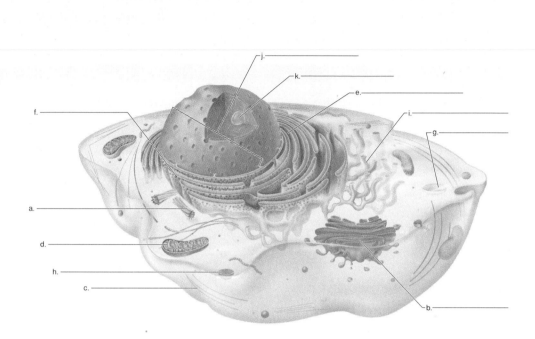

14. Label this diagram of a plant cell
    with the following terms:

    actin filament
    cell wall
    central vacuole
    chloroplast
    chromatin
    cytosol
    Golgi apparatus
    intracellular space
    microtubule
    middle lamella
    mitochondrion
    nuclear envelope
    nuclear pore
    nucleolus
    plasma membrane
    ribosome
    rough ER
    smooth ER

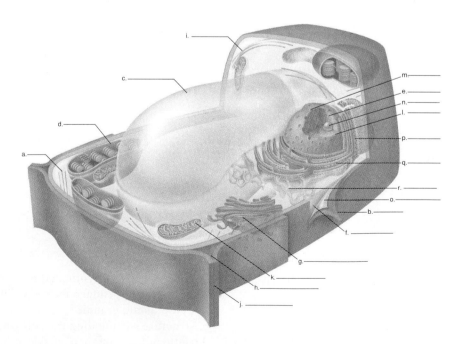

15. Complete this table by writing *yes* (the structure is present) or *no* (it is not present) on the lines provided.

	Prokaryotic	Eukaryotic (animal)
Plasma Membrane		
Cell Wall		
Nuclear Envelope		
Mitochondria		
Endoplasmic Reticulum		
Ribosomes		
Centrioles		

16. Place the following terms in the appropriate column to compare plant and animal cell structures (some terms are used in both columns): *cell wall, centrioles, chloroplasts, large central vacuole, mitochondria, plasma membrane,* and *small vacuoles only.*

Animal	Plant

The Nucleus Stores Genetic Information (p. 66)

• Eukaryotic cells have a membrane-bounded nucleus that contains DNA within chromosomes.

17. The nucleus is enclosed by the a._____, which contains b._____ that open into the cytoplasm. At the time of cell division, chromatin c._____ to form chromosomes. Chromatin has a region called the d._____ , where e._____ is produced.

The Endomembrane System Is Elaborate (p. 67)

• Organelles are membrane-bounded compartments specialized to carry out specific functions.

18. Explain how these organelles work together.

ribosomes and endoplasmic reticulum a._____

_____

endoplasmic reticulum and Golgi apparatus b._____

_____

lysosomes and vacuoles c. _____

_____

chloroplasts and mitochondria d. _____

_____

Energy-Related Organelles (p. 70)

- Chloroplasts use solar energy to produce organic molecules that are broken down, releasing energy in mitochondria.

19. Label this diagram with the following terms:
    ATP
    carbohydrate
    CO₂ and H₂O
    chloroplast
    mitochondrion

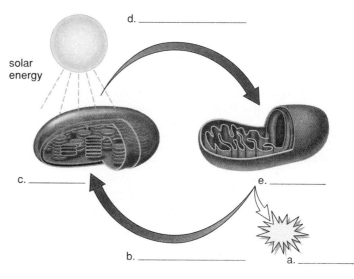

Use this diagram to answer the following: Chloroplasts build up f._____, and mitochondria break it down. Chloroplasts use the molecules that mitochondria give off, namely g._____ and h._____, as raw material for i._____, which utilizes the energy of the j._____. Mitochondria use k._____ produced by chloroplasts to build up a supply of l._____, the energy currency of cells. m._____ is the cellular breakdown of carbohydrate to acquire energy.

20. Label this diagram of a chloroplast with the following terms:
    granum
    inner membrane
    outer membrane
    stroma
    thylakoid space

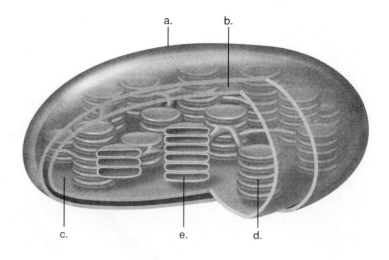

21. Using words, what is the overall equation for photosynthesis? _____

22. Label this diagram of a mitochondrion with the following terms:
    cristae
    inner membrane
    matrix
    outer membrane

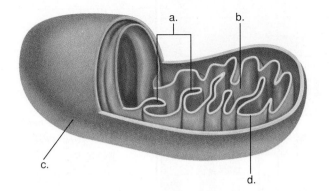

23. Using words, what is the overall equation for aerobic cellular respiration? _____

Cytoskeleton Contains Filaments and Microtubules (p. 72)

- The cytoskeleton, a complex system of filaments and tubules, gives the cell its shape and accounts for the movement of the cell and its organelles.

24. Match these definitions with the following terms: *actin filament, intermediate filament*, and *microtubule*.
    _____ a. small cylinder made of the protein tubulin
    _____ b. long, extremely thin fiber that often interacts with myosin
    _____ c. fibrous polypeptide that varies according to the tissue

25. Microtubules, like actin filaments and intermediate filaments, are able to assemble and ᵃ·_____.
    Microtubules radiate out from the centrosome, the main ᵇ·_____ center in a cell. In animal cells, this
    center contains two ᶜ·_____, which have a 9 + 0 pattern of microtubules. Centrosomes have long
    been associated with the formation of the ᵈ·_____ during cell division. Centrioles are believed to
    give rise to ᵉ·_____, which organize cilia and flagella. Cilia and flagella have
    a(n) ᶠ·_____ pattern of microtubules.

4.4 HOW THE EUKARYOTIC CELL EVOLVED (P. 76)

- The endosymbiotic hypothesis states that certain eukaryotic organelles were originally prokaryotes taken up by a larger cell.

26. Match these definitions with the following terms: *chloroplast, mitochondria, flagellum, eukaryote.*
    _____ a. arose from a photosynthetic cyanobacterial endosymbiont
    _____ b. host cell taking up prokaryotes by endosymbiosis
    _____ c. arose from heterotrophic bacterial endosymbionts
    _____ d. derived from a spirochete prokaryote

Review key terms by completing this crossword puzzle, using the following alphabetized list of terms:

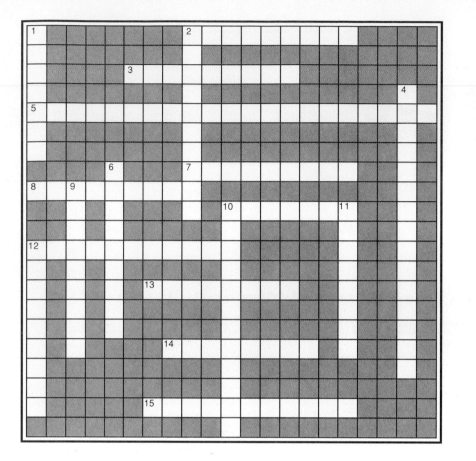

bacterium
cell wall
centriole
chloroplast
chromatin
chromosome
cytoplasm
cytoskeleton
cytosol
endoplasmic reticulum
eukaryotic cell
lysosome
microbody
microtubule
nucleoid region
nucleus
organelle
ribosome

Across

2 contents of a cell between the nucleus (nucleoid region) and the plasma membrane
3 membrane-bounded vesicle containing specific enzymes involved in lipid and alcohol metabolism, photosynthesis, and germination
5 system of membranous saccules and channels in the cytoplasm (two words)
7 small, membranous structure in the cytoplasm having a specific function
8 unicellular organism that lacks a nucleus and cytoplasmic organelles other than ribosomes; reproduces by binary fission and occurs in one of three shapes
10 solution phase of the cytoplasm
12 membrane-bounded organelle with chlorophyll-containing membranous grana; where photosynthesis takes place
13 RNA and protein in two subunits; site of protein synthesis
14 area in prokaryotic cell where DNA is found
15 small, cylindrical organelle that is believed to be involved in maintaining cell shape and is present in cilia and flagella

Down

1 region of a eukaryotic cell, containing chromosomes, that controls the structure and function of the cell
2 association of DNA and proteins in which genes are arranged linearly; visible only during cell division
4 typical of most types of organisms, except bacteria, having a well-defined nucleus and organelles (two words)
6 cell organelle, existing in pairs, that organizes a mitotic spindle for chromosome movement during cell division
9 tough layer of material outside the plasma membrane of a bacterium, a fungal cell, an algal cell, or a plant cell that provides mechanical protection (two words)
10 internal framework of the cell, consisting of microtubules, actin filaments, and intermediate filaments
11 membrane-bounded vesicle that contains hydrolytic enzymes for digesting macromolecules
12 complex of DNA and associated proteins observed within a nucleus that is not dividing

OBJECTIVE QUESTIONS

Do not refer to the text when taking this test. In questions 1–8, match each cell part with the following descriptions:

    a. regulates passage of substances into the cell
    b. processing and transport channel
    c. contains enzymes for digestion
    d. site of protein synthesis
    e. location of the nucleolus
    f. site of aerobic cellular respiration
    g. found in plants, not animals
    h. maintains cell shape

_____ 1. chloroplast

_____ 2. cytoskeleton

_____ 3. endoplasmic reticulum

_____ 4. lysosome

_____ 5. mitochondrion

_____ 6. nucleus

_____ 7. plasma membrane

_____ 8. ribosome

_____ 9. Cells are normally measured in
    a. centimeters.
    b. meters.
    c. micrometers.
    d. millimeters.

_____10. The minimum distance between two objects before they are seen as one object is known as
    a. illumination.
    b. magnification.
    c. resolution.
    d. transmission.

_____11. Select the structure found in eukaryotic cells but not in prokaryotic cells.
    a. plasma membrane
    b. cell wall
    c. mitochondrion
    d. ribosome

_____12. Select the incorrect association.
    a. capsule—covering
    b. cell wall—covering
    c. flagellum—movement
    d. plasmid—movement

_____13. The cytoplasmic structures in a bacterial cell is the
    a. cell wall.
    b. nucleoid.
    c. plasma membrane.
    d. ribosome.

_____14. Which of the following structures is part of the cell's endomembrane system?
    a. chloroplast
    b. endoplasmic reticulum
    c. mitochondrion
    d. nucleolus

_____15. How are mitochondria and chloroplasts similar to bacteria?
    a. They are bounded by a single membrane.
    b. They have a limited amount of genetic material.
    c. They lack ribosomes.
    d. They are larger than normal cells.

_____16. Plant cells
    a. have a cell wall but not plasma membrane.
    b. have chloroplasts but no mitochondria.
    c. do not have any centrioles and yet divide.
    d. have a large central vacuole but do not have endoplasmic reticulum.

_____17. Which of these does NOT contain nucleic acid?
    a. chromosomes
    b. ribosomes
    c. chromatin
    d. centrioles
    e. genes

_____18. How are mitochondria like chloroplasts?
    a. They have the same structure.
    b. They both absorb the energy of the sun.
    c. They both are concerned with energy.
    d. They are both in animal cells.

_____19. Which of the following cell structures within the cytoplasm is connected to the nuclear envelope?
    a. nucleolus
    b. chromatin
    c. endoplasmic reticulum
    d. vacuoles
    e. lysosomes

_____20. Which organelle is used to produce steroid hormones and to detoxify drugs?
    a. lysosomes
    b. Golgi apparatus
    c. mitochondria
    d. rough endoplasmic reticulum
    e. smooth endoplasmic reticulum

CRITICAL THINKING QUESTIONS

Answer in complete sentences.

21. What would be the effect on cell if it were suddenly to lose its mitochondria?

22. How would the destruction of the Golgi apparatus affect a cell?

Test Results: _____   Number right ÷ 22 = _____ × 100 = _____ %

EXPLORING THE INTERNET

Use the Internet to further explore topics in this chapter, such as cells, through downloadable videos, a dictionary of cell biology, or photos and illustrations of different cell types. Go to the Mader Home Page (http://www.mhhe.com/sciencemath/biology/mader/) and click on *Biology,* 6th edition. Go to Chapter 4 and select a Web site of interest.

ANSWER KEY

STUDY EXERCISES

1. a, d   **2. a.** B **b.** T **c.** T **d.** B   **3.** scanning electron microscopy, phase contrast microscopy, video-enhanced contrast microscopy, confocal microscopy   **4. a.** increases **b.** decreases   **5. a.** nutrients **b.** wastes **c.** surface **d.** decreases proportionately **e.** small   **6. a.** cytoplasm **b.** ribosome **c.** nucleoid region **d.** capsule **e.** cell wall **f.** plasma membrane **g.** cytoplasm **h.** thylahoid **i.** slime layer **j.** cell wall **k.** ribosome **l.** plasma membrane **m.** nucleoid region **n.** the one on the right   **7.** c   **8.** e   **9.** a   **10.** f   **11.** b   **12.** d   **13. a.** centriole **b.** Golgi apparatus **c.** microtubule **d.** mitochondrion **e.** rough ER **f.** ribosome **g.** vacuole **h.** lysosome **i.** smooth ER **j.** nucleus **k.** nucleolus   **14. a.** actin filament **b.** cell wall **c.** central vacuole **d.** chloroplast **e.** chromatin **f.** cytosol **g.** Golgi apparatus **h.** intracellular space **i.** microtubule **j.** middle lamella **k.** mitochondrion **l.** nuclear envelope **m.** nuclear pore **n.** nucleolus **o.** plasma membrane **p.** ribosome **q.** rough ER **r.** smooth ER

15.

Prokaryotic	Eukaryotic (animal)
yes	yes
yes	no
no	yes
no	yes
no	yes
yes	yes
no	yes

16.

Animal	Plant
centrioles	cell wall
mitochondria	mitochondria
small vacuoles only	large central vacuole
plasma membrane	plasma membrane
	chloroplasts

17. **a.** nuclear envelope **b.** nuclear pores **c.** condenses **d.** nucleolus **e.** rRNA **18. a.** Proteins are made at the ribosomes located on the endoplasmic reticulum. **b.** Products made at the endoplasmic reticulum are sent to the Golgi apparatus for final processing, packaging, **c.** Vacuoles may contain a substance that can be digested after fusion with lysosomes. **d.** Carbohydrates made in chloroplasts are broken down partly in mitochondria. **19. a.** ATP **b.** CO_2 and H_2O **c.** chloroplast **d.** carbohydrate **e.** mitochondrion **f.** carbohydrate **g.** carbon dioxide **h.** water **i.** photosynthesis **j.** sun **k.** carbohydrate **l.** ATP **m.** Cellular respiration **20. a.** outer membrane **b.** inner membrane **c.** stroma **d.** granum **e.** thylakoid space **21.** solar energy + carbon dioxide + water → carbohydrate + oxygen **22. a.** cristae **b.** matrix **c.** outer membrane **d.** inner membrane **23.** carbohydrate + oxygen → energy + carbon dioxide + water **24. a.** microtubule **b.** actin filament **c.** intermediate filament **25. a.** disassemble **b.** microtubule organizing body **c.** centrioles **d.** spindle **e.** basal bodies **f.** 9 + 2 **26. a.** chloroplast **b.** eukaryote **c.** mitochondria **d.** flagellum

KEYWORD CROSSWORD

Across:
2. CYTOPLASM
3. MICROBODY
5. ENDOPLASMIC RETICULUM
7. ORGANELLE
8. BACTERIUM
10. CYTOSOL
12. CHLOROPLAST
13. RIBOSOME
14. NUCLEOID
15. MICROTUBULE

CHAPTER TEST

1. g **2.** h **3.** b **4.** c **5.** f **6.** e **7.** a **8.** d **9.** c **10.** c **11.** c **12.** d **13.** d **14.** b **15.** b **16.** c **17.** d **18.** c **19.** c **20.** e **21.** The cell would be unable to extract energy from carbohydrates. The ATP harvested by this process would be unavailable for cell functions. Therefore, the cell would die. **22.** The smooth ER packages substances in vesicles. A large portion of these go to the Golgi apparatus for further processing. These vesicles would most likely accumulate in the cell to the point that the cell would be unable to function properly.

5

MEMBRANE STRUCTURE AND FUNCTION

The sandwich model and its associated unit membrane model preceded the currently accepted **fluid-mosaic model** of membrane structure. According to the fluid-mosaic model, **phospholipid** molecules provide a fluid, lipid bilayer with their polar heads at the membrane surfaces. Hydrophobic portions of protein molecules are in the lipid bilayer; their hydrophilic portions are at the surfaces. The proteins form channels and function as receptors, enzymes, and carrier molecules.

Molecules move across a membrane in several ways. By **diffusion,** molecules move down their concentration gradient. **Osmosis** is the diffusion of water through a differentially permeable membrane. When cells are in a **hypotonic solution,** they gain water; when they are in a **hypertonic solution,** they lose water. In **isotonic solutions,** cells neither gain nor lose water. Both diffusion and osmosis are passive processes that do not require energy. Facilitated transport is also passive and involves carrier molecules moving substances from higher to lower concentrations. **Active transport** moves substances in the opposite direction, with the function of a carrier molecule and energy. Larger substances pass through cells by **endocytosis** and **exocytosis.**

An extracellular matrix is a meshwork of insoluble proteins and carbohydrates that is now known to influence animal cell differentiation and cellular metabolism. Plant cells are bounded by a cell wall that is external to the plasma membrane. This boundary is freely permeable. Several types of junctions exist between animal cells: desmosomes, gap junctions, and tight junctions. Between plant cells, plasmodesmata perform this function.

Study the text section by section as you answer the questions that follow.

5.1 MEMBRANE MODELS HAVE CHANGED (P. 82)

- The present-day fluid-mosaic model of membrane structure is less rigid and more dynamic than the previous sandwich model.

1. Indicate whether the following statements are true (T) or false (F):
   _____ a. According to the sandwich model, polar substances enter the cell through channels.
   _____ b. According to the fluid-mosaic model, globular proteins are embedded in the membrane.
   _____ c. According to the unit membrane model, the cell membrane lacks phospholipids.
   _____ d. According to the unit membrane model, membranes differ according to their function.
   _____ e. According to the sandwich model, proteins form an outer and inner layer.
   _____ f. According to the fluid-masaic model, proteins function as receptors, enzymes, and carrier molecules.

• The membrane contains lipids and proteins, each with specific functions.

2. Label this diagram of the plasma membrane with the following terms:
    carbohydrate chain
    cholesterol
    cytoskeleton filaments
    glycolipid
    glycoprotein
    phospholipid bilayer
    protein molecule

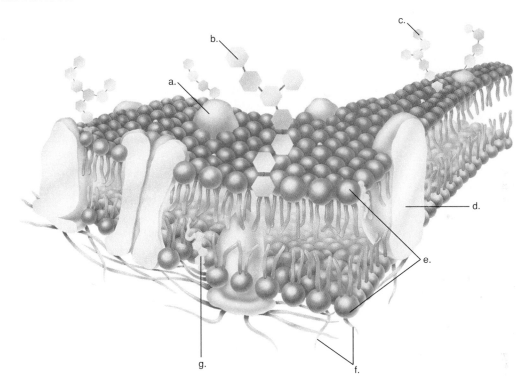

3. The two components of the fluid-mosaic model of membrane structure are ᵃ·_____
   and ᵇ·_____.

4. ᵃ·_____ form a bilayer, in which the ᵇ·_____ heads are at the surfaces of the membranes,
   and the ᶜ·_____ tails face each other, making up the interior of the membrane. The
   lipid ᵈ·_____, which is also in the membrane, ᵉ·_____ the membrane's permeability.

5. Complete the sentences, using the terms *hydrophilic* and/or *hydrophobic:* Transmembrane proteins are found
   within the plasma membrane. ᵃ·_____ regions are embedded within the membrane,
   and ᵇ·_____ regions project from both surfaces of the bilayer.

6. Both glycolipids and glycoproteins have a(n) ᵃ·_____ chain and are active in cell
   to ᵇ·_____ recognition.

7. Label the diagrams of proteins found in the membrane and state a function on the lines provided:

carrier protein _____

cell recognition protein _____

channel protein _____

enzymatic protein_____

receptor protein _____

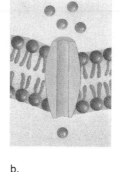

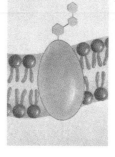

a. _____

_____

b. _____

_____

c. _____

_____

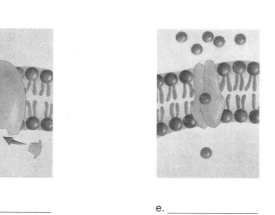

d. _____

_____

e. _____

_____

5.3 HOW MOLECULES CROSS THE PLASMA MEMBRANE (P. 86)

- The plasma membrane regulates the passage of molecules into and out of the cell.
- Small, noncharged molecules tend to pass freely across the plasma membrane.
- Some molecules diffuse (move from an area of higher concentration to an area of lower concentration) across a plasma membrane.
- Water diffuses across the plasma membrane, and this can affect cell size and shape.

8. Label each of the following as diffusion (D) or osmosis (O):

_____ a. Algae in a pond become dehydrated.

_____ b. A hypertonic solution draws water out of cell.

_____ c. A red blood cell bursts in a test tube.

_____ d. Dye crystals spread out in a beaker of water.

_____ e. Gases move across the plasma membrane.

_____ f. Perfume is sensed from the other side of a room.

9. In the following diagram, assume that glucose and water can cross the membrane and that protein cannot.

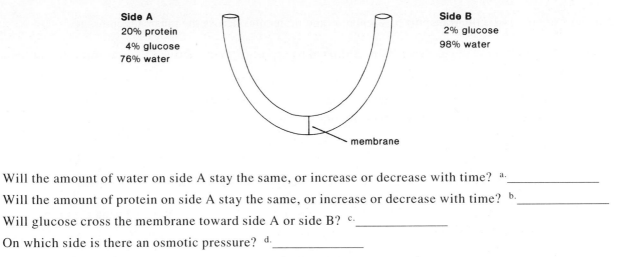

Side A
20% protein
4% glucose
76% water

Side B
2% glucose
98% water

membrane

Will the amount of water on side A stay the same, or increase or decrease with time? a._____

Will the amount of protein on side A stay the same, or increase or decrease with time? b._____

Will glucose cross the membrane toward side A or side B? c._____

On which side is there an osmotic pressure? d._____

What will happen to the level of solution on each side of the membrane? e._____

_____

10. Complete this diagram to describe the effect of tonicity on red blood cells.

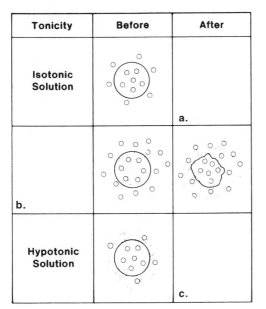

Tonicity	Before	After
Isotonic Solution		a.
b.		
Hypotonic Solution		c.

11. Complete this diagram to describe the effect of tonicity on plant cells.

12. If a solution is 8% solute, it is a._____% solvent.

If a solution is 99.5% solvent, it is b._____% solute.

If solution A is 2% solute and solution B is 3% solute, then solution A is c._____ to solution B which is d._____ to solution A.

Compared to solution A, a solution with 2% solute is e._____.

Tonicity	Before	After
a.	cell wall / water vacuole / plasma membrane	
b.		vacuole
Hypertonic Solution		c.

Transport by Carrier Proteins (p. 90)

- Carrier proteins assist the transport of some ions and molecules across the plasma membrane.

13. Label each of the following as describing facilitated transport (F) only, active (A) transport only, or both (F, A) processes:
    _____ a. Uses a carrier molecule.
    _____ b. Substances travel down a concentration gradient.
    _____ c. Substances travel against a concentration gradient.
    _____ d. Sodium-potassium pump.
    _____ e. Energy is not required.

Use of Membrane-Assisted Transport (p. 92)

- Vesicle formation takes other substances into the cell, and vesicle fusion with the plasma membrane discharges substances from the cell.

14. Label each of the following as describing exocytosis (Ex) or endocytosis (En):
    _____ a. Vesicles formed by Golgi apparatus fuse with plasma membrane.
    _____ b. Materials leave the cell.
    _____ c. Phagocytosis is an example.
    _____ d. Pinocytosis is an example.
    _____ e. Occurs after receptors bind to a ligand.

5.4 THE CELL SURFACE IS MODIFIED (P. 94)

- The cell wall of a plant cell supports the cell. The extracellular matrix of animal cells influences their shape, movement, and function.
- The activities of cells within a tissue are coordinated, in part, because cells are linked and directly communicate with one another.

15. An extracellular matrix is a meshwork of $^{a.}$_____ and $^{b.}$_____. The carbohydrate chains, which allow cells to $^{c.}$_____ one another, are also sometimes $^{d.}$_____ for molecules. They receive molecules in the matrix that affect the cell's development and metabolism.

16. Indicate whether the following statements about the cell wall are true (T) or false (F):
    _____ a. It is found in plants but not in animals.
    _____ b. It interferes with plasma membrane function when present.
    _____ c. It is internal to the plasma membrane.
    _____ d. Some woody plants have a primary and secondary cell wall.

In questions 17–20, match the following descriptions with each type of cell junction:
    a. attached to cytoskeleton
    b. found only in plants
    c. formed from two identical plasma membrane channels
    d. where plasma proteins attach to each other

    _____17. adhesion junction (desmosome)
    _____18. gap junction
    _____19. plasmodesmata
    _____20. tight junction

Review the key terms by completing this crossword puzzle, using the following alphabetized list of terms:

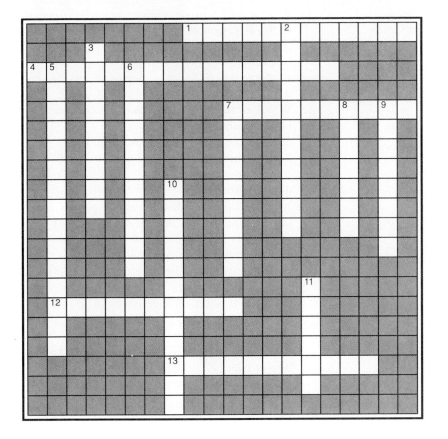

active transport
carrier protein
cholesterol
diffusion
endocytosis
exocytosis
hypertonic
hypotonic
isotonic
osmosis
phagocytosis
phospholipid
pinocytosis
turgor

Across

1   process by which amoeboid-type cells engulf large material, forming an intracellular vacuole

4   use of a plasma membrane carrier protein to move particles from a region of lower to higher concentration; it opposes an equilibrium and requires energy (two words)

7   higher solute concentration (less water) than the cytoplasm of a cell; causes cell to lose water by osmosis

12   process by which vesicles that fuse with the plasma membrane move particles or debris out of the cell

13   process by which vesicles form around and bring macromolecules into the cell

Down

2   steroid that occurs in animal plasma membranes and, in humans, is known to contribute to the development of plaque on blood vessel walls

3   movement of molecules from a region of higher to lower concentration; it requires no energy and tends to lead to an equal distribution

5   protein that combines with and transports a molecule across the plasma membrane (two words)

6   process by which particles or debris is moved into the cell from the environment by phagocytosis or pinocytosis

7   lower solute concentration (more water) than the cytoplasm of a cell; causes cell to gain water by osmosis

8   diffusion of water through a differentially permeable membrane

9   solution that is equal in solute and water concentration to that of the cytoplasm of a cell; causes cell to neither lose nor gain water by osmosis

10   molecule having the same structure as a fat except that a phosphate-containing group replaces one fatty acid; an important component of plasma membranes

11   pressure of the cell contents against the cell wall in plant cells; determined by the water content of the vacuole; gives internal support to the plant cell

Do not refer to the text when taking this test. In questions 1–7, match the following descriptions with each transport process:

   a. small particle or liquid intake into a cell
   b. requires vacuole formation
   c. carrier molecule, no energy
   d. carrier molecule, energy required
   e. water enters a hypertonic solution from a cell
   f. secretion from the cell
   g. dye molecules spread through water

_____ 1. active transport
_____ 2. diffusion
_____ 3. exocytosis
_____ 4. facilitated transport
_____ 5. osmosis
_____ 6. phagocytosis
_____ 7. pinocytosis

_____ 8. Proteins form the nonactive matrix of the plasma membrane.
   a. true
   b. false

_____ 9. Phospholipids are present in the plasma membrane.
   a. true
   b. false

_____ 10. Hydrophilic ends of proteins are oriented toward membrane surfaces.
   a. true
   b. false

_____ 11. Lipid-soluble molecules pass through the plasma membrane by
   a. active transport.
   b. diffusing through it.
   c. facilitated transport.
   d. use of the sodium-potassium pump.

_____ 12. A 2% salt solution is _____ to a 4% salt solution.
   a. hypertonic
   b. hypotonic
   c. isometric
   d. isotonic

_____ 13. Which molecule is directly required for operation of the sodium-potassium pump?
   a. ATP
   b. NAD^+
   c. DNA
   d. water

_____ 14. In cells, which process moves materials opposite to the direction of the other three?
   a. endocytosis
   b. exocytosis
   c phagocytosis
   d. pinocytosis

_____ 15. Which of the following junctions is found only between plant cells?
   a. adhesion junctions (desmosomes)
   b. gap junctions
   c. plasmodesmata
   d. tight junctions

_____ 16. A small lipid-soluble molecule passes easily through the plasma membrane. Which of these statements is the most likely explanation?
   a. A carrier protein must be at work.
   b. The plasma membrane is partially composed of lipid molecules.
   c. The cell is expending energy to do this.
   d. Phagocytosis has enclosed this molecule in a vacuole.

_____ 17. Which of these does NOT require an expenditure of energy?
   a. diffusion
   b. osmosis
   c. facilitated transport
   d. None of these require energy.

_____ 18. Which term refers to the bursting of an animal cell?
   a. plasmolysis
   b. crenation
   c. lysis
   d. turgor pressure

_____ 19. An animal cell always takes in water when placed in a(n) _____ solution.
   a. hypertonic
   b. osmotic
   c. isotonic
   d. hypotonic

_____ 20. Which of the following is actively transported across plasma membranes?
   a. carbon dioxide
   b. oxygen
   c. water
   d. sodium ions

Answer in complete sentences.

21. Why is the plasma membrane considered so important to the cell?

22. What osmotic problem would plant cells experience if they lost their cell walls?

Test Results: _____ Number right ÷ 22 = _____ × 100 = _____ %

EXPLORING THE INTERNET

Use the Internet to further explore topics in this chapter, such as osmosis or membrane structure. Go to the Mader Home Page (http://www.mhhe.com/sciencemath/biology/mader/) and click on *Biology*, 6th edition. Go to Chapter 5 and select a Web site of interest.

ANSWER KEY

STUDY EXERCISES

1. a. T **b.** T **c.** F **d.** F **e.** T **f.** T   **2. a.** glycoprotein **b.** carbohydrate chain **c.** glycolipid **d.** protein molecule **e.** phospholipid bilayer **f.** cytosketon filaments **g.** cholesterol   **3. a.** lipids **b.** proteins   **4. a.** Phospholipids **b.** hydrophilic (polar) **c.** hydrophobic **d.** cholesterol **e.** reduces   **5. a.** hydrophobic **b.** hydrophilic   **6. a.** carbohydrate **b.** cell   **7. a.** receptor protein, shaped in such a way that a specific molecule can bind to it. **b.** channel protein, allows molecules to pass across the plasma membrane. **c.** cell recognition protein, functions in cell to cell recognition. **d.** enzymatic protein, catalyzes a specific reaction. **e.** carrier protein, allows selective passage of molecules across the plasma membrane. **8. a.** O **b.** O **c.** O **d.** D **e.** D **f.** D **9. a** increase **b.** stay the same **c.** toward side B **d.** side A **e.** Side A will rise, and side B will fall.   **10. a.** cell is same size and shape **b.** Hypertonic Solution **c.** cell is bursting   **11. a.** Isotonic Solution **b.** Hypotonic Solution **c.** vacuole is much smaller   **12. a.** 92 **b.** 0.5 **c.** hypotonic **d.** hypertonic **e.** isotonic **13. a.** F, A **b.** F **c.** A **d.** A **e.** F   **14. a.** Ex **b.** Ex **c.** En **d.** En **e.** En   **15. a.** proteins **b.** carbohydrates **c.** recognize **d.** receptors   **16. a.** T **b.** F **c.** F **d.** T   **17.** a   **18.** c   **19.** b   **20.** d

KEYWORD CROSSWORD

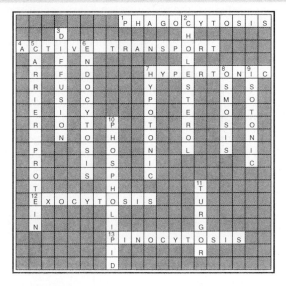

CHAPTER TEST

1. d **2.** g **3.** f **4.** c **5.** e **6.** b **7.** a **8.** b **9.** a **10.** a **11.** b **12.** b **13.** a **14.** b **15.** c **16.** b **17.** d **18.** c **19.** d **20.** d   **21.** The plasma membrane is very important because it is the outer living boundary of the cell, provides and regulates the passage of molecules into and out of the cell.   **22.** In a hypotonic environment, plant cells would continue to gain water until they burst.

METABOLISM: ENERGY AND ENZYMES

Living things can't exhibit any of the characteristics of life without a supply of energy. There are two energy laws that are basic to understanding energy-use patterns in organisms at the cellular level. The first law says that energy cannot be created or destroyed, but can only be transferred or transformed. The second law states that a usable form of energy cannot be converted completely into another usable form. As a result of these laws, we know that the **entropy** of the universe is increasing and that only a constant input of energy maintains the organization of living things.

Metabolism is all the reactions that occur in a cell. Only those reactions that result in a negative free energy difference—that is, the products have less usable energy than the reactants—occur spontaneously. Such reactions, called exergonic reactions, release energy. Endergonic reactions, which require an input of energy, occur because it is possible to **couple** an exergonic process with an endergonic process. For example, glucose breakdown is an exergonic metabolic pathway that drives the buildup of many ATP molecules. These ATP molecules then supply energy for cellular work. Thus, ATP goes through a cycle in which it is constantly being built up from, and then broken down to ADP +Ⓟ.

A metabolic pathway is a series of reactions that proceed in an orderly, step-by-step manner. Each reaction has a specific **enzyme** that speeds the reaction by forming a complex with their substrates. Any environmental factor that affects the shape of a protein also affects the ability of an enzyme to do its job. (Many enzymes have cofactors or coenzymes that help them carry out a reaction.) Photosynthesis is a metabolic pathway in chloroplasts that transforms solar energy to the chemical energy within carbohydrates, and aerobic respiration, which is completed in mitochondria, is a metabolic pathway that transforms the energy of carbohydrates into that of ATP molecules. Eventually the energy within ATP molecules becomes heat. Therefore, the world of living things is dependent on a constant input of solar energy.

Both photosynthesis and aerobic respiration make use of an electron transport system, in which electrons are transferred from one carrier to the next with the release of energy that is ultimately used to produce ATP molecules. The chemiosmotic hypothesis explains how the electron transport system produces ATP. The carriers of this system deposit hydrogen ions (H^+) on one side of a membrane. When the ions flow down an electrochemical gradient through an ATPase complex, ATP is formed from ADP and P.

Study the text section by section as you answer the questions that follow.

6.1 ENERGY (P. 100)

- Energy cannot be created nor destroyed; energy can be changed from one form to another but there is always a loss of usable energy.

1. Indicate whether the following statements, related to the energy laws, are true (T) or false (F) and if the statements are false, change them to true statements:

   _____ a. The chemical energy of ATP cannot be transformed into any other type of energy such as kinetic energy. Rewrite: _____

   _____

   _____ b. A cell produces ATP and therefore cells do not obey the first law of thermodynamics. Rewrite:

   _____

_____ c. Because energy transformations always result in a loss of usable energy, the entropy of the universe is increasing. Rewrite: _____

_____

_____ d. Because our society uses coal as an energy source, it is helping to decrease the entropy of the universe. Rewrite: _____

_____

6.2 METABOLIC REACTIONS AND ENERGY TRANSFORMATIONS (P. 101)

- In cells the breakdown of ATP, which releases energy, can be coupled to reactions that require an input of energy.
- ATP goes through a cycle: energy from glucose breakdown drives ATP buildup and then ATP breakdown provides energy for cellular work.

2. Label each of the following as either an endergonic (EN) or an exergonic (EX) reaction:
   _____ a. energy is released as the reaction occurs.
   _____ b. energy is required to make the reaction go.
   _____ c. reaction used by the body for muscle contraction and nerve conduction.
   _____ d. ATP → ADP + ℗.
   _____ e. ADP + ℗ → ATP.

3. Label this diagram with the following terms:
   ATP
   ADP
   –P
   +P

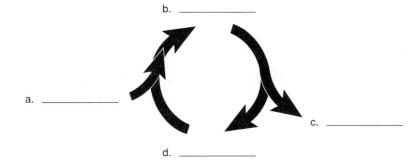

b. _____

a. _____

c. _____

d. _____

4. Label each of the following as pertaining to the left (L) or right (R) side of the diagram. Explain your choice.
   _____ a. aerobic respiration Explain: _____

   _____

   _____ b. muscle contraction Explain: _____

   _____

   _____ c. active transport Explain: _____

   _____

5. ATP is the common a._____ of cells; when cells require energy, they "spend" ATP. ATP breakdown provides energy for b._____ work, such as synthesizing macromolecules; c._____ work, such as pumping substances across plasma membranes; and d._____ work, such as the beating of flagella. Because ATP breakdown is e._____ to endergonic reactions, energy transformation occurs with minimal loss to the cell.

• Cells have metabolic pathways in which every reaction has a specific enzyme.

6. Consider the following diagram of a metabolic pathway:

$$E_1 \quad E_2 \quad E_3 \quad E_4 \quad E_5 \quad E_6$$
$$A \rightarrow B \rightarrow C \rightarrow D \rightarrow E \rightarrow F \rightarrow G$$

A–F are a._____ and B–G are b._____. E_1–E_6 are c._____. A is

a d._____ for the first enzyme and B is the product.

7. Enzymes a._____ the energy of activation. What is the "energy of activation?" b._____

Enzyme-Substrate Complexes (p. 104)

• Enzymes speed reactions because they have an active site where a specific reaction occurs.
• Environmental factors like temperature and pH affect the activity of enzymes.
• Inhibition of enzymes is a common way for cells to control enzyme activity.

8. Label this diagram using the following terms:
   active site
   enzyme (used more than once)
   enzyme-substrate complex
   products
   substrate

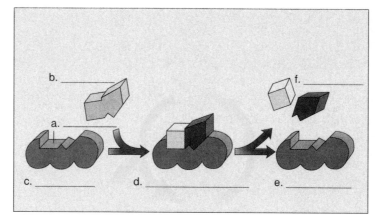

9. Use letters only (rather than a diagram) to show the reaction in question 8. a._____

Is the reaction shown in question 8 a synthetic reaction or a degradative reaction? b._____

How do you know? c._____

The enzyme-substrate complex and the reaction occur at the d._____ site of the enzyme. What is the

significance of using the label "enzyme" twice in the diagram? It shows that e._____

_____

Why are enzymes named for their substrate (e.g., maltase speeds the breakdown of maltose)? f._____

_____

10. Complete each statement with the term *increases* or *decreases*.

Raising the temperature generally ^{a.}_____ the rate of an enzymatic reaction.

Boiling an enzyme drastically ^{b.}_____ the rate of the reaction.

Changing the pH toward the optimum pH for an enzyme ^{c.}_____ the rate of the reaction.

Introducing a competitive inhibitor ^{d.}_____ the availability of an enzyme for its normal substrate.

Due to feedback inhibition, the affinity of the active site for the substrate ^{e.}_____.

11. Enzymes have helpers called ^{a.}_____, which ^{b.}_____

_____

6.4 METABOLIC PATHWAYS AND LIVING THINGS (P. 107)

- Photosynthesis and cellular respiration are metabolic pathways that allow a flow of energy through all living things.

12. Label each of the following as pertaining to aerobic respiration (AR) and/or photosynthesis (P):

_____ a. mitochondria
_____ b. chloroplasts
_____ c. breakdown of carbohydrate by oxidation of glucose
_____ d. synthesis of carbohydrate by reduction of carbon dioxide
_____ e. high-energy electrons pass down an electron transport system, and ATP is produced
_____ f. ATP is utilized to reduce carbon dioxide
_____ g. NADH carries high-energy electrons to the electron transport system
_____ h. solar energy energizes electrons
_____ i. NADPH is utilized to reduce carbon dioxide

13. Trace the energy content of ATP to the sun by arranging these statements in the proper order. _____
    a. Carbohydrates are broken down during cellular respiration.
    b. Solar energy is needed for photosynthesis.
    c. Cellular respiration produces ATP molecules.
    d. Carbohydrates are end products of photosynthesis.

14. Examine this diagram on chemiosmosis and then complete the sentences.

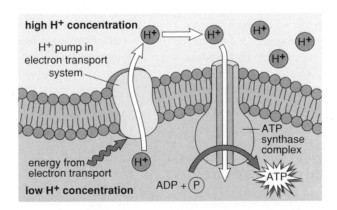

As electrons are passed from carrier to carrier within the electron transport system, energy is released, and some of this is used to ^{a.}_____ hydrogen ions across a membrane. A high H^+ ^{b.}_____ builds up. When H^+ flows down this gradient through a channel in a protein, the energy released is used to form ^{c.}_____ from ^{d.}_____.

Review key terms by completing this crossword puzzle, using the following alphabetized list of terms:

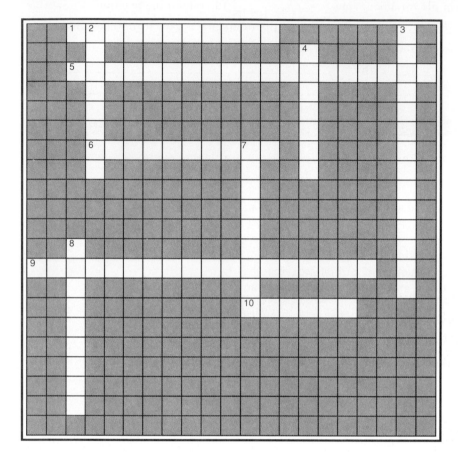

active site
coenzyme
denatured
electron transport
enzyme
feedback inhibition
metabolism
photosynthesis
substrate
vitamin

Across

1   that part of an enzyme molecule where the substrate fits and the chemical reaction occurs (two words)

5   process by which a substance, often an end product of a reaction or a metabolic pathway, controls its own continued production by binding with the enzyme that produced it (two words)

6   all of the chemical reactions that occur in a cell during growth and repair

9   system whereby electrons are passed along a series of carrier molecules, releasing energy for the synthesis of ATP (two words)

10 organic catalyst, usually a protein molecule, that speeds chemical reactions in living systems

Down

2   nonprotein organic part of an enzyme structure, often with a vitamin as a subpart

3   process usually occurring within chloroplasts whereby chlorophyll traps solar energy, and carbon dioxide is reduced to a carbohydrate

4   organic molecule that is required in small quantities for various biological processes and that must be in an organism's diet because the organism cannot synthesize it; becomes part of coenzyme structure

7   reactant in an enzymatic reaction; each enzyme has a specific one

8   condition of an enzyme when its shape is changed so that its active site cannot bind substrate molecules

OBJECTIVE QUESTIONS

Do not refer to the text when taking this test.

_____ 1. The useful energy conversion in photosynthesis is
   a. chemical to solar.
   b. heat to mechanical.
   c. mechanical to heat.
   d. solar to chemical.

_____ 2. Any energy transformation involves the loss of some energy as
   a. electricity.
   b. heat.
   c. light.
   d. motion.

_____ 3. In the enzymatically-controlled chemical reaction A → B + C, A is the
   a. cofactor.
   b. enzyme.
   c. product.
   d. substrate.

_____ 4. An enzyme, functioning best at a pH of 3, is in a neutral solution at a temperature of 40°C. Its activity will increase by
   a. decreasing the amount of substrate.
   b. denaturing the enzyme.
   c. increasing the temperature 10 more degrees.
   d. making the pH more acidic.

_____ 5. In the reaction A + B → C, the reaction rate may slow down through feedback inhibition by
   a. increasing the concentration of A.
   b. increasing the concentration of B.
   c. increasing the concentration of C.
   d. decreasing the concentration of B.

_____ 6. The energy laws
   a. account for why energy does not cycle.
   b. say that some loss of energy always accompanies transformation.
   c. say that energy can be made available to living things.
   d. All of these are correct.

_____ 7. In a metabolic pathway,
   a. A, B, C, and D are substrates.
   b. B, C, D, and E are products.
   c. each reaction requires its own enzyme.
   d. All of these are correct.

_____ 8. The enzyme-substrate complex
   a. indicates that an enzyme has denatured.
   b. accounts for why enzymes lower the energy of activation.
   c. is nonspecific.
   d. All of these are correct.

_____ 9. The tendency for an ordered system to become spontaneously disordered is called
   a. thermodynamics.
   b. entropy.
   c. activation.
   d. energy conversion.

_____10. A coupled reaction occurs when energy released from a(n) _____ reaction is used to drive a(n) _____ reaction.
   a. endergonic; exergonic
   b. breakdown; exergonic
   c. exergonic; endergonic
   d. chemical; mechanical

_____11. NAD^+ and FAD are
   a. dehydrogenases.
   b. proteins.
   c. coenzymes.
   d. Both _a_ and _c_ are correct.

_____12. NADH takes electrons to
   a. ATP.
   b. NADPH.
   c. the electron transport system.
   d. All of these are correct.

_____13. The electron transport system is properly associated with
   a. the production of ATP.
   b. chemiosmosis.
   c. both aerobic respiration and photosynthesis.
   d. All of these are correct.

_____14. ATP is used for
   a. chemical work
   b. transport work
   c. mechanical work
   d. All of these are correct.

_____15. The hydrogen ions that flow across the inner mitochondrial membrane are coupled to the formation of
   a. enzymes.
   b. carbohydrate.
   c. acids.
   d. ATP.

_____16. Which statement is NOT correct about enzymes?
   a. They usually end in the suffix "-ase."
   b. They catalyze only one reaction.
   c. They increase the energy of activation.
   d. They bind temporarily with the substrate.

_____17. Which of these is NOT expected to increase the rate of an enzymatic reaction?
   a. add more enzyme
   b. remove inhibitions
   c. boil rapidly
   d. adjust the pH to optimum level

____18. Which of these will result in a larger supply of ATP for an animal?
  a. muscle contraction
  b. basking in the sun
  c. increased activity of the electron transport system
  d. inhibiting the ATP synthase complex
____19. Since energy does not cycle, animal cells
  a. require a continuing source of glucose.

  b. are dependent on plant cells.
  c. must produce ATP nonstop.
  d. All of these are correct.
____20. Synthetic reactions
  a. require the participation of ATP.
  b. do not require enzymes.
  c. are represented by S + E → ES → P.
  d. are coupled directly to glucose breakdown.

CRITICAL THINKING QUESTIONS

Answer in complete sentences.
21. Why couldn't life exist without a continual supply of solar energy?

22. Why are enzymes absolutely necessary to the continued existence of a cell?

Test Results: _____ Number right ÷ 22 = _____ × 100 = _____ %

EXPLORING THE INTERNET

Use the Internet to further explore topics in this chapter, such as the properties of enzymes, or to quiz yourself about enzymes. Go to the Mader Home Page (http://www.mhhe.com/sciencemath/biology/mader/) and click on *Biology,* 6th edition. Go to Chapter 6 and select a Web site of interest.

ANSWER KEY

STUDY EXERCISES

1. a. F The chemical energy of ATP can be transformed into other types of energy such as kinetic energy (muscle contraction). b. F Cells transform the energy of glucose breakdown into ATP molecules and they do obey the first law of thermodynamics. c. T d. F Because our society uses coal as an energy source, it is increasing the entropy of the universe. 2. a. EX b. EN c. EX d. EX e. EN 3. a. +P b. ATP c. –P d. ADP 4. a. L, because during aerobic respiration the chemical energy within a glucose molecule is converted to the chemical energy within ATP. b. R, because when muscles contract, the chemical energy within ATP is converted to the kinetic energy of muscle contraction. c. R, because when active transport occurs, the energy released by ATP break-down is used to pump a molecule across the plasma membrane. 5. a. energy currency b. chemical c. transport d. mechanical e. coupled 6. a. reactants b. products c. enzymes d. substrate 7. a. lower b. energy that must be added to cause molecules to react with one another. 8. a. active site b. substrate c. enzyme d. enzyme-substrate complex e. enzyme f. products 9. a. E + S → ES → E + P b. degradative c. The reactant is broken down. d. active e. The enzyme is not broken down and can be used over and over again. f. Enzymes are specific to their substrate. 10. a. increases b. decreases c. increases d. decreases e. decreases 11. a. coenzymes b. help enzymes function. 12. a. AR b. P c. AR d. P e. AR, P f. P g. AR h. P i. P 13. b d a c 14. a. pump b. concentration c. ATP d. ADP +Ⓟ.

Crossword answers:

1. ACTIVE SITE
2. COENZYME
3. PHOTOSYNTHESIS
4. VITAMIN
5. FEEDBACK INHIBITION
6. METABOLISM
7. SUBSTRATE
8. DENATURED
9. ELECTRON TRANSPORT
10. ENZYME

1. d **2.** b **3.** d **4.** d 5. c **6.** d **7.** d **8.** b **9.** b **10.** c **11.** d **12.** c **13.** d **14.** d **15.** d **16.** c **17.** c **18.** c **19.** d **20.** a **21.** When chloroplasts carry on photosynthesis, solar energy is converted to the energy of carbohydrates; and when mitochondria complete aerobic respiration, the energy stored in carbohydrates is converted to energy temporarily held by ATP. The energy released by ATP breakdown is used by the cell to do various types of work, and eventually it becomes nonusable heat.   **22.** Enzymes are absolutely essential for the existence of a cell because they lower the energy of activation of a reaction, thereby requiring less heat to bring about the reaction. At high temperatures, proteins would denature.

7

PHOTOSYNTHESIS

Photosynthesis provides food for living organisms and replenishes oxygen in the atmosphere. Photosynthesis utilizes the portion of the electromagnetic spectrum known as visible light. **Chlorophyll**—both chlorophyll *a* and chlorophyll *b*—absorbs violet, blue, and red light better than light of other colors. These pigments are present in the **thylakoid** membrane within the **grana** or **chloroplasts.** They participate in the so-called **light-dependent reactions.**

The light-dependent reactions involve a cyclic electron pathway and a noncyclic electron pathway. Only **photosystem I** is required for the cyclic electron pathway, in which electrons energized by the sun leave the reaction-center chlorophyll *a* and then pass down an **electron transport system** with the concomitant buildup of ATP before returning to chlorophyll *a*. In the noncyclic electron pathway, energized electrons leave chlorophyll *a* of **photosystem II,** pass down an electron transport system, and enter photosystem I, where they are energized once more before being accepted by NADPH. The overall result from the noncyclic pathway is the production of NADPH and ATP. Oxygen is also liberated when water is split and electrons enter chlorophyll *a* (photosystem II) to replace those lost. The NADPH and ATP from the light-dependent reactions of photosynthesis are used to build a carbohydrate in the **light-independent reactions,** which occur in the **stroma** of chloroplasts.

ATP production during the light-dependent reactions requires chemiosmosis. Hydrogen ions are concentrated in the thylakoid space; when water splits, it releases hydrogen ions, and carriers within the cytochrome complex of the electron transport system pump the hydrogen ions to the thylakoid space. The hydrogen ions flow down their concentration gradient through a channel in a protein having an ATP synthase, which forms ATP from ADP and $\textcircled{P}$.

The light-independent reactions occur during the **Calvin cycle:** carbon dioxide is fixed by **RuBP,** it is reduced to PGAL (this requires the ATP and NADPH from the light-dependent reactions), and RuBP is regenerated. One PGAL out of every six joins with another PGAL to form glucose-6-phosphate.

C_3 photosynthesis (the first molecule after fixation is a C_3 molecule) occurs when a plant uses the Calvin cycle directly. Plants have also evolved two other types of photosynthesis: C_4 photosynthesis and **CAM** photosynthesis. C_4 plants fix carbon dioxide in mesophyll cells (which results in a C_4 molecule) and then transport it to bundle sheath cells, where it enters the Calvin cycle. CAM plants fix carbon dioxide at night and then release it during the day to the Calvin cycle. C_4 and CAM photosynthesis are adaptations to hot, dry environments, since these processes allow the stomates to close to conserve water.

STUDY QUESTIONS

Study the text section by section as you answer the questions that follow.

7.1 SUNLIGHT PROVIDES SOLAR ENERGY (P. 114)

- Plants make use of solar energy in the visible light range when they carry on photosynthesis.

1. Indicate whether the following statements about the importance of photosynthesis are true (T) or false (F):
   _____ a. It makes food for animals.
   _____ b. It promotes the breakdown of biodegradable wastes.
   _____ c. It returns carbon dioxide to the atmosphere.
   _____ d. It returns oxygen to the atmosphere.

2. Indicate whether the following statements about solar energy are true (T) or false (F):

_____ a. Chlorophylls *a* and *b* absorb violet, blue, and red light best.

_____ b. Photons of visible light energize electrons without harming cells.

_____ c. Photosynthesis uses infrared light efficiently in the daytime.

_____ d. Photosynthesis uses ultraviolet light efficiently at night.

7.2 PHOTOSYNTHESIS OCCURS IN CHLOROPLASTS (P. 116)

- Photosynthesis takes place in chloroplasts, organelles that contain membranous thylakoids surrounded by a fluid-filled stroma.
- Photosynthesis has two sets of reactions: solar energy is captured by the pigments in thylakoids, and carbon dioxide is reduced by enzymes in the stroma.

3. Photosynthesis refers to the ability of plants, algae, and a few kinds of bacteria to make their own a._____ in the presence of b._____. In plants, photosynthesis is carried on in c._____.

4. The green pigment a._____ is found within the membrane of the b._____, and it is here that c._____ energy is captured.

5. A chloroplast contains flattened, membranous sacs called a._____ that are stacked like poker chips into b._____. The fluid-filled space surrounding the grana is called the c._____.

6. Label this diagram of a chloroplast using the following terms:

   granum
   stroma
   thylakoid

7. From the diagram in question 6, the light-dependent reactions would be associated with the a._____, and the light-independent reactions would be associated with the b._____.

a.

b.

c.

8. The light-dependent reactions drive the light-independent reactions. The light-independent reactions use the NADPH and a._____ from the light-dependent reactions to reduce b._____ to a c._____.

9. Label each of the following as either light-dependent (LD) or light-independent (LI) reactions:

_____ a. energy-capturing reactions

_____ b. synthesis reactions

_____ c. carbon dioxide becomes carbohydrate

_____ d. water gives off oxygen

_____ e. NADPH and ATP are made

_____ f. NADPH and ATP are used

7.3 SOLAR ENERGY IS CAPTURED (P. 118)

- Solar energy energizes electrons that enter an electron transport system, releasing energy as electrons pass from one carrier to the next.

10. The thylakoid membrane has two light-gathering units called a._____ and b._____. Within each unit are green pigments called c._____ and yellow-orange pigments called d._____.

11. Label this diagram of the cyclic electron
    pathway with the following terms:
    ADP
    ATP
    electron acceptor
    light-dependent reactions
    photosystem I
    pigment complex

12. Label this diagram of the noncyclic electron
    pathway with the following terms (some are
    used more than once):
    electron acceptor (used twice)
    electron transport system
    light-dependent reactions
    light-independent reactions
    photosystem I
    photosystem II

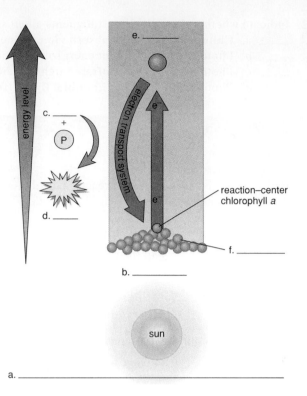

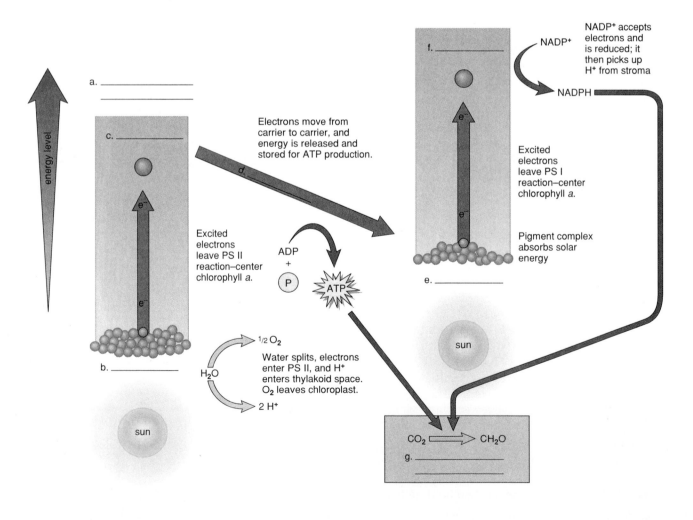

13. What is the role of each of these in the noncyclic electron pathway?

reaction-center chlorophyll *a* a. _____

_____

electron acceptors b. _____

_____

NADP⁺ c. _____

_____

electron transport system d. _____

_____

water e. _____

_____

_____

_____

Production ATP (p. 120)

- Chemiosmosis depends on an electrochemical gradient that the electron transport system establishes.

14. The concentration of H⁺ in the a._____ space is b._____, compared to the lower H⁺ concentration in the c._____. The flow of H⁺ down its concentration gradient provides the energy for an enzyme called d._____ to produce e._____ from ADP + Ⓟ.

The Thylakoid Membrane (p. 120)

15. Match the complexes in the thylakoid membrane with the following functions:
    1 produces ATP from ADP + Ⓟ
    2 transports electrons and stores H⁺ in the thylakoid space
    3 captures solar energy water is split, releasing electrons and oxygen
    4 captures solar energy; NADP⁺ is reduced to NADPH
    _____ a. photosystem II
    _____ b. cytochrome complex
    _____ c. photosystem I
    _____ d. ATP synthase complex

7.4 CARBOHYDRATE IS SYNTHESIZED (P. 121)

- Carbon dioxide reduction requires energized electrons and ATP.

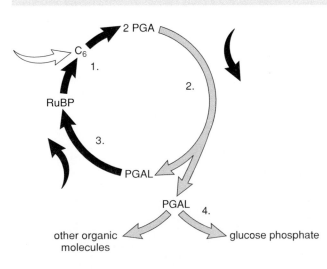

16. Match the numbers in the diagram to the following descriptions of events in the Calvin cycle (some numbers are used more than once):
    _____ a. ATP only required
    _____ b. CO_2 reduction reaction
    _____ c. NADPH and ATP required
    _____ d. CO_2 taken up, CO_2 fixation
    _____ e. glucose formed after six turns of cycle
    _____ f. five PGAL required to form three molecules of product

17. Rearrange the letters to indicate the order that the molecules appear during or as a result of the Calvin cycle. _____

   a. CO_2
   b. glucose phosphate
   c. PGA
   d. PGAL
   e. starch

Photosynthesis Takes Other Routes (p. 124)

• Plants use either C_3, C_4, or CAM photosynthesis, which are distinguishable by the manner in which CO_2 is fixed.

18. Label the following as describing C_3, C_4, and/or CAM plants:
   _____ a. predominate in spring and cooler summer weather
   _____ b. PEPCase
   _____ c. succulent plants, cacti; live in hot, arid regions
   _____ d. what, rice, oats
   _____ e. predominate in hot, dry summer weather
   _____ f. product of CO_2 fixation is PGA
   _____ g. CO_2 fixation occurs at night and C_4 molecules are stored until daylight
   _____ h. photorespiration occurs
   _____ i. stomates are closed *during the day* to conserve water
   _____ j. end product of CO_2 fixation is oxaloacetate
   _____ k. sugarcane, corn, Bermuda grass
   _____ l. chloroplasts only in mesophyll cells
   _____ m. chloroplasts in bundle sheath cells and mesophyll

Photosynthesis: A Play in Two Acts

Photosynthesis, which is now playing in chloroplasts, has two acts. The first act is the light-dependent reactions, and the second act is the light-independent reactions. The theater has a revolving stage of two parts, shown in the diagram.

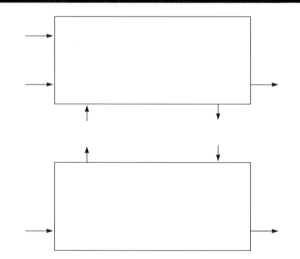

1. Place these "props" on the correct "stage": grana (thylakoids) and stoma.
2. Place these "props" on the correct "stage": Calvin cycle, energy-capturing reactions, and synthesis reactions.
3. Place these "props" on the correct "stage": chlorophyll and RuBP.
4. Certain actors/actresses walk on during either the first act or the second act (not both acts), and certain others walk off during either the first act or the second act. Entrances and exits are represented by the arrows. Show where the following "actresses/actors" either walk on or walk off: CO_2, H_2O, light, O_2, and PGAL.
5. Certain actors/actresses are in the first act, but then they change their costumes and move to the second act. Naturally, they have to get ready again for the first act. Movement of these actors/actresses are indicated by arrows between the acts. Show where the following "actresses/actors" belong: ADP, ATP, $NADP^+$, and NADPH.

Review key terms by completing this crossword puzzle, using the following alphabetized list of terms:

C_3 plant
C_4 plant
CAM plant
chlorophyll
chloroplast
granum
light-dependent
light-independent
photon
photosystem
RuBP
stroma
thylakoid
visible light

Across

3 plant that directly uses the Calvin cycle; the first detected molecule during photosynthesis is PGA, a three-carbon molecule (two words)

5 portion of the electromagnetic spectrum of light that can be seen with the human eye (two words)

7 green pigment that absorbs solar energy and is important in photosynthesis

11 discrete packet of solar energy; the amount of energy is inversely related to the wavelength

12 flattened sac within a granum whose membrane contains the photosynthetic pigments (e.g., chlorophyll); where the light-dependent reactions occur

Down

1 plant that fixes carbon dioxide at night to produce a C_4 molecule that releases carbon dioxide to the Calvin cycle during the day (two words)

2 photosynthetic unit where solar energy is absorbed; contains an antenna (photosynthetic pigments) and an electron acceptor

3 plant that fixes carbon dioxide in bundle sheath cells to produce a molecule that releases carbon dioxide to the Calvin cycle in mesophyll (two words)

4 set of photosynthetic reactions that does not directly require solar energy; it uses the products of the light-dependent reactions to reduce carbon dioxide to a carbohydrate (two words)

6 stack of chlorophyll-containing thylakoids in a chloroplast

7 membrane-bounded organelle with chlorophyll-containing membranous grana; where photosynthesis takes place

8 five-carbon compound that combines with and fixes carbon dioxide during the Calvin cycle and is later regenerated by the same cycle

9 set of photosynthetic reactions that requires solar energy to proceed; it produces ATP and NADPH (two words)

10 large, central space in a chloroplast that is fluid filled and contains enzymes used in photosynthesis

OBJECTIVE QUESTIONS

Do not refer to the text when taking this test. In questions 1–6, match the terms with the following definitions:

a. organic product of photosynthesis
b. released by photosynthesis
c. reactant of photosynthesis
d. site of light-dependent reactions
e. site of light-independent reactions
f. molecule-absorbing solar energy

_____ 1. chlorophyll
_____ 2. oxygen
_____ 3. stroma
_____ 4. sugar
_____ 5. thylakoid membrane
_____ 6. water

_____ 7. Each of the following is a product of photosynthesis EXCEPT
a. carbon dioxide.
b. organic food.
c. oxygen.
d. carbohydrate.

_____ 8. Photosynthesis occurs best at wavelengths that are
a. blue.
b. gamma.
c. infrared.
d. ultraviolet.

_____ 9. Each is a product of light-dependent reactions EXCEPT
a. ATP.
b. NADPH.
c. oxygen.
d. sugar.

_____ 10. The cyclic pathways of photosynthesis produce
a. ATP only.
b. NADPH only.
c. ATP and NADPH.
d. organic sugars only.

_____ 11. Carbon dioxide fixation occurs when CO_2 combines with
a. ATP.
b. NADPH.
c. PGAL.
d. RuBP.

_____ 12. Which of the following pathways uses the enzyme PEPCase?
a. C_2
b. C_3
c. CAM
d. CAP

_____ 13. The enzyme that produces ATP from ADP + P in the thylakoid is
a. RuBP carboxylase.
b. rubisco.
c. ATPase.
d. ATP synthase.
e. coenzyme A.

_____ 14. Which statement is NOT true regarding chemiosmosis?
a. H^+ concentration is higher in the stroma than in the thylakoid space.
b. The electron transport system pumps H^+ from the stroma into the thylakoid space.
c. The ATP synthase complex is present in the thylakoid membrane.
d. All of these are true.

_____ 15. Which of the following is NOT a stage in the Calvin cycle?
a. carbon dioxide fixation
b. carbon dioxide oxidation
c. carbon dioxide reduction
d. ribulose bisphosphate regeneration

_____ 16. Which of these descriptions is NOT true of photosynthesis?
a. not affected by temperature
b. not affected by solar energy
c. requires a supply of oxygen
d. involves a reduction reaction
e. more likely to occur during the day

_____ 17. Which of these descriptions is NOT true of chlorophyll?
a. absorbs solar energy
b. located in the grana
c. located in thylakoid membranes
d. passes electrons directly to $NADP^+$
e. passes electrons to an acceptor molecule

_____ 18. The two major sets of reactions involved in photosynthesis are
a. the cyclic and noncyclic electron pathways.
b. glycolysis and the Krebs cycle.
c. the Calvin and Krebs cycles.
d. the Calvin cycle and the electron transport system.
e. the light-dependent and light-independent reactions.

_____ 19. Which of the following statements is NOT true of the Calvin cycle?
a. RuBP is regenerated with the use of ATP.
b. Glucose phosphate is synthesized from PGAL.
c. NADPH is used to reduce PGAL to PGA.
d. Five molecules of PGAL are used to reform three molecules of RuBP.

_____20. Photosystem II gets replacement electrons from
a. the sun.
b. water molecules.

c. ATP.
d. photosystem I.
e. NADPH.

CRITICAL THINKING QUESTIONS

Answer in complete sentences.

21. How is life dependent on photosynthesis?

22. Why is photosynthesis dependent on the high degree of compartmentalization in cells?

Test Results: _____ Number right ÷ 22 = _____ × 100 = _____ %

EXPLORING THE INTERNET

Use the Internet to further explore topics in this chapter, such as photosynthesis, from a variety of viewpoints. Go to the Mader Home Page (http://www.mhhe.com/sciencemath/biology/mader/) and click on *Biology,* 6th edition. Go to Chapter 7 and select a Web site of interest.

ANSWER KEY

STUDY EXERCISES

1. a. T **b.** F **c.** F **d.** T **2. a.** T **b.** T **c.** F **d.** F **3. a.** food **b.** sunlight **c.** chloroplasts **4. a.** chlorophyll **b.** thylakoids **c.** solar **5. a.** thylakoids **b.** grana **c.** stroma **6. a.** thylakoid **b.** stroma **c.** granum **7. a.** thylakoid and granum **b.** stroma **8. a.** ATP **b.** carbon dioxide **c.** carbohydrate **9. a.** LD **b.** LI **c.** LI **d.** LD **e.** LD **f.** LI **10. a.** photosystem I **b.** photosystem II **c.** chlorophyll **d.** carotenoids **11. a.** light-dependent reactions **b.** photosystem I **c.** ADP **d.** ATP **e.** electron acceptor **f.** pigment complex **12. a.** light-dependent reactions **b.** photosystem II **c.** electron acceptor **d.** electron transport system **e.** photosystem I **f.** electron acceptor **g.** light-independent reactions. **13. a.** releases electrons that become excited from solar energy **b.** accepts energized electrons from the reaction-center chlorophyll *a* and sends them to the electron transport system **c.** accepts electrons and hydrogen and becomes NADPH **d.** stores energy as the electrons fall to a lower energy level **e.** splits releasing oxygen and hydrogen ions **14. a.** thylakoid **b.** higher **c.** stroma **d.** ATP synthase **e.** ATP **15. a.** 3 **b.** 2 **c.** 4 **d.** 1 **16. a.** 2, 3 **b.** 2 **c.** 2 **d.** 1 **e.** 4 **f.** 3 **17.** a, c, d, b, e **18. a.** C_3 **b.** C_4, CAM **c.** CAM **d.** C_3 **e.** C_4 **f.** C_3 **g.** CAM **h.** C_3 **i.** CAM **j.** C_4 **k.** C_4 **l.** C_3 **m.** C_4

PHOTOSYNTHESIS: A PLAY IN TWO ACTS

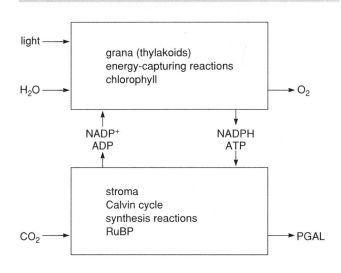

1. f **2.** b **3.** e **4.** a **5.** d **6.** c **7.** a **8.** a **9.** d **10.** a **11.** d **12.** c **13.** d **14.** a **15.** b **16.** c **17.** d **18.** e **19.** c **20.** b **21.** Through photosynthesis, plants (and algae) produce food for themselves and all other living things. These organisms are the producers at the start of food chains of all types. Animals feed directly on photosynthesizers or on other animals that have fed on photosynthesizers. **22.** Chemiosmosis cannot occur without a membrane that maintains a difference in hydrogen ion concentration. In plant cells, hydrogen ions build up within the thylakoid space and then they flow down their concentration gradient through an ATP synthase complex located in the thylakoid membrane.

8

CELLULAR RESPIRATION

Cellular respiration includes aerobic respiration and fermentation. **Aerobic respiration,** the oxidation of glucose to carbon dioxide and water, is an exergonic reaction that drives ATP synthesis, an endergonic reaction. Oxidation involves the removal of hydrogen atoms ($H^+ + e^-$) from substrate molecules, usually by the coenzyme NAD^+, but in one case by FAD. Four events are required: glycolysis, the transition reaction, the Krebs cycle, and the electron transport system.

During **glycolysis,** glucose is converted to pyruvate in the cytosol. Glycolysis produces two ATP by substrate-level phosphorylation. When oxygen is available, pyruvate from glycolysis enters mitochondria. In mitochondria, the **transition reaction** and the **Krebs cycle** are located in the matrix, and the electron transport system is located on the cristae. Both the transition reaction and the Krebs cycle release carbon dioxide as a result of oxidation of carbohydrate breakdown products.

The electrons carried by NADH and $FADH_2$ enter the **electron transport system.** The electrons pass down a chain of carriers until they are finally received by oxygen, which combines with H^+ forming water. As electrons pass down the electron transport system, energy is released and stored for ATP production. The term oxidative phosphorylation is sometimes used for 34 ATPs produced as a result of the electron transport system. The protein complexes of the electron transport system pump H^+ received from NADH and $FADH_2$ into the intermembrane space, setting up an electrochemical gradient. When H^+ flows down this gradient through the ATP synthase complex, energy is released and used to form ATP. This process of producing ATP is called **chemiosmosis.**

Other carbohydrates, as well as protein and fat, can also generate ATP by entering various steps in the degradative paths of glycolysis and the Krebs cycle. These pathways also provide metabolites needed for the synthesis of various important cellular substances.

Fermentation, which occurs when oxygen is not available for aerobic respiration, involves glycolysis followed by the reduction of pyruvate by NADH. The end product can be lactate or alcohol and carbon dioxide. Fermentation produces a net yield of 2 ATP molecules per glucose molecule. Fermentation provides a quick, immediate source of ATP, but lactate build-up is toxic to the cell and creates an **oxygen debt** by the organism.

STUDY EXERCISES

Study the text section by section as you answer the questions that follow.

8.1 HOW CELLS ACQUIRE ATP (P. 130)

- During cellular respiration, the breakdown of glucose drives the synthesis of ATP.
- The coenzymes NAD^+ and FAD accept electrons from substrates and carry them to the electron transport system in mitochondria.

1. Consider the following equation.

$$C_6H_{12}O_6 + 6\,O_2 \rightarrow 6\,H_2O + 6\,CO_2 + energy$$

The molecule glucose is (oxidized or reduced) a._____ while oxygen is (oxidized or reduced)

b._____. This is an (endergonic or exergonic) c._____ reaction and therefore is used by

cells to build up ATP.

2. Complete the adjacent diagram and answer these questions:

The (left or right) e._____ side of the diagram represents oxidation and the (left or right) f._____ side of the diagram represents reduction of NAD. Why is NAD$^+$ called a coenzyme of oxidation-reduction?

g._____

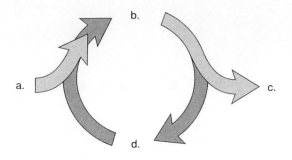

Metabolic Pathways Are Required (p. 131)

- Complete glucose breakdown involves metabolic pathways, and each reaction requires a specific enzyme.

3. Indicate whether the following statements pertain to glycolysis (GL), transition reaction (TR), Krebs cycle (KC), or the electron transport system (ETS). Some items require more than one answer.
   _____ a. Series of carriers that pass electrons from one to the other.
   _____ b. Cyclical series of oxidation reactions that release CO_2
   _____ c. Pyruvate is oxidized to an acetyl group.
   _____ d. Breakdown of glucose to two molecules of pyruvate.
   _____ e. Energy is released and stored for ATP production.
   _____ f. Occurs inside mitochondria.
   _____ g. Occurs outside the mitochondria in the cytosol.
   _____ h. Results in only 2 ATP.

8.2 OUTSIDE THE MITOCHONDRIA: GLYCOLYSIS (P. 132)

- Glycolysis, the breakdown of glucose to pyruvate, is a part of fermentation when oxygen is not available, or a part of aerobic respiration when oxygen is available.

4. Where does glycolysis occur? a._____

Does it require oxygen? b._____

Glycolysis begins with c._____.

Glycolysis ends with d._____.

How many ATP are produced per glucose molecule as a direct result of glycolysis? e._____

What type of phosphorylation occurs during glycolysis? f._____

What coenzyme carries out oxidation of substrates during glycolysis? g._____

Considering your answers to these questions, what is the output of glycolysis? h._____,

_____, and _____

When glycolysis is a part of fermentation what is end product in humans? i._____.

8.3 INSIDE THE MITOCHONDRIA: COMPLETION OF AEROBIC RESPIRATION (P. 134)

- Aerobic respiration continues inside the mitochondria where an electron transport system leads to most of the ATP production from glucose breakdown.

5. Label this diagram of a mitochondrion using the following terms:
   cristae
   cytosol
   inner membrane
   intermembrane space
   matrix
   outer membrane

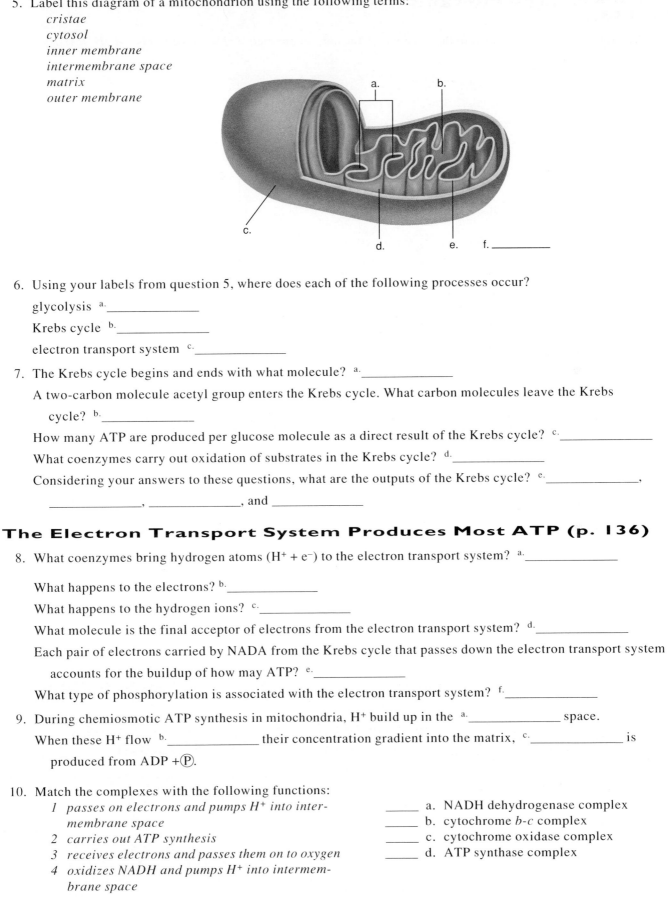

6. Using your labels from question 5, where does each of the following processes occur?

   glycolysis a._____

   Krebs cycle b._____

   electron transport system c._____

7. The Krebs cycle begins and ends with what molecule? a._____

   A two-carbon molecule acetyl group enters the Krebs cycle. What carbon molecules leave the Krebs

   cycle? b._____

   How many ATP are produced per glucose molecule as a direct result of the Krebs cycle? c._____

   What coenzymes carry out oxidation of substrates in the Krebs cycle? d._____

   Considering your answers to these questions, what are the outputs of the Krebs cycle? e._____,

   _____, _____, and _____

The Electron Transport System Produces Most ATP (p. 136)

8. What coenzymes bring hydrogen atoms ($H^+ + e^-$) to the electron transport system? a._____

   What happens to the electrons? b._____

   What happens to the hydrogen ions? c._____

   What molecule is the final acceptor of electrons from the electron transport system? d._____

   Each pair of electrons carried by NADA from the Krebs cycle that passes down the electron transport system

   accounts for the buildup of how may ATP? e._____

   What type of phosphorylation is associated with the electron transport system? f._____

9. During chemiosmotic ATP synthesis in mitochondria, H^+ build up in the a._____ space.

   When these H^+ flow b._____ their concentration gradient into the matrix, c._____ is

   produced from ADP +(P).

10. Match the complexes with the following functions:
    *1 passes on electrons and pumps H^+ into inter-
       membrane space*
    2 carries out ATP synthesis
    3 receives electrons and passes them on to oxygen
    *4 oxidizes NADH and pumps H^+ into intermem-
       brane space*

    _____ a. NADH dehydrogenase complex
    _____ b. cytochrome *b-c* complex
    _____ c. cytochrome oxidase complex
    _____ d. ATP synthase complex

Calculating the Energy Yield from Glucose Metabolism (p. 138)

11. In the following diagram, fill in the blanks with the correct numbers and with the terms *NADH, FADH₂,* and *ATP:*

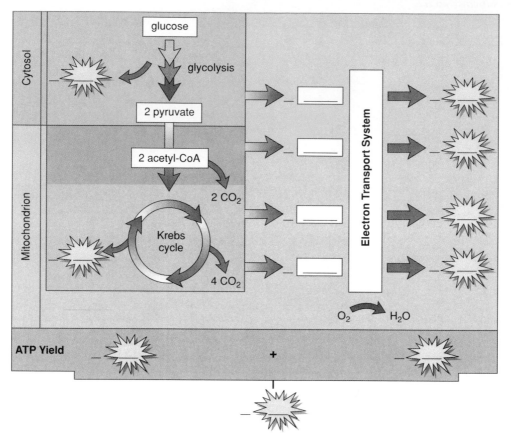

8.4 METABOLIC POOL AND BIOSYNTHESIS (p. 139)

• A number of metabolites in addition to glucose can be broken down to drive ATP synthesis.

12. The carbon skeleton of amino acids can be respired if the amino acid first undergoes ᵃ·_____.
When fats are respired, glycerol is converted to ᵇ·_____, fatty acids are converted to the two-carbon
molecule ᶜ·_____, and the acetyl group enters the Krebs cycle. Excess acetyl groups from glucose
metabolism can be used to build up fat. Explain why the consumption of carbohydrate makes us fat. ᵈ· ____

8.5 FERMENTATION (p. 141)

• Fermentation is a metabolic pathway that partially breaks down glucose under anaerobic conditions.

13. What happens to pyruvate during fermentation? in humans ᵃ·_____ in yeast ᵇ·_____
Why is fermentation wasteful? ᶜ·_____
What is its advantage? ᵈ·_____
What is oxygen debt in humans? ᵉ·_____

14. Label the following processes I, II, and/or III, based on this pyruvate diagram:

_____ a. occurs under anaerobic conditions
_____ b. fermentation
_____ c. glycolysis
_____ d. transition reaction

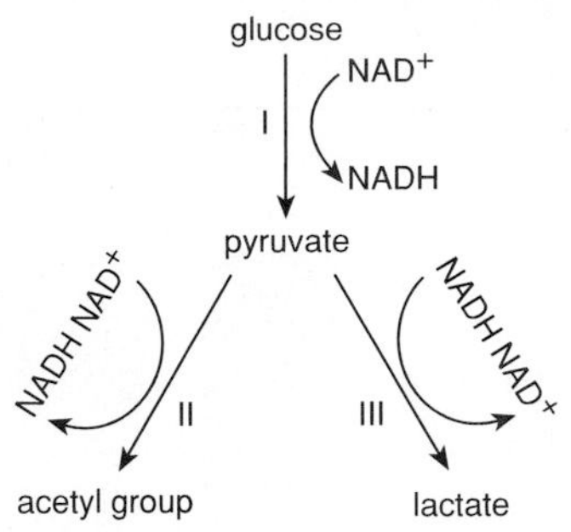

15. Consider III in the diagram for question 17.

Which has more hydrogen atoms, pyruvate or lactate? a._____

In yeast, the product for this reaction is b._____.

What happens to NAD^+ produced by the reaction? c._____

16. Consider II in the diagram for question 17.

What happens to NADH? a._____

What happens to the acetyl group? b._____

glucose
I
NAD^+
NADH
pyruvate
NADH NAD^+
NADH NAD^+
II
III
acetyl group
lactate

On the table before you are three locations to place a bet. These locations are labeled:

G	K	E
Glycolysis	**Krebs cycle**	**Electronic Transport System**

You can place a chip on more than one of these locations. For every chip properly paced, you would hypothetically win $5.00. Place your bets! Where should you place (a) chip(s) for each of the following:

_____ 1. occurs in cytoplasm
_____ 2. occurs in mitochondrion
_____ 3. glucose
_____ 4. oxygen
_____ 5. carbon dioxide
_____ 6. NADH produced
_____ 7. NADH received
_____ 8. water produced
_____ 9. 2 ATP
_____ 10. 32 ATP
_____ 11. product from transition reaction enters here
_____ 12. How much money did you win?

Review the key terms by completing this crossword puzzle, using the following alphabetized list of terms:

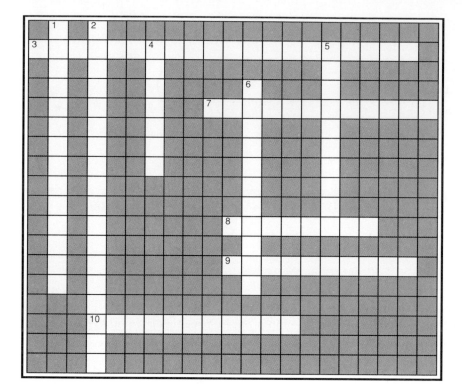

acetyl-CoA
aerobic
cellular respiration
electron transport
fermentation
glycolysis
Krebs cycle
metabolic pool
oxygen debt
pyruvate

Across

3   metabolic reactions that use the energy from carbohydrate or fatty acid or amino acid oxidation to produce ATP molecules; incudes fermentation and aerobic respiration (two words)

7   anaerobic breakdown of glucose that results in two ATP and products such as alcohol and lactate

8   end product of glycolysis; its further fate, involving fermentation or entry into a mitochondrion, depends on oxygen availability

9   pathway of metabolism converting glucose to pyruvate; resulting in a net gain of two ATP and two NADH molecules

10 use of oxygen to metabolize lactate, which builds up due to anaerobic conditions (two words)

Down

1   metabolites that are the products of and/or the substrates for key reactions in cells, allowing one type of molecule to be changed into another type, such as the conversion of carbohydrates to fats (two words)

2   type of system whereby electrons are passed along a series of carrier molecules, releasing energy for the synthesis of ATP (two words)

4   type of process that requires oxygen

5   molecule made up of a two-carbon acetyl group attached to coenzyme A; the acetyl group enters the Krebs cycle for further oxidation (two words)

6   cycle of reactions in mitochondria that begins and ends with citric acid; produces CO_2, ATP, NADH, and $FADH_2$, also called the citric acid cycle (two words)

Do not refer to the text when taking this test.

_____ 1. Fermentation is
   a. glycolysis and the Krebs cycle.
   b. glycolysis and the reduction of pyruvate.
   c. glycolysis only.
   d. the reduction of pyruvate only.

_____ 2. Each of the following is a product of aerobic respiration EXCEPT
   a. ATP.
   b. carbon dioxide.
   c. oxygen.
   d. water.

_____ 3. Per glucose molecule, the net gain of ATP molecules from glycolysis is
   a. two.
   b. four.
   c. six.
   d. eight.

_____ 4. Fermentation supplies
   a. glycolysis with free NAD^+.
   b. hydrogen to the transition reaction.
   c. oxygen as an electron acceptor.
   d. the Krebs cycle with oxygen.

_____ 5. The process that evolved first was
   a. chemiosmosis.
   b. glycolysis.
   c. the electron transport system.
   d. the Krebs cycle.

_____ 6. Which is NOT an event of the transition reaction?
   a. breaks down pyruvate
   b. converts a citrate molecule
   c. oxidizes pyruvate
   d. transfers an acetyl group

_____ 7. Select the incorrect association.
   a. electron transport system—cristae
   b. fermentation—plasma membrane
   c. glycolysis—cytosol
   d. Krebs cycle—matrix

_____ 8. Select the process with the greatest yield per glucose molecule.
   a. glycolysis
   b. Krebs cycle
   c. substrate-level phosphorylation
   d. transition reaction

_____ 9. The energy yield by ATP molecules per glucose molecule is closest to
   a. 25%.
   b. 40%.
   c. 50%.
   d. 60%.

_____10. Inside a cell, glycerol is broken down into
   a. amino acids.
   b. acetyl CoA.
   c. fatty acids.
   d. PGAL.

_____11. Which of the following reactions is NOT a part of aerobic respiration?
   a. glycolysis
   b. Krebs cycle
   c. electron transport system
   d. transition reaction
   e. fermentation

_____12. The coenzyme used in the transition reaction of aerobic respiration is
   a. ATP.
   b. NAD^+.
   c. NADH.
   d. coenzyme A.
   e. RuBP.

_____13. The carbon dioxide given off by aerobic respiration is produced by
   a. glycolysis.
   b. the transition reaction.
   c. the Krebs cycle.
   d. the electron transport system.
   e. Both _b_ and _c_ are correct.

_____14. The final acceptor for electrons in aerobic respiration is
   a. ATP.
   b. NAD^+.
   c. FAD.
   d. oxygen.
   e. carbon dioxide.

_____15. Which of the following reactions occurs on the inner membrane of mitochondria?
   a. the Krebs cycle
   b. the transition reaction
   c. the electron transport system
   d. glycolysis
   e. the Calvin cycle

_____16. The coenzymes NAD^+ and FAD carry hydrogen atoms $(H^+ + e^-)$ to the
   a. glycolysis reactions.
   b. transition reaction.
   c. Krebs cycle.
   d. Calvin cycle.
   e. electron transport system.

_____17. Which of the following statements is NOT true about fermentation?
   a. It is an anaerobic process.
   b. The end products are toxic to cells.
   c. It results in two ATPs per glucose molecule.
   d. In the absence of O_2, muscle cells form CO_2 and alcohol.
   e. It can be used to make bread rise.

_____18. Which of the following statements is NOT true regarding fats?
   a. Fatty acids are converted to acetyl-CoA.
   b. Eighteen-carbon fatty acids are converted to nine acetyl-CoA molecules.
   c. Glycerol is converted to PGAL.
   d. Fats are the least efficient form of stored energy.
   e. Carbohydrates can be converted to fats.

_____19. The process directly responsible for most of the ATP formed during aerobic respiration is
   a. the Krebs cycle.
   b. the transition reaction.
   c. the electron transport system.
   d. chemiosmosis.

_____20. A pathway that begins with glucose and ends with pyruvate is
   a. glycolysis.
   b. the Krebs cycle.
   c. the electron transport system.
   d. the transition reaction.

CRITICAL THINKING QUESTIONS

Answer in complete sentences.

21. Explain how the human body obtains the reactants for aerobic respiration and what happens to the products.

22. In what ways are cellular respiration and photosynthesis similar processes?

Test Results: _____ Number right ÷ 22 = _____ × 100 = _____ %

EXPLORING THE INTERNET

Use the Internet to further explore topics in this chapter, such as glycolysis or cell metabolism. Go to the Mader Home Page (http://www.mhhe.com/sciencemath/biology/mader/) and click on *Biology,* 6th edition. Go to Chapter 8 and select a Web site of interest.

ANSWER KEY

STUDY EXERCISES

1. **a.** oxidized **b.** reduced **c.** exergonic **2. a.** 2H **b.** NADH + H⁺ **c.** 2H **d.** NAD⁺ **e.** right **f.** left **g.** It becomes reduced when it accepts electrons from a substrate and becomes oxidized when it passes electrons on to another carrier. **3. a.** ETS **b.** KC **c.** TR **d.** GL **e.** ETS **f.** TR, KC, ETS **g.** GL **h.** GL, KC (two turns per glucose molecule) **4. a.** cytosol **b.** no **c.** glucose **d.** pyruvate **e.** two ATP **f.** substrate level **g.** NAD⁺ **h.** NADH, ATP, pyruvate **i.** lactate **5. a.** cristae **b.** matrix **c.** outer membrane **d.** intermembrane space **e.** inner membrane **f.** cytosol **6. a.** cytosol **b.** matrix **c.** cristae **7. a.** citrate **b.** CO_2 **c.** two ATP **d.** NAD⁺ and FAD **e.** NADH, FADH₂, ATP, and CO_2 **8. a.** NADH and FADH₂ **b.** pass down the system **c.** pumped into intermembrane space **d.** O_2 **e.** three ATP **f.** oxidative **9. a.** intermembrane **b.** down **c.** ATP **10. a.** 4 **b.** 1 **c.** 3 **d.** 2 **11.** see Figure 8.8, page 138, in text **12. a.** deamination **b.** PGAL **c.** acetyl-CoA **d.** The acetyl groups, which result from carbohydrate breakdown can be used to make fat. **13. a.** reduced to lactate **b.** reduced to alcohol and CO_2 **c.** produces only two ATP **d.** does not require oxygen **e.** O_2 needed to metabolize lactate **14. a.** I, III **b.** III **c.** I **d.** II **15. a.** lactate **b.** alcohol and CO_2 **c.** returns to glycolysis **16. a.** goes to the electron transport system **b.** enters the Krebs cycle

72

GAME III: CELLULAR RESPIRATION ROULETTE

1. G 2. K, E 3. G 4. E 5. K 6. G, K 7. E 8. E
9. G, K 10. E 11. K 12. Calculate your winnings.

KEYWORD CROSSWORD

CHAPTER TEST

1. b 2. c 3. a 4. a 5. b 6. b 7. b 8. b 9. b
10. d 11. e 12. d 13. c 14. d 15. c 16. e
17. d 18. d 19. d 20. a 21. Glucose enters the body at the digestive tract and oxygen enters at the lungs. Glucose and oxygen are delivered to cells by the circulatory system. Water from aerobic respiration enters the blood and is utilized by the body or excreted; we breathe out the carbon dioxide. 22. Both photosynthesis and aerobic respiration consist of a series of reactions that the overall reaction does not indicate. Both pathways make use of an electron transport system located in membrane to build up an electrochemical gradient of H$^+$. When H$^+$ flows down this gradient through an ATP synthase complex, ATP is produced. Both pathways utilize a coenzyme of oxidation/reduction—photosynthesis utilizes NADP and aerobic respiration utilizes NAD. The same molecules (PGA and PGAL) occur in the Calvin cycle and the Krebs cycle but in photosynthesis PGA is reduced to PGAL, and in aerobic respiration PGAL is oxidized to PGA.

9

CELL DIVISION

CHAPTER REVIEW

Prokaryotes divide by **binary fission**—replication of the single chromosome and elongation of the cell that pulls the chromosomes apart. Inward growth of the plasma membrane and formation of new cell wall divide the cell in two.

Each eukaryote has a characteristic number of chromosomes. The chromosomes are visible only when the cell is dividing. In the nondividing cell the genetic material appears as **chromatin.** Mitosis is nuclear division in which the chromosome number stays constant. Mitosis is a part of the cell cycle which also includes interphase. **Interphase** includes the G_1 stage when the organelles increase in number; the S stage when DNA replication occurs; and the G_2 stage when various proteins are synthesized. Control of the cell cycle is an area of intense investigation, particularly because cancer cells divide uncontrollably.

The events of mitosis (or karyokinesis) are studied over five primary phases: prophase, prometaphase, metaphase, anaphase, and telophase. A **spindle** forms and daughter chromosomes derived from the chromatids separate and move to the poles. In the end, each daughter cell has the same number and kinds of chromosomes as does the parent cell. **Cytokinesis** (division of the cytoplasm) in animal cells occurs by furrowing, while in plant cells a **cell plate** forms. Control of the cell cycle is an important area of research today.

Binary fission (in prokaryotes) and mitosis (in unicellular eukaryotic protists and fungi) allow these organisms to reproduce asexually. Mitosis in multicellular eukaryotes is primarily for the purpose of development, growth, and repair of tissues.

STUDY EXERCISES

Study the text section by section as you answer the questions that follow.

9.1 HOW PROKARYOTIC CELLS DIVIDE (P. 148)

• Binary fission allows prokaryotes to reproduce and ensures that each new cell has a chromosome.

1. Indicate whether the following statements about binary fission are true (T) or false (F):
   _____ a. A unicellular organism reproduces by this process.
   _____ b. DNA replicates before the onset of this process.
   _____ c. Elongation of the cell requires that the two circular chromosomes combine.
   _____ d. Eukaryotic cells also divide through this process.
   _____ e. The plasma membrane grows inward when the cell reaches about twice its original length.
   _____ f. Two daughter cells that are genetically identical to the parent cell are produced.

9.2 EUKARYOTIC CHROMOSOMES AND THE CELL CYCLE (P. 149)

• Each eukaryotic species has a characteristic number of chromosomes.

2. Complete each of the following statements with the correct number:

In corn, the haploid chromosome number is 10. Its body cells normally have a._____ chromosomes.

The diploid chromosome number in the domestic cat is 38. Normally, its sex cells have b._____ chromosomes. The horse has a haploid chromosome number of 32. In this animal, 2n = c._____.

The sex cells of a dog normally have 39 chromosomes. In this animal, n = d._____.

3. Label the following diagram:

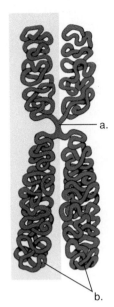

a.

b.

How Eukaryotic Cells Cycle (p. 150)

- Cell division in eukaryotes is a part of the cell cycle. First, cells get ready to divide and then they divide.

4. Study the diagram on page 76 and notice that the center of the diagram pertains to the events of the cell cycle. G_1, S, and G_2 comprise interphase.

Complete the following table:

Stage	Main events
G_1	
S	
G_2	
M	

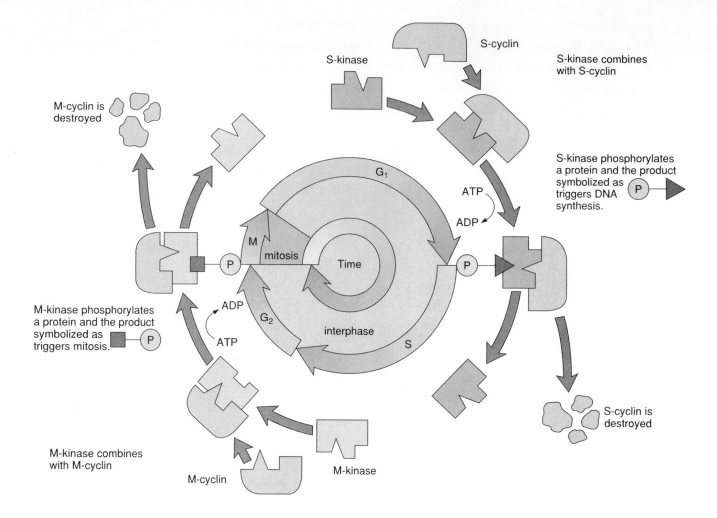

5. What event is triggered by S-kinase after S-kinase combines with S-cyclin? a. _____

   What event is triggered by M-kinase after M-kinase combines with M-cyclin? b. _____

   Why are S-kinase and M-kinase said to be cyclin dependent? c. _____

   Oncogenes cause cancer. Would their presence promote or turn off cyclin-dependent kinases d. _____
   _____

   Tumor-suppressor genes prevent cancer. Would their presence promote or turn off cyclin-dependent kinases?
   e. _____

9.3 HOW EUKARYOTIC CELLS DIVIDE (P. 152)

- Mitosis is a type of nuclear division that ensures that each new eukaryotic cell has a full set of chromosomes.
- Mitosis is necessary to the development, growth, and repair of multicellular organisms.

6. Label the following diagram:

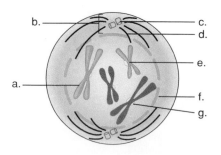

7. Complete the following diagrams to show the arrangement and movement of chromosomes during animal cell mitosis. Briefly describe the events of each phase.

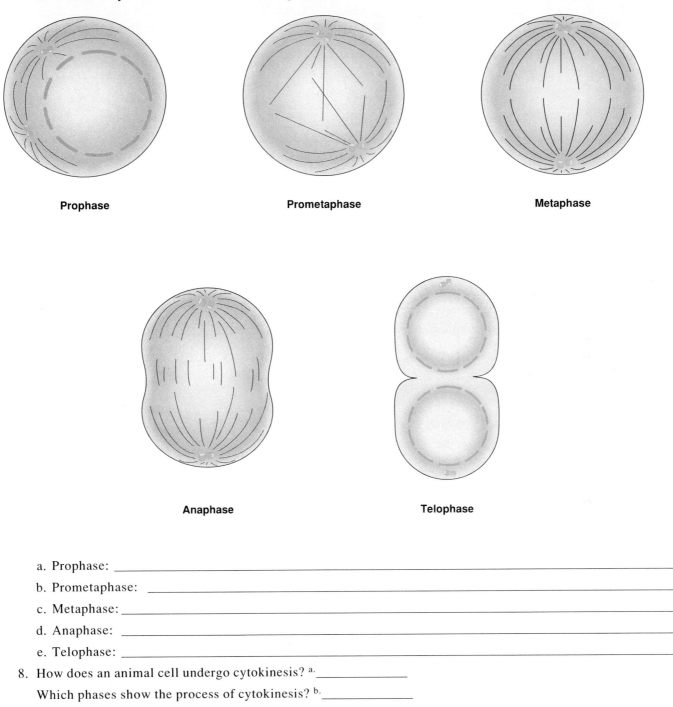

Prophase

Prometaphase

Metaphase

Anaphase

Telophase

a. Prophase: _____

b. Prometaphase: _____

c. Metaphase: _____

d. Anaphase: _____

e. Telophase: _____

8. How does an animal cell undergo cytokinesis? a._____

Which phases show the process of cytokinesis? b._____

9. To show the difference between plant and animal mitosis complete the table by writing *yes* or *no*.

Mitosis	Plant Cell	Animal Cell
same phases		
spindle fibers		
aster		
cell plate		
furrowing		

10. Do plant cells have a centrosome? a._____

    _____

    Do plant cells have centrioles? b._____

    _____

    Are centrioles necessary to spindle formation? Explain. c._____

    _____

9.4 COMPARING PROKARYOTES AND EUKARYOTES (P. 156)

- Prokaryotes differ from eukaryotes by the structure of their chromosomes, the way they divide, and the function of cell division.

11. Indicate whether each statement is true (T) or false (F) and change all false statements to true statements.

    _____a. Binary fission and mitosis ensure that each daughter cell is genetically identical to the parent cell.

    Rewrite: _____

    _____

    _____b. Cell division in unicellular organisms is a form of asexual reproduction. Rewrite: _____

    _____

    _____c. Both binary fission and mitosis are necessary to the growth and repair of multicellular organisms.

    Rewrite: _____

    _____

    _____d. Spindle formation occurs both during binary fission and mitosis. Rewrite: _____

    _____

    _____e. Spindle formation occurs during plant and animal cell division. Rewrite: _____

    _____

Review key terms by completing this crossword puzzle, using the following alphabetized list of terms:

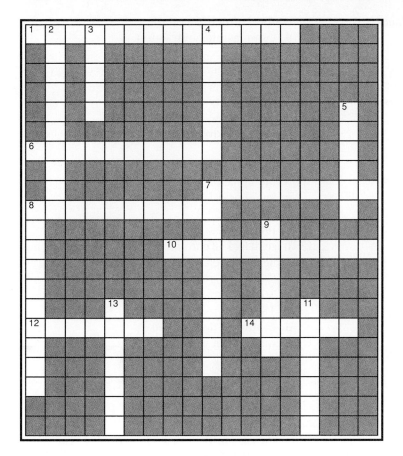

asexual
aster
binary fission
cell plate
centromere
centrosome
chromatin
chromosome
cyclin
cytokinesis
diploid
haploid
interphase
kinase
mitosis
spindle

Across

1 splitting of a parent cell into two daughter cells; an asexual form of reproduction in bacteria (two words)

6 association of DNA and proteins in which genes are arranged linearly; visible only during cell division

7 mass of DNA and associated proteins observed within a nucleus that is not dividing

8 structure across a dividing plant cell that signals the location of new plasma membranes and cell walls (two words)

10 division of the cytoplasm following mitosis and meiosis

12 process in which a parent nucleus reproduces two daughter nuclei, each identical to the parent nucleus; this division is necessary for growth and development

14 any one of several enzymes that phosphorylate their substrates

Down

2 stage of the cell cycle during which DNA synthesis occurs and the nucleus is not actively dividing

3 short, radiating fiber that the centrioles in animal cells produce

4 microtubule structure that brings about chromosomal movement during cell division

5 protein that cycles in quantity as the cell cycle progresses; combines with and activates the kinases that promote the events of the cycle

7 central microtubule organizing center of cells, consisting of granular material; in animal cells, it contains two centrioles

8 constriction where sister chromatids of chromosomes are held together

9 cell condition in which two of each type of chromosome are present

11 cell condition in which only one of each type of chromosome is present

13 reproduction that requires only one parent and does not involve gametes

Do not refer to the text when taking this test. In questions 1–5, match the cell phase to its description.

    a. chromosomes attach to spindle fibers
    b. chromosomes first become visible
    c. chromatids separate at centromere
    d. chromosomes are aligned at the metaphase plate
    e. last phase of nuclear division

_____ 1. anaphase
_____ 2. prometaphase
_____ 3. metaphase
_____ 4. prophase
_____ 5. telophase

_____ 6. Which statement about binary fission is NOT correct?
    a. DNA is replicated before division
    b. exhibits five active phases
    c. occurs in prokaryotic cells
    d. produces two daughter cells

_____ 7. The diploid chromosome number in an organism is 42. The number of chromosomes in its sex cells is normally
    a. 21.
    b. 42.
    c. 63.
    d. 84.

_____ 8. Which statement about mitosis is NOT correct?
    a. does not affect the nuclear envelope
    b. forms four daughter cells
    c. makes diploid nuclei
    d. prophase is the first active phase

_____ 9. How does mitosis in plant cells differ from that in animal cells?
    a. Animal cells do not form a spindle.
    b. Animal cells lack cytokinesis.
    c. Plant cells lack a cell plate.
    d. Plant cells lack centrioles.

_____ 10. Select the incorrect association.
    a. G_1—cell grows in size
    b. G_2—protein synthesis occurs
    c. mitosis—nuclear division
    d. S—DNA fails to duplicate

_____ 11. The phase of cell division in which the nuclear envelope and nucleolus are disappearing as the spindle fibers are appearing is called
    a. anaphase.
    b. prophase.
    c. telophase.
    d. metaphase.

_____ 12. In animal cells, cytokinesis takes place by
    a. membrane fusion.
    b. a furrowing process.
    c. formation of a cell plate.
    d. cytoplasmic contraction.

_____ 13. Cyclin
    a. is a molecule that regulates the cell cycle.
    b. combines with a kinase.
    c. occurs in two different forms.
    d. All of these are correct.

_____ 14. If a cell is to divide, DNA replication must occur during
    a. prophase.
    b. metaphase.
    c. anaphase.
    d. telophase.
    e. interphase.

_____ 15. If a cell had 18 chromosomes, how many chromosomes would each daughter cell have after mitosis?
    a. 9
    b. 36
    c. 18
    d. cannot be determined

_____ 16. Normal growth and repair of the human body requires
    a. mitosis.
    b. binary fission.
    c. both a and b.
    d. neither a nor b.

_____ 17. The cell cycle
    a. incudes mitosis as an event.
    b. includes only the stages G_1, S, and G_2.
    c. is under cellular but not under genetic control.
    d. involves proteins but not chromosomes.

_____ 18. Which of these is involved in asexual reproduction?
    a. mitosis
    b. binary fission
    c. oogenesis
    d. Both a and b are correct.

_____ 19. When do chromosomes move to opposite poles?
    a. prophase
    b. metaphase
    c. anaphase
    d. telophase

_____ 20. Which statement about binary fission is NOT correct?
    a. Unicellular prokaryotes reproduce by binary fission.
    b. Like mitosis, binary fission utilizes a spindle.
    c. Binary fission is a form of asexual reproduction.
    d. Binary fission ensures that daughter cells receive the same genetic material as the parent cell.

Answer in complete sentences.

21. Why might mitosis and multicellularity be considered adaptive for organisms?

22. Why are mutations sometimes particularly beneficial to organisms that reproduce asexually.

Test Results: _____ Number right ÷ 22 = _____ × 100 = _____ %

EXPLORING THE INTERNET

Use the Internet to further explore topics in this chapter, such as binary fission and mitosis. Go to the Mader Home Page (http://www.mhhe.com/sciencemath/biology/mader/) and click on *Biology*, 6th edition. Go to Chapter 9 and select a Web site of interest.

ANSWER KEY

STUDY EXERCISES

1. **a.** T **b.** T **c.** F **d.** F **e.** T **f.** T **2. a.** 20 **b.** 19 **c.** 64 **d.** 39 **3. a.** centromere **b.** sister chromatids **4.** G₁, Organelles begin to double in number; S, Replication of DNA; G₂, Synthesis of proteins; M, events of mitosis

5. **a.** DNA synthesis (replication) **b.** mitosis **c.** They are activated after they combine with a cyclin molecule. **d.** promote **e.** turn off **6. a.** chromatid **b.** centrosome **c.** centriole **d.** aster **e.** centromere **f.** nuclear membrane fragment **g.** kinetochore

Prophase   **Prometaphase**

Metaphase

Anaphase

Telophase

7. **a.** Chromosomes are now distinct; nucleolus is disappearing; centrosomes begin moving apart and nuclear envelope is fragmenting. **b.** Spindle is in process of forming and kinetochores of chromosomes are attaching to kinetochore spindle fibers. **c.** Chromosomes are at the metaphase plate. **d.** Daughter chromosomes are at the poles of the spindle. **e.** Daughter cells are forming as nucler envelopes and nucleoli appear. **8. a.** cleavage furrowing **b.** anaphase and telophase

9.

Plant Cell	Animal Cell
yes	yes
yes	yes
no	yes
yes	no
no	yes

10. **a.** Yes and they form a spindle. **b.** no **c.** It seems not because plant cells have no centrioles, yet they have a spindle. **11. a.** T **b.** T **c.** F Mitosis is necessary (multicellular organisms do not undergo binary fission). **d.** F Spindle formation occurs only during mitosis. **e.** T

KeyWord CrossWord

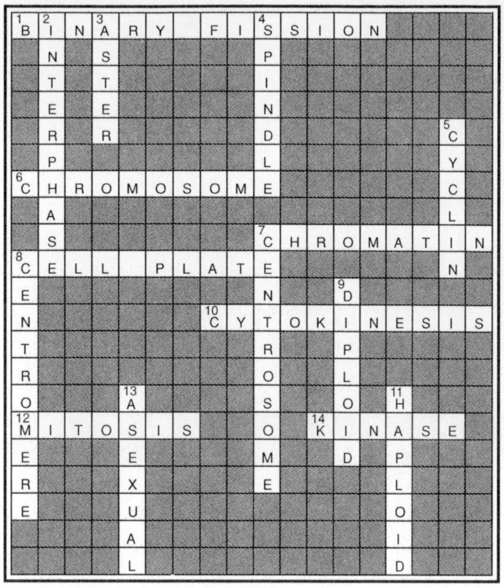
1 BINARY FISSION
2 INTERPHASE
3 ASTER
4 SPINDLE
5 CYCLIN
6 CHROMOSOME
7 CHROMATIN
7 CENTROSOME
8 CELL PLATE
8 CENTROMERE
9 DIPLOID
10 CYTOKINESIS
11 HAPLOID
12 MITOSIS
13 ASEXUAL
14 KINASE

Chapter Test

1. c **2.** a **3.** d **4.** b **5.** e **6.** b **7.** a **8.** b **9.** d **10.** d **11.** b **12.** b **13.** d **14.** e **15.** c **16.** a **17.** a **18.** d **19.** c **20.** b **21.** Complex organisms are multicellular with specialized tissues and organs. In addition, mitosis allows growth and repair of the organism. **22.** Without mutations, asexual reproduction produces offspring that are identical to the parent. With mutations, variations may occur that will be adaptive, particularly if the environment is changing.

10

MEIOSIS AND SEXUAL REPRODUCTION

CHAPTER REVIEW

Working in conjunction with fertilization, **meiosis** ensures the constancy of the chromosome number from generation to generation. In the animal life cycle, meiosis is a part of gametogenesis; in the plant life cycle, meiosis produces spores that develop into a gametophyte generation; and among fungi, meiosis occurring after zygote formation produces spores that develop into a haploid adult.

Prior to meiosis, the parent cell is **diploid.** Replication has occurred, and the chromosomes are duplicated. Meiosis involves two consecutive cell divisions that produce four haploid daughter cells. **Crossing-over** often occurs between nonsister chromatids in prophase I. Dur-

ing anaphase I, the chromosomes of each **homologous** pair separate independently into different daughter cells, thus producing haploid cells. In meiosis II, the separation of chromosomes is similar to the pattern in mitosis except that cells are now **haploid.**

The human life cycle includes mitosis and meiosis (**spermatogenesis** in males and **oogenesis** in females). Only during meiosis do the homologous chromosomes pair and undergo independent separation, resulting in a haploid number of chromosomes in the **gametes.** Both crossing-over and independent separation of homologues account for genetic variability in the four daughter cells. Subsequently, fertilization also accounts for variation.

STUDY EXERCISES

Study the text section by section as you answer the questions that follow.

10.1 HALVING THE CHROMOSOME NUMBER (P. 160)

- Due to meiosis, sex cells contain half the total number of chromosomes.
- Meiosis occurs at varied times during the life cycle of organisms.

1. The nuclear division that reduces the chromosome number from the [a.]_____ number to the

   [b.]_____ number is called meiosis.

2. In a life cycle, the zygote always has the _____ number of chromosomes.

3. In the animal life cycle, meiosis results in haploid [a.]_____; in the plant life cycle, meiosis results in

   haploid [b.]_____; in the fungal life cycle, meiosis results in haploid [c.]_____.

4. A pair of chromosomes having the same length and centromere position are called [a.]_____.

   The [b.]_____, a product of fertilization, is always diploid.

5. Indicate whether the following statements regarding the role of meiosis are true (T) or false (F):
   _____ a. In animals, meiosis forms gametes that fuse to form a zygote.
   _____ b. Meiosis forms haploid cells in the life cycle of animals.
   _____ c. In plants, meiosis produces diploid spores that divide mitotically.
   _____ d. Meiosis produces four diploid cells over two divisions.

- Meiosis requires two cell divisions and results in four daughter cells.
- During meiosis, nonsister chromatids exchange genetic material.

6. Label this summary diagram of meiosis.

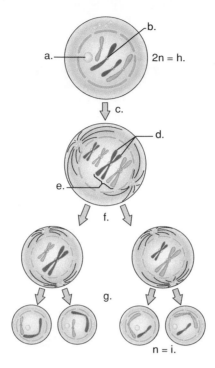

Why is it correct to symbolize meiosis as 2n → n? h. _____

_____

7. What is the diploid number of chromosomes in the diagram in question 6? a. _____

Which structures separate during meiosis I? b. _____

Which structures separate during meiosis II? c. _____

Does chromosome duplication occur between meiosis I and meiosis II? d. _____

Why or why not? e. _____

8. Match the following terms with the appropriate description: *bivalents, crossing-over, genetic variation,* and *synapsis.*

Homologous chromosomes line up side by side. a. _____

Nonsister chromatids exchange genetic material. b. _____

Two chromosomes stay in close association with each other. c. _____

The arrangement of genetic material is new due to crossing-over. d. _____

9. Using ink for one duplicated chromosome and pencil for the other, color this bivalent before and after crossing-over has occurred.

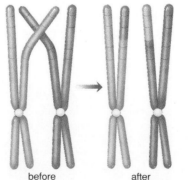

before   after

- Both meiosis I and meiosis II have four phases.

10. Label and complete these diagrams to show the arrangement and movement of chromosomes during meiosis I and meiosis II. (The diagram for meiosis II pertains to only one daughter cell from meiosis I.)

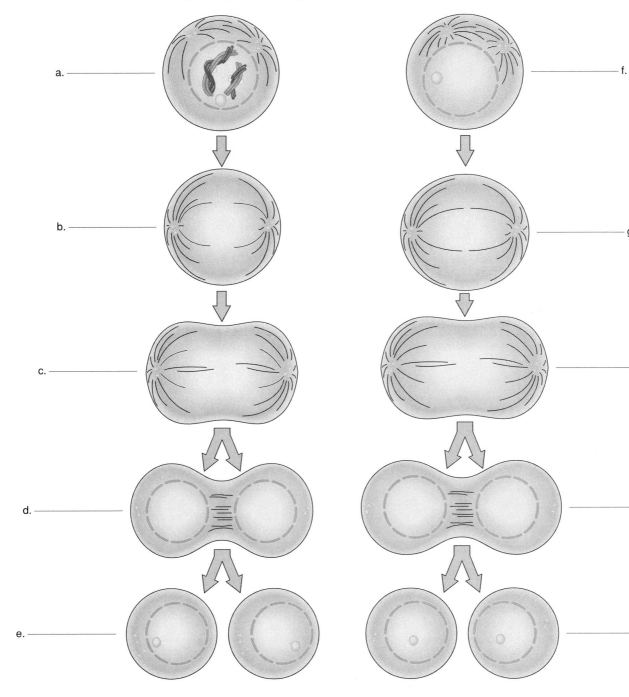

10.4 Viewing the Human Life Cycle (p. 166)

• In humans, meiosis is a part of sperm production in males and egg production in females.

11. Indicate whether the following statements are true (T) or false (F):
    _____ a. Meiosis in human males is a part of spermatogenesis.
    _____ b. Mitosis in human females is a part of oogenesis.
    _____ c. Oogenesis occurs in the testis.
    _____ d. A zygote undergoes mitosis during development of the embryo.
    _____ e. Oogenesis produces four functional egg cells from one cell.

12. State whether the following processes occur in males (M), females (F), or both (B):
    _____ a. gamete formation
    _____ b. spermatogenesis
    _____ c. oogenesis
    _____ d. polar body formation

13. Complete the table by writing *yes* or *no* to distinguish meiosis from mitosis.

	Meiosis	Mitosis
Complete after One Division		
Requires Two Successive Divisions		
During Anaphase, Daughter Chromosomes Separate		
During Anaphase I, Homologous Chromosomes Separate		
Results in Daughter Cells with the Diploid Number of Chromosomes		
Results in Daughter Cells with the Haploid Number of Chromosomes		
In Animals, Is Unique to the Somatic (Body) Cells		
In Animals, Is Unique to Formation of Gametes		

10.5 Significance of Meiosis (p. 169)

• Sexual reproduction, which includes meiosis, brings about variation and contributes to the evolutionary process.

14. Show how genetic recombination occurs as a result of sexual reproduction by matching the following statements:
    1. Zygote carries a unique combination of chromosomes and genes.
    2. Gametes carry different combinations of chromosomes.
    3. Daughter chromosomes carry different combinations of genes.
    _____ a. Homologous chromosomes separate independently.
    _____ b. Crossing-over occurs.
    _____ c. Gametes fuse during fertilization.

1. Make playing cards with the following words or phrases on them:

    1. nucleolus
    2. chromosomes (chromatids held by centromere)
    3. centrosome with centrioles
    4. nucleus (nuclear envelope)
    5. spindle fibers
    6. cell plate
    7. aster
    8. furrowing

    a. From these, select those that have to do with the formation and structure of the spindle.
    b. From the cards remaining, select those that name structures that disappear during mitosis.
    c. Select the cards that have to do with cytokinesis.

2. Make cards with the following phrases on them:
    1. daughter chromosomes separate
    2. distinct chromosomes within daughter nuclei
    3. chromosomes arranged at the metaphase plate
    4. chromosomes are distinct; spindle appears; nucleolus disappears and nuclear envelope fragments
    5. homologous pairs separate

    a. Arrange the cards to describe the events of mitosis or meiosis II.
    b. Arrange the cards to describe the events of meiosis I.

3. Make three cards that are marked as follows:
    16
    8 (diploid number)
    4 (haploid number)

    a. Pick the card that tells how many chromosomes are in the parent nucleus before division.
    b. Pick the card that tells how many chromosomes each daughter nucleus will have after mitosis.
    c. Pick the card that tells how many chromosomes are in the parent nucleus during prophase of mitosis or prophase I of meiosis.
    d. Pick the card that tells how many chromatids are in the parent nucleus during prophase of mitosis or prophase I of meiosis. (For purposes of the game, assume the chromosomes are duplicated.)
    e. Pick the card that tells how many chromosomes are at *both* poles during anaphase of mitosis.
    f. Pick the card that tells how many chromosomes are at *both* poles during anaphase I of meiosis.
    g. Pick the card that tells how many chromosomes are in each daughter nucleus after meiosis I.
    h. Pick the card that tells how many chromosomes are in each daughter nucleus after meiosis II.

Review key terms by completing this crossword puzzle, using the following alphabetized list of terms:

bivalent
crossing-over
diploid
gamete
haploid
homologous chromosome
homologue
meiosis
oogenesis
polar body
secondary oocyte
spermatogenesis

Across

2 member of a pair of chromosomes that carry genes for the same traits and synapse during prophase of the first meiotic division (two words)

9 homologous chromosomes, each having sister chromatids, that are joined by a nucleoprotein lattice during meiosis; also called a tetrad

10 cell condition in which only one of each type of chromosome is present

Down

1 type of nuclear division that occurs as part of sexual reproduction and in which the daughter cells receive the haploid number of chromosomes

3 egg production in females by the process of meiosis and maturation

4 haploid sex cell

5 in oogenesis, the functional product of meiosis I; becomes the egg (two words)

6 exchange of segments between nonsister chromatids of a bivalent during meiosis (two words)

7 sperm production in males by the process of meiosis and maturation

8 cell condition in which two of each type of chromosome is present

10 member of a homologous pair of chromosomes

11 in oogenesis, a nonfunctional product; three of the four meiotic products are of this type (two words)

CHAPTER TEST

OBJECTIVE QUESTIONS

Do not refer to the text when taking this test. In questions 1–8, match each of the descriptions with the following processes:

    a. mitosis only
    b. meiosis only
    c. mitosis and meiosis
    d. neither mitosis nor meiosis

_____ 1. begins with a diploid nucleus
_____ 2. complete after one division
_____ 3. requires two successive divisions
_____ 4. homologous chromosomes separate
_____ 5. produces haploid nuclei
_____ 6. produces diploid nuclei
_____ 7. normally produces triploid cells
_____ 8. results in the somatic (body) cells in eukaryotes

In questions 9–15, label each statement with one of the following choices:

    a. meiosis I
    b. meiosis II

_____ 9. synapsis of homologous chromosomes occurs

_____10. separation of homologous chromosomes occurs

_____11. results in one oocyte and one polar body in human females

_____12. results in four sperm cells in human males

_____13. daughter cells have double-stranded chromosomes

_____14. daughter nuclei produced have single-stranded chromosomes

_____15. crossing-over occurs

_____16. Which of the following is NOT a valid contrast between mitosis and meiosis:

Mitosis	Meiosis
a. requires one set of phases	requires two sets of phases
b. occurs when somatic (body) cells divide	occurs during gamete production
c. results in four daughter nuclei	results in two daughter nuclei
d. results in daughter nuclei with diploid number of chromosomes	results in daughter nuclei with haploid number of chromosomes

_____17. Polar bodies are formed during
    a. meiosis.
    b. mitosis.
    c. oogenesis.
    d. spermatogenesis.
    e. Both *a* and *c* are correct.

_____18. During anaphase of meiosis II,
    a. homologous chromosomes separate.
    b. chromatid pairs separate.
    c. daughter chromosomes separate.
    d. duplicated chromosomes separate.

_____19. During interkinesis
    a. chromosome duplication occurs.
    b. chromosomes consist of two chromatids.
    c. occurs after meiosis I is complete.
    d. Both *b* and *c* are correct.

_____20. By the end of meiosis I,
    a. crossing-over has occurred.
    b. daughter chromosomes have separated.
    c. synapsis of homologous chromosomes has occurred.
    d. each daughter nucleus is genetically identical to the original cell.
    e. Both *a* and *c* are correct.

CRITICAL THINKING QUESTIONS

Answer in complete sentences.

21. How might sexual reproduction be advantageous to the organism?

22. Based on the behavior of chromosomes during meiosis, how does a species with six chromosome pairs have an evolutionary advantage over a species with two chromosome pairs?

Test Results: _____ Number right ÷ 22 = _____ × 100 = _____ %

EXPLORING THE INTERNET

Use the Internet to further explore topics in this chapter, such as meiosis or homologous recombination as it relates to kidney disease. Go to the Mader Home Page (http://www.mhhe.com/sciencemath/biology/mader/) and click on *Biology,* 6th edition. Go to Chapter 10 and select a Web site of interest.

ANSWER KEY

STUDY EXERCISES

1. a. diploid (2n) **b.** haploid (n) **2.** diploid (2n) (or full) **3. a.** gametes **b.** spores **c.** spores **4. a.** homologous chromosomes (or homologues) **b.** zygote **5. a.** T **b.** T **c.** F **d.** F **6. a.** nucleolus **b.** centromere **c.** DNA replication **d.** sister chromatids **e.** synapsis **f.** Meiosis I **g.** Meiosis II **h.** 4 **i.** 2 **j.** A diploid cell becomes haploid. The parent cell is diploid and undergoes meiosis, which results in four daughter cells, each of which is haploid. **7. a.** 4 **b.** homologous chromosomes **c.** daughter chromosomes **d.** no **e.** The chromosomes are already duplicated. **8. a.** synapsis **b.** crossing-over **c.** bivalents **d.** genetic variation **9.** See Fig. 10.2, page 163, in text **10. a.** prophase I **b.** metaphase I **c.** anaphase I **d.** telophase I **e.** interkinesis **f.** prophase II **g.** metaphase II **h.** anaphase II **i.** telophase II **j.** daughter cells. See Fig. 10.7, page 167, in text **11. a.** T **b.** F **c.** F **d.** T **e.** F **12. a.** B **b.** M **c.** F **d.** F
13.

Meiosis	Mitosis
no	yes
yes	no
no	yes
yes	no
no	yes
yes	no
no	yes
yes	no

14. a. 2 **b.** 3 **c.** 1

SOLITAIRE

1. a. 3, 5, 7 **b.** 1, 4 **c.** 6, 8 **d.** 2, move into daughter nuclei **2. a.** 4, 3, 1, 2 **b.** 4, 3, 5, 2 **3. a.** 8 **b.** 8 **c.** 8 **d.** 16 **e.** 16 **f.** 8 **g.** 4 **h.** 4

KEYWORD CROSSWORD

CHAPTER TEST

1. c **2.** a **3.** b **4.** b **5.** b **6.** a **7.** d **8.** a **9.** a **10.** a **11.** a **12.** b **13.** a **14.** b **15.** a **16.** c **17.** e **18.** c **19.** d **20.** e **21.** Sexual reproduction results in genetic recombinations among offspring due to (1) crossing-over of nonsister chromatids, (2) independent separation of homologous chromosomes, and (3) fertilization. Certain recombinations may result in a variation that makes the organism more suited to the environment. **22.** By independent separation of homologous chromosomes, the species with six chromosomes pairs can produce 64 different combinations of chromosomes by meiosis. The species with only two pairs can produce only four and therefore lacks the same potential for variety.

90

11

MENDELIAN PATTERNS OF INHERITANCE

At the time Mendel started his work, the blending theory of inheritance was prevalent. Mendel disproved this theory through well-designed experiments that offered statistical evidence. By analyzing the 3:1 results among the F_2 generation of a monohybrid cross, Mendel arrived at the law of segregation: factors (genes) for a trait occur in pairs in an organism; they separate into different sex cells during gamete formation. This explains why the recessive phenotype—absent in the F_1 generation—reappeared in the F_2 generation.

Solving genetics problems requires distinguishing between the **phenotype** (appearance) and **genotype** (genetic makeup) of an individual. For any pair of **alleles,** the **dominant allele** is given as an uppercase letter, and the **recessive allele** is given as a lowercase letter. A cross is done by using the laws of probability, most often by employing a **Punnett square,** which offers a mechanism whereby all possible types of sperm fertilize all possible types of eggs. The results can be expressed as the phenotypic ratio or can be used to state the chances of an individual having a particular genotype.

Mendel used a monohybrid **testcross** to verify his law of segregation. A cross represented by $Aa \times aa$ offers the best chance of producing a recessive offspring. Today, the testcross is used to determine whether an individual is **heterozygous** or **homozygous** dominant.

The F_2 results of a dihybrid cross allowed Mendel to formulate his law of independent assortment: during gamete formation, the factors of one pair segregate independently from the factors of other pairs. This law explains why the F_2 generation contained four types of genotypes—that is, all possible combinations of dominant and recessive characteristics. The Punnett square can also be used to solve dihybrid problems, including the dihybrid testcross.

Study the text section by section as you answer the questions that follow.

11.1 INTRODUCING GREGOR MENDEL (P. 174)

- Mendel discovered certain laws of heredity after doing experiments with garden peas during the mid-1800s.

1. When Mendel began breeding experiments, other breeders had different ideas about heredity. Check the following statement(s) that represent(s) the ideas at that time:
   _____ a. A cross between a red flower and a white flower results in all offspring having red flowers.
   _____ b. A cross between a red flower and white flower results in some offspring having white flowers.
   _____ c. In a genetic cross, both parents contribute equally to the offspring.
   _____ d. Parents of contrasting appearance will produce offspring of intermediate appearance.
   _____ e. The blending theory of inheritance existed in genetic crosses.
2. Mendel's work reflected several methods and advantages that contributed to his success. Check the following statement(s) that represent(s) those methods and advantages:
   _____ a. Each trait studied (e.g., seed shape, flower color) displayed many different phenotypes.
   _____ b. The breeding experiments had a statistical basis.
   _____ c. The garden pea plants used had a long generation time.
   _____ d. The plants used were easy to cultivate.
   _____ e. The plants used could not self-pollinate.

3. Mendel arrived at the law of segregation by interpreting the results of his monohybrid crosses. Check the interpretation(s) that he used.

_____ a. F_1 organisms contain one copy for each hereditary factor.

_____ b. Factors segregate when gametes form.

_____ c. Gametes fuse randomly during fertilization.

_____ d. Allelic pairs assort in a dependent manner.

4. The length of stem in the plants that Mendel studied had two alleles: T (tall) and t (short). Using these letters, write the alleles for the heterozygous genotype a._____, the homozygous dominant genotype b._____, and the homozygous recessive genotype c._____.

11.2 MENDEL DID A MONOHYBRID CROSS (P. 176)

• The monohybrid cross told Mendel that each organism contains two factors for each trait and the factors segregate during formation of gametes.

• Today, it is known that alleles located on chromosomes control the traits of individuals and homologous pairs of chromosomes separate during meiosis I.

5. When Mendel crossed true breeding tall plants with true breeding short plants, the F_1 generation was

a._____. When he crossed $F_1 \times F_1$, the offspring included b._____ plants for every

c._____ plant. Because some of the F_2 plants were short, he concluded that the F_1 generation was Tt; therefore, each original parent plant had passed on only one factor. Mendel's law of segregation states: d._____

_____

_____

6. a. Complete the following table to show the difference between genotype and phenotype:

Genotype	Genotype	Phenotype
TT	_____	_____
_____	heterozygous	_____
tt	_____	_____

If a plant's phenotype is short, its genotype(s) can be b._____.

If a plant's phenotype is tall, its genotype(s) can be c._____.

7. Among humans, the allele for dark hair (D) is dominant to the allele for blonde hair (d). Consider the cross $Dd \times Dd$. To answer these questions, use fractions except when asked for a percentage.

What is the chance that either parent will produce a gamete with a dominant allele? a._____

Using the multiplicative law of probability, calculate the chance of a homozygous dominant offspring (dark hair). Show your work. b._____

What is the chance this couple will have a homozygous dominant offspring? c._____%

What is the chance either parent will produce a gamete with a recessive allele? d._____

Using the multiplicative law of probability, calculate the chance of a homozygous recessive offspring (blonde hair). Show your work. e._____

What is the chance this couple will have a homozygous recessive offspring? f._____%

Using the multiplicative law and additive law, calculate the chance of a heterozygous offspring (dark hair). [g.]

What is the chance this couple will have a heterozygous offspring? [h.]_____%

Using the additive law, calculate the chance of an offspring with the dominant phenotype (dark hair).

[i.]_____

Your calculations indicate that the phenotypic ratio for this cross is ¾ dark hair to ¼ blonde hair, or a phenotypic ratio of [j.]_____:_____.

8. In peas, yellow seed color is dominant to green. The key is: [a.] $Y =$ _____, $y =$ _____.

Fill in this Punnett square for the cross $Yy \times Yy$. [b.]

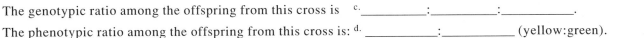

The genotypic ratio among the offspring from this cross is [c.]_____:_____:_____.

The phenotypic ratio among the offspring from this cross is: [d.]_____:_____ (yellow:green).

9. The gametes combine at [a.]_____, and usually, a(n) [b.]_____ number must be counted before a 3:1 ratio can be verified.

Mendel Did a Testcross (p. 180)

• A testcross can determine the genotype of an individual with the dominant phenotype.

10. Researchers do a(n) [a.]_____ (i.e., the dominant phenotype is mated to the recessive phenotype) to determine if the dominant phenotype is homozygous or heterozygous. If the individual is homozygous dominant, the F_1 generation is expected to be [b.]_____. If the individual is heterozygous, a phenotypic ratio of [c.]_____:_____ is expected.

11. In humans, widow's peak (W) is dominant to continuous hairline (w). Consider the cross $Ww \times Ww$. The chance of a child with widow's pea is [a.]_____ %, and the chance of a child with continuous hairline is [b.]_____ %.

12. Consider the cross $Ww \times ww$. The chance of a child with widow's peak is [a.]_____ %, and the chance of a child with continuous hairline is [b.]_____ %.

13. Among humans, dark eyes (B) is dominant to blue eyes (b). In a family, one parent has dark eyes, and the other has blue eyes. Among their offspring, two develop dark eyes, and two develop blue eyes. Most likely, the genotypes of the parents are [a.]_____ (dark-eyed parent) and [b.]_____ (blue-eyed parent).

14. In fruit flies, a cross between long wing (L) flies and short wing (l) flies produces only long wing flies. Most likely, the genotypes of the parental flies are [a.]_____ (long-wing parents) and [b.]_____ (short-wing parents).

- A dihybrid cross told Mendel that every possible combination of factors is present in the gametes.
- Today, it is known that homologous pairs of chromosomes separate independently during meiosis I, producing all possible combinations of alleles in the gametes.

15. In pea plants, T = tall and t = short, G = green pods and g = yellow pods. When Mendel crossed homozygous tall plants having green pods with pure, short plants having yellow pods, the F_1 plants all had the genotype
a._____ and the phenotype b._____. If T always stayed with G and t always stayed with g in the gametes, then how many different phenotypes would be among the F_2 plants? c._____ Mendel observed four different phenotypes and formulated his law of independent assortment, which states: d. _____
_____

16. The process of meiosis explains the law of segregation and the law of independent assortment. Considering the movement of chromosomes, why is only one allele for each trait present in the gametes? a._____ Why are all combinations of alleles present in the gametes? b. _____

Doing Dihybrid Genetics Problems (p. 182)

- A testcross can determine the genotype of an individual who is dominant in two traits.

17. In horses, black (B) is dominant to brown (b), and a trotter (T) is dominant to a pacer (t). Use fractions in your answers.

Consider the cross $Bb \times bb$. Among the offspring, the chance of black coat is a._____, and the chance of brown coat is b._____.

Consider the cross $Tt \times Tt$. Among the offspring, the chance of a trotter is c._____, and the chance of a pacer is d._____.

Consider the cross $BbTt \times bbTt$, and use the multiplicative law of probability to determine the chances of the following:

black trotter e._____ = _____

black pacer f._____ = _____

brown trotter g._____ = _____

brown pacer h._____ = _____

What is the phenotypic ratio expected for the preceding cross? i.

_____:_____:_____:_____

Check your answer by doing a Punnett square. j.

18. Given the cross *BbTt* × *BbTt*, determine the ratio and phenotypes expected._____ _____:

_____ _____:_____ _____:_____ _____

19. Do a Punnett square for the cross *BbTt* × *Bbtt*. a.

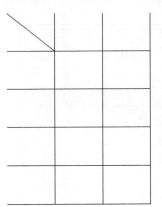

What is the phenotypic ratio among offspring? b._____: _____

_____:_____

20. In rabbits, black (*B*) is dominant to brown (*b*), and spotted coat (*S*) is dominant to solid coat (*s*). A black, spotted rabbit is mated to a brown, solid one, and all ten of their offspring are black and spotted. The genotypes of the parents are a._____ and b._____.

21. In humans, widow's peak (*W*) is dominant to continuous hairline (*w*), and short fingers (*S*) are dominant to long fingers (*s*).

If the two parents are heterozygous in both regards, what is the chance of any offspring having widow's peak and short fingers? a._____

If one parent is heterozygous in both regards and the other is homozygous recessive, what is the chance of an offspring with widow's peak and short fingers? b._____ or c._____%.

Review key terms by completing this crossword puzzle, using the following alphabetized list of terms:

allele
dominant allele
gene locus
genotype
heterozygous
homozygous
phenotype
Punnett square
recessive allele
testcross

Across

2 gridlike graph for calculating the results of simple genetic crosses by lining up alleles within the gametes of two parents on the outside margin and writing their recombination in boxes inside the grid (two words)

5 possessing two identical alleles for a particular trait

7 alleles of an organism for a particular trait or traits; for example, *BB* or *Aa*

8 alternative forms of a gene that occur at the same locus on homologous chromosomes

9 cross between an individual with the dominant phenotype and an individual with the recessive phenotype to see if the individual with the dominant phenotype is homozygous or heterozygous

Down

1 possessing unlike alleles for a particular trait

2 visible expression of a genotype—for example, brown eyes or attached earlobes

3 allele that exerts its phenotypic effect only in the homozygote; its expression is masked by a dominant allele (two words)

4 allele that exerts its phenotypic effect in the heterozygote; it hides the expression of the recessive allele (two words)

6 specific location of a particular gene on homologous chromosomes (two words)

OBJECTIVE QUESTIONS

Do not refer to the text when taking this test.

_____ 1. When Gregor Mendel began crossing plants, most breeders of organisms believed that
   a. dominance was complete.
   b. many genes affected one trait.
   c. red and white flowers produced pink offspring.
   d. the genetic material was always stable.

_____ 2. Select an advantage that made Mendel's work successful.
   a. He used true-breeding members of plants for mating.
   b. He used philosophical laws to interpret his results.
   c. His plants had many phenotypes for a trait.
   d. His plants required many years to develop.

_____ 3. Two different phenotypes result among the offspring from a genetic cross. The genotypes of the parents are
   a. TT and TT.
   b. TT and Tt.
   c. Tt and tt.
   d. tt and tt.

_____ 4. The phenotypic ratio from a genetic cross is 1:1:1:1. The genotypes of the parents are
   a. $TTGG \times TtGg$.
   b. $TtGG \times Ttgg$.
   c. $TtGg \times ttgg$.
   d. $Ttgg \times ttgg$.

_____ 5. What were the genotypes of the parents in the F_1 generation of Mendel's monohybrid cross for stem length?
   a. both TT
   b. both Tt
   c. TT and Tt
   d. Tt and tt

_____ 6. In guinea pigs, the allele for dark color (B) is dominant to the allele for light color (b). In a cross between two heterozygous organisms, the chance for producing a light-colored offspring is
   a. ⅖.
   b. ¾.
   c. ½.
   d. ¼.

_____ 7. The two factors for each trait separate when gametes form, so that each gamete contains only one factor for each trait. This statement is part of Mendel's law of
   a. dominance.
   b. independent assortment.
   c. random recombination.
   d. segregation.

_____ 8. Select the incorrect association.
   a. alleles—A and p
   b. heterozygous—Aa
   c. homozygous—DD
   d. homozygous—pp

_____ 9. An organism has the genotype DD. How many kinds of gametes can this organism produce?
   a. none
   b. one
   c. two
   d. four

_____10. Which of the following crosses generates the largest Punnett square?
   a. $TT \times TT$
   b. $TT \times Tt$
   c. $Tt \times Tt$
   d. $Tt \times tt$

_____11. From the cross $Aa \times Aa$, the probability of producing a homozygous dominant offspring is
   a. 25%.
   b. 33%.
   c. 50%.
   d. 75%.

_____12. From the cross $Dd \times Dd$, the probability of producing the dominant phenotype is
   a. 25%.
   b. 50%.
   c. 75%.
   d. 100%.

_____13. How many kinds of gametes can an organism with genotype $AaBB$ produce?
   a. one
   b. two
   c. three
   d. four

_____14. For a testcross, an organism with a dominant phenotype is mated with a homozygous recessive organism. Hundreds of offspring are produced. Fifty-five percent of the offspring reveal the dominant phenotype; the others show the recessive phenotype. The genotype of the dominant parent is
   a. AA.
   b. definitely Aa.
   c. probably Aa.
   d. aa.

_____15. Members of one pair of factors separate independently of the members of another pair of factors. This is a statement of Mendel's law of
a. dominant factors.
b. independent assortment.
c. random recombination.
d. segregation.

_____16. What are the dimensions of the Punnett square for the cross $TtGG \times TtGg$?
a. 2×2
b. 2×4
c. 4×1
d. 4×5

_____17. Two organisms, each with the genotype $TtGg$, mate. The chance of producing an offspring that has the dominant phenotype for height and the recessive phenotype for color is
a. $\%_{16}$.
b. $\%_{16}$.
c. $\%_{16}$.
d. $\%_{16}$.

_____18. A *Drosophila* fly with the genotype $LlGg$ mates with a fly that is short and black. The phenotypic ratio among the offspring is
a. 9:3:3:1.
b. 3:3:1:1.
c. 1:2:1:2.
d. 1:1:1:1.

_____19. In horses, B = black coat and b = brown coat, T = trotter and t = pacer. A true-breeding horse, which is black and a trotter, is considered for mating. The number of kinds of gametes it can produce is
a. one.
b. two.
c. four.
d. sixteen.

_____20. In humans, B = short fingers and b = long fingers, W = widow's peak and w = continuous hairline. From the cross $BbWW \times Bbww$, the chance of an offspring having both dominant traits is
a. $\%_{16}$.
b. $\frac{3}{4}$.
c. $\frac{3}{8}$.
d. $\frac{1}{4}$.

CRITICAL THINKING QUESTIONS

Answer in complete sentences.

21. The phenotypic ratio of a testcross is 1:1:1:1. Did a monohybrid testcross or a dihybrid testcross produce this ratio? Explain.

22. Consider the cross $TtGg \times ttgg$. The phenotypic ratio produced from this cross is not 1:1:1:1. Instead, only two phenotypes are produced in significant numbers. Explain why this may have occurred.

Test Results: _____ Number right ÷ 22 = _____ × 100 = _____ %

EXPLORING THE INTERNET

Use the Internet to further explore topics in this chapter, such as Mendelian genetics or the genetic makeup of many different organisms. Go to the Mader Home Page (http://www.mhhe.com/sciencemath/biology/mader/) and click on *Biology*, 6th edition. Go to Chapter 11 and select a Web site of interest.

STUDY EXERCISES

1. c, d, e   **2.** b, d   **3.** b, c   **4. a.** *Tt* **b.** *TT* **c.** *tt*   **5. a.** tall
b. three tall **c.** one short **d.** see page 176 in text   **6. a.** see
Table 11.1, page 177, in text **b.** *tt* **c.** *TT* or *Tt*   **7. a.** ½
b. ½ × ½ = ¼ **c.** 1 out of 4, or 25% **d.** ½ **e.** ½ × ½ = ¼
f. 1 out of 4, or 25% **g.** chance of *Dd* = ½ × ½ = ¼; chance
of *dD* = ½ × ½ = ¼; chance of heterozygous offspring is
¼ + ¼ = ½ **h.** 1 out of 2, or 50% **i.** ¼ + ½ = ¾ **j.** 3:1
8. a. *Y* = yellow seed, *y* = green seed
b.

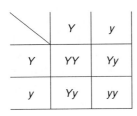

	Y	y
Y	YY	Yy
y	Yy	yy

c. 1:2:1 **d.** 3:1   **9. a.** random **b.** large   **10. a.** testcross **b.** all dominant **c.** 1:1   **11. a.** 75 **b.** 25   **12. a.** 50
b. 50   **13. a.** *Bb* **b.** *bb*   **14. a.** *LL* **b.** *ll*   **15. a.** *TtGg*
b. tall with green pods **c.** two **d.** see page 181 in text
16. a. homologous pairs separate **b.** homologous pairs separate independently   **17. a.** ½ (50%) **b.** ½ (50%) **c.** ¾
(75%) **d.** ¼ (25%) **e.** ½ × ¾ = ⅜ **f.** ½ × ¼ = ⅛ **g.** ½ × ¾ =
⅜ **h.** ½ × ¼ = ⅛ **i.** 3:1:3:1
j.

	bT	bt
BT	BbTT	BbTt
Bt	BbTt	Bbtt
bT	bbTT	bbTt
bt	bbTt	bbtt

18. 9 black trotters: 3 black pacers: 3 brown trotters: 1
brown pacer

19. a.

	Bt	bt
BT	BBTt	BbTt
Bt	BBtt	Bbtt
bT	BbTt	bbTt
bt	Bbtt	bbtt

b. 3 black trotters: 3 black pacers: 1 brown pacer: 1 brown
trotter   **20. a.** *BBSS* **b.** *bbss*   **21. a.** %₁₆ **b.** ¼ **c.** 25%

KEYWORD CROSSWORD

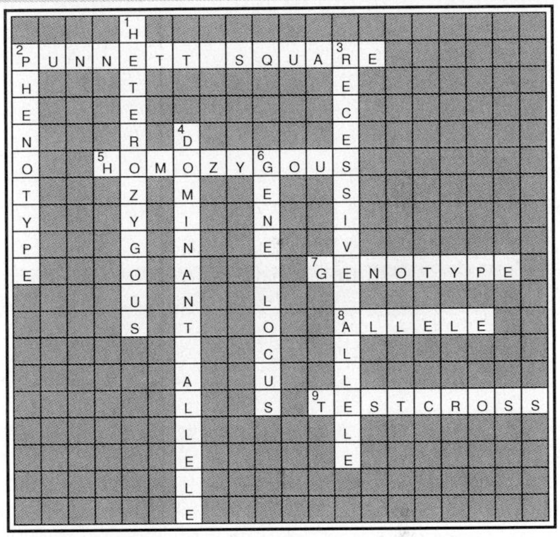

```
²P U N N E T T   S Q U A ³R E
```

(crossword grid with answers: PUNNETT SQUARE, HOMOZYGOUS, GENOTYPE, ALLELE, TESTCROSS, and down words including HETEROTYPE, HETERZYGOUS, and others)

CHAPTER TEST

1. c   **2.** a   **3.** c   **4.** c   **5.** b   **6.** d   **7.** d   **8.** a   **9.** b   **10.** c
11. a   **12.** c   **13.** b   **14.** b   **15.** b   **16.** b   **17.** d   **18.** d
19. a   **20.** c   **21.** It is a dihybrid testcross. The separa-
tion of one pair of alleles (*Tt*) from a heterozygous parent produces a 1:1 ratio. The independent assortment of
two pairs of alleles (*Tt* and *Gg*) from a heterozygous parent produces more variety: four kinds of alleles, and four
different phenotypes among offspring.   **22.** A 1:1:1:1
ratio is produced only if the two gene pairs from the *TtGg*
parent assort independently. They will not assort this
way if they are located on the same chromosome pair. In
this case, only two kinds of gametes, and offspring,
result.

12

CHROMOSOMES AND GENES

The phenotypes of individuals arise from many kinds of genotypes and inheritance patterns. **Dominance,** for example, can be complete or **incomplete. Codominance** can also exist among the offspring of a genetic cross. Genes for some traits have **multiple alleles,** whereas, sometimes, genes interact through pleiotropy or epistasis. On the other hand, **polygenic inheritance** controls some traits. The relative effect of a genotype varies, depending on the influence of the environment.

Genes are located on the chromosomes, as stated by the **chromosomal theory of inheritance.** This explains the similarity of gene behavior during events such as meiosis. All genes on a given chromosome belong to the same **linkage group.** Genes of a linkage group do not obey Mendel's laws. The inheritance patterns of chromosomes explain sex determination in animals, as supported by Morgan's experiments with *Drosophila.* **X-linked** inheritance refers to genes located on the X chromosomes. Solving X-linked genetics problems requires that the Y chromosome be shown as blank for X-linked alleles.

Chromosomal mutations exist in two classes: changes in the number of chromosomes (e.g., **polyploidy,** trisomy, monosomy) and changes in the structure of chromosomes (e.g., inversion, translocation, deletion, and duplication).

Study the text section by section as you answer the questions that follow.

12.1 GOING BEYOND MENDEL (P. 188)

- There are forms of inheritance that involve degrees of dominance, interactions, multiple alleles, and polygenes.
- Environmental conditions can influence gene expression.

1. When a curly-haired person reproduces with a straight-haired person and their children have wavy hair, this is an example of _____.

2. Roan cattle have red hairs and white hairs because of codominance of two alleles. Using the key in the diagram that follows, cross a roan cow and a roan bull, and give the phenotypic ratio. a._____ What ratio would have resulted if red hair was dominant over white hair? b._____

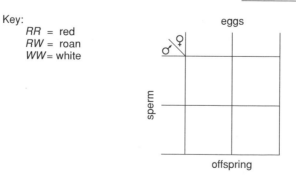

Key:
    RR = red
    RW = roan
    WW = white

3. A gene that affects more than one characteristic is an example of _____.

4. In humans, A = a normal amount of the pigment melanin and a = albinism (absence of pigment), and **B** = brown eyes and b = blue eyes.

   What is the eye color for the genotype $BBAa$? a._____

   What is the eye color for the genotype $bbaa$? b._____

   If a man with the genotype $BBAa$ reproduces with a woman having the genotype $bbaa$, what is the chance (percent) of producing a child with normal amounts of melanin? c._____

   What is the chance of producing a child with albinism? d._____

5. In rabbits there are four alleles for coat color, but each rabbit has only two of these. What type of inheritance pattern is this? _____

6. An investigator notes that a population contains a range of phenotypes that fits a bell-shaped curve. What type of inheritance pattern is this? a._____

   The investigator decides that three pairs of alleles are involved. List all the possible genotypes for an intermediate phenotype. b._____

   Explain your answer. c. _____

   _____

12.2 CHROMOSOMES CONTAIN GENES (P. 192)

- The genes are on the chromosomes; therefore, they behave similarly during mitosis and meiosis.

7. How many chromosomes and alleles are there for each kind in the body cells of an organism?
   a._____

   How many chromosomes and alleles are there for each kind in a gamete? b._____

   In general terms, what different types of combinations of chromosomes and alleles are in the gametes?
   c._____

   In general terms, how does fertilization affect the number of chromosomes and alleles? d._____

   _____

Sex Chromosomes Determine Gender (p. 192)

- Certain chromosomes are called the sex chromosomes because they determine the sex of the individual.

8. Males have what sex chromosomes? a._____

   Females have what sex chromosomes? b._____

   On the basis of your answers, explain why you would expect 50% of all newborns to be males and 50% to be females. c. _____

   _____

Genes That Are on the X Chromosomes (p. 192)

> • Certain traits, unrelated to sex, are controlled by genes located on the sex chromosomes .

9. Indicate whether the following statements about Morgan's findings with *Drosophila* are true (T) or false (F):

_____ a. An allele on the X chromosome was not found on the Y chromosome.

_____ b. *Drosophila* has the same sex chromosome pattern as humans.

_____ c. The behavior of $X^R x^r$ could not be determined.

_____ d. White eyes are dominant to red eyes.

10. Bar eye in *Drosophila* is an X-linked characteristic in which bar eye (*B*) is dominant over nonbar eye (*b*). The genotype of a nonbar-eyed female is ᵃ·_____, and the genotype of a bar-eyed male is ᵇ·_____.

11. a. Draw a Punnett square to show the genotypes among the offspring from a cross of the flies in question 10. Then determine the chance (percent) of each of the following phenotypes:

bar-eyed males ᵇ·_____

bar-eyed females ᶜ·_____

nonbar-eyed males ᵈ·_____

nonbar-eyed females ᵉ·_____

Genes Are Linked (p. 194)

> • Alleles on the same chromosome are said to be linked and it is possible to determine the order of the genes on the chromosomes.

12. All the genes on one chromosome form a linkage group and tend to be inherited together. Mendel's law of independent assortment _____ (does/does not) hold for linked genes.

In questions 13–15, consider that, in humans, arched eyebrow (*E*) is dominant over curved eyebrow (*e*), and hitchhiker thumb (*T*) is dominant over normal thumb (*t*). Imagine that these two genes are linked and that two dihybrids having these gametes reproduce.

13. From the diagram, indicate the phenotype for the following offspring:

a._____

b._____

c._____

d._____

14. What is the phenotypic ratio among the offspring? ᵃ·_____ What would the ratio have been if the genes were on nonhomologous chromosomes, according to Mendel?

b._____

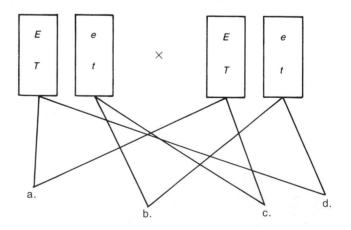

15. What are the chances (percent) that the offspring will have the following? curved eyebrows and normal thumbs ᵃ·_____, arched eyebrows and hitchhiker thumbs ᵇ·_____, arched eyebrows and normal thumbs ᶜ·_____, curved eyebrows and hitchhiker thumbs ᵈ·_____. Is it correct to say that linkage cuts down on the possible number of phenotypes? ᵉ·_____

16. The percentage of crossing-over indicates the distance between two gene loci. For example, *A* and *B* recombine with *a* and *b* in 10% of the offspring, *A* and *C* recombine with *a* and *c* in 20% of the offspring, and *B* and *C* recombine with *a* and *c* in 10% of the offspring.

How many map units are between the following?

A and *C* ᵃ·_____

A and *B* ᵇ·_____

B and *C* ᶜ·_____

d. Draw a line and map the positions of *A*, *B*, and *C*.

12.3 CHROMOSOMES UNDERGO MUTATIONS (P. 196)

- Chromosome mutations are caused by a change in chromosome number and by a change in chromosomal structure.

17. The diploid chromosome number of a species is 24. Give the chromosome number if the species has the following conditions:

pentaploid condition ᵃ·_____

tetraploid condition ᵇ·_____

condition with one trisomy ᶜ·_____

condition with one monosomy ᵈ·_____

18. In the following diagram, write each type of chromosomal mutation illustrated:

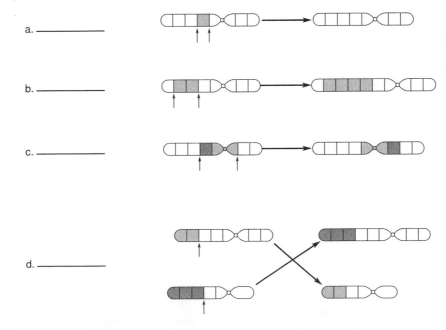

a. _____

b. _____

c. _____

d. _____

RULES AND REGULATIONS

1. Time how long it takes you to answer the questions that follow.
2. Give yourself one point for each correct answer.
3. Add the points for your time and for your correct answers. Did you beat the master?

QUESTIONS

1. If T = tall, t = short, R = round, r = wrinkled, Y = yellow, and y = green, give the genotype for a homozygous tall, round, yellow plant. a._____ Give all the possible gametes for this plant. b._____

2. An offspring of this plant has how many alleles? _____

3. The genotype always has _____ allele(s) for every trait.

4. The gametes always have _____ allele(s) for every trait.

5. A color-blind son received the recessive gene from which parent? _____

For questions 6 and 7, R = red eyes, r = white eyes, L = long wings, and l = vestigial wings.

6. Give the genotype for a white-eyed female fly with vestigial wings. _____

7. Give the genotype for a white-eyed male fly with vestigial wings. _____

8. Give the genotype for a rough guinea pig who is the father of a smooth guinea pig (rough is dominant). _____

9. Give the genotype for a rough, short-haired guinea pig who is homozygous (rough and short are dominant). _____

10. A hidden inherited allele is called _____.

11. A 3:1 ratio results when a heterozygous tall plant is crossed with a plant that is _____.

12. If ¾ of the offspring show the dominant trait, the parents were _____.

13. The cross $AaBb \times AaBb$ results in the appearance of traits in the ratio of _____.

14. Mendel's law of independent assortment is best illustrated by crossing _____.

15. That alleles are inherited individually is stated in Mendel's law of _____.

16. When red and white four-o'clocks are crossed, the color of the offspring is _____.

17. In guinea pigs, black is dominant to white. If two black guinea pigs produce a white offspring, the parents were _____.

18. To determine whether an unknown black guinea pig is pure black or hybrid black, it should be crossed with a(n) _____.

19. A cross of two heterozygous yellow garden peas resulted in 120 offspring. According to the laws of probability, the most likely number of yellow offspring is _____.

20. When true breeding round squash are crossed with true breeding long squash, all offspring are oval in shape. How many phenotypes are produced when pure round squash are crossed with oval squash? _____

21. In fruit flies, white eye is sex-linked. If a white-eyed male is mated with a pure red-eyed female, their offspring will be _____.

22. If the sex is reversed and a white-eyed female is mated with a red-eyed male, their offspring will be _____ males and _____ females.

Master's time	6 minutes	Your time	_____
Master's number correct	22	Your number correct	_____
Master's total	28	Your total	_____

Review key terms by completing this crossword puzzle, using the following alphabetized list of terms.

autosome
codominance
incomplete dominance
linkage group
multiple allele
mutation
polygenic inheritance
polyploid
sex chromosome

Across

2 pattern of inheritance in which several allelic pairs control a trait; each dominant allele contributes in an additive and like manner (two words)

7 alteration in chromosomal structure or number; also an alteration in a gene due to a change in DNA composition

8 pattern of inheritance in which more than two alleles exist for a particular trait (two words)

Down

1 determines the sex of an individual; in many animals, females have two X and males have an X and a Y (two words)

2 condition in which an organism has more than two complete sets of chromosomes

3 alleles of different genes that are located on the same chromosome and tend to be inherited together (two words)

4 pattern of inheritance in which the offspring shows characteristics intermediate between two extreme parental characteristics—for example, a red and a white flower producing pink offspring (two words)

5 any chromosome other than a sex chromosome

6 pattern of inheritance in which both alleles of a gene are expressed equally

OBJECTIVE QUESTIONS

Do not refer to the text when taking this test.

_____ 1. In snapdragons, crossing a pink plant with a white plant produces offspring that are
   a. all red.
   b. ½ red, ½ pink.
   c. ½ pink, ½ white.
   d. all white.

_____ 2. The cross described in number 1 is an example of
   a. multiple alleles.
   b. pleiotropy.
   c. epistasis.
   d. incomplete dominance.

_____ 3. If A = normal pigment, a = albinism (no pigment), B = brown eyes, and b = blue eyes, select the genotype of the person who will NOT develop any pigment for eye color.
   a. _Bbaa_
   b. _BbAa_
   c. _BBAa_
   d. _bbAa_

_____ 4. The cross described in number 3 is an example of
   a. epistasis.
   b. polygenic inheritance.
   c. multiple alleles.
   d. environmental influence.

_____ 5. Select the wheat plant genotype with the darkest-colored seeds (the dominant allele of each gene pair contributes an equal amount of red pigment to the seed).
   a. _AaBbCc_
   b. _AaBBcc_
   c. _AaBbCC_
   d. _AabbCc_

_____ 6. The cross described in number 5 is an example of
   a. polygenic inheritance.
   b. codominance.
   c. X-linkage.
   d. multiple alleles.

_____ 7. Which type of genetic crosses will produce a continuous variation of phenotypes resembling a bell-shaped curve?
   a. codominance
   b. incomplete dominance
   c. multiple alleles
   d. simple dominance
   e. polygenic inheritance

_____ 8. Which of the following statements is NOT true about the chromosomal theory of inheritance?
   a. Genes are on the chromosomes and behave similarly.
   b. The chromosomes, but not the alleles, occur in pairs in diploid cells.
   c. Both the chromosomes and the alleles of each pair separate independently during meiosis.
   d. Fertilization restores the diploid chromosome number and the paired condition for alleles in the zygote.

_____ 9. Who determines the sex of offspring?
   a. male
   b. female
   c. both male and female
   d. alternately male, then female

_____10. If B = normal vision and b = color blindness, then the genotype $X^B X^b$ is a
   a. male with normal vision.
   b. male with color blindness.
   c. female with normal color vision.
   d. carrier female with normal color vision.
   e. female who is color blind.

_____11. Which represents the genotype of a carrier female?
   a. $X^A X^A$
   b. $X^A X^a$
   c. $X^a X^a$
   d. Both _b_ and _c_ are correct.

_____12. If the female in question 11 reproduces with a normal male, then in the F^1 generation,
   a. all males will have the recessive phenotype, and all females will be normal.
   b. a male will have a 50% chance of the recessive phenotype, and a female will have a 50% chance of being a carrier.
   c. 50% of males will have the recessive phenotype, and 50% of females will have the recessive phenotype.
   d. The answer depends on whether the father is heterozygous.

_____13. A male in the P generation has the recessive X-linked condition, but all F_1 offspring are normal. Why would you expect some of the F_2 offspring to have the condition?
   a. The F_1 males and females are heterozygous and carriers.
   b. All of the F_1 females are carriers.
   c. Half of the F_1 females are carriers.
   d. F_2 males always have the condition like their grandfather.

_____14. Genes *A* and *B* are 8 chromosome map units apart. Genes *B* and *C* are 10 units apart. Genes *A* and *C* are 2 map units apart. The order of these genes on the chromosome is
a. *ABC*.
b. *ACB*.
c. *BAC*.
d. *CBA*.

_____15. The diploid number of an organism is 36. Its pentaploid chromosome number is
a. 5.
b. 48.
c. 72.
d. 90.

_____16. The haploid number of an organism is 16. The number of chromosomes in its body cells, if they have one trisomy, is
a. 3.
b. 17.
c. 33.
d. 46.

_____17. The gene arrangement on a chromosome changes from *ABCDEFG* to *ABCDEDEFG*. This is an example of
a. deletion.
b. duplication.
c. inversion.
d. linkage.

_____18. Which of the following conditions is NOT an example of a chromosomal mutation?
a. inversion
b. translocation
c. deletion
d. duplication
e. linkage

_____19. Which chromosomal mutation does NOT require the presence of another chromosome?
a. translocation
b. duplication
c. inversion
d. All of these are correct.

_____20. Which type of chromosomal mutation occurs when two simultaneous breaks in a chromosome lead to the loss of a segment?
a. inversion
b. translocation
c. deletion
d. duplication

CRITICAL THINKING QUESTIONS

Answer in complete sentences.

21. How do genes working together (i.e., polygenic inheritance) to determine a trait produce more variety among the individuals of a population?

22. Why is it evident that a gene for maleness exists on the Y chromosome among humans?

Test Results: _____ Number right ÷ 22 = _____ × 100 = _____ %

EXPLORING THE INTERNET

Use the Internet to further explore topics in this chapter, such as genetic linkage or variation in chromosomal structure and chromosome number. Go to the Mader Home Page (http://www.mhhe.com/sciencemath/biology/mader/) and click on *Biology,* 6th edition. Go to Chapter 12 and select a Web site of interest.

STUDY EXERCISES

1. incomplete dominance **2. a.** 1:2:1 **b.** 3:1
3. pleiotropy **4. a.** brown eyes **b.** pink eyes **c.** 50%
d. 50% **5.** multiple alleles **6. a.** polygenic
b. *AaBbCc, AABbcc, aABBcc, aaBBCc, aabBCC, AAb-bCc* **c.** All capitals have the same quantitative effect.
7. a. two **b.** one **c.** all possible **d.** It restores full number. **8. a.** XY **b.** XX **c.** Fifty percent of male gametes carry X, and 50% carry Y. **9. a.** T **b.** T **c.** F **d.** F
10. a. X^bX^b **b.** X^BY **11. a.**

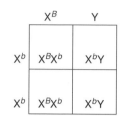

	X^B	Y
X^b	X^BX^b	X^bY
X^b	X^BX^b	X^bY

b. 0% **c.** 100% **d.** 100% **e.** 0% **12.** does not
13. a. arched, hitchhiker **b.** curved, normal **c.** arched, hitchhiker **d.** arched, hitchhiker **14. a.** 3 arched, hitchhiker: 1 curved, normal **b.** 9:3:3:1 **15. a.** 25% **b.** 75%
c. 0% **d.** 0% **e.** yes **16. a.** 20 units **b.** 10 units **c.** 10 units **d.**

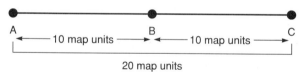

A — 10 map units — B — 10 map units — C

20 map units

17. a. 120 **b.** 72 **c.** 25 **d.** 23 **18. a.** deletion **b.** duplication **c.** inversion **d.** translocation

RAPID FIRE

1. a. *TTRRYY* **b.** *TRY* **2.** six **3.** two **4.** one
5. mother **6.** X^rX^rll **7.** X^rYll **8.** *Rr* **9.** *RRSS*
10. recessive **11.** heterozygous **12.** heterozygous
13. 9:3:3:1 **14.** *AaBb × AaBb* **15.** segregation
16. pink **17.** heterozygous **18.** recessive guinea pig
19. 30 **20.** two **21.** red-eyed **22.** white-eyed, red-eyed

KEYWORD CROSSWORD

(crossword grid with answers: POLYGENIC INHERITANCE, MUTATION, MULTIPLE ALLELE, and down words including POLYPLOIDY, INKAGE(LINKAGE), EXCHROMOSOME, NONCOMPLETE, AUTOSOME, CODOMINANCE, DOMINANCE, MUTATION, DOMINANT GENE, NONDISJUNCTION)

CHAPTER TEST

1. c **2.** d **3.** a **4.** a **5.** c **6.** a **7.** e **8.** b **9.** a **10.** d
11. b **12.** b **13.** c **14.** c **15.** d **16.** c **17.** b
18. e **19.** c **20.** c **21.** One gene pair, with only two alleles, for example, produces only three possible genotypes. Adding more gene pairs increases the possible combination of genes. **22.** The presence of the Y chromosome in humans produces maleness and the absence of this chromosome leads to the absence of maleness.

13

HUMAN GENETICS

CHAPTER REVIEW

Chromosomal abnormalities can be diagnosed through interpreting a **karyotype,** an organized display of paired chromosomes. Chromosomes are often taken from fetal cells recovered through amniocentesis and chorionic villi testing. The chromosomes are treated, photographed, and arranged through karyotyping. Among the well-known chromosomal abnormalities, trisomies include Down syndrome (trisomy 21), Klinefelter syndrome, and triplo-X females and Jacob syndrome males. The extra chromosome inherited for Down syndrome usually arises from a **nondisjunction** during gamete formation. The occurrence of this syndrome is often related to the age of the mother.

Pedigree charts can reveal the inheritance pattern over generations in a family. Inheritance patterns include **autosomal** dominant patterns (neurofibromatosis, Huntington disease), autosomal recessive patterns (phenylketonuria, Tay-Sachs disease), and X-linked patterns (color blindness, hemophilia). Some human inheritance patterns are not this simple; for example, human skin color is a polygenic trait, ABO blood types are produced through multiple alleles, and sickle-cell disease involves incomplete dominance . **Sex-influenced traits** arise when the same genotype leads to a different phenotype due only to the individual's sex.

STUDY EXERCISES

Study the text section by section as you answer the questions that follow.

13.1 CONSIDERING THE CHROMOSOMES (P. 202)

- Normally, humans inherit 22 pairs of autosomes and one pair of sex chromosomes for a total of 46 chromosomes.
- Abnormalities arise when humans inherit an extra chromosome or an abnormal chromosome.

1. Indicate whether the following statements about human karyotypes are true (T) or false (F):
   _____ a. Autosomal chromosomes are ordered from largest to smallest.
   _____ b. Chromosomes are organized into pairs.
   _____ c. A karyotype has 23 pairs of autosomes.
   _____ d. Prophase chromosomes are photographed.
   _____ e. The sex chromosomes are not included.
   _____ f. White blood cells are one source of the chromosomes.

2. a. Illustrate nondisjunction by adding chromosomes where needed to the cells in the following diagram:

   If an abnormal egg with two chromosomes of same kind is fertilized by a normal sperm a (monosomy or trisomy) b._____ results. A monosomy is symbolized by 2n + 1, or 2n − 1? c._____

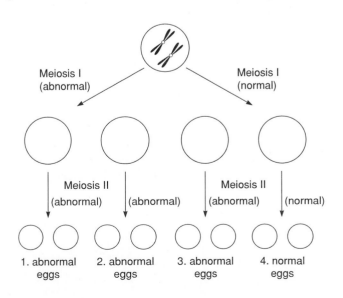

Meiosis I (abnormal)   Meiosis I (normal)

Meiosis II (abnormal)   (abnormal)   Meiosis II (abnormal)   (normal)

1. abnormal eggs   2. abnormal eggs   3. abnormal eggs   4. normal eggs

3. Indicate whether the following statements about Down syndrome are true (T) or false (F):

_____ a. Characteristics include a wide, rounded face and slanting eyelids.

_____ b. In some cases, an extra copy of chromosome 21 is attached to chromosome 16.

_____ c. Children of younger women are more likely to be affected than children of older women.

_____ d. It most often occurs due to a nondisjunction.

_____ e. The *Gart* gene may be involved in the mental retardation that accompanies Down syndrome.

_____ f. Persons with the defect usually have three copies of chromosome 18.

4. Complete each of the following statements with the correct number:

A triplo-X individual has at least ᵃ·_____ X chromosomes.

The number of autosomes in Down syndrome is ᵇ·_____.

The number of autosomes in Klinefelter syndrome is ᶜ·_____.

The number of Y chromosomes in Klinefelter syndrome is ᵈ·_____.

The number of autosomes in Turner syndrome is ᵉ·_____.

The number of X chromosomes in Turner syndrome is ᶠ·_____.

The total number of chromosomes in Jacob (XXY) syndrome is ᵍ·_____.

5. Fragile X syndrome is due to the inheritance of a(n) ᵃ·_____. The fragile location seems to be due to a multiple ᵇ·_____ of the bases CGG.

13.2 CONSIDERING AUTOSOMAL TRAITS (P. 208)

- Many genetic disorders are inherited according to the laws first established by Gregor Mendel.
- The pattern of inheritance indicates whether the disorder is a simple autosomal dominant or simple recessive disorder.
- Polygenic traits include skin color, behavior and various syndromes.
- Blood type is controlled by multiple alleles.
- Some traits like sickle-cell disease are incompletely dominant.

6. A man who is heterozygous for neurofibromatosis disease reproduces with a woman who is normal. The chances (percent) of the offspring having neurofibromatosis disease are ᵃ·_____ and of the offspring being normal are ᵇ·_____.

7. A normal man carrying the allele for PKU reproduces with a normal woman carrying the same allele. The chances (percent) of the offspring having PKU are ᵃ·_____ and of the offspring being normal are ᵇ·_____.

8. Match the descriptions with the disorders.
   1 *cystic fibrosis*
   2 *Huntington disease*
   3 *neurofibromatosis*
   4 *phenylketonuria (PKU)*
   5 *Tay-Sachs disease*

_____ a. lysosomal storage disease

_____ b. benign tumors in skin or deeper

_____ c. progressive nervous system degeneration

_____ d. disorder affecting function of mucous and sweat glands

_____ e. essential liver enzyme deficiency

9. Answer the questions for the following pedigree:

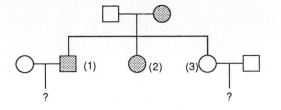

?   ?

What is the mode of inheritance shown in this pedigree? a._____

What is the genotype of person 1? b._____

What are the chances of person 1 having normal children? c._____

What are the chances of person 3 having normal children? d._____

10. Answer the questions for the following pedigree:

What is the mode of inheritance in this pedigree? a._____

?

For person 2, the genotype is b._____, and the phenotype is c._____.

For person 1, the genotype is d._____.

How did you determine this? e. _____

What are the chances that person 3's children will be normal? f._____

11. Consider a model in which there are three gene pairs of alleles; a dominant allele in any pair adds pigment to the skin. Use the letters *A, B, C* to indicate pigment formation and *a, b, c* to indicate lack of pigment formation.

What is the genotype for the darkest individual? a._____

What is the genotype for the lightest individual? b._____

What is the genotype for the offspring from a cross of the individuals from *a* and *b*? c._____

How does the skin color of this person compare to either of the parents? d._____

12. A man with blood type A reproduces with a woman who has blood type B. Their child has blood type O. Give the genotype of all persons involved: man a._____, woman b._____, and child
c._____.

13. If a child has AB blood and the father has type B blood, what could the genotype of the mother be?

_____

14. If a child has BO blood and the father has type O blood, what could the genotype of the mother be?

_____

15. Both a man and a woman have sickle-cell trait. List all phenotypes among the offspring, as well as the chance (percent) of each occurring. a._____, b._____, c._____.

13.3 CONSIDERING SEX-LINKED TRAITS (P. 215)

- Sex-linked traits are usually carried on the X chromosome. Males, with only one X, are more likely to exhibit X-linked disorders.
- The pattern of inheritance can also indicate whether the disorder is an X-linked disorder..
- Some traits are sex-influenced rather than sex-linked.

16. Hemophilia is an X-linked recessive condition. A woman who is a hemophiliac reproduces with a man who is not. The genotype of the woman is a._____ and of the man is b._____.

    What is the genotype of sons from this cross? c._____

    What is the genotype of daughters from this cross? d._____

    What is the chance (percent) of the daughters' sons having hemophilia? e._____ What is the chance

    of the sons' sons (assume noncarrier wife) having hemophilia? f._____

17. Consider this pedigree chart for the family discussed in question 16.

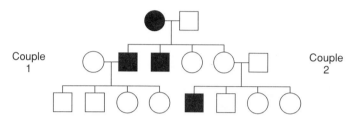

Couple 1   Couple 2

    Based on the genotypes of couple 1, explain why this couple has no hemophilic son. a._____

    _____

    Based on the genotypes of couple 2, explain why this couple has a hemophilic son. b._____

    _____

18. Explain on the basis of the following diagram why you believe baldness to be a sex-influenced characteristic:

Phenotypes	Genotypes	Phenotypes

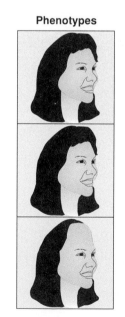

$H^N H^N$

$H^N H^n$

$H^n H^n$

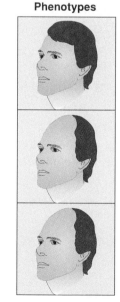

H^N = Normal hair growth
H^n = Pattern baldness

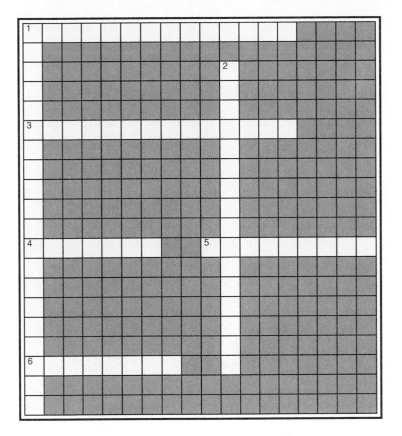

KeyWord CrossWord

Review the key terms by completing this crossword puzzle, using the following alphabetized list of terms:

autosome
carrier
karyotype
multiple alleles
nondisjunction
sex chromosome
sex-influenced trait

Across

1 chromosome that determines the sex of an individual (two words)
3 failure of homologous chromosomes or daughter chromosomes to separate during meiosis II
4 individual who appears incapable but can transmit an infectious or genetic disorder
5 chromosomes arranged by pairs according to their size, shape, and general appearance in mitotic metaphase
6 any chromosome other than a sex chromosome

Down

1 autosomal phenotype controlled by an allele that is expressed differently in the two sexes; for example, the presence of testosterone in males increases the possibility of pattern baldness (three words)
2 pattern of inheritance in which a particular trait has more than two alleles, although each individual has only two of these alleles (two words)

OBJECTIVE QUESTIONS

Do not refer to the text when taking this test.

_____ 1. Select the syndrome in which the person has 45 autosomes.
   a. Down
   b. Klinefelter
   c. Turner
   d. triplo-X

_____ 2. Select the syndrome that is a monosomy.
   a. Down
   b. Klinefelter
   c. Turner
   d. Jacob

_____ 3. Which syndrome affects the sex chromosomes?
   a. Down
   b. Edward
   c. Patau
   d. Turner

_____ 4. From the mating *Pp × pp,* the chance for producing an offspring with PKU is
   a. 0%.
   b. 25%.
   c. 50%.
   d. 75%.

_____ 5. Select the disease caused by an autosomal dominant pattern.
   a. cystic fibrosis
   b. hemophilia
   c. neurofibromatosis
   d. color blindness

_____ 6. Which is NOT involved in producing a karyotype?
   a. arranging chromosomes in pairs
   b. ordering chromosomes by size
   c. photographing chromosomes
   d. removing the pigment from chromosomes

_____ 7. Select the organism with intermediate skin pigmentation.
   a. *AaBbcc*
   b. *AaBBcc*
   c. *Aabbcc*
   d. *AABbCc*

_____ 8. A type O woman has a type O child. The father could have the blood type
   a. A only.
   b. B only.
   c. A or B.
   d. A, B, or AB.

_____ 9. Assuming two alleles (*C* or *c*), the number of possible genotypes for color discrimination in males is
   a. one.
   b. two.
   c. three.
   d. four.

_____10. A woman with sickle-cell trait marries a normal man. The chance for producing a child with sickle-cell disease is
   a. 0%.
   b. 25%.
   c. 50%.
   d. 75%.

In questions 11–12, refer to the following diagram:

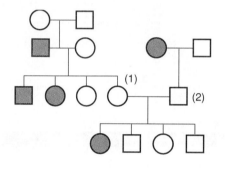

_____11. The shaded individuals are affected with a disorder; the unshaded individuals are not affected. The disorder is
   a. X-linked.
   b. dominant.
   c. recessive.
   d. undetermined.

_____12. Persons 1 and 2 are
   a. *AA × AA.*
   b. *aa × aa.*
   c. *Aa × Aa.*
   d. *Aa × aa.*
   e. *Aa × AA.*

_____13. Which of the following could produce a blue-eyed child (blue eyes being recessive)?
   a. *BB × bb*
   b. *Bb × Bb*
   c. *bb × Bb*
   d. *Bb × BB*
   e. Both *a* and *b* are correct.
   f. Both *b* and *c* are correct.

_____14. Which genotype could NOT be produced if both
parents had type A blood?
   a. type A
   b. type O
   c. type AB
   d. type B
   e. Both c and d are correct.
   f. All of the above are correct.
_____15. Which genotype could NOT be produced from a
parent who is AB?
   a. type A
   b. type B
   c. type AB
   d. type O
_____16. Sickle-cell disease illustrates
   a. Mendelian dominance.
   b. Mendelian recessiveness.
   c. incomplete dominance.
   d. multiple alleles.
_____17. If the husband is a carrier of Tay-Sachs disease
(recessive), but the wife is homozygous normal,
what are the chances of their child having Tay-
Sachs?
   a. 0%
   b. 25%
   c. 50%
   d. 75%

_____18. A person with the sickle-cell trait would have
which genotype?
   a. Hb^AHb^A
   b. Hb^AHb^S
   c. Hb^SHb^S
_____19. Males are more likely to have pattern baldness
because
   a. the allele is carried on the Y chromosome.
   b. they inherit three copies of chromosome 21.
   c. they produce testosterone.
   d. Only males can _ever_ be bald.
_____20. Which genetic disease is characterized by a fail-
ure of the chloride ion membrane channels, resulting in thick mucus in the lungs and digestive
tract?
   a. sickle-cell disease
   b. Tay-Sachs disease
   c. PKU
   d. cystic fibrosis
   e. neurofibromatosis

CRITICAL THINKING QUESTIONS

Answer in complete sentences.

21. What evidence suggests that Huntington disease is not inherited as a simple autosomal dominant disorder?

22. Why are color-blind women rare?

Test Results: _____ Number right ÷ 22 = _____ × 100 = _____ %

EXPLORING THE INTERNET

Use the Internet to further explore topics in this chapter, such as human genes and genetic disorders. Go to the Mader
Home Page (http://www.mhhe.com/sciencemath/biology/mader/) and click on _Biology,_ 6th edition. Go to Chapter 13
and select a Web site of interest.

STUDY EXERCISES

1. a. T **b.** T **c.** F **d.** F **e.** F **f.** T   **2. a.** See Figure 13.2, page 203, in text **b.** trisomy **c.** 2n-1   **3. a.** T **b.** F **c.** F **d.** T **e.** T **f.** F   **4. a.** three **b.** 45 **c.** 44 **d.** one **e.** 44 **f.** one **g.** 47   **5. a.** abnormal X chromosome **b.** repeat   **6. a.** 50% **b.** 50%   **7. a.** 25 % **b.** 75%   **8. a.** 5 **b.** 3 **c.** 2 **d.** 1 **e.** 4   **9. a.** autosomal dominant **b.** *Aa* **c.** 50% **d.** 100%   **10. a.** autosomal recessive **b.** *AA* or *Aa* **c.** normal **d.** *Aa* **e.** because he has an affected child **f.** 0%   **11. a.** *AABBCC* **b.** *aabbcc* **c.** A genotype that has any three capitals and any three lower case letters. **d.** intermediate between the two   **12. a.** AO **b.** BO **c.** OO   **13.** AA or AO   **14.** BB or BO   **15. a.** sickle-cell disease 25 % **b.** sickle-cell trait 50% **c.** normal 25%   **16. a.** X^hX^h **b.** X^HY **c.** X^hY **d.** X^HX^h **e.** 50% **f.** 0%   **17. a.** The wife is not a carrier and a hemophilic father gives his son a Y only. **b.** The wife is a carrier and all her sons have a 50% chance of hemophilia. The father is normal but gives the sons a Y only.   **18.** A man has pattern baldness if his genotype is either *NN* or *Nn;* a woman has pattern baldness only if her genotype is *NN*. This difference is believed to be due to a higher amount of testosterone in the body of a man.

KEYWORD CROSSWORD

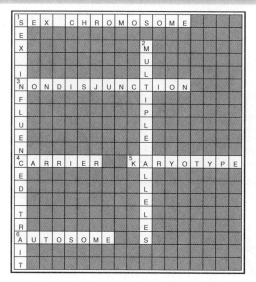

CHAPTER TEST

1. a **2.** c **3.** d **4.** c **5.** c **6.** d **7.** b **8.** c **9.** b **10.** a **11.** c **12.** c **13.** f **14.** e **15.** d **16.** c **17.** a **18.** b **19.** c **20.** d **21.** The severity and time of onset can vary, and it appears that persons most at risk have inherited the disorder from their fathers. Analysis has revealed that Huntington disease is due to many repeats of the base triplet CAG. The more repeats the earlier the onset and the more severe the symptoms.   **22.** For a color-blind female to be produced, the father must be color blind (X^bY) and the mother must be at least a carrier (X^BX^b). This is a very unlikely event.

14

DNA: THE GENETIC MATERIAL

Several experiments proved that **DNA** is the genetic material. Griffith's work revealed the presence of a transforming substance in the pneumococcus infecting mice. Avery and associates reported that the transforming substance was DNA. The results from Hershey and Chase work with a virus offered more convincing evidence for the genetic role of DNA.

Several lines of investigation contributed to a knowledge of DNA structure. Chargaff showed that the amount of **purine** (**adenine** and **guanine**) equals the amount of **pyrimidine** (**cytosine, thymine,** and uracil). Franklin's X-ray diffraction analysis revealed the helical shape of the molecule.

Watson and Crick used the information gained from the experiments of others to build a model of DNA. Alternating sugar-phosphate molecules compose the sides of a ladder, with base pairs composing the rungs. This ladder is twisted into a helix. This model also accurately predicted the mode of DNA replication. As the helix unzips, each parental strand serves as the template for the synthesis of a new daughter strand. Through replication, each duplex produced is identical to the original double helix. This **semiconservative** mode of replication was demonstrated through the experiments of Meselson and Stahl. Replication in prokaryotes and eukaryotes is bidirectional along the chromosome, although the details of the process differ.

STUDY EXERCISES

Study the text section by section as you answer the questions that follow.

14.1 SEARCHING FOR THE GENETIC MATERIAL (P. 222)

- DNA is the genetic material, and therefore, its structure and functions constitute the molecular basis of inheritance.
- DNA stores information that controls both the development and metabolism of a cell.

1. Check the descriptions that are requirements for a substance that is genetic material.
   _____ a. has the constancy to store information and, therefore, serve as a blueprint for each generation
   _____ b. can be replicated and each new cell has a copy
   _____ c. can undergo mutations resulting in variability between species
   _____ d. cannot be transmitted from generation to generation so that veracity exists
   _____ e. conducts photosynthesis ensuring that each organism gets the energy it needs
2. Indicate whether the following statements about Griffith's transformation experiments are true (T) or false (F):
   _____ a. The normal S strain was virulent.
   _____ b. The normal R strain was not virulent.
   _____ c. The heat-killed S strain was not virulent.
   _____ d. A mixture of heat-killed S strain and live R strain was virulent.
3. Based on your answers to question 2, what was Griffith's conclusion? _____

_____

4. Indicate whether the following statements about Avery's transformation experiments are true (T) or false (F):

_____ a. Action of a DNase on the transforming substance prevented transformation.

_____ b. The transforming substance had many nucleotides.

_____ c. Protein from S strain bacteria transformed R strain bacteria.

_____ d. RNA was the transforming substance.

5. Based on your answers to question 4, what was Avery's conclusion? _____

_____

6. The diagram of the Hershey and Chase experiment that follows shows that the two separate experiments used ^{32}P to label a._____ and ^{35}S to label b._____ of viruses. In each experiment, the viruses were allowed to infect bacteria, and then a blender was used to separate the viral coats from the bacteria. Radioactivity was found inside the cell only when c._____ was labeled. Since replication of viruses followed, the hypothesis that d._____ is the genetic material was supported. Label the diagram.

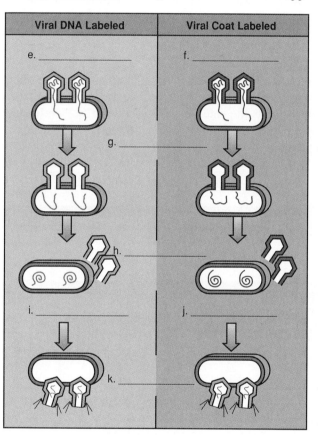

Viral DNA Labeled	Viral Coat Labeled
e. _____	f. _____

g. _____

h. _____

i. _____   j. _____

k. _____

14.2 FINDING THE STRUCTURE OF DNA (P. 225)

- DNA is a double helix; each of the two strands is a polymer of four different nucleotides.
- Hydrogen bonding between complementary bases joins the two strands.
- Four nucleotides permit a great deal of variability, and the sequence of base pairs in DNA varies from gene to gene.

7. Four different nucleotides are found in DNA. Check the way(s) these nucleotides differ.

_____ a. They differ in their sugar content.

_____ b. They differ in their phosphate content.

_____ c. They differ in their base content.

8. What are the four different nucleotide bases in DNA? _____

9. Study the following table and use it to illustrate Chargaff's rules:

Species	A	T	G	C
Homo sapiens	31.0	31.5	19.1	18.4
Drosophila melanogaster	27.3	27.6	22.5	22.5
Zea mays	25.6	25.3	24.5	24.6
Neurospora crassa	23.0	23.3	27.1	26.6
Escherichia coli	24.6	24.3	25.5	25.6
Bacillus subtilis	28.4	29.0	21.0	21.6

Is the amount of each base constant between species? [a.]_____

What is Chargaff's first rule? [b.]_____

_____

With which requirement for the genetic material in question 1 (p. 117) do you associate this rule? [c.]_____

_____

What is constant within each species, as stated in Chargaff's second rule? [d.]_____

_____

With which requirement for the genetic material in question 1 (p. 117) do you associate this rule? [e.] _____

_____

10. Examine the following diagram, which shows the ladder structure of DNA:

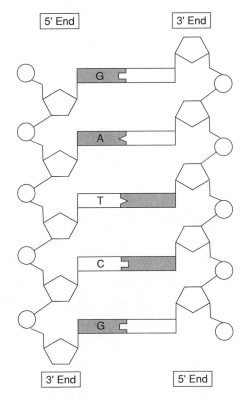

5' End   3' End

G C

A

T

C

G

3' End   5' End

DNA is a polymer of a._____.

Draw a box around one nucleotide. b.

The molecules making up the sides of the ladder are c._____.

Label a sugar and a phosphate. d.

What is meant by the phrase *complementary base pairing?* e._____

Fill in the bases that are complementary to those on the left. f.

What do you have to do to the ladder structure to have it match the Watson and Crick model?

  g._____

Explain what is meant by "double-stranded helix." h._____

_____

Explain what is meant by "antiparallel strands." i._____

_____

14.3 DNA CAN BE REPLICATED (P. 228)

• DNA is able to replicate, and in this way genetic information is passed from one cell generation to the next.

11. Study the following diagram of replication:

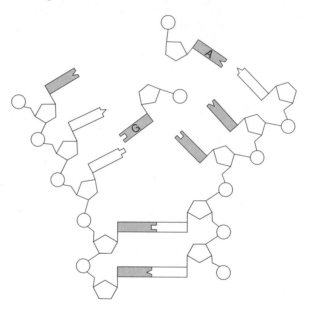

The bases in parental DNA are held together by what type of bond (not shown)? a._____

What happens to these bonds for replication to take place? b._____

During replication, new nucleotides move into proper position by what methodology? c._____

Elongation of DNA is catalyzed by an enzyme called d._____.

Assuming that parental DNA has the base pair sequences shown in the ladder structure (question 10), what
  will be the base pair sequence of the daughter DNA molecule on the left? e._____

_____

What will be the base pair sequence of the daughter DNA molecule on the right? f._____

_____

What do you notice about these sequences? g. _____

12. Use the diagram to help you fill in the blanks below, and complete the explanation of the Meselson and Stahl experiment.

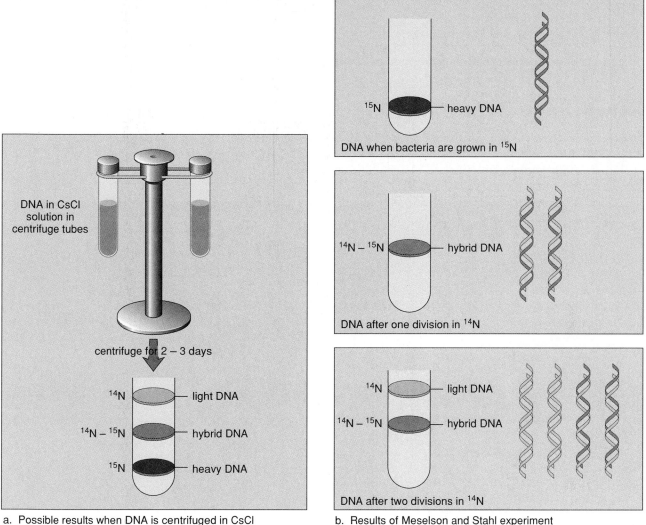

a. Possible results when DNA is centrifuged in CsCl

b. Results of Meselson and Stahl experiment

First, Meselson and Stahl grew bacteria in a medium with a._____ (see upper right). By this step, only b._____ molecules of DNA were in the cells. When they switched the medium to c._____, then d._____ DNA molecules were in the cell after one cell division. After two divisions, half of the DNA molecules were e._____, and the other half were f._____.
Color the DNA molecules to be consistent with the description in the paragraph. g.

13. Meselson and Stahl concluded that DNA replication is a._____, meaning that each daughter molecule contains a(n) b._____ strand and a(n) c._____ strand.

Replication Errors Do Occur (p. 231)

- Mutations occur when there are errors during the replication process.

14. Label each statement as true (T) or false (F) and change all false statements to true statements.

_____ a. A genetic material must be able to undergo rare changes called mutations. Rewrite: _____

_____

_____b. Mutations introduce variations that can possibly cause evolution to occur. Rewrite: _____

_____

_____c. Mutations are rare because RNA polymerase checks to make sure that complementary base pairing

occurs correctly. Rewrite: _____

_____

_____d. This process is called "proofreading." Rewrite: _____

_____

Prokaryotic Versus Eukaryotic Replication (p. 231)

15. Label each statement as indicating DNA replication in prokaryotes (P), eukaryotes (E), or both (P, E).
_____ a. Cells complete replication in a matter of hours.
_____ b. Cells complete replication in a matter of minutes.
_____ c. It begins at numerous origins.
_____ d. It begins at one origin.
_____ e. It is bidirectional.
_____ f. A replication fork is involved.

Review key terms by completing this crossword puzzle, using the following alphabetized list of terms:

adenine
bacteriophage
cytosine
DNA
DNA polymerase
guanine
mutation
nucleic acid
purine
pyrimidine
RNA
thymine

Across

2 one of four nitrogen-containing bases in nucleotides composing the structure of DNA and RNA, pairs with thymine

3 one of four nitrogen-containing bases in nucleotides composing the structure of DNA and RNA, pairs with guanine

4 nucleic acid polymer produced from covalent bonding of nucleotide monomers that contain the sugar; helps carry out protein synthesis

5 type of nitrogen-containing base, such as adenine and guanine, having a double ring structure

7 during replication, an enzyme that joins the nucleotides complementary to a DNA template

10 one of four nitrogen-containing bases in nucleotides composing the structure of DNA, pairs with adenine

11 polymer of nucleotides; both DNA and RNA are this (two words)

Down

1 virus that parasitizes a bacterial cell as its host, often destroying it by lytic action

6 one of four nitrogen-containing bases in nucleotides composing the structure of DNA and RNA, pairs with cytosine

7 nucleic acid polymer produced from covalent bonding of nucleotide monomers that contain the sugar deoxyribose; the genetic material of nearly all organisms

8 type of nitrogen-containing base, such as cytosine, thymine, and uracil, having a single-ring structure

9 alteration in chromosome structure or number and also an alteration in a gene due to a change in DNA composition

OBJECTIVE QUESTIONS

Do not refer to the text when taking this test.

_____ 1. Griffith concluded that
   a. bacteria do not have genetic material.
   b. the genetic material controls the phenotype.
   c. the genetic material can pass from dead bacteria to live bacteria.
   d. Both *b* and *c* are correct.

_____ 2. Which of these would be true of the transforming substance that Avery isolated?
   a. After isolation, it no longer could transform R strain bacteria into S strain bacteria.
   b. Its effect could be destroyed if subjected to ribonuclease, which degrades RNA.
   c. Its effect could be destroyed if subjected to digestion by trypsin, an enzyme that digests protein.
   d. Its effect could be destroyed if exposed to DNAse.

_____ 3. Hershey and Chase found that
   a. the entire virus enters bacteria, so determining whether the protein coat or the DNA controls replication of viruses is difficult.
   b. just the protein coat enters bacteria and controls replication of viruses.
   c. just the DNA enters bacteria and controls replication of viruses.
   d. the protein coat must be digested for DNA to control replication of viruses.

_____ 4. In a DNA molecule, the sugar
   a. bonds covalently to phosphate groups.
   b. bonds covalently to nitrogen-containing bases.
   c. is deoxyribose.
   d. All of these are correct.

_____ 5. Which of these is NOT true of complementary base pairing?
   a. A is always bonded to T.
   b. A pyrimidine is always bonded to a purine.
   c. The amount of A + T is always equal to the amount of G + C.
   d. All of these are true.

_____ 6. If the structure of DNA is compared to a ladder, then the
   a. sides of the ladder consist of phosphate and sugar.
   b. rungs of the ladder are hydrogen-bonded bases.
   c. ladder is twisted.
   d. All of these are correct.

_____ 7. During DNA replication,
   a. the nucleotides separate and reassemble, allowing genetic variability.
   b. the daughter molecules are just like the parental molecule so that constancy is maintained.
   c. one daughter molecule resembles the parental molecule, and one does not, so that variability and constancy are achieved at the same time.
   d. All of these are correct.

_____ 8. Semiconservative replication means that
   a. sometimes DNA can replicate and sometimes it cannot—this accounts for aging.
   b. sometimes daughter DNA molecules are exact copies of parental molecules and sometimes they are not, so that genetic variability may occur.
   c. a new DNA molecule consists of an old strand and a new strand.
   d. All of these are correct.

_____ 9. X-ray diffraction data suggested that, in the ladder structure of DNA,
   a. the sides are composed of bases, and the rungs are composed of phosphate and sugar molecules.
   b. nucleotides have a different composition than previously thought.
   c. DNA has a center from which the ladders project.
   d. the ladder is twisted.

_____ 10. Which is(are) correct regarding DNA?
   a. C is paired with G.
   b. The sugar is deoxyribose.
   c. Hydrogen bonds exist between the bases.
   d. All of these are correct.

_____ 11. Before replication begins,
   a. enzymes must be present.
   b. the parental strands must unzip.
   c. "free" nucleotides must be present.
   d. All of these are correct.

_____ 12. It is NOT required that the genetic material
   a. be replicated.
   b. handle energy.
   c. store information.
   d. undergo mutation.

_____ 13. Griffith found that heat-killed S strains are
   a. mobile.
   b. not mobile.
   c. not virulent.
   d. virulent.

_____14. Hershey and Chase used
   a. C to label nucleic acids.
   b. C to label protein.
   c. N to label protein.
   d. S to label protein.
_____15. By Chargaff's rule,
   a. G = A.
   b. A = T.
   c. C = T.
   d. G = T.
_____16. In the DNA double helix, if 20% of the bases are
   A, then _____ of the bases are G.
   a. 10%
   b. 20%
   c. 30%
   d. 80%
_____17. Franklin offered information about the DNA
   molecule's
   a. base content.
   b. length.
   c. shape.
   d. sugar content.

_____18. Replication of DNA cannot begin until the helix
   a. joins.
   b. transcribes.
   c. transposes.
   d. unwinds.
_____19. Each is true of replication in prokaryotes EX-
   CEPT that it
   a. does not produce replication forks.
   b. is unidirectional.
   c. proceeds from a single loop of DNA.
   d. is relatively rapid.
_____20. Each is true of replication in eukaryotes EX-
   CEPT that it
   a. begins at numerous origins of replication.
   b. begins at replication forks.
   c. is faster than that of prokaryotes.
   d. precedes cell division in eukaryotes.

CRITICAL THINKING QUESTIONS

Answer in complete sentences.

21. What characteristics of proteins do you think might impede their use as the genetic material? Base your answer
   on the three functions of the genetic material listed on page 222 of the text.

22. Why are mutations necessary to the process of evolution?

Test Results: _____ Number right ÷ 22 = _____ × 100 = _____ %

EXPLORING THE INTERNET

Use the Internet to further explore topics in this chapter, such as the famous experiments by Griffith, Beadle and
Tatum, or Hershey and Chase. Go to the Mader Home Page (http://www.mhhe.com/sciencemath/biology/mader/) and
click on *Biology,* 6th edition. Go to Chapter 14 and select a Web site of interest.

ANSWER KEY

STUDY EXERCISES

1. a, b, c   **2. a.** T **b.** T **c.** T **d.** T   **3.** Somehow, the vir-
ulence of the S strain was transferred to the R strain be-
cause the R strain had been transformed.   **4. a.** T
b. T **c.** F **d.** F   **5.** DNA is the transforming substance
and, therefore, the hereditary material.   **6. a.** DNA
b. protein coats **c.** DNA **d.** DNA **e.–k.** see Figure 14.3,
page 224, in text   **7.** c   **8.** adenine (A), guanine (G),
thymine (T), cytosine (C)   **9. a.** no **b.** The quantity of
A, T, C, and G varies from species to species.   **c.** The genetic material can undergo mutations resulting in variability
between species.   **d.** the amount of A = T and the amount
of G = C **e.** The genetic material has the constancy to
store information so it can serve as a blueprint for each
generation.   **10. a.** nucleotides **b.** see figure that

follows **c.** sugar (deoxyribose) and phosphate **d.** see figure that follows **e.** A binds with T, and G binds with C. **f.** see figure that follows **g.** twist it **h.** Each nucleotide polymer is a strand; when the ladder twists, a helix results. **i.** The strands run opposite to one another. One strand ends with an attached phosphate group at the 5′ carbon while the other strand ends with a 3′ carbon which has no attached phosphate group.

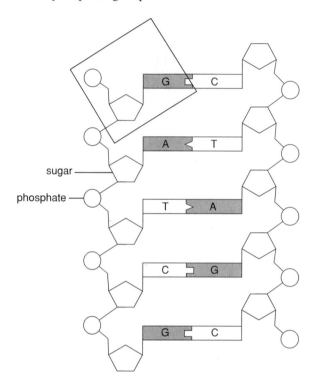

sugar

phosphate

11. a. hydrogen bond **b.** They become unzipped. **c.** complementary base pairing **d.** DNA polymerase **e.** G–C, A–T, T–A, C–G, G–C **f.** same as *e* **g.** They are exactly the same. **12. a.** ¹⁵N **b.** heavy **c.** ¹⁴N **d.** hybrid **e.** light **f.** hybrid **g.** see Figure 14.8, page 229, in text **13. a.** semiconservative **b.** old **c.** new **14. a.** T **b.** T **c.** F Mutations are rare because DNA polymerase . . . **d.** T **15. a.** E **b.** P **c.** E **d.** P **e.** P, E **f.** E

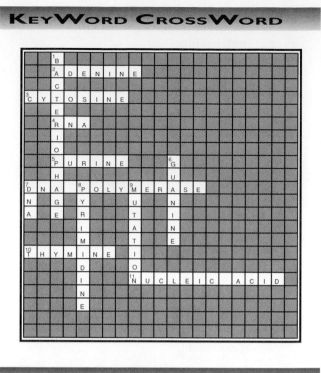

CHAPTER TEST

1. d **2.** d **3.** c **4.** d **5.** c **6.** d **7.** b **8.** c **9.** d **10.** d **11.** d **12.** b **13.** c **14.** d **15.** b **16.** c **17.** c **18.** d **19.** b **20.** c **21.** Proteins have numerous functions in cells; some have a structural role and some have a metabolic role. It seems unlikely, then, that they would also store genetic information. Genetic material should have a means of self replicating and proteins have no such ability. A change in amino acid sequence could be a mutation, but how would such mutations be passed on to offspring? **22.** Mutations are the ultimate means of introducing variation into a population. Recombination that occur during sexual reproduction can produce a different phenotype, but without mutations there could be no changes in the genetic material itself.

15

GENE ACTIVITY

The knowledge of gene activity arose from the experiments of several investigators. Garrod reasoned the basis for inborn errors of metabolism. Beadle and Tatum suggested the one gene—one enzyme hypothesis. Pauling and Itano refined this to the one gene—one polypeptide hypothesis.

RNA differs from DNA in several ways: (1) the pentose sugar is ribose, not deoxyribose; (2) the base uracil replaces thymine; and (3) RNA is single stranded. According to the central dogma of molecular biology, DNA is the template for its own replication and also for RNA formation. The sequence of bases in DNA specifies the proper sequence of amino acids in a polypeptide. The genetic code is a triplet code, and each codon (code word) consists of three bases. The code is just about universal among organisms.

Polypeptide (protein) synthesis requires transcription and translation. **Transcription,** which is the synthesis of an RNA off a DNA template in the nucleus, begins when RNA polymerase attaches to a promoter.

Elongation of an RNA molecule occurs through the process of complementary base pairing until there is a stop DNA sequence. **Messenger RNA (mRNA),** which now carries codons, is processed before it leaves the nucleus; in particular, introns are removed.

Translation, which is the making of a polypeptide in the cytoplasm, requires several types of RNA. **Ribosomal RNA (rRNA)** and various proteins make up a ribosome where a polypeptide is formed. As a ribosome moves down an mRNA strand, the codons pair with the anticodons of **transfer RNAs (tRNA)** which bring amino acids to the ribosomes. Because of this process, the amino acids are joined according to the sequence of bases in DNA.

Mutagens can cause a mutation, which is a change in DNA base sequence leading to noticeable change in protein function. Types of mutations include frameshift and point mutations. The mutation rate of genes is usually low. By producing genetic variety, mutations, along with recombination, are the raw material for evolution.

Study the text section by section as you answer the questions that follow.

15.1 WHAT GENES DO (P. 236)

- Each gene specifies the amino acid sequence of one polypeptide of a protein, molecules that are essential to the structure and function of a cell.

1. Indicate whether the following statements are true (T) or false (F):
   _____ a. Beadle and Tatum induced mutations in asexual haploid spores.
   _____ b. Beadle and Tatum proposed the one gene–one enzyme hypothesis.
   _____ c. Garrod was the first to suggest an association between genes and proteins.
   _____ d. Pauling and Itano showed that a mutation leads to a change in the structure of protein in hemoglobin.
   _____ e. Pauling and Itano proposed the one gene–one enzyme hypothesis.

2. The work of these investigators made it possible to conclude that _____

- The expression of genes leading to a protein product involves two steps, called transcription and translation.
- Three different types of RNA molecules are involved in transcription and translation.

3. Since genes (DNA) reside in the ^{a.}_____ of the cell and polypeptide synthesis occurs in the

   ^{b.}_____, there must be a go-between the two. The most likely molecule to fill this role is

   ^{c.}_____.

4. Indicate whether the following statements about differences between DNA and RNA are true (T) or false (F):
   _____ a. DNA is double stranded; RNA is single stranded.
   _____ b. DNA is a polymer; RNA is a building block of that polymer.
   _____ c. DNA occurs in three forms; RNA occurs in only one.
   _____ d. The sugar of DNA is ribose, which is absent in RNA.
   _____ e. Uracil, in RNA, replaces the base thymine, found in DNA.

5. Complete this table to describe the function of the various types of RNA involved in protein synthesis.

RNA	Function
messenger RNA (mRNA)	a. _____
ribosomal RNA (rRNA)	b. _____
transfer RNA (tRNA)	c. _____

6. Label this diagram which pertains to the central dogma of molecular biology.

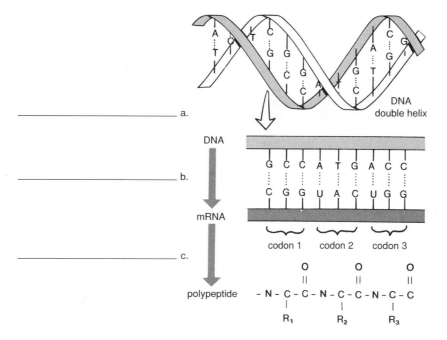

_____ a.

_____ b.

_____ c.

15.3 How Genes Code for Amino Acids (p. 239)

- The genetic code is a triplet code; each code word, called a codon, consisting of three nucleotide bases, stands for a particular amino acid of a polypeptide.

7. Study the following figure which lists the mRNA codons.

First Base	Second Base				Third Base
	U	C	A	G	
U	UUU phenylalanine	UCU serine	UAU tyrosine	UGU cysteine	U
	UUC phenylalanine	UCC serine	UAC tyrosine	UGC cysteine	C
	UUA leucine	UCA serine	UAA *stop*	UGA *stop*	A
	UUG leucine	UCG serine	UAG *stop*	UGG tryptophan	G
C	CUU leucine	CCU proline	CAU histidine	CGU arginine	U
	CUC leucine	CCC proline	CAC histidine	CGC arginine	C
	CUA leucine	CCA proline	CAA glutamine	CGA arginine	A
	CUG leucine	CCG proline	CAG glutamine	CGG arginine	G
A	AUU isoleucine	ACU threonine	AAU asparagine	AGU serine	U
	AUC isoleucine	ACC threonine	AAC asparagine	AGC serine	C
	AUA isoleucine	ACA threonine	AAA lysine	AGA arginine	A
	AUG (*start*) methionine	ACG threonine	AAG lysine	AGG arginine	G
G	GUU valine	GCU alanine	GAU aspartic acid	GGU glycine	U
	GUC valine	GCC alanine	GAC aspartic acid	GGC glycine	C
	GUA valine	GCA alanine	GAA glutamic acid	GGA glycine	A
	GUG valine	GCG alanine	GAG glutamic acid	GGG glycine	G

What does it mean to say that the genetic code is a triplet code? [a] ______________________________

What are the mRNA codons for leucine? [b] ______________________________

____

What does it mean to say that the genetic code is degenerate? [c] ______________________________

What does it mean to say that the genetic code is unambiguous? [d] ______________________________

____

15.4 How Transcription Occurs (p. 240)

- During transcription, a DNA strand serves as a template for the formation of an RNA molecule.

8. Complete this paragraph to describe transcription.

During transcription, the enzyme [a] ______________ attaches to a region called a promoter. An RNA molecule is formed that has a sequence of bases [b] ______________ to a portion of one DNA strand. The bases pair in this manner: A in DNA pairs with [c] ______________ and G pairs with [d] ______________ (and vice versa) in the mRNA being formed. If the sequence of bases in DNA is CGA AGC TCT, then the sequence in mRNA is [e] ______________________________

Why is there a space between every three bases? [f] ______________________________

____

____

Messenger RNA Is Processed (p. 241)

9. Which one, exons or introns, is spliced out when primary RNA is processed? a._____

   Which one, the cap at the 5′ end or the poly-A tail at the 3′ end, tells a ribosome where to attach? b._____

   _____

   Which one, a spliceosome or a ribozyme, is an intron and also an enzyme? c._____

   How is it possible for mRNA processing to produce different products in different cells? d._____

   _____

15.5 HOW TRANSLATION OCCURS (P. 242)

- During translation, the amino acids of a specific polypeptide are joined in the order directed by a type of RNA called messenger RNA.

10. Features of tRNA structure include: At one end an a._____ attaches, and at the other end there is an b._____ which is complementary to a condon in mRNA.

11. Features of rRNA structure include: Each ribosome is composed of a a._____ subunit and a b._____ subunit. Ribosomes have a binding site for c._____ and two d._____ at a time. Several ribosomes moving down the same mRNA plus the mRNA is called a e._____.

12. Label the following diagram which shows the features mentioned in question 11.

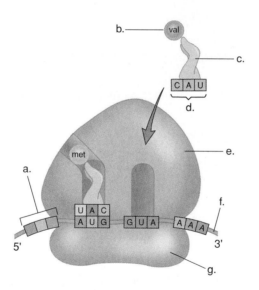

13. What are the three steps of translation? a._____ b._____ c._____

14. Use the diagram in question 11 to help you answer questions with regard to initiation.

   During initiation, two ribosomal subunits come together to form a a._____. An initiator tRNA is at the P site of the ribosome. According to the diagram, the A site is ready for a tRNA that has the anticodon b._____.

15. Use the following diagram to help you answer questions with regard to elongation.

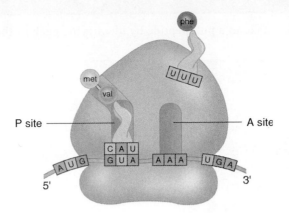

During elongation, the tRNA at the ᵃ·_____ site leaves and its peptide passes to the tRNA-amino acid

at the ᵇ·_____ site. Then ᶜ·_____ occurs, making room for another tRNA-amino acid to

pair with the next codon. This sequence of events reoccurs until the polypeptide is complete.

16. Use the following diagram to help you answer questions with regard to termination.

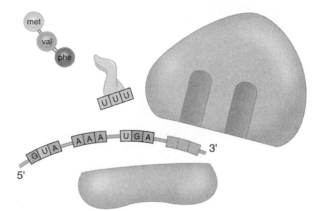

During terminations, the ribosomal ᵃ·_____ dissociate liberating the ᵇ·_____ molecule, and

the ᶜ·_____ is released from the last tRNA before the stop codon UGA.

15.6 MUTATIONS ARE BASE CHANGES (P. 247)

17. The original base sequence is UACUACUAC.

Name the mutation that reads UAUACUACU. ᵃ· _____

Name the mutation that reads UACUAGUAC. ᵇ· _____

Which of these two types of mutations causes sickle-cell disease? ᶜ·_____

18. Aside from replication errors, what affects the rate of mutation? ᵃ· _____

How is DNA protected against mutations due to mutagens? ᵇ· _____

Can you find your way through the maze to a polypeptide by identifying each of the components depicted?

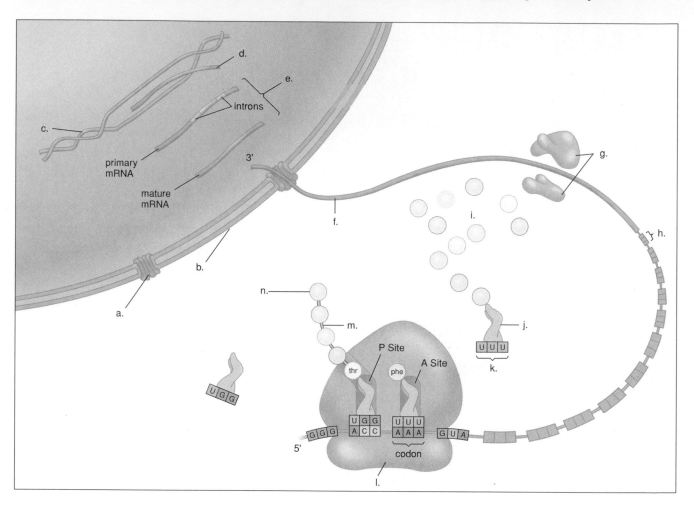

a. _____

b. _____

c. _____

d. _____

e. _____

f. _____

g. _____

h. _____

i. _____

j. _____

k. _____

l. _____

m. _____

n. _____

Review key terms by completing this crossword puzzle, using the following alphabetized list of terms:

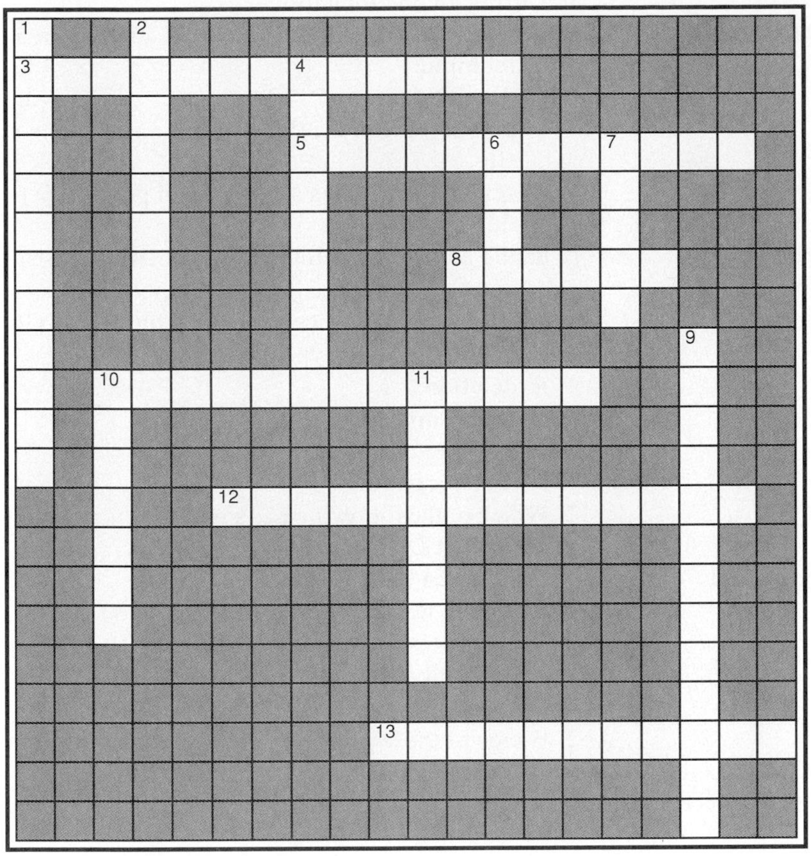

anticodon
codon
exon
intron
messenger RNA
mutagen
polysome
ribosomal RNA
ribozyme
RNA polymerase
transcription
transfer RNA
translation
triplet code

Across

3 type of RNA found in ribosomes that coordinates the coupling of anticodons with codons during polypeptide synthesis (two words)

5 genetic code (mRNA, tRNA) in which sets of three bases call for specific amino acids in the formation of polypeptides (two words)

8 noncoding segments of DNA that are transcribed but removed before mRNA leaves the nucleus

10 type of RNA formed from a DNA template and bearing coded information that directs the amino acid sequence of a polypeptide (two words)

12 enzyme that speeds the formation of RNA from a DNA template (two words)

13 process whereby the sequence of codons in mRNA determines the sequence of amino acids in a polypeptide

Down

1 type of RNA that transfers a particular amino acid to a ribosome during protein synthesis; at one end, it binds to the amino acid, and at the other end, it has an anticodon that binds to an mRNA codon (two words)

2 string of ribosomes that simultaneously translate the same mRNA strand during protein synthesis

4 three nucleotides on a tRNA molecule that are attracted to a complementary codon on mRNA

6 in a gene, the portion of DNA base sequence that is expressed as the result of polypeptide formation

7 three nucleotides of DNA or mRNA; it stands for a particular amino acid

9 process whereby a DNA strand is a template for the formation of mRNA

10 agent, such as radiation or a chemical, that brings about a mutation in DNA

11 enzyme that carries out mRNA processing

OBJECTIVE QUESTIONS

Do not refer to the text when taking this test.

_____ 1. Select the one characteristic that is NOT different between DNA and RNA.
   a. identity of the nucleotide sugar
   b. identity of one of the bases
   c. number of strands in the molecule
   d. solubility in water

_____ 2. Select the incorrect association.
   a. mRNA—takes DNA message to the ribosome
   b. mRNA—takes amino acids to the ribosome
   c. rRNA—combines with protein in ribosomal subunits
   d. tRNA—has an anticodon

_____ 3. Select the incorrect association.
   a. transcription—DNA synthesized
   b. transcription—RNA synthesized
   c. translation—occurs at the ribosome
   d. transition—polypeptide is made

_____ 4. If each codon consisted of two bases, there would be _____ different codons.
   a. 4
   b. 16
   c. 64
   d. 128

_____ 5. The base sequence of DNA is ATAGCATCC. The sequence of RNA transcribed from this strand is
   a. ATAGCATCC.
   b. CCTACGATA.
   c. CCUACGAUA.
   d. UAUCGUAGG.

_____ 6. An mRNA base sequence is UUAGCA. The two anticodons complementary to this are
   a. AAT CGT.
   b. AAU CGU.
   c. TTA GCA.
   d. UUA GCA.

_____ 7. A DNA base sequence is 90 bases long. How many codons can this sequence order?
   a. 270
   b. 180
   c. 90
   d. 30

_____ 8. An RNA base sequence is 120 bases long. How many anticodons can it order?
   a. 240
   b. 180
   c. 120
   d. 40

_____ 9. During chain elongation,
   a. the P site but not the A site of a ribosome is required.
   b. the tRNA at the P site transfers the growing polypeptide to the tRNA–amino acid at the A site.
   c. several ribosomes are involved per polypeptide made.
   d. the amino acids line up and then are joined by peptide bonds.

_____10. A DNA base sequence changes from ATGCGG to ATGCGC. This type of mutation is
   a. deletion.
   b. frameshift.
   c. point.
   d. translocation.

_____11. Which of the following pairs is NOT a valid comparison of DNA and RNA?

	DNA	**RNA**
a.	double helix	single stranded
b.	replicates	replicates
c.	deoxyribose	ribose
d.	thymine	uracil

_____12. Which of these is true of an anticodon but is not true of a codon?
   a. part of an RNA molecule
   b. sequence of three bases
   c. part of a tRNA molecule
   d. part of a mRNA molecule

_____13. If a mutation occurs, then
   a. the code changes
   b. some particular codon or codons changes
   c. some particular anticodon or anticodons changes
   d. Both _a_ and _b_ are correct.
   e. All of these are correct.

_____14. RNA nucleotides are joined during transcription by
   a. helicase.
   b. DNA polymerase.
   c. RNA polymerase.
   d. ribozymes.

_____15. Which statement is NOT true?
   a. Transcription in eukaryotes occurs in the nucleus.
   b. Introns are DNA segments found within a gene but not expressed.
   c. Exons are portions of a gene that are ultimately expressed.
   d. Ribozymes are protein enzymes that remove introns during RNA processing.

_____16. Which of these is happening when translation takes place?

a. mRNA is still in the nucleus

b. tRNAs are bringing amino acids to the ribosomes

c. rRNA is exposing its anticodons

d. DNA is being replicated

e. All of these are correct.

_____17. Which of these is true concerning translation?

a. Each polypeptide is synthesized one amino acid at a time.

b. The amino acids are joined by RNA polymerase at the same time.

c. Each ribosome is responsible for adding a single amino acid to each polypeptide.

d. The same type of polypeptide often contains a different sequence of amino acids.

e. All of these are true.

_____18. Which of the following is NOT correct?

a. mRNA is produced in the nucleus and processed in the cytoplasm.

b. Several ribosomes move along mRNA at a time.

c. DNA has a triplet code, and each triplet stands for an amino acid.

d. tRNA brings amino acids to ribosomes, where they contribute to polypeptide formation.

_____19. If the triplet code in DNA is TAG, what is the anticodon?

a. UTC

b. AUG

c. UAG

d. ATG

_____20. The substitution of histidine for tyrosine will have little effect if

a. the shape of the protein does not change.

b. the active site does not change.

c. histidine and tyrosine have similar properties.

d. All of these are correct.

CRITICAL THINKING QUESTIONS

Answer in complete sentences.

21. What is the significance of a universal genetic code throughout the kingdoms of life?

22. Why is control of protein synthesis advantageous to the cell, compared to other kinds of molecules?

Test Results: _____ Number right ÷ 22 = _____ × 100 = _____ %

EXPLORING THE INTERNET

Use the Internet to further explore topics in this chapter, such as DNA structure and replication, or protein synthesis. Go the Mader Home Page (http://www.mhhe.com/sciencemath/biology/mader/) and click on *Biology,* 6th edition. Go to Chapter 15 and select a Web site of interest.

ANSWER KEY

STUDY EXERCISES

1. a. T **b.** T **c.** T **d.** T **e.** F **2.** the genes determine the proteins of the cell. **3. a.** nucleus **b.** cytoplasm **c.** RNA. **4. a.** T **b.** F **c.** F **d.** F **e.** T **5. a.** takes a message from DNA in the nucleus to the ribosomes in the cytoplasm. **b.** is found in ribosomes, where proteins are synthesized. **c.** transfers amino acids to the ribosomes. **6. a.** replication **b.** transcription **c.** translation **7. a.** Every three bases stands for an amino acid. **b.** UUA, UUG, CUU, CUC, CUA, CUG **c.** There can be more than one codon for each amino acid. **d.** Each codon has only one meaning. **8. a.** RNA polymerase **b.** complementary **c.** U **d.** C **e.** GCU UCG ACA **f.** The code is a triplet code and each codon contains three bases. **9. a.** introns **b.** cap **c.** ribozyme **d.** The product depends on which exons remain and how they are arranged. **10. a.** amino acid **b.** anticodon **11. a.** small **b.** large **c.** mRNA **d.** tRNAs **e.** polysome **12. a.** codon **b.** amino acid **c.** tRNA **d.** anticodon **e.** large ribosomal subunit **f.** mRNA **g.** small ribosomal subunit **13. a.** initiation **b.** elongation **c.** termination **14. a.** ribosome **b.** CAU **15. a.** P **b.** A **c.** translocation **16. a.** subunits **b.** mRNA **c.** polypeptide **17. a.** frameshift **b.** point **c.** point **18. a.** exposure to mutagens **b.** through the action of repair enzymes

PROTEIN SYNTHESIS MAZE

a. nuclear pore **b.** nuclear envelope **c.** DNA **d.** primary mRNA **e.** mRNA processing **f.** mRNA **g.** large and small ribosomal subunits **h.** codon **i.** amino acids **j.** tRNA **k.** anticodon **l.** ribosome **m.** peptide bond **n.** polypeptide

KEYWORD CROSSWORD

3 (across). RIBOSOMAL RNA
5. TRIPLET
7. CODE
8. INTRON
10. MESSENGER RNA
12. RNA POLYMERASE
13. TRANSLATION

CHAPTER TEST

1. d **2.** b **3.** a **4.** b **5.** d **6.** b **7.** d **8.** d **9.** b **10.** c **11.** b **12.** c **13.** b **14.** c **15.** d **16.** b **17.** a **18.** a **19.** c **20.** d **21.** It shows that all organisms have a common origin. Related organisms share genetic characteristics. **22.** Proteins have a wide variety of functions in cells, ranging from structural roles to enzymatic activity. Other molecules are not this varied in their abilities.

16

REGULATION OF GENE ACTIVITY

In prokaryotic cells, gene regulation usually occurs at the level of transcription. Examples are the *lac* **operon,** in which a repressor protein coded by a **regulator gene** ordinarily binds the **operator** so that RNA polymerase is unable to bind and transcription is therefore unable to take place. When lactose is present, it binds to the **repressor,** and then this combination is unable to bind to the operator. The *lac* operon is an **inducible operon.** The *trp* operon is a **repressible operon** because the repressor must bind with a **corepressor** (i.e., tryptophan) before the complex can bind to the operator and stop protein synthesis.

Eukaryotic cells have four levels of gene regulation: transcriptional, posttranscriptional, translational, and posttranslational. Transcriptional control includes the organization of the chromatin and the use of **transcription factors.** Posttranscriptional control includes differences in mRNA processing and the speed with which mRNA leaves the nucleus. Translational control pertains to the life span of mRNA molecules, which can vary; some mRNAs may need modification before they can be translated. Posttranslational control includes feedback control of enzymes, as well as the possible need for additional changes before a protein is functional.

Cancer is due to the disruption of genetic control in cells. **Carcinogens** cause mutations that lead to cancer. These mutations activate **oncogenes** or deactivate **tumor-suppressor genes,** resulting in uncontrolled cell division that leads to a **tumor.** A growth control network includes plasma membrane receptors for growth factors, intracellular reactions, and the genes that code for these. Proper diet can influence events in cells and help prevent cancer.

Study the text section by section as you answer the questions that follow.

16.1 PROKARYOTES UTILIZE OPERONS (P. 252)

• Regulator genes control the expression of genes that code for a protein product.

1. Label this diagram of a *lac* operon using the following terms: a.
   mRNA
   operator
   promoter
   regulator gene
   repressor protein
   structural genes
   transcription is prevented

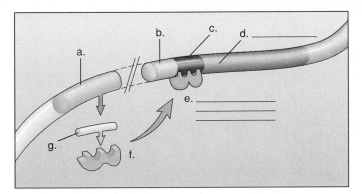

Which of these codes for a repressor? b._____

To which of these does RNA polymerase bind? c._____

To which of these does the repressor bind? d._____

Which of these codes for enzymes of the pathway? e._____

2. Cross out all portions of the diagram that are not in use if the *lac* operon is turned off.

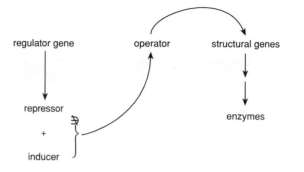

3. Cross out all portions of the diagram that are not in use if the *lac* operon is turned on.

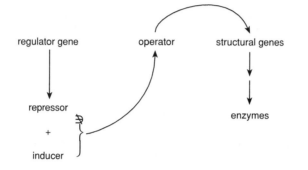

4. Put this sequence of events in order to describe how *E. coli* ensures that the lactose operon is maximally turned on when glucose is absent.

_____ a. Cyclic ATP builds up.

_____ b. Now RNA polymerase is better able to bind to the promoter.

_____ c. Cyclic ATP binds to catabolite activator protein (CAP).

_____ d. The complex attaches to the lac promoter.

5. With the *trp* operon, are the structural genes ordinarily turned on or off? a._____ Why is the *trp*

operon a repressible operon? b. _____

16.2 EUKARYOTES UTILIZE VARIOUS METHODS (P. 254)

- The structural organization of chromatin helps control gene expression in eukaryotes.
- The control of gene expression can occur at all stages from transcription to the activity of proteins in the eukaryotic cell.

6. Complete the following table:

Levels of Control of Gene Activity	Affects the Activity of

7. Indicate whether the following statements about heterochromatin and euchromatin are true (T) or false (F):
_____ a. Highly compacted and condensed heterochromatin is inactive.
_____ b. Heterochromatin is actively being transcribed.
_____ c. Decompacted euchromatin is inactive.
_____ d. Looped euchromatin is actively being transcribed.

8. Which statement in question 6 is supported by knowledge of Barr bodies? a._____ Why? b._____
_____

9. Which statement in question 6 is supported by knowledge of lampbrush chromosomes? a._____
Why? b._____

10. Consider the following diagram:

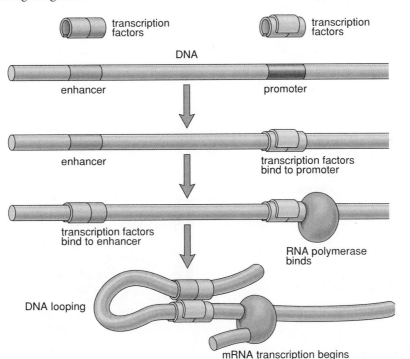

What are transcription factors? a._____
_____
_____

Where do transcription factors bind? b._____

What conformational change occurs before transcription begins? c._____

11. Questions 7–9 pertain to what level of genetic control in eukaryotes? _____

12. Label each of these as either posttranscriptional (PTC), translational control (TL), or posttranslational control (PTL):
    _____ a. The end product of a metabolic pathway binds to enzyme that speeds the first reaction of the pathway.
    _____ b. mRNA persists for different lengths of times in cells.
    _____ c. Estrogen interferes with ribonuclease activity in certain cells. Ribonuclease destroys mRNA.
    _____ d. Different patterns of mRNA splicing.

16.3 CANCER IS A FAILURE IN GENETIC CONTROL (P. 260)

- Cancer cells have characteristics that are consistent with their ability to grow uncontrollably.
- Mutations of proto-oncogenes and tumor-suppressor genes are now known to cause cancer.
- It is possible to avoid certain agents that contribute to the development of cancer and to take protective steps to reduce the risk of cancer.

13. Complete the following table:

Characteristics of Normal Cells	Characteristics of Cancer Cells
controlled growth	
contact inhibition	
one organized layer in tissue culture	
differentiated cells	
normal nuclei	

14. Instead of growing in a._____ layer(s), as normal cells do, cancer cells grow in b._____ layer(s), losing the property of c._____ inhibition. Cancer cells divide to form a growth, or d._____. The cells of e._____ tumors remain in one place. The cells of f._____ tumors wander, a characteristic called g._____.

15. This diagram shows a growth control network in cells. Label the statements as being associated with oncogenes (O) or tumor-suppressor genes (T).
    _____a. receptor capable of binding to a growth factor
    _____b. receptor incapable of binding to a growth factor
    _____c. changes in the growth control network so that cell division is promoted
    _____d. changes in the growth control network so that cell division is inhibited

16. In question 15, where would you place a *T* if your answer pertained to a mutated tumor-suppressor gene? _____

17. In question 15, where would you place a *P* for proto-oncogene? _____

18. By what particular reaction does a cell activate or inactivate signaling proteins? _____

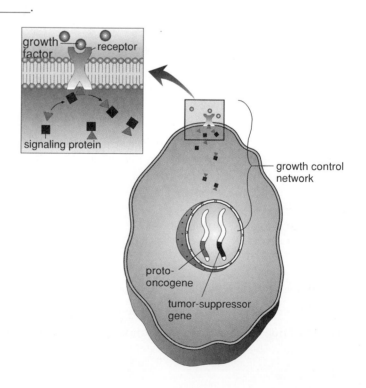

19. What are carcinogens? ª·_____

   Name four environmental factors that are carcinogens. ᵇ·_____

20. The right diet can help reduce the chances of cancer. What would you advise about the following?

   obesity ª·_____

   intake of salt-cured, smoked, or nitrite-cured foods ᵇ·_____

   fat intake ᶜ·_____

   intake of fruits and vegetables containing vitamins A and C ᵈ·_____

   intake of high-fiber foods ᵉ·_____

KEYWORD CROSSWORD

Review key terms by completing this crossword puzzle, using the following alphabetized list of terms:

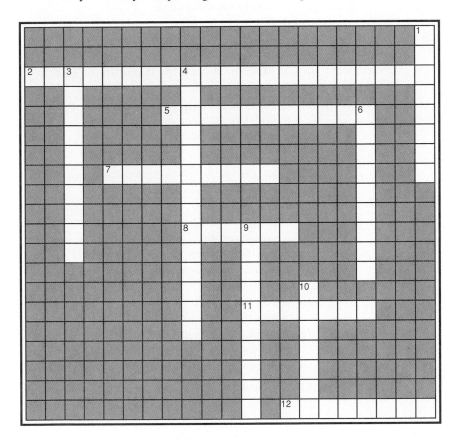

Barr body
cancer
carcinogen
corepressor
inducer
metastasis
mutagen
oncogene
operator
proto-oncogene
repressor
tumor-suppressor gene

Across

2 gene that codes for a protein that ordinarily suppresses cell division (three parts)
5 molecule that binds to a repressor, allowing the repressor to bind to an operator in a repressible operon
7 dark-staining body in the nuclei of female mammals that contains a condensed, inactive X chromosome (two words)
8 malignant tumor whose nondifferentiated cells exhibit loss of contact inhibition, uncontrolled growth, and the ability to invade tissue and metastasize
11 molecule that brings about activity of an operon by joining with a repressor and preventing it from binding to the operator
12 cancer-causing gene

Down

1 in an operon, the sequence of DNA to which the repressor protein binds
3 spread of cancer from the place of origin throughout the body; caused by the ability of cancer cells to migrate and invade tissues
4 normal gene that can become an oncogene through mutation (two parts)
6 in an operon, a protein molecule that binds to an operator, preventing RNA polymerase from binding to the promoter site
9 environmental agent that causes mutations, leading to the development of cancer
10 agent, such as radiation or a chemical, that brings about a mutation in DNA

OBJECTIVE QUESTIONS

Do not refer to the text when taking this test.

_____ 1. A drug prevents the exit of mRNA from the nucleus. This control is
   a. transcriptional.
   b. posttranscriptional.
   c. translational.
   d. posttranslational.

_____ 2. Select the incorrect association.
   a. promoter—accepts RNA polymerase
   b. regulator—makes inducer
   c. repressor—binds to operator
   d. structural gene—transcriptional unit

_____ 3. Select the correct statement about the _lac_ operon.
   a. It involves at least five enzymes.
   b. It is an inducible operon.
   c. It was first studied in _B. subtilis._
   d. Tryptophan is the inducer in this operon.

_____ 4. Select the correct statement about the _trp_ operon.
   a. It is an inducible operon.
   b. It was first studied in _B. subtilis._
   c. Lactose is the inducer.
   d. Tryptophan is a corepressor.

_____ 5. Select the incorrect statement about heterochromatin.
   a. It is found in Barr bodies.
   b. It is genetically inactive.
   c. Its pattern is highly diffuse.
   d. Polytene chromosomes are not in this state.

_____ 6. Chromosome puffs indicate that the
   a. DNA is being destroyed.
   b. DNA is very active.
   c. genetic material is radioactive.
   d. RNA remains bound to DNA.

_____ 7. An enhancer affects what level of genetic control?
   a. transcriptional
   b. posttranscriptional
   c. translational
   d. posttranslational

_____ 8. Which of the following does NOT describe the behavior of cells in a malignant tumor?
   a. carry out metastasis
   b. lose the ability of contact inhibition
   c. multiply rapidly
   d. remain in one site

_____ 9. An agent that contributes to the development of cancer is a(n)
   a. carcinogen.
   b. oncogene.
   c. promoter.
   d. tumor-suppressor gene.

_____10. Which of the following is NOT a suggested measure to prevent cancer?
   a. Avoid foods of the cabbage family.
   b. Cut down on salt-cured foods.
   c. Eat more high-fiber foods.
   d. Increase the intake of vitamins A and C.

_____11. Which of the following will NOT help you to prevent cancer?
   a. Avoid carcinogenic chemicals.
   b. Stop smoking.
   c. Lower total fat intake.
   d. Eat fewer high-fiber foods.
   e. Eat more broccoli and cauliflower.

_____12. A promoter
   a. turns on and off the transcription of a set of structural genes.
   b. binds to RNA polymerase.
   c. codes for the enzymes necessary for the transcription of polypeptides.
   d. is an intron that breaks up a structural gene.

For questions 13–16, match each of the following levels of control to the correct description:
   a. _transcriptional_
   b. _posttranscriptional_
   c. _translational_
   d. _posttranslational_

_____13. Antisense RNA controls the expression of a gene in bacteria.

_____14. Given lactose, _E. coli_ begins to make three enzymes that metabolize this sugar.

_____15. The mRNA leaving the nucleus of the hypothalamus and thyroid gland is different.

_____16. Feedback controls the metabolic activity of genes.

_____17. Which statement is descriptive of euchromatin?
   a. A Barr body is in this form.
   b. It is highly compacted and visible with the light microscope.
   c. Lampbrush chromosomes are an example.
   d. It is diffuse in its pattern when viewed under the microscope.
   e. Both _c_ and _d_ are correct.

For questions 18–20, match the following parts of an operon to the correct description:
   a. _regulator_
   b. _promoter_
   c. _structural genes_
   d. _operator_

_____18. A group of genes that code for enzymes active in a particular metabolic pathway.

_____19. A segment of DNA that acts as an on/off switch for transcription of the structural gene.

_____20. A gene that codes for a protein that either directly combines with the operator or else must first join with a metabolite before joining with the operator.

CRITICAL THINKING QUESTIONS

Answer in complete sentences.

21. How can you reason that a human muscle cell contains a gene to make the polypeptides in hemoglobin?

22. How might cancer be cured through a study of gene control systems?

Test Results: _____ Number right ÷ 22 = _____ × 100 = _____ %

EXPLORING THE INTERNET

Use the Internet to further explore topics in this chapter, such as the eukaryotic cell cycle and cancer, or how oncogenes may trigger cancer development. Go to the Mader Home Page (http://www.mhhe.com/sciencemath/biology/mader/) and click on *Biology,* 6th edition. Go to Chapter 16, and select a Web site of interest.

ANSWER KEY

STUDY EXERCISES

1. a. see page 252 in text **b.** regulator gene **c.** promoter **d.** operator **e.** structural genes **2.** cross out *inducer, structural genes, enzymes* **3.** cross out arrow to operator **4.** a, c, d, b **5. a.** turned on **b.** because the operon is ordinarily turned on, and the corepressor combines with the repressor to turn it off

6.

Levels of Control of Gene Activity	Affects the Activity of
transcriptional	DNA
posttranscriptional	mRNA during formation and processing
translational	mRNA life span during protein synthesis
posttranslational	protein

7. a. T **b.** F **c.** F **d.** T **8. a.** a **b.** because a Barr body is a highly condensed X chromosome that is inactive **9. a.** d **b.** because lampbrush chromosomes are looped, and transcription is actively going on **10. a.** factors that must be in place for transcription to begin **b.** enhancer and promoter **c.** A looping occurs to bring the transcription factors attached to the enhancer and promoter next to one another. **11.** transcriptional **12. a.** PTL **b.** TL **c.** TL **d.** PTC

13.

Characteristics of Cancer Cells

uncontrolled growth

no contact inhibition

disorganized, multilayered

nondifferentiated cells

abnormal nuclei

14. a. one **b.** multiple **c.** contact **d.** tumor **e.** benign **f.** malignant **g.** metastasis **15. a.** O **b.** T **c.** O **d.** T **16.** a, c **17.** b, d **18.** by adding or removing a phosphate **19. a.** environmental factors that can cause mutations **b.** smoking, organic chemicals, radiation, viruses **20. a.** avoid **b.** avoid **c.** reduce **d.** increase **e.** increase

KeyWord CrossWord

Across:
2. TUMOR-SUPPRESSOR GENE
5. COREPRESSOR
7. BARR BODY
8. CANCER
11. INDUCER
12. ONCOGENE

Down:
1. OPERATOR
3. METASTASIS
4. PPRESSOR
6. REPRESSOR
9. CARCINOGEN
10. MUTAGEN
Also: NONCODING GENE

Chapter Test

1. b **2.** b **3.** b **4.** d **5.** c **6.** b **7.** a **8.** d **9.** a **10.** a **11.** d **12.** b **13.** b **14.** a **15.** b **16.** d **17.** e **18.** c **19.** d **20.** a **21.** The muscle cell is derived from the first cell, the zygote, by mitosis. Mitosis assures that all daughter cells receive all chromosomes with copy of each gene. **22.** Cancer might be cured by learning how to suppress the effects of oncogenes, preventing them from promoting uncontrolled cell division. Learning how to activate tumor-suppressor genes can also stabilize cell growth.

17

RECOMBINANT DNA AND BIOTECHNOLOGY

Through biotechnology, natural biological systems are manipulated to make desirable products for human beings. One technological advance involves using a vector to introduce a foreign gene into a cell. Foreign DNA is inserted into a vector, which is either a **plasmid** or a virus. The foreign gene can then be **cloned** in this manner. After receiving the foreign gene through the vector, a cell is transformed and is then capable of making such products as hormones and vaccines. A genomic library can be used as a source of genes to be cloned. Instead of utilizing cloning, the polymerase chain reaction (PCR) can make multiple copies of a DNA segment.

DNA fingerprinting is a way to analyze DNA. If the entire genome is used, radioactive probes are used to mark specific regions of the DNA. If analysis follows PCR, probes are not required because of the limited amount of DNA involved. PCR plus analysis, which may even involve sequencing the bases of a DNA segment has proved to be invaluable.

Organisms that receive a foreign gene are **transgenic.** There are transgenic bacteria, plants, and animals. **Genetically engineered** bacteria protect plants, perform bioremediation, produce chemicals, and help mine various metals. Safeguards are in place to prevent transgenic bacteria from disturbing ecosystems. Plants and animals can be improved or can be used to produce products such as pharmaceuticals.

In ex vivo **gene therapy,** cells are removed, are genetically engineered to control a specific genetic disorder, and are returned to the patient. During in vivo therapy, the gene is delivered directly to the patient, usually using a virus as a vector.

The Human Genome Project is under way to map the human chromosomes. Its goal is to identify the location of all genes and the order of the base pairs on all the human chromosomes.

Study the text section by section as you answer the questions that follow.

17.1 CLONING OF A GENE (P. 270)

- Using recombinant DNA technology, bacteria and viruses can be utilized to clone a gene.
- A genomic library contains bacteria or viruses that carry fragments of all the DNA of a particular organism.
- The polymerase chain reaction (PCR) makes multiple copies of a particular piece of DNA so that it can be analyzed.

1. In the diagram, write the numbers of the following descriptions in the appropriate blanks:
   1 *Cloning occurs when host cell reproduces.*
   2 *Host cell takes up recombined plasmid.*
   3 *DNA ligase seals human gene and plasmid.*
   4 *Restriction enzyme cleaves DNA.*

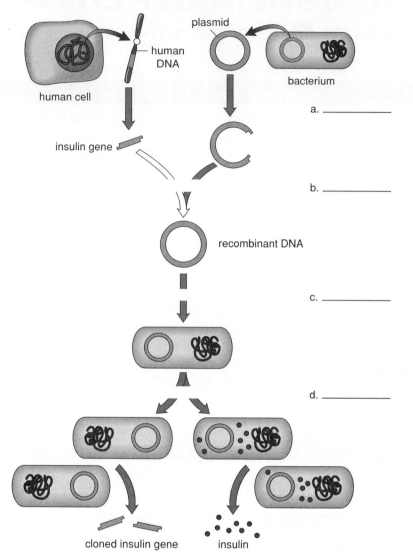

a. _____

b. _____

c. _____

d. _____

2. What is meant by the expression that restriction enzymes produce "sticky ends"? _____

_____

3. Change the following false statements to true statements:

   a. Only plasmids are used as vectors during genetic engineering experiments. _____

   _____

   b. Recombinant DNA contains two types of bacterial DNA recombined together. _____

   _____

   c. Genetic engineering usually means that an organism receives genes from a member of its own species. ____

   _____

   _____

   d. Gene cloning occurs when a gene produces many copies of various genes. _____

   _____

4. Use the following diagram to help you complete this paragraph.

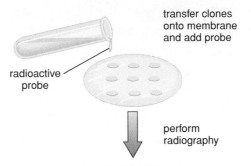

transfer clones
onto membrane
and add probe

radioactive
probe

perform
radiography

The clones on the petri dish are from a genomic library. What is a genomic library? a. _____

If these clones are from a mammalian cell, the genes are accompanied by b. _____ regions that are

necessary for the expression of mammalian genes. If these clones have been made using reverse

transcriptase, then the cDNA contains the c. _____ but not the introns. In the diagram, a

radioactive probe is being added to the petri dish. What is a probe? d. _____

5. Explain the polymerase chain reaction by telling what *polymerase* refers to a. _____, and what chain

reaction means b. _____. At the beginning of the reaction, very little DNA may be available, but at

the end of the reaction c. _____ copies of a segment of DNA are available.

6. In DNA fingerprinting, a. _____ enzymes digest the two samples to be compared. b. _____

separates the fragments, and their different lengths are compared. If the pattern is similar, the samples are

from c. _____.

17.2 BIOTECHNOLOGY PRODUCTS ARE MANY (P. 274)

• Genetically engineered prokaryotic and eukaryotic cells can be utilized to mass-produce products.

7. Theoretically, bacteria can be genetically engineered to produce any a. _____ of interest to humans.
Many products produced to date will be used to b. _____ human disorders—for example,
c. _____ for diabetes and d. _____ hormone for dwarfism. Along the same lines,
e. _____ are produced to immunize people against various possible f. _____. For example,
the g. _____ now in use for Lyme disease and whooping cough are h. _____ products.

17.3 MAKING TRANSGENIC ORGANISMS (P. 275)

• Bacteria, agricultural plants, and farm animals have been genetically engineered to improve the services they perform for humans.

8. Complete the following table on transgenic organisms:

Type of Organism	Engineered for What Purpose

9. The advantage of using bacteria to produce a product is that a. _____.

   The advantage of using plants to produce a product is that b. _____.

   The advantage of using farm animals to produce a product is that c. _____.

10. Should society be concerned about genetically modified organisms in the environment? Suppose wheat modified to resist herbicides were to cross with a weed in the wild, what might happen? a. _____

   _____

   Suppose a freshwater fish modified to grow faster and larger were to invade our rivers. What might happen?
   b. _____

17.4 GENE THERAPY IS A REALITY (P. 278)

- Gene therapy can be used to replace defective genes with healthy genes to cure human ills.

11. In the ex vivo method, which is used for SCID and familial hypercholesterolemia, cells removed from the patient are a. _____ and then b. _____ to the patient. The type of virus employed is a(n) c. _____. During reverse transcription, d. _____

   _____.

12. In the in vivo method, which is used for cystic fibrosis, a viral vector _____.

17.5 MAPPING THE HUMAN CHROMOSOMES (P. 279)

- Various methods are being used to determine the order of the genes (mapping) of the human chromosomes.

13. What are the two purposes of the Human Genome Project? a. _____

   b. _____

Earn a Study Break

You can earn a study break if you choose the right answer 15 times in a row.

1. _____ uses a natural biological system or a genetically engineered organism to produce a product or achieve an end favorable to human beings.

2. Most biotechnology products so far have come from genetically engineered _____.

3. A gene is said to have been _____ when many copies of a foreign gene are produced in a host cell.

4. _____ enzymes cut up DNA molecules into discrete pieces.

5. DNA _____ can be used to determine the guilt or innocence of a suspected rapist or the evolutionary relationship of the quagga to today's mammals.

6. _____ organisms are free-living organisms in the environment that have had a foreign gene inserted into them.

7. Plant cells that have their cell wall removed are termed _____.

8. Plasmids and viruses can be used as _____ for carrying foreign DNA into host cells.

9. A DNA _____ is a machine that joins nucleotides into the correct sequence to form a gene.

10. The _____ reaction can produce millions of copies of a single gene in a test tube.

11. A DNA _____ is a single strand of nucleotides that binds to any complementary DNA strand.

12. _____ transcriptase is an enzyme used to make a copy of DNA from RNA.

13. A _____ is a collection of clones carrying all the genes of an organism.

14. Plasmids are small accessory rings of DNA obtained from _____.

15. _____ is an enzyme used to seal any breaks in DNA or to seal foreign DNA into a vector.

If you selected the right answer 15 times without missing, enjoy your study break!

KEYWORD CROSSWORD

Review key terms by completing this crossword puzzle, using the following alphabetized list of terms:

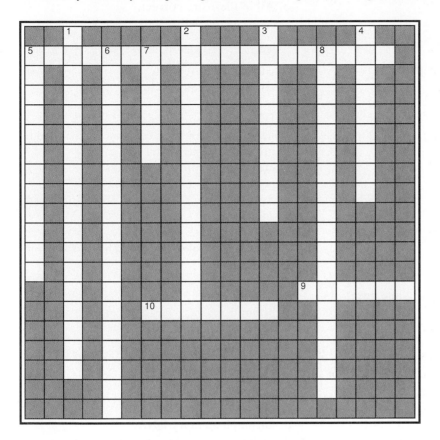

cloned
DNA fingerprinting
DNA ligase
DNA probe
gene therapy
genetic engineering
plasmid
recombinant DNA
restriction enzyme
transgenic organism
vector

Across

5 use of technology to alter the genome of a living cell for medical or industrial use (two words)

9 in genetic engineering, a means to transfer foreign genetic material into a cell—for example, a plasmid

10 self-duplicating ring of accessory DNA in the cytoplasm of bacteria

Down

1 using DNA fragment lengths, resulting from restriction enzyme cleavage, to identify particular individuals (two words)

2 DNA that contains genes from more than one source (two words)

3 enzyme that links DNA fragments; used during production of recombinant DNA to join foreign DNA to the vector DNA (two words)

4 known sequences of DNA that are used to find complementary DNA strands; can be used diagnostically to determine the presence of particular genes (two words)

5 use of bioengineered cells or other biotechnology techniques to treat human genetic disorders (two words)

6 free-living organisms in the environment that have had a foreign gene inserted into them (two words)

7 production of identical copies; in genetic engineering, the production of many identical copies of a gene

8 bacterial enzyme that stops viral reproduction by cleaving viral DNA; used to cut DNA at specific points during production of recombinant DNA (two words)

CHAPTER TEST

OBJECTIVE QUESTIONS

Do not refer to the text when taking this test.

_____ 1. Select the incorrect description of a plasmid.
   a. used as vector
   b. consists of chromosomal DNA
   c. found in some bacteria
   d. small, ringlike structure

_____ 2. Restriction enzymes
   a. cleave DNA into small fragments.
   b. restrict the growth of eukaryotic cells.
   c. seal pieces of DNA together.
   d. serve as introns in cells.

_____ 3. Select the human hormone that is NOT currently produced through genetic engineering.
   a. ADH
   b. growth hormone
   c. insulin
   d. tPA

_____ 4. Interferon holds the potential to treat
   a. anemia.
   b. cancer.
   c. hemophilia.
   d. pituitary dwarfism.

_____ 5. A final step in the use of a plasmid to clone a gene is to
   a. insert a foreign gene into a bacterium.
   b. introduce a plasmid into a treated cell.
   c. remove a plasmid from a bacterium.
   d. reproduce a plasmid in a treated cell.

_____ 6. The bacteriophage lambda is used as a
   a. cleavage agent for DNA in a virus.
   b. cleavage agent for RNA in a virus.
   c. vector to carry rDNA into bacterial cells.
   d. vector to carry rDNA into eukaryotic cells.

_____ 7. A transgenic organism is
   a. free-living and receives a foreign gene.
   b. free-living and transmits a foreign gene.
   c. parasitic and receives a foreign gene.
   d. parasitic and transmits a foreign gene.

_____ 8. A physical map shows the sequence of
   a. DNA bases on a chromosome.
   b. genes on a chromosome.

_____ 9. A major advantage of rDNA biotechnology is to
   a. mass-produce proteins that are hard to obtain.
   b. mass-produce lipids that are hard to obtain.
   c. clone animal cell DNA.
   d. clone plant cell DNA.

_____ 10. Genetically engineered plants have been or will be used to
   a. resist insects.
   b. resist herbicides.

   c. produce protein-enhanced beans, corn, and wheat.
   d. produce animal neuropeptides, blood factors, and growth hormones.
   e. All of these are correct.

_____ 11. _____ is a protein that activates an enzyme to dissolve blood clots.
   a. tPA
   b. Clotting factor VIII
   c. Atrial natriuretic factor
   d. bGH
   e. DNA ligase

_____ 12. Genetically engineered bacteria can be used to
   a. protect plants from frost.
   b. clean up oil spills on beaches.
   c. produce organic chemicals.
   d. extract copper and gold from low-grade sources.
   e. All of these are correct.

_____ 13. A DNA probe will seek out and bind to any complementary
   a. DNA.
   b. RNA.
   c. plasmid.
   d. organoid.
   e. restriction enzyme.

_____ 14. DNA that is made from mRNA is called
   a. nonsense DNA.
   b. antisense DNA.
   c. complementary DNA.
   d. uncomplementary DNA.

_____ 15. If a cell is altered while outside the human body for gene therapy, it is considered _____ therapy.
   a. ex vivo
   b. in vivo
   c. in vitro
   d. extraneous
   e. intravenous

_____ 16. Which of the following is NOT needed to make a recombinant DNA molecule?
   a. foreign DNA
   b. vector DNA
   c. restriction enzymes
   d. DNA ligase
   e. DNA polymerase

_____ 17. Foreign DNA can be inserted into vector DNA because both DNA molecules
   a. have the same genes.
   b. have the same bases.
   c. have "sticky ends."
   d. are not complementary to each other.

_____18. Which enzyme is used to seal breaks in a DNA
molecule?
   a. DNA polymerase
   b. RNA polymerase
   c. restriction enzymes
   d. DNA ligase
   e. RNA ligase
_____19. Possible uses for biotechnology include
   a. production of vaccines.
   b. production of drugs for health.

   c. altered bacteria to clean up oil spills.
   d. study how mammalian genes function.
   e. All of these are correct.
_____20. The gene for _____ will result in in-
creased milk production in cows.
   a. bGH
   b. tPA
   c. insulin
   d. erythropoietin
   e. interferon

CRITICAL THINKING QUESTIONS

Answer in complete sentences.
21. How do studies of genetic engineering prove that the genetic code is nearly universal?

22. What do you think are some objections our society may have regarding genetic engineering?

Test Results: _____ Number right ÷ 22 = _____ × 100 = _____ %

EXPLORING THE INTERNET

Use the Internet to further explore topics in this chapter, such as biotechnology, food biotechnology, or the Human Genome Project. Go to the Mader Home Page (http://www.mhhe.com/sciencemath/biology/mader/) and click on *Biology,* 6th edition. Go to Chapter 17 and select a Web site of interest.

ANSWER KEY

STUDY EXERCISES

1. a. 4 **b.** 3 **c.** 2 **d.** 1   **2.** Cleavage results in unpaired bases. **3. a.** Both plasmids and viruses are used . . . **b.** contains DNA from two different sources **c.** . . . from a member of a different species **d.** . . . many copies of the same gene   **4. a.** a collection of clones that carry all the genes of an organism **b.** regulatory **c.** exons **d.** single-stranded DNA or mRNA that hybridizes (pairs) with a gene of interest **5. a.** DNA polymerase, the enzyme involved in DNA replication **b.** the reaction occurs over and over again **c.** many   **6. a.** restriction **b.** gel electrophoresis **c.** from the same individual **7. a.** protein **b.** treat **c.** insulin **d.** growth **e.** vaccines **f.** diseases **g.** vaccines **h.** biotechnology

8.

Type of Organism	Engineered for What Purpose
bacteria	to protect plants, for bioremediation, to produce chemicals, and to mine metals
plants	to resist insects, pesticides and herbicides, and to make products
animals	to have improved qualities and to make products

9. a. They will take up plasmids. **b.** They will grow from single cells (protoplasts). **c.** The product is easily obtainable in milk. **10. a.** The weed may take over the environment. **b.** The fish may crowd out native fishes. **11. a.** genetically treated **b.** returned **c.** retrovirus **d.** a cDNA copy of RNA genes is made, and this becomes incorporated into the host genome. **12.** infects the patient directly **13. a.** to map the human chromosomes **b.** to determine the base sequence of human DNA

1. Biotechnology **2.** bacteria **3.** cloned **4.** Restriction **5.** fingerprinting **6.** Transgenic **7.** protoplasts **8.** vectors **9.** synthesizer **10.** polymerase chain **11.** probe **12.** Reverse **13.** genomic library **14.** bacteria **15.** DNA ligase

KEYWORD CROSSWORD

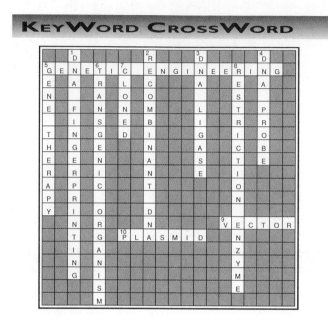

CHAPTER TEST

1. b **2.** a **3.** a **4.** b **5.** d **6.** c **7.** a **8.** a **9.** a **10.** e **11.** a **12.** e **13.** a **14.** c **15.** a **16.** e **17.** c **18.** d **19.** e **20.** a **21.** Genes transmitted to new cells through vectors and other means are still transcribed and translated by the same process and with the same accuracy. **22.** Some people may object to genetic engineering on religious grounds because we are now able to change the inherited characteristics of organisms including human beings. Some scientists have concerns because a disease-causing transgenic bacterium may be produced for which humans have no immunity or a transgenic bacterium, plant, or animal may be produced which could wreak havoc in the environment.

PART III EVOLUTION

18

DARWIN AND EVOLUTION

In the mid-nineteenth century, Charles Darwin's studies led to his hypothesis on **evolution.** Darwin was a student of geology and **paleontology.** His observations on the life-forms of the Galápagos Islands, including their **biogeography,** influenced the formation of his hypothesis.

Darwin's view of evolution, in stark contrast to the pre-Darwinian outlook, supported the common descent of organisms. During this process, members of a species evolve **adaptations** through **natural selection.** Inherited variations in the members of a population establish the raw material for these adaptations. Through potential overpopulation, and the inevitable competition among population members, organisms that are more **fit** through their characteristics are more likely to survive and reproduce. Over generations, this results in the adaptation

of the population to the environment. This change in the population over time is called evolution.

Cuvier and Lamarck, contemporaries of Darwin, expressed ideas about evolution that differed from Darwin's. Cuvier proposed the hypothesis of **catastrophism.** Lamarck correctly recognized the process of descent with modification among organisms in a population, but he explained the mechanism for that process incorrectly.

Numerous lines of evidence currently support Darwin's theory of common descent and evolution through natural selection. Evidence includes studies from fossils, biogeography, comparative anatomy, and comparative biochemistry.

STUDY EXERCISES

Study the text section by section as you answer the questions that follow.

18.1 THE WORLD WAS READY (P. 286)

- In the eighteenth century, scientists became especially interested in classifying and understanding the relationships between the many forms of present and past life.
- Gradually in the eighteenth century, scientists began to accept the view that the earth is very old and that life-forms evolve or change over time.
- Evolution has two aspects: descent from a common ancestor and adaptation to the environment.

1. Before each of the following statements, write *pre* for pre-Darwinian or *post* for post-Darwinian view of evolution:
   _____ a. Adaptation to the environment occurs through the work of a creator.
   _____ b. Hypotheses are tested through observation and experimentation.
   _____ c. Species are related by a common descent.
   _____ d. The earth is relatively young, with an age measured in thousands of years.

Mid-Eighteenth-Century Contributions (p. 287)

2. Indicate whether the following statements, related to the principles of mid-eighteenth-century taxonomy, are true (T) or false (F):

_____ a. A binomial system of nomenclature can be used to classify organisms.

_____ b. Different organisms can be arranged by increasing order of complexity.

_____ c. Each species has an ideal structure and function fixed in the sequential ladder of life.

_____ d. Gradations occur naturally between species.

Late-Eighteenth-Century Contributions (p. 288)

3. Label each of the following as reflecting the thinking of Cuvier (C) or Lamarck (L):

_____ a. A new stratum or mix of fossils in a region signals that a local catastrophe occurred.

_____ b. Members of a population change over time through the inheritance of acquired characteristics.

_____ c. The entire anatomy of an animal can be deduced by studying one of its fossil bones.

_____ d. The increasing complexity of organisms through evolutionary descent is the result of a natural force.

18.2 DARWIN DEVELOPS A THEORY (P. 289)

- Charles Darwin's trip around the Southern Hemisphere aboard the HMS *Beagle* provided him with evidence that the earth is very old and that descent with modification does occur.

4. Indicate whether the following statements are true (T) or false (F):

_____ a. Darwin had no suitable background to be the naturalist on board the HMS *Beagle*.

_____ b. Darwin had taken various science courses and had worked with people who were experts in their fields.

_____ c. The HMS *Beagle* took a trip to South America and then returned.

_____ d. The HMS *Beagle* went around the world in the Southern Hemisphere.

Descent Does Occur (p. 289)

5. **Fossils:** Darwin noticed a close a._____ between modern forms and extinct species known only through fossils. He began to think that these fossil forms might be b._____ to modern species. If so, the implication is that new species appear on earth as a result of biological change.

Biogeography: Darwin noticed that whenever the environment changed, the types of species c._____. He also observed that similar environments have different but d._____ adapted species. This indicates that species are suited to the environment.

Darwin's finches: Darwin speculated that a mainland finch was the e._____ ancestor for all the different species of finches on the Galápagos Islands. This shows that speciation occurs.

Conclusion: Based on his observations, Darwin came to accept the idea of f._____; that is, life-forms change over time.

Natural Selection Provides a Mechanism (p. 292)

- Both Darwin and Alfred Wallace proposed natural selection as a mechanism by which adaptation to the environment occurs. This mechanism is consistent with our present-day knowledge of genetics.

6. Rearrange the letters to indicate the correct order of the statements that describe Darwin's theory of natural selection. _____

a. The result of organic evolution is many different species, each adapted to specific environments.

b. Many more individuals are produced each generation than can survive and reproduce.

c. Gradually, over long periods of time, a population can become well adapted to a specific environment.

d. The members of a population have heritable variations.

e. Some individuals have adaptive characteristics that enable them to survive and reproduce better than others in the environment.

7. In each of the following pairs of situations, place a check beside the members that are more fit:

   a. In a forest, certain ground plants
   _____ (1) are able to grow in the shade.
   _____ (2) require full sunlight.
   b. In the depths of the ocean, certain fishes
   _____ (1) need to eat only infrequently.
   _____ (2) must eat continuously.
   c. In a mountain village, some inhabitants
   _____ (1) get dizzy when the oxygen level falls below normal.
   _____ (2) do not get dizzy when the oxygen level falls below normal.

18.3 EVIDENCE ACCUMULATES (P. 296)

- The fossil record, biogeography, comparative anatomy, and comparative biochemistry support a hypothesis of common descent.

In questions 8–12, match each of the following statements to the type of evidence supporting evolution:

   a. *The succession of life-forms is revealed through preserved remnants.*
   b. *Organisms have similarities and differences in structures.*
   c. *Closely related organisms have high correlations in DNA base sequences.*
   d. *Organisms arise and disperse from place of origin.*
   e. *In their early phases of development, vertebrates show a plan of unity.*
   _____ 8. biogeography
   _____ 9. comparative anatomy
   _____ 10. comparative biochemistry
   _____ 11. comparative embryology
   _____ 12. fossil record

KeyWord CrossWord

Review key terms by completing this crossword puzzle, using the following alphabetized list of terms:

adaptation
biogeography
catastrophism
evolution
fitness
homologous
paleontology
vestigial

Across

1 remains of a structure that was functional in some ancestor but is no longer functional in the organism in question
4 belief espoused by Cuvier that periods of major extinctions occurred, after which surviving species repopulated, giving the appearance of change through time
5 ability of an organism to survive and reproduce in its environment
7 study of the geographical distribution of organisms

Down

2 descent of organisms from common ancestors with the development of genetic and phenotypic changes over time that make the organisms more suited to the local environment
3 organism's modification in structure, function, or behavior that increases the likelihood of continued existence
6 study of fossils that results in knowledge about the history of life
8 in evolution, a structure that is similar in different organisms because these organisms are derived from a common ancestor

OBJECTIVE QUESTIONS

Do not refer to the text when taking this test.

_____ 1. Each is a pre-Darwinian view of evolution EXCEPT
   a. adaptation to the environment comes from a creator.
   b. each species is specially created.
   c. hypotheses regarding species can be tested by experimentation.
   d. the earth is relatively young.

_____ 2. Each is an idea from taxonomy in the mid-eighteenth century EXCEPT
   a. a fixity of species exists.
   b. humans occupy the last rung of a ladder of life.
   c. natural gradations exist between species.
   d. species have a special creation.

_____ 3. The science of paleontology was founded by
   a. Cuvier.
   b. Darwin.
   c. Lamarck.
   d. Lyell.

_____ 4. The Galápagos Islands are off the western coast of
   a. Africa.
   b. Asia.
   c. North America.
   d. South America.

_____ 5. Darwin claimed that the beak size of finch species was related to their
   a. body size.
   b. flight pattern.
   c. food source.
   d. time of reproduction.

_____ 6. Select the statement that is NOT a tenet of Darwin's theory of natural selection.
   a. Members of a population have heritable variations.
   b. Members of a population will compete.
   c. Populations tend to reproduce in small numbers.
   d. Some population members have adaptive characteristics.

_____ 7. Each could be an example of fitness EXCEPT a
   a. plant that has the broadest leaves.
   b. plant that has the greatest height.
   c. predator that has the keenest eyesight.
   d. prey species that runs the slowest.

_____ 8. An adaptation promotes
   a. only the chance to reproduce.
   b. survival only.
   c. the chance to survive and reproduce.
   d. neither the chance to reproduce nor the chance to survive.

_____ 9. Darwin's studies closely matched the independent work of
   a. Cuvier.
   b. Lamarck.
   c. Lyell.
   d. Wallace.

_____10. Vertebrate forelimbs are most likely to be studied in
   a. biogeography.
   b. comparative anatomy.
   c. comparative biochemistry.
   d. ecological physiology.

_____11. Biochemical evidence supporting evolution would show that
   a. there are more base differences between yeasts and humans than between horses and humans.
   b. there are more base differences between apes and humans than between horses and humans.
   c. apes and humans have almost the same sequence of bases.
   d. Both _a_ and _c_ are correct.

_____12. Comparative anatomy demonstrates that
   a. each species has its own structures, indicating no relationship with any other species.
   b. different vertebrates have widely different body plans.
   c. different species can have similar structures that are traceable to a common ancestor.
   d. fossils bear no anatomical similarities to modern-day species.

_____13. The study of biogeography shows that
   a. the same species of plants and animals are found on different continents whenever the environment is the same.
   b. one species can spread out and give rise to many species, each adapted to varying environments.
   c. the structure and function of organisms bear no relationship to the environment.
   d. barriers do not prevent the same species from spreading around the world.

_____14. Which is NOT true of fossils?
   a. They are evidences of life in the past.
   b. They look exactly like modern-day species, regardless of their age.
   c. In general, the older the fossil, the less it resembles modern-day species.
   d. They indicate that life has a history.

_____15. Darwin reasoned that, if the world is very old, then
   a. taxonomy will have to give up the binomial system of nomenclature.
   b. evolution could not have occurred.
   c. geological changes occur in a relatively short period of time.
   d. there was time for evolution to occur.

Answer in complete sentences.

16. A line of talented pianists, each practicing diligently, is found over five generations in a family. Offer a modern-day explanation as opposed to a Lamarckian explanation.

17. In a sample of geological strata, where are the oldest life-forms most likely to be found? Where are the most recent life-forms?

Test Results: _____ Number right ÷ 17 = _____ × 100 = _____ %

EXPLORING THE INTERNET

Use the Internet to further explore topics in this chapter, such as spontaneous generation or the history of the idea of evolution. Go to the Mader Home Page (http://www.mhhe.com/sciencemath/biology/mader/) and click on *Biology,* 6th edition. Go to Chapter 18 and select a Web site of interest.

ANSWER KEY

STUDY EXERCISES

1. a. pre **b.** post **c.** post **d.** pre **2. a.** T **b.** T **c.** T **d.** F **3. a.** C **b.** L **c.** C **d.** L **4. a.** F **b.** T **c.** F **d.** T **5. a.** resemblance or similarity **b.** related **c.** changed **d.** similarly **e.** common **f.** evolution **6.** d, b, e, c, a **7. a.** 1 **b.** 1 **c.** 2 **8.** d **9.** b **10.** c **11.** e **12.** a

KEYWORD CROSSWORD

CHAPTER TEST

1. c **2.** c **3.** a **4.** d **5.** c **6.** c **7.** d **8.** c **9.** d **10.** b **11.** d **12.** c **13.** b **14.** b **15.** d **16.** Phenotypic changes, such as an ability to play the piano, cannot be passed on. Traits are passed on by way of the gametes. It is possible, however, that the genes in a particular family endow recipients with a musical ability, including anatomical characteristics that facilitate playing the piano. **17.** The oldest forms are in the deepest strata. The most recent life-forms are in the more recently added strata, which are not as deep.

PROCESS OF EVOLUTION

CHAPTER REVIEW

Members of a **population** vary. Sources of variation are gene and chromosomal mutations and also recombination, which may produce a more favorable combination of alleles. The **Hardy-Weinberg** equilibrium refers to a constancy of the gene pool as long as there are no mutations, no gene flow, random mating, no genetic drift, and no selection. The reverse of these conditions causes evolution to occur.

Gene flow will cause the **gene pool** of two populations to become similar, and **genetic drift** will cause them to become dissimilar. Today it is possible to see that natural selection occurs when certain alleles become more frequent in a gene pool. **Directional selection** occurs when

the most common phenotype shifts in one direction; **stabilizing selection** occurs when the common phenotype increases in number; and **disruptive selection** occurs when more than one phenotype becomes common.

Mutation and gene flow maintain variation within a population despite natural selection. Balanced polymorphism exists due to a heterozygote that hides the recessive allele from selection.

Speciation occurs when populations become isolated from one another, most often due to a geographic barrier. **Allopatric speciation** requires a barrier; **sympatric speciation** does not. **Species** remain reproductively isolated due to pre- and postmating mechanisms.

STUDY EXERCISES

Study the text section by section as you answer the following questions.

19.1 EVOLUTION IN A GENETIC CONTEXT? (P. 304)

- The raw material for evolutionary change are mutations, both genetic and chromosomal. Recombination of genes is another source in sexually reproducing organisms.

1. Indicate whether the following statements, related to sources of variation among diploid members in a population, are true (T) or false (F).
   _____ a. Gene mutations occur at random.
   _____ b. The only mutations that occur are those that make organisms more fit.
   _____ c. Some chromosomal mutations are simply a change in chromosomal number.
   _____ d. Duplications are important sources of chromosomal mutations that can lead to genotypic diversity.
   _____ e. An offspring receives recombined genes because of the events of meiosis and fertilization.
   _____ f. Recombination is a significant source of variation because many traits are polygenic.

How to Detect Evolution (p. 305)

- The Hardy-Weinberg law defines evolution in terms of allele frequency changes in a population over time.

2. An investigator determines, by inspection, that 4% of a population is albino. Answer the following questions about this population:
   a. $q^2 =$ _____.
   b. This represents the percentage of the population that is _____.
   c. What is the frequency of the recessive allele in this population? $q =$ _____
   d. Considering the frequency of the recessive allele, what is the frequency of the dominant allele?
      $p =$ _____

e. If p = this value, then p^2 = _____.

f. This is the frequency of the population that is _____.

g. The value of $2pq$ = _____.

h. This represents the frequency of the population that is _____.

i. What percentage of the population has normal pigmentation? _____

3. Forty-nine percent of a population cannot taste a chemical called PTC. Presence of a dominant allele is necessary to taste this substance. Complete the following information about the gene pool of the population:

a. q^2 = _____

b. q = _____

c. p = _____

d. p^2 = _____

e. $2pq$ = _____

4. a. Using this Punnett square, show that the next generation of the population in question 3 will have exactly the same composition, assuming a Hardy-Weinberg equilibrium.

	( )T	( )t	
( )T	( )TT	( )Tt
( )t	( )Tt	( )tt

b. The frequency of T = _____.

c. The frequency of t = _____.

d. Describe the gene pool of the next generation. _____

e. What does this prove? _____

f. How would we know when evolution occurs? _____

What Causes Evolution? (p. 307)

- Additional mutations and also gene flow, nonrandom mating, genetic drift, and natural selection can cause allele frequency changes in future generations.

5. Label the statements with the correct agents of evolutionary change: *gene flow, genetic drift, mutations, natural selection, and nonrandom mating.*

Investigators have discovered that multiple alleles are common in a population. [a.]_____

Populations are subject to new alleles entering by migration of organisms between populations.

[b.]_____

Female birds of paradise choose mates with the most splendid feathers. [c.]_____

Investigators discovered that if they randomly picked out a few flies from each generation to start the next generation, gene pool frequency changes appeared. [d.]_____

Giraffes with longer necks get a larger share of resources and tend to have more offspring. [e.]_____

6. Match the following descriptions to one of the agents of evolutionary change listed in question 5 (some agents are used more than once):

Dwarfism is common among the Amish of Lancaster County, Pennsylvania. [a.]_____

Cheetahs are homozygous for a larger proportion of their genes. [b.]_____

This tends to make the members of a population dissimilar to one another. c._____

This tends to make the members of a population similar to one another. d._____

Certain members of a population are more fit than other members. e._____

Bacteria and insects become resistant to agents that formerly killed them. f._____

19.2 ADAPTATION OCCURS NATURALLY (P. 310)

- Natural selection involves changes in allele frequencies in a population due to the differential ability of certain phenotypes to reproduce.
- Natural selection results in adaptation to the environment. The three types of natural selection are: directional selection, stabilizing selection, and disruptive selection.

7. Natural selection can now be understood in terms of genetics. Many of the variations that exist between members of a population are due to differences in a._____. Some of these genotypes result in b._____ that are better adapted to the environment. Individuals that are better adapted to the environment reproduce to a(n) c._____ extent, and therefore, these genotypes and phenotypes become more prevalent in the population.

8. Label the observations with the correct type of natural selection at work: directional selection, disruptive selection, and stabilizing selection.

Trees in a windy area tend to remain the same size each year. a._____

The brain size of hominids steadily increases. b._____

The same species of moths tends to have blue stripes in open areas and orange stripes in forested areas.

c._____

9. Match the types of natural selection listed in question 8 with the following diagrams:

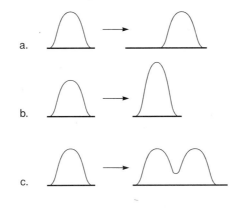

10. Variation is maintained in a population despite directional and stabilizing selection when members have a._____ alleles for every trait. That's because the b._____ allele is hidden by the c._____ allele. In instances such as sickle-cell disease, in which the d._____ genotype is more fit, the two e._____ genotypes are maintained due to the reproductive process, which involves meiosis and fertilization.

19.3 CONSIDERING SPECIATION (P. 314)

- New species come about when populations are reproductively isolated from other, similar populations.
- Adaptive radiation is the rapid development of several species from a single species; each species is adapted in a unique way.

11. Bush babies (a type of primate) living higher in the tropical canopy are a different species from those living lower in the canopy. Answer the following *yes* or *no:*

Would the two species of bush babies reproduce with each other? a._____

Would a premating mechanism separate the two species of bush babies? b._____

Could the two species of bush babies eat the same food? c._____

Would the two species of bush babies have to look dissimilar enough to be distinguishable by the naked eye?
d._____

12. Match the following numbered statements to the letters in the diagram (some numbers are used more than once):

    1 A newly formed barrier comes between the populations.
    2 The barrier is removed.
    3 A species contains one population or several interbreeding populations.
    4 Reproductive isolation has occurred.
    5 Two species now exist.
    6 Reproductive isolation has occurred without benefit of a barrier.
    7 Drift alone can cause gene pools to become dissimilar.
    8 Divergent evolution occurs.
    9 Allopatric speciation.
    10 Sympatric speciation.

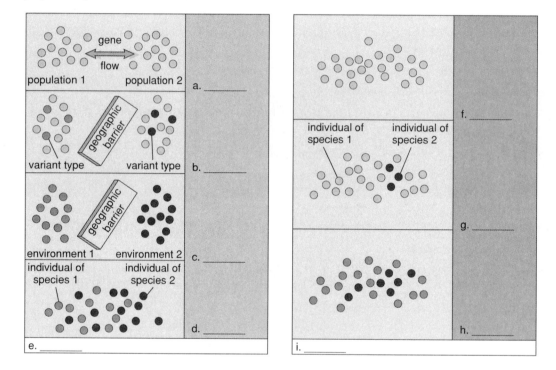

13. Label each of these with *pre* for premating isolating mechanism or *post* for postmating isolating mechanism.
    _____ a. Zygote mortality exists.
    _____ b. Species reproduce at different times.
    _____ c. Species have genitalia that are unsuitable to each other.

Review key terms by completing this crossword puzzle, using the following alphabetized list of terms:

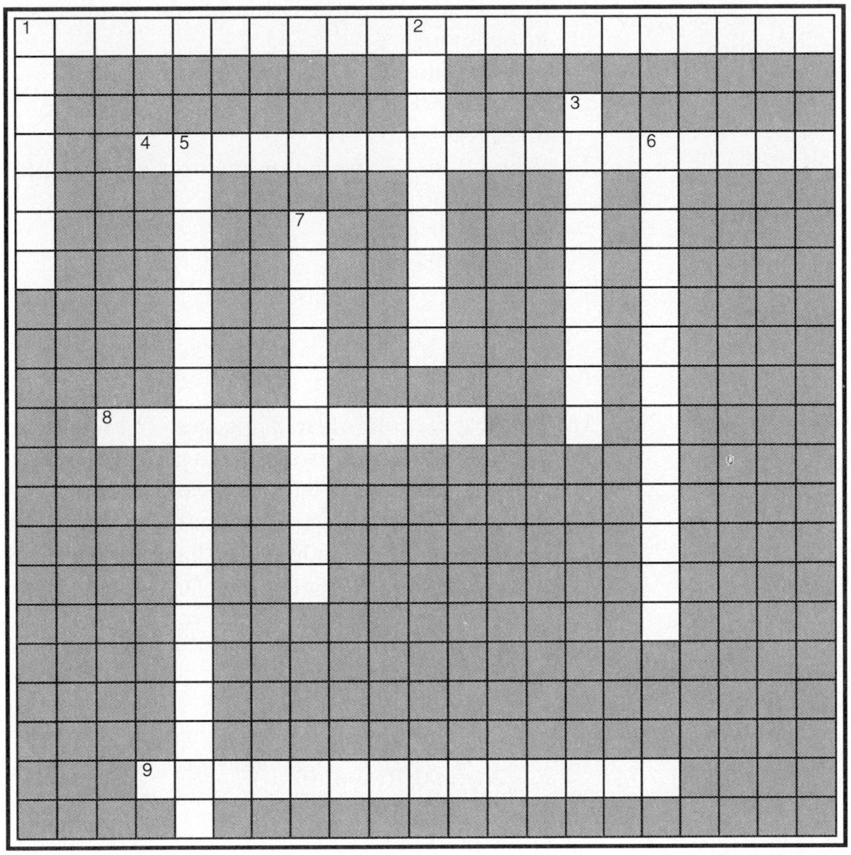

adaptive radiation
founder effect
gene flow
gene pool
genetic drift
Hardy-Weinberg law
population
speciation
species
stabilizing selection

Across

1 outcome of natural selection in which extreme phenotypes are eliminated and the average phenotype is conserved (two words)

4 law stating that the frequency of an allele in a population remains stable under certain assumptions, such as random mating; therefore, no change or evolution occurs (three words)

8 process whereby a new species originates or is produced

9 tendency for a new, small population to experience genetic drift after it has separated from an original, larger population (two words)

Down

1 taxonomic category that is the subdivision of a genus; its members can breed successfully with each other but not with members of another species

2 sharing of genes between two populations through interbreeding (two words)

3 total of all the genes of all the individuals in a population (two words)

5 formation of a large number of species from a common ancestor (two words)

6 change in the genetic makeup of a population due to chance (random) events; important in small populations or when only a few individuals mate (two words)

7 group of organisms of the same species occupying a certain area and sharing a common gene pool

Do not refer to the text when taking this test.

In questions 1–5, assume that 16% of the organisms in a population are homozygous recessive. Describe the current gene pool.

_____ 1. frequency of *aa*

_____ 2. frequency of *a*

_____ 3. frequency of *A*

_____ 4. frequency of *AA*

_____ 5. frequency of *Aa*

_____ 6. Each is a condition of the Hardy-Weinberg law EXCEPT that
   a. gene flow is absent.
   b. genetic drift does not occur.
   c. mutations are lacking.
   d. random mating does not occur.

_____ 7. Establishment of polydactylism among the Amish is an example of
   a. artificial selection.
   b. natural selection.
   c. the bottleneck effect.
   d. the founder effect.

_____ 8. Industrial melanism is an example of selection that is
   a. directional.
   b. disruptive.
   c. sexual.
   d. stabilizing.

_____ 9. In a population of mature trees, it is NOT true that disruptive selection
   a. favors the shortest trees.
   b. favors the tallest trees.
   c. will not occur if the environment is diverse.
   d. will occur in an unchanging environment.

_____ 10. Each factor contributes to the maintenance of variation from a recessive allele EXCEPT
   a. diploidy.
   b. heterozygosity.
   c. homozygosity.
   d. sexual reproduction.

_____ 11. The criterion used to distinguish between two species is based on
   a. geography.
   b. physical traits.
   c. reproduction.
   d. time.

_____ 12. Select the premating isolating mechanism.
   a. F_2 fitness
   b. gamete mortality
   c. habitat type
   d. hybrid sterility

_____ 13. Select the postmating isolating mechanism.
   a. behavior
   b. mechanical differences in genitalia
   c. temporal factors
   d. zygote mortality

_____ 14. Which type of speciation requires a geographical barrier?
   a. allopatric
   b. sympatric

_____ 15. Which type of speciation occurs from polyploidy in plants?
   a. allopatric
   b. sympatric

_____ 16. Two populations of field mice become separated by an interstate highway so that gene flow is impossible. After ten years, a researcher detects an evolutionary change in the populations: mice on the north side of the highway have longer nails than those on the south side. The two habitats, however, appear identical in every respect. The probable reason for the difference is _____ each group.
   a. natural selection within
   b. nonrandom mating among
   c. genetic drift within
   d. mutations in
   e. adaptation of

_____ 17. During the usual process of speciation, a species is first isolated
   a. behaviorally.
   b. geographically.
   c. reproductively.
   d. mechanically.
   e. genetically.

_____ 18. Two species have been observed in nature to copulate successfully with each other yet are unable to produce a hybrid line. This might be due to all of the following EXCEPT
   a. gamete mortality.
   b. hybrid sterility.
   c. zygote mortality.
   d. courtship behavioral differences.

_____ 19. The frequency of the dark form of the peppered moth increased in industrial areas of England during the last century. This is because
   a. predatory birds changed their preference from the light to the dark form.
   b. the light form was more sensitive to deteriorating environmental conditions.
   c. dark colored moths had a better survival rate as the Industrial Revolution progressed.
   d. environmental pollutants became responsible for increased mutation rates.
   e. the allele for dark color is dominant to that for light color.

_____20. Evolution by natural selection requires
    a. variation.
    b. heritable genetic differences.

c. differential adaptedness.
d. differential reproduction.
e. All of these are correct.

CRITICAL THINKING QUESTIONS

Answer in complete sentences.

21. One percent of a population consists of albinos. A nonscientist studies the population and claims that albinism can be removed from the population by preventing the mating of all albinos. Will this approach work?

22. A dominant allele produces a desirable coloration pattern in a fish species. A pond owner stocks a pond with a small number of heterozygous members showing this desirable trait, hoping to maintain it. Will this approach work?

Test Results: _____ Number right ÷ 22 = _____ × 100 = _____ %

EXPLORING THE INTERNET:

Use the Internet to further explore topics in this chapter, such as convergent evolution and animal flight or the Hardy-Weinberg equilibrium. Go to the Mader Home Page (http://www.mhhe.com/sciencemath/biology/mader/) and click on *Biology,* 6th edition. Go to Chapter 19 and select a Web site of interest.

ANSWER KEY

STUDY EXERCISES

1. a. T **b.** F **c.** T **d.** T **e.** T **f.** T   **2. a.** 0.04 or 4% **b.** homozygous recessive **c.** 0.2 **d.** 0.8 **e.** 0.64 or 64% **f.** homozygous dominant **g.** 0.32 or 32% **h.** heterozygous **i.** 0.96 or 96%   **3. a.** 0.49 **b.** 0.7 **c.** 0.3 **d.** 0.09 **e.** 0.42
4.

	(0.3) T	(0.7) t
(0.3) T	(0.09) TT	(0.21) Tt
(0.7) t	(0.21) Tt	(0.49) tt

a. In the generation shown in the Punnett square, $TT = 0.09$, $Tt = 0.42$, $tt = 0.49$; this is exactly the same as the parental generation in question 3. **b.** 0.3 **c.** 0.7 **d.** exactly the same as the previous generation **e.** that sexual reproduction alone does not change allele frequencies **f.** when gene pool frequencies change   **5. a.** mutations **b.** gene flow **c.** nonrandom mating **d.** genetic drift **e.** natural selection   **6. a.** genetic drift (founder effect) **b.** genetic drift (bottleneck effect) **c.** genetic drift **d.** gene flow **e.** natural selection **f.** mutations   **7. a.** genotype **b.** phenotypes **c.** greater   **8. a.** stabilizing **b.** directional **c.** disruptive   **9. a.** directional **b.** stabilizing **c.** disruptive   **10. a.** two **b.** recessive **c.** dominant **d.** heterozygous **e.** homozygous   **11. a.** no **b.** yes **c.** yes **d.** no   **12. a.** 3 **b.** 1 **c.** 8 **d.** 2, 4, 5 **e.** 9 **f.** 3 **g.** 6, 5 **h.** 4, 7 **i.** 10   **13. a.** post **b.** pre **c.** pre

¹S	T	A	B	I	L	I	Z	I	N	G	²G	S	E	L	E	C	T	I	O	N
P											E								
E											N		³G						
C		⁴H	⁵A	R	D	Y	-	W	E	I	N	B	E	R	⁶G		L	A	W
I			D									N		E					
E			A		⁷P		F				E		N						
S			P		O		L				P		E						
			T		P		O				O		T						
			I		U		W				O		I						
			V		L						L		C						
		⁸S	P	E	C	I	A	T	I	O	N								
					T							D							
		R			I							R							
		A			O							I							
		D			N							F							
		I										T							
		A																	
		T																	
		I																	
⁹F	O	U	N	D	E	R		E	F	F	E	C	T						
		N																	

1. $0.16 = 16\%$ **2.** 0.4 **3.** 0.6 **4.** $0.36 = 36\%$ **5.** $0.48 = 48\%$ **6.** d **7.** d **8.** a **9.** d **10.** c **11.** c **12.** c **13.** d **14.** a **15.** b **16.** c **17.** b **18.** d **19.** c **20.** e. **21.** It will not work because a recessive allele causes albinism. Eighteen percent of the population members are heterozygotes and will protect the recessive allele, even though it is hidden from expression phenotypically. **22.** It may not work because of genetic drift—the population may diverge to homozygous forms through random events.

20

ORIGIN AND HISTORY OF LIFE

The primitive atmosphere contained mainly water vapor, nitrogen, and carbon dioxide; since it contained no oxygen, it is known as a reducing atmosphere. As the earth cooled, rains began to fall, and the gases reacted with one another in the original ocean. First, small organic molecules and then macromolecules formed. The RNA-first hypothesis states that RNA could have been the first genetic material because it may have enzymatic properties that allowed it to reproduce itself and form proteins. Alternately, the first macromolecules could have been proteins that carried on metabolism, allowing growth to occur; only later did DNA genes come into being. A plasma membrane is required for the **protocell** to exist. The protocell was a **heterotrophic** fermenter. Later, photosynthesis and then aerobic respiration occurred.

Paleontologists have put together a **fossil** record that sketches the history of life in broad terms. Prokaryotes were alone for at least 1.5 billion years, and they diversified metabolically. Eukaryotes, which may have come about by endosymbiosis, arose at about the time the atmosphere became an oxidizing one because of cyanobacterial release of oxygen. Multicellularity and sexual reproduction began about 600 million years ago. The Cambrian period of the Paleozoic era began with an explosion of animals whose abundance in the fossil record is attributed to their having skeletons.

The swamp forest of the Silurian period contained primitive vascular plants, insects, and amphibians—all of whom lived on land. The Mesozoic era was the Age of Cycads and Reptiles. Twice during this era, dinosaurs of enormous size evolved. Mammals evolved earlier but did not diversify until the Cenozoic era, after the dinosaurs were extinct. The Neogene period of the Cenozoic era is associated with the evolution of primates—first prosimians, then monkeys, apes, and humans.

Many environmental factors influence evolution. Continental drift has affected biogeography and helps explain the distribution pattern of today's land organisms. **Mass extinctions** have played a dramatic role in the history of life. While some mass extinctions may have been caused by meteorite impact, others may be climatic fluctuations due to continental drift.

Changing gene frequencies in local populations as discussed in the previous chapter, may be considered microevolution. Traditional evolutionists believe the same processes are involved in macroevolution, observed changes in lineages. The lack of intermediate fossils that link the various groups together suggests a pattern of **punctuated equilibrium,** as opposed to one of **phyletic gradualism.**

STUDY EXERCISES

Study the text section by section as you answer the questions that follow.

20.1 ORIGIN OF LIFE (P. 325)

- A chemical evolution proceeded from atmospheric gases to small organic molecules to macromolecules to protocells.

1. In the top half of the diagram, place the following labels next to the correct arrows: *cooling, energy capture,* and *polymerization*. Then place the following labels in the boxes: *gases, macromolecules, plasma membrane, primitive earth,* and *small organic molecules.*

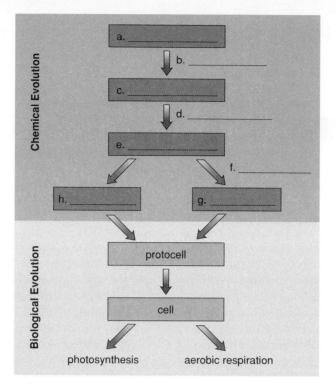

2. A student decides to reproduce Miller's experiment, and she assembles all the necessary tubing and adds the proper gases. What is still needed and why? _____

_____

3. A student decides to reproduce Fox's experiment, and he puts a solution of amino acids on heated rocks. What is still needed and why? _____

_____

4. What is the evidence for suggesting that it was an "RNA world" some 4 billion years ago? _____

_____

A Protocell Evolves (p. 326)

- The primitive atmosphere contained no oxygen, and the first cell was an anaerobic heterotroph.
- The first cell was bounded by a membrane and contained a replication system—that is, DNA, RNA, and proteins.

5. Indicate whether the following statements about the protocell are true (T) or false (F):
_____ a. carried on aerobic respiration
_____ b. was a heterotrophic fermenter
_____ c. contained a self-replication system that allowed it to reproduce
_____ d. had a plasma membrane

A Self-Replication System Evolves (p. 327)

6. To be a true cell, which statement, labeled as false in question 5, must be fulfilled? [a.]_____ Add the label *self-replication system* to the diagram in question 1. [b.]

7. Why does it seem logical that the protocell was heterotrophic? a._____

   Why would the protocell have been a fermenter? b._____

8. Rearrange the letters to indicate the order of events in the evolution of a self-replication system, assuming that it was an "RNA world" at the time. _____
   a. replication of RNA
   b. reverse transcription of DNA
   c. RNA → proteins
   d. DNA → RNA → proteins

9. Label each of the following as describing the *primitive* (P) atmosphere of the earth or the *current* (C) atmosphere of the earth:
   _____ a. It exists without the ozone shield.
   _____ b. It favors the polymerization of organic molecules.
   _____ c. It is a reducing atmosphere.
   _____ d. It is an oxidizing atmosphere.
   _____ e. It tends to break down organic molecules.
   _____ f. Oxygen-producing autotrophs made it.

20.2 HISTORY OF LIFE (P. 328)

- The fossil record allows us to trace the history of life, which is divided into the Precambrian, and the Paleozoic, Mesozoic, and Cenozoic eras.

10. Why do most fossils reveal shells, bones, or teeth? _____

11. Indicate whether the following comparisons between relative dating and absolute dating of fossils are true (T) or false (F):

   Relative Dating

   _____ a. Date such as 3.5 MYA is known.
   _____ b. Strata location must be known.
   _____ c. Only comparative age is known.

   Absolute Dating

   Date such as 3.5 MYA is not known.
   Strata location does not need to be known.
   Age independent of other fossils is known.

How the Story Unfolds (p. 330)

- The first fossils are of prokaryotes and date from about 3.5 billion years ago. Prokaryotes diversified for about 1.5 billion years before the eukaryotic cell and multicellular forms evolved during the Precambrian.
- Fossils of complex marine multicellular invertebrates and vertebrates appeared during the Cambrian period of the Paleozoic era. Swamp forests on land contained nonseed vascular plants, insects, and amphibians.
- The Mesozoic era was the Age of Cycads and Reptiles. Mammals and flowering plants evolved during the Cenozoic era.

12. In the Precambrian, the first cells were prokaryotes that carried on a._____ because the atmosphere contained no b._____. Some of the earliest cells dated 3.5 billion years ago are found in c._____, of which living examples are found in shallow seas today. One of the main events of the Precambrian is the evolution of photosynthesizers, which added d._____ to the atmosphere. The eukaryotic cell, which appeared in the fossil record about 2.1 billion years ago, probably acquired its e._____ gradually. For example, the f._____ were added by the process called g._____. Finally, h._____, which may have been preceded by i._____ reproduction, came into being.

13. Write a sentence based on the text material that includes each term listed.

    Cambrian fossils, invertebrates a._____

    _____

Carboniferous forests, insects, vascular plants, amphibians b. _____

_____

_____

14. Change these false statements concerning the Mesozoic era into true statements.

The dominant plants of this era were flowering plants. a. _____

_____

The dominant animals on land were mammals. b. _____

_____

The dinosaurs lived on to become the dominant animals of the Cenozoic era. c. _____

_____

15. What type of vertebrate diversified during the Cenozoic era? a. _____ What type of plant diversified during the Cenozoic era? b. _____

20.3 FACTORS THAT INFLUENCE EVOLUTION (P. 338)

- Continental drift can explain patterns of past and present distributions of life-forms and may have contributed to several mass extinction episodes during the history of life.

16. Indicate whether the following statements about continent drift and the evolution of life are true (T) or false (F):
    _____ a. The earth existed for some time before Pangaea formed.
    _____ b. The very first continent was Pangaea.
    _____ c. Laurasia and Gondwanaland resulted from the breakup of Pangaea.
    _____ d. South America and Africa have matching coastlines.
    _____ e. Widely separated continents have similar fossils that date from before separation occurred.

17. According to this diagram, the earth's plates move like a(n) a. _____.

    What happens at ocean ridges? b. _____

    What happens at ocean trenches? c. _____

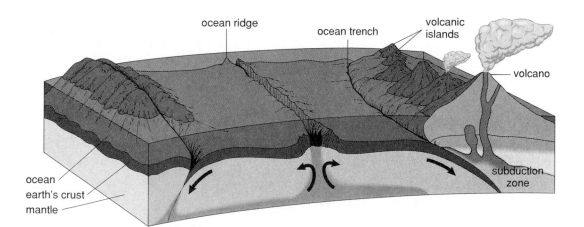

Exploring Mass Extinctions (p. 340)

18. Place a check in front of the statement(s) that contributed to mass extinctions.
    _____ a. The wrath of God showed its power.
    _____ b. Asteroid impact spewed dust into the atmosphere.
    _____ c. Climates changed due to continental drift.
    _____ d. Species have a finite life existence.

Microevolution Versus Macroevolution (p. 342)

> • A new interpretation of the fossil record suggests that relatively rapid evolutionary change, including speciation, followed long periods of stasis (no change).

19. Label each statement as pertaining to microevolution (MI) or macroevolution (MA) or both (B).

_____ a. refers to changes in gene frequencies in a population, as when a peppered moth population changes from mostly light- to mostly dark-colored moths.

_____ b. refers to major transformations, as in the statement that reptiles gave rise to birds and mammals.

_____ c. can be due to natural selection, genetic drift, and other evolutionary forces.

_____ d. can be due to gradual changes as believed by traditionalists, or due to punctuated equilibrium.

_____ e. refers to changes within a lineage, as when the modern horse *Equus* evolved from dog-sized *Hyracotherium*.

20. Indicate whether the following comparisons between the phyletic gradualism and punctuated equilibrium models of evolutionary change are true (T) or false (F):

Phyletic Gradualism	**Punctuated Equilibrium**
_____ a. Speciation occurs gradually.	Speciation occurs rapidly.
_____ b. Transitional links are expected.	Transitional links may not be found.
_____ c. New species are easily recognizable in the fossil record.	New species cannot be recognized.
_____ d. An ancestral species can gradually become a new species.	A subpopulation usually becomes a new species.
_____ e. Speciation is always occurring.	Speciation occurs sporadically.
_____ f. Stasis is rare.	Stasis is common.

KeyWord CrossWord

Review key terms by completing this crossword puzzle, using the following alphabetized list of terms:

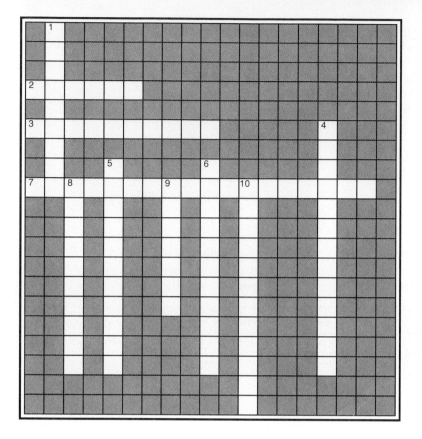

autotroph
chemical evolution
extinction
fossil
heterotroph
lineage
microsphere
ozone shield
proteinoid
sedimentation

Across

2 remains or tangible traces of an ancient organism preserved in sediment or rock

3 abiotically polymerized amino acids that are joined in a preferred manner; possible early step in cell evolution

7 increase in the complexity of chemicals that could have led to the first cells (two words)

Down

1 organism that can make organic molecules from inorganic nutrients

4 process by which particulate material accumulates and forms a stratum

5 formed from proteinoids exposed to water; has properties similar to today's cells

6 organism that cannot synthesize organic compounds from inorganic substances and therefore must take in preformed food

8 total disappearance of a species or higher group

9 line of evolutionary descent from a common ancestor

10 formed from oxygen in the upper atmosphere, it protects the earth from ultraviolet radiation (two words)

OBJECTIVE QUESTIONS

Do not refer to the text when taking this test.

_____ 1. Each of the following was present in the primitive atmosphere of the earth EXCEPT
   a. carbon dioxide.
   b. carbon monoxide.
   c. molecular nitrogen.
   d. molecular oxygen.

_____ 2. Miller's experiments produced
   a. coacervate droplets from macromolecules.
   b. inorganic substances from organic molecules.
   c. organic molecules from inorganic substances.
   d. protocells from macromolecules.

_____ 3. Select the correct sequence that occurred on the primitive earth.
   a. gases, small molecules, macromolecules, protocells
   b. macromolecules, small molecules, protocells, gases
   c. protocells, macromolecules, small molecules, gases
   d. small molecules, gases, macromolecules, protocells

_____ 4. Microspheres formed from the polymerization of
   a. amino acids.
   b. nucleotides.
   c. sugars.
   d. water.

_____ 5. Clay may have promoted the formation of macromolecules because it
   a. attracts small organic molecules.
   b. is dry.
   c. lacks zinc and iron.
   d. wards off energy.

_____ 6. Protocells exhibited each of the following EXCEPT
   a. the ability to separate from water.
   b. a lipid-protein membrane.
   c. conduction of energy metabolism.
   d. means of self-replication.

_____ 7. The most primitive life-forms were
   a. anaerobic photosynthesizers.
   b. eukaryotic plants.
   c. eukaryotic protists.
   d. prokaryotic cells.

_____ 8. Currently, the ozone in the atmosphere
   a. enhances photosynthesis.
   b. promotes the origin of life today.
   c. protects organisms from the effect of ultraviolet rays.
   d. reacts with and destroys pollutants.

_____ 9. Which is NOT a characteristic of the Cenozoic era?
   a. appearance of first hominids
   b. extinction of dinosaurs
   c. dominance on land by flowering plants
   d. increase in number of herbaceous plants

_____10. The term _stasis_ means
   a. convergence of species.
   b. divergence of species.
   c. gradual change.
   d. lack of change.

In questions 11–14, match the descriptions with the following time periods:
   a. Precambrian
   b. Paleozoic
   c. Mesozoic
   d. Cenozoic

_____11. single cells
_____12. mammals
_____13. amphibians
_____14. reptiles

_____15. We know there was a Cambrian explosion because
   a. a mass extinction took place due to all the dust in the air.
   b. the fossil record is very rich.
   c. so many fish were in the seas.
   d. prokaryotes became so structurally diversified.

_____16. Which expression should be associated with the Mesozoic era?
   a. Age of Amphibians
   b. Age of Fishes
   c. Age of Cycads and Dinosaurs
   d. Age of Primates

_____17. What happens when continents collide?
   a. Mountain ranges develop.
   b. The earth moves slightly in the solar system.
   c. Subduction zones appear.
   d. All of these are correct.

_____18. Mass extinctions
   a. refer to loss of mass by many species.
   b. may be due to asteroid impacts.
   c. may be due to climatic changes.
   d. Both _b_ and _c_ are correct.

Answer in complete sentences.

19. How do the currently existing RNA viruses lend support to the hypothesis that RNA could have been the first genetic material?

20. Some scientists hypothesize that birds are dinosaurs. How might biotechnological techniques help settle the question?

Test Results: _____ Number right ÷ 20 = _____ × 100 = _____ %

EXPLORING THE INTERNET

Use the Internet to further explore topics in this chapter, such as chemical evolution, the geologic time scale, or archosaurs. Go to the Mader Home Page (http://www.mhhe.com/sciencemath/biology/mader/) and click on *Biology,* 6th edition. Go to Chapter 20 and select a Web site of interest.

ANSWER KEY

STUDY EXERCISES

1. see figure 20.4, page 327, in text **2.** an energy source, because amino acids do not react unless energy is provided **3.** To obtain microspheres, proteinoids must be placed in water. **4.** discovery of ribozymes, which are nucleotides with enzymatic properties **5. a.** F **b.** T **c.** F **d.** T **6. a.** must contain a self-replication system **b.** add *self-replication system* between protocell and cell **7. a.** The ocean contained organic molecules that could serve as food. **b.** The atmosphere did not contain any oxygen. **8.** a, c, b, d **9. a.** P **b.** P **c.** P **d.** C **e.** C **f.** C **10.** These parts do not decompose. **11. a.** F **b.** T **c.** T **12. a.** anaerobic fermentation **b.** oxygen **c.** stromatolites **d.** oxygen **e.** organelles **f.** mitochondria (chloroplasts) **g.** endosymbiosis **h.** multicellularity **i.** sexual **13. a.** During the Cambrian period, many and various shelled invertebrates appeared. **b.** The vascular plants that characterized the Carboniferous forests are of minor importance today, but at that time, they provided a home for insects and various amphibians—some of whom were very large. **14. a.** . . . were nonflowering plants, or gymnosperms **b.** . . . were reptiles, including dinosaurs **c.** The mammals lived on . . . **15. a.** mammals **b.** flowering plants, or angiosperms **16. a.** T **b.** F **c.** T **d.** T **e.** T **17. a.** conveyor belt **b.** seafloor spreading occurs **c.** subduction occurs **18.** b, c **19. a.** MI **b.** MA **c.** B **d.** MA **e.** MA **20. a.** T **b.** T **c.** F **d.** T **e.** T **f.** T

KEYWORD CROSSWORD

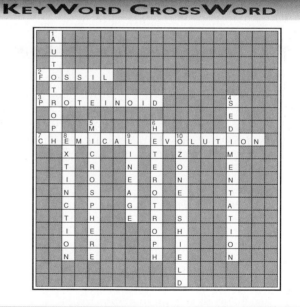

CHAPTER TEST

1. d **2.** c **3.** a **4.** a **5.** a **6.** d **7.** d **8.** c **9.** b **10.** d **11.** a **12.** d **13.** b **14.** c **15.** b **16.** c **17.** a **18.** d **19.** Some RNA viruses exist that manage to replicate without need of DNA. The RNA genome of these viruses can be used as an mRNA to produce protein and additional RNA genomes. This suggests that the first cell would have been able to function without a DNA genome. **20.** The polymerase chain reaction could be used to make multiple copies of dinosaur genes, and then DNA fingerprinting could be used to compare the dinosaur genome to genome of birds. If the two patterns are quite similar, it would lend support to the hypothesis that birds are dinosaurs.

21

HUMAN EVOLUTION

Primates differ from other mammals because they have opposable thumbs and their digits bear nails, not claws. The forebrain is enlarged, and during an extended childhood, they learn much of their behavior.

The classification of humans reflects their evolutionary history. They belong to the order Primates, along with **prosimians,** monkeys, and apes. The superorder Anthropoidea includes monkeys, apes, and humans. The superfamily of **hominoids** includes only apes and humans, and the family of **hominids** includes only aus-

tralopithecines and humans. Finally, the genus *Homo* includes only extinct and living human species.

The australopithecines were diverse, and some species lived at the same time as ***Homo habilis.*** *Australopithecus afarensis,* who walked erect, may have been a common ancestor to these two lineages. *H. habilis* may have been the first to make tools; ***H. erectus*** left Africa and traveled. Modern humans either arose in several different places in Eurasia or else originated in Africa and then migrated to Europe and Asia.

STUDY EXERCISES

Study the text section by section as you answer the questions that follow.

21.1 HUMANS ARE PRIMATES (P. 348)

- Humans (*Homo sapiens*) are in the order Primates, which are mammals adapted to living in trees.
- Primate characteristics include opposable thumbs, an enlarged forebrain, and an emphasis on learned behavior.

1. The invertebrate chordates are believed to have been present in Cambrian seas. They gave rise to the vertebrates.

   Humans are what type of vertebrate? [a.]_____

   Humans are what type of mammal? [b.]_____

   Humans are what type of primate? [c.]_____

   Among anthropoids, what fossil may have been a common ancestor to all apes and humans? [d.]_____

   In addition, there may be a common ancestor for African [e.]_____ and humans.

   The hominid ancestor to humans is believed to have been [f.]_____.

2. List an adaptation for arboreal life in relation to the following:

   vision [a.]_____

   digits [b.]_____

   brain size [c.]_____

   birth number [d.]_____

21.2 Primates Are Diverse (p. 349)

- Prosimians (tarsiers and lemurs) are primates that diverged early from the human line of descent.

3. The tarsier is mouse-sized with large eyes, and lemurs have a squirrel-like appearance. What is the significance of these animals in terms of human evolution? ______________________________

____

Anthropoids Followed (p. 351)

- Humans are in the suborder Anthropoidea (monkeys, apes, and humans), the superfamily Hominoidea (apes and humans), and the family Hominidea (extinct and modern humans).

4. Beside each taxonomic category, place the following terms as appropriate: *apes, humans,* and *monkeys.*
   anthropoids a.______________, ______________, ______________
   hominoids b.______________, ______________
5. In the following chart, list characteristics that distinguish Old-World monkeys from New-World monkeys:

Old-World Monkeys	New-World Monkeys

6. What is the name given to the first hominoid? a.______________
   Which Asian ape is smaller and has long arms? b.______________
   Which Asian ape is larger and still lives in trees? c.______________
   Which African ape is the largest of all the apes? d.______________
   Which African ape is at home in trees and on the ground? e.______________
7. What geographic barrier in Africa may have contributed to the evolution of humans? a.______________
   How so? b.______________________________

21.3 Hominids Break Away (p. 354)

- Australopithecines (about 3 MYA), the first hominids, evolved in eastern Africa, an area whose climate was no longer suitable to the growth of trees. Australopithecines had a small brain, but they walked erect.

8. Australopithecines were the first a.______________. The oldest one, dated about 4.4 MYA in the fossil record and known as b.______________, represents a transitional stage between c.______________ and d.______________. Australopithecines walked e.______________, but their brain was f.______________. They exhibit mosaic evolution, meaning that their g.______________________________

   ______________________________.

   The next australopithecine in the fossil record is h.______________, who was a common ancestor for the rest of the australopithecines and i.______________. *A. afarensis* and *A. africanus* are termed *gracile* because they are slight in appearance. j.______________ and k.______________ are termed l.______________ because they had larger facial bones, most likely due to larger teeth and chewing muscles.

Homo habilis Made Tools (p. 357)

- *Homo habilis* (about 2 MYA), the first hominid to make tools, was most likely a hunter and may have been able to speak.
- *Homo erectus* (about 1 MYA) migrated out of Africa and was a big-game hunter who possessed fire. *Homo erectus* may have evolved into the so-called "archaic *Homo sapiens*."
- According to the out-of-Africa hypothesis, modern humans evolved in Africa, and after migrating to Europe and Asia (about 100,000 BP), they replaced the archaic *Homo* species, including, perhaps, the Neanderthals.
- Cro-Magnon is the name given to modern humans who made sophisticated tools and definitely had culture.

9. Match the *Homo* species with the following phrases that describe their way of life (numbers can be used more than once):
   - *1 brain size less than 1,000 cc*
   - *2 brain size 1,000 cc or larger*
   - *3 more likely scavenged meat*
   - *4 more likely hunted animals*
   - *5 certainly had speech and culture*
   - *6 most likely had speech and culture*
   - *7 perhaps had speech and culture*
   - *8 made tools*
   - *9 had upright posture*

   Homo habilis ᵃ·_____

   Homo erectus ᵇ·_____

   Neanderthals ᶜ·_____

   Cro-Magnons ᵈ·_____

10. Which hypothesis—the out-of-Africa hypothesis or the multiregional continuity hypothesis—states that *H. erectus* and then, later on, humans left Africa? ᵃ·_____ Which hypothesis states that *H. erectus* left Africa and that then modern humans simultaneously arose in Europe, Asia, and Africa? ᵇ·_____ With which hypothesis would you expect more similarity between fossils dated between 300,000 BP and 100,000 BP? ᶜ·_____ The fossil record shows several varieties of humans in Asia and Europe dated prior to 100,000 BP. These are called ᵈ· "_____ *H. sapiens*." One example of an "archaic *H. sapiens*" is ᵉ·_____.

KEYWORD CROSSWORD

Review key terms by completing this crossword puzzle, using the following alphabetized list of terms:

anthropoid
australopithecine
Cro-Magnon
hominid
hominoid
Homo erectus
Homo habilis
mammal
molecular clock
Neanderthal
primate
Proconsul
prosimian

Across

1 group of primates that includes monkeys, apes, and humans

3 member of a class of vertebrates characterized especially by the presence of hair and mammary glands

6 hominid who lived during the last Ice Age in Europe and the Middle East; made stone tools, hunted large game, and lived in a kind of society

9 group of primates that includes lemurs and tarsiers; may resemble the first primates to have evolved

10 hominid who lived 40,000 years ago; accomplished hunter, made compound stone tools, and possibly had a language (two words)

11 hominid who lived during the Pleistocene epoch; had a posture and locomotion similar to modern humans (two words)

Down

1 one of several species of *Australopithecus,* a genus that contains the first generally recognized hominids

2 member of a superfamily containing humans and the great apes

4 idea that the rate at which mutation changes accumulate in certain types of genes is constant over time and is not involved in adaptation to the environment (two words)

5 animal that belongs to the order that includes prosimians, monkeys, apes, and humans

7 member of a family containing humans and their direct ancestors; known only by the fossil record

8 hominid of 2 million years ago; possibly, a direct ancestor of modern humans (two words)

9 possible hominoid ancestor; a forest-dwelling primate with some characteristics of living apes

OBJECTIVE QUESTIONS

Do not refer to the text when taking this test.

_____ 1. Which of these are NOT primates?
a. lemurs
b. monkeys
c. gorillas
d. humans
e. All of these are primates.

_____ 2. Which is NOT true of primates?
a. They have diversified and live in the air, on land, and in the water.
b. They are adapted to life in trees.
c. They have opposable thumbs.
d. They have jointed appendages.

_____ 3. Which is NOT an ape?
a. gibbon
b. gorilla
c. orangutan
d. chimpanzee
e. All of these are apes.

_____ 4. Modern humans are more closely related to
a. monkeys than apes.
b. African apes than Asian apes.
c. Neanderthals than Cro-Magnon.
d. whales than prosimians.

_____ 5. Which of these is NOT a correct contrast between human and ape anatomy?

Human	**Ape**
a. short pelvis	long pelvis
b. long legs	short legs
c. bipedal	knuckle walking
d. sloping face	straight face

_____ 6. Australopithecines
a. were remarkable for their lack of body hair.
b. may have lived at the same time as _H. habilis._
c. were robust and most closely related to the Neanderthals.
d. had dentition similar to that of modern humans.

_____ 7. Australopithecines
a. were apelike below the waist and humanlike above the waist.
b. were humanlike below the waist and apelike above the waist.
c. were generally apelike.
d. were generally humanlike.

_____ 8. In baboons, males are larger than females, and
a. in australopithecines, females are larger than males.
b. this is unique among primates.
c. this is found in australopithecines also.
d. None of these are correct.

_____ 9. Dentition tells us much about
a. the brain size of hominoids.
b. how long ago modern humans left Africa.
c. the foods hominids ate.
d. Both _a_ and _c_ are correct.

In questions 10–14, match the descriptions with the following hominids:
a. _australopithecines_
b. _H. habilis_
c. _H. erectus_
d. _Cro-Magnon_

_____10. The species most likely NOT to have tools.

_____11. The species most likely to have traveled out of Africa.

_____12. The species most likely to have been able to control fire first.

_____13. The species most likely to have made tools first.

_____14. The species known to have painted and sculpted.

_____15. It has been proposed that _A. afarensis_ is a common ancestor to
a. modern African apes and humans.
b. _H. erectus_ and _H. habilis._
c. other austropithecines and _H. habilis._
d. It could not have been a common ancestor to any other species.

_____16. A likely hypothesis is that
a. _H. erectus_ never migrated out of Africa; Lucy's son did.
b. _H. erectus_ still climbed trees and ate only fruit.
c. _H. erectus_ hunted animals and had a home base.
d. All of these are likely.

_____17. The multiregional continuity hypothesis says that
a. modern humans arose in several different places.
b. no interbreeding took place between different types of humans.
c. Neanderthals, and not _H. erectus,_ migrated out of Africa.
d. the Neanderthals were more modern in appearance than once thought.

_____18. The fact that humans adapted to various climates shows that
a. not all humans can reproduce with one another.
b. humans are adaptable.
c. we need to rethink some of the tenets of human evolution.
d. All of these are correct.

Answer in complete sentences.

19. In what way do australopithecines illustrate mosaic evolution?

20. What types of evidence would convince you that a particular fossil should be classified in the genus *Homo?*

Test Results: _____ Number right ÷ 20 = _____ × 100 = _____ %

EXPLORING THE INTERNET

Use the Internet to further explore topics in this chapter, such as fossil hominids and human evolution in Africa. Go to the Mader Home Page (http://www.mhhe.com/sciencemath/biology/mader/) and click on *Biology,* 6th edition. Go to Chapter 21 and select a Web site of interest.

ANSWER KEY

STUDY EXERCISES

1. a. mammal **b.** primate **c.** human **d.** *Proconsul* **e.** apes **f.** *Australopithecus afarensis* **2. a.** eyes forward with stereoscopic vision **b.** nails, not claws, and opposable thumb **c.** large, well developed **d.** single offspring at a time **3.** They are most like the mammal from which all primates evolved. **4. a.** monkeys, apes, humans **b.** apes, humans
5.

Old-World Monkeys	New-World Monkeys
no prehensile tail	prehensile tail
snout	flat face

6. a. *Proconsul* **b.** gibbon **c.** orangutan **d.** gorilla **e.** chimpanzee **7. a.** rift valley **b.** Dry environmental conditions caused hominid ancestors to come down out of trees. **8. a.** hominids **b.** *A. ramidus* **c.** apes **d.** humans **e.** erect **f.** small **g.** body parts evolved at different rates **h.** *A. afarensis* **i.** humans **j.** *A. robustus* **k.** *A. boisei* **l.** robust **9. a.** 1, 3, 7, 8, 9 **b.** 2, 4, 6, 8, 9 **c.** 2, 4, 6, 8, 9 **d.** 2, 4, 5, 8, 9 **10. a.** out-of-Africa **b.** multiregional continuity **c.** multiregional continuity **d.** archaic **e.** Neanderthal

KEYWORD CROSSWORD

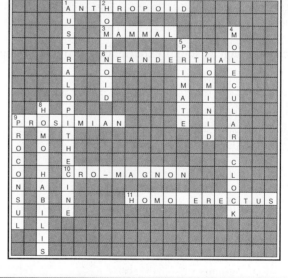

CHAPTER TEST

1. e **2.** a **3.** e **4.** b **5.** d **6.** b **7.** b **8.** c **9.** c **10.** a **11.** c **12.** c **13.** b **14.** d **15.** c **16.** c **17.** a **18.** b **19.** Mosaic evolution occurs when various parts evolve at different rates. Australopithecines walked erect but had a small brain; therefore, the lower half of their body was more like that of modern humans than the upper half. **20.** A hominid should be classified in the genus *Homo* if it has erect posture, dentition like that of modern humans, a brain of 1,000 cc or more, a high forehead, and a projecting chin.

PART IV BEHAVIOR AND ECOLOGY

22

ANIMAL BEHAVIOR

CHAPTER REVIEW

Biologists ask causal questions and survival value questions about **behavior.** Causal questions pertain to mechanisms of behavior, and survival value questions pertain to the adaptive nature of behavior. Hybrid studies with warblers show that behavior has a genetic basis. The nervous and endocrine systems control behavior, as shown by garter snake experiments and snail (*Aplysia*) DNA studies.

A behavior sometimes undergoes development after birth, as exemplified by improvement in laughing gull chick begging behavior. **Learning** occurs when a behavior changes with practice. Experiments teaching male birds to sing in their species dialect show that various factors—such as social experience—influence whether or not learning takes place.

Since genes influence behavior, it is reasonable to assume that adaptive behavioral traits will evolve. Both sexes are expected to behave in a manner that will raise their reproductive success. Females who produce only one egg a month are expected to choose the best mate, and males who produce many sperm are expected to inseminate as many females as possible. **Sexual selection** is natural selection due to mate choice by females and competition among males. Do females choose mates who have the best traits for survival or simply the ones to

whom they are attracted? Or are these hypotheses one and the same? Experiments with satin bowerbirds and birds of paradise were inconclusive. Food sources can influence reproductive behavior, however, as shown by observations of birds of paradise.

A cost-benefit analysis is particularly applicable to male competition. A **dominance hierarchy,** as seen in baboons, and establishment of a **territory,** as seen in red deer, are two ways in which strong males get to reproduce more than weaker males. Do the nonmating males receive a benefit? And are the costs within reason for the mating males? Experiments are still being conducted.

Communication between animals consists of chemical, auditory, visual, and tactile signals. Social living can help an animal avoid predators, rear offspring, and find food. Disadvantages include fighting among members, spread of a contagious disease, and the possibility of subordination to others.

Altruistic behavior seems self-sacrificing until we consider the concept of **inclusive fitness,** which includes personal reproductive success and the reproductive success of relatives. Among social insects, sisters share 75% of their genes rather than 50%. This makes it more likely that they will help raise siblings.

STUDY EXERCISES

Study the text section by section as you answer the questions that follow.

22.1 BEHAVIOR HAS A GENETIC BASIS (P. 368)

- Behaviors, any actions of an animal that can be observed and described, are inherited and have at least a partial genetic basis.
- The nervous and endocrine systems have immediate control over behaviors.

1. Label each of the following as describing a mechanistic question (M) or a survival value question (S):
   _____ a. How do insects spread their wings before they begin to fly?
   _____ b. Do male robins attack any other male that attempts to mate with their partner?
   _____ c. How do garter snakes sense slugs?
   _____ d. Why do some garter snakes eat slugs and others eat frogs?

2. Describe Berthold's experiment and results concerning Cape Verde blackcap warblers (those that do not migrate) and German blackcap warblers (that migrate to Africa).

experiment a. _____

results b. _____

conclusion c. _____

3. Inland garter snakes eat frogs, and coastal garter snakes eat slugs. Arnold discovered that inland snakes do not respond to the smell of slugs, and hybrids generally have only an intermediate ability to respond to the smell of slugs. What did he conclude? _____

4. Egg-laying behavior of *Aplysia* involves a set sequence of movements. Investigators found that the gene that controls behavior codes for hormones. What is the conclusion? _____

22.2 BEHAVIOR UNDERGOES DEVELOPMENT (P. 370)

- Behaviors sometimes undergo development after birth, as when learning affects behavior.

5. Indicate whether the following statements about Hailman's experiment with laughing gull chicks are true (T) or false (F):
_____ a. Laughing gull chicks seek their own food.
_____ b. Motor development helps explain why the pecking behavior of chicks improves.
_____ c. Operant conditioning—a form of learning—helps explain why older chicks choose a model that looks more like the parent.

6. Explain question 5c here. _____

_____

7. Due to imprinting, chicks follow the first moving object they see. In relation to this observation, explain the following:

sensitive period a. _____

_____

need for social interaction b. _____

_____

8. The following diagram illustrates experiments studying how birds learn to sing:

Explain each of the frames.

first a. _____

second b. _____

third c. _____

What conclusion is appropriate? d. _____

22.3 BEHAVIOR IS ADAPTIVE (p. 372)

- Natural selection influences such behaviors as methods of feeding, selecting a home, and reproducing.
- Environmental correlation and cost-benefit analysis are tools for testing adaptive responses about behavior.

9. Indicate whether the following statements about the adaptive nature of behavior are true (T) or false (F):
   _____ a. Behavior has a genetic basis.
   _____ b. Certain behaviors can improve reproductive success.
   _____ c. The nervous and endocrine systems control behavior.

10. Borgia observed the reproductive behavior of satin bowerbirds. Females chose males with well-kept bowers that contained blue objects. Why might this be supportive of the good genes hypothesis? _____ _____

11. Beehler studied the reproductive behavior of birds of paradise. Perhaps females choose the males with spectacular plumes because it signifies a._____ or because their sons will be b._____ to females also. He also found that raggiana offspring are fed a more c._____ food than those of the related species, the trumpet manucode. This seems to correlate with the fact that the birds of paradise are d._____, while the trumpet manucode birds are e._____. Birds are monogamous when it takes two parents to f._____ the offspring.

12. In terms of a cost-benefit analysis, what is the benefit to dominant males in a baboon troop? a._____ _____

    What are the costs? b. _____ _____

    What is the benefit to subordinate males in a baboon troop? c. _____

    What are the costs? d. _____

    Why do you predict that the benefits for each must outweigh the costs? e. _____

22.4 ANIMALS ARE SOCIAL (p. 376)

- Animals living in societies have various means of communicating with one another.

13. Match the descriptions with the following terms:
    1 chemical communication
    2 auditory communication
    3 visual communication
    4 tactile communication
    _____ a. Honeybees do a waggle dance in dark hive.
    _____ b. Male raggiana birds of paradise do spectacular courtship dances.
    _____ c. Birds sing songs.
    _____ d. Cheetahs spray a pheromone onto a tree.

22.5 SOCIOBIOLOGY AND ANIMAL BEHAVIOR (p. 378)

- Group living is adaptive in some situations and not in others.
- Behaviors that appear to reduce fitness may be found to increase fitness on closer examination.

14. Indicate whether the statements that follow are true (T) or false (F). Change all false statements to true statements.

_____ a. Subordinate males have less chance to mate, but group living may help them survive. Rewrite: _____

_____

_____ b. Animals that live alone may have to spend less time grooming. Rewrite: _____

_____

_____ c. Animals that capture large prey tend to live alone. Rewrite: _____

_____

_____ d. The cost of social living outweighs the benefits, but animals like being with others. Rewrite: _____

_____

15. Match the statements with the following terms (multiple answers are possible):

   1 altruism
   2 inclusive fitness
   3 helpers at the nest
   4 reciprocity

_____ a. Males do not prevent receptive female chimpanzees from copulating with several members of a group.
_____ b. A behavior seems to be self-sacrificing.
_____ c. Older siblings take care of younger siblings.
_____ d. Worker bees do not reproduce and instead help raise siblings.
_____ e. A younger bird helps an older bird raise its young but takes over the territory when the older bird dies.

Review key terms by completing this crossword puzzle, using the following alphabetized list of terms:

altruism
behavior
communication
dominance hierarchy
imprinting
learning
operant conditioning
pheromone
sexual selection
society
sociobiology
territoriality

Across

1 social ranking within a group in which a higher-ranking individual acquires more resources than a lower-ranking individual (two words)

7 observable, coordinated responses to environmental stimuli

9 behavior related to the act of marking or defending a particular area against invasion by another species member; area often used for the purpose of feeding, mating, and caring for young

10 chemical released by the body that causes a predictable reaction from another member of the same species

11 group in which species members are organized in a cooperative manner, extending beyond sexual and parental behavior

12 relatively permanent change in an animal's behavior that results from practice and experience

Down

2 form of learning that results from rewarding or reinforcing a particular behavior (two words)

3 form of learning that occurs early in the lives of animals; a close association is made that later influences sexual behavior

4 signal by a sender that influences the behavior of a receiver

5 social interaction that has the potential to decrease the lifetime reproductive success of the member exhibiting the behavior

6 changes in males and females due to male competition and female selectivity (two words)

8 application of evolutionary biological principles to the study of social behavior in animals

OBJECTIVE QUESTIONS

Do not refer to the text when taking this test.

_____ 1. Which of these pertain(s) to behavior?
  a. The heart pumps blood into the arteries.
  b. Ants lay a pheromone trail to guide other ants.
  c. Birds have warning calls.
  d. Both *b* and *c* are correct.

_____ 2. A mechanistic question
  a. is the same as a survival value question.
  b. pertains to a mechanism of behavior.
  c. pertains to behavior that results from evolution.
  d. Both *b* and *c* are correct.

For questions 3–7, match the statements to the following descriptions of behavior:
  a. Behavior has a genetic basis.
  b. The nervous and endocrine systems control behavior.
  c. Behavior undergoes development.

_____ 3. Hybrid studies with warblers reveal this.

_____ 4. Garter snakes differ in their ability to smell slugs.

_____ 5. Laughing gull chicks improve in their ability to recognize their parent.

_____ 6. Egg-laying behavior in *Aplysia* reveals this.

_____ 7. Caged birds can learn to sing their species' song if they hear a recording of it during a sensitive period.

_____ 8. The pecking improvement of laughing gull chicks
  a. can be explained by operant conditioning.
  b. correlates with improved motor skills.
  c. is a form of learning.
  d. All of these are correct.

_____ 9. A sensitive period for learning was observed when
  a. hybrid garter snakes were intermediate in their ability to smell slugs.
  b. captive birds learned to sing a more developed song by hearing a recording.

  c. imprinting occurred.
  d. Both *b* and *c* are correct.

_____ 10. The adaptiveness of behavior may be associated with which statement(s)?
  a. Behavior has a genetic basis.
  b. The nervous and endocrine systems control behavior.
  c. Behaviorists ask causal questions.
  d. All of these are correct.

_____ 11. Which of these is NOT consistent with reproduction in females?
  a. selecting the best mate possible
  b. having a higher potential to produce many offspring
  c. nurturing offspring until they can care for themselves
  d. producing few eggs over a lifetime

_____ 12. Male competition leads to
  a. dominance hierarchies and reduction in fighting.
  b. defense of a territory.
  c. neglect of the young.
  d. Both *a* and *b* are correct.

_____ 13. A cost-benefit analysis can explain
  a. why subordinate males remain in a group.
  b. why red deer males are large despite the chances of it shortening their life span.
  c. why older siblings take care of younger siblings.
  d. All of these are correct.

_____ 14. Inclusive fitness explains
  a. seemingly altruistic behavior.
  b. why older siblings help raise younger siblings.
  c. the benefit of being a worker bee.
  d. All of these are correct.

CRITICAL THINKING QUESTIONS

Answer in complete sentences.

15. What evidence shows that behavior is inherited?

16. According to the tenets of sociobiology, is the behavior of animals altruistic?

Test Results: _____ Number right ÷ 16 = _____ × 100 = _____ %

Use the Internet to further explore topics in this chapter, such as examples of animal behavior and the significance of animal behavior research. Go to the Mader Home Page (http://www.mhhe.com/sciencemath/biology/mader/) and click on *Biology,* 6th edition. Go to Chapter 22 and select a Web site of interest.

ANSWER KEY

STUDY EXERCISES

1. a. M **b.** S **c.** M **d.** S **2. a.** Mate the two types of warblers. **b.** Hybrids show migratory restlessness. **c.** Hybrids inherit genes from both parents and therefore show behavior intermediate between the two. **3.** The nervous system controls the eating behavior of garter snakes. **4.** Hormones also control behavior. **5. a.** F **b.** T **c.** T **6.** Due to operant conditioning, chicks learn to peck correctly (i.e., only at models that closely resemble the parent) because in that way they are rewarded with food. **7. a.** Behavior is best learned during a sensitive period immediately after birth. **b.** Clucking by a hen that has recently had chicks can bring about the behavior even outside the sensitive period. **8. a.** Isolated bird sings but does not learn to sing the species' song. **b.** Bird learns to sing the song if a recording is played during a sensitive period. **c.** Bird learns to sing the song of a social tutor of another species outside a sensitive period. **d.** Social interactions help learning take place. **9. a.** T **b.** T **c.** T **10.** Aggressive males are able to have well-kept bowers, and this behavior, which may be inherited, may lead to reproductive success. **11. a.** health **b.** attractive **c.** nutritious **d.** polygamous **e.** monogamous **f.** feed **12. a.** first chance to mate **b.** might be injured protecting the troop **c.** protection **d.** less frequent chance to mate **e.** because the behavior evolved through natural selection **13. a.** 4 **b.** 3 **c.** 2 **d.** 1 **14. a.** T **b.** T **c.** F; . . . tend to live in a group **d.** F; The benefits of social living outweigh the costs or else animals would not live in a group. **15. a.** 2 **b.** 1, 3 **c.** 1, 2, 3 **d.** 1, 2, 3 **e.** 4

KEYWORD CROSSWORD

CHAPTER TEST

1. d **2.** d **3.** a **4.** b **5.** c **6.** b **7.** c **8.** d **9.** d **10.** a **11.** b **12.** d **13.** d **14.** d **15.** Experimentation has shown that behavior has a genetic basis. Hybrid warblers show migratory restlessness, a trait intermediate to both parents, indicating that behavior is inherited. Hybrid garter snakes generally have an intermediate ability to smell slugs. Since behavior has a genetic basis, it has to be inherited. **16.** It may appear to be altruistic but may be explainable by inclusive fitness—which depends not only on the number of direct descendants due to personal reproduction but also on the number of offspring produced by relatives that the individual has helped nurture.

23

ECOLOGY OF POPULATIONS

Ecology is the study of the interactions of organisms with other organisms and with the physical environment. Ecology encompasses several levels of study: organism, **population, community, ecosystem,** and finally, the **biosphere.** The interactions of organisms with the abiotic and biotic environment affect their distribution and abundance.

Populations have a certain size that depends, in part, on their **net reproductive rate** (r). There are two patterns of population growth: **exponential growth** results in a J-shaped growth curve, and **logistic growth** results in an S-shaped growth curve. Exponential growth can only occur when resources are abundant; otherwise, logistic growth occurs. When population size reaches the **carrying capacity** of the environment, environmental resistance opposes **biotic potential.**

A **survivorship** curve describes the mortality (deaths per capita) of a population. There are three idealized survivorship curves: with type I, most individuals survive well past the midpoint of the life span; with type II, survivorship decreases at a constant rate throughout the life span; and with type III, most individuals die young. **Age structure diagrams** tell what proportion of the population is prereproductive, reproductive and postreproductive.

Density-dependent and density-independent factors regulate population size. Density-independent factors, such as weather and fire, and density-dependent factors, such as predation and competition, are both extrinsic factors Intrinsic factors such as territoriality may also be involved.

Life history patterns have been related to the logistic growth curve. So-called *r*-selection occurs in unpredictable environments (density-independent factors regulate population size) and favors small adults that reproduce early and do not invest in parental care. So-called *K*-selection occurs in stable environments (density-dependent factors regulate population size) and favors large adults that reproduce repeatedly during a long life span and invest much energy in parental care.

The human population is currently in the exponential part of its growth curve. **MDCs (more developed countries)** experienced **demographic transition** some time ago, and the populations of most are either not growing or are decreasing. **LDCs (Less developed countries)** are only now undergoing demographic transition but will still experience much growth because of their pyramid-shaped age structure diagram. To preserve the environment and the human population, a **sustainable world** philosophy is a necessity. Control of population size in developing countries while meeting economic needs and protecting the environment are all components of this philosophy.

Study the text section by section as you answer the questions that follow.

23.1 SCOPE OF ECOLOGY (P. 384)

- Ecology is the study of the interactions of organisms with other organisms and with the physical environment.
- The interactions of organisms with the abiotic and biotic environment affect their distribution and abundance.

1. Match the statements to the following levels of ecological study:

   1 community
   2 population
   3 ecosystem
   4 biosphere

   _____ a. a group of populations interacting in an area
   _____ b. a community interacting with its physical environment

_____ c. all the individuals of the same species in an area

_____ d. portion of earth's surface where living things exist

_____ e. focus of ecological study is growth and regulation of size

_____ f. focus of ecological study is interactions such as predation and competition between populations

2. To describe patterns of distribution of individuals within a population, place the words *uniform, random,* or *clumped* beneath the following diagrams:

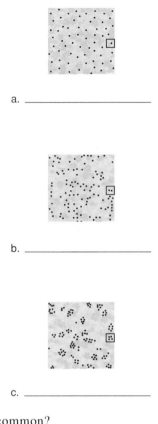

a. _____

b. _____

c. _____

3. Which pattern of distribution is most common? _____

4. a._____ factors determine where an individual organism can live. Temperature is an example of a(n) b._____ factor, and availability of prey is an example of a(n) c._____ factor that can limit where types of organisms are found.

23.2 CHARACTERISTICS OF POPULATIONS (P. 386)

- Population size depends on natality, mortality, immigration, and emigration.
- Population growth models predict changes in population size over time under particular conditions.

5. Considering natality (birthrate), mortality (death rate), immigration, and emigration, which two lead to an increase in population size, and which two lead to a decrease in population size?

Increase	Decrease
a._____	c._____
b._____	d._____

6. Calculate the net reproductive rate (r) when the birthrate is .06 per capita per unit time, and the death rate is .04 per capita per unit time.

$r =$ a._____ $-$ b._____ $=$ c._____ per capita unit time

Given a population of panthers in the Florida Everglades, and per unit time = 1 year and population = 50 panthers, how many panthers would there be after a year? d._____

Questions 7–12 pertain to the following two population growth curves:

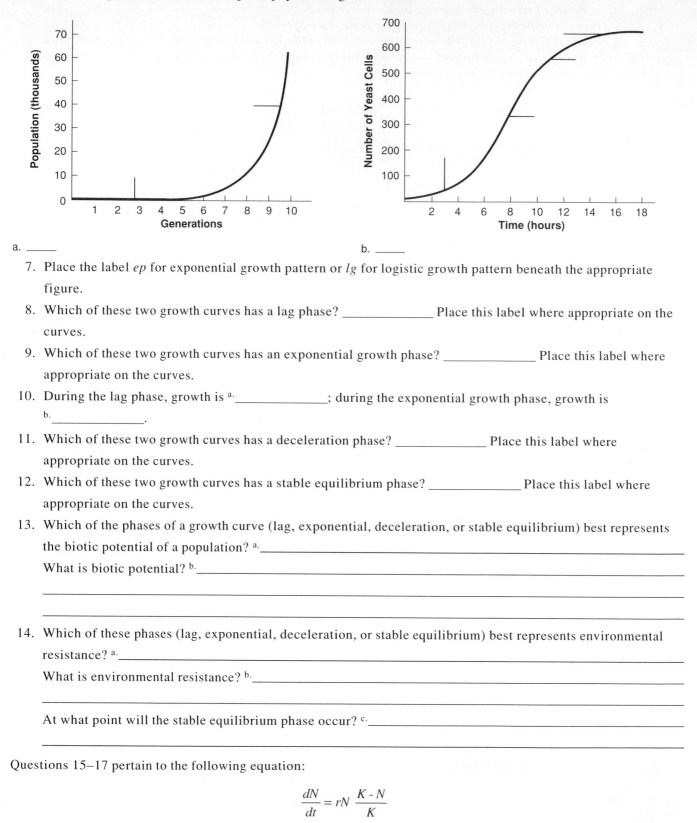

a. _____

b. _____

7. Place the label *ep* for exponential growth pattern or *lg* for logistic growth pattern beneath the appropriate figure.

8. Which of these two growth curves has a lag phase? _____ Place this label where appropriate on the curves.

9. Which of these two growth curves has an exponential growth phase? _____ Place this label where appropriate on the curves.

10. During the lag phase, growth is [a.]_____; during the exponential growth phase, growth is [b.]_____.

11. Which of these two growth curves has a deceleration phase? _____ Place this label where appropriate on the curves.

12. Which of these two growth curves has a stable equilibrium phase? _____ Place this label where appropriate on the curves.

13. Which of the phases of a growth curve (lag, exponential, deceleration, or stable equilibrium) best represents the biotic potential of a population? [a.]_____

    What is biotic potential? [b.]_____

    _____

    _____

14. Which of these phases (lag, exponential, deceleration, or stable equilibrium) best represents environmental resistance? [a.]_____

    What is environmental resistance? [b.]_____

    _____

    At what point will the stable equilibrium phase occur? [c.]_____

    _____

Questions 15–17 pertain to the following equation:

$$\frac{dN}{dt} = rN \; \frac{K - N}{K}$$

15. When N is much smaller than K, the term $K - N/K$ is approximately 1. Is the opportunity for population growth maximal or minimal? _____

16. When N is about equal to K, the term $K - N/K$ is zero. Is the opportunity for population growth maximal or minimal? _____

17. Which of the following can be associated with biotic potential, and which can be associated with carrying capacity?

K a._____

r b._____

Mortality Patterns (p. 390)

- Mortality within a population is recorded in a life table and illustrated by a survivorship curve.

18. Study the following diagram of survivorship curves and then answer the questions:

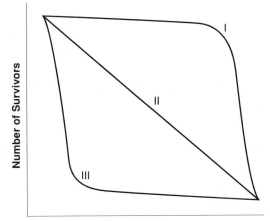

Which curve shows that the members of a cohort die at a constant rate? a._____

Which curve shows that the members of a cohort tend to die early in life? b._____

Which curve shows that the members of a cohort usually live through their entire allotted life span?

    c._____

19. What is a cohort? _____

Age Distribution (p. 391)

- Populations have an age distribution consisting of prereproductive, reproductive, and postreproductive portions.

20. If the age structure diagram has a pyramid shape and the prereproductive population is largest, what do you predict about population growth? a._____

Why? b._____

21. If the age structure diagram has an urn shape and the postreproductive group is largest, what do you predict about population growth? a._____

Why? b._____

23.3 REGULATION OF POPULATION SIZE (P. 392)

- Factors that limit population size are classified as density-independent and density-dependent.

22. In general, density-independent factors are a._____ (*abiotic or biotic*), such as b._____, and density-dependent factors are c._____ (*abiotic or biotic*), such as d._____. Intrinsic factors such as e._____ may also be involved in regulating population size.

- Life histories range from discrete reproduction with intermittent rapid population growth to repeated reproduction but a stable population size.

For questions 23–26, match the phrases to the following types of environments:

    1 unpredictable environment and density-independent regulation of population size
    2 stable environment and density-dependent regulation of population size

23. large adults, long life span, slow to mature, repeated reproduction, and much care of offspring _____

24. *r*-selection is expected. _____

25. *K*-selection is expected. _____

26. small adults, short life span, fast to mature, many offspring during a burst of reproduction, and little or no care of offspring _____

23.5 HUMAN POPULATION GROWTH (P. 399)

- The human population is still growing exponentially, and how long this can continue is not known.

27. If the human population outstrips its carrying capacity, what will happen to the size of the population? _____
_____

28. If the human population is curtailed by environmental resistance, what will happen to the size of the population? _____

For the short answers in questions 29–32, use the following:

    1 MDCs (More developed countries)
    2 LDCs (Less developed countries)

29. Which type of country has a pyramid-shaped age structure diagram? [a.]_____ With such an age distribution, growth is expected for some time. Why? [b.]_____
_____

30. Which type of country overconsumes resources and thus does not follow the sustainable world philosophy? ___
_____

31. Which type of country has undergone demographic transition? [a.]_____ What is demographic transition? [b.]_____

32. Which type of country has a high net reproductive rate and thus does not follow the sustainable world philosophy? _____

Review key terms by completing this crossword puzzle, using the following alphabetized list of terms:

age structure diagram
biotic potential
carrying capacity
ecology
exponential growth
population
r-*strategist*
survivorship

Across

1 representation of the number of individuals in each age group in a population (three words)

8 group of organisms of the same species occupying a certain area and sharing a common gene pool

Down

2 study of the interaction of organisms with other organisms and with the physical environment

3 percentage of survivors of a population over time; usually shown graphically, it can be used to depict death rates

4 species that has evolved characteristics that maximize its net reproductive rate—for example, high birthrate

5 maximum size of a population that can be supported by the environment in a particular locale (two words)

6 accelerating population growth (two words)

7 maximum net reproductive rate of a population that can occur under ideal circumstances (two words)

CHAPTER TEST

OBJECTIVE QUESTIONS

Do not refer to the text when taking this test.

____ 1. Which of these is mismatched?
   a. population—all the members of a species in same area
   b. community—populations interacting with the physical environment
   c. biosphere—surface of the earth where organisms live
   d. ecosystem—energy flow and chemical cycling occur

____ 2. Distribution of organisms tends to be
   a. clumped.
   b. determined by limiting factors.
   c. the same as the population density.
   d. Both *a* and *b* are correct.

____ 3. If the birthrate is 10 per capita per unit time and the death rate is 10 per capita per unit time, then the net reproductive rate is
   a. 0.
   b. 10.
   c. 20.
   d. 100.

_____ 4. If the net reproductive rate is positive, then
   a. population growth will occur.
   b. the size of the population will increase.
   c. environmental resistance is likely to come into play.
   d. All of these are correct.

_____ 5. In the equation $N_{t+1} = rN_t$, r equals
   a. environmental resistance.
   b. biotic potential.
   c. net reproductive rate.
   d. Both b and c are possible.

_____ 6. To calculate r,
   a. assume immigration = emigration.
   b. subtract death rate per capita per unit time from birthrate per capita per unit time.
   c. Both a and b are correct.
   d. Neither a nor b is correct.

_____ 7. During exponential growth,
   a. growth remains steady.
   b. growth is accelerating.
   c. growth is declining.
   d. growth depends on the environment.

_____ 8. During the stable equilibrium phase of logistic growth,
   a. the term $(K-N)/K = 0$.
   b. the term $(K-N)/K = 1$.
   c. the population has outstripped the carrying capacity.
   d. biotic potential is in full force.

_____ 9. Which sentence is most appropriate?
   a. Environmental resistance encourages biotic potential.
   b. If population size is at carrying capacity, growth is unlikely.
   c. Environmental resistance consists only of density-independent factors.
   d. Exponential growth can usually occur indefinitely.

_____10. Which is true of an S-shaped growth curve?
   a. represents the exponential growth pattern
   b. represents the logistic growth pattern
   c. does not usually occur in nature
   d. Both b and c are correct.

_____11. Survivorship in a population is related to
   a. age of death.
   b. biotic potential.
   c. age structure diagram.
   d. All of these are correct.

_____12. If the survivorship curve is a straight diagonal line, then
   a. the rate of death is constant, regardless of age.
   b. most individuals live out the expected life span.
   c. most individuals die early.
   d. environmental resistance has occurred.

_____13. Select the density-dependent effect.
   a. climate
   b. predation
   c. natural disaster
   d. weather

_____14. Density-dependent effects
   a. increase as density increases.
   b. tend to be biotic factors.
   c. tend to be abiotic factors.
   d. Both a and b are correct.

_____15. K-strategists tend to have a(n) _____ growth curve.
   a. J-shaped
   b. S-shaped

_____16. Select the characteristic that is NOT consistent with r-selection.
   a. large body size
   b. many offspring
   c. short life span
   d. fast to mature

_____17. The countries in Asia and Africa are
   a. MDCs that are experiencing rapid growth.
   b. LDCs that are experiencing rapid growth.
   c. MDCs that are experiencing slow growth.
   d. LDCs that are experiencing slow growth.

_____18. The doubling time for the world's population will most likely
   a. always remain the same.
   b. become longer because of demographic transition.
   c. become shorter and shorter regardless.
   d. fluctuate because of depressions.

_____19. The world population increases by the number of people found in a medium-size city (200,000) every
   a. year.
   b. six months.
   c. month.
   d. day.

Answer in complete sentences.

20. Under what conditions could the growth of a population be infinite?

21. How is the exponential growth of a population similar to the effect of compound interest on money saved in a bank?

Test Results: _____ Number right ÷ 21 = _____ × 100 = _____ %

EXPLORING THE INTERNET

Use the Internet to further explore topics in this chapter, such as naturalist John Muir or renewable energy. Go to the Mader Home Page (http://www.mhhe.com/sciencemath/biology/mader/) and click on *Biology*, 6th edition. Go to chapter 23 and select a Web site of interest.

ANSWER KEY

STUDY EXERCISES

1. a. 1 **b.** 3 **c.** 2 **d.** 4 **e.** 2 **f.** 1 **2. a.** uniform **b.** random **c.** clumped **3.** clumped **4. a.** Limiting **b.** abiotic **c.** biotic **5. a.** natality **b.** immigration **c.** mortality **d.** emigration. **6. a.** .06 **b.** .04 **c.** .02 **d.** 51 **7. a.** ep **b.** lg **8.** both; see figures 23.4*b* and 23.5*b*, pages 387–88, in text **9.** both; see figures 23.4*b* and 23.5*b*, pages 387–88, in text **10. a.** slow **b.** accelerating **11.** b; see figure 23.5*b*, page 388, in text **12.** b; see figure 23.5*b*, page 388, in text **13. a.** exponential **b.** the maximum population growth that can possibly occur under ideal circumstances of unlimited resources, plenty of room, and no hindrances **14. a.** deceleration **b.** encompasses all environmental factors that oppose biotic potential **c.** when biotic potential and environmental resistance are equal **15.** maximum **16.** minimal **17. a.** carrying capacity **b.** biotic potential **18. a.** II **b.** III **c.** I **19.** an original group of individuals born at the same time **20. a.** It will continue for some time. **b.** A large number of women will be entering their reproductive years. **21. a.** It will decline. **b.** Most of the population is postreproductive. **22. a.** abiotic **b.** weather, fire **c.** biotic **d.** predation, competition **e.** territoriality **23.** 2 **24.** 1 **25.** 2 **26.** 1 **27.** A crash will occur. **28.** It will become stable. **29. a.** 2 **b.** A large number of women are entering their reproductive years. **30.** 1 **31. a.** 1 **b.** decreased death rate followed by decreased birthrate **32.** 2

KEYWORD CROSSWORD

CHAPTER TEST

1. b **2.** d **3.** a **4.** d **5.** d **6.** c **7.** b **8.** a **9.** b **10.** b **11.** a **12.** a **13.** b **14.** d **15.** b **16.** a **17.** b **18.** b **19.** d **20.** If environmental resistance were absent, the population size could continue to increase without end. This is unlikely, because the increase in population size without an increase in resources would force environmental resistance to be present. **21.** Interest in the bank is paid on both the principal (initial amount of money) and also on the interest generated from and added to that base amount. During exponential growth, new individuals are generated from the original base population, from their descendants, and so on.

24

COMMUNITY ECOLOGY

A **community** is an assemblage of populations interacting with one another within the same environment. Communities are characterized by their composition (types of species) and by their diversity, which includes richness (number of species) and evenness (relative abundance). Investigators are trying to determine if species co-occur in communities because their tolerance ranges for some abiotic factor(s) overlap or because they are part of a superorganism. In any case, richness seems to depend on the size of the community.

In a community, each population occupies a **habitat** and also has an **ecological niche,** which is the role an organism plays in its community, including its habitat and its interactions with other organisms. Relationships between populations in a community are defined by such interactions as **competition, predation, parasitism, commensalism,** and **mutualism.** The **competitive exclusion principle** states that no two species can occupy the same niche at the same time. **Resource partitioning** is observed when **character displacement** occurs, as in Galápagos finches, but is also believed to be present whenever similar species feed on slightly different foods or occupy slightly different habitats. Predation reduces the size of the **prey** population but can have a feedback effect that limits the **predator** population. Prey species have evolved various means to escape predators—for example, chemical defenses in plants and **mimicry** in animals. **Coevolution** is observed between predators and prey, and between **parasite** and **host.**

Species in a community may exhibit several types of **symbiotic** relationships. In parasitism, the fitness of the parasite increases, and that of the host decreases. Commensalism has a neutral effect. In mutualism, the fitness of both species increases.

Communities are dynamic and undergo **ecological succession,** a change in a community following a disturbance. The process of succession is complex and may not always reach particular end points of community composition and diversity. Habitat patchiness at different stages of succession produces greater species diversity within the community.

To increase biodiversity, an intermediate level of disturbance may be desirable, predation and competition may be beneficial (except when exotic species are introduced), and a size large enough for greater degree of diversity is helpful.

Study the text section by section as you answer the questions that follow.

24.1 WHAT IS A BIOLOGICAL COMMUNITY? (P. 406)

- Communities are assemblages of interacting populations that differ in composition and diversity.
- Environmental factors influence community composition and diversity.

1. Draw a line between the terms in the second column that pertain to those in the first column, and a line between those in the third column that pertain to those in the second column.

   a. composition   c. richness   e. relative abundance

   b. diversity   d. evenness   f. number of species

2. Label each of these findings with (1) for the individualistic model of community structure and (2) for the interactive model of community structure.

   _____ a. Five different coral reefs all contain the same species in the same relative numbers.

   _____ b. There was so much overlapping between species between the forest and field that determining where one ended and the other began was impossible.

3. Use these terms to label the following diagram:
   immigration, near small island
   immigration, far large island
   immigration, near large island
   immigration, far small island

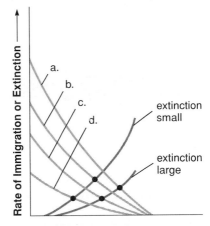

Use the equilibrium point between immigration and extinction to explain why a small island will have less

species richness than a large island. e. _____

24.2 COMMUNITIES ARE ORGANIZED (P. 409)

- Community organization involves the interactions among species, such as competition, predation, parasitism, and mutualism.
- The ecological niche is the role an organism plays in its community, including its habitat and its interactions with other organisms.
- Competition leads to resource partitioning, which reduces competition between species.
- Predation reduces prey population density but also can lead to a reduction in predator population density.
- There are a number of different kinds of prey defenses, including mimicry.
- Symbiotic relationships include parasitism, commensalism, and mutualism.

4. The habitat of an organism is simply a._____,

   but the ecological niche of an organism includes its habitat and its interactions with other organisms. What

   type of interactions? b._____

   _____

5. Which would you expect to be larger—the fundamental niche of an organism or its realized niche?

   a._____

   Why? b._____

6. You would expect competition to be a (− −) interaction because both species are a._____. Gause's

   laboratory experiments supported the b. _____,

   which states that no two species can occupy the same niche. c. _____

   is a way for two species to ensure different niches. For example, five species of warblers can coexist because

   each species d. _____.

7. Study this graph, which describes experimental results obtained by G. F. Gause, and then answer the questions that follow.

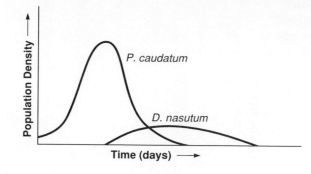

What happened to the prey population of *Paramecium?* a._____

What happened to the predator population of *Didinium?* b._____

In nature, both predator and prey populations continue to exist but in reduced densities. Explain. c._____

_____

8. Cycling between the lynx and snowshoe hare populations has been studied in detail. One experiment showed that when the hare population was given a constant supply of food, cycling between the lynx and hare populations continued. What does this tell you? a._____

In another experiment, the hare population was maintained separately (predators were excluded), but no food was added to the environment. The hare population continued to cycle. What does this tell you? b._____

_____

9. Identify the antipredator device in the following:

Inchworms resemble twigs. a._____

Dart-poison frogs are brightly colored. b._____

Frilled lizards open up folds of skin around the neck. c._____

10. If appropriate, label the following as describing Batesian (B) or Müllerian (M) mimicry:
_____ a. A predator mimics another species that has a successful predatory style.
_____ b. A prey mimics another species that has a successful defense.
_____ c. A predator captures food.
_____ d. Several different species with the same defense mimic one another.

11. a._____ occurs when two species evolve in response to one another. Give an example from the text.
   b._____

_____

12. Commensalism, mutualism, and parasitism are all different types of _____ relationships.

13. Complete this table to compare types of symbiosis by marking a plus (+) if the species *benefits,* a minus (−) if the species is *harmed,* and a zero (0) if the symbiotic relationship has *no effect* on the species.

	First Species	Second Species
Parasitism		
Commensalism		
Mutualism		

14. Label each of the following as describing commensalism (C), mutualism (M), or parasitism (P):
_____a. The clownfish lives safely within the poisonous tentacles of the sea anemone, which other fish avoid.

_____ b. Certain bacteria cause pneumonia.

_____ c. Humans get a tapeworm from eating raw pork.

_____ d. Epiphytes grow in branches of trees but get no nourishment from the trees.

_____ e. Flowers provide nourishment to a pollinator, and the pollinator carries pollen to another flower.

15. Label these symbiotic relationships of species A to species B with the following terms: *commensalism, competition, mutualism, parasitism,* and *predation.*

    Species A consumed more of the resource than species B. a._____

    Species A eats species B. b._____

    Species A is cultivated by species B as a source of food. c._____

    Species A infects species B. d._____

    Species A rides along with species B to get food while species B hunts. e._____

24.3 COMMUNITY STRUCTURE CHANGES OVER TIME (P. 420)

- Ecological succession is a change in species composition and community structure and organization over time.

16. Draw a series of stages that illustrate the changes in plant species composition during secondary succession.

    early→ late-climax community

17. Label each of the following as being characteristic of an early successional stage (E) or a late successional stage (L):

    _____ a. equilibrium species

    _____ b. opportunistic species

    _____ c. *K*-strategists

    _____ d. *r*-strategists

    _____ e. few species present

    _____ f. many species present

    _____ g. climax community

24.4 HOW TO INCREASE COMMUNITY BIODIVERSITY (P. 422)

- The intermediate disturbance hypothesis suggests that the presence of patches that contain various species increases biodiversity.
- Predation and competition can help maintain biodiversity, and island biogeography suggests how to maintain species richness.

18. Place a check by each factor that increases community diversity.

    _____ a. high or severe levels of disturbance

    _____ b. low levels of disturbance

    _____ c. intermediate levels of disturbance

    _____ d. uniformity of habitat

    _____ e. patchiness of habitat

    _____ f. competition between species

    _____ g. human interference

Review key terms by completing this crossword puzzle, using the following alphabetized list of terms:

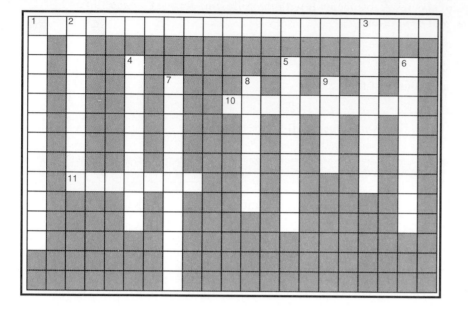

commensalism
community
competitive exclusion
disturbance
diversity
habitat
mimicry
mutualism
niche
parasitism
stability
symbiosis

Across

1 theory that no two species can occupy the same niche (two words)

10 symbiotic relationship in which one species benefits in terms of growth and reproduction to the harm of the other species

11 superficial resemblance of one organism to another organism of a different species; often used to avoid predation

Down

1 symbiotic relationship in which one species is benefited and the other is neither harmed nor benefited

2 symbiotic relationship in which both species benefit

3 relationship that occurs when two different species live together in a unique way; it may be beneficial, neutral, or detrimental to one and/or the other species

4 measure of the number and evenness of species in a community

5 allows the community to be resistant to change

6 group of many different populations that interact with one another

7 floods, fires, and storms are examples

8 conditions of the environment that influence an organism's life activities and describe the location where the organism is able to survive and reproduce

9 role an organism plays in its community; includes its habitat and its interactions with other organisms

Chapter Test

Objective Questions

Do not refer to the text when taking this test.

_____ 1. A community is made up of

    a. all the members of a given population.

    b. all of the plant populations of a given area.

    c. all of the populations of a given area.

    d. all of the populations of a given area plus the abiotic habitat in which they live.

_____ 2. Which is a facet of species diversity?

    a. species richness

    b. species evenness

    c. composition only

    d. Both *a* and *b* are correct.

_____ 3. Which of these is likely to have the greatest number of species?

    a. a small island with many patches

    b. a small, homogenous island

    c. a large island with many patches

    d. a large, homogenous island

_____ 4. Gause showed that two paramecia species

    a. cannot occupy the same test tube.

    b. can exist in the same test tube.

    c. can exist in two different areas of the same test tube.

    d. None of these are correct.

_____ 5. Competition
   a. always eliminates one or the other species.
   b. widens niche breadth.
   c. narrows niche breadth and increases species diversity.
   d. None of these are correct.

_____ 6. The niche that an organism occupies while interacting with all others in its community is its
   a. realized niche.
   b. fundamental niche.
   c. habitat.
   d. patch.

_____ 7. Predator population size is limited in part by available _____, while prey population size is limited by _____.
   a. living space; food
   b. predators; prey
   c. food; predators
   d. food; food

_____ 8. Plants produce hormone analogues that
   a. interfere with metabolism of the adult insect.
   b. inhibit egg production in insects.
   c. interfere with the development of insect larvae.
   d. None of these are correct.

_____ 9. Antipredator defenses may include
   a. camouflage.
   b. fright.
   c. warning.
   d. All of these are correct.

_____10. Mimicry can help
   a. a predator capture food.
   b. prey avoid capture.
   c. Both a and b are correct.
   d. None of these are correct.

_____11. Bees, wasps, and hornets are examples of
   a. Batesian mimicry.
   b. Müllerian mimicry.
   c. mimicry for predation.
   d. Both a and c are correct.

For questions 12–14, match the organisms with the following terms:
   a. parasitism
   b. commensalism
   c. mutualism

_____12. virus
_____13. termites and protozoa
_____14. barnacle

_____15. In which relationship do both species benefit?
   a. mutualism
   b. commensalism
   c. symbiosis
   d. Both b and c are correct.

_____16. Which can be a parasite?
   a. bacteria
   b. plants
   c. animals
   d. All of these are correct.

_____17. What parasite is a vector for Lyme disease?
   a. virus
   b. bacterium
   c. tick
   d. fungus

_____18. Choose the scenario that best represents secondary succession.
   a. trees—shrubs—grasses—perennial grasses
   b. annual weeds and grasses—perennial grasses—shrubs—trees
   c. shrubs—annual weeds—perennial grasses—trees
   d. All of these are correct.

_____19. Which characteristic is typical of a late successional community?
   a. comprised of K-strategists
   b. many species present
   c. climax community
   d. All of these are correct.

_____20. Which of the following factors increases the diversity of a community?
   a. patchiness
   b. high levels of disturbance
   c. little or no competition
   d. All of these are correct.

CRITICAL THINKING QUESTIONS

Answer in complete sentences.

21. How does niche diversity affect species diversity in a community?

22. Explain how intermediate levels of disturbance maintain diversity.

Test Results: _____ Number right ÷ 22 = _____ × 100 = _____ %

Use the Internet to further explore topics in this chapter, such as disturbance experiments or predation, or look at a guide to outdoor and environmental careers. Go to the Mader Home Page (http://www.mhhe.com/sciencemath/biology/mader/) and click on *Biology,* 6th edition. Go to Chapter 24 and select a Web site of interest.

ANSWER KEY

STUDY EXERCISES

1. Draw lines between: *b* and *c, b* and *d, e* and *d, f* and *c*
2. a. 2 **b.** 1 **3. a.** immigration, near large island **b.** immigration, near small island **c.** immigration, far large island **d.** immigration, far small island **e.** Small island has less immigration and more extinction. **4. a.** where it lives **b.** predation, competition, symbiosis (parasitism, commensalism, mutualism) **5. a.** fundamental **b.** because it includes the full range of species potential **6. a.** competing for the same resource **b.** competitive exclusion principle **c.** Resource partitioning **d.** occupies a different spruce tree zone **7. a.** died out **b.** died out **c.** prey defenses reduce the number of prey **8. a.** The predator can cause cycling. **b.** The lack of food also causes cycling. **9. a.** camouflage **b.** warning coloration **c.** fright **10. b.** B **d.** M (both *a* and *c* should be left blank) **11. a.** Coevolution **b.** The cuckoo lays its eggs in the nests of other birds. To do so, it must lay an egg

similar in appearance to that of the host and do so rapidly, and it must leave most of the host bird's eggs in the nest so the cuckoo egg goes unnoticed. The cuckoo hatches first and removes the host's eggs from the nest. **12.** symbiotic
13.

First Species	Second Species
+	−
+	0
+	+

14. a. C **b.** P **c.** P **d.** C **e.** M **15. a.** competition **b.** predation **c.** mutualism **d.** parasitism **e.** commensalism **16.** see figure 24.19, page 421, in text **17. a.** L **b.** E **c.** L **d.** E **e.** E **f.** L **g.** L **18.** c, e, f

KEYWORD CROSSWORD

CHAPTER TEST

1. c **2.** d **3.** c **4.** a **5.** c **6.** a **7.** c **8.** c **9.** d **10.** c **11.** b **12.** a **13.** c **14.** b **15.** a **16.** d **17.** c **18.** b **19.** d **20.** a **21.** The greater the number of niches, the greater the number of possible species that can fill them, and therefore, the greater the diversity. **22.** At low levels of disturbance, the organisms that dominate the community (*K*-strategists) become more abundant, and other species have fewer opportunities to become established. At high levels of disturbance, only the *r*-strategists, which reproduce quickly, survive. At intermediate levels of disturbance, both *r*- and *K*-strategists maintain their populations at a smaller size, but overall diversity increases.

25

ECOSYSTEMS

An **ecosystem** consists of the living organisms in an ecological community, together with their chemical and physical environment. A pond or a forest could be an ecosystem. Every ecosystem has inputs from other ecosystems and outputs to other ecosystems. All the ecosystems of the world comprise the **biosphere.** The biosphere consists of the hydrosphere, the atmosphere, and the lithosphere.

Producers, consumers (**herbivores** and **carnivores**), **omnivores,** and **decomposers** are part of the biotic portion of an ecosystem. They are related through the flow of energy and the cycling of materials. **Food chains** have several forms, including **grazing food** chains and **detritus food** chains. Food chains form an intricate web of trophic levels. A **trophic level** is all the organisms that feed at a particular link in a food chain. Energy passes through the various links of a food chain and does not cycle. As a rule of thumb, only about 10% of the available energy is assimilated into the tissues of the organisms at the next trophic level.

Inorganic nutrients do cycle through an ecosystem. The actions of decomposers on the dead organisms (organic matter) in an ecosystem make inorganic nutrients available for recycling and reuse.

The global cycling of inorganic elements involves the biotic and abiotic parts of an ecosystem. Cycles usually contain (1) a reservoir (a source normally unavailable to organisms), (2) a pool (a source available to organisms), and (3) the biotic community. In gaseous cycles exemplified by the **carbon** and **nitrogen cycles,** the elements return and are withdrawn from the atmosphere. In a sedimentary cycle, exemplified by the **phosphorus cycle,** elements are absorbed from the soil by plant roots, passed to heterotrophs, and eventually returned to the soil by decomposers. Human activities transfer nutrients out of reservoirs and pools, making nutrients available at a higher-than-normal rate.

Study the text section by section as you answer the questions that follow.

25.1 THE NATURE OF ECOSYSTEMS (P. 428)

- An ecosystem is a community of organisms and the physical environment with which the organisms interact.
- In an ecosystem organisms interact with each other and the physical environment.
- Autotrophs are self-feeders: photoautotrophs capture solar energy and produce organic nutrients. Heterotrophs, on the other hand, take in preformed organic nutrients.

1. Match the descriptions with the following terms:
   1 lithosphere
   2 hydrosphere
   3 atmosphere
   4 biosphere
   _____ a. contains gases; extends from the earth's surface to 1,000 km
   _____ b. rocky surface of the earth extending to 100 m deep
   _____ c. water layer covering 75% of the earth's surface
   _____ d. layer of life at the earth's surface

2. Match the descriptions with the following terms:

1 carnivores
2 consumers
3 decomposers
4 herbivores
5 omnivores
6 autotrophs

_____ a. organisms of decay
_____ b. feed only on other animals
_____ c. producers in an ecosystem
_____ d. heterotrophs eating preformed food
_____ e. feed directly on green plants
_____ f. feed on both plants and animals

25.2 ENERGY FLOW AND NUTRIENT CYCLING (P. 430)

- Solar energy enters ecosystems via photosynthesis, and as organic nutrients pass from one organism to another, heat is returned to the atmosphere.
- Nutrients cycle within and between ecosystems in global cycles.

3. Examine the following diagram and then answer the questions:

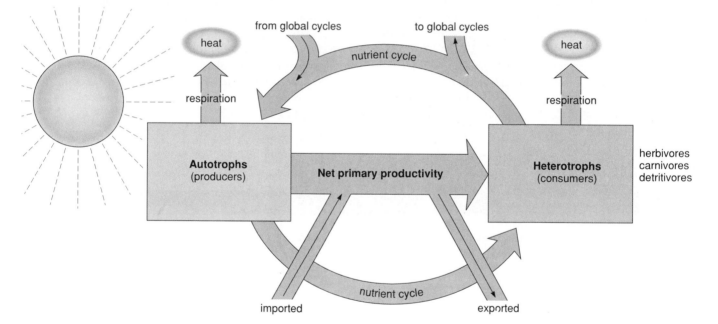

Solar energy enters an ecosystem when ^{a.} _____

_____.

In what other way do nutrients and energy enter a particular ecosystem? ^{b.} _____

_____

Net primary productivity is ^{c.} _____

_____.

What happens to the energy (except the portion exported) that enters an ecosystem? ^{d.} _____

_____

Nutrients cycle back to producers because ^{e.} _____

_____.

Questions 4–10 are based on the following diagram:

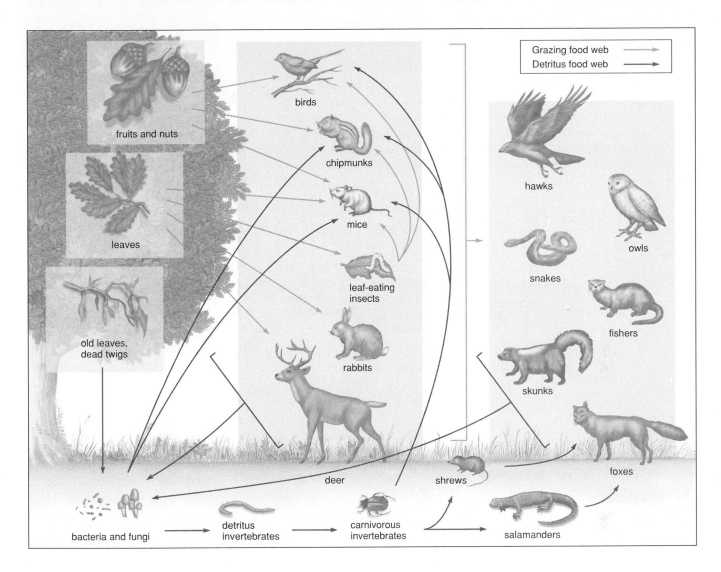

4. From this food web, formulate a grazing food chain.

_____

5. From this food web, formulate a detritus food chain.

_____

6. Explain one way in which the detritus food web and the grazing food web are always connected.

_____

7. Name an organism that is at the first trophic level of the grazing food web.

_____

8. Name two organisms that are at the second trophic level of the grazing food web.

_____

9. Name two organisms that are at the third trophic level of the grazing food web.

_____

10. Why is the number of trophic levels in an ecosystem limited?

_____

- Biogeochemical cycles involve the biosphere, hydrosphere, lithosphere, and atmosphere.
- Human activities alter biogeochemical cycles. One of the goals of ecology is to predict how our activities will affect ecosystems.

11. Place a check in front of the statement(s) pertaining to freshwater.
    _____ a. renewable resource and therefore we cannot run out of it
    _____ b. finite resource but we can run out of it
    _____ c. renewable resource but we can run out of it
    _____ d. finite resource and therefore we cannot run out of it

12. Examine the following diagram and then answer the questions:

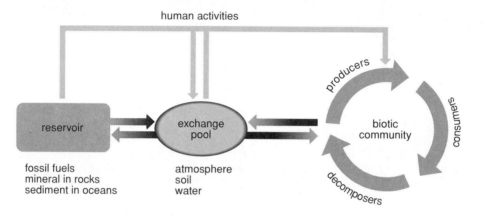

What is a reservoir? a. _____

What is an exchange pool? b. _____

What is a biotic community? c. _____

Explain the arrows labeled *human activities* .d. _____

_____

13. In the carbon cycle, carbon dioxide is removed from the atmosphere by the process of a._____

but is returned to the atmosphere by the process of b._____. Living things and dead matter in

soil are carbon c._____ and so are the d._____ because of shell accumulation. In

aquatic ecosystems, carbon dioxide from the air combines with water to produce e._____ that

algae can use for photosynthesis. In what way do humans alter the exchange rates in the carbon cycle?

f._____

Questions 14–16 are based on the following diagram:

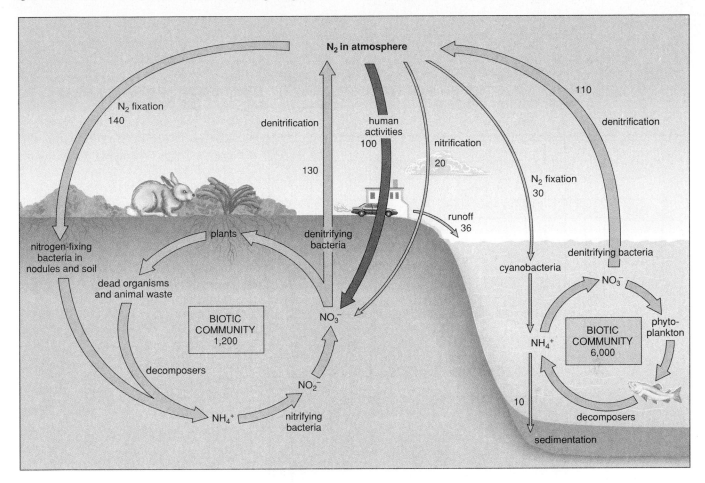

14. Match the definitions with the following terms:

    1 denitrifying bacteria
    2 nitrifying bacteria
    3 nitrogen-fixing bacteria

    _____ a. bacteria that convert nitrate to nitrogen gas
    _____ b. bacteria that convert ammonium to nitrate
    _____ c. bacteria in legume nodules that convert nitrogen gas to ammonium

15. Add the amounts of nitrogen gas (in 10^{12}g N/yr) that are removed from the atmosphere.

    a._____ And the amounts that are returned to the atmosphere. b._____ Which

    is larger? c._____ If human activities were not contributing nitrogen to the atmosphere, which

    amount would be larger? d._____

16. Plants cannot utilize nitrogen gas. What are two ways in which plants receive a supply of nitrogen for

    incorporation into proteins and nucleic acids? _____

17. Place a check in front of the statement(s) that describe(s) the results when producers take up phosphate.

    _____ a. becomes a part of phospholipids
    _____ b. becomes a part of ATP
    _____ c. becomes a part of nucleotides
    _____ d. becomes a part of the atmosphere

18. Indicate whether the statements that follow are true (T) or false (F). Rewrite all false statements to be true
    statements.

    _____ a. Excess phosphate in bodies of water may cause radiation poisoning. Rewrite: _____

    _____

    _____ b. Most ecosystems have plenty of phosphate. Rewrite:_____

    _____

_____ c. The phosphorus cycle is a sedimentary cycle. Rewrite: _____

_____

_____ d. Phosphate enters ecosystems by being taken up by animals. Rewrite:_____

_____

KeyWord CrossWord

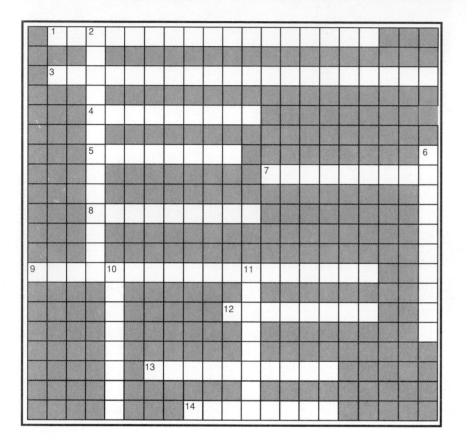

Review key terms by completing this crossword puzzle, using the following alphabetized list of terms:

biogeochemical cycle
carnivore
consumer
decomposer
detritus
ecological pyramid
ecosystem
food chain
food web
herbivore
nitrogen fixation
omnivore
producer
trophic level

Across

1 process whereby soil bacteria convert free atmospheric nitrogen into compounds, such as ammonium and nitrates (two words)
3 circulating pathway of an element through the biotic and abiotic components of an ecosystem (two words)
4 primary consumer in a food chain; plant eater
5 organism that feeds on another organism in a food chain
7 secondary or higher consumer in a food chain; eats other animals
8 biological community together with the associated abiotic environment
9 pictorial graph representing biomass, organism number, or energy content of each trophic level in a food web—from the producer to the final consumer populations (two words)

12 complex pattern of interlocking and crisscrossing food chains (two words)
13 succession of organisms in an ecosystem that are linked by an energy flow and by the order of who eats whom (two words)
14 partially decomposed remains of plants and animals found in soil and on the beds of bodies of water

Down

2 feeding level of one or more populations in a food web (two words)
6 organism, usually a bacterial or fungal species, that breaks down large organic molecules into elements that can be recycled in the environment
10 organism in a food chain that feeds on both plants and animals
11 organism at the start of a food chain that makes its own food

Do not refer to the text when taking this test.

_____ 1. The biosphere includes
   a. all life on the earth.
   b. the atmosphere and the lithosphere.
   c. the hydrosphere and lithosphere.
   d. None of these are correct.

In questions 2–11, indicate whether the statements are true (T) or false (F).

_____ 2. Both herbivores and carnivores are producers in a food chain.

_____ 3. Energy flows through a food chain because it is constantly lost from organic food as heat.

_____ 4. A food web contains many food chains.

_____ 5. An ecological pyramid is usually broadest at the bottom and narrowest at the top.

_____ 6. Generally, the third link in a food chain has about one-half the available energy as the second link.

_____ 7. The weathering of rocks is one way that phosphate ions are made available to plants.

_____ 8. Photosynthesis incorporates carbon from the atmosphere into biomass.

_____ 9. Respiration returns carbon to the atmosphere.

_____10. Nitrogen fixation is the return of nitrogen to the atmosphere.

_____11. Denitrifying bacteria convert atmospheric nitrogen into the bodies of organisms.

_____12. About _____ of the energy available at a particular trophic level is incorporated into the tissues at the next trophic level.
   a. 1%
   b. 10%
   c. 25%
   d. 50%
   e. 75%

_____13. Gross primary production refers to
   a. the amount of weight primary consumers gain.
   b. the amount of weight all consumers gain.
   c. the rate of production by all producers in a community.
   d. the amount of plant production available to consumers.

Questions 14–16 refer to the following food chain: grass → rabbits → snakes → hawks.

_____14. Each population
   a. is always larger than the one before it.
   b. supports the next level.
   c. is an herbivore.
   d. is a carnivore.

_____15. Rabbits are
   a. consumers.
   b. herbivores.
   c. more plentiful than snakes.
   d. All of these are correct.

_____16. Hawks
   a. contain phosphate taken up by grass.
   b. give off O_2 that will be taken up by rabbits.
   c. die and decompose and because of this they cannot contribute to a grazing food chain.
   d. All of these are correct.

_____17. Which of the following contribute(s) to the carbon cycle?
   a. respiration
   b. photosynthesis
   c. fossil fuel combustion
   d. All of these are correct.

_____18. The largest reserve of unincorporated carbon is in
   a. the soil.
   b. the atmosphere.
   c. the ocean.
   d. deep sediments.

_____19. The greenhouse effect
   a. is caused by particles in the air.
   b. is caused in part by carbon dioxide.
   c. will cause temperatures to increase.
   d. will cause temperatures to decrease.
   e. Both _b_ and _c_ are correct.

_____20. The form of nitrogen most plants make use of is
   a. atmospheric nitrogen.
   b. nitrogen gas.
   c. organic nitrogen.
   d. nitrates.

Answer in complete sentences

21. Why is a food chain normally limited to four or five links?

22. How would shortage of an element in the exchange pool affect an ecosystem? Explain.

Test Results: _____ Number right ÷ 22 = _____ × 100 = _____ %

EXPLORING THE INTERNET

Use the Internet to further explore topics in this chapter, such as the Florida Everglades and their destruction and rehabilitation, or a listing of environmental resources. Go to the Mader Home Page (http://www.mhhe.com/science-math/biology/mader/) and click on *Biology,* 6th edition. Go to Chapter 25 and select a Web site of interest.

ANSWER KEY

STUDY EXERCISES

1. a. 3 **b.** 1 **c.** 2 **d.** 4 **2. a.** 3 **b.** 1 **c.** 6 **d.** 2 **e.** 4 **f.** 5 **3. a.** autotrophs carry on photosynthesis and produce organic food **b.** imported from other ecosystems **c.** that portion of gross primary productivity (photosynthesized food) made available to heterotrophs **d.** exits as heat **e.** decomposers break down dead organisms and organic wastes **4.** Example: nuts from tree → birds → hawks **5.** Example: old leaves and dead twigs → bacteria and fungi of decay → mice → hawks **6.** members of the grazing food web die and are decomposed by bacteria and fungi. **7.** In the diagram, a tree is the producer. **8.** Example: rabbits and deer **9.** Example: foxes and snakes **10.** As a rule of thumb, only 10% of the energy available in the previous level is passed on to the next level, and eventually, there is not enough energy to support another level. **11. c 12. a.** a source that is usually unavailable to the biotic community **b.** a source that is usually available to the biotic community **c.** producers, consumers, and decomposers that interact through nutrient cycling and energy flow **d.** Humans remove elements from reservoirs and exchange pools and make them available to producers. For example, humans convert nitrogen in the air to make fertilizer, and they mine phosphate to make fertilizer. **13. a.** photosynthesis **b.** cellular respiration **c.** reservoirs **d.** oceans **e.** bicarbonate **f.** by burning fossil fuels that add carbon to the atmosphere **14. a.** 1 **b.** 2 **c.** 3 **15. a.** 290 **b.** 240 **c.** amount removed from atmosphere **d.** amount returned to atmosphere **16.** nitrogen-fixing bacteria in nodules and nitrate in soil **17.** a, b, c **18. a.** F; . . . may cause algal bloom **b.** F, . . . have a limited supply of phosphate **c.** T **d.** F, . . . taken up by plants

KEYWORD CROSSWORD

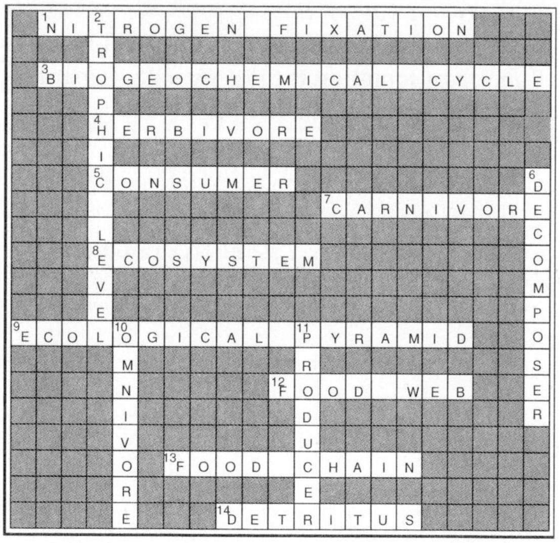

CHAPTER TEST

1. a **2.** F **3.** T **4.** T **5.** T **6.** F **7.** T **8.** T **9.** T **10.** F **11.** F **12.** b **13.** c **14.** b **15.** d **16.** a **17.** d **18.** c **19.** e **20.** d **21.** By the laws of thermodynamics, energy conversion at each link of a food chain results in nonusable heat. Too little useful energy remains for more links. **22.** A shortage of an element such as nitrogen or phosphorus would reduce the biomass of the producer population. Therefore, the biomass of each succeeding population in the ecosystem would most likely be smaller than it otherwise would be.

26

THE BIOSPHERE

Because the earth is a sphere, the sun's rays are vertical only at the equator and temperature decreases from the equator to the poles. The tilt of the earth on its axis along with the earth's rotation about the sun creates the seasons. Because the oceans are warmer at the equator than the poles, air rises at the equator and moves toward the poles; these air currents in turn cause ocean currents that affect climate about the world.

Warm air rising at the equator loses its moisture and then descends at about 30° north and south latitude and so forth to the poles. This movement of air in general accounts for different amounts of rainfall at different latitudes. Topography also plays a role in the distribution of rainfall.

Just south of the North Pole, the tundra has cold winters and short summers; the vegetation consists largely of short grasses and sedges and dwarf woody plants. Proceeding southward, the taiga is a coniferous forest, the temperate deciduous forest has seasons, and the tropical rain forest is a broad-leaved evergreen forest.

Among grasslands, which have less rainfall than forests, the savanna is a tropical grassland which supports the greatest number of different types of large herbivores. The prairie found in the United States has a limited variety of vegetation and animal life. In deserts some plants, such as cacti, are succulents, and others are shrubs with thick leaves they often lose during dry periods.

Among aquatic biomes, freshwater communities include streams, rivers, lakes, and ponds. Lakes experience spring and fall overturns. Lakes and ponds have rooted plants in the littoral zone, plankton and fishes in the sunlit limnetic zone, and bottom-dwelling organisms in the profundal zone. Estuaries near the mouth of rivers are the nurseries of the sea. Marine communities include coastal communities and the oceans. An ocean has a pelagic division (open waters) and benthic division (ocean floor). Coral reefs are productive communities found in shallow tropical waters.

STUDY EXERCISES

Study the text section by section as you answer the questions that follow.

26.1 CLIMATE AND THE BIOSPHERE (P. 444)

- Solar radiation provides the energy that drives climate differences in the biosphere.
- Global air circulation patterns, ocean currents, and physical features produce the various patterns of temperature and rainfall about the globe.

1. Place a check in front of the statements that are true.
   _____ a. Because the earth is a sphere, solar energy hitting earth is uniformly distributed.
   _____ b. The distribution of rainfall is partially due to topography.
   _____ c. Heat always passes from warm areas to colder areas.
   _____ d. The great deserts of the world lie at the equator.
   _____ e. Warm air moves from the equator to the poles.
   _____ f. Arctic winds across the Great Lakes produce lake-effect snows.
   _____ g. Rain shadows always form on the leeward side of the mountains.

- Ecosystems can be divided into a few major classes of terrestrial and aquatic biomes.
- Terrestrial and aquatic biomes are linked and interact with one another.

2. Label this diagram that compares the effects of altitude and latitude on vegetation with the following terms (some are used more than once):
   coniferous forest
   deciduous forest
   tropical forest
   tundra

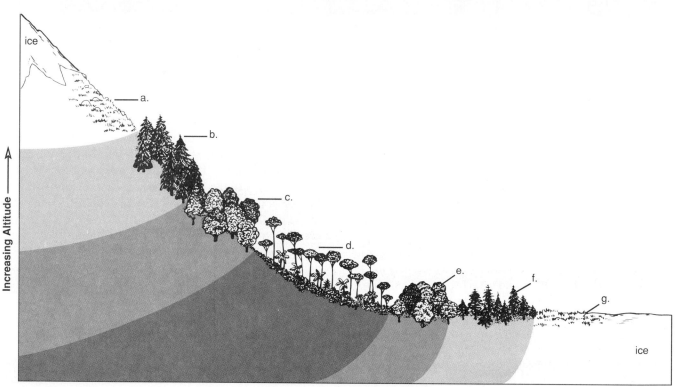

3. The diagram from question 2 emphasizes that vegetation is determined in part by ᵃ·_____.
   ᵇ·_____ also plays a major role and, therefore, tropical rain forests are found at the equator where
   both ᶜ·_____ and ᵈ·_____ are maximal.

4. For each biome listed, write a one- or two-word description for the temperature and rainfall.

Biome	Temperature	Rainfall
tundra		
desert		
grassland		
taiga		
temperate deciduous forest		
tropical rain forest		

5. Label the soil diagram with the following terms:
   leaching
   parent material
   topsoil
   subsoil

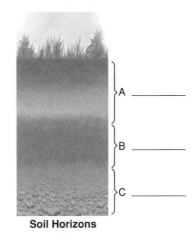

A _____

B _____

C _____

Soil Horizons

6. Because of limited leaching (due to limited rainfall), the A horizon is deep in a. _____ and this made the prairies of the United States good agricultural lands. Generally, in b. _____ both the A and B horizons supply inorganic nutrients for tree root growth. In tropical rain forests, however, because leaching is extensive there is only a shallow c. _____ horizon; therefore, these forests (can, cannot) d. _____ support crops for many years.

26.3 TERRESTRIAL BIOMES (P. 451)

- The earth's major biomes are forests (broad-leaf and coniferous), scrublands, grasslands (tropical savannah and temperate grasslands), tundra, and deserts.

Tundra (p. 451)

7. For each comparison select the one that applies to the tundra.
   _____ a. light—dark
   _____ b. cold—hot
   _____ c. short grasses—trees
   _____ d. musk-ox—horses
   _____ e. epiphytes—permafrost

Coniferous Forests (p. 452)

8. For each comparison select the one that applies to the taiga.
   _____ a. broad-leaf trees—narrow-leaf trees
   _____ b. cold—hot
   _____ c. cool lakes—pools and mires
   _____ d. zebras—moose
9. For each comparison select the one that applies to the temperate rain forest on the west coast of Canada and the United States.
   _____ a. short trees—tall trees
   _____ b. old trees—young trees
   _____ c. ferns and mosses—sedges and grasses

Temperate Deciduous Forests (p. 453)

10. For each comparison select the one that applies to temperate deciduous forests.
    _____ a. conifers only—oak and maple trees
    _____ b. flowering shrubs—short grasses
    _____ c. caribou—white-tail deer
    _____ d. rabbits and skunks—lemmings and prairie chickens

Tropical Forests (p. 454)

11. For each comparison select the one that applies to tropical rain forests.
    _____ a. deciduous broad-leafed trees—evergreen broad-leafed trees
    _____ b. lianas and epiphytes—pine needles
    _____ c. few insects—many insects
    _____ d. colorful birds—drab birds
    _____ e. horses and zebras—monkeys and large cats

Shrublands (p. 456)

12. For each comparison select the one that applies to shrublands.
    _____ a. rainfall in summer—rainfall in winter
    _____ b. shrubs with thick roots—trees with shallow roots

Grasslands (p. 456)

13. For each comparison select the one that applies to United States prairies.
    _____ a. rabbits—prairie dogs
    _____ b. hawks—parakeets
    _____ c. trees—grasses
14. For each comparison select the one that applies to the African savanna
    _____ a. elephants—moose
    _____ b. even rainfall—severe dry season
    _____ c. herds of herbivores—large primates

Deserts (p. 456)

15. For each comparison select the one that applies to North American deserts.
    _____ a. cool days—cool nights
    _____ b. cacti,—broad-leafed evergreen trees
    _____ c. lizards and snakes—elephants and zebras

Hoop Dreams

Each biome is a hoop. The plants and animals are balls. Try to get the balls in the right hoops.

Hoops (biomes)	Plants (balls)	Animals (balls)
desert	lichens	moose
taiga	spruce trees	beaver and muskrat
U.S. prairie	epiphytes	lemming
temperate deciduous forest	oak trees	monkey
tundra	grasses	lizard
African savanna	acacia trees	buffalo
tropical rain forest	cacti	wildebeest

Possible number of baskets is 14. How many baskets did you make? _____

26.4 Aquatic Biomes (p. 459)

- The earth's major aquatic biomes are of two types: freshwater and saltwater.

16. Aquatic communities can be divided into two major types: the a._____ communities that consist of lakes, ponds, rivers, and streams, and the b._____ communities along the coast and in the ocean itself.

Lakes (p. 460)

17. Lakes occur as nutrient-poor or a._____ lakes and nutrient-rich or b._____ lakes. In the temperate zone, deep lakes are stratified. In the fall, as the top layer called c._____ cools, and in the spring as it warms, a d._____ occurs. During this time, a mixing of e._____ and f._____ take place.

18. List and describe the three life zones of a lake, noting the types of organisms found in each.

    a. _____

    b. _____

    _____

    c. _____

    _____

Coastal Communities (p. 462)

19. Label these statements as true (T) or false (F):

    _____ a. Salt marshes in the tropics and mangrove swamps in the temperate zone occur at the mouth of a river.

    _____ b. Estuaries offer protection and nutrients to immature forms of marine life.

    _____ c. Rocky coasts are protected, but sandy shores are bombarded by the seas as the tides roll in and out.

    _____ d. There are different types of shelled and algal organisms at the upper, middle, and lower portions of the littoral zone of a rocky coast.

Oceans (p. 464)

20. Label each of the following as describing the pelagic divison (P) or the benthic division (B):

    _____ a. has the sublittoral and abyssal zones

    _____ b. has the greater overall diversity of organisms

    _____ c. includes neritic and oceanic provinces

    _____ d. includes organisms living on the continental shelf and slope

    _____ e. has organisms that depend on floating debris from above for food

    _____ f. is penetrated by sunlight

21. Complete the following table by noting the amount of light present (bright/semidark/dark) and the types of organisms found (phytoplankton/strange-looking fish/filter feeders/carnivores/sea urchins) in these ocean zones:

Ocean Zone	Amount of Light	Organisms
epipelagic		
mesopelagic		
bathypelagic		
abyssal		

22. What supports life in the epipelagic zone? a._____

    What supports life in the abyssal zone? b._____

Review key terms by completing this crossword puzzle, using the following alphabetized list of terms:

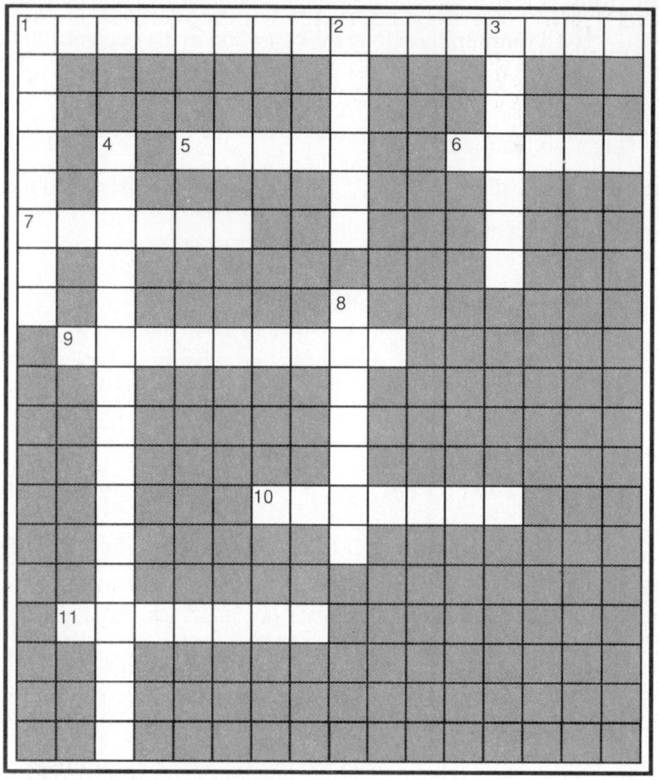

benthic division
biome
biosphere
climate
desert
estuary
pelagic division
plankton
prairie
savanna
taiga
tundra

Across

1 open portion of the sea (two words)
5 major terrestrial community characterized by certain climatic conditions and dominated by particular types of plants
6 terrestrial biome that is a coniferous forest extending in a broad belt across northern Eurasia and North America
7 treeless terrestrial biome of cold climates; found on high mountains and in polar regions
9 zone of air, land, and water at the surface of the earth in which living organisms are found
10 major factor determining biome distribution across the earth
11 end of a river where freshwater and saltwater mix as they meet

Down

1 freshwater and marine organisms that float on or near the surface of the water
2 treeless biome where the annual rainfall is less than 25 cm; the rain that does fall is subject to rapid runoff and evaporation
3 terrestrial biome that is a tropical grassland in Africa; characterized by a few trees and a severe dry season
4 ocean floor, which supports a unique set of organisms (two words)
8 terrestrial biome that is a temperate grassland

Chapter Test

Objective Questions

Do not refer to the text when taking this test.
For questions 1–10, indicate whether the statements are true (T) or false (F).

____ 1. Climate determines the geographic location of a biome.

____ 2. Grasslands usually receive a greater annual rainfall than deserts.

____ 3. The taiga is the northernmost forested biome.

____ 4. Temperate deciduous forests show the greatest species diversity of all forested biomes.

____ 5. The leaves of tropical rain forest evergreen trees are needlelike.

_____ 6. The profundal zone of a lake is the zone closest to the shore.

_____ 7. An estuary acts as a nutrient trap, existing where a large river flows into an ocean.

_____ 8. The solid part of a coral reef consists of the skeletons of dead coral.

_____ 9. A food chain in the pelagic division could be: phytoplankton, zooplankton, small fish, herring.

_____10. The benthic division receives less light penetration than the pelagic division.

_____11. Which of the following phrases is NOT true of the tundra?
a. low-lying vegetation
b. northernmost biome
c. few large mammals
d. short growing season
e. many different types of species

_____12. A temperate deciduous forest will
a. be warm and moist.
b. be hot and dry.
c. be cold and have limited rain.
d. have moderate temperatures and moderate rain.
e. have moderate temperatures and little rain.

_____13. A tropical rain forest will typically
a. be warm and moist.
b. be hot and dry.
c. be cold and have limited rain.
d. be moderate temperatures and moderate rain.
e. be moderate temperatures and little rain.

_____14. A desert will typically
a. be warm and moist.
b. be hot and dry.
c. be cold and have limited rain.
d. have moderate temperatures and moderate rain.
e. have moderate temperatures and little rain.

_____15. The biome that best supports grazing animals is
a. a tropical rain forest.
b. a coniferous forest.
c. a grassland.
d. a desert.

_____16. Which biome has most of the animals living in trees?
a. taiga
b. temperate deciduous forest
c. tropical rain forest
d. savanna
e. grassland

_____17. Which type of biome has succulent, leafless plants that have stems that store water and roots that can absorb great quantities of water in a brief period of time?
a. tropical rain forest
b. tundra
c. temperate deciduous forest
d. desert
e. savanna

_____18. Large grazing animals are most numerous in which biome?
a. tundra
b. grassland
c. coniferous forest
d. deciduous forest
e. tropical rain forest

_____19. Which zone of the ocean is the deepest?
a. epipelagic
b. mesopelagic
c. bathypelagic
d. abyssal
e. estuarial

_____20. Which zone in the ocean receives the most sunlight?
a. epipelagic
b. mesopelagic
c. bathypelagic
d. abyssal
e. estuarial

CRITICAL THINKING QUESTIONS

Answer in complete sentences.

21. Both the temperate rain forest and the chaparral occur in California. Explain various differences in climate and vegetation.

22. Explain why estuaries are the nurseries of the sea.

Test Results: _____ Number right ÷ 22 = _____ × 100 = _____ %

Use the Internet to further explore topics in this chapter, such as deforestation in rain forests or satellite imaging of environmental change. Go to the Mader Home Page (http://www.mhhe.com/sciencemath/biology/mader/) and click on *Biology*, 6th edition. Go to Chapter 26 and select a Web site of interest.

ANSWER KEY

STUDY EXERCISES

1. b, c, e, f, g   2. See Fig. 26.7, page 449, in text.
3. a. temperature b. Rainfall c. temperature d. rainfall
4.

Temperature	Rainfall
cold	little
hot	little
moderate	limited
cool	moderate
moderate	rather high
hot	high

5. a. topsoil, leaching b. subsoil c. parent material 6. a. temperate grasslands b. forests c. A d. cannot 7. a. dark b. cold c. short grasses d. mosk-ox e. permafrost 8. a. narrow-leaf trees b. cold c. cool lakes d. moose 9. a. tall trees b. old trees c. ferns and mosses 10. a. oak and maple trees b. flowering shrubs c. white-tail deer d. rabbits and skunks 11. a. evergreen broad-leafed trees b. lianas and epiphytes, c. many insects, d. colorful birds e. monkeys and large cats 12. a. rainfall in winter b. shrubs with thick

roots 13. a. prairie dogs b. hawks c. grasses 14. a. elephants b. severe dry season c. herds of herbivores 15. a. cool nights b. cacti c. lizards, and snakes Hoop Dreams desert: cacti, lizard; taiga: spruce trees, moose; U.S. prairie: grasses, buffalo; temperate deciduous forest: oak trees, beaver and muskrat; tundra: lichens, lemming; African savanna: acacia trees, wildebeest; tropical rain forest: epiphytes, monkey 16. a. freshwater b. saltwater 17. a. oligotrophic b. eutrophic c. epilimnion d. overturn e. oxygen f. nutrients 18. shore—aquatic plants, microscopic organisms b. *limnetic zone,* sunlit main body—some surface organisms and plankton c. *profundal zone,* depths where sunlight does not reach—mollusks, crustacea, worms 19. a. F b. T c. F d. T   20. a. B b. P c. P d. B e. B f. P
21.

Amount of Light	Organisms
bright	phytoplankton
semidark	carnivores
dark	strange-looking carnivores
dark	filter feeders and sea urchins

22. a. photosynthesis by algae b. debris floating down from above

KEYWORD CROSSWORD

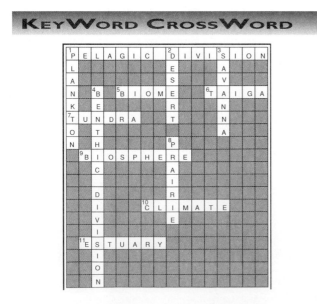

CHAPTER TEST

1. T   2. T   3. T   4. F   5. F   6. F   7. T   8. T   9. T 10. T   11. e   12. d   13. a   14. b   15. c   16. c   17. d 18. a   19. d   20. a   21. The temperate rain forest lies along the coast and has much rainfall; the old trees are covered by ferns and mosses and grow very tall. The chaparral occurs among hills; has limited rainfall and the shrubs that occur there are adapted to arid consditions and regrowth after fire.   22. An estuary which is a partially enclosed body of water where freshwater and seawater meet is a nutrient trap. They offer a protective environment where larval marine forms can mature before moving out to other coastal areas and the open sea.

27

HUMAN IMPACT ON THE GLOBAL ENVIRONMENT

CHAPTER REVIEW

The human population has increased steadily since industrialization and the advent of modern medicine. The resulting large population has had negative impacts on the global environment. The so-called more developed countries (MDCs) use 80% of the world's energy yet have only 22% of the total population. Most of the population increase into the twenty-first century will be in less developed countries (LDCs), all of which will desire an increased standard of living.

Emissions from automobile exhaust and the burning of **fossil fuels** have increased carbon dioxide, nitrous oxide, methane, and **chlorofluorocarbons (CFCs)** that trap solar heat, leading to global warming due to the **greenhouse effect. Pollution** of ecosystems is resulting from the increase in human population size. Global warming, destruction of the **ozone shield, acid deposition,** and **photochemical smog** are results of air pollution. Ozone shield destruction is particularly associated with CFCs. CFCs rise into the stratosphere and release chlorine, which causes ozone to break down. Sulfur dioxide and

nitrogen oxide react with water vapor to form acids that contribute to acid deposition. Hydrocarbons and nitrogen oxides react to form smog, which contains ozone and **PAN (peroxyacetyl).**

Clean supplies of fresh water are now in short supply. Pesticides and heavy metals contaminate waterways and concentrate as they move through food chains, resulting in **biological magnification.** Solid wastes, including hazardous wastes, are deposited on land and may contaminate the water supply. The ocean is the final recipient of wastes.

Soil erosion reduces land quality and leads to **desertification.** The Canadian forest and tropical rain forests are foremost among those being cut to provide wood for export. Loss of biological diversity due to tropical rain forest destruction will be immense.

Human activities have brought about the rapid extinction of many species. Conservation biology is a new discipline that incorporates a number of areas in biology to manage ecosystems for sustainability.

STUDY EXERCISES

Study the text section by section as you answer the questions that follow.

27.1 HUMAN POPULATION AND INDUSTRIALIZATION (P. 472)

- The human population rate of increase and continued industrialization impact the environment on a global scale.

1. Place a check beside the statements that are true.
   _____ a. People in industrialized countries use a greater share of natural resources, even though they have fewer people than nonindustrialized countries.
   _____ b. People in more developed countries cause more pollution per person than those in less developed countries.
   _____ c. The survival rate of people declined when modern medicine came into being.
   _____ d. Industrialization has lead to greatly increased use of fossil fuels, which will contribute greatly to global environmental change.

2. What type of environmental impact do you associate with each of the following?

less developed countries   a._____

more developed countries   b._____

27.2 GLOBAL CLIMATE CHANGE (P. 474)

• An increase in certain atmospheric gases, such as carbon dioxide, is expected to cause some degree of global warming.

3. Explain why the gases that cause global warming are known as the greenhouse gases.

_____

_____

4. What gases are implicated in global warming?

_____

27.3 GLOBAL CHEMICAL CLIMATE (P. 476)

• Sulfur and nitrogen compound deposits have negatively affected the quality of surface waters, forests, and human health.
• Air pollutants lead to photochemical smog which contains ozone that can be damaging to plants and human health.

5. When nitrogen oxides and sulfur dioxide react with water vapor, what results?_____

_____

27.4 STRATOSPHERIC OZONE DEPLETION (P. 478)

• A depletion in stratospheric ozone is expected to raise ultraviolet radiation levels at the earth's surface.

6. What is the ozone shield, and why is it important? _____

_____

7. Explain the significance of the following:

$$Cl + O_3 \rightarrow ClO + O_2$$

_____

8. What are some of the possible effects of increased ultraviolet radiation on humans and other organisms?_____

_____

9. Complete the table by listing the sources for these air pollutants and associating each with one or more of the following conditions: *acid deposition, global warming, ozone shield destruction,* and *photochemical smog.*

Pollutant	Sources	Conditions
No_x		
CO		
CO_2		
CFCs		

10. Match the situations with the following terms:

    1 acid deposition
    2 global warming
    3 ozone shield destruction
    4 photochemical smog

    _____ a. increase incidence of skin cancer
    _____ b. rise in sea level and loss of coastal cities
    _____ c. breathing difficulties
    _____ d. thermal inversions
    _____ e. loss of oceanic plankton
    _____ f. dead or dying lakes and forests
    _____ g. ozone and PAN

27.5 SURFACE WATERS, AQUIFERS, AND OCEANS (P. 479)

- Fresh water from surface waters is used for various purposes. Pollutants from the land run off into waters and make their way to the oceans, which are also direct receptacles for many wastes.

11. List three reasons why we might be running out of fresh water.

    a. _____

    b. _____

    c. _____

12. What is the effect of each of the following?

    excess nutrients in bodies of water a. _____

    organochlorides in drinking water b. _____

    aluminum and iron leached from soil by acid rain c. _____

13. Aquifers are polluted when a._____ percolates into the underground water supply. Chemical wastes are sometimes b._____ into deep wells or dumped into the c._____. Sometimes, these wastes can be prevented by d._____. In any case, the ocean is the final resting place for all types of wate e._____.

14. Indicate whether the following statements about biological magnification are true (T) or false (F):

    _____ a. Poisons such as DDT decrease as they pass upward from one trophic level to another.
    _____ b. Biological magnification is more likely in aquatic food chains.
    _____ c. Humans are not affected by biological magnification.
    _____ d. Poisons like DDT become more magnified (concentrated) as they pass upward from one trophic level to another.

27.6 SOIL EROSION, DESERTIFICATION, AND DEFORESTATION (P. 482)

- Expanding arid lands and diminishing forests are expected to cause the loss of much biodiversity.

15. Complete the following phrases to explain how land is being degraded today:

    Soil erosion causes a loss of a._____.

    Desertification means b._____.

    Forests are c._____.

16. Explain how forest destruction causes each of the following:

    loss of a CO_2 sink a._____

    loss of biodiversity b._____

    loss of medicinal plants c._____

soil erosion ^{d.}_____

water pollution ^{e.}_____

ecosystem destruction ^{f.}_____

27.7 HUMAN IMPACT ON BIODIVERSITY (P. 484)

- Conservation biology is the scientific study of biodiversity and ecosystem management for the preservation of all species, including *Homo sapiens*.

17. What three levels interplay to make up biodiversity? _____

_____

18. List four human activities that lead to extinction of other organisms. _____

_____

19. What new area of biology is concerned with the preservation and management of ecosystems for

sustainability?_____

Review key terms by completing this crossword puzzle, using the following alphabetized list of terms:

acid deposition
aquifer
desertification
greenhouse effect
ozone shield
photochemical smog
pollutant
sustainable world
thermal inversion

Across

1. return to earth as rain or snow of the sulfate or nitrate salts of acids produced by commercial and industrial activities (two words)
4. substance that is added to the environment and leads to undesirable effects for living organism
7. reradiation of solar heat toward the earth, caused by gases in the atmosphere (two words)

Down

1. rock layers that contain water and will release it in appreciable quantities to wells or springs
2. transformation of marginal lands to desert conditions
3. formed from oxygen in the upper atmosphere, it protects the earth from ultraviolet radiation (two words)
5. temperature inversion that traps cold air and its pollutants near the earth with the warm air above it (two words)
6. air pollution that contains nitrogen oxides and hydrocarbons which react to produce ozone and PAN (peroxylacetyl nitrate) (two words)
8. global way of life that can continue indefinitely because the economic needs of all people are met while still protecting the environment (two words)

OBJECTIVE QUESTIONS

Do not refer to the text when taking this test.

For questions 1–4, match the air pollutants with the following conditions:

    a. ozone shield destruction
    b. global warming
    c. acid deposition
    d. photochemical smog

_____ 1. CFCs

_____ 2. SO_2

_____ 3. CO

_____ 4. CO_2

_____ 5. The major greenhouse gas(es) is (are)
    a. SO_2.
    b. CO_2.
    c. CO.
    d. Both *b* and *c* are correct.

_____ 6. UV radiation
    a. causes mutations.
    b. impairs crop growth.
    c. kills plankton.
    d. All of these are correct.

_____ 7. Nitrogen oxides and hydrocarbons react in the presence of sunlight to produce
    a. acid particles.
    b. ground level ozone.
    c. greenhouse gases.
    d. All of these are correct.

_____ 8. What may occur as a result of the greenhouse effect?
    a. coastal flooding
    b. loss of food
    c. excess plant growth
    d. Both *a* and *b* are correct.

_____ 9. What contributes to the greenhouse effect?
    a. nuclear power
    b. burning of fossil fuels
    c. geothermal energy
    d. Both *a* and *c* are correct.

_____ 10. Which is the cause of stratospheric ozone depletion?
    a. chlorine
    b. PANs
    c. nitrates
    d. Both *b* and *c* are correct.

_____ 11. Freon contributes to
    a. acid rain.
    b. stratospheric ozone depletion.
    c. photochemical smog.
    d. All of these are correct.

_____ 12. Acid deposition is associated with
    a. dying lakes.
    b. dying forests.
    c. dissolving of copper from pipes.
    d. All of these are correct.

_____ 13. Aluminum and iron leach from the soil due to
    a. cultural eutrophication.
    b. ozone.
    c. acid deposition.
    d. All of these are correct.

_____ 14. Which is helpful against acidification of a lake?
    a. lime
    b. sulfur
    c. nitrates
    d. organochlorides

_____ 15. Nutrients such as nitrates and phosphates can enter waterways via
    a. sewage treatment plants.
    b. fertilizer runoff.
    c. soil erosion.
    d. All of these are correct.

_____ 16. Cultural eutrophication is caused by
    a. an excess of CO_2.
    b. PAN.
    c. acid deposition.
    d. excess nutrients.

_____ 17. Ammonium enters the water from
    a. industrial waste.
    b. human waste.
    c. pesticides.
    d. Both *a* and *b* are correct.

_____ 18. Biological magnification indicates that certain toxic chemicals
    a. replicate.
    b. cannot be broken down.
    c. spread rapidly.
    d. become less toxic in the body.

_____ 19. DDT will be most concentrated in
    a. producers.
    b. primary consumers.
    c. tertiary consumers.
    d. All of these are correct.

_____ 20. Tropical rain forests are being cut down for
    a. furniture.
    b. farming.
    c. cattle ranching.
    d. All of these are correct.

Answer in complete sentences.

21. Explain why the slash-and-burn agriculture used in tropical rain forests is not a good long-term investment for productivity.

22. How do pesticides and heavy metals become concentrated through biological magnification?

Test Results: _____ Number right ÷ 22 = _____ × 100 = _____ %

EXPLORING THE INTERNET

Use the Internet to further explore topics in this chapter, such as endangered species, ozone depletion, or tips to save the environment. Go to the Mader Home Page (http://www.mhhe.com/sciencemath/biology/mader/) and click on *Biology,* 6th edition. Go to chapter 27 and select a Web site of interest.

ANSWER KEY

STUDY EXERCISES

1. a, b, d **2. a.** increasing population size **b.** increasing pollution and resource use **3.** These gases act like the glass of a greenhouse because they allow sunlight to pass through and trap heat inside. **4.** carbon dioxide, nitrous oxide, methane, chlorofluorocarbons, halons **5.** Acid forms and is deposited on earth. **6.** Ozone is a layer within the stratosphere that protects the earth's surface from ultraviolet radiation. Organisms evolved in the presence of this ozone layer. **7.** the chlorine breaks down the ozone and the UV radiation is not absorbed **8.** It will increase the incidence of skin cancer and decrease the productivity of living systems. Loss of oceanic plankton will disrupt marine ecosystems.

9.

Sources	Conditions
vehicle exhaust fossil fuel burning	photochemical smog acid deposition global warming
vehicle exhaust deforestation	photochemical smog
vehicle exhaust fossil fuel burning deforestation	global warming
refrigerants plastic foam	global warming ozone shield destruction

10. a. 3 **b.** 2 **c.** 4 **d.** 4 **e.** 3 **f.** 1 **g.** 4 **11. a.** excess use **b.** human waste **c.** industrial waste **12. a.** cultural eutrophication **b.** cancer **c.** death of fish and aquatic life **13. a.** soluble nitrate **b.** injected **c.** ocean **d.** recycling **e.** pollution **14. a.** F **b.** T **c.** F **d.** T **15. a.** productivity **b.** transformation of marginal land to desert **c.** rapidly cut down **16.** See Figure 27.10, page 483, in text **17.** genetic diversity, species diversity, community diversity **18.** hunting, habitat disturbance, introduction of new species, pollution **19.** conservation biology

Crossword solution:
- 1 Across: ACID DEPOSITION
- 4 Across: POLLUTANT
- 7 Across: GREENHOUSE EFFECT
- 1 Down: AQUIFER
- 2 Down: DESERTIFICATION
- 3 Down: OZONE
- 5 Down: THERMAL INVERSION
- 6 Down: PHOTOCHEMICAL SMOG
- 8 Down: SUSTAINABLE WORLD
- SHIELD

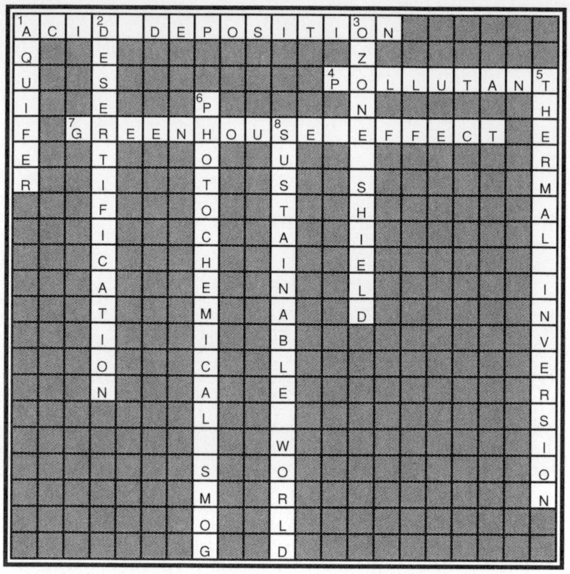

Chapter Test

1. a **2.** c **3.** d **4.** b **5.** b **6.** d **7.** b **8.** d **9.** b **10.** a **11.** b **12.** d **13.** c **14.** a **15.** d **16.** d **17.** b **18.** b **19.** c **20.** d **21.** The soil is nutrient-poor and will not sustain crops over many years. Once unproductive, it must be abandoned. **22.** Producers pick up certain toxins that are in low levels in the environment. As consumers eat the producers, the toxins become more concentrated because they do not break down. The toxins continue to concentrate (magnify) with each step in the food chain.

28

CLASSIFICATION OF LIVING THINGS

CHAPTER REVIEW

Taxonomy deals with the naming of organisms; each species is given a binomial name consisting of the genus and the specific epithet. Members of the same species share anatomical similarities and reproduce only with each other.

Systematics includes taxonomy and **classification.** The seven obligatory classification categories are: species, genus, family, order, class, phylum, and kingdom.

Classification should reflect **phylogeny,** which can be described in terms of **phylogenetic trees.** Homology—determined by similarity in structure due to a **common ancestor,** molecular data, and the fossil record—helps decipher phylogenies. The traditional school of systemat-

ics uses common ancestry and the degree of structural difference to construct trees. The **cladistic** school analyzes primitive and derived characters to construct **cladograms. Convergent evolution** can make it seem as if groups share derived characters when they actually do not. The numerical phenetic school clusters species on the basis of shared similarities, regardless of whether the similarities are due to convergent evolution.

The five-kingdom classification system recognizes **Plantae, Animalia, Fungi, Protista,** and **Monera.** Molecular data indicate that there are three evolutionary domains: **bacteria, archaea,** and **Eukarya.**

STUDY EXERCISES

Study the text section by section as you answer the questions that follow.

28.1 NAMING AND CLASSIFYING ORGANISMS (P. 492)

- Each known species has been given a binomial name consisting of the genus and species epithet.
- Species are distinguished on the basis of structure, reproductive isolation, and evolutionary relatedness. This chapter stresses evolutionary relatedness.

1. The branch of biology concerned with identifying and naming organisms is called _____.

2. The a._____ system of naming species contains two parts. The first part of the name is the b._____. The second part of the name is the c._____. Both names together is the d._____ name. The e._____ name can be used alone to refer to a group of related species.

3. A species can be distinguished by its distinctive structural a._____, even though members of a species show b._____. The biological definition of species states that members of a species c._____ and share the same gene pool. But we know that d._____ occurs between members of different species. In this chapter, we define a species as a(n) e._____ category below the rank of genus. All species within a genus share a recent f._____.

Now Let's Classify (p. 494)

- Classification involves the assignment of species to a genus, family, order, class, phylum, and kingdom (the largest classification category).

4. Create a mnemonic device that will help you remember the order of the classification categories. a._____

   _____

   Which category is just below family? b. _____

   Which category is just above class? c._____

   Which category is just below class? d. _____

   Which two categories are used in a binomial name? e._____ , f._____

5. What is a structural, chromosomal, or molecular feature that distinguishes one group of organisms from another? a._____

   Which taxonomic category has the most general characters in common? b._____

   Which category has the most specific characters in common? c._____

28.2 CONSTRUCTING PHYLOGENETIC TREES (P. 496)

- Systematics encompasses both taxonomy (the naming of organisms) and classification (placing species in the proper categories).
- Homology, molecular data, and the fossil record are used to decide the evolutionary relatedness of species and the construction of phylogenetic trees, diagrams that show their relatedness.
- There are three main schools of systematics: the traditional, the cladistics, and the numerical phenetic school.

6. The goal of systematics is to determine a._____ , which is the evolutionary history of a group of organisms. Common ancestors and lines of descent are found in diagrams called b._____ .

7. A(n) a._____ character is one that is present in ancestral forms; a(n) b._____ character is one that is found in descendants.

8. To determine phylogeny, systematists rely on a._____, b._____, and the c._____ to tell primitive from derived characters.

9. Similarity in structure due to descent from a common ancestor defines a._____ structures. Analogous structures have the same b._____, but there is no recent c._____ ancestor for the groups being studied. d._____ structures reveal that groups are closely related. e._____ structures appear in groups not closely related.

10. Sometimes, the fossil record reveals how a._____ a particular group is. Some fossils are intermediate enough to show possible b._____ between two groups. In regard to molecular data, the more closely related the two groups of animals, the c._____ the differences between their genes.

11. The three primary schools of systematics are a._____, b._____, and numerical c._____. In the traditional school, the d._____ of structural difference is important. Therefore, a traditionalist does not group dinosaurs and birds together. In the cladistic school, the common ancestor is included in the group; therefore, dinosaurs are e._____ with birds.

12. To construct a cladogram, a cladist determines which characters are a._____ and which are b._____. A cladogram is composed of c._____, each of which contains a common ancestor and species derived from that ancestor.

13. In the diagram that follows, *a* is a(n) ᵃ·_____
    and *b* is a(n) ᵇ·_____.

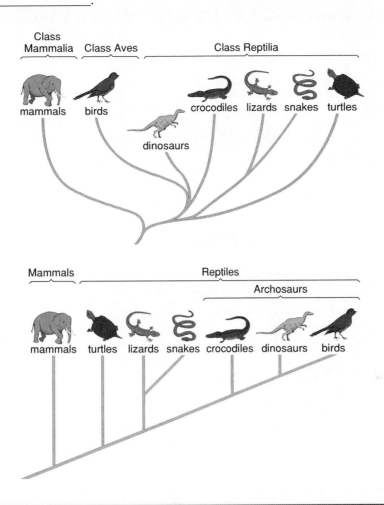

- The five-kingdom system contains: Plantae, Animalia, Fungi, Protista, and Monera.
- Recently, three domains have been recognized: Bacteria, Archaea, and Eukarya.

14. Match the five kingdoms to the proper description.
    1 Monera
    2 Protista
    3 Fungi
    4 Plantae
    5 Animalia
    _____ a. eukaryotic, multicellular, motile, and ingest their food.
    _____ b. eukaryotic, unicellular or multicellular, absorb, ingest, or photosynthesize their food.
    _____ c. prokaryotic, unicellular, usually absorb or photosynthesize their food, motile or nonmotile.
    _____ d. eukaryotic, multicellular, absorb food, nonmotile.
15. Using the same listing of kingdoms as in question 14, match the five kingdoms to these organisms.
    _____ a. includes algae, protozoa, water molds, and slime molds
    _____ b. includes bacteria
    _____ c. includes yeasts, mushrooms, and molds
    _____ d. includes trees, grasses, and vines
16. The three domains of life are a. _____, _____, _____. Why are archaea placed in their
    own domain? _____

229

Review key terms by completing this crossword puzzle, using the following alphabetized list of terms:

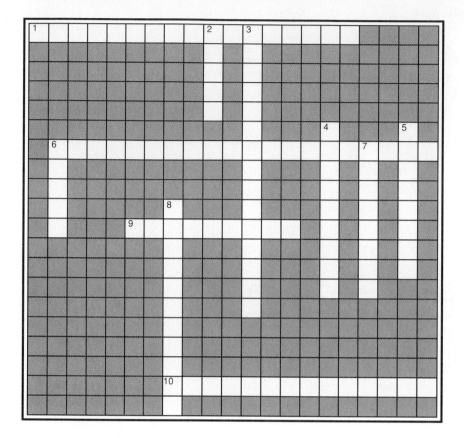

clade
cladogram
classification
common ancestor
convergent evolution
homology
phylogenetic tree
phylogeny
systematics
taxon
taxonomy

Across

1   diagram that indicates common ancestors and lines of descent (two words)
6   similarity in structure in distantly related groups due to adaptation to the environment (two words)
9   evolutionary history of a group of organisms
10   set of categories to which species are assigned on the basis of their relationship to other species

Down

2   group of organisms that fills a particular classification category
3   ancestor shared by at least two lines of descent (two words)
4   in cladistics, a branching diagram that shows the relationship among species in regard to their shared, derived characters
5   similarity in structure due to having a common ancestor
6   in cladistics, a common ancestor and all the species descended from this common ancestor
7   branch of biology concerned with identifying and naming organisms
8   study of the diversity of organisms at all levels of organization, from the cellular level to the population level

OBJECTIVE QUESTIONS

Do not refer to the text when taking this test.

_____ 1. Which of the following sequences is in correct order, starting from the most specific but fewest in number of species?
   a. class, family, kingdom, order, phylum
   b. family, order, class, phylum, kingdom
   c. order, family, kingdom, class, phylum
   d. phylum, order, kingdom, family, class

_____ 2. In the scientific name *Elaphe obsoleta,* which is the genus name?
   a. *Elaphe*
   b. *obsoleta*
   c. *bairdi*
   d. *Elaphe obsoleta*

_____ 3. In the scientific name *Elaphe obsoleta,* which name is the specific epithet?
   a. *Elaphe*
   b. *obsoleta*
   c. *bairdi*
   d. *Elaphe obsoleta*

_____ 4. Structures having the same makeup but different functions are _____; structures having different makeup but similar functions are _____.
   a. analogous; homologous
   b. homologous; analogous

_____ 5. Members of the same _____ are most similar to each other.
   a. species
   b. genus
   c. class
   d. family

_____ 6. Organisms that can interbreed and bear fertile offspring are in the same
   a. order.
   b. family.
   c. class.
   d. species.

_____ 7. Insect wings and bird wings are examples of _____ structures.
   a. homologous
   b. analogous
   c. vestigial
   d. None of these are correct.

_____ 8. The presence of _____ structures strongly indicates that organisms are related.
   a. homologous
   b. analogous
   c. vestigial
   d. None of these are correct.

_____ 9. Taxonomy is the branch of biology concerned with the
   a. interaction of living organisms.
   b. identifying, naming, and classifying living organisms.
   c. history of humans.
   d. history of dinosaurs.
   e. interaction of living organisms with the inorganic environment.

_____10. According to traditionalists, which of the following are descended from amphibians?
   a. birds
   b. reptiles
   c. mammals
   d. fish
   e. plants

_____11. Bacteria including cyanobacteria belong to the kingdom
   a. Monera.
   b. Protista.
   c. Fungi.
   d. Plantae.
   e. Animalia.

_____12. Molds and mushrooms belong to the kingdom
   a. Monera.
   b. Protista.
   c. Fungi.
   d. Plantae.
   e. Animalia.

_____13. Which of the following statements is false?
   a. Taxonomists are biologists who classify living things.
   b. Moving from genus to kingdom, more different types of species are included in each higher category.
   c. Species that are in the same genus share very specific characteristics.
   d. Organisms placed in the same genus are least closely related.

_____14. In which kingdom are the members unicellular and without a nucleus?
   a. Monera
   b. Protista
   c. Fungi
   d. Plantae
   e. Animalia
   f. Both *b* and *e* are correct.

_____15. Whenever a phylogenetic tree branches, there is assumed to be
   a. no living member of that group.
   b. always a living member of that group.
   c. a common ancestor.
   d. an embryo only.

_____16. Those who believe that the ancestor for all mammals is a mammal, not a reptile, are in the _____ school.
   a. traditional
   b. cladistic
   c. phylogenetic

_____17. When determining phylogeny, systematists use
   a. homology.
   b. the fossil record.
   c. molecular data.
   d. All of these are correct.
   e. None of these are correct.

_____18. Acquisition of the same or similar characteristics in distantly related lines of descent is called
   a. parallel evolution.
   b. convergent evolution.
   c. evolution by natural selection.
   d. evolution by mutation.

_____19. A similar banding pattern that is found in almost all species of moths is an example of
   a. parallel evolution.
   b. convergent evolution.
   c. evolution by natural selection.
   d. evolution by mutation.

_____20. Analyzing molecular data to determine phylogeny involves which of the following techniques?
   a. comparing the base sequences of DNA and RNA
   b. immunological studies
   c. DNA fingerprinting
   d. Both a and b are correct.
   e. All of these are correct.

_____21. The degree of relatedness of species can be indicated by
   a. the fossil record.
   b. homology.
   c. analyzing molecular data.
   d. All of these are correct.

_____22. The fossil record is incomplete because
   a. not every organism becomes a fossil.
   b. most organisms decay before they become buried.
   c. fossils must survive intense geological processes.
   d. All of these are correct.

_____23. The traditional school of systematics
   a. came after the cladistic school.
   b. stresses common ancestry.
   c. stresses the degree of structural difference among divergent groups.
   d. Both b and c are correct.
   e. All of these are correct.

_____24. Cladists
   a. agree with the traditional approach to systematics.
   b. believe that any group must contain the ancestor to that group.
   c. believe that the common ancestor for mammals is a reptile.
   d. All of these are correct.

_____25. A clade is a
   a. tool used to excavate archeological sites.
   b. piece of laboratory equipment used to sterilize glassware.
   c. division of a cladogram.
   d. common ancestor, with its descendent species, on a cladogram.
   e. Both c and d are correct.
   f. None of these are correct.

CRITICAL THINKING QUESTIONS

Answer in complete sentences.

26. Why is it imperative that organisms be given a scientific name in Latin, rather than simply using common names?

27. Why do you think the species concept can often be difficult to test in wild populations?

Test Results: _____ Number right ÷ 27 = _____ × 100 = _____ %

Use the Internet to further explore topics in this chapter, such as phylogenetic systematics or cladistics. Go to the Mader Home Page (http://www.mhhe.com/sciencemath/biology/mader/) and click on *Biology,* 6th edition. Go to Chapter 28 and select a Web site of interest.

ANSWER KEY

STUDY EXERCISES

1. taxonomy 2. a. binomial b. genus c. specific epithet d. species e. genus 3. a. characteristics b. variations c. interbreed d. hybridization e. taxonomic f. common ancestor 4. a. Example: Karen Pushed Cans Off Friendly Grandmother's Stove (kingdom, phylum, class, order, family, genus, species) b. genus c. phylum d. order e. genus f. species 5. a. character b. kingdom c. species 6. a. phylogeny b. phylogenetic trees 7. a. primitive b. derived 8. a. homologous structures b. molecular data c. fossil record 9. a. homologous b. function c. common d. Homologous e. Analogous 10. a. old b. relationships c. fewer 11. a. traditional b. cladistics c. phenetics d. degree e. classified 12. a. primitive b. derived c. clades 13. a. phylogenetic tree b. cladogram 14. a. 5 b. 2 c. 1 d. 3 15. a. 2 b. 1 c. 3 d. 4 16. a. bacteria, archaea, eukarya b. The archaea have nucleotide sequences that are unique and do not match those of eukarya or bacteria.

KEYWORD CROSSWORD

```
 1                          2       3
[P][H][Y][L][O][G][E][N][E][T][I][C][ ][T][R][E][E]
                           [A]   [O]
                           [X]   [M]
                           [O]   [M]
                           [N]   [O]
                    4                             5
                           [N]   [N]       [C]       [H]
 6                                 7
[C][O][N][V][E][R][G][E][N][T][ ][E][V][O][L][U][T][I][O][N]
[L]                        [A]   [A][A]       [M]
[A]                        [N]   [D][X]       [O]
[D]               8 [S]          [C][D][O]    [L]
[E]            9 [P][H][Y][L][O][G][E][N][Y][G][N][O]
                   [S]          [S][R][O][G]
                   [T]          [T][A][M][Y]
                   [E]          [O][M][Y]
                   [M]          [R]
                   [A]
                   [T]
                   [I]
               10[C][L][A][S][S][I][F][I][C][A][T][I][O][N]
                   [S]
```

CHAPTER TEST

1. b 2. a 3. b 4. b 5. a 6. d 7. b 8. a 9. b 10. b 11. a 12. c 13. d 14. a 15. c 16. b 17. d 18. b 19. a 20. e 21. d 22. d 23. d 24. b 25. e 26. The common name for organisms will vary from country to country because of language differences. Even among those speaking the same language, different common names are sometimes used for the same organism. However, with the scientific Latin name, we know we are referring to the same organism. 27. Two species may never meet to test whether or not they can effectively interbreed.

29

VIRUSES, BACTERIA, AND ARCHAEA

CHAPTER REVIEW

Viruses are noncellular entities consisting of an outer capsid and an inner core of nucleic acid. They are obligate parasites that reproduce inside cells. **Bacteriophages** undergo either a **lytic cycle,** in which they break out of the host cell, or a **lysogenic cycle,** in which viral DNA is integrated into bacterial DNA. Animal viruses have a membranous envelope they acquire when they bud from the host cell; some RNA viruses are **retroviruses** that transcribe RNA into DNA, which then becomes incorporated into the host genome.

Bacteria are prokaryotic. They lack a nucleus and most other cytoplasmic organelles found in eukaryotic cells. Bacteria reproduce asexually by **binary fission,** but genetic recombination occurs by **conjugation, transfor-**

mation, and **transduction.** Bacteria differ in their need for oxygen, but most are aerobic heterotrophs that act as **decomposers.** Some heterotrophs are **symbiotic** and others are **parasitic.** Other bacteria acquire energy and nutrients by using photosynthetic or **chemosynthetic** processes.

There are two types of prokaryotes: bacteria and archaea. On the basis of molecular evidence, it is suggested that there are three evolutionary domains: Bacteria, Archaea, and Eukarya. It appears that the archaea are more closely related to eukarya than to bacteria. Archaea do not have peptidoglycan in their cell walls, as do the bacteria, and they share genes with the eukarya.

STUDY EXERCISES

Study the text section by section as you answer the questions that follow.

29.1 VIRUSES ARE PARTICLES (P. 508)

- Viruses are noncellular, while bacteria are fully functioning cellular organisms.
- All viruses have an outer capsid composed of protein and an inner core of nucleic acid. Some have an outer membranous envelope.
- Viruses are obligate intracellular parasites, including bacteriophages (reproduce inside bacteria), and plant and animal viruses.

1. Fill in the following table to contrast viruses and bacteria:

	Viruses	Bacteria
Structure		
Life Cycle, Where?		
Parasitic?		

Viruses Replicate (p. 510)

2. a. Label the diagram, which describes how viruses replicate, with the following terms:

attachment
biosynthesis
integration
lysogenic cycle
lytic cycle
maturation
penetration
release

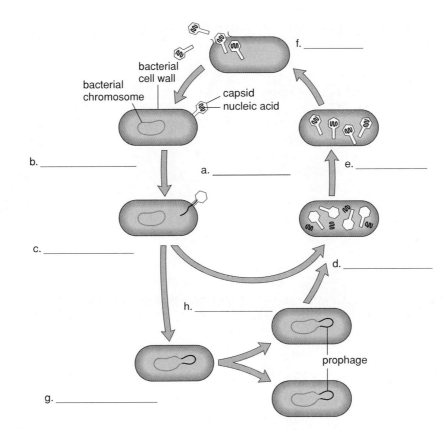

Which cycle produces viruses? b._____

Which cycle is dormant? c._____

Which cycle kills, or lyses, the host? d._____

3. Place the correct number from the following diagram next to its description:

_____ a. reverse transcription
_____ b. integration
_____ c. biosynthesis
_____ d. attachment
_____ e. penetration
_____ f. maturation
_____ g. release
_____ h. replication
_____ i. transcription

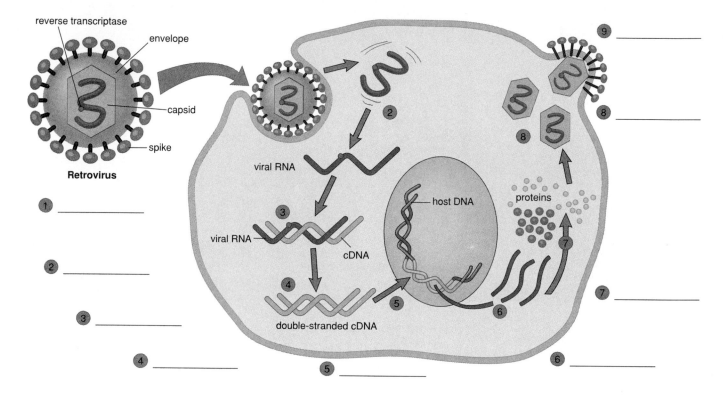

4. The life cycle shown in question 3 is that of a(n) a._____. In this life

cycle, b._____ integrates into the host genome until transcription occurs. Then translation

provides three types of proteins: c._____, d._____,

and e._____. When the viruses leave the cell, they are surrounded by

a(n) f._____.

5. Indicate whether the following statements are true (T) or false (F):
_____ a. Antibiotics are helpful for viral infections.
_____ b. Antiviral drugs act by interfering with viral replication.
_____ c. There are no vaccines for viral infections.
_____ d. Prions are neither viruses nor bacteria; they are protein particles.

- Bacterial cells lack a nucleus and most other cytoplasmic organelles found in eukaryotic cells.

6. Label this diagram of a bacterial cell with the following terms:

   capsule
   cell wall
   cytosol
   fimbriae
   flagellum
   nucleoid
   plasma membrane
   plasmid
   ribosome

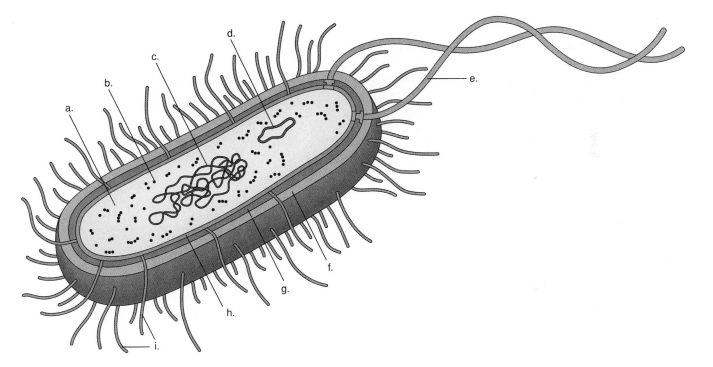

7. Based on the diagram you labeled in question 6, which of these structures are present in eukaryotic animal/plant cells but are not in a bacterial cell?

   _____ a. plasma membrane
   _____ b. nucleus
   _____ c. ribosomes
   _____ d. mitochondria
   _____ e. cell wall
   _____ f. chloroplasts
   _____ g. flagella

8. Based on the diagram you labeled in question 6, what two structures are present in a bacterial cell but absent from a eukaryotic cell? What are their functions?

Structure	Function
a. _____	_____
b. _____	_____
c. _____	_____

Bacteria Reproduce Asexually (p. 515)

- Bacteria reproduce asexually by binary fission. Mutations and genetic recombinations by various means introduce variability.

9. Match the descriptions with the following terms:
   1 binary fission
   2 conjugation
   3 transformation
   4 transduction
   5 endospores
   _____ a. bacteria picks up free pieces of DNA
   _____ b. a means of survival
   _____ c. asexual division
   _____ d. male passes DNA to female
   _____ e. bacteriophages carry DNA from one cell to the next

Bacterial Nutrition Is Diverse (p. 516)

- Some bacteria require oxygen; others are obligate anaerobes or facultative anaerobes.
- Some bacteria are autotrophs. They are photosynthetic bacteria (cyanobacteria give off oxygen, and purple and green sulfur bacteria do not) and chemosynthetic bacteria.
- Most bacteria are aerobic heterotrophs, just as animals are. However, many heterotrophic bacteria are symbiotic, being mutualistic, commensalistic, or parasitic.

10. Match the descriptions with the following organisms:
    1 chemosynthetic bacteria
    2 cyanobacteria
    3 parasitic bacteria
    4 saprotrophic bacteria
    _____ a. decomposers
    _____ b. O_2 given off
    _____ c. $NH_3 \rightarrow NO_3^-$
    _____ d. disease
11. Match the relationships with the following terms:
    1 commensalism
    2 mutualism
    3 parasitism
    4 symbiotic
    _____ a. includes all the others
    _____ b. bacteria living in nodules of legumes
    _____ c. bacteria living on your skin
    _____ d. bacteria that cause strep throat

29.3 HOW BACTERIA ARE CLASSIFIED (P. 517)

- Traditionally, Gram staining is one laboratory method used to differentiate bacteria which may be rod, round, or spiral-shaped.

12. Label the three shapes of bacteria in the following diagram:

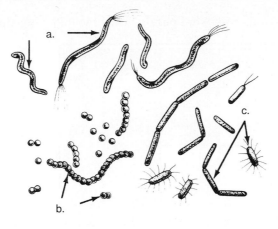

13. Place a check next to all characteristics that are typical of cyanobacteria.
    _____ a. many forms of nutrition
    _____ b. always photosynthetic
    _____ c. have flagella
    _____ d. form lichens
    _____ e. associated with algal bloom
    _____ f. nitrogen fixing

29.4 ARCHAEA COMPARED TO BACTERIA (P. 519)

- Three evolutionary domains are now recognized; Bacteria, Archaea, and Eukarya.
- The archaea are quite specialized and live in extreme habitats.

14. Archaea are able to live in extreme environments. Name the type of archaea that live in the following habitats:

swamps and marshes; produce methane a._____

salty environments (Great Salt Lake in Utah) b._____

hot and acidic environments (hot sulfur springs of Yellowstone National Park) c._____

Review the key terms by completing this crossword puzzle, using the following alphabetized list of terms:

archaea
bacterium
chemosynthesis
commensalism
decomposer
endospore
lichen
nitrogen fixation
prion
retrovirus
saprotroph
symbiotic
virus

Across

2 one of the three domains of life, often found living in extreme habitats; prokaryotic cells that have unique genetic, biochemical, and physiological characteristics

5 bacterium that has shrunk its cell, rounded up within the former plasma membrane, and secreted a new and thicker cell wall in the face of unfavorable environmental conditions

7 close relationship between two species; includes parasitism, mutualism, and commensalism

8 symbiotic relationship in which one species is benefited, and the other is neither harmed nor benefited

9 organism, usually a bacterial or fungal species, that breaks down large organic molecules into elements that can be recycled in the environment

12 symbiotic relationship between certain fungi and algae that has long been thought to be mutualistic; the fungi provide inorganic food, and algae provide organic food

13 non-living, obligate, intracellular parasite consisting of an outer capsid and an inner core of nucleic acid

Down

1 unicellular organism that lacks a nucleus and cytoplasmic organelles other than ribosomes; reproduces by binary fission and occurs in one of three shapes (rod, spherical, spiral)

3 process of making food by using energy derived from the oxidation of inorganic compounds in the environment

4 protein particles that possibly can cause other proteins in the cell to convert to their shape

6 process whereby free atmospheric nitrogen is converted into compounds, such as ammonium and nitrates, usually by soil bacteria (two words)

10 organism, usually a bacterium or fungus, that digests dead organic matter; secretes digestive enzymes and absorbs the resulting nutrients across the plasma membrane

11 RNA virus containing the enzyme reverse transcriptase that carries RNA/DNA transcription; for example, the AIDS virus

Do not refer to the text when taking this test.

_____ 1. Which is NOT generally true of viruses?
   a. consist of a nucleic acid core
   b. consist of a protein coat
   c. have a specific host range
   d. reproduce independently

_____ 2. Which viral life cycle does NOT immediately rupture the bacterial cell?
   a. lysogenic
   b. lytic

_____ 3. Which is true concerning animal viruses?
   a. lack an envelope when they leave the host cell
   b. attack the host cell by exocytosis
   c. have an outer coat of nucleic acid
   d. some have RNA genomes

_____ 4. In the lytic cycle, the term _maturation_ refers to the
   a. translation of RNA.
   b. integration of cDNA.
   c. assembly of parts into new viruses.
   d. All of these are correct.

_____ 5. Which shape is NOT representative of bacteria?
   a. bacillus
   b. coccus
   c. flagellar
   d. spirillum

_____ 6. Which of the following is NOT a form of genetic recombination in bacteria?
   a. binary fission
   b. conjugation
   c. transduction
   d. transformation

_____ 7. The function of the bacterial endospore is to
   a. increase the rate of anaerobic respiration.
   b. promote asexual reproduction.
   c. protect against attack from immune systems.
   d. withstand harsh environmental conditions.

_____ 8. A bacterium that can exist in the presence or absence of oxygen is a(n)
   a. autotroph.
   b. facultative anaerobe.
   c. obligate anaerobe.
   d. saprotroph.

_____ 9. A bacterium produces vitamins for a host while gaining a habitat. This relationship is
   a. commensalism.
   b. mutualism.
   c. parasitism.
   d. predation.

_____10. Which of these is NOT a correct contrast between bacteria and eukaryotes?

	Bacteria	**Eukaryotic**
a.	binary fission	mitotic cell division
b.	nucleoid	nucleus
c.	asexual only	asexual and sexual
d.	nonmotile	motile

_____11. The cyanobacteria differ from other bacteria in which of the following ways?
   a. They are unicellular, and other bacteria are filamentous.
   b. They are able to form spores, whereas other bacteria cannot.
   c. They are autotrophic, whereas other bacteria never are.
   d. They release oxygen during photosynthesis, whereas other bacteria do not.

_____12. A virus infecting a bacterium injects its _____ and leaves behind its _____.
   a. protein coat; outer capsule
   b. nucleic acid; capsid
   c. nucleus; nucleoplasm
   d. genes; metabolic enzymes

_____13. Bacteria have
   a. a cell wall with a construction similar to that of plants.
   b. flagella with a construction different from that of eukaryotes.
   c. mitochondria but not chloroplasts.
   d. All of these are correct.

_____14. Viruses are not in the classification system because
   a. they are obligate parasites.
   b. they are noncellular.
   c. they can integrate into the host genome.
   d. All of these are correct.

_____15. Chemosynthetic bacteria
   a. give off oxygen just like plants do.
   b. are exemplified by the nitrifying bacteria that oxidize ammonia (NH_3) to nitrites (NO_2^-).
   c. are decomposers like all bacteria.
   d. Both _b_ and _c_ are correct.

_____16. Why can't cyanobacteria be classified with the eukaryotic algae?
   a. They fix atmospheric nitrogen.
   b. They form a symbiotic relationship with fungi.
   c. They cause disease.
   d. They do not have a nucleus.

___17. Which of these is (are) a true statement(s)?
  a. Archaea are in a separate kingdom.
  b. Archaea are in their own domain.
  c. Archaea are found in most every habitat.
  d. Archaea are found in extreme habitats like swamps, salty lakes, hot, acidic aquatic habitats.
  e. Both *b* and *d* are correct.

___18. How are archaea different from bacteria?
  a. Archaea have a nucleus and bacteria do not.
  b. Archaea live in extreme habitats and bacteria do not.
  c. Archaea have nucleotide sequences not found in bacteria.
  d. Archaea have a cell wall and bacteria do not.
  e. Both *b* and *c* are correct.

CRITICAL THINKING QUESTIONS

Answer in complete sentences.

19. Taking into consideration the specificity of viruses, explain how HIV (the AIDS virus) may have come into being.

20. Bacteria have diverse lifestyles. Give examples.

Test Results: _____ Number right ÷ 20 = _____ × 100 = _____ %

EXPLORING THE INTERNET

Use the Internet to further explore topics in this chapter, such as bringing ancient bacteria to life or learning more about viruses. Go to the Mader Home Page (http://www.mhhe.com/sciencemath/biology/mader/) and click on *Biology,* 6th edition. Go to Chapter 29 and select a Web site of interest.

ANSWER KEY

STUDY EXERCISES

1.

Viruses	Bacteria
capsid plus nucleic acid core	prokaryotic cell
in host cell	independently
always	sometimes

2. a. See Figure 29.3, page 511, in text. **b.** lytic **c.** lysogenic **d.** lytic **3. a.** 3. **b.** 5 **c.** 7 **d.** 1 **e.** 2 **f.** 8 **g.** 9 **h.** 4 **i.** 6 **4. a.** retrovirus **b.** cDNA **c.** coat protein **d.** reverse transcriptase **e.** envelope protein **f.** envelope **5. a.** F **b.** T **c.** F **d.** T **6. a.** cytosol **b.** ribosome **c.** nucleoid **d.** plasmid **e.** flagellum **f.** capsule **g.** cell wall **h.** plasma membrane **i.** fimbriae **7.** b, d, f **8. a.** plasmid, accessory ring of DNA **b.** fimbriae, attachment to a substratum **c.** capsule, protection **9. a.** 3 **b.** 5 **c.** 1 **d.** 2 **e.** 4 **10. a.** 4 **b.** 2 **c.** 1 **d.** 3 **11. a.** 4 **b.** 2 **c.** 1 **d.** 3 **12. a.** spirillum **b.** coccus **c.** baccillus **13.** b, d, e, f **14. a.** methanogens **b.** halophiles **c.** thermoacidophiles

1. d 2. a 3. d 4. c 5. c 6. a 7. d 8. b 9. b 10. d 11. d 12. b 13. b 14. b 15. b 16. d 17. e 18. c 19. HIV attacks a particular immune cell. Therefore, the RNA found in these viruses must be derived from this type of cell. 20. Bacteria carry on various means of nutrition: saprotrophic, chemosynthetic, and photosynthetic. Bacteria are symbiotic: mutualistic, commensalistic, or parasitic. Bacteria vary in their need for oxygen and can be anaerobic, facultative, or aerobic. Saprotrophic bacteria can digest almost any type of material and can live and survive under all sorts of conditions.

30

THE PROTISTS

Algae are not plants because they do not protect the zygote from desiccation. Algae are a part of **plankton,** aquatic organisms that drift along. **Green algae,** which have biochemical characteristics in common with plants, exist as flagellated cells, colonies, filaments, and multicellular sheets. Life cycles are equally diverse. **Brown algae** and **golden brown algae** share chemical characteristics, although brown algae are complex, and golden brown algae include **diatoms,** which are box-shaped single cells. **Dinoflagellates** have cellulose plates and two flagella and, along with diatoms, are plentiful photosynthesizers. **Euglenoids** are also flagellated single cells,

but the cell wall is flexible. Both red algae and brown algae are called **seaweeds;** brown algae is seen in the north temperate zone, and red algae usually grows in warmer waters.

Protozoa, which are usually single cells, are the animal-like protists with unique organelles. **Amoeboids** move by **pseudopods, ciliates** move by cilia, and **zooflagellates** have flagella.

Both **slime molds** and **water molds** have some characteristics in common with fungi and some characteristics that separate them from fungi.

STUDY EXERCISES

Study the text section by section as you answer the questions that follow.

30.1 ALGAE ARE PLANTLIKE (p. 524)

- Algae are adapted to an aquatic environment and do not protect the gametes and zygote from drying out, as do plants, which are adapted to a terrestrial environment.
- Like plants, green algae possess chlorophylls *a* and *b,* have a cell wall of cellulose, and store reserve food as starch inside chloroplasts.

1. Match the organisms with the following phyla:
   1 phylum Chlorophyta
   2 phylum Phaeophyta
   3 phylum Chrysophyta
   4 phylum Dinoflagella
   5 phylum Euglenophyta
   6 phylum Rhodophyta
   _____ a. dinoflagellates
   _____ b. euglenoids
   _____ c. brown algae
   _____ d. red algae
   _____ e. green algae
   _____ f. golden brown algae

Green Algae Are Most Plantlike (p. 524)

2. Green algae are believed to be related to plants because they have a cell wall that

   contains ^{a.}_____, they possess chlorophylls ^{b.}_____

   and ^{c.}_____, and they store reserve food as ^{d.}_____.

3. Complete the table describing the algae by placing the following terms in the appropriate columns (some terms are used more than once):

I	II
unicellular	isogametes
filamentous	heterogametes
colonial	conjugation
multicellular	alternation of generations
	daughter colonies
	zoospores

Algae	I.	II.
Volvox		
Chlamydomonas		
Spirogyra		
Ulva		

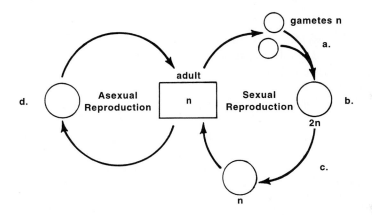

4. Label this diagram of the life cycle of *Chlamydomonas* with the following terms: *fertilization, meiosis, zoospores,* and *zygote.*

   Which portions of this life cycle are haploid? e. _____

   Which portion is diploid? f. _____

   What type of life cycle is this? g. _____

5. Label this diagram of the life cycle of *Ulva* with the following terms: *fertilization, gametophyte, meiosis,* and *sporophyte.*

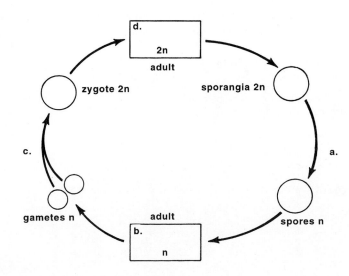

What type of life cycle is this? e. _____

_____

Brown Algae and Golden Brown Algae Are Biochemically Alike (p. 527)/Dinoflagellates Have Two Flagella (p. 528)/ Euglenoids Are Flexible (p. 528)/ Red Algae Are Sources of Agar (p. 529)

- Brown algae (e.g., seaweeds) and golden brown algae (e.g., diatoms) have chlorophylls *a* and *c* plus a brownish carotenoid.
- Diatoms, along with dinoflagellates, are significant producers in marine and freshwater habitats.
- Euglenoids are flagellated cells with both animal-like and plantlike characteristics, typifying the difficulty of classifying protists.
- Red algae are filamentous or multicellular seaweeds that are more delicate and grow in warmer waters than brown algae.

6. Match the traits with the following algae (some numbers are used more than once):

   1 brown algae
   2 diatoms
   3 euglenoids
   4 dinoflagellates

   _____ a. are numerous photosynthesizers in ocean
   _____ b. have animal-like and plantlike characteristics
   _____ c. have chlorophylls *a* and *c,* and carotenoid pigment
   _____ d. have silica-impregnated valves
   _____ e. are used as filtering agents and scouring powders
   _____ f. cause red tide
   _____ g. have a symbiotic relationship with corals
   _____ h. are seaweeds

7. Label each of the following descriptions as identifying brown algae (B) or red algae (R):
   _____ a. *Fucus,* a rockweed
   _____ b. *Laminaria,* a kelp
   _____ c. adapted to cold, rough water
   _____ d. adapted to warm, gentle water
   _____ e. economically important as source of agar

30.2 PROTOZOA ARE ANIMAL-LIKE (P. 530)

- While algae are the phytoplankton, protozoa are the zooplankton of aquatic habitats.
- Protozoa are not considered animals because animals are multicellular, have more than one kind of nonreproductive cell, and undergo embryonic development.
- Amoeboids move by pseudopods, ciliates move by cilia, and zooflagellates have flagella. Sporozoa are nonmotile parasites that form spores; *Plasmodium* causes malaria.

8. Match the organisms with the following phyla:

   1 phylum Sarcodina
   2 phylum Ciliophora
   3 phylum Zoomastigophora
   4 phylum Sporozoa

   _____ a. *Paramecium*
   _____ b. foraminifera
   _____ c. trypanosome
   _____ d. *Plasmodium vivax*
   _____ e. radiolaria

9. Protozoa are typically ᵃ·_____, ᵇ·_____, and ᶜ·_____

organisms. Some protozoa ᵈ·_____ and engulf their food; others are ᵉ·_____

and absorb nutrients; others are ᶠ·_____ and cause disease.

10. Complete the following table, classifying the protozoa by means of locomotion and giving an example organism of each:

Classes	Organelle of Locomotion	Example
amoeboids		
ciliates		
zooflagellates		
sporozoa		

11. Label this diagram of *Paramecium* with the following terms:

anal pore
contractile vacuole
food vacuole
macronucleus
micronucleus
oral groove
pellicle

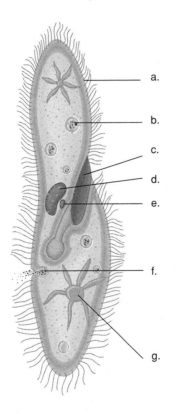

a.

b.

c.

d.

e.

f.

g.

12. Ciliates, such as *Paramecium,* have hundreds of ᵃ·_____ that extend through a pellicle. Beneath the pellicle are numerous oval capsules that contain ᵇ·_____, which are used for defense. Food is swept down a(n) ᶜ·_____, at the end of which food vacuoles form. Ciliates have two nuclei: a large ᵈ·_____ that controls normal metabolism and one or more micronuclei used during conjugation.

13. a. Label this diagram of the life cycle of *Plasmodium vivax* with the following terms: *gametes, sporozoites,* and *zygote*.

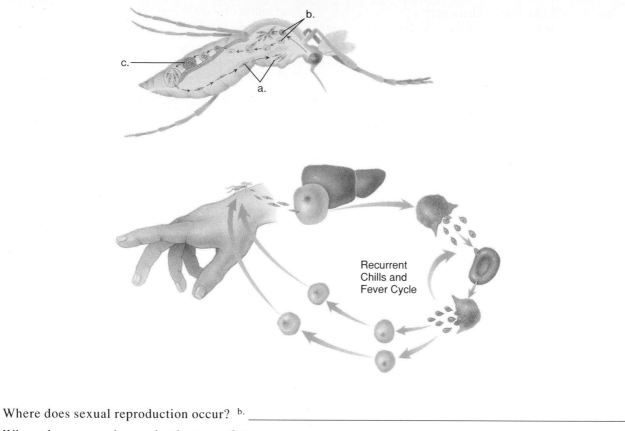

Where does sexual reproduction occur? b. _____

Where does asexual reproduction occur? c. _____

What causes the cycle of recurring chills and fever? d. _____

_____

30.3 SLIME MOLDS AND WATER MOLDS ARE FUNGUSLIKE (P. 535)

- Like fungi, slime molds produce nonmotile spores, but unlike fungi, they have an amoeboid stage that ingests food.
- Like fungi, water molds are filamentous and saprotrophic, but unlike fungi, they produce 2n zoospores.

14. Complete this table to describe slime molds and water molds.

Type of Mold	Body Organization	Nutrition	Reproduction
plasmodial slime molds			
cellular slime molds			
water molds			

Review key terms by completing this crossword puzzle, using the following alphabetized list of terms:

alga
amoeboid
conjugation
diatom
euglenoid
phytoplankton
plankton
protozoan
pseudopod
spore
trypanosome
zooflagellate
zooplankton

Across

1. member of a genus of parasitic zooflagellates that cause severe disease in human beings and domestic animals, including a condition called sleeping sickness
3. asexual reproductive structure that is resistant to unfavorable environmental conditions and develops into a haploid generation
5. freshwater or marine unicellular golden brown alga, with a cell wall consisting of two silica-impregnated valves, that is extremely numerous in phytoplankton
10. protozoan that moves by means of flagella
11. freshwater and marine organisms that are suspended on or near the surface of the water
13. union that results in the transfer of genetic material from one cell to another

Down

2. cytoplasmic extension of amoeboid protists; used for locomotion and engulfing food
4. animal-like, heterotrophic, unicellular organism
6. aquatic, plantlike organism carrying out photosynthesis and belonging to the kingdom Protista
7. flagellated and flexible freshwater unicellular organism that usually contains chloroplasts and is often characterized as having both animal-like and plantlike characteristics
8. part of plankton containing organisms that (1) photosynthesize and produce much of the oxygen in the atmosphere and (2) serve as food producers in aquatic ecosystems
9. part of plankton containing protozoa and microscopic animals
12. protist that moves and engulfs prey with pseudopods; amoebalike in movement

OBJECTIVE QUESTIONS

Do not refer to the text when taking this test.

_____ 1. Green algae
   a. store reserve food as lipid.
   b. do not give off oxygen.
   c. possess chlorophylls *a* and *b*.
   d. have a cell wall that contains pectin.

_____ 2. Classification of algae according to color
   a. can no longer be justified.
   b. is based on the type of pigments they contain.
   c. suggests that they do not have chlorophyll.
   d. means that some algae are colorless.

_____ 3. Which is NOT true of *Chlamydomonas?*
   a. has an eyespot
   b. produces zoospores
   c. is multicellular
   d. All of these are true.

_____ 4. *Volvox* is a colonial alga that
   a. does not reproduce.
   b. produces heterogametes.
   c. produces daughter colonies.
   d. Both *b* and *c* are correct.

_____ 5. Which of these is NOT true of *Spirogyra?*
   a. has a spiral chloroplast
   b. is filamentous
   c. carries out conjugation
   d. reproduces asexually by forming spores

_____ 6. Some brown algae
   a. live at sea.
   b. are quite large.
   c. produce algin.
   d. All of these are correct.

_____ 7. Diatoms
   a. reproduce sexually.
   b. have a cell wall impregnated with cellulose.
   c. are flagellated.
   d. resemble a pill box.

_____ 8. Which of these is NOT true of dinoflagellates?
   a. are numerous in the ocean
   b. have the same pigments as brown algae
   c. protected by cellulose plates
   d. have two flagella

_____ 9. Which is (are) true of euglenoids?
   a. They have flagella.
   b. Some have chloroplasts.
   c. They reproduce asexually.
   d. All of these are correct.

_____ 10. Both red algae and brown algae
   a. have the same pigments.
   b. are delicate in appearance.
   c. are seaweeds.
   d. are economically unimportant.

_____ 11. Protozoa are not animals because they are
   a. pigmented.
   b. motile.
   c. unicellular.
   d. All of these are correct.

_____ 12. Amoebas
   a. have pseudopods.
   b. never have a shell.
   c. always live in fresh water.
   d. All of these are correct.

_____ 13. Ciliates
   a. have a macronucleus and a micronucleus.
   b. do not move.
   c. are parasitic.
   d. are usually saprotrophic.

_____ 14. A trypanosome causes
   a. malaria.
   b. trichinosis.
   c. an intestinal infection.
   d. African sleeping sickness.

_____ 15. Which one of these is NOT an alga?
   a. *Chlamydomonas*
   b. *Volvox*
   c. *Paramecium*
   d. All of these are algae.

_____ 16. In the life cycle of *Plasmodium vivax,* a cause of malaria,
   a. sexual reproduction occurs in a mosquito.
   b. red blood cells burst causing chills and fever.
   c. spores and gametes form.
   d. All of these are correct.

_____ 17. Slime molds
   a. are exactly like fungi.
   b. have a body composed of hyphae.
   c. produce spores.
   d. All of these are correct.

18. How does the versatility of a protozoan cell (i.e., *Paramecium*) compare to that of a multicellular organism cell?

19. Algae and protozoa are in the same kingdom. Do they seem closely related? Why or why not?

Test Results: _____ Number right ÷ 19 = _____ × 100 = _____ %

EXPLORING THE INTERNET

Use the Internet to further explore topics in this chapter, such as algal diversity or the bizarre slime molds. Go to the Mader Home Page (http://www.mhhe.com/sciencemath/biology/mader/) and click on *Biology,* 6th edition. Go to Chapter 30 and select a Web site of interest.

ANSWER KEY

STUDY EXERCISES

1. a. 4 **b.** 5 **c.** 2 **d.** 6 **e.** 1 **f.** 3   **2. a.** cellulose **b.** *a* **c.** *b* **d.** starch
3.

I.	II.
colonial	heterogametes, daughter colonies
unicellular	isogametes, zoospores
filamentous	conjugation
multicellular	isogametes, alternation of generations, zoospores

4. a. fertilization **b.** zygote **c.** meiosis **d.** zoospores **e.** zoospores, adult, gametes **f.** zygote **g.** haplontic **5. a.** meiosis **b.** gametophyte **c.** fertilization **d.** sporophyte **e.** alternation of generations **6. a.** 2, 4 **b.** 3 **c.** 1, 2 **d.** 2 **e.** 2 **f.** 4 **g.** 4 **h.** 1 **7. a.** B **b.** B **c.** B **d.** R **e.** R **8. a.** 2 **b.** 1 **c.** 3 **d.** 4 **e.** 1 **9. a.** heterotrophic **b.** unicellular **c.** motile **d.** capture **e.** saprotrophic **f.** parasitic **10.** See page 530 in text. **11.** See Figure 30.10*c*, page 531, in text. **12. a.** cilia **b.** trichocysts **c.** gullet **d.** macronucleus **13. a.** See Figure 30.12, page 533, in text. **b.** in the mosquito **c.** in the human **d.** Toxins, or poisons, enter the blood when red blood cells release spores.

14.

Body Organization	Nutrition	Reproduction
2n plasmodium	phagocytosis	sporangium produces spores by meiosis, which produce flagellated haploid cells that fuse
individual amoeboid cells	phagocytosis	sporangium produces spores
2n filamentous, cell walls are cellulose	parasitism	meiosis produces haploid gametes; otherwise asexual by zoospores

1. c **2.** b **3.** c **4.** d **5.** d **6.** d **7.** d **8.** b **9.** d **10.** c **11.** c **12.** a **13.** a **14.** d **15.** c **16.** d **17.** c **18.** The versatility of the protozoan cell is greater, because it's capable of many more functions. In multicellular organisms, cells are generally specialized and carry out a specific function. **19.** They do not seem related in that algae are photosynthetic and protozoa are heterotrophic. They do seem related in that some of the algae are motile in the same way protozoa are.

3 1

THE FUNGI

Fungi are saprotrophic multicellular eukaryotes. The body of a fungus is composed of **hyphae,** collectively called a **mycelium.** Hyphae produce nonmotile and often windblown **spores** during both asexual and sexual reproduction.

During sexual reproduction, hyphae tips fuse; **dikaryotic** hyphae result before zygote formation and zygotic meiosis occur. The **zygospore** fungi are **non-septate,** and during sexual reproduction, they form a thick-walled **zygospore.** The sac fungi are **septate,** and during sexual reproduction, dikaryotic hyphae end in saclike cells (**asci**) within a **fruiting body** that produces spores. The club fungi are septate, and during sexual reproduction, dikaryotic hyphae end in club-shaped structures called **basidia** that produce spores. Sexual reproduction has not been observed in imperfect fungi.

Fungi form symbiotic relationships with algae in **lichens** and with seed plants in **mycorrhizae.**

Study the text section by section as you answer the questions that follow.

31.1 WHAT FUNGI ARE LIKE (P. 540)

- Fungi are saprotrophic decomposers that aid the cycling of inorganic nutrients in ecosystems.
- The body of a fungus is multicellular; it is composed of thin filaments called hyphae.
- As an adaptation to life on land, fungi produce nonmotile and often windblown spores during asexual and sexual reproduction.

1. Indicate whether the following statements about fungi are true (T) or false (F):
   _____ a. usually multicellular
   _____ b. usually unicellular
   _____ c. composed of hyphae
   _____ d. saprotrophic
   _____ e. can be parasitic
   _____ f. can be photosynthetic
   _____ g. cell wall contains cellulose
   _____ h. cell wall contains chitin
   _____ i. have flagella at some time in their life cycle
   _____ j. do not have flagella at any time in their life cycle
   _____ k. form spores only during asexual reproduction
   _____ l. form spores during both asexual and sexual reproduction

2. Fungi are mostly ᵃ·_____ decomposers that assist in the recycling of nutrients in ecosystems.
   The bodies of most fungi are made up of filaments called ᵇ·_____, a collection of which are
   called a(n) ᶜ·_____. They reproduce in accordance with the ᵈ·_____ life cycle.
   Classification is largely based on the mode of ᵉ·_____.

31.2 How Fungi Are Classified (p. 542)

- Fungi are classified according to aspects of their sexual life cycle. Zygospore fungi have a dormant stage consisting of a thick-walled zygospore.

3. Match the types of mushrooms with the following divisions:

   1 division Zygomycota
   2 division Ascomycota
   3 division Basidiomycota
   4 division Deuteromycota

   _____ a. club fungi
   _____ b. zygospore fungi
   _____ c. sac fungi
   _____ d. imperfect fungi
   _____ e. mushrooms
   _____ f. cup fungi
   _____ g. bread mold
   _____ h. *Penicillium*

Zygospore Fungi Form Zygospores (p. 542)

4. Label this diagram of the life cycle of black bread mold with the following terms (some are used more than once):

   asexual reproduction
   gametangia fuse
   meiosis
   mycelium
   nuclear fusion
   sexual reproduction
   sporangiophore
   sporangium
   spores
   zygospore
   zygote

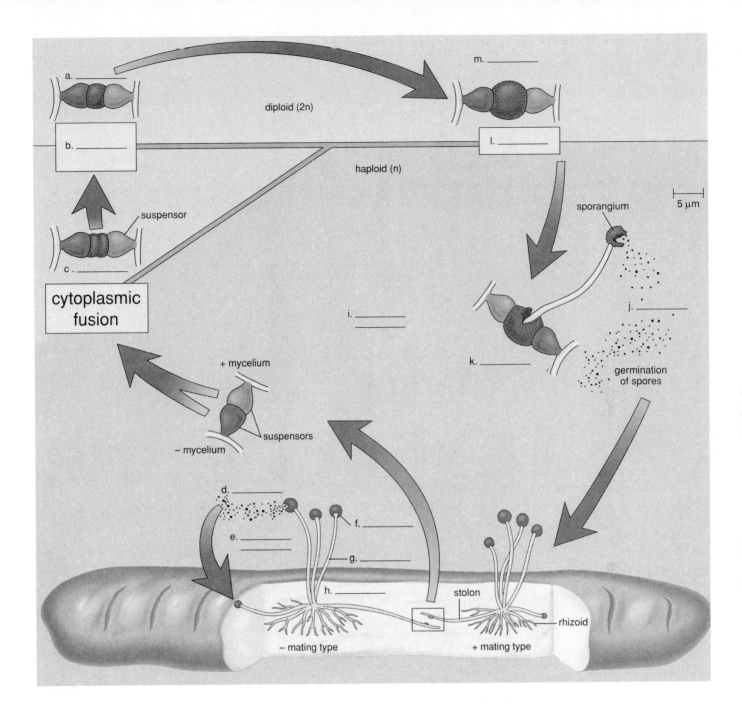

diploid (2n)

haploid (n)

a. _____
m. _____
b. _____
l. _____
c. _____
suspensor
5 μm
sporangium
cytoplasmic fusion
i. _____
j. _____
k. _____
germination of spores
+ mycelium
suspensors
– mycelium
d. _____
e. _____
f. _____
g. _____
h. _____
stolon
rhizoid
– mating type
+ mating type

5. Answer these questions based on the life cycle of the black bread mold.

Is the adult diploid or haploid? a._____

In which cycle (asexual or sexual) are haploid spores produced? b._____

Where are the spores produced? c._____

What is the name of the enlarged diploid zygote formed in sexual reproduction? d._____

How are the spores dispersed from the sporangium? e._____

Sac Fungi Form Ascospores (p. 545)

• During sexual reproduction of sac fungi, saclike cells (asci) produce spores. Asci are located in fruiting bodies.

6. Label each of the following as describing a free-living sac fungi (F) or a parasitic sac fungi (P):
   _____ a. powdery mildew that grows on leaves
   _____ b. red mold that grows on bread
   _____ c. cup fungi that grows on the forest floor
   _____ d. chestnut blight that grows on chestnut trees
   _____ e. ergot that grows on rye plants
   _____ f. unicellular yeasts

7. Why are all these fungi classified as sac fungi? _____
   _____

8. Explain what is happening in each of the following sequential drawings of asci:

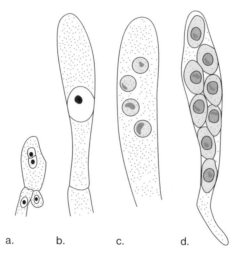

   a.   b.   c.   d.

Club Fungi Have Basidiospores (p. 547)

• During sexual reproduction of club fungi, club-shaped structures (basidia) produce spores. Basidia are located in fruiting bodies.

9. What do mushrooms, puffballs, bird's nest fungi, stinkhorn fungi, and bracket fungi have in common?
   _____

10. Name two well-known parasites of cereal crops. _____

11. Label this diagram of the life cycle of a mushroom with the following terms:

basidiospores	*gill (portion of)*
basidium	*meiosis*
cap	*monokaryotic*
cytoplasmic fusion	*nuclear fusion*
dikaryotic (n+n)	*nuclei*
dikaryotic mycelium	*spore germination*
diploid (2n)	*spore release*
fruiting body	*stalk*
gill	*zygote*

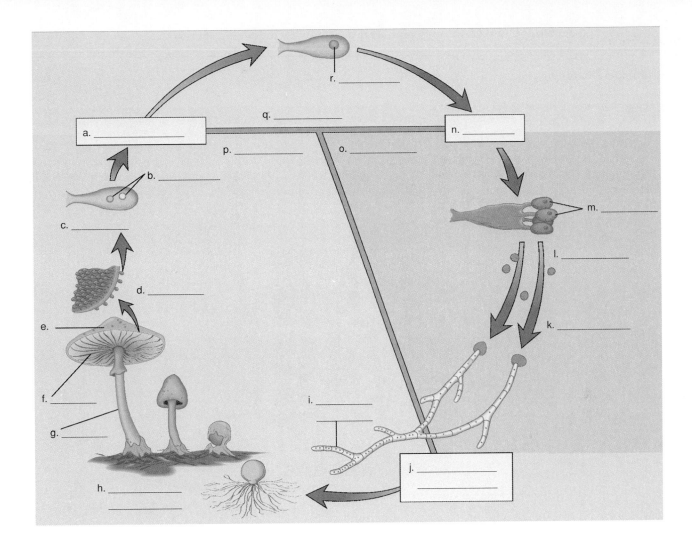

12. In the life cycle of a mushroom, the basidiocarp is a(n) ^{a.}_____ in which club-shaped structures
    called ^{b.}_____ form where ^{c.}_____ are produced. Beneath each mushroom is a
    dikaryotic ^{d.}_____ that exists for years.

Imperfect Fungi Reproduce Asexually Only (p. 549)

- The fungi imperfecti always reproduce asexually by conidiospores; sexual reproduction has not yet been
  observed in these organisms.

13. Complete the following table:

Fungus	Significance	Associated Disease
Penicillium		
Aspergillus		
Candida albicans		

14. Like sac and club fungi, imperfect fungi reproduce asexually by producing spores
called a._____. Unlike sac and club fungi, however, sexual reproduction b._____
in imperfect fungi.

31.3 FUNGI FORM SYMBIOTIC RELATIONSHIPS (P. 549)

- Lichens, which may live in stressful environments, are an association between a fungus and a cyanobacterium
  or a green alga. The fungus may be somewhat parasitic on the alga.
- Mycorrhizae is an association between a fungus and the roots of a plant, such that the fungus helps the plant
  absorb minerals, and the plant supplies the fungus with carbohydrates.

15. Label this diagram of a lichen with the following terms: *algal cells* and *hyphae of fungus*.

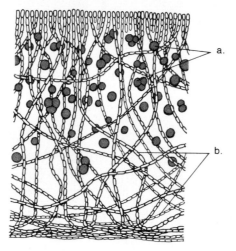

a.

b.

16. Match the type of lichen with the following descriptions:
    1 compact
    2 leaflike
    3 shrublike
    _____ a. crustose
    _____ b. fruticose
    _____ c. foliose

17. a._____ (fungus roots), which are b._____ relationships between

    a(n) c._____ and d._____ roots, help plants acquire e._____

    nutrients.

Review key terms by completing this crossword puzzle, using the following alphabetized list of terms:

ascus
basidium
conidiospore
fruiting body
fungus
hypha
lichen
mycelium
mycorrhiza
sporangium
zygospore

Across

1 fingerlike sac in which nuclear fusion, meiosis, and ascospore formation occur during the sexual reproduction of the sac fungi

4 symbiotic relationship between fungal hyphae and roots of vascular plants; the fungus allows the plant to absorb more mineral ions and obtains carbohydrates from the plant

6 clublike structure in which nuclear fusion and meiosis occur and basidiospores are produced during the sexual reproduction of club fungi

8 spore produced by sac and club fungi during asexual reproduction

9 symbiotic relationship between certain fungi and algae, which has long been thought to be mutualistic, in which the fungi provide inorganic food and the algae provide organic food

10 tangled mass of hyphal filaments composing the vegetative body of a fungus

11 saprotrophic decomposer; the body is made up of filaments called hyphae that form a mass called a mycelium

Down

2 capsule that produces sporangiospores

3 filament of the vegetative body of a fungus

5 thick-walled, resting cell formed during sexual reproduction of zygospore fungi

7 spore-producing and spore-disseminating structure found in sac and club fungi (two words)

OBJECTIVE QUESTIONS

Do not refer to the text when taking this test.

_____ 1. Most fungi
  a. are plant parasites.
  b. form mycorrhizae.
  c. are saprotrophic.
  d. are deuteromycetes.

_____ 2. Which terms are mismatched?
  a. hyphae—mycelium
  b. ascocarp—fruiting body
  c. basidiospore—sporangium
  d. zygomycete—bread mold

_____ 3. Yeasts
  a. usually reproduce by budding.
  b. never form spores.
  c. are dikaryotic.
  d. All of these are correct.

_____ 4. Nonseptate describes a fungus
  a. whose means of sexual reproduction is unknown.
  b. whose hyphae do not have cross walls.
  c. whose hyphae are dikaryotic.
  d. that is parasitic.

_____ 5. Club fungi
  a. include the mushrooms.
  b. have a basidiocarp that looks like a cup.
  c. include more parasites than all the other types of fungi.
  d. All of these are correct.

_____ 6. Which of these is mismatched?
  a. red bread molds—zygomycete
  b. bracket fungi—basidiomycete
  c. yeasts—ascomycete
  d. rust and smuts—basidiomycetes

_____ 7. Conidiospores are
  a. formed asexually.
  b. formed sexually.
  c. formed either asexually or sexually.
  d. never formed.

_____ 8. In fungi, the gametes are
  a. heterogametes.
  b. flagellated.
  c. the ends of hyphae.
  d. produced by meiosis.

_____ 9. Rusts and smuts
  a. parasitize cereal crops.
  b. are found infrequently.
  c. do not form basidiocarps.
  d. Both _a_ and _c_ are correct.

For questions 10–15 match the terms with the following types of fungi (fungi types are used more than once; each question can have more than one answer):
  a. bread mold
  b. sac fungi
  c. club fungi
  d. other fungi

_____10. conidiospores

_____11. athlete's foot

_____12. sporangia

_____13. fruiting bodies

_____14. cup fungi

_____15. bracket fungi

_____16. Which of the following is NOT characteristic of lichens?
  a. soil formers
  b. algal cells and fungal hyphae
  c. form a type of moss
  d. can live in extreme conditions

_____17. Which of the following is NOT true of fungi?
  a. saprotrophic nutrition
  b. eukaryotic cells
  c. reproduce by means of spores
  d. are always multicellular

_____18. A fruiting body is
  a. a special type of vacuole found in fungi.
  b. a symbiotic relationship between algae and bacteria.
  c. a reproductive structure found in fungi.
  d. always the same shape.

_____19. Sexual reproduction in a bread mold involves the production of
  a. a sperm and an egg.
  b. flagellated zoospores.
  c. zygospores.
  d. fruiting bodies.

_____20. In a mushroom, the _____ is (are) analogous to the asci of a sac fungus.
  a. stalk
  b. cap
  c. basidia
  d. spores

Answer in complete sentences.

21. How have yeasts proven invaluable to human civilization?

22. How do you think the earth would change ecologically if fungi were not present?

Test Results: _____ Number right ÷ 22 = _____ × 100 = _____ %

EXPLORING THE INTERNET

Use the Internet to further explore topics in this chapter, such as edible and poisonous mushrooms or lichens. Go to the Mader Home Page (http://www.mhhe.com.sciencemath/biology/mader) and click on *Biology,* 6th edition. Go to Chapter 31 and select a Web site of interest.

ANSWER KEY

STUDY EXERCISES

1. a. T **b.** F **c.** T **d.** T **e.** T **f.** F **g.** F **h.** T **i.** F **j.** T **k.** F **l.** T **2. a.** saprotrophic **b.** hyphae **c.** mycelium **d.** haplontic **e.** sexual reproduction **3. a.** 3 **b.** 1 **c.** 2 **d.** 4 **e.** 3 **f.** 2 **g.** 1 **h.** 4 **4.** See Figure 31.3, page 543, in text. **5. a.** haploid **b.** both **c.** in the sporangia **d.** zygospore **e.** by the wind **6. a.** P **b.** F **c.** F **d.** P **e.** P **f.** F **7.** because they form asci during sexual reproduction **8. a.** Ascus with two nuclei is forming. **b.** Nuclei have fused, and zygote has formed. **c.** Meiosis has occurred. **d.** A mitotic division has resulted in eight ascospores **9.** They are all basidiomycetes. **10.** rust and smuts **11.** See Figure 31.6, page 546, in text. **12. a.** fruiting body **b.** basidia **c.** basidiospores **d.** mycelium

13.

Significance	Associated Disease
makes penicillin	none
makes various chemicals	none
yeastlike	vaginal infections

14. a. conidiospores **b.** has never been observed **15. a.** algal cells **b.** hyphae of fungus **16. a.** 1 **b.** 3 **c.** 2 **17. a.** Mycorrhizae **b.** symbiotic **c.** fungus **d.** plant **e.** mineral

KEYWORD CROSSWORD

CHAPTER TEST

1. c **2.** c **3.** a **4.** b **5.** a **6.** a **7.** a **8.** c **9.** a **10.** b, c **11.** d **12.** a **13.** b, c **14.** b **15.** c **16.** c **17.** d **18.** c **19.** c **20.** c **21.** Yeast makes bread rise, and bread is the staff of life in many parts of the world. Yeast is also used to make wine, and in some countries where the purity of the drinking water is in question, wine is the preferred drink at meals. Today, yeast is used for recombinant DNA experiments that require a eukaryote as the experimental material. **22.** Recycling would falter, and organic waste would accumulate. Without efficient recycling, the carrying capacities of ecosystems would diminish.

32

THE PLANTS

Plants are multicellular photosynthetic organisms living on land that protect the developing embryo from desiccation. All plants utilize the alternation of generations life cycle.

The nonvascular plants include the **liverworts** and **mosses** in which the **gametophyte** is dominant. Flagellated sperm swim from the **antheridia** to the **archegonia,** and in mosses the **sporophyte** is a stalk plus a capsule where spores form.

The extinct rhyniophytes may be ancestral to such seedless vascular plants as **whisk ferns, club mosses, horsetails,** and **ferns.** Ferns have a separate and water-dependent gametophyte. The zygote develops into the dominant sporophyte with large fronds.

Seed plants produce heterospores; therefore, microgametophytes and megagametophytes are separate. The microgametophyte is the mature **pollen grain** that produces sperm, and the megagametophyte produces an egg. Fertilization results in an embryo enclosed within a seed. **Gymnosperms** produce naked seeds; **angiosperms** produce seeds covered by **fruit** derived from an **ovary,** which is part of the flower. Development of the flower, which attracts insects that carry out cross-fertilization, allowed angiosperms to spread and become the dominant plant today.

STUDY EXERCISES

Study the text section by section as you answer the questions that follow.

32.1 WHAT IS A PLANT? (P. 554)

- Plants are photosynthetic organisms adapted to living on land. Among various adaptations, all plants have an alternation of generations life cycle.
- The presence of vascular tissue and reproductive strategy are used to compare plants.

1. Indicate whether the following statements about plants are true (T) or false (F):
   - _____ a. adapted to living on land
   - _____ b. diploid sporophyte produces diploid spores
   - _____ c. haploid gametophyte, which produces sex cells
   - _____ d. photosynthetic organisms
2. Match the plants to the following plant categories (the categories can be used more than once):
   1 bryophytes
   2 seedless vascular plants
   3 gymnosperms
   4 angiosperms
   - _____ a. club mosses
   - _____ b. conifers
   - _____ c. mosses
   - _____ d. division Magnoliophyta
   - _____ e. ferns
   - _____ f. cycads

- The nonvascular plants are the bryophytes (e.g., liverworts and mosses), which are low-growing. In bryophytes, the gametophyte (haploid generation) is dominant, and windblown spores disperse the species.

3. Label this diagram of part of a moss life cycle with the following terms: *antheridium, archegonium, egg,* and *sperm.*

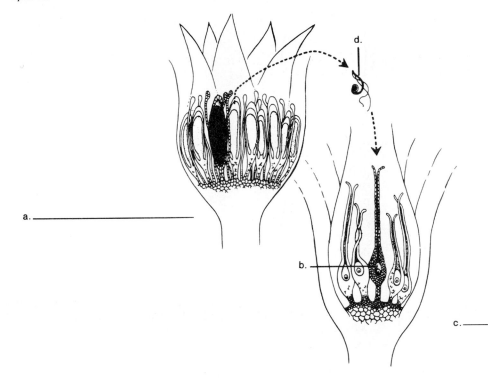

a._____

b._____

c._____

d._____

4. In the diagram in question 3, the antheridium and archegonium are part of what

   generation? a._____

   Do mosses have flagellated sperm? b._____

   Do mosses protect the zygote? c._____

5. Is the sporophyte generation dependent on the gametophyte generation in the moss? a._____

   Do either of these generations have vascular tissue? b._____ The capsule contains the

   sporangium where the cellular process of c._____ occurs during the production

   of d._____. The latter disperse the species. When they germinate,

   a(n) e._____ forms to begin the f._____ generation.

6. The a._____ anchor the moss gametophyte plant in the soil while absorbing minerals and

   water. There must be an external source of b._____ for the sperm to move from

   the c._____ to the eggs found in the d._____.

7. Label this diagram of part of the moss life cycle with the following terms: *capsule, gametophyte generation, rhizoids,* and *sporophyte generation.*

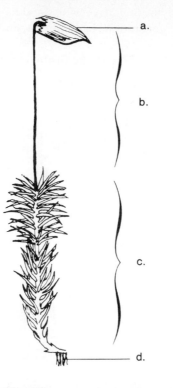

a. _____

b. _____

c. _____

d. _____

32.3 VASCULAR PLANTS INCLUDE SEEDLESS AND SEED PLANTS (P. 558)

- In vascular plants, the dominant sporophyte (diploid generation) has transport tissue.
- In seedless vascular plants, windblown spores disperse the species, and in seed plants, seeds disperse the species.

8. In all vascular plants, the a._____ generation is the dominant generation, and it is b._____ (*haploid/diploid*). c._____ vascular tissue conducts water and minerals up from the soil. d._____ vascular tissue transports organic nutrients from one part of the body to another. An advantage of a diploid plant is that a functional gene can e._____ a faulty gene.

9. Indicate whether the statements that follow are true (T) or false (F). Rewrite the false statement(s) to be true.

_____ a. All vascular plants produce pollen grains and seeds. _____

_____

_____ b. Spores disperse seedless vascular plants, while seeds disperse seed plants. _____

_____

_____ c. In all vascular plants, the gametophyte generation is dependent on the sporophyte. _____

_____

- The seedless vascular plants were much larger and extremely abundant during the Carboniferous period.
- The fern sporophyte is the familiar plant with large fronds that produces windblown spores; the independent gametophyte is a heart-shaped structure that produces flagellated sperm.

10. Indicate whether the following descriptions of rhyniophytes are true (T) or false (F):

    _____ a. had true stem, roots, and leaves

    _____ b. spores were produced without benefit of sporangia

    _____ c. had a forked stem, no roots or leaves

11. Match the descriptions to the following plants:

    1 whisk ferns
    2 club mosses
    3 horsetails
    4 ferns

    _____ a. Scalelike leaves cover stems and branches; there are terminal strobili.

    _____ b. Whorls of slender branches form at the nodes of the stem, where the leaves are; they are sometimes called scouring rushes.

    _____ c. These plants, alive today, best resemble *Rhynia*.

    _____ d. Large fronds subdivide into leaflets.

12. Label this diagram of part of the fern life cycle with the following terms: *antheridium, archegonium,* and *rhizoid.*

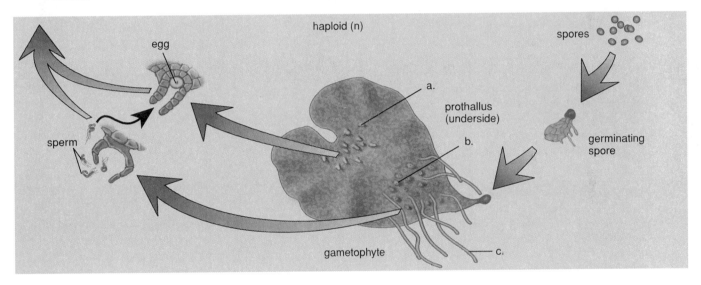

13. In the diagram in question 12, this entire structure is called the a._____. This structure has

    a(n) b._____ shape and represents the c._____ generation.

    It d._____ (*does/does not*) have vascular tissue and e._____ (*does/does not*)

    have flagellated sperm. The sporophyte f._____ (*is/is not*) the dominant

    generation. g._____ disperse the species.

14. Label this diagram of part of the life cycle of a fern with the following terms: *fiddlehead, frond, rhizome,* and *sorus.*

wood fern, *Dryopterus*

diploid (2n)

15. The frond is part of the ª._____ generation in the fern, and it ᵇ._____ (*does/does not*) have vascular tissue. This generation is ᶜ._____ (*diploid/haploid*).

16. Label the following as a bryophyte (B) or fern (F):
    _____ a. peat moss
    _____ b. ornamental
    _____ c. Native Americans used this during childbirth

32.5 GYMNOSPERMS HAVE NAKED SEEDS (P. 564)

- There are four divisions of gymnosperms; the familiar conifers and the little-known cycads, ginkgo, and gnetophytes.
- The conifer sporophyte is usually a cone-bearing tree (e.g., pine tree). The pollen cones produce pollen (male gametophyte), which is windblown to the seed cone, where windblown seeds are produced.

17. Label the following diagram, showing the alternation of generations in seed plants with the notation n or 2n:

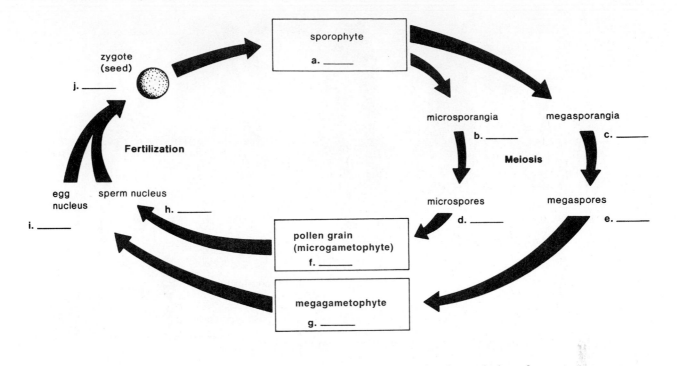

18. Is the gametophyte generation dependent on the sporophyte generation in seed plants?
a._____ Does the sporophyte generation have vascular tissue? b._____ What structure in seed plants replaces flagellated sperm in nonseed plants? c._____ What structure disperses the species in seed plants? d._____

19. Match the descriptions with the following types of gymnosperms:
   1 conifer
   2 cycad
   3 ginkgo
   4 gnetophytes
   _____ a. includes *Ephedra,* the gymnosperm most closely related to angiosperms
   _____ b. stout, unbranched stem with large, compound leaves
   _____ c. fan-shaped leaves shed in autumn; planted in parks
   _____ d. pine trees, hemlocks, spruces

20. Study this diagram of the life cycle of a pine tree and then describe the numbered events.

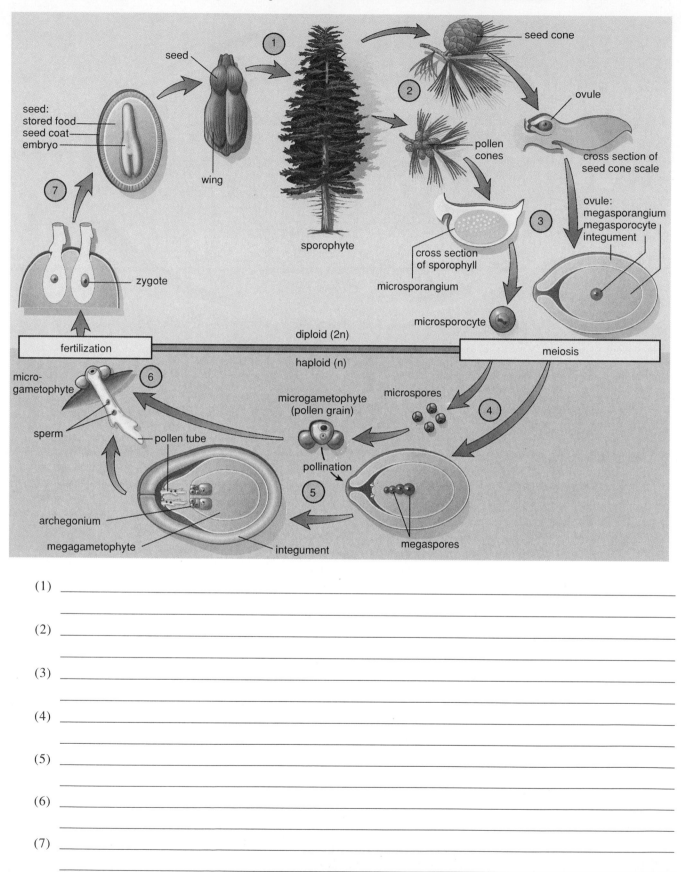

(1) _____

_____

(2) _____

_____

(3) _____

_____

(4) _____

_____

(5) _____

_____

(6) _____

_____

(7) _____

_____

21. Gymnosperms have an alternation of generations life cycle. Which structure in the diagram in question 20 is described in each of the following?

is the sporophyte ᵃ·_____

produces the microspore ᵇ·_____

produces the megaspore ᶜ·_____

is the microgametophyte ᵈ·_____

contains the megagametophyte ᵉ·_____

contains the sperm ᶠ·_____

contains the egg ᵍ·_____

contains the embryonic sporophyte ʰ·_____

32.6 ANGIOSPERMS HAVE COVERED SEEDS (P. 567)

- Angiosperms are the very diversified flowering plants, which may depend on an animal pollinator to carry pollen to another flower. The seeds are enclosed within a fruit, which often assists dispersal of seeds.

22. Label each of the following statements as describing either a monocot (M) or a dicot (D):
    _____ a. almost always herbaceous
    _____ b. either woody or herbaceous
    _____ c. flower parts in fours or fives
    _____ d. flower parts in threes
    _____ e. net-veined leaves
    _____ f. parallel-veined leaves
    _____ g. vascular bundles arranged in a circle in the stem
    _____ h. vascular bundles scattered in the stem

23. Label this diagram of the structures of a flower with the following terms: *anther, ovary,* and *ovule.*

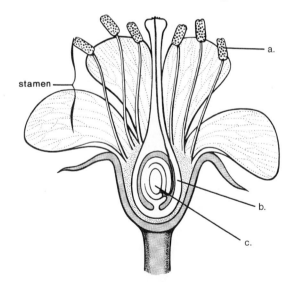

stamen

a.

b.

c.

24. Study this diagram of the life cycle of a flowering plant and then describe the numbered events.

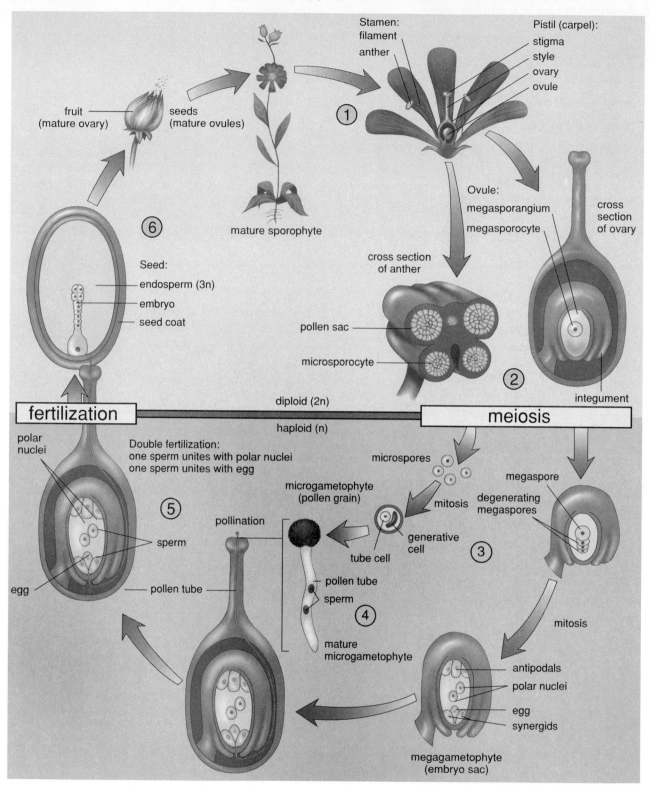

(1) _____
_____

(2) _____
_____

(3) _____
_____

(4) _____
_____

(5) _____
_____

(6) _____
_____

25. Flowering plants have an alternation of generations life cycle. Which structure in the diagram in question 24 is described in each of the following?

is the sporophyte a._____

produces the microspore b._____

produces the megaspore c._____

is the microgametophyte d._____

contains the megagametophyte e._____

contains the sperm f._____

contains the egg g._____

contains the embryonic sporophyte h._____

matures to become a fruit i._____

26. The color and arrangement of flower parts are designed to a._____.

A flower, which is necessary to the reproduction of flowering plants, contains b._____
_____.

A flower produces seeds enclosed by c._____, which helps d._____.

27. Complete the following table to compare the different plants:

Plant	Vascular Tissue (yes or no)	Dominant Generation	Spores or Seeds Disperse Species	Fruit (yes or no)
mosses				
ferns				
gymnosperms				
angiosperms				

1. Players are given a set of cups of different colors and sizes.
   a. Sort these cups according to size as quickly as you can. Each different size represents a category in the classification system.
   b. Sort the cups according to color as quickly as you can. The different colors represent the different kingdoms (and the organisms within) of the classification system.

   Cups

plants	*cyanobacteria*	*slime mold*
protozoa	*algae*	*protists*
viruses	*mosses*	*bacteria*
flowers	*nonvascular plants*	*vascular plants*
monera	*fungi*	*fern*
pine		

2. Players are given disks and required to flip them into the correct cup. A small disk goes into a small cup, and a large disk goes into a large cup. (More than one disk can go into a cup.)

   Disks

   a. *toxins*
   b. *red, brown, golden brown, green, multicolored*
   c. *single cell, motile, food vacuoles*
   d. *live on the land*
   e. *trees*
   f. *vascular tissue*
   g. *lack nucleus*
   h. *protect the embryo*
   i. *saprotrophic*
   j. *photosynthesis*
   k. *alternation of generations*
   l. *haplontic cycle*
   m. *alive?*
   n. *malaria*
   o. *bacteriophage*
   p. Amoeba, Paramecium, Euglena
   q. *zygospore, sac, club, imperfect*
   r. *heterospores*
   s. *fruit*
   t. *fruiting body*
   u. *hyphae*
   v. *rhizoids, shoot, leaflets*
   w. *zoospores*
   x. *naked seeds*
   y. *pollen carried by insects*
   z. *endospores*
   aa. *plasmodium*
   bb. *monocot and dicot*
   cc. *fronds*

Review key terms by completing this crossword puzzle, using the following alphabetized list of terms:

angiosperm
antheridium
archegonium
conifer
dicotyledon
fruit
gametophyte
gymnosperm
herbaceous
monocotyledon
phloem
pollen
rhizoid
sporophyte
woody
xylem

Across

2 flowering plant group; members show one embryonic leaf, parallel-veined leaves, scattered vascular bundles, and other characteristics

6 reproductive organ found in bryophytes and some vascular plants that produces an egg

7 flowering plant structure, consisting of one or more ripened ovaries, that usually contains seeds

10 vascular tissue that transports water and mineral solutes upward through the plant body

11 plant that contains wood; types include gymnosperms and angiosperms

12 vascular plant producing naked seeds, as in conifers

14 plant that lacks persistent woody tissue

15 microgametophyte in seed plants

Down

1 flowering plant; the seeds are borne within a fruit

3 one of the four groups of gymnosperm plants; cone-bearing trees that include pine, cedar, and spruce

4 flowering plant group; members show two embryonic leaves, net-veined leaves, cylindrical arrangement of vascular bundles, and other characteristics

5 diploid generation of the alternation of generations life cycle of a plant; meiosis produces haploid spores that develop into the haploid generation

6 reproductive organ, found in bryophytes and some vascular plants, that produces flagellated sperm

8 rootlike hair that anchors a plant and absorbs minerals and water from the soil

9 haploid generation of the alternation of generations life cycle of a plant; it produces gametes that unite to form a diploid zygote

13 vascular tissue that conducts organic solutes in plants; it contains sieve-tube cells and companion cells

OBJECTIVE QUESTIONS

Do not refer to the text when taking this test.

_____ 1. Select the incorrect association.
   a. gametophyte—diploid generation
   b. gametophyte—produces sex cells
   c. sporophyte—diploid generation
   d. sporophyte—produces haploid spores

_____ 2. Select the nonvascular plant.
   a. bryophyte
   b. cycad
   c. fern
   d. rosebush

_____ 3. The antheridium is part of the
   a. megagametophyte.
   b. megasporophyte.
   c. microgametophyte.
   d. microsporophyte.

_____ 4. Rhyniophytes are significant because they
   a. are currently the most successful conifers.
   b. are currently the most successful flowering plants.
   c. were the first to evolve flowers.
   d. were the first to evolve vascular tissue.

_____ 5. Xylem and phloem are
   a. the covering tissues on roots, stems, and leaves.
   b. the male and female parts of a flower.
   c. two kinds of flowering plants.
   d. two types of vascular tissue.

_____ 6. Ferns are plants that are
   a. nonvascular with seeds.
   b. nonvascular without seeds.
   c. vascular with seeds.
   d. vascular without seeds.

_____ 7. Which structure develops into a pollen grain?
   a. antheridium
   b. archegonium
   c. megaspore
   d. microspore

_____ 8. Select the characteristic NOT descriptive of conifers.
   a. can withstand cold winters
   b. can withstand hot summers
   c. needlelike leaves
   d. reproduce through flowers

_____ 9. Select the incorrect statement about angiosperms.
   a. contain only tracheids in their vascular tissue
   b. did not diversify until the Cenozoic era
   c. include tiny plants living on pond surfaces
   d. the most successful group of plants

_____10. Select the incorrect association.
   a. dicot—woody or herbaceous
   b. dicot—vascular bundles arranged in a circle within the stem
   c. monocot—almost always herbaceous
   d. monocot—net-veined leaf

_____11. In comparing alternation of generations for non-seed and seed plants, it is apparent that seed plants have
   a. flowers only.
   b. heterospores.
   c. flagellated sperm.
   d. megagametophytes and microgametophytes.
   e. Both _b_ and _d_ are correct.

_____12. The fern is a nonseed plant and
   a. is a bryophyte.
   b. has flagellated sperm.
   c. lacks vascular tissue.
   d. All of these are correct.

_____13. The dominant generation in the seed plants is the
   a. sporophyte.
   b. gametophyte.
   c. green leafy shoot.
   d. flower only.

_____14. Ferns are restricted to moist places because
   a. of the sporophyte generation called the frond.
   b. of a sensitive type of chlorophyll.
   c. of the water-dependent gametophyte generation.
   d. they never grow very tall.

_____15. In the life cycle of seed plants, meiosis
   a. produces the gametes.
   b. produces microspores and megaspores.
   c. does not occur.
   d. produces spores.

_____16. Double fertilization refers to the fact that in angiosperms
   a. two egg cells are fertilized within an ovule.
   b. a sperm nucleus fuses with an egg cell and with polar nuclei.
   c. two sperm are required for fertilization of one egg cell.
   d. a flower can engage in both self-pollination and cross-pollination.

____17. Identify the correct order of life cycle stages in a moss.
  a. gametophyte—sporophyte—spores—zygote—protonema
  b. sporophyte—spores—protonema—gametes—zygote
  c. gametophyte—spores—sporophyte—gametes—zygote
  d. zygote—sporophyte—gametophyte—spores—protonema
____18. The sporangia of a fern is generally
  a. at the tips of the rhizomes.
  b. on the bottom surface of the prothallus.
  c. inside the fiddleheads.
  d. at the point where leaves join the stem.
  e. on the undersides of fronds.

____19. In which of these groups is the gametophyte nutritionally dependent upon the sporophyte?
  a. ferns
  b. angiosperms
  c. gymnosperms
  d. Both *b* and *c* are correct.
  e. All of these are correct.
____20. In pine trees, _____ develop in separate types of cones.
  a. microgametophytes and megagametophytes
  b. pollen and ovules
  c. microspores and megaspores
  d. Both *a* and *b* are correct.
  e. All of these are correct.

CRITICAL THINKING QUESTIONS

Answer in complete sentences.

21. What do you think will be the impact on human life if there is a major extinction of plants during the next century?

22. Should algae be considered plants? Offer reasons why they should and should not be classified this way.

Test Results: _____ Number right ÷ 22 = _____ × 100 = _____ %

EXPLORING THE INTERNET

Use the Internet to further explore topics in this chapter, such as the plant families and the ecology of cycads. Go to the Mader Home Page (http://www.mhhe.com/sciencemath/biology/mader/) and click on *Biology*, 6th edition. Go to Chapter 32 and select a Web site of interest.

ANSWER KEY

STUDY EXERCISES

1. a. T **b.** F **c.** T **d.** T **2. a.** 2 **b.** 3 **c.** 1 **d.** 4 **e.** 2 **f.** 3 **3. a.** antheridium **b.** egg **c.** archegonium **d.** sperm **4. a.** gametophyte **b.** yes **c.** yes **5. a.** yes **b.** no **c.** meiosis **d.** spores **e.** protonema **f.** gametophyte **6. a.** rhizoids **b.** water **c.** antheridia **d.** archegonia **7. a.** capsule **b.** sporophyte generation **c.** gametophyte generation **d.** rhizoids **8. a.** sporophyte **b.** diploid **c.** Xylem **d.** Phloem **e.** mask **9. a.** F. Only gymnosperms and angiosperms produce pollen grains and seeds. **b.** T **c.** F. In most seed vascular plants, the gametophyte generation is dependent on the sporophyte. **10. a.** F **b.** F **c.** T **11. a.** 2 **b.** 3 **c.** 1 **d.** 4 **12. a.** archegonium **b.** antheridium **c.** rhi-

zoid **13. a.** prothallus **b.** heart **c.** gametophyte **d.** does not **e.** does **f.** is **g.** Spores **14. a.** frond **b.** sorus **c.** fiddlehead **d.** rhizome **15. a.** sporophyte **b.** does **c.** diploid **16. a.** B **b.** F **c.** F **17. a.** 2n **b.** 2n **c.** 2n **d.** n **e.** n **f.** n **g.** n **h.** n **i.** n **j.** 2n **18. a.** yes **b.** yes **c.** pollen grain **d.** seed **19. a.** 4 **b.** 2 **c.** 3 **d.** 1 **20.** (1) Sporophyte is dominant. (2) pollen cones and seed cones (3) microsporangia on lower surface of pollen cone; megasporangia on upper surface of seed cone inside ovule (4) Meiosis produces microspores/megaspores. (5) Each microspore develops in a microgametophyte (pollen grain); one megaspore develops into a megagametophyte. (6) Pollen tube delivers sperm to egg. (7) Ovule becomes seed. **21. a.** tree **b.** microsporangium on scale of pollen cone **c.** megasporangium inside ovule on scale of seed cone **d.** pollen grain **e.** ovule **f.** mature microgametophyte (pollen grain) **g.** megagametophyte inside ovule **h.** seed   **22. a.** M **b.** D **c.** D **d.** M **e.** D **f.** M **g.** D **h.** M   **23. a.** anther **b.** ovary **c.** ovule   **24.** (1) Flower contains stamens and pistil. (2) Megasporocyte produces four haploid megaspores; microsporocyte produces four haploid microspores. (3) One functional megaspore survives and divides mitotically; microgametophyte contains generative cell nucleus and tube cell nucleus. (4) Megagametophyte results and consists of eight haploid nuclei; pollen grain germinates and produces a pollen tube. (5) Double fertilization occurs; one sperm fertilizes the egg, and the other joins with the polar nuclei. (6) Seed contains endosperm, embryo, and seed coat.   **25. a.** flowering plant **b.** pollen sac **c.** megasporangium inside ovule **d.** pollen grain **e.** ovule **f.** pollen tube **g.** megagametophyte (embryo sac) **h.** seed **i.** ovary   **26. a.** attract pollinators **b.** micro- and megasporangia where microspores and megaspores are produced **c.** fruit **d.** disperse the species

27.

Vascular Tissue (yes or no)	Dominant Generation	Spores or Seeds Disperse Species	Fruit (yes or no)
no	gametophyte	spores	no
yes	sporophyte	spores	no
yes	sporophyte	seeds	no
yes	sporophyte	seeds	fruit

CLASSIFICATION TIDDLEDYWINKS

1. a. Size: largest: kingdoms = monera, protists, plants next: groups = bryophytes, vascular plants; next: organisms = all the rest **b.** Colors: **1.** monera: bacteria, including cyanobacteria **2.** protists: algae, protozoa, slime mold **3.** fungi **4.** plants: nonvascular plants (mosses), vascular plants (includes all others)

2. a. bacteria **b.** algae **c.** protozoa **d.** plants **e.** pine, flower **f.** vascular plants **g.** monera **h.** plants **i.** fungi **j.** plants, algae **k.** plants **l.** protists **m.** viruses **n.** protozoa **o.** viruses **p.** protozoa **q.** fungi **r.** pine, flower **s.** flower **t.** fungi **u.** fungi **v.** mosses **w.** algae **x.** pine **y.** flower **z.** bacteria **aa.** slime mold **bb.** flower **cc.** fern

KEYWORD CROSSWORD

CHAPTER TEST

1. a **2.** a **3.** c **4.** d **5.** d **6.** d **7.** d **8.** d **9.** a **10.** d **11.** e **12.** b **13.** a **14.** c **15.** b **16.** b **17.** b **18.** e **19.** d **20.** e **21.** The ecologic and economic contributions of plants will be lost. Examples include loss of food production and inability to maintain a balance of gases in the atmosphere.   **22.** They are photosynthetic producers, so in this way, they should be considered plants. However, they lack the adaptations for terrestrial life so in this way, they should not be considered plants.

33

ANIMALS: INTRODUCTION TO INVERTEBRATES

Animals are multicellular, locomote by contracting fibers, and ingest their food. They all have the diplontic life cycle, but differ in a number of ways by which they are classified. Many animals, such as those discussed in this chapter, are **invertebrates.**

Sponges have the cellular level of organization and lack tissues and symmetry. Sponges are **sessile filter feeders** and depend on a flow of water through the body to acquire food which is digested in vacuoles within color cells that line a central cavity.

Cnidaria and **comb jellies** have two tissue layers and are radially symmetrical. Cnidaria have a sac body plan and exist as either polyps (e.g., *Hydra*) of medusae, (e.g., jellyfishes) or they can alternate between the two (e.g., *Obelia*).

Flatworms and **ribbon worms** have **bilateral symmetry** and the organ level of organization. Flatworms may be free living or parasitic. Freshwater planaria have muscles, a ladder-type nervous organization, and **cephalization** consistent with a predatory way of life. Parasitic flatworms; namely, tapeworms and flukes, lack cephalization and are otherwise modified for a parasitic lifestyle.

Roundworms and rotifers are **pseudocoelomates** and have a **tube-within-a-tube** body plan. Many roundworms, ranging form pinworms to *Ascaris* and *Trichinella* are parasitic.

Study the text section by section as you answer the questions that follow.

33.1 HOW ANIMALS EVOLVED AND ARE CLASSIFIED (P. 576)

- Animals are mulitcellular heterotrophs that move about and ingest their food. They have the diplontic life cycle.
- Animals are classified according to certain criteria, including type of coelom, symmetry, body plan, development, and presence of segmentation.

1. The phylogenetic tree of animals shows that all animals are believed to have evolved

   from a_____ ancestors, most likely b._____.
2. Beside the letters, write the names of the animal phyla depicted in the phylogenetic tree that follows. Beside the numbers, write the level of organization.

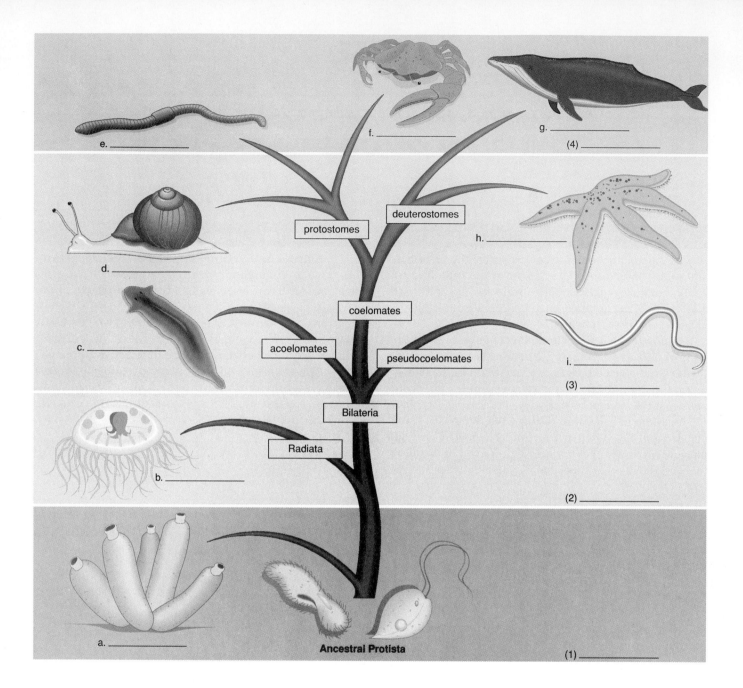

protostomes

deuterostomes

coelomates

acoelomates

pseudocoelomates

Bilateria

Radiata

Ancestral Protista

e. _____

f. _____

g. _____

(4) _____

d. _____

h. _____

c. _____

i. _____

(3) _____

b. _____

(2) _____

a. _____

(1) _____

3. Place a check in front of those phrases that correctly describe animal characteristics.

_____ a. autotrophic nutrition

_____ b. haplontic life cycle

_____ c. ingest food

_____ d. meiosis produces gametes

_____ e. multicellular organisms

4. Match the definitions with the following types of symmetry: *asymmetry, bilateral symmetry,* and *radial symmetry.*

_____ a. A definite right and left half; one longitudinal cut down the center of the animal produces two equal halves.

_____ b. Animal has no particular symmetry.

_____ c. Animal is organized circularly; two identical halves are obtained no matter how the animal is sliced longitudinally.

5. The three germ layers are called ᵃ·_____, ᵇ·_____, and ᶜ·_____.

6. Animals with the tissue level of organization have ^a._____ germ layers. Animals with

the ^b._____ level of organization have three germ layers.

7. Match the definitions with the following terms: *acoelomate, pseudocoelomate, protostome,* and *deuterostome.*
   _____ a. A cavity is incompletely lined with mesoderm.
   _____ b. The blastopore becomes the mouth.
   _____ c. A coelom is lacking.
   _____ d. The blastopore becomes the anus, and a second opening becomes the mouth.

33.2 MULTICELLULARITY EVOLVES (P. 578)

- Sponges have the cellular level of organization and lack tissues and symmetry. They depend on a flow of water through the body to acquire food.

8. Label the cells in this diagram of the body wall of the sponge with the following terms: *amoeboid cell, collar cell, epidermal cell, pore,* and *spicule.* Write the function of each cell next to its label.

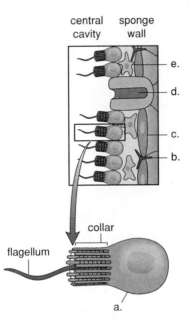

9. Sponges are the only animals to have the ^a._____ level of organization. Their bodies are

perforated by many ^b._____; the phylum name Porifera means ^c._____. The beating

of the flagella of ^d._____ creates water currents, which flow through the pores into the central

cavity and out through the ^e._____. Food particles brought in by water are digested in food

vacuoles and ^f._____ cells. The result of sexual reproduction is a ciliated larva that moves

(disperses) by ^g._____. The two methods of asexual reproduction of sponges are

called ^h._____ and fragmentation. If a sponge fragments, it can grow whole again by a process

called ^i._____. The classification of sponges is based on the type of ^j._____ they

have.

33.3 TWO TISSUE LAYERS EVOLVE (P. 580)

- Cnidaria and comb jellies have a radially symmetrical saclike body consisting of two tissue layers from the germ layers ectoderm and endoderm.
- Cnidaria typically are either polyps (e.g., *Hydra*) or medusa (e.g., jellyfishes) or alternate between these two forms, the polyp being an asexual state and the medusa being a sexual state.

10. Embryonic comb jellies and cnidaria have ^{a.}_____ germ layers, the ^{b.}_____ and the ^{c.}_____. Because of this, they are said to be ^{d.}_____. They exhibit ^{e.}_____ symmetry.

11. What is the function of a nematocyst? _____

12. Label this diagram with the following terms: *hydra, jellyfish, medusa,* and *polyp.*

a._____

b._____

_____ c.

_____ d.

13. In cnidaria, which demonstrate the alternation of generations life cycle, the polypoid stage is sessile and produces ^{a.}_____. The medusan stage is motile and produces ^{b.}_____.

14. The hydra is a solitary ^{a.}_____ that lives in ^{b.}_____. Because they contain muscle fibers, the cells of the epidermis of the hydra are called ^{c.}_____. Cells capable of becoming other types of cells, allowing the animal to regenerate, are called ^{d.}_____. ^{e.}_____ secrete digestive juices. The main type of gastrodermal cell is the ^{f.}_____ cell. Hydras can reproduce either asexually by ^{g.}_____ or sexually.

15. Cnidaria, whose calcium-carbonate skeletons provide a major ocean habitat for thousands of other animals, are the _____.

33.4 BILATERAL SYMMETRY EVOLVES (P. 584)

- Flatworms and ribbon worms have tissues and organs derived also from mesoderm, the third germ layer. They have the organ level of organization and are bilaterally symmetrical.
- Planaria are free-living predators, but flukes and tapeworms are animals adapted to a parasitic way of life.

16. Animals with three germ layers are said to be ^{a.}_____, and they exhibit ^{b.}_____ symmetry.

17. Flatworms have the ^{a.}_____ body plan; ribbon worms have a ^{b.}_____ body plan.

Of the two types of body plans, which is the most advanced? ^{c.}_____

Why? ^{d.}_____

_____

18. Complete the following table to compare a hydra and a planarian:

	Hydra	Planarian
Body Plan		
Cephalization		
Number of Germ Layers		
Organs		
Symmetry		

Parasitic Flatworms Cause Serious Illnesses (p. 586)

19. The condition schistosomiasis is caused by a(n) a._____. The Chinese liver fluke requires two hosts, the snail and the fish. Humans contract liver flukes when they eat b._____.

20. The body of the tapeworm is made up of a head region called a(n) a._____ and numerous segments called b._____. Each segment is a(n) c._____ factory and produces many fertilized d._____.

21. Label this diagram of the life cycle of a human tapeworm with the following terms: *humans, meat,* and *pigs/cattle.*

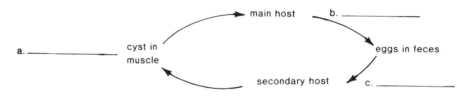

22. Complete the following table to compare the structure of the parasitic tapeworm with that of the planarian:

Body Structure	Tapeworm	Planarian
eyes		
nervous system		
digestive system		
reproductive system		

33.5 A Pseudocoelom Evolves (p. 588)

- Roundworms and rotifers have a coelom, a body cavity where organs are found and that can serve as a hydrostatic skeleton. Their coelom is a pseudocoelom because it is not completely lined by mesoderm.
- Roundworms take their name from a lack of segmentation; they are very diverse and include some well-known parasites.

23. Two animal phyla that consist of pseudocoelomates are a.____________________ and b.____________________.

24. Complete the following table to compare the structure of flatworms and roundworms:

	Flatworms	Roundworms
Number of Germ Layers		
Organs		
Sexes Separate		
Pseudocoelom		
Body Plan		

25. Trichinosis is a condition humans get by eating rare a.____________________ containing b.____________________.

26. Complete the following table to compare the four animal phyla discussed in this chapter:

	Sponges	Cnidaria	Flatworms	Roundworms
Symmetry				
Body Plan				
Number of Germ Layers				
Level of Organization				
Body Cavity				

Review key terms by completing this crossword puzzle, using the following alphabetized list of terms:

hydra
invertebrate
mesoglea
nematocyst
pseudocoelom
radially symmetrical
sac body plan
sessile filter feeder
spicule

Across

4 in cnidaria, a capsule that contains a threadlike fiber whose release aids in the capture of prey

6 skeletal structure of sponges composed of calcium carbonate or silicate

7 freshwater cnidarian with only a polyp stage that reproduces both sexually and asexually

9 jellylike layer between the epidermis and the gastrodermis of cnidaria

10 organism that stays in one place and filters its food from the water (three words)

Down

1 referring to an animal without a serial arrangement of vertebrae, or a backbone

2 body cavity lying between the digestive tract and the body wall; incompletely lined by mesoderm

3 describes body plan in which similar parts are arranged around a central axis, like spokes of a wheel (two words)

8 body with a digestive cavity that has only one opening, as in cnidaria and flatworms (three words)

OBJECTIVE QUESTIONS

Do not refer to the text when taking this test.
In questions 1–10, match each description with the following animals:

    a. sponges
    b. cnidaria
    c. flatworms
    d. roundworms

_____ 1. tube-within-a-tube body plan

_____ 2. below the tissue level of organization

_____ 3. two germ layers present

_____ 4. tissue level of organization

_____ 5. pseudocoelom present

_____ 6. include planaria

_____ 7. include *Ascaris*

_____ 8. have collar cells and spicules

_____ 9. feed by nematocysts

_____10. some cause elephantiasis

_____11. Select the incorrect association.
    a. amoeboid cell—digestion
    b. collar cell—water current
    c. epidermal cell—covering
    d. spicule cell—reproduction

_____12. The gastrovascular cavity functions for
    a. digestion only.
    b. transport only.
    c. digestion and transport.
    d. neither digestion nor transport.

_____13. Which of the following is NOT an embryonic germ layer among cnidaria?
    a. ectoderm
    b. endoderm
    c. mesoderm

_____14. In cnidaria, the epidermis is separated from the cell layers lining the internal cavity by
    a. mesoderm.
    b. mesoglea.
    c. a coelom.
    d. a pseudocoelom.
    e. endoderm.

_____15. Which statement is NOT true of *Hydra's* life cycle?
    a. It reproduces asexually by means of budding.
    b. It alternates between the polyp form and the medusa form.
    c. The polyp produces the egg and sperm.
    d. Only the polyp form is ever haploid.

_____16. In contrast to cnidaria, flatworms have
    a. a complete digestive tract.
    b. sexual reproduction.

    c. a mesoderm layer that gives rise to organs.
    d. a nervous system.
    e. specialized tissues for gas exchange.

_____17. Cephalization means that
    a. a definite head develops.
    b. reproduction is sexual.
    c. the nervous system is ladderlike.
    d. wastes are excreted through flame cells.

_____18. A fluke is responsible for the condition of
    a. pinworms.
    b. schistosomiasis.
    c. trichinosis.
    d. elephantiasis.

_____19. A parasitic worm living in a vertebrate intestine probably has little need for
    a. a high degree of tolerance to pH changes.
    b. a digestive tract.
    c. reproductive organs.
    d. a means of attachment to the host.
    e. glycolysis.

_____20. A true coelom differs from a pseudocoelom in that it
    a. has a body cavity for internal organs.
    b. is lined completely by mesoderm.
    c. is incompletely lined by mesoderm.
    d. is found only in segmented worms.

_____21. The distinction between protostomes and deuterostomes is based on differences in their
    a. digestive tracts.
    b. nervous systems.
    c. embryonic development.
    d. circulatory systems.
    e. Both *a* and *c* are correct.

_____22. Humans may become infected with *Ascaris* by
    a. soil which contains eggs.
    b. consuming muscle tissue that contains a cyst.
    c. drinking water contaminated with eggs.
    d. Both *a* and *c* are correct.

In questions 23–25, match the descriptions with the following organisms (some are used more than once):

    a. cnidaria
    b. flatworms
    c. roundworms

_____23. sac body plan, radial symmetry

_____24. alternation of generations

_____25. some are parasitic

Answer in complete sentences.

26. From sponges to roundworms, evolution has produced a more complex body form. What evidence supports this?

27. A loss of body complexity accompanies parasitism among flatworms. What evidence supports this?

Test Results: _____ Number right ÷ 27 = _____ × 100 = _____ %

EXPLORING THE INTERNET

Use the Internet to further explore topics in this chapter, such as cnidaria and sponges. Go to the Mader Home Page (http://www.mhhe.com/sciencemath/biology/mader/) and click on *Biology,* 6th edition. Go to Chapter 33 and select a Web site of interest.

ANSWER KEY

STUDY QUESTIONS

1. a. protistan **b.** protozoa   **2. a.** Porifera (sponges) **b.** Cnidaria (cnidaria)   **c.** Platyhelminthes (flatworms) **d.** Mollusca (mollusks) **e.** Annelida (annelids) **f.** Arthropoda (arthropods) **g.** Chordata (chordates) **h.** Echinodermata (echinoderms) **i.** Nematoda (roundworms) (1) cellular level (2) tissue level (3) organ level (4) segmentation; see Figure 33.2, page 577, in text.   **3.** c, d, e **4. a.** bilateral symmetry **b.** asymmetry **c.** radial symmetry   **5. a.** ectoderm **b.** mesoderm **c.** endoderm   **6. a.** two **b.** organ   **7. a.** pseudocoelomate **b.** protostome **c.** acoelomate **d.** deuterostome **8. a.** collar— produces water currents and captures food **b.** spicule—internal skeleton **c.** epidermal—protection **d.** pore—entrance of water **e.** amoeboid—distributes nutrients and produces gametes   **9. a.** cellular **b.** pores **c.** pore bearing **d.** collar cells **e.** osculum **f.** amoeboid **g.** swimming **h.** budding **i.** regeneration **j.** skeleton **10. a.** two **b.** ectoderm **c.** endoderm **d.** diploblasts **e.** radial   **11.** to trap or paralyze prey   **12. a., b.** polyp, hydra **c., d.** medusa, jellyfish   **13. a.** medusae **b.** eggs and sperm   **14. a.** polyp **b.** freshwater **c.** epitheliomuscular cells **d.** interstitial (embryonic) **e.** Gland cells **f.** nutritive-muscular **g.** budding   **15.** corals **16. a.** triploblasts **b.** bilateral   **17. a.** sac **b.** tube-within-a-tube **c.** tube-within-a-tube **d.** With a one-way flow of contents, each part can take on a particular function.

18.

Hydra	Planarian
sac	sac
no	yes
two	three
no	yes
radial	bilateral

19. a. blood fluke **b.** raw fish **c.** reproductive **d.** eggs   **20. a.** scolex **b.** proglottids **c.** pigs/cattle   **21. a.** meat **b.** humans

22.

Tapeworm	Planarian
no	yes
much reduced	extensive
not present	branches
well developed	present

23. a. Nematoda (roundworms) **b.** Rotifera (rotifers)

24.

Flatworms	Roundworms
three	three
yes	yes
no	yes
no	yes
sac	tube-within-a-tube

25. **a.** pork **b.** encysted roundworm larvae **26.** See Table 33.3, page 590, in text.

KEYWORD CROSSWORD

Across:
4. NEMATOCYST
5. SPICULE
6. HYDRA
8. MESOGLEA
9. SESSILE FILTER FEEDER

Down:
1. INVERTEBRATE
2. PSEUDOCOELOM
3. RADIALLY SYMMETRICAL
7. SAC BODY PLAN

CHAPTER TEST

1. d **2.** a **3.** b **4.** b **5.** d **6.** c **7.** d **8.** a **9.** b
10. d **11.** d **12.** c **13.** c **14.** b **15.** b **16.** c
17. a **18.** b **19.** b **20.** b **21.** c **22.** d **23.** a
24. a **25.** b, c **26.** Among roundworms, there is a tube-within-a-tube body plan, with bilateral symmetry and an organ level of organization. Also, a pseudocoelom develops. **27.** Organ systems may be lost, partially or completely in parasites. Only the reproductive system remains well developed. The head region bears hooks and/or suckers instead of sense organs.

34

ANIMALS: THE PROTOSTOMES

The **protostomes** (and **deuterostomes**) have a **coelom** completely lined with mesoderm. In protostomes, the mouth appears at or near the blastopore, the first embryonic opening. The body of a **mollusk** is composed of a foot, a visceral mass, and a **mantle** cavity. Mollusks are adapted to various ways of life; for example, clams are sessile filter feeders, squids are active predators of the open ocean, and snails are terrestrial. **Annelids** are the segmented worms. Polychaetes (e.g., clam worms, tube worms) are marine animals with parapodia for gas exchange; earthworms live on land; and the **leech** is parasitic. In the earthworm, the coelom and the nervous, excretory, and circulatory systems all provide evidence of **segmentation.**

Arthropods have a ventral nerve cord and an external **exoskeleton** made of **chitin,** which is periodically shed by **molting;** this is different from the internal skeleton of **vertebrates.** Like vertebrates, however, arthropods are segmented and have **jointed appendages.** This combination has led to specialization of parts, and in some arthropods, the body is divided into special regions, each with its own particular type of appendages. Whereas the crayfish, a **crustacean,** is adapted to a marine existence, the grasshopper, an **insect,** is adapted to a terrestrial existence. Insects have wings and breathe by means of air tubes called **trachea.** Their circulatory system does not contain a respiratory pigment.

STUDY EXERCISES

Study the text section by section as you answer the questions that follow.

34.1 A COELOM (P. 594)

- A coelom has many advantages: the digestive system can become more complex, coelomic fluid assists body processes and acts as a hydrostatic skeleton.
- In protostomes, the mouth appears at or near the blastopore, the first embryonic opening, and the coelom develops by a splitting of the mesoderm.

1. What are the advantages of having a coelom in regard to the following?

   the digestive tract a. _____

   locomotion b. _____

   circulation c. _____

   reproduction d. _____

2. Label each of the following statements as describing a deuterostome (D) or protostome (P):
   - _____ a. A schizocoelom develops.
   - _____ b. The blastopore becomes the anus.
   - _____ c. The blastopore becomes the mouth.
   - _____ d. The coelom develops from mesodermal pouches.
   - _____ e. The fate of developing cells is fixed and determinate.
   - _____ f. The fate of developing cells is indeterminate.
   - _____ g. Radial cleavage occurs.
   - _____ h. Spiral cleavage occurs.

34.2 A THREE-PART BODY PLAN (P. 596)

- The body of a mollusk typically contains a visceral mass, a mantle, and a foot.
- Clams are adapted to a sedentary coastal life, squids to an active life in the sea, and snails are adapted to a life on land.

3. All mollusks have a(n) ᵃ·_____, a(n) ᵇ·_____, and a(n) ᶜ·_____. Another feature often present is a(n) ᵈ·_____, an organ that bears rows of teeth. The nervous system is one of ᵉ·_____ connected by nerve cords. Slow-moving mollusks tend to lack a(n) ᶠ·_____, but the active ones do undergo ᵍ·_____.

4. Give an example of each of the following animals:

   bivalve ᵃ·_____

   cephalopod ᵇ·_____

   gastropod ᶜ·_____

5. State the manner in which a clam, a squid, and a snail are adapted to their way of life.

   clam ᵃ·_____

   _____

   squid ᵇ·_____

   _____

   snail ᶜ·_____

   _____

   _____

   _____

6. Complete the following table to compare the clam, the squid, and the snail:

Characteristic	Clam	Squid	Snail
skeleton			
food procurement			
locomotion			
cephalization			
reproduction			

34.3 SEGMENTATION EVOLVES (P. 600)

- Annelids are the segmented worms with a well-developed coelom, a closed circulatory system, a ventral solid nerve cord, and paired nephridia in each segment.
- Polychaetes include marine predators with a definite head region, and filter feeders with terminal tentacles to filter food from the water.
- Oligochaetes include the earthworms that burrow in the soil and use a moist body wall as a respiratory region.

7. Annelids are the ᵃ·_____ worms. The tube-within-a-tube body plan has resulted in a digestive system with ᵇ·_____ parts. Annelids have an extensive ᶜ·_____ circulatory system. The nervous system is a brain and ᵈ·_____ nerve cord. Paired ᵉ·_____ in each segment collect and excrete waste.

8. Complete the following table to compare annelids:

Class	Representative Organism	Setae	Parapodia
Polychaeta			
Oligochaeta			
Hirudinea			

9. Describe the following systems to show that an earthworm is segmented:

nervous system ᵃ·_____

excretory system ᵇ· _____

circulatory system ᶜ· _____

10. Place a check in front of the item(s) that pertain(s) to earthworm reproduction.
    _____ a. Worms are hermaphroditic.
    _____ b. Worms have separate sexes.
    _____ c. Glands in every segment provide mucus.
    _____ d. The clitellum provides mucus.
    _____ e. Worms exchange sperm and eggs.
    _____ f. Worms exchange sperm.
    _____ g. The embryo develops externally.

34.4 JOINTED APPENDAGES EVOLVE (P. 603)

- Arthropods are segmented with specialized body regions and an external skeleton that includes jointed appendages.
- Among the many kinds of arthropods, crustacea are adapted to a life at sea, and insects are adapted to a terrestrial existence.

11. Like the annelids, arthropods are ᵃ·_____, but there is specialization of parts. The segments

    are fused into three regions: ᵇ·_____, ᶜ·_____, and ᵈ·_____.

    The arthropods have an exoskeleton that contains ᵉ·_____, and there

    are ᶠ·_____ appendages. Because they have an external skeleton, arthropods have

    to ᵍ·_____ to grow larger. Arthropods have a(n) ʰ·_____ nerve

    cord; ⁱ·_____ is apparent, and the head bears sense organs, including ʲ·_____

    eyes in most species.

12. Label the following organisms as chelicerates (CH), crustacea (CR), or uniramia (U):
    _____ a. copepods and krill
    _____ b. scorpions
    _____ c. centipedes
    _____ d. insects
    _____ e. lobsters and crayfish
    _____ f. spiders
    _____ g. horseshoe crabs

13. Which subphylum of arthropods lacks antennae, mandibles, and maxillae, and instead has pincerlike

    appendages and pedipalps for feeding? ᵃ·_____

    Which subphylum of arthropods has an exoskeleton hardened by the addition of calcium and biramous

    appendages? ᵇ·_____

    Which subphylum of arthropods has only one pair of antennae and appendages with only one

    branch? ᶜ·_____

14. Label these diagrams of the grasshopper with the following terms (some are used more than once):

antenna
compound eye
crop
Malpighian tubules
spiracle(s)
tracheae
tympanum

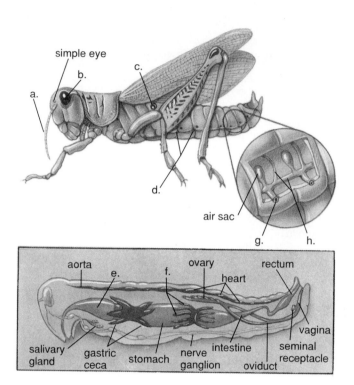

15. Give the function of each of the following structures:

crop and gizzard ᵃ· _____

Malpighian tubules ᵇ· _____

tracheae ᶜ· _____

hemocoel ᵈ·_____

ovipositor ᵉ· _____

16. Complete the following table to compare the crayfish to the grasshopper, indicating how each is adapted to its way of life:

System	Crayfish	Grasshopper
locomotion		
excretion		
digestion		
reproduction		
respiration		

Review key terms by completing this crossword puzzle, using the following alphabetized list of terms:

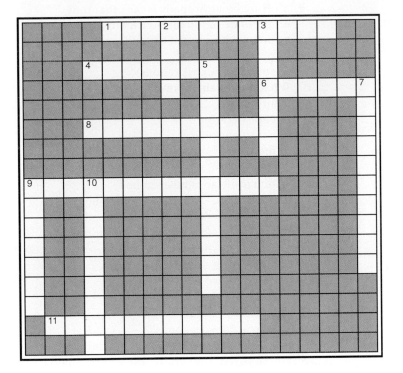

annelid
arthropod
chitin
deuterostome
exoskeleton
metamorphosis
mollusk
molt
nephridium
protostome
segmentation
trachea

Across

1 repetition of body units as is seen in the earthworm

4 member of a phylum, which includes clam worms, tube worms, earthworms, and leeches; characterized by a segmented body

6 strong but flexible nitrogenous polysaccharide found in the exoskeleton of arthropods

8 group of coelomate animals in which the first embryonic opening (the blastopore) is associated with the mouth

9 change in shape and form that some animals, such as insects, undergo during development

11 protective external skeleton, as in arthropods

Down

2 periodic shedding of the exoskeleton in arthropods

3 air tube in insects located between the spiracles and the air sacs

5 group of coelomate animals in which the second embryonic opening is associated with the mouth; the first embryonic opening, the blastopore, is associated with the anus

7 segmentally arranged, paired excretory tubules of many invertebrates, as in the earthworm

9 member of a phylum, which includes squids, clams, snails, and chitons; characterized by a visceral mass, a mantle, and a foot

10 member of a phylum, which includes lobsters, insects, and spiders; characterized by jointed appendages

Do not refer to the text when taking this test.

_____ 1. A true coelom differs from a pseudocoelom in that the latter
   a. has a body cavity for internal organs.
   b. is lined completely by mesoderm.
   c. is incompletely lined by mesoderm.
   d. is found only in segmented worms.

_____ 2. The distinction between protostomes and deuterostomes is based on differences in their
   a. digestive tracts.
   b. nervous systems.
   c. embryonic development.
   d. circulatory systems.
   e. Both *a* and *c* are correct.

_____ 3. The digestive and reproductive systems of a mollusk are located within the
   a. mantle cavity.
   b. visceral mass.
   c. gastrovascular cavity.
   d. highly branched coelom.
   e. water vascular cavity.

_____ 4. A common feature of all classes of mollusks is
   a. a muscular foot.
   b. a coiled shell, either internal or external.
   c. obvious segmentation.
   d. their carnivorous nature.
   e. All of these are correct.

_____ 5. Earthworms are incompletely adapted to life on land because
   a. their reproduction takes place in the water.
   b. they have to exchange gases with water.
   c. they tend to dry out if exposed to dry air.
   d. their setae have to be kept wet.

_____ 6. What type of skeleton helps an earthworm to move?
   a. an exoskeleton
   b. a bony endoskeleton
   c. a hydrostatic skeleton
   d. spiny plates

_____ 7. The _____ in the earthworms secretes mucus for deposition of eggs and sperm.
   a. typhlosole
   b. nephridia
   c. clitellum
   d. setae
   e. gizzard

_____ 8. Select the statement NOT descriptive of annelids.
   a. excretion by nephridia
   b. sac body plan
   c. segmented body
   d. well-developed coelom

_____ 9. Molting by arthropods means that they
   a. circulate blood through a closed system.
   b. move with jointed appendages.
   c. reproduce sexually.
   d. shed their exoskeletons.

_____10. What do a crab, an insect, and a spider have in common?
   a. cephalization
   b. external skeleton
   c. molting
   d. All of these are correct.

_____11. Which of these is mismatched?
   a. chelicerate—pincerlike appendages
   b. uniramia—one branch on appendages
   c. crustacea—calcified exoskeleton
   d. crustacea—insects
   e. chelicerate—spiders

_____12. Which of these is mismatched?
   a. insect—scorpion
   b. arachnid—spider
   c. crustacea—decapods
   d. insect—grasshopper

_____13. Which is NOT generally true of arthropods?
   a. exoskeleton contains chitin
   b. breathe with tracheae
   c. have jointed appendages
   d. have compound eyes

_____14. Which of these is mismatched?
   a. annelid—earthworm
   b. mollusk—spider
   c. arthropod—grasshopper
   d. annelid—clam worm, *Nereis*

_____15. Which is NOT a general feature of insects?
   a. body divided into head, thorax, and abdomen
   b. three pairs of legs
   c. respiration typically by book lungs
   d. one or two pairs of wings

_____16. Which of these is NOT a mollusk?
   a. squid
   b. chiton
   c. leech
   d. clam

_____17. Which of these is NOT a characteristic of mollusks?
   a. body in three parts—head, thorax, and abdomen
   b. a foot modified in various ways
   c. a visceral mass that contains the internal organs
   d. usually an open circulatory system

_____18. Which of these is mismatched?
    a. clam—sessile filter feeder
    b. squid—closed circulatory system
    c. snail—shell and broad foot
    d. clam—well-developed brain

_____19. What do a scallop, a chambered nautilus, and a chiton have in common?
    a. cephalization
    b. vertebrate-type eyes
    c. a mantle cavity
    d. a jointed external skeleton

_____20. What do an earthworm, a clam worm, and a leech have in common?
    a. a clitellum
    b. parapodia
    c. a closed circulatory system
    d. All of these are correct.

CRITICAL THINKING QUESTIONS

Answer in complete sentences.

21. The arthropods are considered the most successful animal phylum inhabiting the earth. What justifies this claim?

22. What evidence suggests that mollusks are ancestral to annelids and that annelids are ancestral to arthropods?

Test Results: _____ Number right ÷ 22 = _____ × 100 = _____ %

EXPLORING THE INTERNET

Use the Internet to further explore topics in this chapter, such as aquatic organisms or insects. Go to the Mader Home Page (http://www.mhhe.com/sciencemath/biology/mader/) and click on *Biology,* 6th edition. Go to Chapter 34 and select a Web site of interest.

ANSWER KEY

STUDY EXERCISES

1. a. The digestive tract can move independently of the body wall. The coelom allows specialization in that the tract has room to coil. **b.** With a hydrostatic skeleton, muscular contractions allow the animal to move. **c.** Coelomic fluid can substitute for a circulatory system. **d.** The coelomic cavity can provide room for storage of eggs/sperm. **2. a.** P **b.** D **c.** P **d.** D **e.** P **f.** D **g.** D **h.** P **3. a.** mantle **b.** visceral mass **c.** foot **d.** radula **e.** ganglia **f.** head **g.** cephalization **4. a.** clam, oyster, mussel, scallop **b.** squid, cuttlefish, octopus, nautilus **c.** snail, whelk, conch, periwinkle, sea slug **5. a.** A clam has a hatchet foot for burrowing in the sand and is a sessile filter feeder that lacks cephalization. **b.** A squid has a head-foot—that is, tentacles about the head with vertebrate-type eyes that help the squid actively capture food. **c.** A snail has a broad, flat foot for moving over flat surfaces and a head with a radula for scraping up food from a surface.

6.

Clam	Squid	Snail
external shell	no external skeleton	external shell
filter feeder	active predator	garden snail is herbivorous
hatchet foot	jet propulsion and fins	broad, flat foot
no	yes	yes
separate sexes	separate sexes	hermaphroditic

7. a. segmented **b.** specialized **c.** closed **d.** ventral **e.** nephridia

8.

Representative Organism	Setae	Parapodia
clam worm	many	yes
earthworm	few	no
leech	no	no

9. a. ganglia and lateral nerves in every segment **b.** paired nephridia in every segment **c.** branched blood vessels in every segment **10.** a, d, f, g **11. a.** segmented **b.** head **c.** thorax **d.** abdomen **e.** chitin **f.** jointed **g.** molt **h.** ventral **i.** cephalization **j.** compound **12. a.** CR **b.** CH **c.** U **d.** U **e.** CR **f.** CH **g.** CH **13. a.** chelicerates **b.** crustacea **c.** uniramia **14.** See Figure 34.14, page 609, in text. **15. a.** crop

stores food, and gizzard grinds it **b.** excretory tubules that concentrate nitrogenous waste **c.** air tubes that deliver oxygen to muscles **d.** cavity where blood is found **e.** special female appendage for depositing eggs in soil **16.**

Crayfish	Grasshopper
swimmerets	hopping legs, wings
liquid	solid
gastric mill	crop
male uses swimmeret to pass sperm	male uses penis to pass sperm
gills	trachea

KeyWord CrossWord

Chapter Test

1. c **2.** c **3.** b **4.** a **5.** c **6.** c **7.** c **8.** b **9.** d **10.** d **11.** d **12.** a **13.** b **14.** b **15.** c **16.** c **17.** a **18.** d **19.** c **20.** c **21.** They are the most diversified phylum with a wide variety of species filling numerous ecological niches. Insects far outnumber any other type of animal. **22.** Mollusks are not segmented except for *Neopilina,* and the segmentation seen in this animal suggests that mollusks could be ancestral to annelids. *Peripatus,* the walking worm, has both annelid and arthropod characteristics, which suggests that annelids could be ancestral to arthropods.

35

ANIMALS: THE DEUTEROSTOMES

In **deuterostomes,** the blastopore develops into an anus. Cleavage is radial, and an enterocoelom develops.

The **echinoderms** have evolved radial symmetry, an internal skeleton, **gills,** a nerve ring, and a **water vascular system.** The sea star is a major echinoderm showing these specializations.

Chordates have evolved a **notochord,** a dorsal hollow nerve cord, and pharyngeal pouches at some point in their life history. Only **lancelets** show all of these characteristics as adults. The **vertebrates** develop a vertebral column in place of a notochord.

Vertebrates are divided into superclasses: the agnathans (jawless fishes) and the gnathostomes (jawed vertebrates). There are six classes of jawed vertebrates: cartilaginous fishes (e.g. shark); bony fishes (e.g. trout, cod, tuna); amphibians (e.g. frogs and salamanders); reptiles (e.g. snakes, lizards, turtles); aves (birds); mammals (e.g. dogs, cats, humans)

The evolution of vertebrates is still being studied. The **hagfishes** and **lampreys** are descendants of the original jawless fishes. Sharks are modern representatives of the cartilaginous fishes. The original bony fishes diverged into two groups: the **ray-finned fishes** and the **lobe-finned fishes.**

Amphibians which evolved from lobe-finned fishes during the Devonian period reached their greatest size and diversity in the swamp forests of the Carboniferous period. Most amphibians return to the water to reproduce.

Reptiles, which are believed to have evolved from the amphibians, have a shelled amniote egg. A shelled egg along with extraembryonic membranes makes reproduction on land possible. Stem reptiles gave rise to dinosaurs and birds. The mammals trace their ancetry to another reptilian line of descent.

While amphibians and reptiles are ectothermic—their body temperature is the same as the environment, both birds and mammals are homeothermic—they metabolically produce a constant body temperature. Adaptations of **birds** include feathers and hollow bones both adaptations for flight. **Mammals** have evolved hair and mammary glands. **Monotremes** are egg-laying mammals, and **marsupials** are pouched mammals which give birth to very immature young. While the young of placental mammals are more developed at birth, they still require parental care to survive.

Study the text section by section as you answer the questions that follow.

- In deuterostomes, the blastopore is associated with the anus, and the coelom develops by outpocketing from the primitive gut.
- Echinoderms (e.g., sea star) and chordates (e.g., vertebrates) are both related to the hemichordates (e.g., acorn worms).
- Echinoderms have radial symmetry and a unique water vascular system for locomotion.

1. Complete the following table to describe the characteristics of echinoderms:

Characteristic	Description
type of symmetry	
skeletal system	
respiration	
nervous system	
water vascular system	

2. Complete the following table to describe types of echinoderms:

Class Name	Examples	Distinctive Features
Crinoidea		
Holothuroidea		
Echinoidea		
Ophiuroidea		
Asteroidea		

3. Label this diagram of a sea star with the following terms (some are used more than once):
   ampulla
   anus
   arm
   cardiac stomach
   central disk
   coelomic cavity
   digestive gland
   endoskeletal plates
   eyespot
   gonads
   pyloric stomach
   radial canal
   sieve plate
   skin gill
   spine
   tube feet

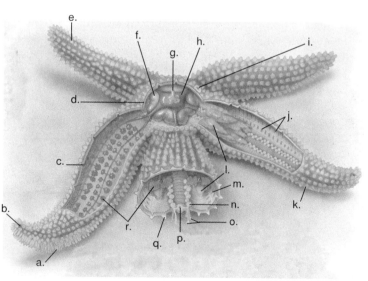

4. Trace the path of water in the water vascular system: sieve plate to a._____canal to b._____canal to radial canal to c._____feet. Each of these feet has a(n) d._____. The function of the water vascular system is e._____.

5. A sea star has a two-part stomach. Describe how the sea star feeds on a clam, mentioning both parts of the stomach. _____

_____

- Lancelets are invertebrate chordates with the three chordate characteristics: a notochord, a dorsal hollow nerve cord, and pharyngeal pouches.

6. Label this diagram with the three primary chordate characteristics, plus another that also distinguishes chordates.

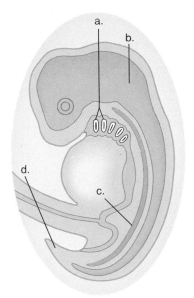

7. Which two chordate characteristics do hemichordates have? a._____

and b._____

What evidence suggests that hemichordates and echinoderms are related? c._____

8. Complete the following table to describe the invertebrate chordates:

Name	Chordate Characteristics	Appearance
tunicates (subphylum Urochordata)		
lancelets (subphylum Cephalochordata)		

35.3 THE VERTEBRATE BODY PLAN EVOLVES (P. 619)

- In vertebrates, the notochord is replaced by the vertebral column. Most vertebrates also have a head region, endoskeleton, and paired appendages.

9. Place a check in front of the characteristics that distinguish the vertebrates.
    _____ a. bilaterial symmetry in all
    _____ b. radial symmetry in some
    _____ c. tube-within-a-tube plus coelom
    _____ d. segmented

_____ e. vertebral column replaces embryonic notochord
_____ f. open/closed circulatory system
_____ g. cephalization with compound eyes
_____ h. living endoskeleton

10. Label each of the following as being in superclass Agnatha or superclass Gnathostomata, and as being a fish or a tetrapod:

lampreys and hagfishes a._____, _____

class Chondrichthyes b._____, _____

class Osteichthyes c._____, _____

class Amphibia d._____, _____

class Reptilia e._____, _____

class Aves f._____, _____

class Mammalia g._____, _____

11. To what class do each of these belong?

frogs and salamanders a._____

snakes and lizards b._____

sharks and rays c._____

storks and robins d._____

horses and giraffes e._____

Jaws Evolve (p. 620)

- There are three groups of fishes: jawless (e.g., hagfishes and lampreys), cartilaginous (sharks and rays), and bony fishes (ray-finned and lobe-finned). Most modern-day fishes are ray-finned (e.g., trout, perch, etc.).

12. Label each of the following as characterizing cartilaginous fishes (C) and/or bony fishes (B):
_____ a. lateral line system
_____ b. placoid (toothlike) scales
_____ c. operculum
_____ d. scales of bone
_____ e. swim bladder

13. What is the significance of ostracoderms (Cambrian period) in the history of vertebrates? a._____

What is the significance of placoderms (Devonian period) in the history of vertebrates? b._____

What is the significance of lobe-finned fishes (coelacanths and lungfishes) in the history of vertebrates?

c._____

What is the significance of amphibians in the history of vertebrates? d._____

What is the significance of reptiles in the history of vertebrates? e._____

Limbs Evolve (p.622)

- Amphibians (e.g., frogs and salamanders), who were more numerous during the Carboniferous period, evolved from lobe-finned fishes.

14. Describe each of these features of amphibians.

skin ᵃ·_____

lungs ᵇ·_____

body temperature ᶜ·_____

life cycle ᵈ·_____

heart ᵉ·_____

35.4 THE AMNIOTE EGG EVOLVES (P. 624)

- Modern-day reptiles (e.g., snakes, lizards, turtles) are the remnants of an ancient group that evolved from amphibians.
- The shelled egg of reptiles, which contains extraembryonic membranes, is an adaptation for reproduction on land.

15. Study this phylogenetic tree and then answer the questions that follow.

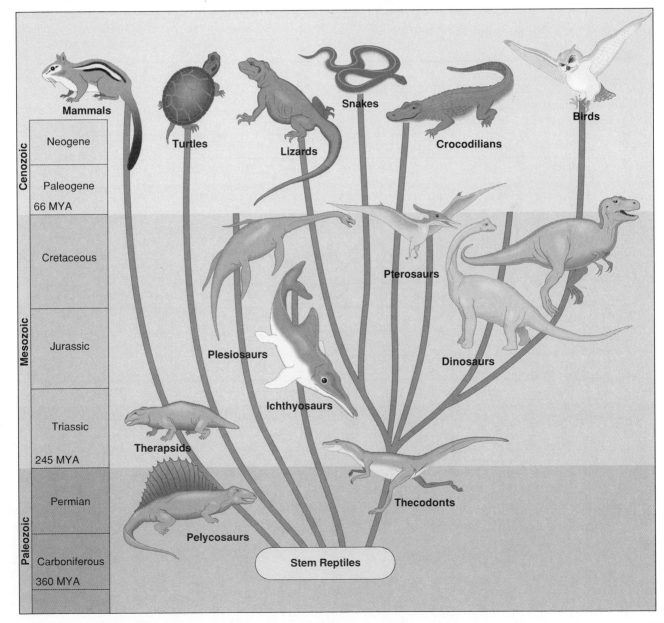

Does this tree support the hypothesis that birds are closely related to dinosaurs? a._____ Explain. b._____

_____

_____

Trace the evolution of mammals from reptiles. c._____

_____

_____

Does the tree suggest that lizards are more closely related to snakes than turtles? d._____ Explain. e._____

_____

_____

Many lines of descent seem to stop at the end of the Cretaceous period. Why? f._____

_____

_____

What type of reptiles are alive today? g._____

_____

16. Describe each of these features of reptiles.

skin a._____

lungs b._____

body temperature c._____

type of egg d._____

heart e._____

35.5 WINGS AND FEATHERS EVOLVE (P. 629)

- Birds have feathers and skeletal adaptations that enable them to fly.

17. How do the following characteristics of birds contribute to their ability to fly?

feathers a._____

horny beak b._____

keel c._____

four-chambered heart d._____

one-way flow of air in lungs e._____

35.6 HOMEOTHERMY PAYS OFF (P. 629)

- Mammals, which evolved from reptiles, were present when the dinosaurs existed. They did not diversify until the dinosaurs became extinct.
- Mammals are vertebrates with hair and mammary glands. The former helps them maintain a constant body temperature.
- Mammals are classified according to methods of reproduction: monotremes lay eggs, marsupials have a pouch in which newborn mature, and placental mammals retain the offspring in a uterus until birth.

18. Match the types of mammals to the following descriptions (some descriptions are used more than once):

    1 All have hair and mammary glands.
    2 All lay eggs.
    3 All have pouches.
    4 All have internal development to term.

    _____ a. monotremes
    _____ b. marsupials
    _____ c. placental mammals

19. Name a type of mammal adapted to each of the following:

    flying in air ᵃ· _____

    running on land ᵇ· _____

    swimming in the ocean ᶜ· _____

    preying on other animals ᵈ· _____

    living in trees ᵉ· _____

Constructing Office Buildings

The object of this game is to construct an office building by matching the numbered terms with the organisms in the key (some numbers should be matched to more than one letter). Five correct answers in a row gives you one story. Any wrong answer is a natural disaster that forces you to start from the ground again.

A fourteen story office building is possible.

Key One

    a. *Protozoa*
    b. *Porifera*
    c. *Cnidaria*
    d. *Platyhelminthes*
    e. *Nematoda*
    f. *Annelida*
    g. *Mollusca*
    h. *Arthropoda*
    i. *Echinodermata*

_____ 1. sea star (starfish)
_____ 2. clitellum
_____ 3. flame cells
_____ 4. egg—nymph—adult
_____ 5. organ system level of organization
_____ 6. ampulla
_____ 7. fluke
_____ 8. jellyfish
_____ 9. leech
_____10. octopus
_____11. jointed appendages
_____12. tube feet
_____13. elephantiasis
_____14. soft body
_____15. five hearts
_____16. bilateral symmetry
_____17. muscles
_____18. water vascular system

_____19. medusa
_____20. cellular level of organization
_____21. muscular foot
_____22. five arms
_____23. earthworm
_____24. nerve net
_____25. clam
_____26. setae
_____27. *Trichinella*
_____28. ladder-type nervous organization
_____29. horseshoe crab
_____30. stone canal
_____31. pseudocoelom
_____32. coelom
_____33. mesoglea
_____34. pore bearers
_____35. polychaete
_____36. squid
_____37. segmentation
_____38. closed circulatory system
_____39. open circulatory system
_____40. mesoderm
_____41. collar cells
_____42. trachea
_____43. trochophore larva
_____44. hydra
_____45. *Hirudo*
_____46. Malpighian tubules
_____47. mantle
_____48. *Dirofilaria*—filarial worm
_____49. nematocysts

_____50. metamorphosis
_____51. gills
_____52. typhlosole
_____53. *Ascaris*
_____54. sieve plate (madreporite)
_____55. hermaphroditic
_____56. acoelomate
_____57. pseudocoelomate
_____58. pyloric stomach
_____59. worms
_____60. molting
_____61. nephridia
_____62. visceral mass
_____63. cephalization
_____64. spicules
_____65. green gland
_____66. exoskeleton
_____67. wings
_____68. sessile
_____69. sac body plan
_____70. tube-within-a-tube
How many stories is your building? _____

_____20. skin gills
_____21. spicules
_____22. shell
_____23. carapace
_____24. "spiny skin"
_____25. planula larva
_____26. metamorphosis
_____27. nymph
_____28. molt
_____29. ovipositor
_____30. asexual reproduction
_____31. alternation of generations
_____32. clitellum
_____33. bilateral larva but radial adult
_____34. nerve ring
_____35. ganglia in foot and visceral mass
_____36. dorsal hollow nerve cord
_____37. ventral solid nerve cord
_____38. no nervous system
_____39. nerve net
_____40. ladder-type nervous organization
How many stories is your building? _____

OFFICE BUILDING TWO

An eight-story office building is possible.
Key Two
    a. sponge
    b. hydra
    c. planarian
    d. Ascaris
    e. clam
    f. earthworm
    g. lobster
    h. sea star
    i. grasshopper
    j. Obelia
_____ 1. diploblastic
_____ 2. coelomate
_____ 3. segmented
_____ 4. nematocyst
_____ 5. sac body plan
_____ 6. tube-within-a-tube body plan
_____ 7. bilateral symmetry
_____ 8. radial symmetry
_____ 9. organs
_____10. closed circulatory system
_____11. insect
_____12. belong to the same phylum
_____13. flame cells
_____14. Malpighian tubules
_____15. green gland
_____16. nephridia
_____17. tracheal tubes
_____18. gills
_____19. body wall for respiration

OFFICE BUILDING THREE

A ten-story office building is possible.
Key Three
    a. jawless fishes
    b. cartilaginous fishes
    c. bony fishes
    d. amphibians
    e. reptiles
    f. birds
    g. mammals
_____ 1. four-chambered heart
_____ 2. frogs and salamanders
_____ 3. air sacs
_____ 4. lampreys and hagfish
_____ 5. infant dependency
_____ 6. Chondrichthyes
_____ 7. hair
_____ 8. smooth, nonscaly skin
_____ 9. ectothermic
_____10. two-chambered heart
_____11. differentiated teeth
_____12. some are parasitic
_____13. highly developed brain
_____14. feathers
_____15. fish, but no operculum
_____16. evolved from amphibians
_____17. homeothermic
_____18. snakes, lizards
_____19. primates
_____20. epidermal placoid (toothlike) scales
_____21. shelled egg
_____22. whales and dolphins

_____23. class aves
_____24. lateral line system
_____25. mammary glands
_____26. some are filter feeders
_____27. metamorphosis
_____28. sharks, rays, and skates
_____29. marsupials
_____30. Osteichthyes
_____31. ray-finned fishes
_____32. monotremes
_____33. scales of bone
_____34. dinosaurs
_____35. operculum
_____36. evolved from reptiles
_____37. lobe-finned fishes

_____38. double circulatory loop
_____39. paired pelvic and pectoral fins
_____40. one-way path through lungs
_____41. three-chambered heart
_____42. lungs
_____43. expandable rib cage
_____44. gills as an adult
_____45. wings
_____46. single circulatory loop
_____47. molt
_____48. usually four limbs
_____49. amniote egg
_____50. cartilaginous skeleton
How many stories is your building? _____

Review key terms by completing this crossword puzzle, using the following alphabetized list of terms:

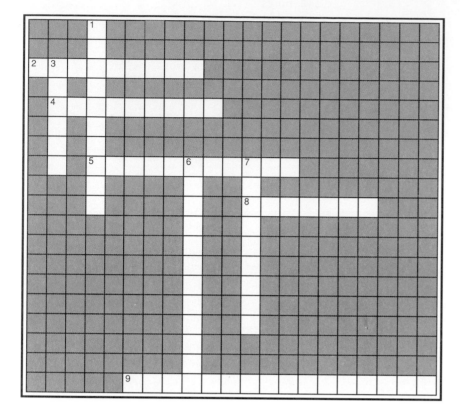

amphibian
echinoderm
ectothermic
homeothermic
mammal
marsupial
monotreme
placental mammal
reptile

Across

2 member of a class of terrestrial vertebrates that includes frogs, toads, and salamanders; they are still tied to a watery environment for reproduction

4 egg-laying mammal—for example, duckbill platypus and spiny anteater

5 having a body temperature that varies according to the environmental temperature

8 member of a class of terrestrial vertebrates with internal fertilization, scaly skin, and an egg with a leathery shell; incudes snakes, lizards, turtles, and crocodiles

9 member of a mammalian subclass characterized by a placenta, an organ of exchange between maternal and fetal blood that supplies nutrients to the growing offspring (two words)

Down

1 member of a phylum of marine animals that includes sea stars, sea urchins, and sand dollars; characterized by radial symmetry and a water vascular system

3 member of a class of vertebrates characterized especially by the presence of hair and mammary glands

6 describing an animal (bird or mammal) that maintains a uniform body temperature independent of the environmental temperature

7 mammal bearing immature young nursed in a marsupium, or pouch—for example, kangaroo and opossum

OBJECTIVE QUESTIONS

Do not refer to the text when taking this test.

_____ 1. Each is a vertebrate characteristic EXCEPT
  a. bilateral symmetry.
  b. coelom development.
  c. open circulatory system.
  d. segmentation.

_____ 2. The earliest vertebrate fossils came from the
  a. amphibians.
  b. bony fishes.
  c. cartilaginous fishes.
  d. jawless fishes.

_____ 3. Select the INCORRECT association.
  a. Cenozoic—humans evolve
  b. Mesozoic—dinosaurs dominate
  c. Paleozoic—amphibians live in swamp forests
  d. Cenozoic—fishes evolve

_____ 4. The skin of amphibians functions mainly for
  a. circulation.
  b. excretion.
  c. reproduction.
  d. respiration.

_____ 5. The extraembryonic membrane in the reptile egg promotes
  a. additional reinforcement from drying out.
  b. complete independence from the water for reproduction.
  c. enhanced elimination of wastes from the embryo.
  d. increased hardness to prevent breakage.

_____ 6. Bird feathers are modified
  a. fish fins.
  b. mammalian hair.
  c. reptilian scales.
  d. vertebrate teeth.

_____ 7. The hair of mammals is an adaptation for
  a. camouflage in all species.
  b. control of body temperature.
  c. faster locomotion.
  d. regulation of waste elimination.

_____ 8. The most successful mammals are the
  a. marsupials.
  b. monotremes.
  c. lancelets.
  d. placentals.

_____ 9. Which is true of echinoderms?
  a. contain a dorsal hollow nerve cord
  b. have internal organs in a visceral mass
  c. move by a water vascular system
  d. All of these are true.

_____ 10. Which is found only among echinoderms?
  a. deuterostome developmental pattern
  b. radial symmetry
  c. exoskeleton
  d. tube feet
  e. ventral mouth

_____ 11. Which feature is NOT found among fishes?
  a. endoskeleton
  b. closed circulatory system
  c. warm blood
  d. dorsal hollow nerve cord

_____ 12. The most important reason amphibians are incompletely adapted to life on land is that
  a. they depend on water for external fertilization.
  b. they must reproduce in water.
  c. the skin is more important than the lungs for gas exchange.
  d. their means of locomotion is poorly developed.

_____ 13. A four-chambered heart is seen among
  a. fishes.
  b. amphibians.
  c. birds.
  d. mammals.
  e. Both _c_ and _d_ are correct.

_____ 14. Which pair of statements correctly contrasts birds and mammals?
  a. Birds are cold-blooded. Mammals are warm-blooded.
  b. Birds are egg-laying. No mammals are egg-laying.
  c. Birds have air sacs in addition to lungs. Mammals have no such sacs.
  d. Birds lack a septum between the ventricles. Mammals have such a septum.

_____ 15. What do echinoderms and chordates have in common?
  a. radial symmetry
  b. pharyngeal pouches
  c. second embryonic opening is the mouth
  d. All of these are correct.

_____ 16. Extraembryonic membranes
  a. are found during the development of all vertebrates.
  b. are found during the development of reptiles, birds, and mammals.
  c. have exactly the same function in all vertebrates.
  d. Both _a_ and _c_ are correct.
  e. Both _a_ and _b_ are correct.

_____17. Which is NOT a distinguishing feature of vertebrates?
   a. dorsal notochord
   b. jointed internal skeleton
   c. extreme cephalization
   d. open circulatory system
   e. efficient respiration

_____18. The type of mammal that lays eggs while nourishing its young with milk is called
   a. a monotreme.
   b. a marsupial.
   c. placental.
   d. hermaphroditic.

_____19. Which is NOT true of echinoderms?
   a. external skeleton
   b. tube feet
   c. skin gills
   d. gonads in arms

_____20. Which is NOT an echinoderm?
   a. sea lily
   b. sea urchin
   c. sea cucumber
   d. sea horse

CRITICAL THINKING QUESTIONS

Answer in complete sentences.

21. Compare the success of chordate evolution to arthropod evolution. What are the similarities and differences?

22. Compare the adaptations of amphibians and reptiles to a land existence.

Test Results: _____ Number right ÷ 22 = _____ × 100 = _____ %

EXPLORING THE INTERNET

Use the Internet to further explore topics in this chapter, such as mammalian evolution, fish topics, and snake evolution. Go to the Mader Home Page (http://www.mhhe.com/sciencemath/biology/mader/) and click on *Biology,* 6th edition. Go to Chapter 35 and select a Web site of interest.

ANSWER KEY

STUDY EXERCISES

1.

Description
radial
spine-bearing, calcium-rich plates in an endoskeleton
gas exchange across skin gills and tube feet
central nerve ring plus radial nerves
a series of canals that ends at tube feet; a means of locomotion

2.

Examples	Distinctive Features
sea lilies, feather stars	branched arms for filter feeding
sea cucumbers	resemble cucumber, have tentacles for feeding
sea urchins, sand dollars	spines for locomotion, defense, burrowing
brittle stars	long, flexible arms
sea stars	five arms

3. See Figure 35.1, page 615, in text.   **4. a.** stone **b.** ring **c.** tube **d.** ampulla **e.** locomotion   **5.** The sea star everts its cardiac stomach, puts it in the shell, and secretes enzymes; partly digested food is taken up, and digestion is completed in the pyloric stomach.   **6.** See page 616 in text.   **7. a.** dorsal nerve cord in collar and trunk **b.** gill slits in pharynx **c.** The larvae of hemichordates and echinoderms are similar.
8.

Chordate Characteristics	Appearance
all three (larva); gill slits (adult)	thick-walled, squat sac
all three	lancet

9. a, c, d, e, h   **10. a.** Agnatha, fish **b.** Gnathostomata, fish **c.** Gnathostomata, fish **d.** Gnathostomata, tetrapod **e.** Gnathostomata, tetrapod **f.** Gnathostomata, tetrapod **g.** Gnathostomata, tetrapod   **11. a.** Amphibia **b.** Reptilia **c.** Chondrichthyes **d.** Aves **e.** Mammalia   **12. a.** C, B **b.** C, B **c.** B **d.** B **e.** B   **13. a.** first vertebrates **b.** first jawed vertebrates **c.** closest living relatives of modern amphibians **d.** first vertebrates to live on land **e.** first vertebrates to reproduce on land   **14. a.** smooth, nonscaly, and used for respiration **b.** small and poorly developed **c.** ectothermic **d.** undergo metamorphosis from tadpole to adult **e.** three chambers   **15. a.** yes **b.** One branch from the stem reptiles leads to birds. **c.** stem reptiles, pelycosaurs, therapsids, mammals **d.** yes **e.** Snakes and lizards have a common ancestor after the stem reptiles. **f.** The dinosaurs became extinct then. **g.** turtles, lizards, snakes, crocodiles   **16. a.** thick, dry, scaly **b.** more developed than in amphibians **c.** ectothermic **d.** amniote **e.** nearly or completely four chambered   **17. a.** provide broad, flat surfaces **b.** reduces weight **c.** attaches flight muscles **d.** provides good delivery of oxygenated blood to muscles **e.** provides good oxygenation of blood   **18. a.** 1, 2 **b.** 1, 3 **c.** 1, 4   **19. a.** bat **b.** horse **c.** whale **d.** lion **e.** monkey

OFFICE BUILDING ONE

1. i **2.** f **3.** d **4.** h **5.** d, e, f, g, h **6.** i **7.** d **8.** c **9.** f **10.** g **11.** h **12.** i **13.** e **14.** c, d, f, g **15.** f **16.** d, e, f, g, h **17.** d, e, f, g, h, i **18.** i **19.** c **20.** a, b **21.** g **22.** i **23.** f **24.** c **25.** g **26.** f **27.** e **28.** d **29.** h **30.** i **31.** e **32.** e, f, g, h, i **33.** c **34.** b **35.** f **36.** g **37.** f, g, h **38.** f **39.** g, h, i **40.** d, e, f, g, h, i **41.** b **42.** h **43.** f, g, h **44.** c **45.** f **46.** h **47.** g **48.** e **49.** c **50.** h **51.** g, h, i **52.** f **53.** e **54.** i **55.** d, f **56.** b, c **57.** e **58.** i **59.** d, e, f **60.** h **61.** f **62.** g **63.** d, h **64.** b **65.** h **66.** g, h **67.** h **68.** b, c **69.** c, d **70.** e, f, g, h, i

OFFICE BUILDING TWO

1. b, j **2.** d, e, f, g, h, i **3.** f, g, i **4.** b **5.** b, c **6.** d, e, f, g, h, i **7.** c, d, e, f, g, i **8.** b, h, j **9.** c, d, e, f, g, h, i **10.** f **11.** i **12.** b and j; g and i **13.** c **14.** i **15.** g **16.** f **17.** i **18.** e, g, h **19.** f **20.** h **21.** a **22.** e **23.** g **24.** h **25.** b **26.** i **27.** i **28.** g, i **29.** i **30.** b **31.** j **32.** f **33.** h **34.** h **35.** e **36.** none **37.** f, g **38.** a **39.** b, j **40.** c

OFFICE BUILDING THREE

1. e, f, g **2.** d **3.** f **4.** a **5.** g **6.** b **7.** g **8.** a, d **9.** a, b, c, d, e **10.** a, b, c **11.** g **12.** a **13.** g **14.** f **15.** a, b **16.** e **17.** f, g **18.** e **19.** g **20.** b **21.** e, f **22.** g **23.** f, g **24.** b, c **25.** g **26.** b, g **27.** d **28.** b **29.** g **30.** c **31.** c **32.** g **33.** c **34.** e **35.** c **36.** f, g **37.** c **38.** c, d, e, f, g **39.** c **40.** f **41.** d **42.** d, e, f, g **43.** e, f, g **44.** a, b, c **45.** f **46.** a, b, c **47.** e **48.** d, e, f, g **49.** e, f **50.** a, b

KEYWORD CROSSWORD

CHAPTER TEST

1. c **2.** d **3.** d **4.** d **5.** b **6.** c **7.** b **8.** d **9.** c **10.** d **11.** c **12.** a **13.** e **14.** c **15.** c **16.** b **17.** d **18.** a **19.** a **20.** d **21.** Each phylum contains numerous diversified species adapted to a variety of environments. Arthropods have more species.   **22.** Amphibians reproduce in the water and have a larval stage that develops in the water. The skin must be kept moist because it supplements the lungs for gas exchange. Reptiles reproduce on land because they lay a shelled egg with extraembryonic membranes. The skin can prevent desiccation because it is dry and scaly. The lungs are moderately developed, and a rib cage helps ventilate the lungs.

36

PLANT STRUCTURE

CHAPTER REVIEW

A flowering plant has three vegetative organs: roots, stems, and leaves. A **root** anchors a plant, absorbs water and minerals, and stores the products of photosynthesis. **Stems** support leaves, conduct materials to and from roots and leaves, and help store plant products. **Leaves** carry on photosynthesis.

Three types of tissue are found in each organ: dermal, **ground,** and **vascular. Epidermis** is the dermal tissue in most parts of the plant. **Parenchyma, collenchyma,** and **sclerenchyma** are the types of ground tissue. **Xylem,** which transports water and minerals, and **phloem,** which transports organic solutes, are the two types of vascular tissue.

Root tissues can be studied in longitudinal and cross section. There are several types of roots: **taproot, fibrous,** and **adventitious.** The layers and organization of vascular tissue differ in the roots of the **monocot,** the herbaceous **dicot,** and the woody dicot. The stems of woody, temperate plants experience pronounced secondary growth, developing **annual rings** of xylem.

The cross section of a leaf shows **mesophyll** between upper and lower layers of epidermis. The venation differs between monocots and dicots. Leaves can be simple or compound. Specializations of the leaf include **epidermis, stomates,** and mesophyll cells.

STUDY EXERCISES

Study the text section by section as you answer the questions that follow.

36.1 PLANTS HAVE ORGANS (P. 638)

- In a plant, the roots anchor, the stems support, and the leaves photosynthesize.

1. Flowering plants are adapted to living on land. The root system a._____ the plant in the soil and takes up b._____ and c._____, especially by means of d._____. Stems lift the leaves and e._____ water and minerals to the leaves. The leaves carry on f._____ after receiving water from the roots and g._____ from the air.

36.2 MONOCOT VERSUS DICOT PLANTS (P. 640)

- Flowering plants are classified into two groups: the monocots and the dicots.

2. Complete the following table to indicate the differences between monocot and dicot plants:

Plant Part	Monocot	Dicot
leaf veins		
vascular bundles in stem		
cotyledons in seed		
parts in a flower		
vascular tissue in root		

36.3 PLANT ORGANS HAVE TISSUES (P. 641)

- In a plant, epidermal tissue protects, ground tissue fills spaces, and vascular tissue transports water, along with ions and organic nutrients.

3. Match the cell types with the following tissue types:

   1 epidermal tissue
   2 ground tissue
   3 vascular tissue

   _____ a. sclerenchyma cells
   _____ b. tracheids
   _____ c. root hair cells
   _____ d. parenchyma cells
   _____ e. sieve-tube cells
   _____ f. vessel elements

4. Indicate whether each of the following statements is true (T) or false (F):

Epidermal Tissue:

   _____ a. Epidermis covers the entire body of nonwoody plants.
   _____ b. Epidermis covers the entire body of young woody plants.
   _____ c. Epidermis replaces cork in the stems of older plants.
   _____ d. Guard cells regulate the entrance of water into the roots.

Ground Tissue:

   _____ e. Collenchyma cells are a major site of photosynthesis.
   _____ f. Collenchyma has thinner primary walls than parenchyma.
   _____ g. Parenchyma is the least specialized cell type.
   _____ h. Sclerenchyma secondary walls are impregnated with lignin.
   _____ i. Sclereids give pears their gritty texture.

Vascular Tissue:

   _____ j. Phloem transports organic nutrients from leaves to roots.
   _____ k. Sieve-tube cells are found in xylem.
   _____ l. Tracheids are a type of cell in phloem.
   _____ m. Xylem transports water from roots to leaves.

36.4 HOW ROOTS ARE ORGANIZED (P. 644)

- In longitudinal section, a dicot root tip has a zone where new cells are produced, another where they elongate, and another where they mature.
- In cross section, dicot and monocot roots differ in the organization of their vascular tissue.
- Some plants have a taproot, others a fibrous root, and others have adventitious roots.

5. Label this diagram of a dicot root tip with the following terms:

cortex
endodermis
epidermis
pericycle
phloem
root cap
root hair
vascular cylinder
xylem
zone of cell division
zone of elongation
zone of maturation

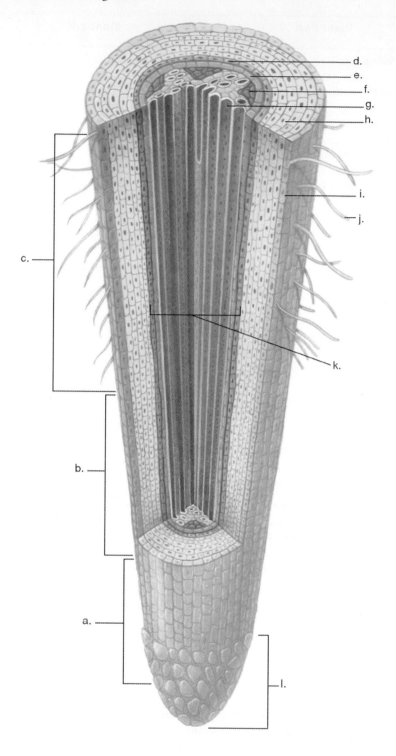

d.

e.

f.

g.

h.

i.

j.

c.

k.

b.

a.

l.

6. Explain what is happening in each of these zones of a root tip.

cell division a. _____

elongation b. _____

maturation c. _____

7. Complete the following table to describe and give a function for the specific tissues within a root:

Tissue	Description	Function
epidermis		
cortex		
endodermis		
vascular tissue		

8. Label each type of root shown and describe its special function.

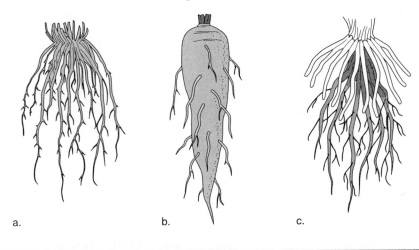

a.　　　　　b.　　　　　c.

36.5 HOW STEMS ARE ORGANIZED (P. 648)

- All stems grow in length, but some stems are woody and grow in girth also.
- In cross section, dicot and monocot herbaceous stems differ in the organization of their vascular tissue.
- Stems are modified in various ways, and some plants have horizontal aboveground or underground stems.

9. Study the diagram and write the term *herbaceous* or *woody* on the lines provided.

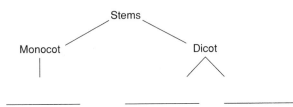

10. Label these diagrams of stems with the following terms (some are used more than once):

bark
cortex
epidermis
phloem
pith
vascular bundle
wood
xylem

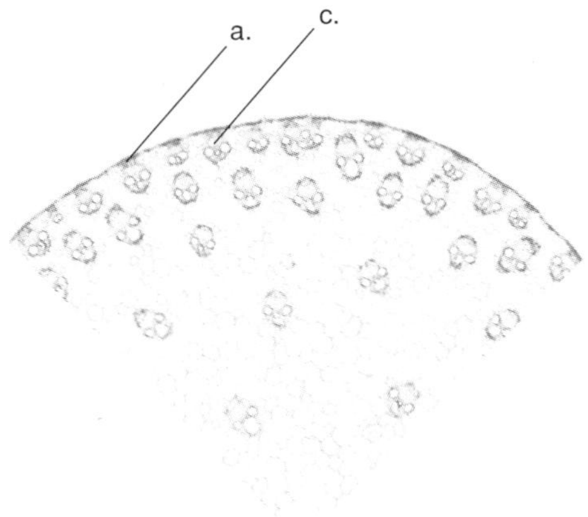

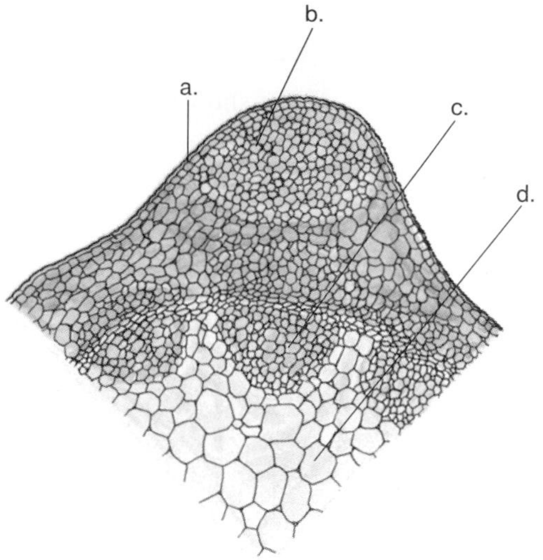

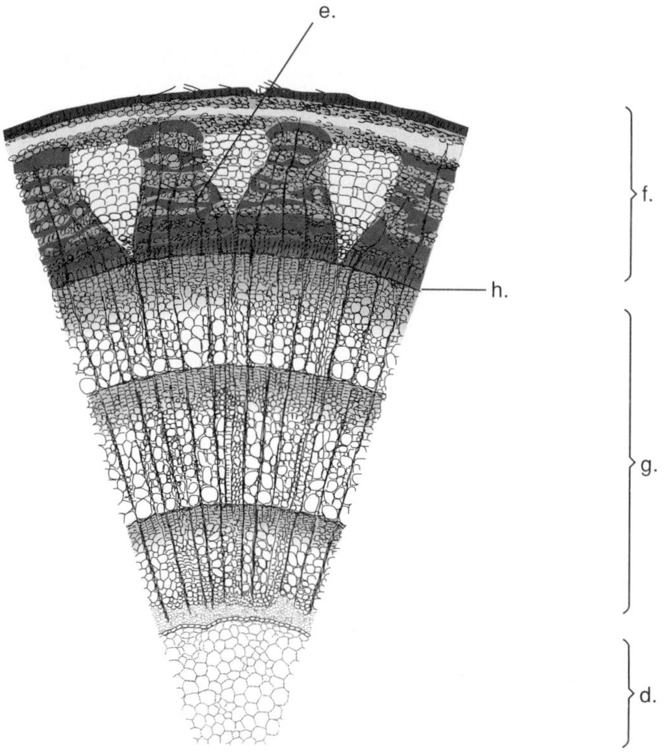

11. Based on your drawings in question 9, how would you describe the arrangement of vascular bundles in a herbaceous monocot stem?

a._____

In a herbaceous dicot stem? b._____

Annual rings appear in which of your drawings? c._____

What causes annual rings? d._____

12. Match the descriptions to the following types of stems:

    1 corm
    2 rhizome
    3 stolon
    4 tuber

    _____ a. bulbous underground stem

    _____ b. enlarged area of an underground stem that serves as storage area

    _____ c. underground stem that survives the winter

    _____ d. runner; new plants start from nodes

36.6 HOW LEAVES ARE ORGANIZED (P. 654)

- The bulk of a leaf is composed of cells that perform gas exchange and carry on photosynthesis.
- Leaves are modified in various ways; some conserve water, some help a plant climb, and some help a plant capture food.

13. a–g. Label this diagram of a leaf with the following terms (some are used more than once):

    epidermis
    guard cell
    leaf vein
    mesophyll
    palisade mesophyll
    spongy mesophyll
    stomate

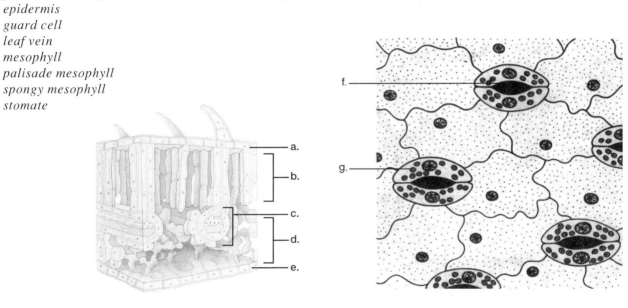

An extension of vascular bundles of stem is the h._____. The i._____

protects the leaf from drying out. The j._____ allow gas exchange. Longitudinal cells that

photosynthesize are the k._____. Loosely arranged cells that photosynthesize and

exchange gases are the l._____.

14. Place a check in front of the correct descriptions of leaves.

    _____ a. spines of a cactus

    _____ b. tendrils of a cucumber

    _____ c. trap of a Venus's-flytrap

    _____ d. stolon of a strawberry plant

Review key terms by completing this crossword puzzle, using the following alphabetized list of terms:

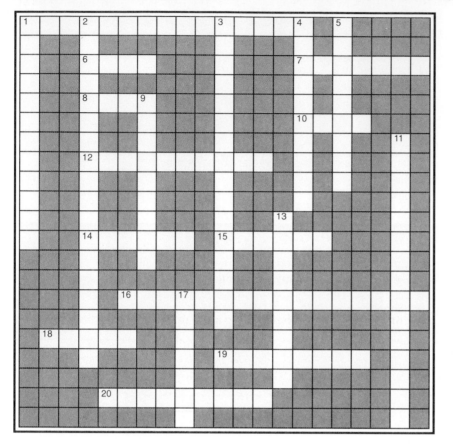

Casparian strip
cork
cork cambium
cotyledon
cuticle
endodermis
epidermis
herbaceous stem
leaf
meristem
mesophyll
palisade mesophyll
parenchyma
phloem
rhizome
root hair
spongy mesophyll
stem
stolon
vascular cambium
xylem

Across

1 layer of impermeable lignin and suberin bordering four sides of root endodermal cells; prevents water and solute transport between adjacent cells (two words)

6 usually broad, flat structure of a plant shoot system, containing cells that carry out photosynthesis

7 rootlike, underground stem

8 usually, the upright, vertical portion of a plant, which transports substances to and from the leaves

10 outer covering of bark of trees; made of dead cells that may be sloughed off

12 internal plant root tissue forming a boundary between the cortex and the vascular cylinder

14 stem that grows horizontally along the ground and establishes plantlets periodically when it contacts the soil (e.g., the runners of a strawberry plant)

15 vascular tissue that conducts organic solutes in plants; contains sieve-tube cells and companion cells

16 lateral meristem that produces secondary phloem and secondary xylem (two words)

18 vascular tissue that transports water and mineral solutes upward through the plant body; it contains vessel elements and tracheids

19 undifferentiated embryonic tissue in the active growth regions of plants

20 seed leaf for embryonic plant, providing nutrient molecules for the developing plant before its mature leaves begin to photosynthesize

Down

1 lateral meristem that produces cork (two words)

2 in a plant leaf, the layer containing elongated cells with many chloroplasts (two words)

3 in a plant leaf, the layer containing loosely packed, irregularly spaced cells that increase the amount of surface area for gas exchange (two words)

4 least specialized of all plant cell or tissue types; contains plastids and is found in all organs of a plant

5 in plants, the covering tissue of roots, leaves, and also stems of nonwoody organisms

9 inner, thickest layer of a leaf consisting of palisade and spongy; the site of most photosynthesis

11 nonwoody stem (two words)

13 extension of a root epidermal cell that collectively increases the surface area for the absorption of water and minerals (two words)

17 waxy layer covering the epidermis of plants that protects the plant against water loss and disease-causing organisms

OBJECTIVE QUESTIONS

Do not refer to the text when taking this test.

_____ 1. Each is an adult tissue in plants EXCEPT
   a. epidermal.
   b. ground.
   c. meristem.
   d. vascular.

_____ 2. Select the incorrect association.
   a. collenchyma—flexible support
   b. parenchyma—unspecialized
   c. sclerenchyma—tough and hard
   d. sieve tube—mechanical strength

_____ 3. Select the correct association.
   a. phloem—minerals
   b. phloem—photosynthesis
   c. xylem—sugar
   d. xylem—water

_____ 4. The zone farthest from the root cap is the zone of
   a. cell division.
   b. elongation.
   c. maturation.
   d. primary growth.

_____ 5. The cortex of the root mainly functions for
   a. entrance of substances into the root.
   b. photosynthesis.
   c. protection.
   d. starch storage.

_____ 6. The root type in the carrot is the
   a. adventitious root.
   b. fibrous root.
   c. taproot.
   d. prop root.

_____ 7. In the vascular bundles of a herbaceous stem,
   a. phloem develops to the inside.
   b. xylem develops to the outside.
   c. Both _a_ and _b_ are correct.
   d. Neither _a_ nor _b_ is correct.

_____ 8. A stolon is a(n)
   a. aboveground stem.
   b. cork covering on a stem.
   c. specialized type of leaf.
   d. underground stem.

_____ 9. The palisade mesophyll
   a. stores food in the form of starch for the rest of the plant.
   b. absorbs water and minerals.
   c. contains elongated cells where photosynthesis takes place.
   d. opens to allow gases to move in and out.

_____ 10. The wood portion of a woody stem is composed of
   a. pith.
   b. cambium.
   c. bark.
   d. secondary xylem.
   e. secondary phloem.

_____ 11. Trace the path of water from the roots to the leaves.
   a. root hairs→cortex→vascular cylinder→ vascular bundles→leaf veins
   b. root hairs→pith→xylem→phloem→ wood→leaf veins
   c. cortex→endodermis→xylem→tracheids→ parenchyma→leaf veins
   d. root hairs→sclerenchyma→vascular cylinder→cortex→leaf veins

_____ 12. Stomates are
   a. a type of transport tissue.
   b. openings in leaf epidermis.
   c. found in woody trees only.
   d. a universal type of cell.
   e. All of these are correct.

_____ 13. Which of these comparisons of monocots and dicots is NOT correct?

_____ | **Monocots** | **Dicots** |
   a. net veined—parallel veined
   b. one cotyledon—two cotyledons
   c. scattered vascular bundles—circular pattern
   d. flower parts in threes—flower parts in fours/fives

_____ 14. The root cap is produced from the zone of
   a. cell division.
   b. elongation.
   c. maturation.
   d. pericycle.
   e. vascular bundle.

_____ 15. A cross section through the zone of maturation of a dicot root would show
   a. cells of the root cap.
   b. the apical meristem.
   c. transport tissues.
   d. greatly elongated, undifferentiated cells.
   e. All of these are correct.

_____ 16. Annual rings in woody stems are caused by an increase in rings of the
   a. primary phloem.
   b. secondary phloem.
   c. primary xylem.
   d. secondary xylem.

____17. The point of a stem at which leaves or buds are attached is termed the
a. node.
b. internode.
c. lenticel.
d. endodermis.
e. plasmodesmata.

____18. Which of these is mismatched?
a. monocot stem—vascular bundles scattered
b. dicot herbaceous stem—vascular bundles in a ring
c. dicot woody stem—no vascular tissue
d. All of these are properly matched.

____19. Water taken up by root hairs has to enter the vascular cylinder because
a. osmosis draws it in.
b. guard cells regulate the opening of stomates.
c. the Casparian strip prevents anything else.
d. Both a and c are correct.

____20. A leaf is like a root because they both
a. photosynthesize.
b. store the products of photosynthesis in bad times.
c. have vascular tissue.
d. have a double layer of epidermis.

CRITICAL THINKING QUESTIONS

Answer in complete sentences.

21. Do plants have a true organ structure, just as animals do? What characteristics of their anatomy support your answer?

22. Why is the evolution of xylem such an important adaptation for the success of plants on land?

Test Results: _____ Number right ÷ 22 = _____ × 100 = _____%

EXPLORING THE INTERNET

Use the Internet to further explore topics in this chapter, such as plant morphology and anatomy. A listing of careers in botany is also available. Go to the Mader Home Page (http://www.mhhe.com/sciencemath/biology/mader) and click on *Biology,* 6th edition. Go to Chapter 36 and select a Web site of interest.

ANSWER KEY

STUDY EXERCISES

1. a. anchors b. water c. minerals d. root hairs e. transport f. photosynthesis g. carbon dioxide
2.

Monocot	Dicot
parallel pattern	net pattern
scattered	in a ring
one	two
in threes	in fours and fives
in a ring	in a vascular cylinder

3. a. 2 b. 3 c. 1 d. 2 e. 3 f. 3   4. a. T b. T c. F d. F e. F f. F g. T h. T i. T j. T k. F l. F m. T   5. See Figure 36.8, page 000, in text.   6. a. New cells are appearing. b. Cells are getting longer. c. Cells are mature and specialized.
7.

Description	Function
outer single layer of cells	root hairs, especially, absorb water and minerals
thin-walled parenchyma cells	food storage
single layer of rectangular cells	regulates entrance of minerals into vascular cylinder
xylem and phloem	transport water, minerals, and organic nutrients

8. a. fibrous root; holds soil **b.** taproot; stores **c.** prop root; anchors in marshy soil   **9.** herbaceous, herbaceous, woody   **10. a.** epidermis **b.** cortex **c.** vascular bundle **d.** pith **e.** phloem **f.** bark **g.** xylem **h.** vascular cambium   **11. a.** scattered **b.** ring **c.** woody stem **d.** summer xylem vessels are small, and spring vessels are large   **12. a.** 1 **b.** 4 **c.** 2 **d.** 3   **13. a.** epidermis **b.** palisade mesophyll **c.** leaf vein **d.** spongy mesophyll **e.** epidermis **f.** stomate **g.** guard cell **h.** leaf veins **i.** cuticle **j.** stomates **k.** palisade mesophyll **l.** spongy mesophyll   **14.** a, b, c

KeyWord CrossWord

Across and down answers:
- CASPARIAN STRIP
- LEAF
- RHIZOME
- STEM
- CORK
- ENDODERMIS
- STOLON
- PHLOEM
- VASCULAR CAMBIUM
- XYLEM
- MERISTEM
- COTYLEDON

Chapter Test

1. c **2.** d **3.** d **4.** c **5.** d **6.** c **7.** d **8.** a **9.** c **10.** d **11.** a **12.** b **13.** a **14.** a **15.** c **16.** d **17.** a **18.** c **19.** c **20.** c **21.** Several specialized tissues (epidermal, ground, vascular) are integrated structurally in the leaf, stem, and root. All are organs, consisting of two or more tissues working together.   **22.** Xylem allows plants to transport water against gravity, from roots to leaves. Without water transport, plants have to be low lying.

37

NUTRITION AND TRANSPORT IN PLANTS

The growth requirements of plants include water, carbon dioxide, oxygen, and some minerals. Plants require eighteen different elements, with carbon, hydrogen, and oxygen making up a substantial amount of a plant's body weight. Each mineral is essential for plant growth. The availability of various minerals in the soil depends on the soil's acidity. **Root hairs** enhance the uptake through active transport. **Nodules** in the roots of leguminous plants facilitate **nitrogen fixation.**

Water and minerals are transported in **xylem,** and organic nutrients are transported in **phloem. Water potential,** which is dependent upon pressure potential and osmotic potential, accounts for the development of turgor pressure, as well as for the movement of water and organic substances in vascular tissue.

Water and minerals pass from the soil through the various layers of the root, eventually entering the vascular cylinder. Positive pressure (due to the lower osmotic potential of root cells) cannot account for water movement in xylem. Rather, water enters and ascends through the xylem because of negative pressure potential caused by **transpiration** at the leaves. Both cohesion and adhesion prevent water molecules from breaking apart in the water column. Transpiration occurs through the **stomates** of leaves. **Guard cells** regulate the opening and closing of stomates in response to various environmental conditions.

Organic solutes pass through the phloem of the plant from a source to a sink, according to the **pressure-flow model.** The active transport of sucrose at the source causes water to enter the phloem, creating a positive pressure. This causes sap to flow from the area of greater solute concentration to the area of lower solute concentration at the sink.

Study the text section by section as you answer the questions that follow:

37.1 PLANTS REQUIRE INORGANIC NUTRIENTS (P. 660)

- Certain inorganic nutrients (e.g., NO_3^-, K^+, Ca^{2+}) are essential to plants; others that are specific to a type of plant are termed beneficial.
- Mineral ions cross plasma membranes by a chemiosmotic mechanism.

1. Label each of the following as either a macronutrient (MA) or micronutrient (MI):
   _____ a. carbon
   _____ b. hydrogen
   _____ c. iron
   _____ d. manganese
   _____ e. potassium
   _____ f. boron

2. An investigator burns a plant, examines the ashes, and finds a synthetic element such as plutonium in the ash. What should he conclude? _____

_____

3. An investigator is studying plant nutrition by means of hydroponics. She finds that the plant apparently is thriving, even though no manganese has been added to the culture water. What should she conclude?

_____

4. The lower the pH, the a._____ the leaching power of water. Aluminum and iron become available to plants in very b._____ soils. Clay particles in the soil have numerous c._____ charges that attract minerals with d._____ charges.

How Minerals Are Taken in and Distributed (p. 662)

- Plants have various adaptations that assist them in acquiring nutrients. For example, symbiotic relationships are of special interest.

5. The _____ of the root regulates the entrance of minerals into the vascular cylinder.
6. Describe the adaptations for each of the following regarding nutrient uptake at the roots:

   root hairs a._____

   nodules in leguminous plants b._____

   mycorrhizae c._____

37.2 HOW WATER MOVES THROUGH A PLANT (P. 664)

- The vascular system in plants is an adaptation to living on land.

7. Indicate whether the statements that follow are true (T) or false (F). Change all false statements to true statements.

   _____ a. Xylem is composed of sieve-tube cells and tracheids. Rewrite:_____

   _____

   _____ b. Xylem is an open pipeline from the roots to the leaves. Rewrite:_____

   _____

   _____ c. Phloem is composed of sieve-tube cells which are connected by strands called fibers. Rewrite:_____

   _____

   _____ d. Sieve-tube cells have a nucleus, but companion cells do not. Rewrite:_____

   _____

   _____ e. Water but not organic nutrients can move from the leaves to the roots through phloem. Rewrite:_____

   _____

8. Study this diagram and then answer the questions that follow.

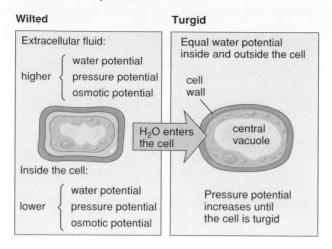

Water potential is based on a._____ potential and b._____ potential. Water

flows from the c._____ pressure potential to the lower pressure potential and from

the d._____ osmotic potential to the lower osmotic potential. As water flows into a wilted

cell, the pressure potential builds, and the flow of water ceases when the cell is e._____.

Xylem Transports Water (p. 666)

- Xylem is the vascular tissue that transports water and minerals; phloem is the vascular tissue that transports organic nutrients.

9. Rearrange the letters of the root structures to show the path of water as it enters the vascular cylinder.
   _____

   a. Casparian strip
   b. cortex
   c. endodermis
   d. epidermis
   e. xylem

10. Water enters the cells of roots by a._____. b._____ pressure pushes sap in the

xylem in a(n) c._____ direction. This movement and pressure account

for d._____ along the edges of leaves.

When Is Water Available? (p. 666)

- The tissues of a root are organized so that water entering between or at the root hairs will eventually enter the xylem.

11. Indicate whether the following statements are true (T) or false (F):
    _____ a. Clay soil is more permeable than sandy soil.
    _____ b. Gravity drains water away from plant roots.
    _____ c. Sandy soil has the largest field capacity.
    _____ d. The permanent wilting point determines the availability of water to plant roots.

To the Leaves (p. 667)

- Because water molecules are cohesive and adhere to xylem walls, the water column in xylem is continuous.
- Transpiration (evaporation) creates a negative pressure that pulls water and minerals from the roots to the leaves in xylem.

12. Study this diagram and then answer the questions that follow.
Explain why transpiration occurs.

a._____

_____

_____

What type of pressure does this create?

b._____

_____

_____

Why doesn't the water column in xylem break?

c._____

_____

_____

The lower water potential in roots is due to the lower (negative) pressure potential and the lower osmotic potential. Which of these causes water to rise from the roots to the leaves?

d._____

_____

_____

Explain what is meant by *cohesion-tension model of xylem transport?*

e._____

_____

_____

_____

_____

_____

The Driving Force—Transpiration:

Energy ultimately comes from the sun.

Evaporation from leaves creates a negative pressure potential.

H_2O

Cohesion in Xylem:

Water column is held together by cohesion.

Adhesion to cell walls keeps water column in place.

Water Uptake from Soil:

H_2O

Negative pressure potential is transferred to root cells, and water enters roots.

Opening and Closing of Stomates (p. 668)

• Stomates must be open for evaporation to occur.

13. Stomates open during photosynthesis when? a._____ ions are actively transported b._____ (*into/out of*) the guard cells. Water now enters the guard cells by c._____, causing the cells to buckle out due to their d._____ (*thick/thin*) inner walls.

14. Rearrange the letters of steps *a–e* to demonstrate how stomates proceed from closed to open positions. _____
    _____
    a. CO_2 decreases in leaf.
    b. K^+ enters guard cells.
    c. Stomates are closed.
    d. Stomates are open.
    e. Water enters guard cells.

15. What two important events are occurring when stomates are open?
    a._____
    b._____

37.3 HOW ORGANIC NUTRIENTS ARE TRANSPORTED (P. 670)

• Active transport of sucrose into phloem creates a positive pressure that causes organic nutrients to flow in phloem from a source (where sucrose enters) to a sink (where sucrose exits).

16. Study the diagram on page 323 and then answer the questions that follow.

What is the "active" part of phloem transport? a._____

_____

When water enters phloem at the leaves, what type of pressure potential is created? b._____

As water flows from the area of higher pressure potential to the area of lower pressure potential, what happens? c._____ Phloem sap moves from a source to a sink. In the summer, what organ is the source of sucrose? d._____ In the spring, before leaves begin to photosynthesize, what organ is the source? e._____

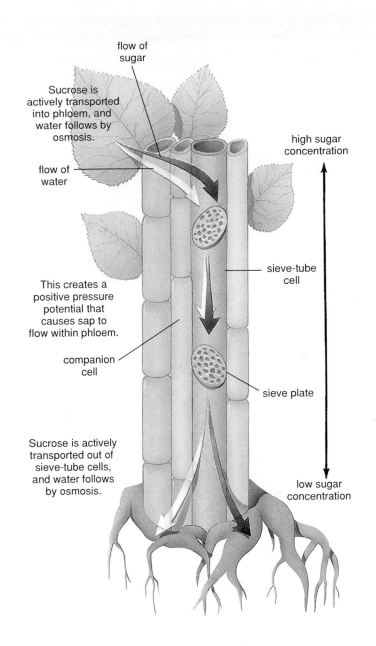

flow of
sugar

Sucrose is
actively transported
into phloem, and
water follows by
osmosis.

flow of
water

This creates a
positive pressure
potential that
causes sap to
flow within phloem.

companion
cell

Sucrose is actively
transported out of
sieve-tube cells,
and water follows
by osmosis.

high sugar
concentration

sieve-tube
cell

sieve plate

low sugar
concentration

Review key terms by completing this crossword puzzle, suing the following alphabetized list of terms:

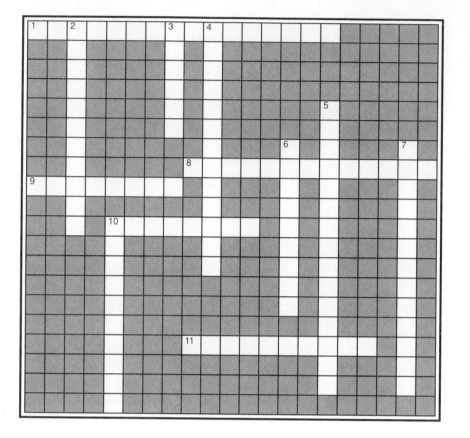

cohesion-tension
epiphyte
girdling
guard cell
guttation
hydroponics
mycorrhiza
nodule
pressure-flow
root pressure
transpiration
water potential

Across

1 explanation for the transport of water to great heights in a plant due to a negative water potential (compared to the roots); this movement is brought about by transpiration and depends on the ability of water molecules to cohere and to adhere to cell walls (two words)

8 model explaining transport through phloem sieve tubes by a positive pressure potential (compared to a sink) due to the active transport of sucrose and the passive transport of water (two words)

9 plant that takes its nourishment from the air because its attachment to other plants gives it an aerial position

10 removing a strip of bark from around a tree

11 symbiotic relationship between fungal hyphae and roots of vascular plants; the fungus allows the plant to absorb more mineral ions and obtains carbohydrates from the plant.

Down

2 water culture method of growing plants that allows an experimenter to vary the nutrients and minerals provided so as to determine the essential nutrients

3 structure on plant roots that contains nitrogen-fixing bacteria

4 plant's loss of water to the atmosphere, mainly through evaporation at leaf stomates

5 potential energy of water; it is a measure of the capability to release or take up water (two words)

6 liberation of water droplets from the edges and tips of leaves

7 force generated by an osmotic gradient that elevates sap through xylem for a short distance (two words)

10 type of plant cell found in pairs, with one on each side of a leaf stomate; changes in the turgor pressure of these cells regulate the size and passage of gases through the stomate (two words)

OBJECTIVE QUESTIONS

Do not refer to the text when taking this test.

In questions 1–10, indicate whether the statement is true (T) or false (F).

_____ 1. Water moves through the layers of a root by osmosis.

_____ 2. The tracheids of xylem are actively metabolizing cells.

_____ 3. Guttation mainly accounts for the upward pull of water through the xylem of a stem.

_____ 4. The activity of guard cells regulates the opening and closing of stomates.

_____ 5. Calcium is a plant micronutrient.

_____ 6. Sulfur is a plant macronutrient.

_____ 7. Increased acidity leaches more elements from the soil.

_____ 8. The cortex is the second root layer that water encounters as it passes through the root toward the vascular cylinder.

_____ 9. By the pressure-flow model of phloem transport, substances travel from the source to the sink.

_____10. Epiphytes are a specialized type of plant root system.

_____11. What role does transpiration play in water transport?
   a. no role
   b. pushes the water
   c. pulls the water

_____12. For transpiration to occur in the leaves,
   a. water must exhibit cohesiveness.
   b. the stomates must be open.
   c. water must evaporate.
   d. All of these are correct.

_____13. If the water potential is higher outside the cell than inside the cell, most likely
   a. water will flow into the cell.
   b. the cell contents have the lower pressure potential.
   c. the solute concentration is higher inside the cell.
   d. All of these are correct.

_____14. Which is the incorrect association?
   a. xylem—transport of water and minerals
   b. phloem—transport of sucrose
   c. mycorrhizae—atmospheric nitrogen uptake
   d. mineral uptake—ATP required

_____15. Turgor pressure is important to
   a. stomate opening and closing.
   b. plant cell rigidity.
   c. water flow in xylem.
   d. Both a and b are correct.
   e. All of these are correct.

_____16. The Casparian strip causes
   a. water to enter the vascular cylinder.
   b. sucrose to enter phloem.
   c. water to stay within xylem during transport.
   d. All of these are correct.

_____17. During transpiration, the negative pressure potential is due to the
   a. cohesion of water molecules.
   b. active transport of sucrose into root cells.
   c. evaporation of water from the leaves.
   d. All of these are correct.

_____18. Which is the incorrect association?
   a. xylem transport—negative pressure potential
   b. phloem transport—positive pressure potential
   c. xylem transport—positive pressure potential
   d. phloem transport—active transport needed

_____19. When stomates are open,
   a. carbon dioxide enters leaves.
   b. potassium and water have entered guard cells.
   c. negative pressure potential pulls water upward.
   d. All of these are correct.

_____20. During phloem transport, the sink has
   a. the higher solute concentration, accounting for why water flows to it.
   b. the lower solute concentration, due to the active transport of sucrose out of it.
   c. the higher solute concentration because that is where sucrose is needed.
   d. Both a and c are correct.

Answer in complete sentences.

21. Physical and chemical laws explain many of the phenomena in biological systems. How is this demonstrated in the ascent of sap through xylem?

22. How are physical and chemical laws demonstrated in the opening and closing of stomates?

Test Results: _____ Number right ÷ 22 = _____ × 100 = _____ %

EXPLORING THE INTERNET

Use the Internet to further explore topics in this chapter, such as the nature of phloem and the essential nutrients for plants. Go to the Mader Home Page (http://www.mhhe.com/sciencemath/biology/mader/) and click on *Biology,* 6th edition. Go to Chapter 37 and select a Web site of interest.

ANSWER KEY

STUDY EXERCISES

1. a. MA b. MA c. MI d. MI e. MA f. MI 2. The plant probably does not require the plutonium, which it acquired accidentally. 3. Manganese probably is already in the water. 4. a. greater b. acidic c. negative d. positive 5. endodermis 6. a. increase surface area for more uptake b. facilitate fixation of nitrogen c. increase surface area and facilitate the breakdown of organic matter for nutrient availability 7. a. F; . . . composed of vessel elements and tracheids b. T c. F; . . . strands called plasmodesmata connect d. F; Companion cells have a nucleus, but sieve-tube cells do not. e. F; Organic nutrients can move from . . .

8. a. pressure b. osmotic c. higher d. higher e. turgid 9. d, b, a, c, e 10. a. osmosis b. Root c. upward d. guttation 11. a. F b. T c. F d. T 12. a. The sun causes water to evaporate at leaves. b. negative pressure c. Water molecules cling to one another (cohesion) and to sides of vessels (adhesion). d. negative pressure potential e. Cohesion refers to water molecules clinging together, and tension refers to negative pressure potential. Consequently, water flows upward along the length of the plant. 13. a. potassium b. into c. osmosis d. thick 14. c, a, b, e, d 15. a. Carbon dioxide is being absorbed. b. Water is lost in transpiration. 16. a. active transport of sucrose into phloem b. positive c. Sucrose moves with it. d. leaves e. roots

KEYWORD CROSSWORD

¹C	O	²H	E	S	I	O	³N	-	⁴T	E	N	S	I	O	N			
	Y			O		R												
	D			D		A												
	R			U		N												
	O			L		S				⁵W								
	P			E		P				A								
	O					I		⁶G		T		⁷R						
	N		⁸P	R	E	S	S	U	R	E	-	F	L	O	W			
⁹E	P	I	P	H	Y	T	E		A		T		R		O			
	C					A			T		T		O		T			
	S	¹⁰G	I	R	D	L	I	N	G		A		P		P			
	U				O				T		I		O		R			
	A				N				I		O		R		E			
	R								O		N		E		S			
	D								N		T				S			
						¹¹M	Y	C	O	R	R	H	I	Z	A	U		
	C										A				U			
	E										L				E			
	L																	
	L																	

CHAPTER TEST

1. T 2. F 3. F 4. T 5. F 6. T 7. T 8. T 9. T 10. F 11. c 12. d 13. d 14. c 15. d 16. a 17. c 18. c 19. d 20. b 21. The evaporation of water and the cohesion between water molecules bring about this process. 22. Osmosis and the mechanical strength of cell walls are involved in this process.

38

GROWTH AND DEVELOPMENT IN PLANTS

Like animals, plants utilize a reception-transduction-response pathway when they respond to a stimulus. **Tropisms** are growth responses toward or away from unidirectional stimuli. Positive **phototropism** of stems is growth toward light. Negative **gravitropism** of stems is growth away from the direction of gravity. **Thigmotropism** occurs when a plant makes contact with an object. Nastic movements are not directional.

Plants exhibit **circadian rhythms** such as the sleep movements of prayer plants and beans and the closing of stomates. A **biological clock** most likely controls these circadian rhythms.

Both stimulatory and inhibitory **hormones** help control growth patterns. Some hormones stimulate growth (**auxins, gibberellins, and cytokinins**), and some inhibit growth (**ethylene and abscisic acid**).

Photoperiodism is the response to the relative length of daylight and darkness. Flowering in plants is a photoperiodic event, leading to the classification of plants as **short-day, long-day,** or **day-neutral.** The response of the pigment **phytochrome** is believed to be involved in the flowering event.

STUDY EXERCISES

Study the text section by section as you answer the questions that follow.

38.1 PLANT RESPONSES TO STIMULI (P. 676)

- Similar to animals, plants use a reception-transduction-response pathway when they respond to a stimulus similar to animals.
- Tropisms are growth responses in plants toward or away from unidirectional stimuli such as light or gravity.
- Plants sometimes exhibit circadian rhythms (e.g., closing of stomates) that reoccur every 24 hours.

1. Match each description with the following terms:
   1 reception
   2 transduction
   3 response
   _____ a. The stimulus is changed into a form meaningful to the organism.
   _____ b. The organism reacts to the stimulus.
   _____ c. The organism perceives the stimulus.
   _____ d. Plants have a pigment that detects far-red light.
   _____ e. When far-red light is present, genes produce an enzyme.
   _____ f. When the enzyme is present, chlorophyll is produced, and the plant turns green.

2. Identify the type of response described, and add the word *positive* or *negative* if appropriate.

   A plant tendril encircles an object. a._____

   A root grows down into the soil. b._____

   When sensitive hairs are touched, the leaves of a Venus's-flytrap snap shut. c._____

   Leaves track the sun, and the stem bends toward the light. d._____

   Stomates open and close every 24 hours. e._____

- Some plant hormones stimulate growth, and other plant hormones inhibit growth.
- The biochemical manner in which auxin and gibberellin function has been studied.
- It now appears that various plant hormones interact to bring about a response to a stimulus.

3. Complete the following table of stimulatory plant hormones:

Name	Function

4. Indicate whether the statements that follow, concerning oat seedling experiments, are true (T) or false (F). Change all false statements to true statements.

_____ a. Oat seedlings with tips removed still bend toward the light. _____

_____ b. When an agar block (containing auxin) is placed on one side of a tipless coleoptile, the shoot curves toward that side. _____

_____ c. Auxin normally moves to the shady side, and thereafter, the stem bends toward the light. _____
_____

5. a Label the diagrams with the following terms: *ATP, auxin, H+,* and *receptor* (some are used more than once).

   b. Explain what is happening in each diagram.

_____
_____
_____

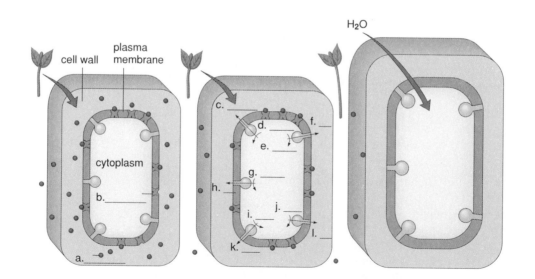

Gibberellins and Stem Elongation (p. 682)

6. What effect do gibberellins have on the following?

   stems a._____

   dormancy of seeds and buds b._____

   dwarf plants c._____

7. Study this diagram and then answer the questions that follow concerning how gibberellin stimulates growth of a plant embryo.

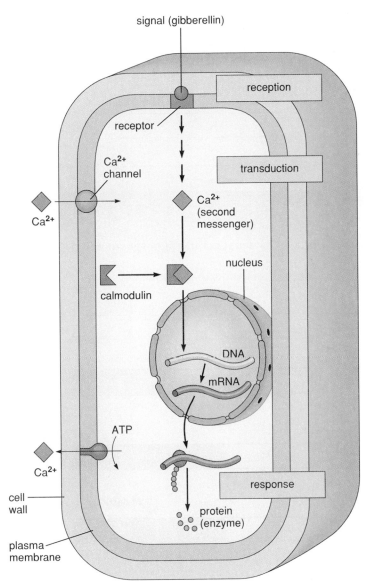

What happens after gibberellin attaches to the plasma membrane? a._____

How does calcium (Ca^{2+}) enter a cell? b._____

What does the calcium-calmodulin complex do? c._____

_____

How does this help the embryo grow? d._____

_____

8. Indicate whether the following statements about tissue culture experiments that demonstrate plant hormone interaction are true (T) or false (F):

_____ a. Cellular enzymes affect the activity of plant hormones.

_____ b. Oligosaccharins function in animals but not in plants.

_____ c. The acidity of the culture medium affects cell differentiation.

_____ d. The ratio of auxin to cytokinin affects cell differentiation.

Plant Hormones That Inhibit (p. 687)

9. What effect does abscisic acid have on the following?

seed and bud dormancy a._____

stomates b._____

a bud in the fall c._____

10. What effect does ethylene have on the following?

ripening of fruit a._____

growth of house plants b._____

abscission c._____

38.3 THE PHOTOPERIOD CONTROLS SEASONAL CHANGES (P. 688)

• Plant responses that are controlled by the length of daylight (photoperiod) involve the hormone phytochrome.

11. Study the diagram and then answer the questions that follow.

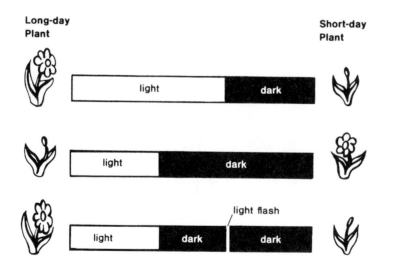

Long-day Plant   Short-day Plant

light   dark

light   dark

light   dark   dark   light flash

A long-day (short-night) plant flowers when the night is a._____ than a critical length. A short-day (long-night) plant will not flower when the night is b._____ than a critical length.

A long-day (short-night) plant will not flower when the night is c._____ than a critical length. A short-day (long-night) plant will flower when the night is d._____ than a critical length.

A long-day (short-night) plant will flower if a flash of light interrupts a night that is [e.]_____ than a critical length. A short-day (long-night) plant will not flower if a flash of light interrupts a night that is [f.]_____ than a critical length.

The conclusion is that it is the length of the [g.]_____, and not the [h.]_____, controls flowering.

12. a. Label the three arrows in the diagram with the following terms: *metabolic conversion, absorbs red light,* and *absorbs far-red light.*

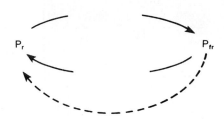

b. Place the following terms above and below the arrows as appropriate: *daytime,* and *shade and evening.*

c. Place the following terms to one side of P_r or P_{fr} as appropriate: *flowering is stimulated* and *stem elongation is inhibited.*

d. The conclusion is that P_{fr} _____

_____.

Review key terms by completing this crossword puzzle, using the following alphabetized list of terms:

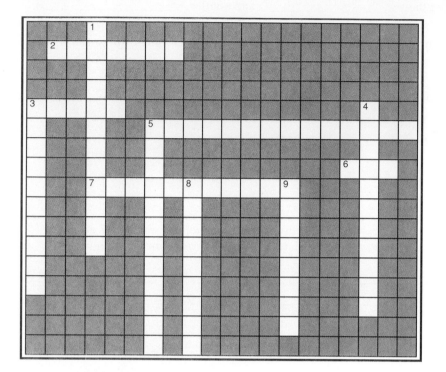

ABA
abscission
auxin
cytokinin
ethylene
gibberellin
gravitropism
hormone
photoperiodism
phototropism
phytochrome

Across

2 chemical messenger produced in one part of the body that controls the activity of other parts

3 plant hormone regulating growth, particularly cell elongation; most often indoleacetic acid (IAA)

5 relative lengths of daylight and darkness that affect the physiology and behavior of an organism

6 plant hormone that causes stomates to close and that initiates and maintains dormancy

7 photoreversible plant pigment whose active form seems to be involved in regulating transcription of certain genes

Down

1 directional growth of plants in response to the earth's gravity

3 dropping of leaves, fruits, or flowers from a plant

4 plant hormone producing increased stem growth; also involved in flowering and seed germination

5 directional growth of plants in response to light

8 plant hormone that promotes cell division; often works in combination with auxin during organ development in plant embryos

9 plant hormone that causes ripening of fruit and is also involved in abscission

CHAPTER TEST

OBJECTIVE QUESTIONS

Do not refer to the text when taking this test.

____ 1. The main site of hormone production in plants is in the
a. epidermis.
b. ground tissue.
c. meristem.
d. vascular tissue.

____ 2. Select the incorrect statement about auxins.
a. They cause breakdown of polysaccharides in the cell wall.
b. Their concentration in leaves and fruits prevents leaves and fruits from falling to the ground.
c. They are produced in the shoot apex of the plant.
d. They are transported to the side of the plant receiving light.

_____ 3. The main effect of gibberellins is to
   a. hasten the ripening of fruits.
   b. inhibit the flowering process.
   c. prevent leaf abscission.
   d. promote cell division and enlargement.

_____ 4. Senescence is the
   a. aging of the overall plant.
   b. loss of leaf color.
   c. propagation of cuttings.
   d. process of flowering.

_____ 5. Ethylene increases the ripening of fruit by stimulating
   a. cell wall production.
   b. enzyme activity.
   c. pigment production.
   d. RNA synthesis.

_____ 6. Another name for ABA is the
   a. dormancy hormone.
   b. flowering inhibitor.
   c. growth inhibitor.
   d. stress hormone.

_____ 7. Select the incorrect association.
   a. positive gravitropism—response to gravity
   b. phototropism—response to light stimulus
   c. negative gravitropism—response to gravity
   d. thigmotropism—response to chemical stimulus

_____ 8. Which of the following is NOT a response to primarily an internal stimulus?
   a. contraction movement
   b. nastic movement
   c. phototropic movement
   d. twining movement

_____ 9. Which of the following is NOT classified as a short-day plant?
   a. barley
   b. cocklebur
   c. poinsettia
   d. chrysanthemum

_____ 10. Interrupting the dark period with a flash of white light prevents flowering in a
   a. long-day plant.
   b. short-day plant.

_____ 11. Which of these would represent transduction following perception of a stimulus?
   a. The stem bends toward the light.
   b. An enzyme is made.
   c. The cell wall weakens.
   d. The cell takes in water.

_____ 12. Which of these is an example of thigmotropism?
   a. A dwarf bean becomes a pole bean.
   b. The prayer plant performs a sleep movement.
   c. When tendrils are touched, they begin to curve.
   d. All of these are correct.

_____ 13. Stomates close every 24 hours because
   a. auxin moves to the shady side of a stem.
   b. cytokinins and auxin are in balance.
   c. plants have a biological clock.
   d. All of these are correct.

_____ 14. Oat seedlings will NOT bend
   a. when exposed to artificial plant hormones.
   b. when coleoptile tips are cut off.
   c. when P_r has become P_{fr}.
   d. All of these are correct.

_____ 15. The reception of auxin leads to
   a. the removal of H^+ from the cell.
   b. $ATP \rightarrow ADP + P$.
   c. the weakening of plant cell walls.
   d. All of these are correct.

_____ 16. When calcium combines with calmodulin,
   a. the amount of amylase in embryonic cells decreases.
   b. the amount of amylase in embryonic cells increases.
   c. a gene is activated.
   d. Both _b_ and _c_ are correct.

_____ 17. Which of these is mismatched?
   a. abscisic acid—stomates close
   b. ethylene—fruits ripen
   c. cytokinin—stems elongate
   d. auxin—stems bend toward the light

_____ 18. Photoperiodism is a
   a. nastic response.
   b. circadian rhythm.
   c. tropism.
   d. light/dark response.

_____ 19. Phytochrome
   a. stimulates the genes directly.
   b. produces an enzyme directly.
   c. is involved in perception of stimulus.
   d. All of these are correct.

_____ 20. In a short-day plant, flowering is believed to depend on
   a. proper lighting.
   b. the presence of phytochrome.
   c. the proper hormonal balance.
   d. All of these are correct.

CRITICAL THINKING QUESTIONS

Answer in complete sentences.

21. Based on their response to photoperiod, many plant species are classified as short-day or long-day. Do you think that these are the best titles for these plant categories?

22. Explain what is meant by a reception-transduction-response pathway.

Test Results: _____ Number right ÷ 22 = _____ × 100 = _____ %

EXPLORING THE INTERNET

Use the Internet to further explore topics in this chapter, such as means of vegetative propagation or the role of IAA in apical dominance and how it can be exploited for plant sculpture techniques. Go to the Mader Home Page (http://www.mhhe.com/sciencemath/biology/mader/) and click on *Biology*, 6th edition. Go to Chapter 38 and select a Web site of interest.

ANSWER KEY

STUDY EXERCISES

1. **a.** 2 **b.** 3 **c.** 1 **d.** 1 **e.** 2 **f.** 3   **2. a.** thigmotropism **b.** positive gravitropism **c.** nastic movement **d.** positive phototropism **e.** circadian rhythm

3.

Name	Function
auxin	phototropism, gravitropism, apical dominance
gibberellin	stem elongation, growth of dwarf plants, seed and bud dormancy broken
cytokinin	cell division, prevention of leaf senescence, initiation of growth

4. a. F; . . . do not bend toward . . . **b.** F; . . . curves away from that side **c.** T   **5. a.** See Figure 38.8, page 681, in text. **b.** Auxin is attaching to receptors. Proton pump is breaking down ATP and pumping H^+ out of the cell. H^+ causes the cell wall to break down, water enters, and the cell increases in size.   **6. a.** makes them grow **b.** breaks dormancy **c.** makes them grow   **7. a.** Ca^{2+} enters the cell and attaches to calmodulin. **b.** through a channel in the plasma membrane **c.** activates a gene and amylase is produced **d.** Amylase breaks down starch, providing glucose as a source of energy.   **8. a.** F **b.** F **c.** T **d.** T   **9. a.** promotes it **b.** closes them **c.** promotes formation of bud scales   **10. a.** promotes it **b.** retards it **c.** promotes it   **11. a.** shorter **b.** shorter **c.** longer **d.** longer **e.** longer **f.** longer **g.** night **h.** day   **12. a.–b.** See Figure 38.15, page 689, in text. **c.** Place both labels beside P_{fr} **d.** is the metabolically active form

KEYWORD CROSSWORD

CHAPTER TEST

1. c **2.** d **3.** d **4.** b **5.** b **6.** d **7.** d **8.** c **9.** a **10.** b **11.** b **12.** c **13.** c **14.** b **15.** d **16.** d **17.** c **18.** d **19.** c **20.** d   **21.** The category titles are somewhat misleading, because the plants are responding mainly to the length of darkness as opposed to the length of daylight.   **22.** During reception, a plasma membrane receptor receives the hormone, such as gibberellin; during transduction, a cellular signal such as a second messenger forms; during the response, DNA is activated and a protein, such as amylase, is made so that growth and elongation occur. See also figure on page 329 of Study Guide.

39

REPRODUCTION IN PLANTS

Angiosperms reproduce sexually, and many species require an animal **pollinator** for seed and fruit production. By an alternation of generations life cycle, flowering plants develop a **microgametophyte (pollen grain)** and a **megagametophyte (embryo sac)**. The megagametophyte remains within the **sporophyte**. The diploid sporophyte is the dominant generation.

To carry out its role as the reproductive organ of the plant, the **flower** has many specialized parts, including an outer whorl, an inner whorl, the **pistil,** and an **ovary** (containing **ovules**). **Double fertilization** occurs in angiosperms, producing a 2n zygote and a 3n **endosperm** cell. The zygote becomes the sporophyte **embryo.** The ovule of the ovary matures into a **seed.** The ovary becomes the **fruit.** There can be fleshy, dry, aggregate, or multiple fruits.

Angiosperms have several means of seed dispersal, including wind, water, or animal transport. The dicot embryo, derived from the zygote, eventually develops a shoot apex, root apex, and other parts that become visible during development.

Asexual means of reproduction in flowering plants include propagation from cuttings, grafting, and budding, as well as **tissue culture** techniques.

STUDY EXERCISES

Study the text section by section as you answer the questions that follow.

39.1 FLOWERING PLANTS UNDERGO ALTERNATION OF GENERATIONS (P. 694)

- Flowering plants have an alternation of generations life cycle. The plant that bears flowers is the sporophyte.

1. What role does the sporophyte play in the plant life cycle?   a._____

_____

What role does the gametophyte play in the plant life cycle?   b._____

_____

What role does a pollen grain play in the flowering plant life cycle?   c._____

_____

What role does an ovule play in the flowering plant life cycle?   d._____

_____

2. a. Label this diagram of the life cycle of a flowering plant with the following terms:
   anther
   megagametophyte
   megaspore
   microgametophyte
   microspore
   ovary
   seed
   sporophyte
   zygote

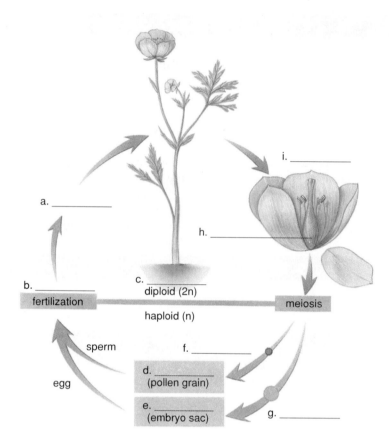

Which generation is dominant? b._____ Flowering plants produce two different types of spores: c._____ and d._____.

3. Label this diagram of a flower with the following terms:
   anther
   filament
   ovary
   ovule
   petal
   pistil
   pollen grain
   pollen tube
   sepal
   stamen
   stigma
   style

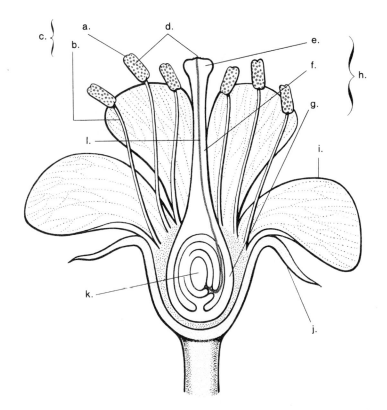

4. Name the following parts of a flower:

   green leaves that form a whorl ^{a.}_____

   colored leaves of a flower ^{b.}_____

   a vaselike structure ^{c.}_____that consists of:

      a sticky enlarged knob ^{d.}_____

      a slender stalk ^{e.}_____

      an enlarged base containing ovules ^{f.}_____

   stamen components include:

      a saclike container that produces pollen grains ^{g.}_____

      a slender stalk ^{h.}_____

The Gametophytes Are Separate (p. 697)

* Flowering plants have two types of gametophytes: the microgametophyte (male) and the megagametophyte (female).

5. In the pistil, a megasporocyte undergoes $^{a.}$_____to produce one $^{b.}$_____megaspore. This megaspore divides by $^{c.}$_____ $^{d.}$_____times, resulting in a megagametophyte with $^{e.}$_____cells and $^{f.}$_____nuclei. This is called the $^{g.}$_____sac. One cell will be the $^{h.}$_____, and one cell will have $^{i.}$_____polar nuclei.

6. In the $^{a.}$_____, many $^{b.}$_____undergo $^{c.}$_____, each producing $^{d.}$_____ haploid microspores. Each microspore divides once by $^{e.}$_____, forming a two-celled $^{f.}$_____. This is the $^{g.}$_____, which contains the $^{h.}$_____cell and the tube cell.

Pollination Precedes Fertilization (p. 700)

* Pollen grains (microgametophytes) carry sperm to the megagametophyte, which produces an egg. This is an adaptation to a land environment.

7. Label each of the following statements as describing pollination (P) or fertilization (F):
   _____ a. can be assisted by the wind
   _____ b. sperm and egg nuclei unite
   _____ c. transfer from anther to stigma
   _____ d. 3n endosperm cell forms

8. $^{a.}$_____occurs when a pollen grain lands on the sticky part of the $^{b.}$_____. One pollen cell will form the $^{c.}$_____, which dissolves a path to the ovary. The other pollen cell divides by $^{d.}$_____ to form $^{e.}$_____ sperm nuclei. One will fertilize the egg, forming a(n) $^{f.}$_____. The other will unite with two polar nuclei, forming a(n) $^{g.}$_____ endosperm. This process is unique to flowering plants and is called $^{h.}$_____.

39.2 THE EMBRYO DEVELOPS IN STAGES (P. 701)

* The dicot embryo goes through a series of stages; once the cotyledons appear, it is possible to distinguish the shoot apex and the root apex.

9. Indicate whether the following statements about the development of the dicot embryo are true (T) or false (F):
   _____ a. Early division of the embryo produces two parts.
   _____ b. Root apical meristem produces underground growth.
   _____ c. Shoot apical meristem produces aboveground growth.
   _____ d. The early embryo is torpedo shaped.

39.3 THE SEEDS ARE ENCLOSED BY FRUIT (P. 702)

* A seed has a seed coat, an embryo, and stored food.
* In flowering plants, seeds are enclosed by fruits that develop from the ovary and accessory organs of a flower.
* Fruits aid the dispersal of seeds.

10. The zygote develops into a(n) a._____ enclosed in a seed coat surrounded by

the b._____ wall and is called a(n) c._____. The endosperm

forms d._____ food within the seed, which will then germinate to produce a new

e._____.

11. Label the type of fruit depicted with the following terms:

achene
berry
capsule
drupe
follicle
legume
nut
pome

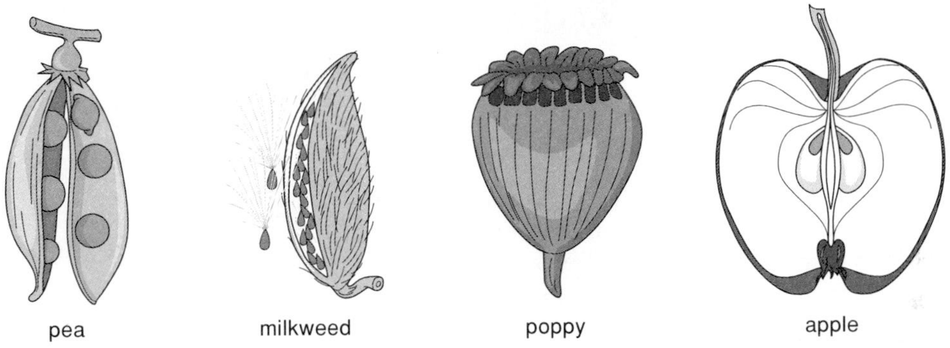

| pea | milkweed | poppy | apple |

a. _____   b. _____   c. _____   d. _____

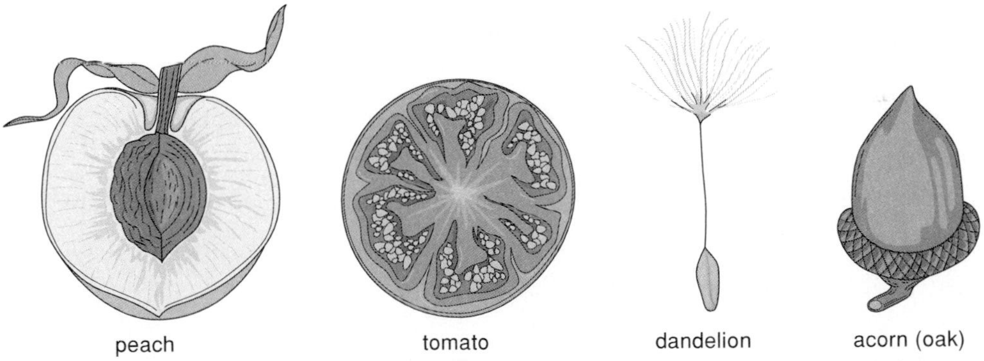

| peach | tomato | dandelion | acorn (oak) |

e. _____   f. _____   g. _____   h. _____

12. What is the pericarp? a._____

Explain the term *simple fruit*. b._____

Explain the term *dry fruit*. c._____

Explain the term *compound fruit*. d._____

A peach is a simple fruit with a(n) e._____ pericarp, while a nut is a simple fruit with a(n)

f._____, hard pericarp.

13. List four ways that seeds and fruits are dispersed.

a._____

b._____

c._____

d._____

14. Label each statement as describing the structure and germination of either the bean seed (B) or the corn kernel (C).

_____ a. It is actually a fruit.

_____ b. The plumule is enclosed in a sheath called the coleoptile.

_____ c. Most of the food storage tissue is endosperm.

_____ d. Shoot is hook shaped.

39.4 PLANTS CAN REPRODUCE ASEXUALLY (P. 708)

- Many flowering plants have an asexual means of propagation (i.e., from nodes of stems or from roots).
- Laboratory means of propagating plants from meristem, anther, culture, or from protoplasts (cells that lack cell walls) have been developed. Protoplasts lend themselves to genetic engineering.

15. Place a check in front of the example(s) of vegetative propagation.

_____ a. strawberry plants grown from the nodes of stolons

_____ b. potato plants grown from the eyes of a potato

_____ c. ornamental plants grown from stem cuttings

16. Place a check in front of the characteristics of vegetative propagation.

_____ a. sexual reproduction

_____ b. asexual reproduction

_____ c. new plant genetically identical to original plant

_____ d. new plant genetically dissimilar to original plant

17. Micropropagation is a commercial way to produce thousands of a._____

(*identical/dissimilar*) seedlings utilizing b._____ culture. Somatic embryos can be grown

from flower c._____, which is free of viruses. Anther culture, which allows the production of

plants that express d._____ alleles, uses the tube cell of e._____ grains. The

process of culturing individual cells—derived from root, stem, or leaf—to produce desirable chemicals is

called f._____. A protoplast is a(n) g._____ that can go on to develop into an

entire plant.

Genetic Engineering of Plants (p. 710)

18. Indicate whether the following statements are true (T) or false (F):

_____ a. It is possible to produce transgenic animals but not transgenic plants.

_____ b. Fertile transgenic corn and wheat plants can be grown from protoplasts.

_____ c. A particle gun bombards plant cells with DNA-coated metal particles.

_____ d. Propagation of plants from single cells is a form of asexual reproduction.

Review key terms by completing this crossword puzzle, using the following alphabetized list of terms:

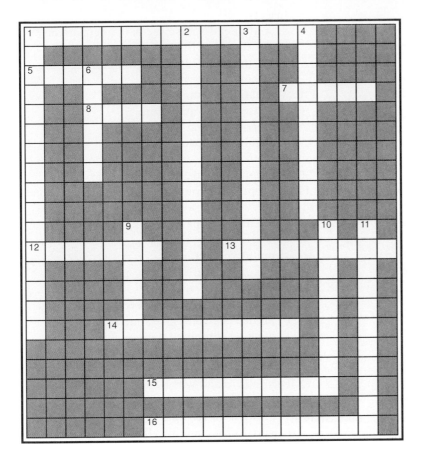

carpel
cotyledon
embryo sac
flower
fruit
hybridization
megagametophyte
megaspore
microgametophyte
microspore
pistil
plumule
pollen grain
pollination
protoplast
seed
tissue culture

Across

1 in seed plants, the gametophyte that produces an egg; in flowering plants, an embryo sac

5 in flowering plants, a reproductive unit of a pistil

7 flowering plant structure consisting of one or more ripened ovaries

8 mature ovule that contains an embryo and stored food enclosed in a protective coat

12 in flowering plants, the embryonic plant shoot that bears young leaves

13 seed leaf for the embryo of a flowering plant; provides nutrient molecules for the developing plant before it begins to photosynthesize

14 plant cell from which the cell wall has been removed

15 spore produced by a microsporocyte of a seed plant; it develops into a pollen grain

16 sperm-bearing structure in seed plants (two words)

Down

1 in seed plants, the gametophyte that produces sperm; a mature pollen grain

2 process of growing tissue artificially, usually in a liquid medium in laboratory glassware (two words)

3 crossing of different varieties or species

4 megagametophyte of flowering plants that contains an egg cell (two words)

6 flower structure consisting of an ovary, a style, and a stigma

9 reproductive organ of a flowering plant, consisting of several kinds of modified leaves arranged in concentric rings and attached to a modified stem called the receptacle

10 spore produced by the megasporocyte of a seed plant

11 in seed plants, the transfer of pollen from the microsporangium to the ovule, which by this time contains a megagametophyte

OBJECTIVE QUESTIONS

Do not refer to the text when taking this test.

_____ 1. Which of these is a true statement?
   a. A microspore develops into an immature microgametophyte.
   b. The dominant generation of the angiosperm is the haploid gametophyte.
   c. Pollination is the union of male and female sex cells.
   d. Most fruits are compound fruits.

_____ 2. Which of these is a false statement?
   a. Flower structures are modified leaves.
   b. The hypocotyl is the portion of the stem above the attachment of the cotyledons.
   c. Hooks and spines of clover are a means of dispersal.
   d. A fruit is the mature ovary containing seeds.

_____ 3. In the life cycle of flowering plants, there are
   a. two types of spores.
   b. microspores and megaspores.
   c. two types of pollen grains.
   d. Both a and b are correct.
   e. All of these are correct.

_____ 4. The ovule is to the pistil as the
   a. anther is to the stamen.
   b. anther is to the filament.
   c. filament is to the anther.
   d. All of these are correct.

_____ 5. The structure immediately preceding the megagametophyte is the
   a. microgametophyte.
   b. ovule.
   c. megaspore.
   d. pistil.

_____ 6. Pollination
   a. precedes fertilization.
   b. is the transfer of pollen to the pistil.
   c. requires the presence of water.
   d. Both a and b are correct.
   e. All of these are correct.

_____ 7. The dicot embryo begins as
   a. two cotyledons.
   b. a single-celled zygote.
   c. a heart-shaped single cell.
   d. All of these are correct.

_____ 8. What do a tomato, a peach, and an apple have in common?
   a. They are all fruits.
   b. They are all fleshy fruits.
   c. They are all drupes.
   d. Both a and b are correct.
   e. All of these are correct.

_____ 9. Insects
   a. routinely disperse seeds in angiosperms.
   b. are flower pollinators.
   c. are the only flower pollinators.
   d. All of these are correct.

_____10. Vegetative propagation
   a. is asexual propagation.
   b. can occur from stems.
   c. requires the use of leaves.
   d. Both a and b are correct.
   e. All of these are correct.

_____11. Micropropagation takes its name from the use of
   a. the microscope.
   b. single cells or tissues.
   c. culture media.
   d. All of these are correct.

_____12. Anther culture
   a. produces homozygous recessive genotypes.
   b. produces genetically similar plants.
   c. must be combined with ovule culture.
   d. Both a and b are correct.
   e. All of these are correct.

_____13. Fertile corn and wheat plants cannot be
   a. genetically engineered.
   b. grown from genetically engineered protoplasts.
   c. grown from single cells.
   d. All of these are correct.

_____14. In the life cycle of flowering plants, the embryo sac
   a. is the equivalent of the pollen grain.
   b. has ten cells.
   c. contains an embryo.
   d. All of these are correct.

_____15. A(n) _____ produces four pollen grains.
   a. microspore
   b. microsporocyte
   c. anther
   d. microsporangium

_____16. Fertilization in flowering plants
   a. results in a 2n zygote and 3n endosperm.
   b. results in a 3n embryo and 2n endosperm.
   c. involves the polar nuclei but not the egg nucleus.
   d. occurs rarely.

_____17. Fruits are classified according to whether they are
   a. big or small.
   b. dry or fleshy.
   c. simple or compound.
   d. Both b and c are correct.
   e. All of these are correct.

_____18. The pollen grain contains
   a. the sperm.
   b. the egg.
   c. the embryo.
   d. It depends on the photoperiod.
_____19. Fertilization in flowering plants occurs
   a. in the flower.
   b. prior to seed formation.
   c. in the ovary.
   d. All of these are correct.

_____20. A seed typically
   a. contains an embryo and stored food.
   b. germinates before it starts to grow.
   c. has cotyledons.
   d. All of these are correct.

CRITICAL THINKING QUESTIONS

Answer in complete sentences.

21. What is one advantage and one disadvantage of asexual plant reproduction, compared to sexual plant reproduction?

22. Aside from pollination, how does seed dispersal by birds and mammals represent another example of coevolution?

Test Results: _____ Number right ÷ 22 = _____ × 100 = _____ %

EXPLORING THE INTERNET

Use the Internet to further explore topics in this chapter, such as hydroponics or flower structure. Go to the Mader Home Page (http://www.mhhe.com/sciencemath/biology/mader/) and click on *Biology,* 6th edition. Go to Chapter 39 and select a Web site of interest.

ANSWER KEY

STUDY EXERCISES

1. a. The sporophyte produce spores; in flowering plants, the sporophyte produces microspores and megaspores. **b.** The gametophyte produces gametes; in flowering plants, the microspore becomes the sperm-bearing pollen grain (microgametophyte) and the megaspore becomes the egg-bearing embryo sac (megagametophyte). **c.** Pollen grain carries sperm to the embryo sac. **d.** Ovule first contains the megaspore and then the embryo sac and then develops into the seed. **2. a.** See Figure 39.1, page 694, in text. **b.** sporophyte **c.** megaspores **d.** microspores **3. a.** anther **b.** filament **c.** stamen **d.** pollen grain **e.** stigma **f.** style **g.** ovary **h.** pistil **i.** petal **j.** sepal **k.** ovule **l.** pollen tube **4. a.** sepals **b.** petals **c.** pistil **d.** stigma **e.** style **f.** ovary **g.** anther **h.** filament **5. a.** meiosis **b.** haploid **c.** mitosis **d.** four **e.** seven **f.** eight **g.** embryo **h.** egg **i.** two **6. a.** anther **b.** microsporocytes **c.** meiosis **d.** four **e.** mitosis **f.** pollen grain **g.** microgametophyte **h.** generative **7. a.** P **b.** F **c.** P **d.** F **8. a.** Pollination **b.** pistil **c.** pollen tube **d.** mitosis **e.** two **f.** zygote **g.** 3n **h.** double fertilization **9. a.** T **b.** T **c.** T **d.** F **10. a.** embryo **b.** ovary **c.** fruit **d.** stored **e.** sporophyte **11. a.** legume **b.** follicle **c.** capsule **d.** pome **e.** drupe **f.** berry **g.** achene **h.** nut **12. a.** thickened ovary wall **b.** developed from an individual ovary **c.** pericarp is dry **d.** developed from a group of individual ovaries **e.** fleshy **f.** dry **13. a.** hooks and spines **b.** defecation by birds and mammals **c.** squirrel activity **d.** wind and ocean currents **14. a.** B **b.** C **c.** C **d.** B **15.** a, b, c **16.** b, c **17. a.** identical **b.** tissue **c.** meristem **d.** recessive **e.** pollen **f.** cell suspension culture **g.** naked cell **18. a.** F **b.** F **c.** T **d.** T

Crossword solution (across):
1. MEGAGAMETOPHYTE
5. CARPEL
7. FRUIT
8. SEED
12. PLUMULE
13. COTYLEDON
14. PROTOPLAST
15. MICROSPORE
16. POLLEN GRAIN

Crossword solution (down):
1. MICROGAMETOPHYTE
2. TISSUE CULTURE
3. HYBRIDIZATION
4. EMBRYO SAC
6. PISTIL
9. FLOWER
10. MEGASPORANGIUM
11. POLLINATION

1. a 2. b 3. d 4. a 5. c 6. d 7. b 8. d 9. b 10. d 11. b 12. d 13. b 14. a 15. b 16. a 17. d 18. a 19. d 20. d 21. Asexual reproduction offers a quick, effective means of reproducing plants; however, it lacks the mechanism for genetic variability available through sexual reproduction. Through the latter, more adaptive forms of the organism can be produced and survive, especially if the environment is changing. 22. The seeds are dispersed over wide distances, promoting their range of survival. The birds and mammals gain a food source while eating the fruit with the seed.

40

ANIMAL ORGANIZATION AND HOMEOSTASIS

CHAPTER REVIEW

Three embryonic germ layers (ectoderm, endoderm, and mesoderm) form the four main categories of **tissue** types in the animal body. **Epithelial tissue** covers the body and lines body cavities. Its cells exist in several shapes, and it can be either simple or stratified. **Connective tissue** exists in many forms: **loose, fibrous, adipose, cartilage,** and **blood.** Each type has a specialized function. **Muscular tissue** contracts. Its forms are **skeletal** (attached to bone), **cardiac** (in the heart), and **smooth** (in all other internal organs). **Nervous tissue,** consisting of

neurons, sends signals. Neuroglial cells support and protect neurons.

Tissues work together as **organs.** The skin is one good example. Many of the organs in the human body are in two body cavities, the dorsal and the ventral. Several related organs form an **organ system.**

Regulation of pH, body temperature, and blood glucose level are good examples **homeostasis.** Through **negative feedback,** the body maintains a relatively constant internal environment.

STUDY EXERCISES

Study the text section by section as you answer the questions that follow.

40.1 ANIMALS ARE ORGANIZED (P. 718)

- Animals have the following levels of organization: molecules—cells—tissues—organs—organ systems—organism.
- Animal tissues can be organized into four major types: epithelial, connective, muscular, and nervous tissue.

1. What four categories of tissues does the text recognize? _____

_____

Epithelial Tissue Covers (p. 718)

- Epithelial tissues, which line body cavities and cover surfaces, are specialized in structure and function.

2. a. Draw a diagram of squamous epithelium.

Name one place in the human body where squamous epithelial tissue can be found. b._____

What is the function of this tissue? c._____

3. a. Draw a diagram of cuboidal epithelial tissue.

Name one place in the human body where cuboidal epithelial tissue can be found. b._____

What is the function of this tissue? c._____

4. a. Draw a diagram of simple columnar epithelial tissue.

Name one place in the human body where simple columnar epithelial tissue can be found. b._____

What is the function of this tissue? c._____

5. The windpipe is lined by pseudostratified ciliated columnar epithelium. Describe this tissue._____

_____

Connective Tissue Connects (p. 720)

- Connective tissues, which protect, support, and bind other tissues, include cartilage and bone and also blood, the only liquid tissue.

6. a. Draw a diagram of loose connective tissue, and include fibroblasts and fibers.

Where in the body do you find this type of tissue? b._____

7. Which type of fiber predominates in fibrous connective tissue? a._____

Tendons are a type of fibrous connective tissue that join b._____ to

c._____.

Ligaments join d._____ to e._____.

8. a. Draw a diagram of cartilage, and label lacunae and the matrix.

Name one place in the human body where cartilage can be found. b._____

9. Draw a diagram of compact bone, and label lacunae, osteons, and central canals.

10. a. Draw a diagram of blood, and include red blood cells, white blood cells, and platelets.

One function of red blood cells is to b._____; one function of white blood cells is to c._____; and one function of platelets is to d._____.

Muscular Tissue Contracts (p. 722)

- Muscular tissues, which contract, make body parts move.

11. Complete the following table to compare types of muscular tissue:

	Fiber Appearance	Location	Control
Skeletal			
Cardiac			
Smooth			

Nervous Tissue Conducts (p. 723)

12. The brain and spinal cord are made up of cells called ^{a.}_____. Outside the central

nervous system, connective tissue binds the long fibers of these cells to form ^{b.}_____.

The function of a neuron is to ^{c.}_____.

The other type of cells in nervous tissue are ^{d.}_____ cells.

This type of cell provides ^{e.}_____ to neurons and keeps tissue free of debris.

Neuroglial cells outnumber neurons ^{f.}_____ to one and take up more than

^{g.}_____ the volume of the brain.

40.2 ORGANS HAVE STRUCTURE AND FUNCTIONS (P. 724)

- Organs usually contain several types of tissues. For example, although skin is composed primarily of epithelial tissue and connective tissue, it also contains muscle and nerve fibers.
- Organs are grouped into organ systems, each of which has specialized functions.
- The coelom, which arises during development, is later divided into various cavities where specific organs are located.

13. Label this diagram of skin with the following terms:

   adipose tissue
   arrector pili muscle
   artery
   connective tissue
   dermis
   epidermis
   hair root
   hair shaft
   nerve
   oil gland
   sense organs
   subcutaneous layer
   sweat gland
   vein

14. Name the system that performs each of the following functions:

   transports materials by the blood ^{a.}_____

   breaks down substances in the diet ^{b.}_____

   distributes and exchanges gases ^{c.}_____

   pulls on bones to produce movements ^{d.}_____

   controls and coordinates through hormones ^{e.}_____

15. Label the following as located in the thoracic cavity (T) or the abdominal cavity (A):

_____ a. small intestine
_____ b. ovaries
_____ c. bladder
_____ d. heart
_____ e. lungs
_____ f. stomach
_____ g. liver
_____ h. kidneys

40.3 HOMEOSTASIS IS NECESSARY (P. 728)

- Homeostasis is the relative constancy of the internal environment. All organ systems contribute to homeostasis in animals.

16. What is homeostasis? a._____

What is the internal environment? b._____

Give an example of homeostasis. c._____

17. How does each of the following systems contribute to homeostasis?

digestive system a._____

respiratory system b._____

urinary system (i.e., the kidneys) c._____

18. The two systems of the body that control homeostasis are a._____

and b._____.

19. Put the following terms in the proper sequence to describe a negative feedback cycle: *effector, receptor, regulator center,* and *response.* _____

_____

20. The body maintains a relatively steady body temperature. If the body cools, what events raise body

temperature? a._____

_____

If the body heats up, what events lower body temperature? b._____

_____

Review key terms by completing this crossword puzzle, using the following alphabetized list of terms:

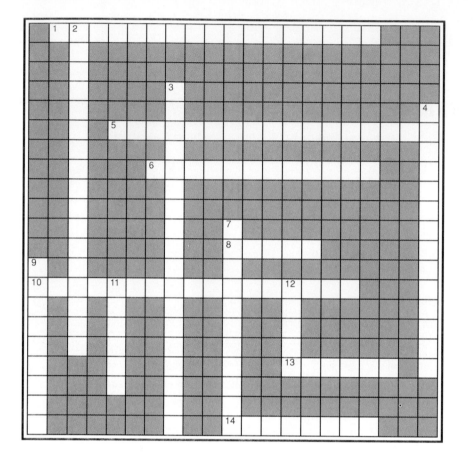

blood
connective tissue
contractile tissue
dermis
epidermis
epithelial tissue
homeostasis
negative feedback
nervous tissue
organ
organ system
positive feedback
striated
tissue

Across

1 mechanism of homeostatic response in which the output is counter to and cancels the input (two words)

5 type of animal tissue that binds structures together, provides support and protection, fills spaces, stores fat, and forms blood cells (two words)

6 group of related organs working together (two words)

8 combination of two or more different tissues performing a common function

10 mechanism of homeostatic response in which the output intensifies and increases the likelihood of response, instead of countering it and canceling it (two words)

13 deeper, thicker layer of the skin that consists of fibrous connective tissue and contains various structures such as sense organs

14 having bands; cardiac and skeletal muscle have bands of light and dark

Down

2 type of animal tissue forming a continuous layer over most body surfaces (i.e., skin) and inner cavities (two words)

3 type of animal tissue composed of fibers that shorten and lengthen to produce movements (two words)

4 type of animal tissue that contains nerve cells (neurons), which conduct impulses, and neuroglial cells, which support, protect, and provide nutrients to neurons (two words)

7 maintenance of internal conditions in a cell or an organism by means of a self-regulation mechanism

9 outer, protective layer of the skin

11 group of similar cells combined to perform a common function

12 type of connective tissue in which cells are separated by a liquid called plasma

Do not refer to the text when taking this test.

_____ 1. Cells working together form
   a. organs.
   b. tissues.
   c. systems.
   d. organisms.

_____ 2. Which of these is true of humans?
   a. They have a vertebral column.
   b. The ventral cavity is divided into two cavities.
   c. The endocrine and nervous systems help coordinate the internal organs.
   d. Muscle and bones make up most of the body weight.
   e. All of these are true.

_____ 3. Which of these pairs is mismatched?
   a. fat—subcutaneous layer
   b. sense organs—dermis
   c. keratinization—epidermis
   d. nerves and blood vessels—epidermis

_____ 4. Which type of epithelial tissue is composed of flat cells?
   a. squamous
   b. cuboidal
   c. columnar
   d. striated

_____ 5. What type of epithelial cells are found in the epidermis?
   a. squamous
   b. columnar
   c. cuboidal
   d. Both _b_ and _c_ are correct.

_____ 6. Which of these tissues lines body cavities?
   a. muscular
   b. epithelial
   c. connective
   d. tendons

_____ 7. Both cartilage and bone
   a. have a flexible matrix.
   b. have cells within lacunae.
   c. contain calcium salts.
   d. are a type of epithelial tissue.

_____ 8. Which of these is a connective tissue?
   a. bone
   b. cartilage
   c. blood
   d. All of these are correct.

_____ 9. Which of these is a loose connective tissue?
   a. tendons
   b. ligaments
   c. adipose tissue
   d. All of these are correct.

_____ 10. Which of these contains blood vessels?
   a. lacuna
   b. matrix
   c. central canal
   d. Both _a_ and _b_ are correct.

_____ 11. Which of the following are cell fragments?
   a. platelets
   b. red blood cells
   c. white blood cells
   d. Both _a_ and _b_ are correct.

_____ 12. What type of tissue does the dermis consist of?
   a. epithelial
   b. connective
   c. muscle
   d. All of these are correct.

_____ 13. A muscle tissue that is both striated and involuntary is
   a. smooth.
   b. skeletal.
   c. cardiac.
   d. All of these are correct.

_____ 14. Which of these types of muscles helps maintain posture?
   a. skeletal
   b. smooth
   c. cardiac
   d. involuntary

_____ 15. Which of these is a nerve cell?
   a. neuroglial cell
   b. dendrite
   c. cell body
   d. neuron

_____ 16. Which of these is the uppermost layer of skin?
   a. fat
   b. subcutaneous
   c. dermis
   d. epidermis

_____ 17. Adipose tissue is found in the
   a. dermis.
   b. epidermis.
   c. subcutaneous.
   d. All of these are correct.

_____ 18. Which of these is located in the abdominal cavity?
   a. heart
   b. digestive system
   c. much of the reproductive system
   d. Both _b_ and _c_ are correct.

_____19. Which of these is an example of homeostasis?
   a. Muscle tissue is specialized to contract.
   b. Normal body temperature is always about 37° C.
   c. There are more red blood cells than white blood cells.
   d. All of these are correct.
_____20. In a negative feedback control system,
   a. homeostasis is impossible.
   b. there is a constancy of the internal environment.
   c. there is a fluctuation about a mean.
   d. Both *a* and *c* are correct.

_____21. When body temperature rises, sweat glands become _____ and blood vessels _____.
   a. active; constrict
   b. inactive; dilate
   c. active; dilate
   d. inactive; constrict

CRITICAL THINKING QUESTIONS

Answer in complete sentences.

22. How is each level of organization of the human body more than merely the sum of its parts?

23. Why is it important to body health to maintain a relatively constant environment?

Test Results: _____ Number right ÷ 23 = _____ × 100 = _____ %

EXPLORING THE INTERNET

Use the Internet to further explore topics in this chapter, such as skin cancer or plastic surgery. Go to the Mader Home Page (http://www.mhhe.com/sciencemath/biology/mader/) and click on *Biology,* 6th edition. Go to Chapter 40 and select a Web site of interest.

ANSWER KEY

STUDY EXERCISES

1. epithelial, connective, muscular, nervous   2. a. See Figure 40.2, page 719, in text. b. blood vessels, esophagus c. protection   3. a. See Figure 40.2, page 719, in text. b. kidney tubules c. absorption   4. a. See Figure 40.2, page 719, in text. b. lining of intestine c. protection and absorption   5. appears to be many layers but is actually only one; cells have little hairs   6. a. See Figure 40.3, page 720, in text. b. beneath skin and most epithelial layers   7. a. collagen fibers b. muscles c. bones d. bones e. bones   8. a. See Figure 40.3, page 720, in text. b. nose, ears, ends of bones   9. See Figure 40.3, page 720, in text.   10. a. See Figure 40.4, page 721, in text. b. carry oxygen c. fight infection d. aid in blood clotting

11.

Fiber Appearance	Location	Control
striated	skeleton	voluntary
striated	heart	involuntary
spindle shaped	internal organs	involuntary

12. a. neurons b. nerves c. transmit nerve impulses d. neuroglial e. support and protection f. nine g. half   13. a. epidermis b. dermis c. subcutaneous layer d. hair shaft e. arrector pili muscle f. sense organs g. oil gland h. hair root i. adipose tissue

j. connective tissue **k.** vein **l.** artery **m.** sweat gland **n.** nerve **14. a.** cardiovascular **b.** digestive **c.** respiratory **d.** skeletal **e.** endocrine **15. a.** A **b.** A **c.** A **d.** T **e.** T **f.** A **g.** A **h.** A **16. a.** the relative constancy of the internal environment **b.** tissue fluid **c.** body temperature remaining around 37° C **17. a.** provides nutrient molecules **b.** removes carbon dioxide and adds oxygen to the blood **c.** eliminates wastes and salts **18. a.** nervous **b.** endocrine **19.** receptor, regulator center, effector, response **20. a.** Blood vessels constrict and sweat glands become inactive. **b.** Blood vessels dilate and sweat glands become active.

KEYWORD CROSSWORD

Across
1. NEGATIVE FEEDBACK
5. CONNECTIVE TISSUE
6. ORGAN SYSTEM
8. ORGAN
10. POSITIVE FEEDBACK
13. DERMIS
14. STRIATED

Down
2. EPITHELIAL TISSUE
3. CONTRACTILITY
4. NERVOUS TISSUE
7. HOMEOSTASIS
9. EPIDERMIS
11. TISSUES
12. BLOOD

CHAPTER TEST

1. b **2.** e **3.** d **4.** a **5.** a **6.** b **7.** b **8.** d **9.** c **10.** c **11.** a **12.** b **13.** c **14.** a **15.** d **16.** d **17.** c **18.** d **19.** b **20.** c **21.** c **22.** The parts are integrated, interacting to form a more complex structure. For example, cardiac tissue functions in a way that the individual cells cannot function. **23.** A constant environment refers to the optimal conditions at which the body functions best, such as body temperature or glucose concentration in the blood.

41

CIRCULATION

Among invertebrates, cnidaria and flatworms supply cells with oxygen through diffusion in a gastrovascular cavity. An internal transport system is lacking. Other invertebrates have such a circulatory system, which may be either internal or external.

Among vertebrates, fish have a single circulatory loop that works with the gills to form the **cardiovascular system.** The other vertebrates have both **pulmonary** and **systemic** circulation. In either type of circuit, blood flows through the following series of vessels: **arteries, arterioles, capillaries, venules,** and **veins.** The oxygenation of blood is most efficient in the four-chambered **heart** of birds and mammals.

In humans, the SA node of the conduction system, initiates the heartbeat by stimulating the **atria.** The AV node signals the **ventricles. Valves** prevent the backward flow of blood through this pump.

The blood consists of the **plasma** and cells. The plasma is mostly water with dissolved substances. Red blood cells transport oxygen. Several types of white blood cells fight infection and establish immunity. One type, **neutrophils,** have phagocytic ability. **Platelets** promote the clotting of blood. Their activity leads to the formation of fibrin, which traps red blood cells, forming the clot.

Blood can be typed by the ABO system. The four types, based on the **antigen** content of the blood, are: A, B, AB, and O.

Study the text section by section as you answer the questions that follow.

41.1 TRANSPORT IN INVERTEBRATES (P.734)

• Some invertebrates do not have a circulatory system, and others have an open, as opposed to a closed, system.

1. Match the animals with the following means of circulation:
   1 gastrovascular cavity
   2 open circulatory system
   3 closed circulatory system
   _____ a. hydra
   _____ b. earthworm
   _____ c. insect
2. Match the animals with the following types of blood:
   1 colorless
   2 pigmented
   3 none
   _____ a. earthworm
   _____ b. insect
   _____ c. planarian

41.2 TRANSPORT IN VERTEBRATES (P. 736)

- Vertebrates have a closed circulatory system: arteries take blood away from the heart to the capillaries, where exchange occurs, and veins take blood to the heart.
- Fishes have a single circulatory loop, whereas the other vertebrates have a double circulatory loop—to and from the lungs and also to and from the tissues.

3. Label this diagram of the blood vessels with the following terms:

arterioles
artery
capillaries
heart
vein
venules

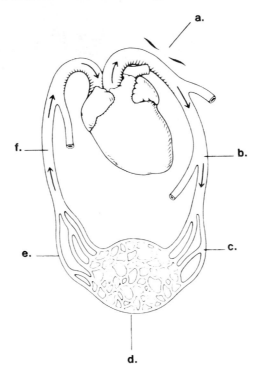

4. Match the animals with the following types of vertebrate hearts:

1 one atrium and one ventricle
2 two atria and one ventricle
3 two atria and two ventricles

_____ a. frog
_____ b. fish
_____ c. mammal

41.3 TRANSPORT IN HUMANS (P. 738)

- The right side of the heart pumps blood to the lungs, and the left side pumps blood to the tissues.

5. Label this diagram of the heart with the following terms (some are used more than once):

aorta
atrioventricular (mitral) valve
atrioventricular (tricuspid) valve
chordae tendineae
inferior vena cava
left atrium
left ventricle
left pulmonary artery
left pulmonary veins
pulmonary trunk
right atrium
right ventricle
right pulmonary arteries
right pulmonary veins
semilunar valves
septum
superior vena cava

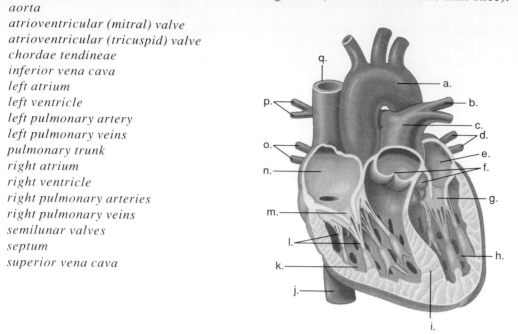

6. Trace the path of blood through the heart.

from the vena cava to the lungs. a._____

_____

from the lungs to the aorta. b._____

_____

7. Use the numbers 1–10 to trace the sequence of blood flow throughout the body. The first one has been marked for you.

_____ a. left atrium
_____ b. left ventricle
_____ c. pulmonary artery
_____ d. pulmonary vein
_____ e. lungs
_____ f. right atrium
_____ g. right ventricle
_____ h. systemic artery
_____ i. systemic capillary
_____ j. systemic vein

How the Heartbeat Occurs (p. 740)

8. The heart beats about 70 times a minute. The a._____ node initiates the contraction of the b._____ (chambers). This stimulus is picked up by the c._____ node, which initiates the contraction of the d._____ (chambers). When the chambers are not contracting, they are relaxing. Contraction is scientifically termed e._____, and the resting is termed f._____ . Contraction of the atria forces the blood through the g._____ valves into the h._____. The closing of these valves is the *lub* sound. Next, the ventricles contract and force the blood into the arteries. Now the i._____ valves close; this is the *dub* sound.

9. Complete the following table with the words *systole* and *diastole* to show what occurs during the 0.85 second of one heartbeat:

Time	Atria	Ventricles
0.15 sec		
0.30 sec		
0.40 sec		

The Vessels Conduct Blood (p. 742)

- Blood pressure causes blood to flow in the arteries and arterioles. Skeletal muscle contraction causes blood to flow in the venules and veins, and valves prevent backflow of blood.

10. How does the hepatic portal circulation differ from the systemic and pulmonary circuits? _____

_____

Questions 11–14 are based on the following diagram:

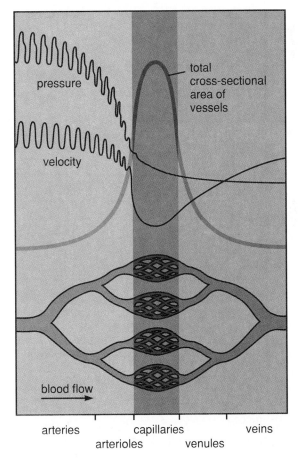

11. What force accounts for blood flow in arteries? _____

_____

12. Why does this force fluctuate? _____

_____

_____

13. What causes the pressure and velocity to drop off? _____
_____

14. What force accounts for blood flow in the veins? _____
_____

41.4 CARDIOVASCULAR DISORDERS IN HUMANS (P. 744)

- Although the circulatory system is very efficient, it is still subject to degenerative disorders.

15. Place a check in front of each example of hypertension.
_____ a. Male, age 39, blood pressure is 120/80.
_____ b. Male, age 46, blood pressure is 140/95.
_____ c. Female, age 50, blood pressure is 160/95.
_____ d. Female, age 25, blood pressure is 160/95.

16. Match the cardiovascular disorders to the following terms:

1 myocardial infarction   *5 angina pectoris*
2 hypertension   *6 familial hypercholesterolemia*
3 varicose veins   *7 embolus in cranial artery*
4 hemorrhoids

_____ a. heart attack
_____ b. varicose veins in rectum
_____ c. weakened valves in legs
_____ d. elevated blood pressure
_____ e. inherited condition leading to atherosclerosis
_____ f. stroke
_____ g. chest pain

41.5 BLOOD IS TRANSPORT MEDIUM (P. 747)

- In humans, blood is composed of cells and a fluid containing proteins and various other molecules and ions.

17. Plasma is mostly a. _____ and b. _____.

18. Match the functions with the following plasma proteins:

1 fibrinogen
2 albumin
3 globulins
4 all plasma proteins

_____ a. transports cholesterol
_____ b. helps blood clot
_____ c. transports bilirubin
_____ d. helps maintain the pH and the osmotic pressure of blood

19. Place a check in front of the items that correctly describe hemoglobin.
_____ a. heme contains iron
_____ b. globin contains iron
_____ c. becomes oxyhemoglobin in the tissues
_____ d. loses oxygen in the tissues
_____ e. makes red blood cells red
_____ f. makes eosinophils red

20. The red blood cells, scientifically called a. _____, are made in the b. _____.
Upon maturation, they are small, biconcave disks that lack a c. _____ and contain
d. _____. After about 120 days, red blood cells are destroyed in the e. _____
and f. _____. An insufficient number of red blood cells or not enough hemoglobin
characterizes the conditon of g. _____.

21. What is erythropoietin? _____
_____

22. White blood cells, scientifically called a._____, are made in the b._____.

23. Three differences between red blood cells and white blood cells are that white blood cells
are a._____ in size than red blood cells, have a(n) b._____, and do not
contain c._____.

24. Match the descriptions with the following types of white blood cells:
    1 basophil
    2 lymphocyte
    3 monocyte
    4 neutrophil
    _____ a. an agranular leukocyte with a large, round nucleus; the B cells produce antibodies, and the T cells
    destroy cells that contain viruses
    _____ b. an abundant granular leukocyte with a multilobed nucleus that phagocytizes foreign material
    _____ c. a large agranular leukocyte that transforms into a macrophage
    _____ d. a granular leukocyte with dark blue staining granules

Platelets Assist Blood Clotting (p. 748)

- Blood clotting is a series of reactions that produce a clot—fibrin threads in which red blood cells are trapped.

25. The following shows the reactions that occur as blood clots:
    platelets → prothrombin activator

    prothrombin → thrombin

    fibrinogen → fibrin threads

    Does the left side or the right side list substances that are always present in the blood? a._____

    Which substances are enzymes? b._____

    Which substance is the actual clot? c._____

Exchanges Between Blood and Tissue Fluid (p. 749)

- Exchange of substances between blood and tissue fluid across capillary walls supplies cells with nutrients and removes wastes.

26. Label this diagram of capillary exchange with the following terms:
    arteriole
    blood pressure, nutrients
    capillary
    osmotic pressure, wastes
    tissue fluid
    venule

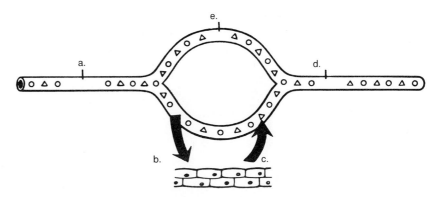

Know Your Blood Type (p. 750)

27. This diagram shows the results of typing which blood type? _____

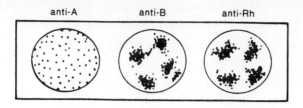

28. Draw a similar diagram to the one in question 27, showing the results of someone with AB⁺ blood.

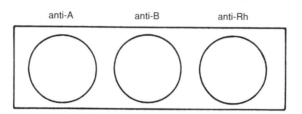

29. The table that follows indicates the blood types. Fill in the last two columns by using this formula:
    The donor's antigen(s) must not be of the same type letter as the recipient's antibody (antibodies).

Blood Type	Antigen	Antibody	Can Receive from	Can Donate to
A	A	Anti-B		
B	B	Anti-A		
AB	A, B	—		
O	None	Anti-A and Anti-B		

Review key terms by completing this crossword puzzle, using the following alphabetized list of terms:

agglutination
artery
AV valve
blood pressure
capillary
cardiovascular system
diastole
heart
hemoglobin
plasma
portal system
pulmonary circuit
systemic circuit
systole
tissue fluid
vein

Across

1 circulatory pathway between the lungs and the heart (two words)
4 blood vessel that transports blood away from the heart
7 filtrate containing all the molecules of blood plasma; bathes the cells of the body (two words)
8 blood vessel that arises from venules and transports blood toward the heart
9 contraction period of a heart during the cardiac cycle
11 microscopic blood vessel; gas and nutrient exchange occurs across its walls
12 clumping of red blood cells due to a reaction between antigens on red blood cell plasma membranes and antibodies in the plasma
14 force of blood pushing against the inside wall of an artery (two words)
15 circulatory pathway of blood flow between the tissues and the heart (two words)

Down

1 pathway of blood flow that begins and ends in capillaries, such as the one found between the small intestine and liver (two words)
2 heart valve located between an atrium and a ventricle (two words)
3 organ system consisting of the blood, heart, and a series of blood vessels that distributes blood under the pumping action of the heart (two words)
5 liquid portion of blood; contains nutrients, wastes, salts, and proteins
6 red respiratory pigment of erythrocytes for transport of oxygen
10 relaxation period of a heart during the cardiac cycle
13 muscular organ that pumps the blood, propelling it through blood vessels

OBJECTIVE QUESTIONS

Do not refer to the text when taking this test.

_____ 1. Which organism transports by a gastrovascular cavity?
   a. cnidarian
   b. earthworm
   c. insect
   d. mollusk

_____ 2. Indicate the correct pathway of blood flow.
   a. arteries, capillaries, veins
   b. arteries, veins, capillaries
   c. veins, arteries, capillaries
   d. veins, capillaries, arteries

_____ 3. The function of the heart valves is to
   a. prevent the backward flow of blood.
   b. pump the blood.
   c. separate the two sides of the heart.
   d. signal the chambers to contract.

_____ 4. When the atria contract, the ventricles are in
   a. diastole.
   b. systole.

_____ 5. Which chamber has the thickest walls?
   a. right atrium
   b. right ventricle
   c. left atrium
   d. left ventricle

_____ 6. The heart sounds are due to
   a. blood flowing.
   b. the closing of the valves.
   c. the heart muscle contracting.
   d. Both _a_ and _c_ are correct.

_____ 7. The chamber of the heart that receives blood from the pulmonary veins
   a. is the right atrium.
   b. is the left atrium.
   c. contains oxygenated blood.
   d. contains deoxygenated blood.
   e. Both _a_ and _d_ are correct.
   f. Both _b_ and _c_ are correct.

_____ 8. The SA node
   a. works only when it receives a nerve impulse.
   b. is located in the left atrium.
   c. initiates the heartbeat.
   d. All of these are correct.

_____ 9. Arteries
   a. carry blood away from the heart.
   b. carry blood toward the heart.
   c. have valves.
   d. Both _b_ and _c_ are correct.

_____ 10. All arteries carry oxygenated blood, and all veins carry blood low in oxygen.
   a. true
   b. false

_____ 11. Which of these vessels have the weakest walls?
   a. arteries
   b. veins
   c. Both are the same.

_____ 12. The venae cavae
   a. carry blood to the right atrium.
   b. carry blood away from the right atrium.
   c. join with the aorta.
   d. have a high blood pressure.

_____ 13. The coronary arteries carry blood
   a. from the aorta to the heart tissues.
   b. from the heart to the brain.
   c. directly to the heart from the pulmonary circuit.
   d. from the lungs directly to the left atrium.

_____ 14. At the capillary, fluid is forced out of the vessel by the
   a. blood pressure.
   b. osmotic pressure.

_____ 15. Gas exchange occurs in
   a. pulmonary capillaries.
   b. renal capillaries.
   c. coronary capillaries.
   d. all capillaries.

_____ 16. For a blood pressure reading of 130/90, 130 is the
   a. diastolic pressure.
   b. systolic pressure.

_____ 17. Select the incorrect statement about red blood cells.
   a. contain hemoglobin
   b. contain iron
   c. respond during inflammation
   d. transport oxygen

_____ 18. Select the incorrect statement about white blood cells.
   a. activate prothrombin
   b. exist in agranular and granular forms
   c. lymphocyte is one type
   d. neutrophil is one type

_____ 19. For the coagulation of blood, fibrinogen is converted to
   a. calcium.
   b. fibrin.
   c. prothrombin.
   d. thrombin.

_____ 20. Type B blood contains _____ antigen(s) and _____ antibody(s).
   a. 0; 1
   b. 1; 0
   c. 1; 1
   d. 2; 2

Answer in complete sentences.

21. How do you think lower osmotic pressure would affect capillary exchange?

22. What do you think would happen to the heartbeat if the SA node did not stimulate the AV node?

Test Results: _____ Number right ÷ 22 = _____ × 100 = _____ %

EXPLORING THE INTERNET

Use the Internet to further explore topics in this chapter, such as heart disease and high cholesterol. Go to the Mader Home Page (http://www.mhhe.com/sciencemath/biology/mader/) and click on *Biology*, 6th edition. Go to Chapter 41 and select a Web site of interest.

ANSWER KEY

STUDY EXERCISES

1. a. 1 **b.** 3 **c.** 2 **2. a.** 2 **b.** 1 **c.** 3 **3. a.** heart **b.** artery **c.** arterioles **d.** capillaries **e.** venules **f.** vein **4. a.** 2 **b.** 1 **c.** 3 **5. a.** aorta **b.** left pulmonary artery **c.** pulmonary trunk **d.** left pulmonary veins **e.** left atrium **f.** semilunar valves **g.** atrioventricular (mitral) valve **h.** left ventricle **i.** septum **j.** inferior vena cava **k.** right ventricle **l.** chordae tendineae **m.** atrioventricular (tricuspid) valve **n.** right atrium **o.** right pulmonary veins **p.** right pulmonary arteries **q.** superior vena cava; see also Figure 41.6, page 739, in text **6. a.** vena cava, right atrium, atrioventricular valve, right ventricle, pulmonary semilunar valve, pulmonary artery, lungs **b.** lungs, pulmonary veins(s), left atrium, atrioventricular valve, left ventricle, aortic semilunar valve, aorta **7. a.** 10 **b.** 1 **c.** 7 **d.** 9 **e.** 8 **f.** 5 **g.** 6 **h.** 2 **i.** 3 **j.** 4 **8. a.** SA **b.** atria **c.** AV **d.** ventricles **e.** systole **f.** diastole **g.** atrioventricular **h.** ventricles **i.** semilunar

9.

Atria	Ventricles
systole	diastole
diastole	systole
diastole	diastole

10. Blood in the capillaries of several organs flows to a second capillary bed in the liver before release into the systemic veins. **11.** blood pressure due to systole of left ventricle **12.** systole is followed by diastole of left ventricle **13.** distance from heart and increase in cross-sectional area of blood vessels **14.** skeletal muscle contraction **15.** a, c, d **16. a.** 1 **b.** 4 **c.** 3 **d.** 2 **e.** 6 **f.** 7 **g.** 5 **17. a.** water **b.** plasma proteins **18. a.** 3 **b.** 1 **c.** 2 **d.** 4 **19.** a, d, e **20. a.** erythrocytes **b.** red bone marrow **c.** nucleus **d.** hemoglobin **e.** liver **f.** spleen **g.** anemia **21.** a molecule that stimulates production of red blood cells **22. a.** leukocytes **b.** bone marrow **23. a.** larger **b.** nucleus **c.** hemoglobin **24. a.** 2 **b.** 4 **c.** 3 **d.** 1 **25. a.** left side **b.** prothrombin activator and thrombin **c.** fibrin threads **26. a.** arteriole **b.** blood pressure, nutrients **c.** osmotic pressure, wastes **d.** venule **e.** capillary **f.** tissue fluid **27.** B

28. The diagram should show clumping for anti-A and anti-B and anti-Rh.

29.

Can Receive from	Can Donate to
A, O	A, AB
B, O	B, AB
A, B, AB, O	AB
O	A, B, AB, O

Across/filled crossword answers:

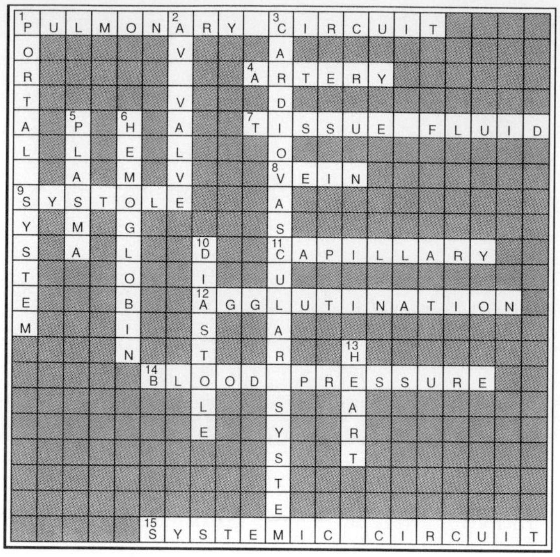

- 1. PULMONARY CIRCUIT
- 4. ARTERY
- 7. TISSUE FLUID
- 8. VEIN
- 9. SYSTOLE
- 11. CAPILLARY
- 12. AGGLUTINATION
- 14. BLOOD PRESSURE
- 15. SYSTEMIC CIRCUIT

Down/filled crossword answers:

- 1. PORTAL SYSTEM
- 2. AVVVAGE (AV...)
- 3. CARDIAC
- 5. PLLEAM (PLEL...)
- 6. HEMGLOBIN
- 10. DISASTER (DIS...)
- 13. HEART

1. a **2.** a **3.** a **4.** a **5.** d **6.** b **7.** f **8.** c **9.** a **10.** b **11.** b **12.** a **13.** a **14.** a **15.** d **16.** b **17.** c **18.** a **19.** b **20.** c **21.** Tissue fluid would not be returned as efficiently to the venous end of the capillary. It would remain in the tissue spaces, and edema would result. **22.** The ventricles would not be signaled to contract. Therefore, ventricular systole would not take place, and oxygenated blood would not effectively flow to body's tissues.

42

LYMPH TRANSPORT AND IMMUNITY

CHAPTER REVIEW

Functions of the **lymphatic system** include collecting excess tissue fluid, absorbing the products of fat digestion, and defending against disease.

The body has several general lines of defense: entry barriers, phagocytic white blood cells, and protective barriers.

Two types of white blood cells are involved in the **immune** response. **B lymphocytes** (B cells) carry out antibody-mediated immunity, in which an **antibody** reacts with an **antigen**. **T lymphocytes** (T cells) carry out cellular immunity. Each of the several types of T cells has a specific role in this immune mechanism.

Vaccines (active immunity) and administration of antibodies (passive immunity) are two examples of immunotherapy. Undesirable side effects of immunity include allergies and autoimmunity.

STUDY EXERCISES

Study the text section by section as you answer the questions that follow.

42.1 LYMPHATIC SYSTEM HELPS CARDIOVASCULAR SYSTEM (P. 756)

- The lymphatic vessels form a one-way system, which transports lymph from the tissues and fat from the lacteals to certain cardiovascular veins.

1. Give three functions of the lymphatic system.

   a._____

   _____

   b._____

   _____

   c._____

   _____

2. Indicate whether the following statements about the structure/function of lymphatic vessels and lymphoid organs are true (T) or false (F):

   _____ a. Bone marrow lacks lymphoid tissue.

   _____ b. Lymph lobules are subdivided into sinus-containing nodes.

   _____ c. The contraction of skeletal muscles blocks the return of lymph to the bloodstream.

   _____ d. The sinuses of the spleen are filled with lymph.

   _____ e. Lymphatic vessels are similar to systemic veins.

   _____ f. Lymphatic vessels contain valves.

3. Indicate whether the statements that follow are true (T) or false (F). Rewrite any false statements to make them true.

   _____ a. Vessels of the lymphatic system begin with systemic capillaries.

   _____ b. Lymph most closely resembles arterial blood.

   _____ c. The right thoracic duct serves the lower extremities, abdomen, one arm, and one side of the head and neck.

   _____ d. Lymphatic capillaries merge directly to form a particular lymphatic duct.

4. Label each of the following statements as describing the thymus (T), spleen (S), or red bone marrow (RBM):

_____ a. contains red pulp and white pulp
_____ b. contains stem cells
_____ c. is located along the trachea
_____ d. is located in the upper left abdominal cavity
_____ e. produces hormones believed to stimulate the immune system
_____ f. contains sinuses filled with blood
_____ g. site of origin for all types of blood cells

42.2 SOME DEFENSES ARE NONSPECIFIC (P. 758)

- Immunity consists of nonspecific and specific defenses to protect the body against disease.
- Nonspecific defenses consist of barriers to entry, the inflammatory reaction, and protective proteins.

5. Match each of the descriptions with the following defense mechanisms:
   1 barrier to entry
   2 inflammatory response
   3 complement protein

_____ a. accompanied by swelling and redness
_____ b. cilia action in the respiratory tract
_____ c. produces holes in bacterial cell walls
_____ d. stomach secretions
_____ e. histamine increases capillary permeability
_____ f. injured cells release bradykinin
_____ g. inhabitation of normal body bacteria
_____ h. interferon action
_____ i. neutrophils and macrophages carry out phagocytosis
_____ j. secretions of the oil, or sebaceous, glands

42.3 OTHER DEFENSES ARE SPECIFIC (P. 760)

- Specific defenses require two types of lymphocytes: B lymphocytes and T lymphocytes.

6. The lymphocytes responsible for antibody-mediated immunity are
   a. T cells.
   b. B cells.
7. According to the clonal selection theory,
   a. B cells make plasma cells.
   b. plasma cells make B cells.
8. The type of cell engulfing a bacterium is the
   a. B cell.
   b. macrophage.
   c. memory cell.
   d. T cell.
9. Antibodies
   a. are responsible for allergic reactions.
   b. are involved in humoral immunity.
   c. function as antigen receptors on lymphocytes.
   d. function mainly in the saliva.
10. T cells are responsible for
    a. antibody-mediated immunity.
    b. cell-mediated immunity.

11. Complete the following table with *yes* or *no:*

	Cytotoxic T Cell	B Cell
Ultimately Derived from Stem Cells in Bone Marrow		
Pass Through Thymus		
Carry Receptors on Membrane		
Cell-Mediated Immunity		
Antibody-Mediated Immunity		

12. According to the clonal selection theory, when membrane-bound antibodies of a B cell combine with specific
    a._____ in a(n) b._____ manner, this brings about
    c._____. This process uses antibody-secreting cells called d._____
    and e._____, which can produce this antibody in the future.

How Antibodies Work (p. 762)

13. a. Label this diagram of an antibody molecule with the following terms: *antigen-binding site, constant regions, heavy chain, light chain,* and *variable region.*

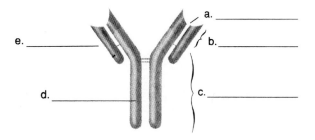

e. _____

a. _____

b. _____

d. _____

c. _____

What is the function of antibodies? b._____

T Cells Become Cytotoxic, Helper, Memory, or Suppressor Cells (p. 764)

14. Study the diagram and then rearrange the letters to put steps a–f in order. _____

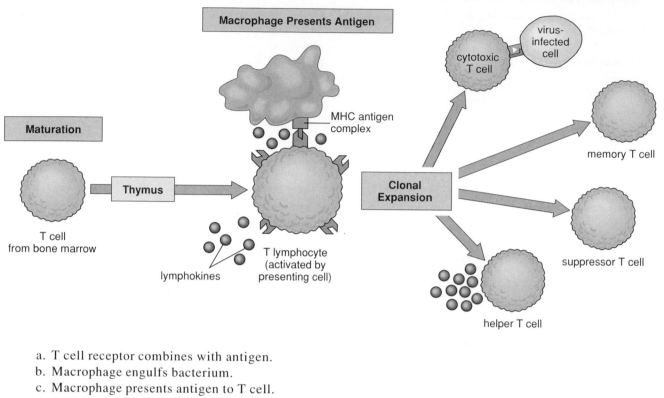

a. T cell receptor combines with antigen.
b. Macrophage engulfs bacterium.
c. Macrophage presents antigen to T cell.
d. Antigen is linked to an MHC protein.
e. Bacterium is digested to release peptide fragments.
f. T cell is now activated.

15. Give a function for each type of T cell.

cytotoxic T cells a._____

helper T cells b._____

suppressor T cells c._____

memory T cells d._____

42.4 IMMUNITY CAN BE INDUCED (P. 767)

• Induced immunity for medical purposes involves the use of vaccines to achieve long-lasting immunity and the use of antibiotics to provide temporary immunity.

16. Classify each of the following as an example of active (A) or passive (P) immunity:
_____ a. occurs from vaccinations
_____ b. can lead to serum sickness
_____ c. primary response occurs
_____ d. antibodies given to combat diseases
_____ e. booster shot enhances the secondary response
_____ f. longer-lived immunity

17. a. Label this diagram of the development of antibody titer during active immunity with the following terms: *first exposure to vaccine, primary response, secondary response,* and *second exposure to vaccine.*

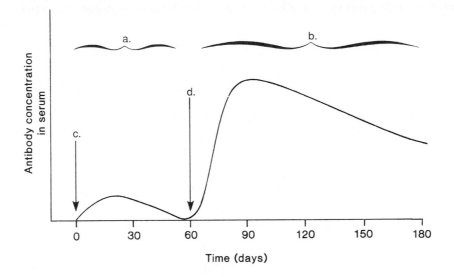

In the diagram, why is the secondary response so much greater than the primary response?

b. _____

_____

18. Answer the following about monoclonal antibodies.

The meaning of *mono* is ᵃ·_____ and of *clonal* is ᵇ·_____. The term

monoclonal antibody means ᶜ·_____. The meaning of *hybrid* is ᵈ·_____ and of

oma is ᵉ·_____. A *hybridoma* is a fusion between a(n) ᶠ·_____ cell and

a(n) ᵍ·_____ cell. Hybridomas are used to produce monoclonal antibodies because ʰ·_____

_____.

42.5 IMMUNITY HAS SIDE EFFECTS (P. 769)

- While immunity preserves our existence, it also is responsible for certain undesirable effects, such as tissue rejection, allergies, and autoimmune diseases.

19. Match the descriptions with the numbered terms. Then explain your choice.
    1 allergy
    2 tissue rejection
    3 autoimmune disease
    _____ a. foreign MHC proteins_____
    _____ b. the body attacks itself_____
    _____ c. overactive immune system_____

Review key terms by completing this crossword puzzle, using the following alphabetized list of terms:

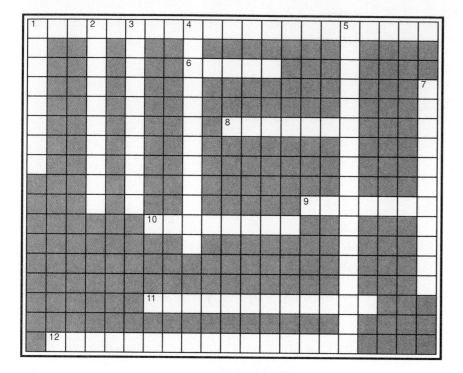

antibody
antigen
B lymphocyte
complement system
immunity
inflammatory reaction
lymph
lymphatic system
lymph nodes
lymphokine
macrophage
T lymphocyte
vaccine

Across

1 tissue response to injury that is characterized by redness, swelling, pain, and heat (two words)
6 fluid, derived from tissue fluid, that is carried in lymphatic vessels
8 antigens prepared in such a way that they can promote active immunity without causing disease
9 foreign substance, usually a protein or polysaccharide, that stimulates the immune system to react, such as to produce antibodies
10 protein produced in response to the presence of an antigen; each combines with a specific antigen
11 lymphocyte that matures in the bone marrow and, when stimulated by the presence of a specific antigen, gives rise to antibody-producing plasma cells (two words)
12 mammalian organ system consisting of lymphatic vessels and lymphoid organs (two words)

Down

1 ability of the body to protect itself from foreign substances and cells, including infectious agents
2 molecule that T cells secrete that can affect the activity of all types of immune cells
3 large phagocytic cell derived from a monocyte that ingests viruses and bacteria and debris
4 lymphocyte that matures in the thymus and exists in four types, one of which kills antigen-bearing cells outright (two words)
5 series of proteins in plasma that forms a nonspecific defense mechanism against a microbe invasion; it complements the antigen-antibody reaction (two words)
7 masses of lymphoid tissue located along the course of a lymphatic vessel (two words)

OBJECTIVE QUESTIONS

Do not refer to the text when taking this test.

_____ 1. The two collecting ducts of the lymphatic system empty into
   a. systemic arteries.
   b. systemic veins.
   c. pulmonary arteries.
   d. pulmonary veins.

_____ 2. The structure of a lymphatic vessel is most similar to that of a
   a. cardiovascular artery.
   b. cardiovascular arteriole.
   c. cardiovascular vein.
   d. skeletal muscle fiber.

_____ 3. Lymph is _____ in lymphatic vessels.
   a. blood
   b. serum
   c. tissue fluid
   d. plasma

_____ 4. Edema occurs when
   a. the lymph nodes are not functioning properly.
   b. too much tissue fluid is being made.
   c. the lymphatic vessels are draining away tissue fluid.
   d. All of these are correct.

For questions 5–8, match the descriptions with the following terms:.
   a. thymus gland
   b. spleen
   c. lymph node
   d. red bone marrow

_____ 5. causes differentiation of T cells

_____ 6. purifies lymph

_____ 7. contains red pulp and white pulp

_____ 8. formation of agranular and granular leukocytes

_____ 9. The spleen
   a. contains stem cells from the bone marrow.
   b. is located along the trachea.
   c. produces a hormone believed to stimulate the immune system.
   d. is a blood reservoir.

_____10. The thymus
   a. contains stem cells from the bone marrow.
   b. is located along the trachea.
   c. produces a hormone believed to stimulate the immune system.
   d. Both _b_ and _c_ are correct.

_____11. Activity of the complement system is an example of nonspecific defense by
   a. barriers to entry.
   b. phagocytic cells.
   c. protective proteins.
   d. Both _a_ and _c_ are correct.

_____12. Secretions of the oil glands are an example of nonspecific defense by a
   a. barrier to entry.
   b. protective protein.
   c. phagocytic cell.
   d. All of these are correct.

_____13. Cells produce interferon in response to the presence of
   a. chemical irritants.
   b. viruses.
   c. bacterial infection.
   d. malarial parasites in the blood.

_____14. White blood cell phagocytes are
   a. neutrophils and macrophages.
   b. neutrophils and eosinophils.
   c. lymphocytes and macrophages.
   d. lymphocytes and neutrophils.

_____15. The white blood cells that are primarily responsible for specific immunity are
   a. neutrophils.
   b. eosinophils.
   c. macrophages.
   d. lymphocytes.

_____16. Which of these is NOT a valid contrast between T cells and B cells?

   T cells   **B cells**
   a. mature in the thymus—mature in the bone marrow
   b. antibody-mediated immunity—cell-mediated immunity
   c. antigen must be presented—direct recognition by antigen-presenting cell
   d. produce lymphokines—do not produce lymphokines

_____17. A particular antibody can
   a. attack any type of antigen.
   b. attack only a specific type of antigen.
   c. be produced by any B cell.
   d. be produced by any T cell.

_____18. The clonal selection theory refers to the
   a. presence of four different types of T cells in the blood.
   b. response of only one type of B cell to a specific antigen.
   c. occurrence of many types of plasma cells, each producing many types of antigens.

_____19. IgG antibody
   a. attacks microbes and enhances phagocytosis.
   b. is the main form of antibodies in the circulation.
   c. has both constant and variable regions.
   d. All of these are correct.

_____20. Which of these is mismatched?
  a. helper T cells—orchestrate the immune response
  b. cytotoxic T cells—stimulate B cells to produce antibodies
  c. memory T cells—long-lasting active immunity
  d. suppressor T cells—shut down the immune response

_____21. An injection of gamma globulin as a protection against hepatitis provides
  a. naturally acquired active immunity.
  b. naturally acquired passive immunity.
  c. artificially acquired passive immunity.
  d. artificially acquired active immunity.

_____22. A vaccination to produce immunity to the flu provides
  a. naturally acquired active immunity.
  b. naturally acquired passive immunity.
  c. artificially acquired passive immunity.
  d. artificially acquired active immunity.

_____23. Monoclonal antibodies are
  a. produced by hybridomas.
  b. available for detection of diseases.
  c. used in pregnancy tests.
  d. All of these are correct.

_____24. Which is NOT true of an autoimmune response?
  a. responsible for such diseases as multiple sclerosis and myasthenia gravis and perhaps type I diabetes
  b. occurs when self-antibodies attack self-tissues
  c. interferes with the transplantation of organs between one person and another
  d. Autoimmune responses are easily cured.

CRITICAL THINKING QUESTIONS

Answer in complete sentences.

25. How is the functioning of the immune system another example of homeostasis?

26. How can the functioning of the immune system hold the key to protecting against AIDS?

Test Results: _____ Number right ÷ 26 = _____ × 100 = _____ %

EXPLORING THE INTERNET

Use the Internet to further explore topics in this chapter, such as AIDS, allergies, and asthma. Go to the Mader Home Page (http://www.mhhe.com/sciencemath/biology/mader/) and click on _Biology,_ 6th edition. Go to Chapter 42 and select a Web site of interest.

ANSWER KEY

STUDY EXERCISES

1. a. return of excess tissue fluid to bloodstream **b.** absorption of fats at intestinal villi **c.** defense against disease **2. a.** F **b.** F **c.** F **d.** F **e.** T **f.** T **3. a.** F; . . . begin with lymph capillaries **b.** F; . . . resembles tissue fluid that has entered the lymph vessels **c.** F; The right lymphatic duct serves the right arm, the right side of the head and neck, and the right thoracic area. **d.** F; . . . capillaries form lymphatic vessels first and these merge before entering a particular lymphatic duct **4. a.** S **b.** RBM **c.** T **d.** S **e.** T **f.** S **g.** RBM **5. a.** 2 **b.** 1 **c.** 3 **d.** 1 **e.** 2 **f.** 2 **g.** 1 **h.** 3 **i.** 2 **j.** 1 **6.** b **7.** a **8.** b **9.** b **10.** b

11.

Cytotoxic T Cell	B Cell
yes	yes
yes	no
yes	yes
yes	no
no	yes

12. a. antigens **b.** lock-and-key **c.** clonal expansion **d.** plasma cells **e.** memory cells   **13. a.** See Figure 42.7a, page 762, in text. **b.** to mark an antigen for destruction by phagocytes or complement   **14.** b, e, d, c, a, f   **15. a.** attack and destroy antigen-bearing cells **b.** stimulate other cells to perform their function; secrete lymphokines **c.** stop the immune response **d.** retain sensitivity to particular antigen   **16. a.** A **b.** P **c.** A **d.** P **e.** A **f.** A   **17. a.** See Figure 42.10, page 767, in text. **b.** the plasma and memory cells are already present.

18. a. one **b.** branch or clone **c.** they all came from the same source **d.** joining of two dissimilar entities **e.** cancer cell **f.** plasma **g.** cancer **h.** a cancer cell divides without stopping and the plasma cell produces the same type of antibody.   **19. a.** 2, The MHC proteins mark a cell as being foreign. **b.** 3, Antibodies are produced against the body's own cells. **c.** 1, The body produces antibodies against substances that the immune systems of most people ignore.

KEYWORD CROSSWORD

```
 1                2      3         4                          5
 I  N  F  L  A  M  M  A  T  O  R  Y     R  E  A  C  T  I  O  N
 M           Y        A                          O
 M           M        C        6 L  Y  M  P  H    M
 U           P        R        Y                  P           7 L
 N           H        O        M                  L           Y
 I           O        P        P     8 V  A  C  C  I  N  E     M
 T           K        H        H                  M           P
 Y           I        A        O                  E           H
             N        G        C                  N
             E        E        Y              9 A  N  T  I  G  E  N
             10 A  N  T  I  B  O  D  Y                        O
                     E                            S           D
                                                  Y           E
             11 B   L  Y  M  P  H  O  C  Y  T  E               S
                                                  E
 12 L  Y  M  P  H  A  T  I  C     S  Y  S  T  E  M
```

CHAPTER TEST

1. b **2.** c **3.** c **4.** b **5.** a **6.** c **7.** b **8.** d **9.** d
10. d **11.** c **12.** a **13.** b **14.** a **15.** d **16.** b
17. b **18.** b **19.** d **20.** b **21.** c **22.** d **23.** d
24. d   **25.** The immune system protects the body from disease, making it possible for other systems to function properly.   **26.** Researchers may eventually combat AIDS by developing a vaccine to stimulate the production of T cells or by finding a way to prevent the infecting retrovirus from attacking T cells.

43

DIGESTION AND NUTRITION

As feeders, animals can be continuous or discontinuous. Throughout the animal kingdom, the digestive tract is either incomplete (e.g., planaria) or complete (e.g., earthworms). The teeth are an important digestive structure in all mammals. The several different shapes of teeth are each specialized for a different function. Specializations develop throughout the digestive system, such as the varying length of the intestine, which is shorter in carnivores and longer in herbivores.

In humans, food passes through a series of chambers: mouth, pharynx, **esophagus,** stomach, **small intestine,** and **large intestine.** In the mouth, chewing breaks down food, and **salivary amylase** initiates the chemical digestion of carbohydrates. The chemical digestion of proteins begins in the stomach through the action of **pepsin.** Food is also stored there. The chemical and physical breakdown of food produces chyme. The action of other enzymes and **bile** in the small intestine finishes the chemical breakdown of all food molecules. The products of chemical digestion (fatty acids, amino acids, monosaccharides) are absorbed in this region. Water and minerals are reabsorbed in the large intestine. Wastes are eliminated from the body after passing through the large intestine, or **colon.**

Several structures near the small intestine produce substances that are secreted into the digestive tract and influence its activity: the **liver** (bile production), the **gallbladder** (bile storage), and the **pancreas** (enzyme production). The pancreas also produces the hormones insulin and glucagon to regulate carbohydrate metabolism.

Several hormones—gastrin, secretin, and CCK—regulate digestive processes.

Along with ingested carbohydrates, proteins, and fats, minerals and **vitamins** contribute to the well-balanced diet of an individual.

STUDY EXERCISES

Study the text section by section as you answer the questions that follow.

43.1 COMPARING DIGESTIVE TRACTS (P. 774)

* An incomplete digestive tract with only one opening has little specialization of parts; a complete digestive tract with two openings does have specialization of parts.
* Discontinuous feeders, rather than continuous feeders, need a storage area for food.
* The dentition of herbivores, carnivores, and omnivores is adapted to the type of food they eat.

1. Label each of the following as describing a planarian (P) or an earthworm (E):
   _____ a. incomplete tract
   _____ b. pharynx, intestine
   _____ c. complete tract
   _____ d. pharynx, crop, gizzard, intestine
2. A complete gut has both a(n) ᵃ⁻_____ and a(n) ᵇ⁻_____.
3. Label each of the following as describing a clam (C) or a squid (S):
   _____ a. siphons
   _____ b. no jaws
   _____ c. stomach only
   _____ d. tentacles
   _____ e. jaws
   _____ f. stomach and cecum

4. Which type of feeder tends to take in small particles or, in the case of parasites, food that needs no digestion? a._____

   Which type of feeder is more likely to require a storage area for food? b._____

5. Label each of the following as describing an herbivore (H) or a carnivore (C):

   _____ a. large, flat molars
   _____ b. chew thoroughly
   _____ c. sharp canines
   _____ d. bolt food

6. On what type of food do herbivores feed? a._____ carnivores? b._____

   Which type of food is harder to digest? c._____

   Which type of feeder needs to chew food thoroughly and requires a more complicated digestive tract with accessory parts? d._____

43.2 HUMANS HAVE A COMPLETE TRACT (P. 777)

- The human digestive tract has many specialized parts and three accessory organs of digestion, which contribute in their own way to the digestion of food.
- The digestive enzymes are specific and have an optimum temperature and pH at which they function best.
- The products of digestion are small molecules, such as amino acids and glucose, that can cross plasma membranes.

7. Rearrange the letters to indicate the order in which food passes through these organs of the digestive tract.

   _____

   a. esophagus
   b. large intestine
   c. mouth
   d. pharynx
   e. small intestine
   f. stomach

8. Use the letters in the diagram of the human digestive system to indicate where each of the events that follow occurs. (Some letters are used more than once.)

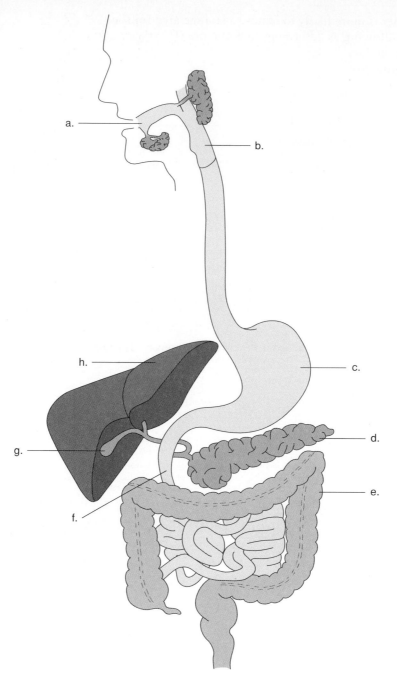

_____ a. A swallowing reflex begins here to prevent food from entering the trachea.

_____ b. Absorption of nutrients occurs here.

_____ c. Chyme passes into this region.

_____ d. This structure makes gastric juice.

_____ e. Large quantities of food are stored here.

_____ f. The chemical breakdown of carbohydrates begins here.

_____ g. The chemical breakdown of lipids begins here.

_____ h. The chemical breakdown of proteins begins here.

_____ i. The salivary glands are found here.

_____ j. Water and minerals are reabsorbed here.

_____ k. This structure conducts food to the stomach.

_____ l. This structure makes bile.

_____ m. This structure secretes enzymes into the small intestine.

_____ n. This structure stores bile.

_____ o. Villi are found on the inside surface of this structure.

9. Name the region where each of the following enzymes functions in the human digestive tract and note the chemical reaction that it affects:

   lipase ^{a.} _____

   pancreatic amylase ^{b.} _____

   pepsin ^{c.} _____

   salivary amylase ^{d.} _____

   trypsin ^{e.} _____

10. List the final molecules produced by enzymatic hydrolysis of each of the following products of digestion:

    peptides ^{a.} _____

    maltose ^{b.} _____

11. Starch digestion begins in the ^{a.}_____. Here, the ducts empty from the ^{b.}_____ glands. The salivary juice contains the enzyme ^{c.}_____, and this enzyme breaks down starch to the disaccharide ^{d.}_____. Starch is also acted on in the ^{e.}_____. Here, a duct empties from the ^{f.}_____. Pancreatic juice contains the enzyme ^{g.}_____, which breaks down starch to the disaccharide ^{h.}_____. Starch digestion is complete when this disaccharide is broken down to ^{i.}_____, a monosaccharide, which intestinal villi can absorb. The enzyme that converts maltose to glucose is called ^{j.}_____, ^{k.}_____ cells of the intestinal villi secrete this enzyme.

12. Protein digestion begins in the ^{a.}_____. The ^{b.}_____ glands line the wall of the stomach. They secrete the enzyme ^{c.}_____, which breaks down protein to ^{d.}_____. Another enzyme called ^{e.}_____ is secreted by the ^{f.}_____, and this enzyme acts on protein in the ^{g.}_____, also breaking down protein to ^{h.}_____. Protein digestion is complete when peptides are broken down to ^{i.}_____, molecules small enough for the villi to absorb. This is achieved by the enzyme ^{j.}_____ that the epithelial cells of the intestinal villus produce.

13. Fat is first emulsified by ^{a.}_____, a substance made by the liver and stored in the ^{b.}_____. The contents of the latter enter the small intestine by way of the ^{c.}_____ duct. After the fat has been emulsified, it is broken down by the enzyme ^{d.}_____, also found in pancreatic juice, which enters the small intestine by way of the pancreatic duct. Fats are broken down to ^{e.}_____ and fatty acids, molecules small enough for intestinal villi to absorb. After resynthesis, fats enter the ^{f.}_____, which are a part of the lymphatic system.

Two Accessory Organs Help Out (p. 782)

14. Label each of the following as a function of the liver (L) or pancreas (P):

_____ a. makes blood proteins

_____ b. makes enzymes that work in the small intestine

_____ c. makes insulin

_____ d. produces bile

_____ e. secretes sodium bicarbonate

_____ f. stores glucose as glycogen

15. Name the hormone that produces each of the following effects:

release of bile a._____

secretion of bicarbonate ions b._____

secretion of hydrochloric acid and pepsin c._____

16. Complete the following table:

Hormone	Where Produced	Cause of Release	Affects What Organ	Affected Organ Releases
gastrin				
secretin				
CCK				

43.3 Nutrition Affects Health (p. 784)

- Proper nutrition supplies the body with energy and nutrients, including the essential amino acids and fatty acids, and all vitamins and minerals.

17. Indicate whether the following statements are true (T) or false (F):

_____ a. A daily diet should contain at least six servings of the bread, cereal, rice, and pasta group.

_____ b. Fats and oils are not necessary to a properly balanced diet.

_____ c. Vitamins are inorganic compounds that provide the body with needed calories.

_____ d. Citrus fruits are natural sources of vitamin A.

_____ e. Vitamins A and C may help guard against the development of cancer.

18. Indicate whether the following statements are true (T) or false (F):

_____ a. Macrominerals include calcium, sodium, and potassium.

_____ b. Microminerals are recommended in amounts of more than 100 mg per day.

_____ c. Microminerals are recommended in amounts of less than 20 mg per day.

_____ d. Microminerals include iron, copper, iodine, and zinc.

_____ e. Adult females require less iron in their diet than males.

_____ f. Safeguards against osteoporosis include excess sodium intake.

Review key terms by completing this crossword puzzle, using the following alphabetized list of terms:

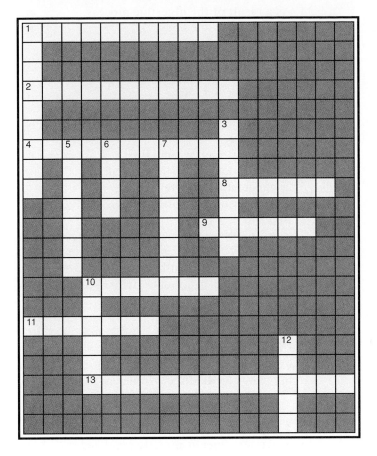

amylase
bile
colon
duodenum
epiglottis
esophagus
gallbladder
lacteal
lipase
pepsin
peristalsis
salivary gland
trypsin
villus
vitamin

Across

1 structure that covers the glottis, the air-tract opening, during swallowing
2 rhythmic, wavelike contraction that moves food through the digestive tract
4 organ attached to the liver that serves as a storage organ for bile
8 protein-digesting enzyme secreted by gastric glands
9 fat-digesting enzyme secreted by the pancreas
10 essential requirement in the diet, needed in small amounts; often part of coenzymes
11 starch-digesting enzyme secreted by salivary glands and the pancreas
13 gland that is associated with the mouth and that secretes saliva (two words)

Down

1 muscular tube for moving swallowed food from the pharynx to the stomach
3 protein-digesting enzyme secreted by the pancreas
5 lymphatic vessel in an intestinal villus; aids in the absorption of fats
6 secretion of the liver that is temporarily stored in the gallbladder before being released into the small intestine, where it emulsifies fat
7 first part of the small intestine, where chyme enters from the stomach
10 small, fingerlike projection of the inner small-intestine wall
12 large intestine

Do not refer to the text when taking this test.

_____ 1. Select the correct terms to describe digestion in planaria.
  a. complete, saclike
  b. complete, tubelike
  c. incomplete, saclike
  d. incomplete, tubelike

_____ 2. Select the incorrect association.
  a. canine—tearing
  b. incisor—biting
  c. molar—crushing
  d. premolar—swallowing

_____ 3. Salivary amylase speeds up the conversion of
  a. protein to amino acids.
  b. protein to peptides.
  c. starch to glucose.
  d. starch to maltose.

_____ 4. Select the correct sequence for the passage of food.
  a. pharynx, esophagus, stomach
  b. large intestine, small intestine, stomach
  c. pharynx, stomach, esophagus
  d. stomach, large intestine, small intestine

For questions 5–7, select from the following options:
  a. mouth
  b. esophagus
  c. stomach
  d. small intestine
  e. large intestine

_____ 5. Protein digestion begins here.

_____ 6. Nutrients are absorbed here.

_____ 7. Starch is digested here.

_____ 8. Villi serve to
  a. increase surface area for absorption.
  b. increase the synthesis of enzymes.
  c. speed up elimination of wastes.
  d. speed up loss of water from the body.

_____ 9. Select the function NOT performed by the pancreas.
  a. detoxifies poisons
  b. makes enzymes
  c. makes insulin
  d. secretes sodium bicarbonate

_____ 10. Select the function NOT performed by the liver.
  a. makes blood proteins
  b. makes new red blood cells
  c. produces bile
  d. stores glucose as glycogen

_____ 11. As a result of the digestive process, _____ are absorbed into the body.
  a. proteins
  b. fats
  c. starches
  d. proteins and fats
  e. amino acids, glucose, and fatty acids

_____ 12. The two enzymes involved in the digestion of proteins are
  a. salivary amylase and lipase.
  b. trypsin and hydrochloric acid.
  c. pancreatic amylase and bile.
  d. pepsin and trypsin.

_____ 13. Bile
  a. is an important enzyme for the digestion of fats.
  b. is made by the gallbladder.
  c. contains products from hemoglobin breakdown.
  d. emulsifies fat.
  e. Both _c_ and _d_ are correct.

_____ 14. HCl
  a. is an enzyme.
  b. creates an acidic environment necessary for pepsin to work.
  c. is found throughout the intestinal tract.
  d. digests fats.

_____ 15. Pancreatic juice is directly regulated by
  a. the presence of food in the intestine.
  b. the sight of food.
  c. the thought of food.
  d. the smell of food.
  e. secretin.

_____ 16. The large intestine
  a. digests all types of food.
  b. is the longest part of the intestinal tract.
  c. absorbs water.
  d. is connected to the stomach.

_____ 17. Which of the following organs does NOT produce digestive enzymes?
  a. salivary glands
  b. stomach
  c. pancreas
  d. small intestine
  e. large intestine

_____ 18. Essential amino acids
  a. are not easily absorbed.
  b. cannot be made by the body.
  c. lack nitrogen.
  d. make an incomplete protein.

19. The greatest storage capacity of calories per gram occurs with
    a. carbohydrates.
    b. lipids.
    c. minerals.
    d. proteins.

20. Select the mineral that can help develop strong bones in young persons.
    a. calcium
    b. magnesium
    c. potassium
    d. sodium

CRITICAL THINKING QUESTIONS

Answer in complete sentences.

21. The well-preserved skull of a mammal shows well-developed molars and poorly developed canine teeth. What can you conclude about the probable diet of this organism?

22. Why is it advantageous for the human body to have a variety of hormones to control digestion?

Test Results: _____ Number right ÷ 22 = _____ × 100 = _____ %

EXPLORING THE INTERNET

Use the Internet to further explore topics in this chapter, such as colorectal cancer and nutrition for health. Go to the Mader Home Page (http://www.mhhe.com/sciencemath/biology/mader/) and click on *Biology,* 6th edition. Go to Chapter 43 and select a Web site of interest.

ANSWER KEY

STUDY EXERCISES

1. a. P b. P c. E d. E 2. a. mouth b. anus
3. a. C b. C c. C d. S e. S f. S 4. a. continuous
b. discontinuous 5. a. H b. H c. C d. C 6. a. vegetation b. meat c. vegetation d. herbivore 7. c, d, a, f, e, b 8. a. b b. f c. f d. c e. c f. a g. f h. c i. a j. e k. b l. h m. d n. g o. f 9. a. small intestine, lipids to glycerol and fatty acids b. small intestine, starch to maltose c. stomach, protein to peptides d. mouth, starch to maltose e. small intestine, protein to peptides
10. a. amino acids b. glucose 11. a. mouth b. salivary c. salivary amylase d. maltose e. small intestine f. pancreas g. pancreatic amylase h. maltose i. glucose j. maltase k. epithelial 12. a. stomach b. gastric c. pepsin d. peptides e. trypsin f. pancreas g. small intestine h. peptides i. amino acids j. peptidase
13. a. bile b. gallbladder c. bile d. lipase e. glycerol f. lacteals 14. a. L b. P c. P d. L e. P f. L
15. a. CCK b. secretin c. gastrin

16.

Where Produced	Cause of Release	Affects What Organ	Affected Organ Releases
stomach	protein	stomach	gastric juice
duodenum	hydrochloric acid	pancreas, liver, gallbladder	pancreatic juice, bile
duodenum	protein, fat	pancreas, liver, gallbladder	pancreatic juice, bile

17. a. F b. F c. F d. F e. T 18. a. T b. F c. T d. T e. F f. F

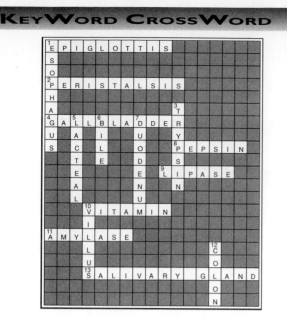

1. c **2.** d **3.** d **4.** a **5.** c **6.** d **7.** a **8.** a **9.** a **10.** b **11.** e **12.** d **13.** e **14.** b **15.** e **16.** c **17.** e **18.** b **19.** b **20.** a **21.** Molars are adapted for grinding, the kind of action needed to break down plant food. The animal was a herbivore. Canine teeth, seen in carnivores, are needed more for the tearing of flesh. **22.** Digestion does not need to occur continuously. Certain digestive responses are needed when food intake warrants it (e.g., pepsin secretion in the stomach with the arrival of protein there, signaled by gastrin secretion).

44

RESPIRATION

For some aquatic organisms (i.e., hydra), the entire body surface functions for gas exchange. More advanced animals have evolved specialized respiratory organs. **Gills** in the water and **tracheal** systems on land are two examples. **Lungs** are another gas exchange structure among some species of land animals. Muscular contractions usually produce pressure changes that either draw air into the lungs or force air out of the lungs. As another solution for gas exchange, birds have evolved a series of air sacs for the one-way flow of air.

The breathing cycle of humans begins with the contraction of the **diaphragm** and rib-elevating muscles. Their contraction creates a negative pressure, drawing air into the lungs (**inspiration**). A reverse of this process drives air out of the lungs (**expiration**). The rate of the breathing cycle depends on the level of carbon dioxide in the blood, as detected by chemoreceptors.

Once in the **alveoli** of the lungs, carbon dioxide and oxygen are exchanged with the blood by diffusion. Diffusion is also the process whereby body cells receive oxygen and give up carbon dioxide. Oxygen is mainly transported in the blood through association with **hemoglobin.** Carbon dioxide is mainly transported as part of the **bicarbonate ion.**

The respiratory tract can become infected with viruses or bacteria. Pneumonia and tuberculosis are infections that can be controlled with antibiotics. Cigarette smoking is the primary cause of the lung diseases **emphysema** and **lung cancer.**

STUDY EXERCISES

Study the text section by section as you answer the questions that follow.

44.1 HOW ANIMALS EXCHANGE GASES (P. 790)

- Respiration comprises breathing, external and internal respiration, and cellular respiration.
- Most animals have a special, localized gas exchange area, such as the gills in aquatic animals and lungs in terrestrial animals.
- Amphibians use positive pressure, but other vertebrates use negative pressure, to ventilate the lungs.
- Birds have a complete ventilation system in that there is a one-way flow of air over the gas-exchange area.

1. Match the processes with the following:
   1 inspiration and expiration
   2 exchange at respiratory surface
   3 exchange in tissues
   _____ a. breathing
   _____ b. external respiration
   _____ c. internal respiration
2. Label each of the following as characteristic of air (A) or water (W):
   _____ a. Mammals use 1–2% of their energy to breathe here.
   _____ b. It is more difficult for animals to obtain oxygen here.
   _____ c. More energy for breathing is required here.
   _____ d. The hydra carries out respiration in this environment.
   _____ e. This is the less dense medium.

3. Which of the classes of vertebrates use(s) positive pressure to fill their lungs with air? _____

4. Which of the classes use(s) negative pressure to fill their lungs with air? _____

5. Contrast ventilation by negative pressure with ventilation by positive pressure. _____
_____

6. How is the means of ventilation more complete in birds, compared to the incomplete means in amphibians, reptiles, and mammals? _____
_____

7. Complete the following table to summarize the means of ventilation in the adult animals listed:

Class	Organ(s) of Exchange	Special Features
hydra		
planarian		
fish		
amphibian		
reptile		
bird		
mammal		

44.2 HOW HUMANS EXCHANGE GASES (P. 794)

- There is a continuous pathway for air from the nose (or mouth) to the lungs in humans.
- The breathing rate is regulated and increases when there is a greater demand of exchange of gases in the lungs.

8. Label this diagram with the following terms:
   epiglottis
   glottis
   larynx
   nasal cavity
   pharynx
   trachea

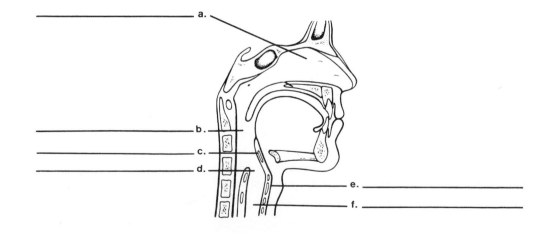

9. Name the structure that functions for each of the following:

gas exchange with blood flowing to and from the heart a._____

sound production b._____

filtering, moistening, and warming the air c._____

conduction of air into the thoracic cavity d._____

passage of air into the lung e._____

10. Indicate whether each of the following phrases is an example of inspiration (I) or expiration (E):

_____ a. lungs expanded
_____ b. muscles (diaphragm and ribs) relaxed
_____ c. dome-shaped diaphragm
_____ d. enlarged chest
_____ e. less air pressure in lungs than in outside environment

11. Indicate whether the following statements, about the control of breathing rate, are true (T) or false (F):

_____ a. Chemoreceptors are sensitive to changes in carbon dioxide in the blood.
_____ b. Chemoreceptors are sensitive to changes in hydrogen ions in the blood.
_____ c. The concentration of oxygen in arterial blood is a major stimulus.
_____ d. The respiratory center is located in the hypothalamus of the brain.

Exchanging and Transporting Gases (p. 797)

- The respiratory pigment hemoglobin transports oxygen from the lungs to the tissues and aids the transport of carbon dioxide from the tissues to the lungs.

12. Write the equation that describes how oxygen is transported in the blood. Label one arrow *lungs* and the reverse arrow *tissues*. a.

Write the equation that describes how most of the carbon dioxide is transported in the blood. Label one arrow *lungs* and the reverse arrow *tissues*. b.

What is the name of the enzyme that speeds up this reaction? c._____

Carbon dioxide transport produces hydrogen ions. Why does this production not form an acidic blood?

d._____

13. How is hemoglobin remarkably suited to the transport of oxygen in animals? a._____
_____

How does hemoglobin transport carbon dioxide? b._____
_____

44.3 KEEPING THE RESPIRATORY TRACT HEALTHY (P. 798)

- The respiratory tract is especially subject to infections. Cigarette smoking contributes to two major lung disorders—emphysema and cancer.

14. Indicate whether the following statements are true (T) or false (F):

_____ a. A sneeze can transfer bacteria or viruses.
_____ b. Emphysema develops from a lung infection.
_____ c. Antibiotics cannot normally control pneumonia.
_____ d. The moist mucous membrane of the respiratory tract is normally exposed to environmental air.

Review key terms by completing this crossword puzzle, using the following alphabetized list of terms:

alveolus
bicarbonate ion
bronchiole
bronchus
carbonic anhydrase
diaphragm
exhalation
gills
glottis
inhalation
larynx
lung
pharynx
rib cage
thoracic cavity
trachea
vocal chord

Across

1   internal body space of some animals that contains the lungs and the heart, and protects them from desiccation; the chest (two words)
6   top and side of the thoracic cavity in vertebrates; contains ribs and intercostal muscles (two words)
8   cartilaginous organ between the pharynx and the trachea in tetrapods that contains the vocal cords; voice box
9   respiratory organ in most aquatic animals; in fish, an outward extension of the pharynx
10 fold of tissue within the larynx; creates vocal sounds when it vibrates (two words)
11 common passageway for both food intake and air movement, located between the mouth and the esophagus
12 dome-shaped, muscularized sheet separating the thoracic cavity from the abdominal cavity in mammals
13 form in which most of the carbon dioxide is transported in the bloodstream; HCO_3^- (two words)
14 stage during respiration when air is pushed out of the lungs; expiration
16 opening for airflow in the larynx

Down

1   air tube (windpipe) in tetrapod vertebrates that runs between the larynx and the bronchi
2   enzyme in red blood cells that speeds the formation of carbonic acid from water and carbon dioxide (two words)
3   terminal, microscopic, grapelike air sac in vertebrate lungs
4   stage during respiration when air is drawn into the lungs; inspiration
5   small tube that conducts air from a bronchus to the alveoli
7   one of two main branches of the trachea in vertebrates that have lungs
15 internal respiratory organ containing moist surfaces for gas exchange

OBJECTIVE QUESTIONS

Do not refer to the text when taking this test.

_____ 1. Oxygen is more difficult to obtain by respiratory organs in the
   a. air.
   b. water.

_____ 2. A major adaptation for gas exchange in planaria is the
   a. countercurrent exchange in the lungs.
   b. lack of a gastrovascular cavity.
   c. presence of a thin, flattened body.
   d. thin surface in parapodia.

_____ 3. The major respiratory organ of the earthworm is the
   a. entire body surface.
   b. nephridia.
   c. parapodia.
   d. tracheae with spiracles.

_____ 4. The frog inhales air by a _____ pressure.
   a. negative
   b. positive

_____ 5. During inspiration, contractions
   a. raise the diaphragm and lower the ribs.
   b. raise the diaphragm and raise the ribs.
   c. lower the diaphragm and lower the ribs.
   d. lower the diaphragm and raise the ribs.

_____ 6. Air is exhaled from the body by passing through which order of structures?
   a. alveolus, bronchiole, bronchus, trachea
   b. bronchus, bronchiole, trachea, pharynx
   c. pharynx, larynx, trachea, bronchus
   d. trachea, alveolus, bronchus, bronchiole

_____ 7. Ventilation in birds is complete because inhaled air
   a. does not meet exhaled air.
   b. does not pass through all structures of the tract.
   c. passes through all structures of the tract.
   d. passes through the lungs by a positive pressure.

_____ 8. The structure(s) that receive(s) air after the bronchi is (are) the
   a. pharynx.
   b. trachea.
   c. bronchioles.
   d. villi.

_____ 9. Select the incorrect association.
   a. alveolus—gas exchange
   b. bronchus—air enters the lungs
   c. larynx—sound production
   d. nasal cavity—air dried and cooled

_____ 10. External respiration is defined as
   a. an exchange of gases in the lungs.
   b. breathing.
   c. an exchange of gases in the tissues.
   d. cellular respiration.

_____ 11. When the lungs recoil,
   a. inspiration occurs.
   b. external respiration occurs.
   c. internal respiration occurs.
   d. expiration occurs.
   e. All of these are correct

_____ 12. The chest is
   a. expanded during inspiration.
   b. closed off from the abdominal cavity by the diaphragm.
   c. divided into an area for the lungs and an area for the heart.
   d. All of these are correct.

_____ 13. The crossing of the digestive and respiratory tracts in the pharynx creates a need for
   a. swallowing.
   b. external nares.
   c. an epiglottis.
   d. a diaphragm.
   e. olfactory epithelium.

_____ 14. Chemoreceptors in the body are sensitive to
   a. carbon dioxide.
   b. hydrogen ions.
   c. Both _a_ and _b_ are correct.
   d. Neither a nor b is correct.

_____ 15. Most carbon dioxide in the blood is transported in the
   a. bicarbonate ion.
   b. carbon dioxide molecule.
   c. hemoglobin molecule.
   d. oxygen molecule.

_____ 16. Which of the following statements is NOT true?
   a. The respiratory center is located in the medulla oblongata.
   b. Breathing increases with exercise because of the reduced amount of oxygen in the blood.
   c. The chemoreceptors communicate with the respiratory center.
   d. When appropriate, the respiratory center increases the breathing rate.

_____ 17. Carbon dioxide is largely carried in the plasma
   a. in combination with hemoglobin.
   b. as the bicarbonate ion.
   c. combined with carbonic anhydrase.
   d. in red blood cells.
   e. Both _a_ and _b_ are correct.

_____18. Hemoglobin combines with _____ in the _____.
   a. oxygen; lungs
   b. carbon dioxide; tissues
   c. oxygen; tissues
   d. carbon dioxide; lungs
   e. Both *a* and *b* are correct.
_____19. _____ is a condition in which the lungs are inflated due to trapped air caused by bronchiole destruction.
   a. Pneumonia
   b. Tuberculosis

   c. Emphysema
   d. Lung cancer
   e. Pulmonary fibrosis
_____20. Smoking cigarettes
   a. causes tuberculosis.
   b. leads to emphysema and cancer.
   c. increases the vital capacity of the lungs.
   d. All of these are correct.

CRITICAL THINKING QUESTIONS

Answer in complete sentences.

21. How are the alveoli examples of a structure admirably suited to function?

22. The lungs of mammals do not contain any muscle tissue. How do they passively respond to the pressure changes around them?

Test Results: _____ Number right ÷ 22 = _____ × 100 = _____ %

EXPLORING THE INTERNET

Use the Internet to further explore topics in this chapter, such as the dangers of tobacco and lung cancer. Go to the Mader Home Page (http://www.mhhe.com/sciencemath/biology/mader/) and click on *Biology*, 6th edition. Go to Chapter 44 and select a Web site of interest.

ANSWER KEY

STUDY EXERCISES

1. a. 2 b. 1 c. 3 **2.** a. A b. W c. W d. W e. A **3.** amphibians **4.** reptiles, birds, mammals **5.** With positive pressure, the air is being forced into the lungs; with negative pressure, the air is being drawn in. **6.** Free, oxygen-rich air passes through the lungs in a one-way direction in birds. This incoming air does not mix with outgoing air, as it does in amphibians, reptiles, and mammals.

7.

Organ(s) of Exchange	Special Features
diffusion of gases across body layers	gastrovascular cavity
diffusion of gases across body layers	flattened, thin body
gills	countercurrent exchange
lungs and skin	use of positive pressure to fill lungs
lungs	jointed ribs, use of negative pressure to fill lungs
lungs	air sacs allow a one-way flow of air
lungs	diaphragm, use of negative pressure to fill lungs

8. a. nasal cavity **b.** pharynx **c.** epiglottis **d.** glottis **e.** larynx **f.** trachea **9. a.** alveolus **b.** larynx **c.** nose **d.** trachea **e.** bronchus **10. a.** I **b.** E **c.** E **d.** I **e.** I **11. a.** T **b.** T **c.** F **d.** F

12. a. $Hb + O_2 \underset{tissues}{\overset{lungs}{\rightleftharpoons}} HbO_2$

b. $CO_2 + H_2O \underset{lungs}{\overset{tissues}{\rightleftharpoons}} H_2CO_3 \underset{lungs}{\overset{tissues}{\rightleftharpoons}} H^+ + HCO_3^-$

c. carbonic anhydrase **d.** Hemoglobin combines with the excess hydrogen ions. **13. a.** It easily combines with oxygen in the lungs, and it easily gives up oxygen in the tissues. **b.** It combines with carbon dioxide somewhat, forming carbaminohemoglobin; it also picks up hydrogen ions **14. a.** T **b.** F **c.** F **d.** T

KEYWORD CROSSWORD

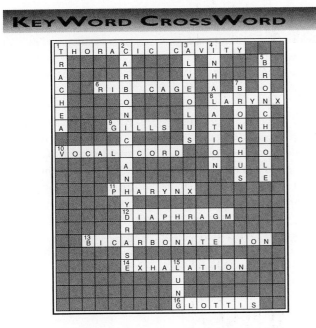

CHAPTER TEST

1. b **2.** c **3.** a **4.** b **5.** d **6.** a **7.** a **8.** c **9.** d **10.** a **11.** d **12.** d **13.** c **14.** c **15.** a **16.** b **17.** b **18.** e **19.** c **20.** b **21.** They are numerous, providing a greater total surface area for gas exchange. Their thin, moist surfaces maximize the diffusion for gas exchange. **22.** The pressure inside the lungs drops below atmospheric pressure when the diaphragm lowers and the rib cage rises. Then air rushes into lungs. The pressure inside of the lungs becomes greater than atmospheric pressure when the diaphragm rises and the rib cage lowers. Then air is forced out of lungs.

45

OSMOTIC REGULATION AND EXCRETION

CHAPTER REVIEW

Most animals have a means to maintain normal solute and water concentration in body fluids. Marine fishes constantly drink water, excrete salt at the gills, and pass an isotonic urine. Freshwater fishes never drink water; they take in salt at the gills and pass a hypotonic urine. The form in which animals excrete nitrogen depends on the type of environment inhabited. In a water environment, the form is usually **ammonia.** On land, it is either **urea** or **uric acid.**

Different groups of animals have evolved different excretory organs (i.e., Malpighian tubules in insects). Humans have a **urinary system** that includes the **kidneys** as the excretory organs. Microscopically, a kidney is made up of microscopic units called nephrons. A nephron makes **urine** through the processes of glomeru-

lar filtration, tubular reabsorption, and tubular secretion. Humans excrete a hypertonic urine through the action of the loop of the nephron.

Three hormones are involved in maintaining the blood volume and blood pressure. **Antidiuretic hormone (ADH)** regulates the reabsorption of water by regulating the permeability of the collecting duct. **Aldosterone** causes the reabsorption of sodium (Na^+) and therefore water. **Atrial natriuretic hormone (ANH)** opposes the action of both these hormones by blocking their secretion.

The kidneys control the pH of the blood by regulating the excretion of hydrogen ions (H^+) and ammonia (NH_3), together with the reabsorption of sodium (Na^+) and bicarbonate ions (HCO_3^-).

STUDY EXERCISES

Study the text section by section as you answer the questions that follow.

45.1 OSMOTIC REGULATION (P. 804)

- The mechanism for maintaining osmotic balance differs according to the environment of the organism.

1. Indicate whether the following statements are true (T) or false (F):
   _____ a. Birds and reptiles living near the sea excrete a concentrated salt solution through salt glands.
   _____ b. Cartilaginous fish live in an environment that is nearly isotonic to their internal body fluids.
   _____ c. Freshwater bony fish are prone to gaining body water.
   _____ d. Freshwater bony fish live in an environment that is hypertonic to their internal body fluids.
   _____ e. Marine bony fish actively transport salt into the seawater through their gills.
   _____ f. Marine bony fish are prone to losing water.
   _____ g. Marine bony fish live in an environment that is hypotonic to their internal body fluids.
   _____ h. The kangaroo rat forms a very dilute urine.

45.2 NITROGENOUS WASTE PRODUCTS (P. 806)

- Nitrogenous waste products differ as to the amount of water and energy required to excrete them.

2. a. Beneath the nitrogenous wastes listed, draw an arrow pointed in the direction of the waste that requires the most water to excrete.

    ammonia   urea   uric acid

   b. Beneath these wastes, draw an arrow pointed in the direction of the waste that requires the most energy for an animal to produce.

    ammonia   urea   uric acid

45.3 ORGANS OF EXCRETION (P. 807)

- Complex animals have organs of excretion that maintain the osmotic balance of the body and rid the body of waste molecules.

3. Explain the action of flame cells in planaria. _____

_____

4. Explain the action of nephridia in earthworms. _____

_____

5. Explain the action of Malpighian tubules in insect. _____

_____

6. Associate the excretory organs mentioned in questions 3–5, with these phrases:
   - _____ a. usually gets rid of excess water.
   - _____ b. usually conserves water.
   - _____ c. excretes uric acid
   - _____ d. present in each segment

45.4 HUMANS HAVE A URINARY SYSTEM (P. 808)

- The urinary system of humans consists of organs that produce, store, and rid the body of urine.
- The work of an organ is dependent on its microscopic anatomy; nephrons within the human kidney produce urine.

7. Rearranging the letters of structures *a–d* to indicate the direction that urine is transported through the human urinary system. _____
   a. bladder
   b. kidney
   c. ureter
   d. urethra

8. Label this diagram of the kidney with the following terms:
   collecting duct
   nephrons
   renal cortex
   renal medulla
   renal pelvis
   renal pyramid
   ureter

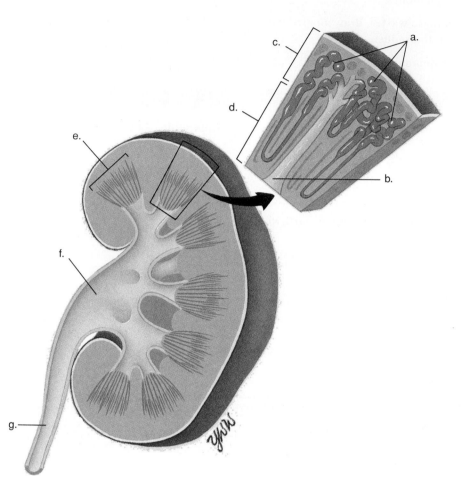

9. Label this diagram of the nephron and associated blood vessels with the following terms:
   afferent arteriole
   collecting duct
   distal convoluted tubule
   efferent arteriole
   glomerular capsule
   loop of the nephron
   peritubular capillaries
   proximal convoluted tubule

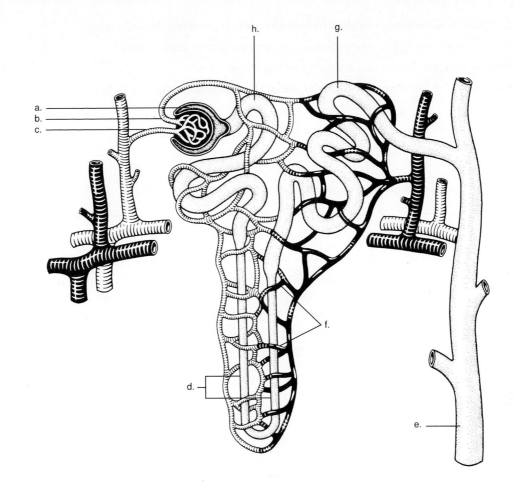

How Urine Is Made (p. 810)

- Like many physiological processes, urine formation in humans is a multistep process.
- In addition to ridding the body of waste molecules and maintaining osmotic balance, the human kidneys adjust the pH of the blood.

10. Label this diagram to indicate the steps of urine formation.

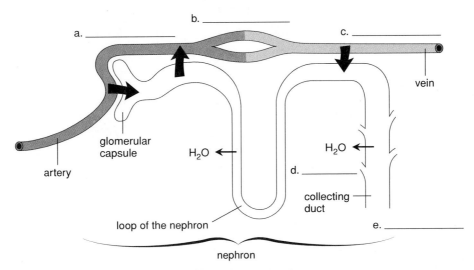

11. Blood approaches the glomerulus in the afferent arteriole. It contains the following:

    small materials—nutrients (glucose, amino acids), wastes (urea), salts, water

    other materials—formed elements, proteins, hydrogen ions

    Will the *small materials* or the *other materials* enter the glomerular capsule to become the

    filtrate? a._____

    Which of the molecules in the filtrate will probably be absorbed? b._____

    Which of the *other materials* will enter the tubule during the process called tubular

    secretion? c._____

12. According to the diagram in question 8, where is water primarily reabsorbed? a._____

    _____

    What effect does this high degree of reabsorption have on the composition of urine? b._____

    _____

13. In the diagram in question 8, darken the portion of the loop of the nephron that is impermeable to water. Add to the diagram one set of colored arrows to indicate the active transport of sodium out of the ascending limb. Color the arrows that indicate the movement of water out of the loop and the collecting duct.

Hormones Maintain Water Balance (p. 812)

14. Examine the following diagram and answer the questions that follow:

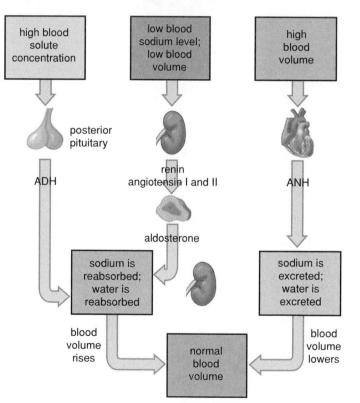

    Name three hormones involved in regulating blood volume and blood pressure? a._____

    Which two hormones act to increase blood volume and blood pressure? b._____

    How does ADH function? c._____

    After ADH is secreted, the volume of urine produced (increases or decreases)? d._____

    How does aldosterone function? e._____

    Which hormone opposes the action of ADH and aldosterone? f._____

How the pH Is Adjusted (p. 813)

15. If the blood is acidic, a._____ ions are excreted in combination with b._____, while c._____ and bicarbonate ions are reabsorbed. If the blood is basic, fewer d._____ ions are excreted, and fewer e._____ and bicarbonate ions are reabsorbed.

Excretion Elimination

In the table, place an X beside the component of blood if the following descriptions pertain to it:

    a. *in the afferent arteriole*
    b. *in the filtrate*
    c. *in the efferent arteriole*
    d. *reabsorbed into the peritubular capillary*
    e. *secreted from the peritubular capillary*
    f. *present in urine*
    g. *absent from urine*
    h. *in venous blood*

	a	b	c	d	e	f	g	h
1. Plasma Proteins								
2. Red Blood Cells								
3. White Blood Cells								
4. Glucose								
5. Amino Acids								
6. Sodium Chloride								
7. Water								
8. Urea								
9. Uric Acid								
10. Creatinine								

There are 45 correct answers. There are 80 possible errors of omission or commission. Any 10 errors and you're ELIMINATED!

Review key terms by completing this crossword puzzle, using the following alphabetized list of terms:

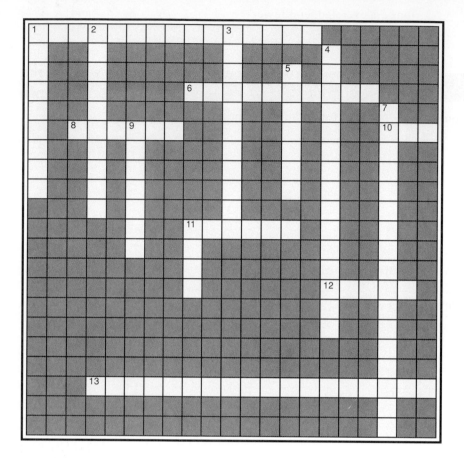

ADH
aldosterone
collecting duct
glomerular capsule
glomerulus
kidney
Malpighian tubule
nephridium
nephron
urea
ureter
urethra
uric acid
urinary bladder
urine

Across

1 organ where urine is stored (two words)

6 capillary network within a glomerular capsule of a nephron

8 one of the paired organs of the urinary system that regulates the chemical composition of the blood and produces a waste product called urine

10 hormone secreted by the posterior pituitary that increases the permeability of the collecting ducts in a kidney

11 tubular structure conducting urine from the kidney to the urinary bladder

12 liquid waste product made by the nephrons of the kidney through the processes of glomerular filtration and tubular reabsorption

13 cuplike structure that is the initial portion of a nephron; where pressure filtration occurs (two words)

Down

1 main nitrogenous waste of insects, reptiles, birds, and some dogs (two words)

2 segmentally arranged, paired, excretory tubules of many invertebrates, such as the earthworm, where the contents are released through a nephridiopore

3 hormone secreted by the adrenal cortex that regulates the sodium and potassium ion balance of the blood

4 duct within the kidney that receives fluid from several nephrons; water is absorbed (two words)

5 tubular structure that receives urine from the bladder and carries it to the outside of the body

7 blind, threadlike, excretory tubule near the anterior end of an insect hindgut (two words)

9 microscopic kidney unit that regulates blood composition by glomerular filtration, tubular reabsorption, and tubular secretion; each human kidney has over a million

11 main nitrogenous waste of terrestrial amphibians and mammals

OBJECTIVE QUESTIONS

Do not refer to the text when taking this test.

_____ 1. Uric acid is _____ soluble in water and _____ toxic.
   a. highly; highly
   b. highly; slightly
   c. slightly; highly
   d. slightly; slightly

_____ 2. Ammonia is the main means of excreting nitrogen in each of the following groups EXCEPT
   a. amphibian adults.
   b. amphibian larvae.
   c. aquatic invertebrates.
   d. bony fishes.

_____ 3. Marine fish face the problem of water loss from the body.
   a. true
   b. false

_____ 4. Select the incorrect association.
   a. flame cell—hydra
   b. kidney—human
   c. Malpighian tubule—insect
   d. nephridia—earthworm

_____ 5. The innermost hollow chamber of the kidney is the
   a. renal cortex.
   b. glomerulus.
   c. renal medulla.
   d. renal pelvis.

_____ 6. The collecting ducts are primarily found in the
   a. renal cortex.
   b. renal medulla.
   c. renal pelvis.
   d. afferent arteriole.

_____ 7. Kidneys are organs of homeostasis because they
   a. regulate the blood volume.
   b. regulate the pH of the blood.
   c. help maintain the correct concentration of ions in the blood.
   d. excrete nitrogenous wastes.
   e. All of these are correct.

_____ 8. Nitrogenous wastes are
   a. metabolic wastes.
   b. toxic.
   c. formed from the breakdown of amino acids.
   d. All of these are correct.

_____ 9. Glomerular filtration occurs in the _____, and reabsorption occurs in the _____.
   a. glomerular capsule; nephron tubule
   b. nephron tubule; glomerular capsule

_____ 10. By tubular reabsorption, substances pass from the
   a. blood into the tubule.
   b. tubule into the blood.

_____ 11. The hormone aldosterone promotes the
   a. excretion of potassium only.
   b. reabsorption of sodium only.
   c. excretion of potassium and reabsorption of sodium.
   d. elimination of water.

_____ 12. The kidneys oppose an acidic blood condition by _____ hydrogen ions and _____ sodium and bicarbonate ions.
   a. excreting; reabsorbing
   b. reabsorbing; excreting

_____ 13. Tubular secretion occurs at the
   a. glomerular capsule.
   b. proximal convoluted tubule.
   c. loop of the nephron.
   d. distal convoluted tubule.

_____ 14. Glucose
   a. is in the filtrate and urine.
   b. is in the filtrate and not in the urine.
   c. undergoes tubular secretion and is in the urine.
   d. undergoes tubular secretion and is not in urine.

_____ 15. A person who lacks ADH
   a. has low blood volume and pressure.
   b. will have sugar in the urine.
   c. has diabetes mellitus.
   d. All of these are correct.

_____ 16. Which of the following describes the contents of the renal vein that leaves the kidney?
   a. low in oxygen, low in urea
   b. high in carbon dioxide, high in urea
   c. high in oxygen, high in urea
   d. low in carbon dioxide, high in urea

_____ 17. Sodium is removed from the nephron tubule by
   a. passive reabsorption.
   b. active reabsorption.
   c. an attraction to Cl^-.
   d. tubular secretion.

_____ 18. The region between the base of the loop of the nephron and the collecting duct has a(n)
   a. very low solute concentration.
   b. intermediate solute concentration.
   c. very high solute concentration.
   d. very high water concentration.

Answer in complete sentences.

19. Glomerular filtration is unselective; tubular reabsorption is very selective. Support this statement.

20. How are mitochondria and microvilli major cellular adaptations of the cells of the proximal convoluted tubule of the nephron?

Test Results: _____ Number right ÷ 20 = _____ × 100 = _____ %

EXPLORING THE INTERNET

Use the Internet to further explore topics in this chapter, such as kidney disease and urinary bladder cancer. Go to the Mader Home Page (http://www.mhhe.com/sciencemath/biology/mader/) and click on *Biology,* 6th edition. Go to Chapter 45 and select a Web site of interest.

ANSWER KEY

STUDY EXERCISES

1. **a.** T **b.** T **c.** T **d.** F **e.** T. **f.** T **g.** F **h.** F **2. a.** Arrow should be pointed left. **b.** Arrow should be pointed right. **3.** Planaria live in freshwater. The movement of flame-cell cilia propels hypotonic fluid through excretory canals and out of body **4.** Fluid from the coelom is propelled through the nephridia by beating cilia; certain substances are reabsorbed by a network of capillaries. **5.** Malpighian tubules take up water and uric acid from the hemolymph and pass them to the gut where water is reabsorbed. **6. a.** flame cells **b.** Malpighian tubules **c.** Malpighian tubules **d.** nephridia. **7.** b, c, a, d **8.** See Figure 45.6, p. 808, in text. **9.** See Figure 45.7, page 809, in text. **10. a.** glomerular filtration **b.** tubular reabsorption **c.** tubular secretion **d.** reabsorption of water **e.** excretion **11. a.** small materials **b.** nutrients, salts, water **c.** hydrogen ions **12. a.** descending limb of the loop of the nephron and collecting duct. **b.** The urine is more concentrated. **13.** See Figure 45.10, p. 812, in text. **14. a.** antidiuretic hormone (ADH), aldosterone, atrial natriuretic hormone (ANH) **b.** antidiuretic hormone (ADH) and aldosterone **c.** Increases permeability of collecting duct so that water is reabsorbed. **d.** decreases **e.** Cause sodium to be reabsorbed and water follows **f.** ANH **15. a.** hydrogen **b.** ammonia **c.** sodium **d.** hydrogen **e.** sodium

GAME X: EXCRETION ELIMINATION

	a	b	c	d	e	f	g	h
1. Plasma Proteins	x		x				x	x
2. Red Blood Cells	x		x				x	x
3. White Blood Cells	x		x				x	x
4. Glucose	x	x		x			x	x
5. Amino Acids	x	x		x			x	x
6. Sodium Chloride	x	x		x		x		x
7. Water	x	x	x	x		x		x
8. Urea	x	x				x		
9. Uric Acid	x	x			x	x		
10. Creatinine	x	x	x		x	x		

KEYWORD CROSSWORD

Across: 1. URINARY BLADDER 6. GLOMERULUS 8. KIDNEY 10. ADH 11. URETER 12. URINE 13. GLOMERULAR CAPSULE

Down answers include: URIC ACID, NEPHRON, BLADDER, COLLECTING, MALPIGHIAN TUBULE, and related terms.

CHAPTER TEST

1. d **2.** a **3.** a **4.** a **5.** d **6.** b **7.** e **8.** d **9.** a **10.** b **11.** c **12.** a **13.** d **14.** b **15.** a **16.** a **17.** b **18.** c **19.** With the exception of the blood cells and plasma proteins, all smaller components of the blood are forced out of the glomerulus in large quantities. Reabsorption returns them to the blood in varying amounts, however, depending on the needs of the body. **20.** The mitochondria increase the energy capacity for the active transport mechanisms carried out by the tubule cells. The microvilli increase the surface area of the cells to make contact with and return materials to the blood by reabsorption.

46

NEURONS AND NERVOUS SYSTEMS

CHAPTER REVIEW

There are three types of **neurons: sensory, motor,** and **interneuron.** As in the motor neuron, each neuron has a cell body, axon, and dendrites. When an axon is not conducting a nerve impulse, the inside of the fiber is negative compared to the outside. This is the **resting potential,** when there is a concentration of Na+ outside and a concentration of K+ inside the axon due to the work of the sodium-potassium pump. When a nerve impulse occurs an **action potential** travels along an axon. Depolarization (inside becomes positive) is due to the movement of Na+ to the inside, and then repolarization (inside becomes negative again) is due to the movement of K+ to the outside.

Transmission of the nerve impulse from one neuron to another takes place across a **synapse.** Synaptic vesicles release a neurotransmitter that binds to receptors in the postsynaptic membrane, causing either stimulation or inhibition.

A comparative study of the invertebrates shows a gradual increase in the complexity of the nervous system. The vertebrate nervous system, like that of the earthworn, is divided into the central and peripheral nervous systems.

The **peripheral nervous system** consists of cranial and spinal nerves. In spinal nerves, reflex actions occur when nerve impulses begin at a receptor and then move from a sensory neuron to an interneuron to a motor neuron, which stimulates an effector to react. In the **autonomic system,** the sympathetic system is associated with reactions to stress, and the **parasympathetic system** is associated with maintenance during relaxation.

The **central nervous system** consists of the spinal cord and brain. Humans have the most well-developed cerebral cortex of all the vertebrates. Each lobe contains association areas for more complex levels of consciousness. The lobes of the cortex can be mapped for sensory and motor functions.

STUDY EXERCISES

46.1 NERVOUS TISSUE (P. 818)

- Nervous tissue is made up of cells called neurons, which are specialized to carry nerve impulses and neuroglial cells that support and protect neurons.

1. Label this diagram of a motor neuron with the following terms:
   dendrite
   cell body
   axon
   myelin sheath
   neurofibril node
   muscle fiber

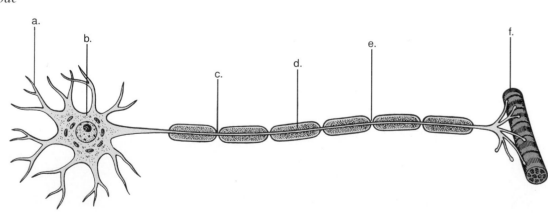

2. Match the terms listed in question 1 with these phrases:
   _____ a. membranes of tightly spiraled neurolemmocytes
   _____ b. conducts signals toward the cell body
   _____ c. conducts nerve impulses away from the cell body
   _____ d. contains the nucleus
   _____ e. gap along the myelin sheath

3. a._____ neurons take messages from sensory receptors to the central nervous system.

   b._____ neurons take messages from the central nervous system to effectors.

   c._____ occur within the CNS and convey messages between neurons.

Transmitting the Nerve Impulse (p. 820)

> • A nerve impulse is an electrochemical change that travels along the length of a neuron.

4. Examine this diagram depicting the resting potential and then answer the questions that follow:

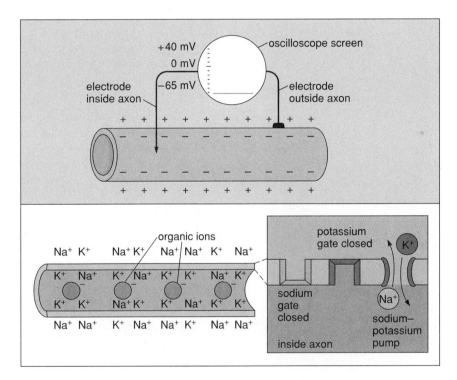

What is an oscilloscope? a._____

_____

The oscilloscope is reading −65 mV. Why is the inside of an axon negative compared to the outside? b._____

_____

At the time of the resting potential, are there more or less Na$^+$ ions outside the axon than inside the axon?

c._____

At the time of the resting potential, are there more or less K$^+$ ions outside the axon than inside the axon?

d._____

What mechanism accounts for the unequal distribution of ions across the axomembrane? e._____

_____

5. Use these terms to label this diagram depicting the trace on the oscilloscope screen as an action potential occurs.

   action potential
   depolarization
   resting potential
   repolarization
   threshold

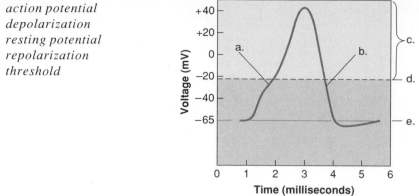

6. Examine this diagram depicting an action potential and then answer the questions that follow.

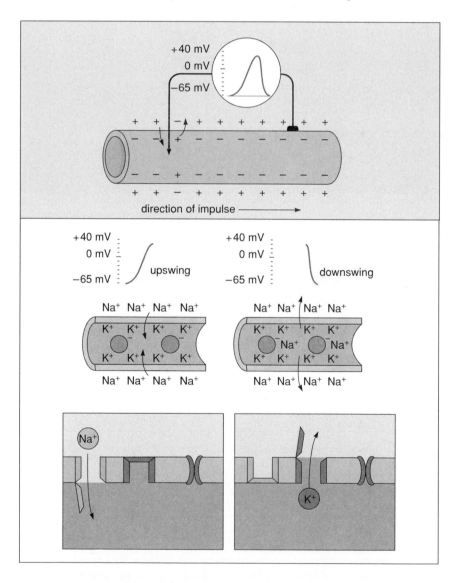

What does the expression depolarization refer to? a._____

_____

What does the expression repolarization refer to? b._____

_____

In the top portion of the diagram on the adjacent page, there is an arrow leading from a plus sign (+) to the interior of the axon and an arrow leading from a minus sign (−) to the exterior of the axon. Explain with relation to the trace on the oscilloscope screen. c._____

_____

In the middle portion of the diagram to the left, there is an arrow leading from Na⁺ to the interior of the axon. Relate this arrow to the "upswing" of the action potential. d._____

_____

By what means does Na⁺ cross the axomembrane? e._____

_____

In the middle portion of the diagram to the right, there is an arrow leading from K⁺ to the exterior of the axon. Relate this arrow to the "downswing" of the action potential. f._____

_____

By what means does K⁺ cross the axomembrane? g._____

_____

Transmitting at Synapses (p. 822)

- Transmission of impulses between neurons is usually accomplished by means of chemicals called neurotransmitters.

7. Label this diagram of a synapse with the following terms:

axon bulbs
dendrite
neurotransmitter
synaptic cleft
synaptic vesicles

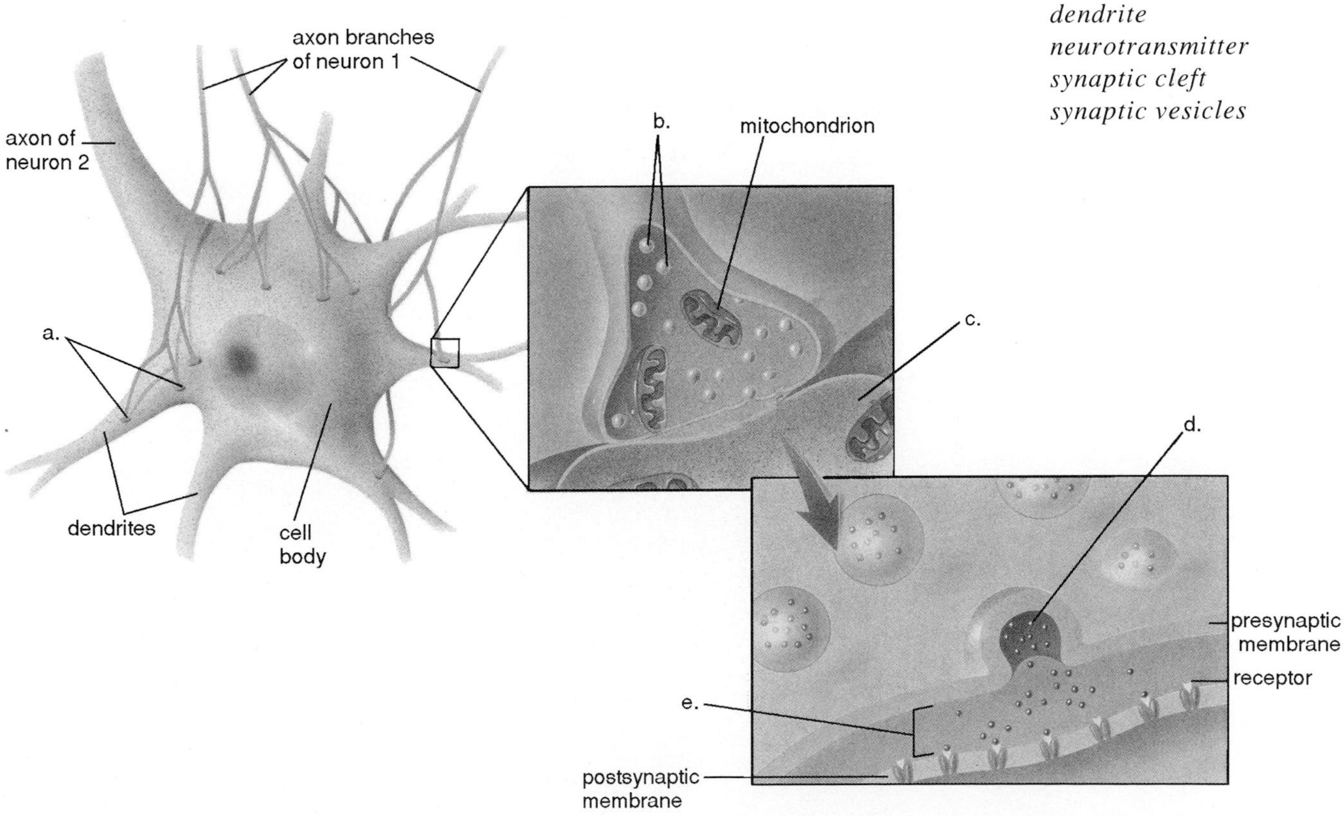

8. What causes transmission of the nerve impulse across a synapse?

a._____

What is integration? b._____

46.2 HOW THE NERVOUS SYSTEM EVOLVED (P. 823)

- A survey of invertebrates shows a gradual increase in the complexity of the nervous system.
- All vertebrates have a well-developed brain, but the forebrain is the largest in mammals, particularly humans.

9. Match the phrases with the following animals:
   1 hydra
   2 planaria
   3 earthworm
   4 squid
   5 cat
   _____ a. ladder organization
   _____ b. dorsal solid nerve cord
   _____ c. nerve net
   _____ d. dorsal hollow nerve cord
   _____ e. giant nerve fibers

10. Why is it said that planaria have cephalization? _____

_____

11. In what way does the nervous organization in these animals suggest a central and peripheral nervous system?

_____

46.3 THE PERIPHERAL NERVOUS SYSTEM CONTAINS NERVES (P. 825)

- The peripheral nervous system contains nerves that conduct nerve impulses between the central nervous system and all body parts.

12. In the peripheral nervous system, the cranial nerves are attached to the a._____ and the spinal nerves are attached to the b._____. Nerves are bundles of c._____ neuron d._____ held together by connective tissue. Mixed nerves contain both e._____ and f._____ fibers.

Somatic System Serves Skin and Muscles (p. 827)

13. Label this diagram of the reflex arc with the following terms:

   central canal
   dorsal-root ganglion
   effector
   gray matter
   interneuron
   motor neuron
   receptor
   sensory neuron
   ventral horn of gray matter
   white matter

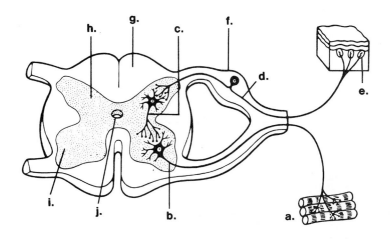

14. During a spinal reflex, a stimulus is received by a(n) ^{a.}_____, which initiates an impulse in the ^{b.}_____ neuron. The sensory neuron takes the message to the spinal cord and transmits it to the ^{c.}_____. This neuron passes the impulse to the ^{d.}_____ neuron, which takes the message from the cord and innervates a muscle, causing a reaction to the stimulus.

Autonomic System Serves Internal Organs (p. 829)

15. Indicate three ways in which the sympathetic and parasympathetic systems are similar.

   a._____

   b._____

   c._____

16. Complete the following table to show how the two systems differ:

	Sympathetic	Parasympathetic
Type of Situation		
Neurotransmitter		
Ganglia Near Cord, or Ganglia Near Organ?		
Spinal Nerves Only, or Spinal Nerves Plus Vagus?		

17. Label each of the following as somatic system (S) or autonomic system (A):
_____ a. activation of skeletal muscles
_____ b. parasympathetic and sympathetic systems
_____ c. control of internal organs

46.4 CENTRAL NERVOUS SYSTEM: BRAIN AND SPINAL CORD (P. 830)

- The central nervous system controls the other systems of the body and coordinates body functions.

18. The central nervous system consists of the ᵃ·_____ and ᵇ·_____.

19. Provide the functions for these parts of the brain.

cerebrum ᵃ·_____

_____

thalamus ᵇ·_____

hypothalamus ᶜ·_____

cerebellum ᵈ·_____

medulla oblongata ᵉ·_____

20. The outer part of the cerebrum is called the ᵃ·_____, and the two halves of the cerebrum are called the ᵇ·_____.

21. Label this diagram of the brain with the parts listed in question 19.

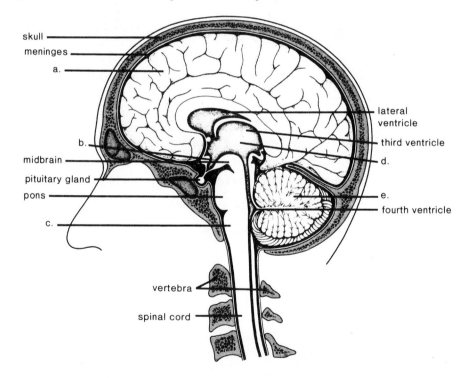

22. Indicate whether the following statements about learning and memory are true (T) or false (F):
_____ a. Learning does not involve gene regulation in the neuron.
_____ b. The number of synapses in the brain decreases during learning.
_____ c. The limbic system is involved in these processes.
_____ d. The limbic system communicates with sensory areas.

For each correct answer, Simon says, "You may move one step forward." Total possible number of steps forward is 10 steps.

1. Which of these would NOT be used when studying nerve conduction?
   a. voltmeter
   b. oscilloscope
   c. electron microscope
   d. electrodes
   e. electric current

2. Which one is NOT *directly* needed for nerve conduction?
   a. dendrites
   b. axons
   c. plasma membrane
   d. nucleus
   e. cytoplasm of the axon
   f. ions

3. Which one does NOT move during nerve conduction?
   a. sodium
   b. potassium
   c. plus charges
   d. minus charges

4. Which one does NOT accurately describe a resting neuron?
   a. positive on the outside of the membrane and negative on the inside
   b. Na^+ on the outside of the membrane and K^+ on the inside
   c. -65 mV inside
   d. negative on both sides of the membrane

5. Which one is NOT involved with an action potential?
   a. resting potential
   b. permeability
   c. sodium-potassium pump
   d. plasma membrane
   e. acetylcholine
   f. ions
   g. glycogen

6. Which one does NOT conduct a nerve impulse?
   a. sensory neurons
   b. osteocytes
   c. motor neurons
   d. sensory nerves
   e. motor nerves

7. Which one is improperly matched?

a. $\int$ Na^+ b. $\big\}$ K^+ c. $\int$ K^+ d. $\dfrac{Na^+}{K^+}$ $\dfrac{Na^+}{K^+}$

8. Which number could NOT be associated with an action potential?
   a. –65 millivolts
   b. 0 millivolts
   c. +40 millivolts
   d. –40 watts

9. Which one is improperly matched?
   a. (e⁻) (nerve impulse)
   b. sodium-potassium pump) (resting potential)
   c. (+) (Na⁺)
   d. (–) (K⁺)
   e. (plasma membrane) (semipermeable)

10. Which one is NOT true?

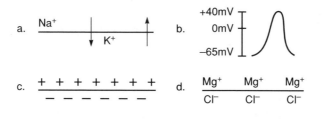

How many steps were you allowed by Simon? _____

Review key terms by completing this crossword puzzle, using the following alphabetized list of terms:

axon
cerebellum
cerebrum
dendrite
ganglion
hypothalamus
limbic system
medulla oblongata
meninges
midbrain
myelin sheath
nerve
neuron
neurotransmitter
pons
reflex
salutatory conduction
synapse
thalamus
ventricle

Across

1 movement of nerve impulses from one neurofibril node to another along a myelinated axon (two words)

5 portion of the brain that coordinates skeletal muscles to produce smooth, graceful motions

8 main part of the brain consisting of two large masses, or cerebral hemispheres; the largest part of the brain in mammals

9 knot or bundle of neuron cell bodies, usually outside the central nervous system

11 white, fatty material—derived from the membrane of neurolemmocytes—that forms a covering for nerve fibers (two words)

13 part of a neuron that conducts impulses from the cell body to the synapse

14 part of the brain that is the integrating center for sensory input; it plays a role in arousing the cerebral cortex

16 protective membranous coverings about the central nervous system

18 part of a neuron that sends impulses toward the cell body

Down

1 junction between neurons consisting of the presynaptic (axon) membrane, the synaptic cleft, and the postsynaptic (usually dendrite) membrane

2 pathways linking the hypothalamus to some areas of the cerebral cortex; governs learning and memory and various emotions, such as pleasure, fear, and happiness (two words)

3 chemical made at the ends of axons that is responsible for transmission across a synapse

4 nerve cell that characteristically has three parts: dendrites, cell body, and axon

6 part of the brain stem controlling heartbeat, blood pressure, breathing, and other vital functions (two words)

7 part of the brain that helps regulate the internal environment of the body; involved in control of heart rate, body temperature, water balance, and glandular secretions of the stomach and pituitary gland

10 cavity in an organ, such as in the brain

11 part of the brain located below the thalamus and above the pons

12 bundle of long axons and/or dendrites outside the central nervous system

15 automatic, involuntary response of an organism to a stimulus

17 part of the brain stem above the medulla oblongata and below the midbrain; it also serves to connect the cerebral hemispheres

OBJECTIVE QUESTIONS

Do not refer to the text when taking this test.

_____ 1. Which of these contains the nucleus?
    a. axon
    b. dendrite
    c. cell body
    d. Both _a_ and _b_ are correct.

_____ 2. The neuron found wholly and completely within the CNS is the
    a. motor neuron.
    b. sensory neuron.
    c. interneuron.
    d. All of these are correct.

In questions 3–6, match the functions to the following structures (some letters are not used):
    a. dendrites
    b. axons
    c. synaptic vesicles
    d. neurofibril
    e. ganglia
    f. motor neurons

_____ 3. contain neurotransmitters
_____ 4. are nerve cell bodies outside the CNS
_____ 5. terminate at muscles
_____ 6. are gaps in the myelin sheath.

_____ 7. Synaptic vesicles are
    a. at the ends of dendrites and axons.
    b. at the ends of axons only.
    c. along the length of all long fibers.
    d. All of these are correct.

_____ 8. The sodium-potassium pump maintains the resting potential.
    a. true
    b. false

_____ 9. What is involved in a nerve impulse?
    a. ions
    b. electrons
    c. atoms
    d. molecules

_____10. The downswing of the nerve impulse is caused by the movement of
    a. sodium ions to the inside of a neuron.
    b. sodium ions to the outside of a neuron.
    c. potassium ions to the inside of a neuron.
    d. potassium ions to the outside of a neuron.

_____11. Rapid conduction of a nerve impulse in vertebrates is due to
    a. the large diameters of the axons.
    b. gaps in the myelin sheath.
    c. an abundance of synapses.
    d. the high permeability of neuronal membranes to ions.
    e. All of these are correct.

_____12. Acetylcholine
    a. is a neurotransmitter.
    b. crosses the synaptic cleft.
    c. is broken down by acetylcholinesterase.
    d. All of these are correct.

_____13. From an evolutionary perspective, which group of animals is the first to exhibit a central nerve cord system?
    a. cnidaria
    b. planaria
    c. annelids and arthropods
    d. vertebrates

_____14. A spinal nerve is
    a. a motor nerve.
    b. a sensory nerve.
    c. a mixed nerve.
    d. All of these are correct.

_____15. The autonomic system has two divisions called the _____ systems.
    a. central nervous and peripheral nervous
    b. somatic and skeletal
    c. efferent and afferent
    d. sympathetic and parasympathetic

_____16. Which of the following motor neurons would be found in the autonomic division of the peripheral nervous system?
    a. motor neurons ending at skeletal muscle
    b. motor neurons leading to the esophagus
    c. motor neurons at the surface of the skin
    d. All of these are correct.

_____17. Sensory neurons
    a. take impulses to the CNS.
    b. have a long dendrite and a short axon.
    c. take impulses away from the CNS.
    d. Both _b_ and _c_ are correct.

_____18. Which system is involved during stress?
    a. parasympathetic
    b. sympathetic
    c. somatic
    d. Both _a_ and _b_ are correct.

_____19. The neurotransmitter of the parasympathetic system is
    a. norepinephrine.
    b. acetylcholine.
    c. cholinesterase.
    d. Both _a_ and _b_ are correct.

_____20. Automatic responses to specific external stimuli require
    a. rapid impulse transmission along the spinal cord.
    b. the involvement of the brain.
    c. simplified pathways called reflex arcs.
    d. the involvement of the autonomic system.

____21. What portion of the nervous system is required for a reflex arc?
  a. mixed spinal nerve
  b. gray matter of spinal cord
  c. cerebrum
  d. Both *a* and *b* are correct.
  e. All of these are correct.
____22. Which is the largest part of the human brain?
  a. cerebrum
  b. cerebellum
  c. medulla oblongata
  d. thalamus
____23. The function of the cerebellum is
  a. consciousness.
  b. motor coordination.
  c. homeostasis.
  d. sense reception.

____24. Which portion of the brain is involved in judgment?
  a. cerebellum
  b. frontal lobe of cerebrum
  c. medulla oblongata
  d. parietal lobe of cerebrum
____25. Drugs of abuse primarily affect the
  a. cerebellum.
  b. medulla oblongata.
  c. limbic system.
  d. thalamus.

CLINICAL THINKING QUESTIONS

Answer in complete sentences.

26. How is the structure of the neuron well suited for its functions?

27. How does motor control of internal organs differ from motor control of skeletal muscles?

Test Results: _____ Number right ÷ 27 = _____ × 100 = _____ %

EXPLORING THE INTERNET

Use the Internet to further explore topics in this chapter, such as brain imaging, sleep medicine, and multiple sclerosis. Go to the Mader Home Page (http://www.mhhe.com/sciencemath/biology/mader/) and click on *Biology,* 6th edition. Go to Chapter 46 and select a Web site of interest.

ANSWER KEY

STUDY EXERCISES

1. a. dendrite **b.** cell body **c.** neurofibril node (or axon) **d.** myelin sheath **e.** axon (or neurofibril node) **f.** muscle fiber **2. a.** myelin sheath **b.** dendrite **c.** axon **d.** cell body **e.** neurofibril node **3. a.** Sensory **b.** Motor **c.** Interneurons **4. a.** an instrument that measures potential differences in millivolts **b.** Large organic ions are inside the membrane (also there is a slow leakage of K^+ to outside). **c.** more Na^+ outside than inside **d.** less K^+ outside than inside **e.** sodium-potassium pump **5. a.** depolarization **b.** repolarization **c.** action potential **d.** threshold **e.** resting potential **6. a.** change from a negative potential to a positive potential inside the axon **b.** change from a positive potential inside the axon back to negative again **c.** refers to the reversal of potential that occurs during the action potential **d.** The movement of Na^+ to the inside of the axon causes the inside to become positive compared to outside. **e.** gate of Na^+ channel opens **f.** The movement of K^+ to the outside causes the inside to become negative again. **g.** gate of K^+ channel opens **7. a.** axon bulbs **b.** synaptic vesicles **c.** dendrite **d.** neurotransmitter **e.** synaptic cleft **8. a.** neurotransmitter is received by receptor of the next neuron **b.** a summing up of the effects of various neurotransmitters—some are stimulatory and some are inhibitory **9. a.** 2 **b.** 3 **c.** 1 **d.** 5 **e.** 4 **10.** Cephalization is a definite head region that bears sense organs.

11. The ganglia or a brain and a longitudinal nerve cord suggest a central nervous system; transverse nerves suggest a peripheral nervous system. **12. a.** brain **b.** spinal cord **c.** long **d.** fibers **e.** sensory **f.** motor **13.** See Figure 46.7, page 827, in text. **14. a.** receptor **b.** sensory **c.** interneuron **d.** motor **15. a.** function automatically and involuntarily **b.** innervate internal organs **c.** use two motor neurons and one ganglion for each impulse

16.

Sympathetic	Parasympathetic
emergency activity	normal activity
norepinephrine (NE)	acetylcholine (ACH)
near cord	near organ
spinal nerves only	spinal and vagus nerves

17. a. S **b.** A **c.** A   **18. a.** brain **b.** spinal cord **19. a.** consciousness and all higher activities like intelligence and reason; reception of sensory data and initiation of motor responses **b.** gatekeeper of the brain; alerts higher centers to receive information **c.** brings about homeostasis; has centers for hunger, sleep, body temperature **d.** motor coordination, muscle tone, posture **e.** control of internal organs   **20. a.** cortex **b.** cerebral hemispheres   **21. a.** cerebrum **b.** hypothalamus **c.** medulla oblongata **d.** thalamus **e.** cerebellum **22. a.** F **b.** F **c.** T **d.** T

SIMON SAYS ABOUT NERVOUS CONDUCTION

1. c **2.** d **3.** d **4.** d **5.** g **6.** b **7.** c **8.** d **9.** a **10.** d

KEYWORD CROSSWORD

¹S	A	L	²T	A	T	O	R	Y		C	³O	N	D	U	C	T	I	O	⁴N
Y			I								E								E
N			⁵C	E	R	E	B	E	L	L	U	M							U
A			B								R		⁶M						R
P			I								O		E		⁷H				O
⁸S	C	E	R	E	B	R	U	M			T		D		Y				N
E									⁹G	A	N	G	L	I	O	N			
	S				¹⁰V					N			L		T				
	Y		¹¹M	Y	E	L	I	¹²N		S	H	E	A	T	H				
	S		I		N			E		M				¹³A	X	O	N		
	T		N		D			R		I			O	L					
	E		B		R			V		T			B	A					
	M		R		I		¹⁴T	H	A	L	A	M	U	S					
			A		C			E		E			N	S					
	¹⁵R		I		L			R		N			G						
¹⁶M	E	N	I	N	G	E	S		¹⁷P			A							
	F		L						O										
	L					¹⁸D	E	N	D	R	I	T	E						
	E								S			A							
	X																		

CHAPTER TEST

1. c **2.** c **3.** c **4.** e **5.** f **6.** d **7.** b **8.** a **9.** a **10.** d **11.** b **12.** d **13.** c **14.** c **15.** d **16.** b **17.** a **18.** b **19.** b **20.** c **21.** d **22.** a **23.** b **24.** b **25.** c **26.** It is a long, thin cell that reaches over distances in the body and is capable of delivering signals to a body region rapidly. **27.** Internal organs are controlled by two branches of the autonomic system which have opposite effects; for example, the sympathetic system causes the heart to speed up and the parasympathetic system causes the heart to slow down. In the somatic system, motor impulses always cause skeletal muscles to contract.

47

SENSE ORGANS

Sense organs detect changes in the environment and generate nerve impulses that travel along sensory neural pathways to reach the brain where they are interpreted. This chapter discusses chemoreceptors, photoreceptors and mechanoreceptors.

Chemoreception is almost universally found in animals. Human **olfactory cells** and **taste buds** are **chemoreceptors** sensitive to chemicals in water and air.

Eyes are **photoreceptors.** The compound eye of arthropods is made up of many individual units, whereas the human eye is a camera-type eye with a single lens. The receptors for sight in humans are the **rod cells** and the **cone cells** located in the retina of the eye. The rods work in minimum light and detect motion, but they do not detect color. The cones require bright light and do detect color.

Rhodopsin, the pigment found in rod cells, is a molecule composed of opsin and retinal. When light strikes rhodopsin, retinal changes shape and opsin is activated. Chemical changes that lead to nerve impulses follow. There are three kinds of cones, containing blue, green, or red pigments each composed of retinal and a particular opsin.

Mechanoreceptors are varied but many are hair cells with cilia, such as those found in the lateral line of fishes as well as the inner ear of humans. The inner ear contains sense organs for balance as well as hearing. The stereocilia of hair cells located within the **cochlea** are embedded in the tectorial membrane. When we hear, pressure waves cause these cilia to bend and nerve impulses are carried by the auditory nerve to the brain.

STUDY EXERCISES

Study the text section by section as you answer the questions that follow.

47.1 SENSING CHEMICALS (P. 840)

- Chemoreceptors are almost universally found in animals for sensing chemical substances in food, liquids, and air.
- Human taste buds and olfactory cells are chemoreceptors.

1. Indicate whether the statements that follow are true (T) or false (F). Change any false statements to make them true statements.

_____ a. Taste is only dependent on chemical substances in food. Rewrite: _____

_____

_____ b. There are four types of tastes and four types of smell. Rewrite: _____

_____

_____ c. Taste and smell combine to give one sensational effect. Rewrite: _____

_____

_____ d. Microvilli on taste cells bear plasma membrane receptors that combine with chemicals in food. _____

Rewrite: _____

_____ e. Olfactory receptors, like touch and temperature receptors, adapt to outside stimuli. Rewrite: _____

_____

2. Match the receptors with the terms below.
   1. Taste Buds
   2. Olfactory cells
   3. Both
   _____ a. Found along walls of papillae
   _____ b. Ends in a tuft of cilia.
   _____ c. Information goes directly to the cerebrum and also to the brain stem.
   _____ d. Plasma membrane receptors
   _____ e. Processing begins outside the brain.

47.2 SENSING LIGHT (P. 842)

3. Label each of the following as describing the arthropod eye (A) or the human eye (H):
   _____ a. consists of three layers
   _____ b. contains one lens for image formation
   _____ c. has many independent visual units
   _____ d. is a compound eye
4. If image-forming eyes are found only among cnidaria, annelids, mollusks, and arthropods what do the "eyespots" of planaria do?

   _____

5. Why is the eye of vertebrates and certain mollusks (squid and octopus) called a camera-type of eye?

   _____

6. Label and give a function on the next page for each part of the eye indicated in this diagram, using the following terms:
   choroid
   ciliary body
   cornea
   fovea centralis
   iris
   lens
   optic nerve
   retina
   sclera

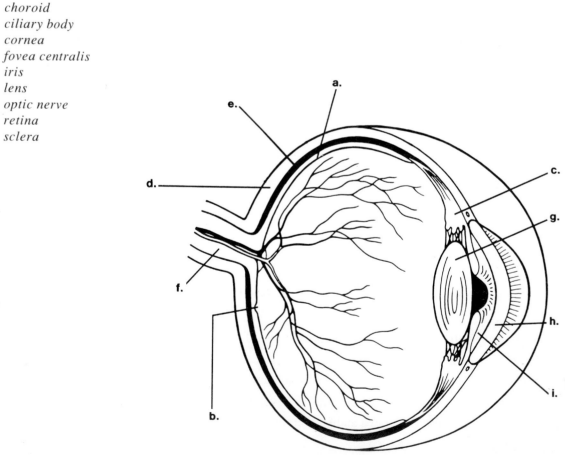

	Structure	Function
a.		
b.		
c.		
d.		
e.		
f.		
g.		
h.		
i.		

7. In the retina of the eye, the rods and cones are closest to the choroid. They pass nerve impulses to a._____ cells which pass them to b._____ cells. There are many more rods and cones than c._____ cells. Therefore, some d._____ occurs in the retina before nerve impulses reach the optic nerve. Where the optic nerve passes through the retina, there is a e._____ spot.

8. The lens is a._____ for distant objects and b._____ for near objects. This is called c._____.

9. Complete the following table:

Name	Description	Where Is Image Focused?	Correction
nearsightedness	see nearby objects	a.	concave lens
farsightedness	b.	c.	d.
astigmatism	cannot focus	image not focused	e.

Seeing Uses Chemistry (p. 846)

10. Put these in the proper order to describe generation of nerve impulses resulting in sight.
    _____ a. Activation of rhodopsin leads to reduction in cGMP and closure of sodium ion channels.
    _____ b. When light strikes retinal, it changes shape and rhodopsin is activated.
    _____ c. Rhodopsin contains a pigment called retinal and opsin.
    _____ d. Ganglionic cells send messages to the brain.

11. Only dim light is required to stimulate a._____ and therefore they are responsible for b._____ vision. The c._____ located primarily in the d._____ of the retina detect the detail and e._____ of an object. There are three different kinds of cones which contain pigments called the B (f._____), G (g._____), and R (h._____) pigments. Each pigment is made up of retinal and opsin but the opsin in each is slightly different. i._____ of cones are stimulated for particular in between shades of color.

- Many mechanoreceptors are ciliated cells, such as those in the lateral line of fishes and inner ear of humans.
- The inner ear of humans contains receptors for a sense of balance and for hearing.

12. Which of these pairs is true about the lateral line of fishes?
    Structure:
    _____ a. Like a Pacinian corpuscle, a lateral line receptor is concentric layers of connective tissue wrapped around the end of a sensory neuron.
    _____ b. Collection of hair cells with cilia embedded in a mass of gelatinous material known as a cupula.
    Function:
    _____ c. Detects currents and pressure waves from nearby objects.
    _____ d. Is more sensitive to temperature or chemicals than mechanical stimuli.

13. Label and give a function below for each part of the ear indicated in this diagram, using the following terms:

    auditory canal
    auditory tube
    cochlea
    cochlear nerve
    malleus
    pinna
    semicircular canal
    stapes
    tympanic membrane
    vestibule

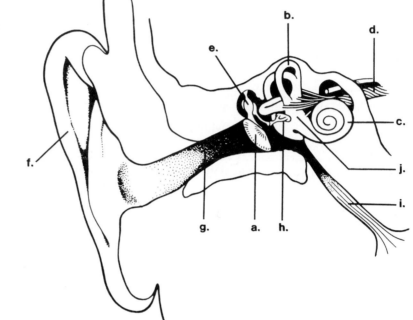

Structure	Function
a.	
b.	
c.	
d.	
e.	
f.	
g.	
h.	
i.	
j.	

14. Match the descriptions with the following structures:

    1 semicircular canals
    2 utricle and saccule

    _____ a. contains otoliths
    _____ b. dynamic equilibrium
    _____ c. static equilibrium

15. Label this diagram of the cochlea (as it might appear if unwound) with the following terms:

    basilar membrane
    cochlear canal
    cochlear nerve
    hair cell in spiral organ
    tectorial membrane
    tympanic canal
    vestibular canal

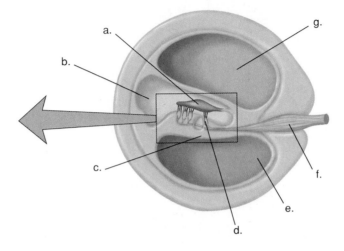

16. What happens when the basilar membrane moves up and down? _____

    _____

17. Rearrange the letters of items *a–f* to describe how we hear. _____

    a. nerve impulses
    b. tympanic membrane oscillates
    c. fluid pressure waves in cochlear canal
    d. stapes hits oval window
    e. temporal lobe of brain
    f. stimulation of spiral organ

Review key terms by completing this crossword puzzle, using the following alphabetized list of terms:

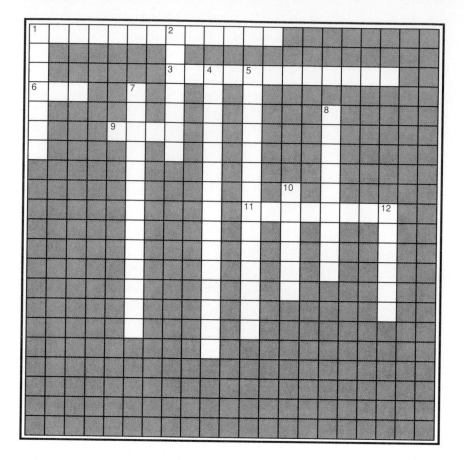

chemoreceptor
choroid
cochlea
compound eye
cone
mechanoreceptor
olfactory cell
photoreceptor
receptor
retina
rhodopsin
rod
sclera

Across

1 receptor that is sensitive to chemical stimulation—for example, receptors for taste and smell

3 type of eye found in arthropods; it is composed of many independent visual units (two words)

6 photoreceptor in vertebrate eyes that responds to dim light

9 photoreceptor in vertebrate eyes that responds to bright light and allows color vision

11 portion of a sensory neuron that responds to an external stimulus

Down

1 vascular, pigmented middle layer of the eyeball

2 spiral-shaped structure of the inner ear containing the receptors for hearing

4 receptor that is sensitive to mechanical stimulation, such as that from pressure, sound waves, and gravity

5 modified neuron that is a receptor for the sense of smell (two words)

7 light-sensitive receptor

8 light-absorbing molecule in rods that contains a pigment and the protein opsin

10 outer, white, fibrous layer that surrounds the eye except for the transparent cornea

12 innermost layer of the eyeball containing the photoreceptors—rods and cones

CHAPTER TEST

OBJECTIVE QUESTIONS

Do not refer to the text when taking this test.

_____ 1. Taste cells and olfactory cells are both
    a. somatic senses.
    b. mechanoreceptors.
    c. pseudociliated epithelium.
    d. chemoreceptors.

_____ 2. Which of these is mismatched?
    a. compound eye—one lens, insect
    b. camera type eye—one lens, squid
    c. compound eye—many lenses, arthropods
    d. photoreceptor—eyespot, planaria

_____ 3. The blind spot is
    a. a nontransparent area on the lens.
    b. a nontransparent area on the cornea.
    c. the area on the retina where there are no rods and cones.
    d. called the fovea centralis.

In questions 4–7, match the questions to the following structures:
    a. retina
    b. optic nerve
    c. lens
    d. cerebrum
    e. all of these

_____ 4. Which is (are) necessary to proper vision?

_____ 5. Which contain(s) the receptors for sight?

_____ 6. Which focus(es) light?

_____ 7. In which is the sensation of sight realized?

_____ 8. The current theory of color vision proposes that
    a. three primary colors are associated with color vision.
    b. cones respond selectively to different wavelengths of light.
    c. rods are responsible for nighttime color vision.
    d. Both _a_ and _b_ are correct.
    e. All of these are correct.

_____ 9. Acute vision is made possible by the
    a. choroid.
    b. fovea centralis.
    c. ciliary muscle.
    d. ciliary body.

_____10. If you are nearsighted, the image is focused
    a. in front of the retina.
    b. behind the retina.
    c. on the retina.
    d. at the blind spot.

_____11. The disorders of nearsightedness and farsightedness are due to
    a. an eyeball of incorrect length.
    b. a cloudy lens.
    c. pressure increase.
    d. a torn retina.

_____12. The lateral line of fishes
    a. has receptors with cilia embedded in a cupula.
    b. detects water currents and pressure waves
    c. is a mechanoreceptor
    d. All of these are correct

_____13. Which of these is mismatched?
    a. outer ear—auditory canal
    b. middle ear—otoliths
    c. inner ear—spiral organ
    d. inner ear—semicircular canals

_____14. The cochlear nerve is associated with the
    a. spiral organ.
    b. ossicles.
    c. tympanic membrane.
    d. auditory tube.

In questions 15–17, match the questions to the following structures (some are used more than once):
    a. ossicles
    b. otoliths
    c. cochlea
    d. auditory canal

_____15. Which has (have) nothing to do with hearing?

_____16. In which do you find the receptors for hearing?

_____17. Which of these is (are) concerned with balance?

_____18. In the utricle and saccule
    a. stereocilia of hair cells are embedded in otolithic membrane.
    b. bending of stereocilia tells direction of head movement.
    c. stereocilia of hair cells are embedded in tectorial membrane.
    d. Both _a_ and _b_ are correct.

_____19. Which part of the ear has receptors for hearing?
    a. outer
    b. middle
    c. inner
    d. All of these are correct.

_____20. When we hear,
    a. the basilar membrane vibrates.
    b. stereocilia of hair cells embedded in tectorial membrane bend.
    c. nerve impulses travel in the cochlear nerve to the brain.
    d. All of these are correct.

Answer in complete sentences.

21. Damage to the retina, optic nerve, and brain prevents vision in a person. Only one is a sense organ. Why are all three necessary?

22. The cochlea, vestibule, and semicircular canals are three distinct structures of the inner ear. How are they remarkably similar at the receptor cell and stimulus level?

Test Results: _____ Number right ÷ 22 = _____ × 100 = _____ %

EXPLORING THE INTERNET

Use the Internet to further explore topics in this chapter, such as radial keratotomy and the aging eye. Go to the Mader Home Page (http://www.mhhe.com/sciencemath/biology/mader/) and click on *Biology,* 6th edition. Go to Chapter 47 and select a Web site of interest.

ANSWER KEY

STUDY EXERCISES

1. a. F Taste is dependent on chemical substances in food and in the air. **b.** F . . . many types of smell **c.** T **d.** T **e.** T **2. a.** 1 **b.** 2 **c.** 1 **d.** 3 **e.** 2 **3. a.** H **b.** H **c.** A **d.** A **4.** seek light **5.** They use a single adjustable lens to bring images into focus. **6. a.** retina; photoreceptor sight **b.** fovea centralis; greatest visual acuity, color vision **c.** ciliary body, adjust lens **d.** sclera; protection and support **e.** choroid; absorbs stray light **f.** optic nerve; transmission of nerve impulse **g.** lens; focusing **h.** cornea; refraction **i.** iris; regulates light entrance **7. a.** bipolar cells **b.** ganglionic **c.** ganglionic cells **d.** integration **e.** blind **8. a.** flat **b.** rounded **c.** accommodation **9. a.** in front of retina **b.** see distant objects **c.** behind retina **d.** convex lens **e.** irregular lens **10.** c, b, a, d **11. a.** rods **b.** night **c.** cones **d.** fovea **e.** color **f.** blue **g.** green **h.** red **i.** Combinations **12.** b, c **13. a.** tympanic membrane; amplication of sound waves **b.** semicircular canal; dynamic equilibrium **c.** cochlea; transmission of pressure waves **d.** cochlear nerve; transmission of nerve impulses **e.** malleus; amplication of sound **f.** pinna, collection of sound waves **g.** auditory canal; filters air **h.** stapes; amplification of sound **i.** auditory tube; equalizes air pressure **j.** vestibule; static equilibrium **14. a.** 2 **b.** 1 **c.** 2 **15. a–e.** See Figure 47.14, page 851, in text. **f.** hair cell in spiral organ **16.** Stereocilia of hair cells embedded in tectorial membrane bend, and nerve impulses begin. **7.** b, d, c, f, a, e

KeyWord CrossWord

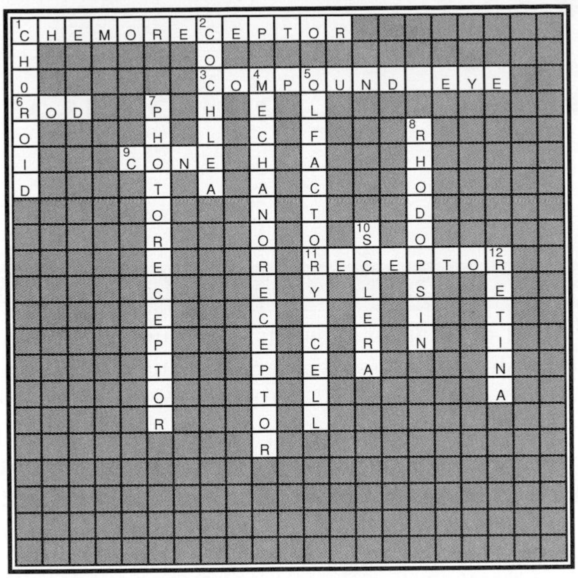
1 CHEMORECEPTOR
1 CHOROID
2 COCHLEA
3 COMPOUND EYE
4 MECHANORECEPTOR
5 OLFACTORY CELL
6 ROD
7 PHOTORECEPTOR
8 RHODOPSIN
9 CONE
10 SCLERA
11 RECEPTOR
12 RETINA

Chapter Test

1. d **2.** a **3.** c **4.** e **5.** a **6.** c **7.** d **8.** d **9.** b **10.** a **11.** a. **12.** d **13.** d **14.** a **15.** b **16.** c **17.** b **18.** d **19.** c **20.** d **21.** The receptor cells of the retina generate nerve impulses. A sensory pathway along the optic nerve must deliver a signal to the brain. The brain (third component) must interpret this input for the sense of vision to occur. **22.** All three structures have sensory hair cells that must be disturbed to create the necessary stimulus for hearing (cochlea), dynamic equilibrium (semicircular canals), and static equilibrium (vestibule).

48

SUPPORT SYSTEMS AND LOCOMOTION

Three types of skeletons have evolved among the different species of the animal kingdom: the hydrostatic skeleton, the exoskeleton, and the endoskeleton. Skeletons generally provide support, protection, and assistance in movement. Additional functions in the human skeleton are mineral storage and blood cell formation.

The human skeleton is divided into two parts: (1) the **axial skeleton,** which is made up of the skull, the **ribs,** the **sternum,** and the **vertebrae;** and (2) the **appendicular skeleton,** which is composed of the girdles and their appendages. **Joints** are regions where bones are linked. Bone is constantly being renewed: **osteoclasts** break down bone, and **osteoblasts** build new bone. **Osteocytes** are found in the lacunae of osteons.

Whole skeletal muscles get shorter when they contract; therefore, muscles work in antagonistic pairs. Muscle fibers are cells that contain **myofibrils** in addition to the usual cellular components. Longitudinally, myofibrils are divided into **sarcomeres,** where it is possible to note the arrangements of **actin** and **myosin** filaments. When a sarcomere contracts, the actin filaments slide past the myosin filaments, and the H zone all but disappears. Myosin has cross-bridges, which attach to and pull the actin filaments along. ATP breakdown by myosin is necessary for detachment to occur.

Innervation of a muscle fiber begins at a **neuromuscular junction.** Here, synaptic vesicles release acetylcholine into the synaptic cleft. When the **sarcolemma** receives acetylcholine, a **muscle action potential** moves down the T system to calcium storage sites. The muscle fiber contracts when calcium ions (Ca^{2+}) are released. When calcium ions are actively transported back into the storage sites, the muscle fiber relaxes.

Study the text section by section as you answer the questions that follow.

- Animals have one of three types of skeletons: a hydrostatic skeleton, an exoskeleton, or an endoskeleton.
- All types of skeletons give support to the body and assist movement. An exoskeleton and endoskeleton also protect internal organs.

1. Earthworms have ª-_____ skeletons. With this type of skeleton, muscles contract against ᵇ-_____ compartments. A limitation of this type of skeleton is that it does not provide ᶜ-_____.

   Arthropods have another type of skeleton called a(n) ᵈ-_____. Although this offers protection similar to a suit of ᵉ-_____, it must be ᶠ-_____ periodically, allowing the animal to grow. Vertebrates have a(n) ᵍ-_____, which is primarily made of ʰ-_____ and ⁱ-_____. This type of skeleton protects ʲ-_____, can ᵏ-_____ with the animal and also allows ˡ-_____ movements.

- Humans have a bony endoskeleton; bone is rigid, but living, tissue.
- The human skeleton is divided into two parts: the axial skeleton consists of the skull, the ribs, the sternum, and the vertebrae, and the appendicular skeleton contains the girdles and the limbs.

2. List five functions of the human skeletal system.

   a. _____

   b. _____

   c. _____

   d. _____

   e. _____

3. Label this diagram of a long bone with the following terms:
   cartilage
   compact bone
   medullary cavity
   spongy bone

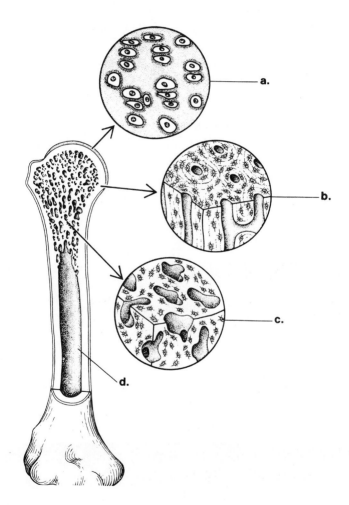

4. Which part of the long bone is associated with red bone marrow? a._____

   What is the flexible layer of connective tissue covering spongy bone? b._____

   Which part of a bone contains osteons, blood vessels, and nerves? c._____

   Which part of a long bone is associated with yellow bone marrow? d._____

5. What is the relationship between osteoblasts and osteocytes? a._____

What role do the cartilaginous disks of long bones play? b._____

What is the function of osteoclasts? c._____

6. Label each of the following as belonging to the axial skeleton (ax) or the appendicular skeleton (ap), and when appropriate, as belonging to the pectoral girdle (pec) or the pelvic girdle (pel):

coxal bone a._____

sternum b._____

humerus c._____

scapula d._____

skull e._____

femur f._____

ribs g._____

radius h._____

clavicle i._____

tibia j._____

fibula k._____

ulna l._____

7. The radius and ulna are to the lower arm as the a._____ and b._____ are to the lower leg. The femur is to the upper leg as the c._____ is to the upper arm. The metacarpals are to the palm as the d._____ are to the foot.

8. Give the scientific terms for these common names.

shinbone a._____

collarbone b._____

hipbone c._____

thighbone d._____

Joints Join Bones (p. 863)

- The human skeleton is jointed; the joints differ in movability.

9. Complete the following table to describe the shoulder and elbow joints:

Joint	Anatomical Type	Degree of Movement
shoulder joint		
elbow joint		

48.3 HOW MUSCLES FUNCTION (P. 865)

- Macroscopically, human skeletal muscles work in antagonistic pairs and exhibit certain physiological characteristics.
- Microscopically, muscle fiber contraction is dependent on filaments of both actin and myosin, and a ready supply of calcium ions (Ca^{2+}) and ATP.

10. Label this diagram of muscles and bones in the arm with the following terms:
    biceps brachii
    humerus
    radius
    scapula
    triceps brachii
    ulna

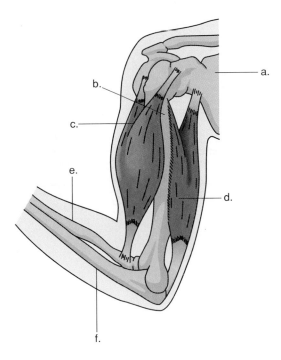

11. Why are the biceps brachii and triceps brachii antagonistic pairs? _____

_____

12. Label this diagram of a portion of a muscle fiber with the following terms:
    myofibrils
    sarcolemma
    T tubules

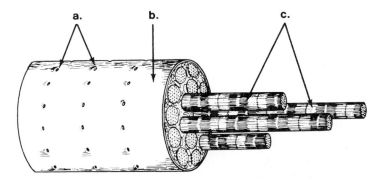

13. Label this diagram of a sarcomere with the following terms:
    actin filament
    H zone
    myosin filament
    Z line

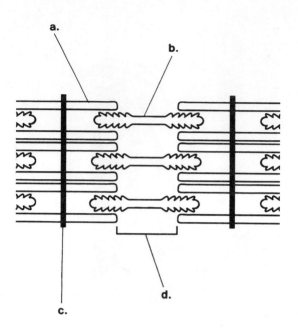

14. Which component in question 13 is a thin filament? a._____

    Which component is a thick filament? b._____

    Which component shrinks when a sarcomere contracts? c._____

    Which component has cross-bridges? d._____

    Which component is the filament that moves when the sarcomere contracts? e._____

15. What molecule immediately supplies energy for muscle contraction? a._____

    What molecule is a storage form of high-energy phosphate in muscles? b._____

At the Neuromuscular Junction (p. 868)

16. Rearrange the letters *a–h* to describe the innervation of muscle contraction. _____
    a. sarcolemma
    b. depolarization (muscle action potential)
    c. acetylcholine
    d. nerve
    e. calcium storage sites
    f. neuromuscular junction
    g. sacroplasmic reticulum
    h. sarcomeres

17. Complete this diagram by matching the phrases below to the appropriate box.

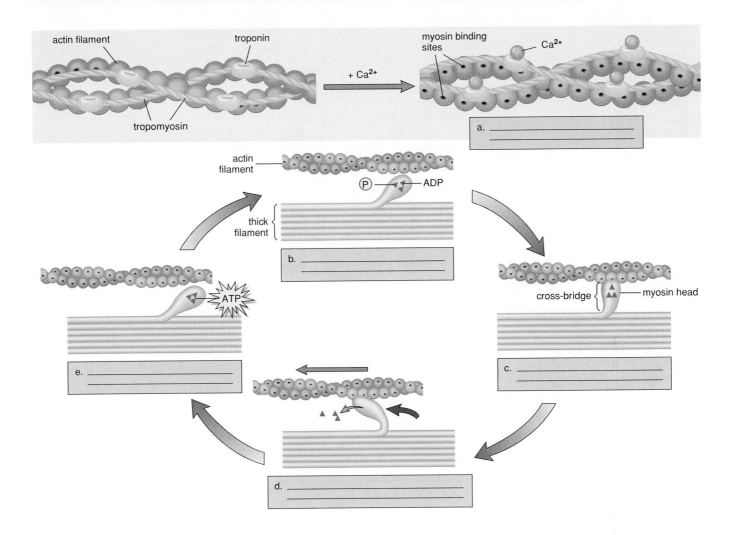

1. ADP + P release causes head to change position and actin filament to move.
2. Troponin-Ca²⁺ complex pulls tropomyosin away, exposing myosin binding sites.
3. ATP is hydrolyzed when myosin head is unattached.
4. Binding of ATP causes myosin head to return to resting position.
5. ADP + P are bound to myosin as myosin head attaches to actin.

Review key terms by completing this crossword puzzle, using the following alphabetized list of terms:

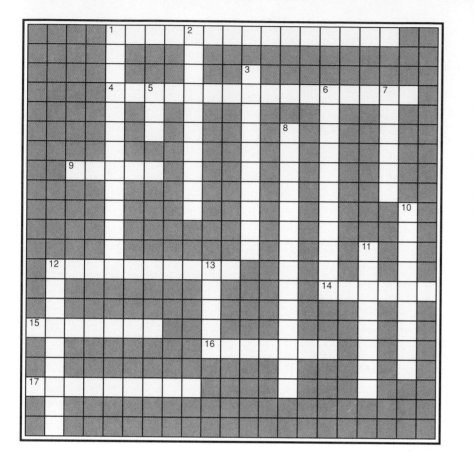

digit
foramen magnum
mandible
menisci
myofibril
myosin
osteoblast
osteoclast
osteocyte
oxygen debt
pectoral girdle
pelvic girdle
rib
sarcolemma
sarcomere
sinus
sternum
tendon
vertebral column

Across

1 portion of the skeleton that provides support and attachment for the arms (two words)
4 backbone of vertebrates through which the spinal cord passes (two words)
9 finger or toe
12 cell that causes erosion of bone
14 strap of fibrous connective tissue that joins skeletal muscle to bone
15 fibrocartilage that separates the surfaces of bones in the knee
16 breastbone, to which the ribs are ventrally attached
17 specific muscle cell organelle containing a linear arrangement of sarcomeres, which shorten to produce muscle contraction

Down

1 portion of the skeleton to which the legs are attached (two words)
2 bone-forming cell
3 plasma membrane of a muscle fiber that forms the tubules of the T system involved in muscular contraction
5 bone hinged to the vertebral column and sternum, which, with muscle, defines the top and sides of the chest cavity
6 use of oxygen to metabolize lactate, which builds up due to anaerobic conditions (two words)
7 muscle protein making up the thick filaments in a sarcomere; it pulls actin to shorten the sarcomere, yielding muscle contraction
8 opening in the occipital bone of the skull through which the spinal cord passes (two words)
10 one of many units arranged linearly within a myofibril, whose contraction produces muscle contraction
11 lower jaw; contains tooth sockets
12 mature bone cell
13 cavity, as in the human skull

Do not refer to the text when taking this test.

_____ 1. Which of these contains osteons?
    a. compact bone
    b. spongy bone
    c. red bone marrow
    d. yellow bone marrow

_____ 2. Which of these is a function of the skeleton?
    a. support
    b. protection
    c. production of red blood cells
    d. All of these are correct.

_____ 3. Which of these is NOT in the appendicular skeleton?
    a. clavicle
    b. coxal bone
    c. metatarsals
    d. vertebrae

_____ 4. Facial bones include the
    a. frontal bone.
    b. occipital bone.
    c. mandible.
    d. All of these are correct.

_____ 5. Ligaments join
    a. bone to bone.
    b. muscle to muscle.
    c. muscle to bone.
    d. All of these are correct.

_____ 6. Vertebrae have
    a. immovable joints.
    b. freely movable joints.
    c. slightly movable joints.
    d. joints that vary according to the person.

_____ 7. Which type of cell is found in lacunae of osteons?
    a. osteoblasts
    b. osteoclasts
    c. osteocytes
    d. Any of these are correct.

_____ 8. Which two of the following are antagonistic?
    a. triceps brachii—gastrocnemius
    b. biceps brachii—triceps brachii
    c. external oblique—quadriceps femoris
    d. rectus abdominus—quadriceps femoris

_____ 9. When sarcomeres contract, they get shorter, and this requires that muscles work in antagonistic pairs.
    a. true
    b. false

_____10. Myosin is
    a. the thick filament of a sarcomere.
    b. a protein.
    c. an ATPase enzyme.
    d. All of these are correct.

_____11. According to the sliding filament theory,
    a. actin moves past myosin.
    b. myosin moves past actin.
    c. actin and myosin move past each other.
    d. actin both moves and breaks down ATP.
    e. None of these are correct.

_____12. The release of calcium from the T system
    a. causes sarcomeres to relax.
    b. causes sarcomeres to contract.
    c. is the end result of a muscle action potential.
    d. Both _b_ and _c_ are correct.
    e. All of these are correct.

_____13. Which of these is the smallest unit?
    a. muscle fiber
    b. myofibril
    c. sarcomere
    d. actin

_____14. The junction between nerve and muscle is
    a. called the neuromuscular junction.
    b. where a neurotransmitter travels from the nerve fiber to a muscle fiber.
    c. the region where nerves innervate muscles.
    d. All of these are correct.

_____15. Creatine phosphate
    a. is used by sarcomeres.
    b. is used to change ADP to ATP.
    c. is a molecule found in DNA.
    d. All of these are correct.

_____16. Muscle fatigue
    a. follows summation and tetanus.
    b. involves the buildup of lactate.
    c. occurs only in the laboratory.
    d. Both _a_ and _b_ are correct.
    e. All of these are correct.

In questions 17–20, match the descriptions to the following structures:
    a. ligament
    b. tendon
    c. knee
    d. Z line
    e. sacroplasmic reticulum

_____17. a part of the T system

_____18. stabilizes bones at joints

_____19. synovial joint

_____20. an organelle of a muscle fiber

Answer in complete sentences.

21. Support the following statement: Contraction of a skeletal muscle is a good example of a whole structure working through the collection of its parts.

22. Support the following statement: A motion such as bending the forearm is not as simple as it appears to be.

Test Results: _____ Number right ÷ 22 = _____ × 100 = _____ %

EXPLORING THE INTERNET

Use the Internet to further explore topics in this chapter, such as proper back care and arthritis. Go to the Mader Home Page (http://www.mhhe.com/sciencemath/biology/mader/) and click on *Biology,* 6th edition. Go to Chapter 48 and select a Web site of interest.

ANSWER KEY

STUDY EXERCISES

1. a. hydrostatic **b.** fluid-filled **c.** protection **d.** exoskeleton **e.** armor **f.** shed **g.** endoskeleton **h.** cartilage **i.** bone **j.** internal organs **k.** grow **l.** flexible **2. a.** support **b.** protection of internal organs **c.** flexible movement **d.** blood formation **e.** mineral storage **3. a.** cartilage **b.** compact bone **c.** spongy bone **d.** medullary cavity **4. a.** spongy bone **b.** cartilage **c.** compact bone **d.** medullary cavity **5. a.** Osteoblasts become the osteocytes of osteons. **b.** They increase in length and allow bone to grow longer. **c.** They break down bone and remove worn cells. **6. a.** ap, pel **b.** ax **c.** ap **d.** ap, pec **e.** ax **f.** ap **g.** ax **h.** ap **i.** ap, pec **j.** ap **k.** ap **l.** ap **7. a.** tibia **b.** fibula **c.** humerus **d.** metatarsals **8. a.** tibia **b.** clavicle **c.** coxal bone **d.** femur

9.

Anatomical Type	Degree of Movement
ball and socket	freely movable
hinge	freely movable

10. a. scapula **b.** humerus **c.** biceps brachii **d.** triceps brachii **e.** radius **f.** ulna **11.** The biceps brachii raises and the triceps brachii lowers the lower arm. **12. a.** T tubules **b.** sarcolemma **c.** myofibrils **13. a.** actin filament **b.** myosin filament **c.** Z line **d.** H zone **14. a.** actin filament **b.** myosin filament **c.** H zone **d.** myosin **e.** actin filament **15. a.** ATP **b.** creatine phosphate **c.** Oxygen is required to complete breakdown of lactate accumulation from exercise. **16.** d, c, f, a, b, g, e, h **17. a.** 2 **b.** 3 **c.** 5 **d.** 1 **e.** 4

Crossword solution

Across:
1. PECTORAL GIRDLE
4. VERTEBRAL COLUMN
9. DIGIT
12. OSTEOCLAST
14. TENDON
15. MENISCI
16. STERNUM
17. MYOFIBRIL

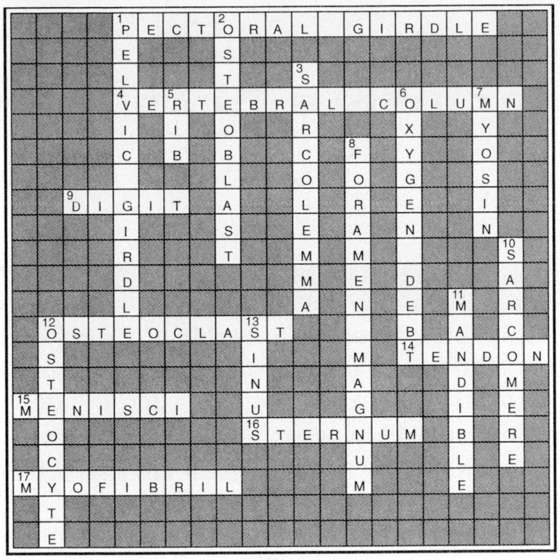

1. a **2.** d **3.** d **4.** c **5.** a **6.** c **7.** c **8.** b **9.** a **10.** d **11.** a **12.** d **13.** d **14.** d **15.** b **16.** d **17.** e **18.** a **19.** c **20.** e **21.** Several levels of organization are involved. A muscle shortens through the shortening of its cells. At the subcellular level, thousands of sarcomeres containing actin/myosin filaments shorten to shorten the cell and produce the contraction of the entire muscle. **22.** It is complex because a number of muscles interact to bring this about. As one muscle contracts, an opposing muscle must relax. Other muscles work to support the major contracting muscle.

49

HORMONES AND ENDOCRINE SYSTEMS

A few **hormones** are **steroids** but most hormones are **nonsteroid** hormones. The steroid hormones are lipid soluble and can pass through membranes. Once inside the nucleus, they combine with a receptor molecule and the complex attaches to transcription factors which activate DNA. The nonsteroid hormones are usually received by a plasma membrane receptor. Most often their reception leads to activation of an enzyme that changes ATP to **cyclic AMP** (cAMP). cAMP initiates a cascade of metabolic reactions.

The **endocrine system** in humans consists of endocrine glands that secrete hormones into the bloodstream. The **hypothalamus** plays a major role in the endocrine system. Neurosecretory cells in the hypothalamus produce **antidiuretic hormone (ADH)** and **oxytocin,** which are stored in axon endings in the **posterior pituitary** until they are released. The hypothalamus also produces **hypothalamic-releasing** and **hypothalamic-release-inhibiting hormones,** which pass to the anterior pituitary by way of a portal system.

Hormones from the **anterior pituitary** include growth hormone (GH), **melanocyte-stimulating hormone** (MSH), and **prolactin.** The anterior pituitary is sometimes called the master gland because it controls the secretion of some other endocrine glands: the **thyroid** (produces **thyroxine** and **triiodothyronine**) the **adrenal cortex** (produces **glucocorticoids** and **mineralocorticoids**) and the **gonads** (produces sex hormones). The **parathyroids** (produces **parathyroid hormone**), **adrenal medulla** (produces **epinephrine** and **norepinephrine**), the pancreas (produces **insulin** and **glucagon**) function independently.

There are three categories of chemical messengers: those that act at a distance between individuals (e.g., **pheromones**); those that act at a distance within the individual (e.g., hormones) and local messengers (e.g., neurotransmitters).

Study the text section by section as you answer the questions that follow.

49.1 HORMONES AFFECT CELLULAR METABOLISM (P. 874)

- Hormones influence the metabolism of their target cells.

1. Place a check in front of the phrases that describe hormones.
   - _____ a. can be any type of chemical
   - _____ b. steroid or nonsteroid
   - _____ c. usually produced by cell in which it is active
   - _____ d. often produced by one set of cells but affects a different set
   - _____ e. secreted by exocrine glands
   - _____ f. secreted by endocrine glands
   - _____ g. secreted into bloodstream
   - _____ h. secreted into a cavity

2. Write either *nonsteroid hormone* or *steroid hormone* on the line above each diagram. Label the remainder of the diagram with the following terms:

    active
    cyclic AMP
    hormone receptor
    hormone-receptor complex
    protein synthesis

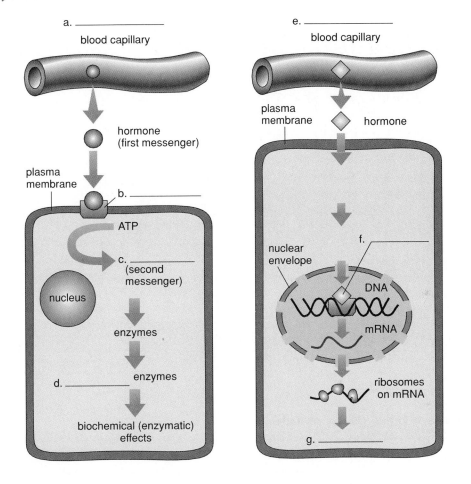

3. You would place a G protein in the diagram in question 2 labeled ᵃ·_____. G proteins are located in the membrane and regulate the action of other ᵇ·_____ in the membrane. They are named for their ability to bind to and break down ᶜ·_____.

4. Label this diagram of endocrine glands with the terms that follow.
   adrenal cortex
   adrenal medulla
   anterior pituitary
   hypothalamus
   pancreas
   parathyroid
   pineal gland
   posterior pituitary
   thymus
   thyroid

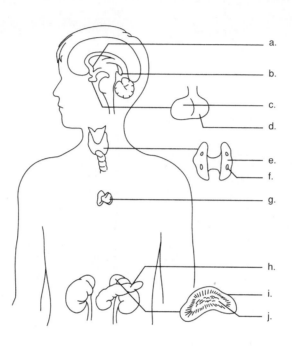

a.

b.

c.

d.

e.

f.

g.

h.

i.

j.

5. List as many hormones as you can for each gland.

Gland	Hormones
Hypothalamus	
Posterior pituitary	
Anterior pituitary	
Thyroid	
Parathyroids	
Adrenal medulla	
Adrenal cortex	
Pancreas	
Thymus	
Pineal gland	

6. The blood level of a product increases enough to slow the release of the hormone causing its production. This type of control is termed a._____. One hormone raises blood calcium, while a second hormone lowers blood calcium. These two hormones are referred to as b._____ hormones.

Hypothalamus Controls the Pituitary Gland (p. 878)

- The hypothalamus controls the function of the pituitary gland, which, in turn, controls several other glands.

7. Add dotted lines to this line diagram wherever feedback control is usually exerted.

   Hypothalamus—Releasing Hormone—Anterior Pituitary Hormone—Gland—Hormone
       (1)   **(2)**   **(3)**

8. If the "gland" in the diagram in question 7 is the thyroid, then the first hormone is a._____, the second is b._____, and the third is c._____. If the "gland" in the diagram in question 7 is the adrenal cortex, then the first hormone is d._____, the second is e._____, and the third is f._____.

9. Label each of the following as describing the anterior pituitary (AP) or the posterior pituitary (PP):

   _____ a. connected to hypothalamus by nerve fibers
   _____ b. connected to hypothalamus by blood vessels
   _____ c. secretes hormones that the hypothalamus produces
   _____ d. controlled by releasing hormones that hypothalamus produces

10. Complete the following table to show why the anterior pituitary is sometimes called the master gland:

Anterior Pituitary Produces	Gland Controlled	Hormone That Gland Produces
TSH		
ACTH		
female gonadotropic hormone		
male gonadotropic hormone		

11. What causes the hypothalamus to stop producing releasing hormones and the anterior pituitary to stop producing its hormones? _____

Thyroid Gland Speeds Metabolism (p. 880)

_____12. Thyroxine production requires the element
    a. calcium.
    b. chloride.
    c. iodine.
    d. magnesium.

_____13. A low level of thyroxine in the blood causes
    a. albinism.
    b. Cushing syndrome.
    c. diabetes mellitus.
    d. goiter.

_____14. A case of hypothyroidism since birth causes
    a. cretinism.
    b. exothalamic goiter.
    c. acromegaly.
    d. thyroxemia.

_____15. Thyroxine
    a. elevates blood calcium levels.
    b. increases metabolic rate.
    c. lowers blood sugar.
    d. promotes kidney reabsorption.

Parathyroid Glands Regulate Calcium (p. 881)

> • Parathyroid glands are embedded in the thyroid but have an entirely separate structure and function.

16. The hormone opposing the effects of calcitonin is
    a. ACTH.
    b. ADH.
    c. oxytocin.
    d. parathyroid hormone (PTH).

17. PTH acts to increase blood concentrations of a._____. PTH b._____

    phosphate levels in the blood and c._____the reabsorption rate of calcium from the gut.

    Tetany develops when blood calcium concentration d._____.

Adrenal Glands Contain Two Parts (p. 882)

> • The adrenal medulla and the adrenal cortex are separate parts of the adrenal glands that have functions in relation to stress.

18. The adrenal medulla secretes two hormones: a._____ and b._____. These

    hormones cause the blood glucose level to c._____ and the metabolic rate

    to d._____; cause the bronchioles to e._____ and the breathing rate

    to f._____; cause the blood vessels to the digestive tract and skin to g._____

    and those to the skeletal muscles to h._____; cause cardiac muscle to i._____

    and the heart rate to j._____.

19. The adrenal cortex secretes two classes of hormones: a._____

    and b._____. c._____ which is the glucocorticoid responsible for the greatest

    amount of activity aids various conditions because it reduces d._____.

    e._____ which is the most important of the mineralocorticoids affects the kidneys by

    promoting the absorption of f._____ and the excretion of g._____. When

    there is a low level of adrenal cortex hormone, a person develops h._____ disease and when

    there is a high level the condition i._____ syndrome results.

Pancreas Produces Two Hormones (p. 885)

> • The pancreas secretes hormones that help control the blood glucose level.

20. a._____ and b._____ are produced by the pancreatic c._____.

21. Complete each of the following statements with the term *increases* or *decreases:*

    Glucagon a._____ blood sugar concentration. In type I diabetes, insulin production from the

    pancreas b._____. In type II diabetes, the response of body cells to the influence of

    insulin c._____.

Testes Are in Males and Ovaries Are in Females (p. 887)

> • The gonads produce the sex hormones that control secondary sexual characteristics.

22. Match the terms below to the two sexes:
    1 male
    2 female
    _____ a. testosterone
    _____ b. ovaries
    _____ c. estrogen
    _____ d. androgens
    _____ e. facial hair
    _____ f. breast development

Thymus Is Most Active in Children (p. 888)
Pineal Gland and Daily/Yearly Rhythms (p. 888)

23. Indicate whether the following statements are true (T) or false (F):
    _____ a. The pineal gland secretes MSH.
    _____ b. The pineal gland secretes melatonin.
    _____ c. The thymus gland contributes to cell-mediated immunity.
    _____ d. The thymus gland increases in size with maturity.

49.3 ENVIRONMENTAL SIGNALS IN THREE CATEGORIES (P. 888)

- In general, there are three types of environmental signals, and hormones are one of these types.
- Many tissues secrete hormones aside from those that are traditionally considered endocrine glands.

24. Give an example of an environmental signal that acts at a distance between individuals. a._____

Give an example of an environmental signal that acts at a distance between body parts. b._____

_____

Give an example of an environmental signal that acts locally between adjacent cells. c._____

_____

_____25. Which is both a neurotransmitter and a hormone?
    a. cortisone
    b. norepinephrine
    c. ACTH
    d. thyroxine

For every 5 correct answers in sequence, you have scored one goal.

First goal: Match the hormone to the glands (a–i).

Glands:

    a. anterior pituitary

    b. thyroid

    c. parathyroids

    d. adrenal cortex

    e. adrenal medulla

    f. pancreas

    g. gonads

    h. pineal gland

    i. posterior pituitary

Hormones:

_____ 1. insulin

_____ 2. oxytocin

_____ 3. melatonin

_____ 4. cortisol

_____ 5. thyroxine

Second goal: Match the condition to the glands (a–i).

Conditions:

_____ 6. diabetes mellitus

_____ 7. creatinism

_____ 8. addison disease

_____ 9. hypertension

_____ 10. giant

Third goal: Match the function to the hormones.

    a. melatonin

    b. estrogens

    c. androgens

    d. insulin

    e. glucagon

    f. epinephrine

    g. aldosterone

    h. cortisol

    i. parathyroid hormone

    j. thyroxine

    k. calcitonin (lowers)

    l. antidiuretic hormone

Functions

_____ 11. raises blood calcium level

_____ 12. reduces stress

_____ 13. maintain secondary female sex characteristics

_____ 14. involved in circadian rhythms

_____ 15. stimulates water reabsorption by kidneys

Fourth goal: Match the glands to the hormones (a–l). Some glands require two answers.

Glands

_____ 16. testes

_____ 17. adrenal cortex

_____ 18. pancreas

_____ 19. thyroid

_____ 20. adrenal medulla

Fifth goal: Select five hormones secreted by the anterior pituitary by answering yes or no to each of these.

_____ 21. thyroid stimulating hormone

_____ 22. androgens

_____ 23. gonadotropic hormones

_____ 24. glucagon

_____ 25. oxytocin

_____ 26. growth hormone

_____ 27. prolactin

_____ 28. antidiuretic hormone

_____ 29. estrogens

_____ 30. adrenocorticotropic hormone

How many goals did you make? _____

Review key terms by completing this crossword puzzle, using the following alphabetized list of terms:

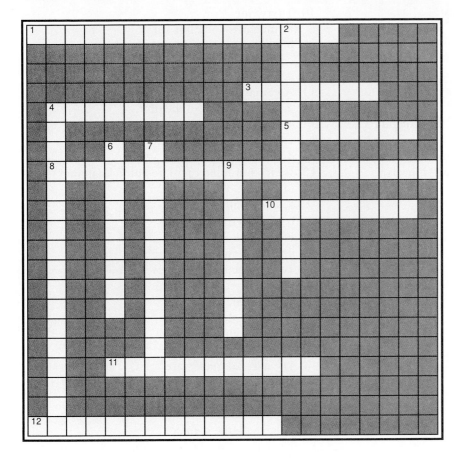

adrenal gland
aldosterone
antidiuretic hormone
endocrine system
glucagon
hormone
insulin
pancreas
parathyroid gland
pineal gland
pituitary
thyroid gland
thyroxine

Across

1 one of the major systems involved in the coordination of body activities; uses messengers called hormones, which are secreted into the bloodstream (two words)

3 chemical produced in one part of the body that controls the activity of other parts

4 abdominal organ that produces digestive enzymes and the hormones insulin and glucagon

5 hormone secreted by the pancreas that lowers the blood glucose level by promoting the uptake of glucose by cells and the conversion of glucose to glycogen by the liver

8 hormone secreted by the posterior pituitary that promotes the reabsorption of water from the collecting ducts of nephrons within the kidneys (two words)

10 hormone secreted by the pancreas that causes the liver to break down glycogen and raises the blood glucose level

11 hormone secreted by the adrenal cortex that regulates the sodium and potassium balance of the blood

12 gland that lies atop a kidney that produces the hormones epinephrine and norepinephrine and produces the corticoid hormones (two words)

Down

2 large gland in the neck that produces several important hormones, including thyroxine and calcitonin (two words)

4 gland embedded in the posterior surface of the thyroid gland that produces a hormone involved in blood calcium regulation

6 small gland composed of two parts that lies just inferior to the hypothalamus

7 gland—either at the skin surface (fish, amphibians) or in the third ventricle of the brain (mammals)—that produces melatonin (two words)

9 substance (also called T_4) secreted from the thyroid gland that promotes growth and development in vertebrates; in general, it increases the metabolic rate in cells

Do not refer to the text when taking this test.

_____ 1. All hormones are believed to
   a. have membrane receptors.
   b. affect cellular metabolism.
   c. increase the amount of cAMP.
   d. increase the amount of protein synthesis.

_____ 2. Steroid hormones
   a. combine with receptors in the plasma membrane.
   b. pass through the nuclear membrane.
   c. activate genes leading to protein synthesis.
   d. Both *b* and *c* are correct.

_____ 3. ADH and oxytocin are
   a. produced by the hypothalamus.
   b. secreted by the posterior pituitary.
   c. secreted by the thyroid gland.
   d. Both *a* and *b* are correct.

_____ 4. Which hormone is involved with milk production and nursing?
   a. prolactin
   b. oxytocin
   c. ADH
   d. Both *a* and *b* are correct.

_____ 5. Too much urine matches with too
   a. little ADH.
   b. much ADH.
   c. little ACTH.
   d. much ACTH.

_____ 6. The hypothalamus controls the anterior pituitary via
   a. nervous stimulation.
   b. the midbrain.
   c. vasopressin.
   d. releasing hormones.

_____ 7. The anterior pituitary stimulates the
   a. thyroid.
   b. adrenal cortex.
   c. adrenal medulla.
   d. pancreas.
   e. Both *a* and *b* are correct.

_____ 8. Acromegaly might be due to a tumor of the
   a. pancreas.
   b. anterior pituitary.
   c. thyroid.
   d. adrenal cortex.

_____ 9. Due to negative feedback control, as the level of thyroxine increases in the blood,
   a. more TSH is produced.
   b. less TSH is produced.
   c. less hypothalamic-releasing hormone is produced.
   d. Both *b* and *c* are correct.

_____ 10. Thyroxine
   a. increases metabolism.
   b. stimulates the thyroid gland.
   c. lowers oxygen uptake.
   d. All of these are correct.

_____ 11. A goiter is caused by
   a. too much salt in the diet.
   b. too little iodine in the diet.
   c. too many sweets in the diet.
   d. a bland diet.

_____ 12. Which hormone regulates blood calcium levels in the blood?
   a. calcitonin
   b. parathyroid hormone
   c. cortisol
   d. Both *a* and *b* are correct.

_____ 13. Tetany occurs when there is too _____ in the blood.
   a. little calcium
   b. much calcium
   c. little sodium
   d. much sodium

_____ 14. The adrenal glands are
   a. at the base of the brain.
   b. on the trachea.
   c. on the kidney.
   d. beneath the stomach.

_____ 15. The adrenal medulla is associated with the nervous system since it
   a. is located at the base of the brain.
   b. produces norepinephrine.
   c. produces acetylcholine.
   d. Both *b* and *c* are correct.

_____ 16. The adrenal cortex produces hormones affecting
   a. glucose metabolism.
   b. stress.
   c. sodium balance.
   d. All of these are correct.

_____ 17. A person suffering from insulin shock should
   a. be given some sugar.
   b. sit with the head down.
   c. be given insulin.
   d. not eat fatty foods.

_____ 18. Glucagon
   a. is produced by the pancreas.
   b. raises blood glucose.
   c. stores glucose as glycogen.
   d. Both *a* and *b* are correct.

___19. In which case is insulin not produced?
   a. type I diabetes
   b. type II diabetes
   c. type III diabetes
   d. Both *a* and *b* are correct.

___20. One of the chief differences between pheromones and local hormones is
   a. that one is a chemical messenger and the other is not.
   b. the distance over which they act.
   c. that one is made by invertebrates and the other is made by vertebrates.
   d. All of these are correct.

CRITICAL THINKING QUESTIONS

Answer in complete sentences.

21. How does the endocrine system contribute to homeostasis?

22. How has the understanding of environmental signaling changed over the last few years?

Test Results: _____ Number right ÷ 22 = _____ × 100 = _____ %

EXPLORING THE INTERNET

Use the Internet to further explore topics in this chapter, such as muscle-building anabolic steroids and diabetes. Go to the Mader Home Page (http://www.mhhe.com/sciencemath/biology/mader/) and click on *Biology,* 6th edition. Go to Chapter 49 and select a Web site of interest.

ANSWER KEY

STUDY EXERCISES

1. a. b, d, f, g **2. a.** nonsteroid hormone **b.** hormone receptor **c.** cyclic AMP **d.** active **e.** steroid hormone **f.** hormone-receptor complex **g.** protein synthesis **3. a.** nonsteroid hormone **b.** proteins **c.** GTP **4. a.** hypothalamus **b.** pineal gland **c.** anterior pituitary **d.** posterior pituitary **e.** thyroid **f.** parathyroid **g.** thymus **h.** pancreas **i.** adrenal cortex **j.** adrenal medulla **5.** See Table 49.1, p. 876, of the text. **6. a.** negative feedback **b.** contrary **7.** Dotted line should be drawn between positions (1) and (2) and between (2) and (3) to indicate negative feedback. **8. a.** TRH (thyroid-releasing hormone) **b.** TSH (thyroid stimulating hormone **c.** thyroxine **d.** ACRH (adrenocorticoid-releasing hormone) **e.** ACTH (adrenocorticotropic hormone) **f.** cortisol **9. a.** PP **b.** AP **c.** PP **d.** AP

10.

Gland Controlled	Hormone That Gland Produces
thyroid	thyroxine
adrenal cortex	cortisol
ovaries	estrogen, progesterone
testes	testosterone

11. negative feedback mechanism **12.** c. **13.** d **14.** a **15.** b **16.** d **17. a.** calcium **b.** decreases **c.** increases **d.** decreases **18. a.** norepinephrine **b.** epinephrine **c.** rise **d.** increase **e.** dilate **f.** increase **g.** constrict **h.** dilate **i.** contract **j.** increase **19. a.** glucocorticoids **b.** mineralocorticoids **c.** Cortisol **d.** inflammation **e.** Aldosterone **f.** sodium **g.** potassium **h.** Addison **i.** Cushing **20. a.** insulin **b.** glucagon **c.** islets **21. a.** increases **b.** decreases **c.** decreases **22. a.** 1 **b.** 2 **c.** 2 **d.** 1 **e.** 1 **f.** 2 **23. a.** F **b.** T **c.** T **d.** F **24. a.** pheromones **b.** insulin (any endocrine gland hormone) **c.** neurotransmitter **25.** b

First goal: **1.** f **2.** i **3.** h **4.** d **5.** b. Second goal: **6.** f **7.** b **8.** d **9.** d **10.** a. Third goal: **11.** i **12.** h **13.** b **14.** a **15.** l. Fourth goal: **16.** c **17.** g and h **18.** d and e **19.** j **20.** f. Fifth goal: **21.** yes **22.** no **23.** yes **24.** no **25.** no **26.** yes **27.** yes **28.** no **29.** no **30.** yes

KEYWORD CROSSWORD

Across:
1. ENDOCRINE SYSTEM
3. HORMONE
4. PANCREAS
5. INSULIN
8. ANTIDIURETIC HORMONE
10. GLUCAGON
11. ALDOSTERONE
12. ADRENAL GLAND

Down:
1. PARATHYROID GLAND
2. THYROID
6. PITUITARY
7. PINEAL GLAND
9. GONAD / GLYCOGEN / THYROXINE

1. b **2.** d **3.** d **4.** d **5.** a **6.** d **7.** e **8.** b **9.** d **10.** a **11.** b **12.** d **13.** a **14.** c **15.** b **16.** d **17.** a **18.** d **19.** a **20.** b **21.** It controls a wide variety of body responses, maintaining an optimal state for such characteristics as heart rate, blood sugar concentration, sodium reabsorption, and calcium storage in the bones. **22.** The concept has expanded the traditional story of hormone signaling via blood. Signaling can also be local between cells and can occur in the outside environment between organisms via pheromones.

50

REPRODUCTION IN ANIMALS

Asexual reproduction involves one parent producing a large number of offspring in a constant environment. **Sexual reproduction** produces genetic variations because two parents contribute genes to the offspring. Therefore, it has advantages in a changing environment. Fertilization tends to be external in aquatic species; it is internal for land species.

In the human male, gametes are produced in the **seminiferous tubules** of the **testis.** This process is regulated by **follicle-stimulating hormone (FSH).** Interstitial cells of the testis produce **testosterone.** This production is regulated by **luteinizing hormone (LH).** **Sperm** cells mature in the **epididymis** and pass through the **vas deferens** and urethra during **ejaculation.** The seminal vesicles, the prostate gland, and the bulbourethral glands add fluid to **seminal fluid.**

In human females, eggs are produced in the **ovary.** Fertilization of a secondary oocyte, released from the ovary into the **oviduct** during **ovulation** stimulates completion of oogenesis and produces a fertilized egg cell (zygote). The **follicle** remaining in the ovary is eventually converted to a **corpus luteum** and produces **estrogen** and **progesterone** through the **ovarian** and **uterine cycles.** Fluctuating levels of FSH and LH are important events of these cycles.

The oviduct leads to the **uterus,** which opens into the **vagina.** If fertilization occurs, the developing embryo implants in the **endometrium,** which lines the uterus. The corpus luteum is maintained through **(human chorionic gonadotropin) (HCG)** production.

Numerous methods of birth control are available. Alternative methods of reproduction are available to help infertile couples.

Many sexually transmitted diseases (STDs) are easily transferred from one person to the next through sexual contact. Some STDs can lead to discomfort, others to sterility or even death.

Study the text section by section as you answer the questions that follow.

50.1 HOW ANIMALS REPRODUCE (P. 894)

- Among animals, there are two patterns of reproduction: asexual reproduction and sexual reproduction.
- Sexually reproducing animals have gonads for the production of gametes, and many have accessory organs for the storage and passage of gametes into or from the body.
- Animals have various means of assuring fertilization of gametes and protecting immature stages.

1. Label each of the following as describing asexual reproduction (A) or sexual reproduction (S):
   _____ a. Budding is one type.
   _____ b. Gametes are produced by the same or different individuals.
   _____ c. Offspring have a different combination of genes than either parent.
   _____ d. Offspring tend to have the same genotype and phenotype as the parents.
   _____ e. Earthworms that are hermaphrodites practice it.
   _____ f. It produces offspring that may be better adapted to a new environment.
   _____ g. Regeneration is one type.
   _____ h. Usually, a large number of offspring are produced.

2. Complete the following statements:

Yolk is ^{a.}_____.

Metamorphosis is ^{b.}_____.

Extraembryonic membranes are ^{c.}_____.

Ovoviviparous means ^{d.}_____.

Viviparous means ^{e.}_____.

50.2 MALES HAVE TESTES (P. 898)

- The human male reproductive system is designed for the continuous production of a large number of sperm that are transported within a fluid medium.

3. Use these terms to label the diagram.

> *bulbourethral gland*
> *epididymis*
> *penis*
> *prostate gland*
> *seminal vesicle*
> *testis*
> *urethra*
> *urinary bladder*
> *vas deferens*

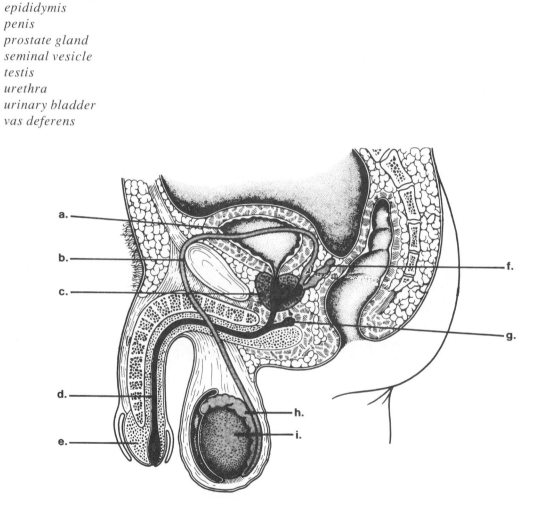

4. Complete this table of the male reproductive system.

Organ	Function
testes (pl)	
epididymides (pl)	
vasa deferentia (pl)	
seminal vesicles (pl)	
prostate gland	
urethra	
bulbourethral glands (pl)	
penis	

5. Trace the path of sperm in the genital tract of males: testis, a._____, b._____, and c._____.

6. The three organs that add secretions to seminal fluid are a._____, b._____, and c._____.

   Do they also produce hormones? d._____

7. Indicate whether the statements that follow are true (T) or false (F). Rewrite the false statements to make them true statements.

   _____ a. Testosterone exerts negative feedback control over the anterior pituitary secretion of LH. Rewrite: __

   _____

   _____ b. Inhibin exerts negative feedback control over anterior pituitary secretion of FSH. Rewrite: _____

   _____

Testes Produce Sperm and Hormones (p. 901)

- Hormones control the production of sperm and maintain the primary and secondary sexual characteristics of males.

8. Label the following as describing the seminiferous tubules (ST) or the interstitial cells (IC):
   _____ a. produce androgens
   _____ b. produce sperm
   _____ c. controlled by FSH
   _____ d. controlled by LH

9. Describe the effect of testosterone on the following:

   sexual organs a._____

   facial hair b._____

   larynx c._____

   muscular strength d._____

   oil and sweat glands e._____

10. Complete each of the following statements with the term *increases* or *decreases*:

    As the level of testosterone rises in the blood, the secretion of LH a._____. As the level of

    testosterone falls in the blood, the hypothalamus b._____ the secretion of the gonadotropic-

    releasing hormone. Secretion of inhibin c._____ FSH secretion. Greatly decreased

    testosterone secretion d._____ beard and pubic hair growth. The presence of

    testosterone e._____ secretion of oil and sweat glands.

• The female reproductive system is designed for the monthly production of an egg and preparation of the uterus to house the developing fetus.

11. Use these terms to label the diagram.
    cervix
    ovary
    oviduct
    urethra
    urinary bladder
    uterus
    vagina

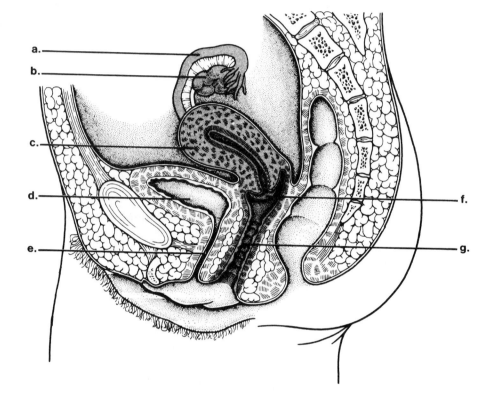

12. Complete this table of the female reproductive system.

Organ	Function
ovaries	
oviducts	
uterus	
cervix	
vagina	

Ovaries Produce Oocytes and Hormones (p. 903)

> • Hormones control the monthly reproductive cycle in females and play a significant role in maintaining pregnancy, should it occur.

13. Each ª·_____ in the ovary contains an oocyte. The secondary follicle contains the b·_____and produces the female sex hormones. A secondary follicle develops into a(n) c·_____follicle. d·_____is the release of the secondary oocyte (egg) from the ovary. A follicle that has lost its oocyte becomes a(n) e·_____.

14. Rearrange the letters to indicate the sequence of organs along the female reproductive tract.

    _____
    a. oviduct
    b. ovary
    c. vagina
    d. uterus

15. Match the phrases to the following hormones (some are used more than once):
    1 FSH
    2 LH
    3 progesterone
    4 estrogen
    _____ a. gonadotropic hormones
    _____ b. female sex hormones
    _____ c. primarily secreted by follicle
    _____ d. primarily secreted by corpus luteum

16. Complete the following table to describe the events in the ovarian and uterine cycles:

Anterior Pituitary	Ovarian Cycle Phases	Events	Uterine Cycle Phases	Events
FSH	Follicular (days 1–13)	a.	b. (days 1–5)	c.
			d. (days 6–13)	e.
Ovulation (day 14*)				
LH	Luteal (days 15–28)	f.	g. (days 15–28)	h.

*Assuming a 28-day cycle.

17. What hormonal changes occur if pregnancy takes place? _____
_____

18. Complete each of the following statements with the term *increase(s)* or *decrease(s):*
    During days 6–13, estrogen production ª·_____. A buildup in blood estrogen during the first half of the ovarian cycle b·_____ FSH secretion. Ovulation is keyed by c·_____ in LH. In the second half of the ovarian cycle, the developing corpus luteum d·_____ its secretion of progesterone. Increased progesterone production e·_____ LH production. During menstruation, blood flow from the vagina f·_____.

If pregnancy occurred HCG ᵍ·_____ the life span and activity of the corpus luteum. The level of estrogen and progesterone during pregnancy ʰ·_____ the activity of the anterior pituitary. Estrogen ⁱ·_____ breast development. Responsiveness of the ovaries to gonadotropic hormones ʲ·_____ during menopause.

19. Describe the effect of the female sex hormones on the following:

    body fat ᵃ·_____

    sex organs ᵇ·_____

    breast development ᶜ·_____

50.4 HUMANS VARY IN FERTILITY (P. 906)

- There are alternative methods of reproduction today, including in vitro fertilization followed by introduction to the uterus.
- Birth-control measures vary in effectiveness from those that are very effective to those that are minimally effective.

20. Match the birth control method to the methodology.
    1 vasectomy
    2 oral contraception
    3 diaphragm
    4 male condom
    5 coitus interruptus
    _____ a. blocks entrance of sperm to uterus
    _____ b. traps sperm
    _____ c. penis withdrawn before ejaculation
    _____ d. anterior pituitary does not release FSH and LH
    _____ e. no sperm in seminal fluid

21. The two major causes of female infertility are ᵃ·_____ and ᵇ·_____. Three methods of alternative reproduction include ᶜ·_____, ᵈ·_____, and ᵉ·_____.

Review key terms by completing this crossword puzzle, using the following alphabetized list of terms:

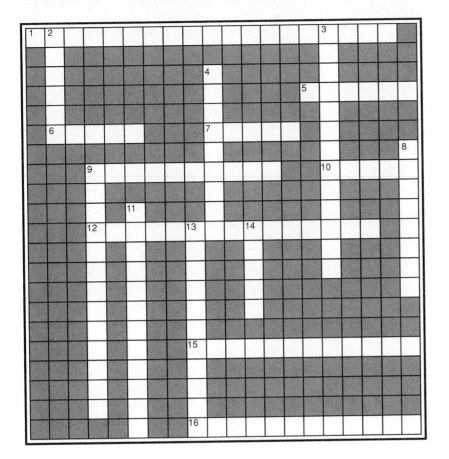

copulation
corpus luteum
endometrium
estrogen
gonad
larva
luteinizing hormone
menstruation
metamorphosis
ovulation
parthenogenesis
penis
progesterone
semen
testosterone
uterus
vagina

Across

1 gonadotropic hormone secreted by the anterior pituitary that stimulates the production of sex hormones in males and females (two words)

5 muscular tube leading from the uterus; the female copulatory organ and the birth canal

6 thick, whitish fluid consisting of sperm and secretions from several glands of the male reproductive tract

7 immature form in the life cycle of some animals; stage of development between the embryo and the adult form; it undergoes metamorphosis to become the adult form

9 sexual union to facilitate the reception of sperm by a partner, usually a female

10 male copulatory organ

12 development of an egg cell into a whole organism without fertilization

15 male sex hormone produced by interstitial cells in the testis; it maintains secondary sexual characteristics in males

16 periodic shedding of tissue and blood from the inner lining of the uterus

Down

2 pear-shaped portion of the female reproductive tract that lies between the oviducts and the vagina; site of embryonic and fetal development

3 change in shape and form that some animals, such as insects, undergo during development

4 bursting of a follicle when an oocyte is released from the ovary

8 one of several female ovarian sex hormones that causes the endometrium of the uterus to proliferate during the uterine cycle; along with progesterone, it maintains secondary sexual characteristics in females

9 follicle after release of an oocyte; increases its secretion of progesterone (two words)

11 one of several female ovarian sex hormones that causes the endometrium of the uterus to become secretory during the uterine cycle; along with estrogen, it maintains secondary sexual characteristics in females

13 mucous membrane lining the interior surface of the uterus

14 organ that produces sex cells; the ovary, which produces eggs, and the testis, which produces sperm

Do not refer to the text when taking this test.

_____ 1. The interstitial cells
    a. are located in the testes.
    b. secrete male sex hormones.
    c. store sperm.
    d. Both *a* and *b* are correct.

_____ 2. The vas deferens
    a. becomes erect.
    b. carries sperm.
    c. is surrounded by the prostate gland.
    d. All of these are correct.
    e. None of these are correct.

_____ 3. The prostate gland
    a. is removed when a vasectomy is performed.
    b. is not needed to maintain the secondary sexual characteristics.
    c. receives urine from the bladder.
    d. All of these are correct.
    e. None of these are correct.

_____ 4. Which gland is an endocrine gland?
    a. seminal vesicles
    b. prostate gland
    c. bulbourethral gland
    d. testes
    e. All of these are correct.

_____ 5. FSH
    a. stimulates sperm production.
    b. is found in the female.
    c. is produced by the anterior pituitary gland.
    d. All of these are correct.

_____ 6. Gonadotropic hormones are produced by the
    a. testes.
    b. ovaries.
    c. anterior pituitary.
    d. Both *a* and *b* are correct.

_____ 7. Which of these is a gonadotropic hormone?
    a. testosterone
    b. FSH
    c. estrogen
    d. All of these are correct.

_____ 8. In the human male, hormones from the _____ stimulate production of testosterone by secreting _____.
    a. testis; seminal fluid
    b. hypothalamus; tropic hormones
    c. pituitary gland; luteinizing hormone
    d. seminal vesicles; follicle-stimulating hormone
    e. prostate gland; releasing factors

_____ 9. Testosterone is necessary for
    a. the development of the male sex organs.
    b. sperm maturation.
    c. the development of the secondary sexual characteristics.
    d. All of these are correct.

_____10. The urethra is part of the reproductive tract in
    a. the female.
    b. the male.
    c. Both *a* and *b* are correct.
    d. None of these are correct.

_____11. The endometrium
    a. lines the vagina.
    b. breaks down during menstruation.
    c. produces estrogen.
    d. Both *a* and *b* are correct.

_____12. The uterus
    a. is connected to both the oviducts and vagina.
    b. is not an endocrine gland.
    c. contributes to the development of the placenta.
    d. All of these are correct.

_____13. Which structure is present after ovulation?
    a. primary follicle
    b. secondary follicle
    c. Graafian follicle
    d. corpus luteum

_____14. Ovulation occurs
    a. due to hormonal changes.
    b. always on day 14.
    c. in postmenopausal women.
    d. as a result of sexual intercourse.
    e. Both *a* and *b* are correct.

_____15. Which of these secretes hormones involved in the ovarian cycle?
    a. hypothalamus
    b. anterior pituitary gland
    c. ovary
    d. All of these are correct.

_____16. Follicle-stimulating hormone stimulates the
    a. release of the oocyte from the follicle.
    b. development of a follicle.
    c. development of the endometrium.
    d. beginning of the menstrual flow.
    e. Both *a* and *c* are correct.

_____17. Secretions from which of the following structures are required before implantation can occur?
    a. the ovarian follicle
    b. the pituitary gland
    c. the corpus luteum
    d. Both *a* and *b* are correct.
    e. All of these are correct.

____18. Human chorionic gonadotropin (HCG) is different from other gonadotropic hormones because it
   a. is produced by the maternal part of the placenta.
   b. is not produced by a female endocrine gland.
   c. does not act upon the ovaries or the corpus luteum.
   d. does not stimulate any tissue in the body.
   e. does not enter the bloodstream.

____19. What do FSH, LH, testosterone, progesterone, and estrogen have in common?
   a. They occur only in the female.
   b. They occur only in the male.
   c. All of them directly affect the uterine lining.
   d. All of them are necessary for sexual reproduction.
   e. Both *a* and *c* are correct.

____20. Menstruation begins in response to
   a. an increase in circulating estrogen levels.
   b. a decrease in circulating progesterone levels.
   c. rupture of the ovarian follicle.
   d. changes in the blood CO_2 level.
   e. secretion of FSH by the pituitary.

____21. In vitro fertilization takes place in
   a. the vagina.
   b. a surrogate mother.
   c. laboratory glassware.
   d. the uterus.

____22. What do all methods of birth control have in common?
   a. They all use some device.
   b. They all interrupt sexual intercourse.
   c. They are all fairly expensive.
   d. None of these are correct.

____23. A vasectomy
   a. prevents the egg from reaching the oviduct.
   b. prevents sperm from reaching seminal fluid.
   c. prevents the release of seminal fluid.
   d. inhibits sperm production.

____24. Which of these means of birth control prevents implantation?
   a. diaphragm
   b. IUD
   c. cervical cap
   d. female condom

____25. Which method of birth control also gives 100% assurance of protection from sexually transmitted diseases?
   a. diaphragm and spermicide
   b. birth control pill
   c. condom and spermicide
   d. None of these offer 100% protection from sexually transmitted diseases.

CRITICAL THINKING QUESTIONS

Answer in complete sentences.

26. Speculate on the benefits and drawbacks of hermaphroditism.

27. Contrast aspects of external fertilization with internal fertilization.

Test Results:_____ Number right ÷ 27 = _____ × 100 = _____ %

EXPLORING THE INTERNET

Use the Internet to further explore topics in this chapter, such as AIDS, breast cancer, or prostate cancer. Go to the Mader Home Page (http://www.mhhe.com/sciencemath/biology/mader/) and click on *Biology*, 6th edition. Go to Chapter 50 and select a Web site of interest.

STUDY QUESTIONS

1. **a.** A **b.** S **c.** S **d.** A **e.** S **f.** S **g.** A **h.** A 2. **a.** stored food for embryo **b.** a dramatic change in shape **c.** membranes that serve the needs of the embryo **d.** eggs are retained in the body until they hatch **e.** offspring are born alive 3. **a.** urinary bladder **b.** vas deferens **c.** prostate gland **d.** urethra **e.** penis **f.** seminal vesicle **g.** bulbourethral gland **h.** epididymis **i.** testis
4.

Organ	Function
testes	produce sperm and sex hormones
epidymides	maturation and some storage of sperm
vasa deferentia	conduct and store sperm
seminal vesicles	contribute fluid to semen (seminal fluid)
prostate gland	contribute fluid to semen
urethra	conducts sperm
bulbourethral glands	contribute fluid to sperm
penis	organ of copulation

5. **a.** epididymis **b.** vas deferens **c.** urethra 6. **a.** seminal vesicles **b.** prostate gland **c.** bulbourethral glands **d.** no 7. **a.** T **b.** T 8. **a.** IC **b.** ST **c.** ST **d.** IC 9. **a.** maturation and maintenance **b.** causes growth **c.** enlarges **d.** increases **e.** activates 10. **a.** decreases **b.** increases **c.** decreases **d.** decreases **e.** increases 11. **a.** oviduct **b.** ovary **c.** uterus **d.** urinary bladder **e.** urethra **f.** cervix **g.** vagina
12.

Organ	Function
ovaries	produce eggs and sex hormones
oviducts	conduct eggs; location of fertilization
uterus	houses developing embryo and fetus
cervix	contains opening of uterus
vagina	receives penis during copulation and serves as birth canal

13. **a.** follicle **b.** secondary oocyte **c.** Graafian **d.** Ovulation **e.** corpus luteum 14. b, a, d, c 15. **a.** 1,2 **b.** 3,4 **c.** 4 **d.** 3 16. **a.** Follicle matures and produces eggs and estrogen **b.** menstruation **c.** Endometrium breaks down. **d.** prolifertive **e.** Endometrium rebuilds. **f.** Corpus luteum produces progesterone. **g.** secretory **h.** Endometrium thickens, and glands are secretory. 17. The placenta adds to the production of estrogen and progesterone. It also produces HCG. 18. **a.** increases **b.** decreases **c.** increase **d.** increases **e.** decreases **f.** increases **g.** increases **h.** decreases **i.** increases **j.** decreases 19. **a.** increases **b.** maturation and maintenance **c.** promotes 20. **a.** 3 **b.** 4 **c.** 5 **d.** 2 **e.** 1 21. **a.** blocked oviducts **b.** failure to ovulate **c.** artificial insemination **d.** in vitro fertilization **e.** surrogate motherhood

KEYWORD CROSSWORD

CHAPTER TEST

1. d 2. b 3. b 4. d 5. d 6. c 7. b 8. c 9. d 10. b 11. b 12. d 13. d 14. a 15. d 16. b 17. e 18. b 19. d 20. b 21. c 22. d 23. b 24. b 25. d 26. When animals are hermaphroditic, its easier to find a partner because any two animals that meet can reproduce sexually. In some instances hermaphroditic animals self fertilize (e.g. tapeworm) and then variability would most likely be reduced in the next generation. 27. External fertilization, which usually occurs in aquatic or moist habitats, requires that males and females release their gametes at the same time. Many offspring are produced at the same time. Internal fertilization requires compatible copulatory organs and fewer offspring are produced. Typically the embryo is protected and the offspring is well cared for.

51

DEVELOPMENT

Development requires three processes: growth, cellular differentiation, and morphogenesis. Development of the lancelet, frog, and chick over the first three stages of embryo formation (**cleavage, blastulation, gastrulation**) differs due to the amount of yolk in the egg.

    Cellular differentiation begins with cleavage. Several factors influence the activation of genes to bring this about. **Induction** is a major process determining the specialization of cells. The establishment of three **germ layers (ectoderm, mesoderm, endoderm)** in the **gastrula** leads to the formation of organs. **Morphogenesis** depends on environmental factors as well as on genetic ones.

    Human development consists of the **embryo** (first two months) and the fetus (last seven months). Early events include **fertilization** in the oviduct, cleavage of the early embryo in the oviduct, **morula** formation, **blastocyst** formation, gastrulation, and formation of three germ layers.

    Several embryonic membranes function in human development, including the **chorion** (maternal-fetal exchange) and the **amnion** (protection). Organ development begins with the formation of the **neural tube** and heart.

STUDY EXERCISES

Study the text section by section as you answer the questions that follow.

51.1 DEVELOPMENT HAS STAGES (P. 914)

- Development begins when a sperm fertilizes an egg.
- The first stages of embryonic development in animals lead to the establishment of the embryonic germ layers.
- The presence of yolk affects the manner in which animal embryos go through the early developmental stages.

1. Put these events in order to describe fertilization.
   a. The vitelline envelope becomes the fertilization envelope, which prohibits any more sperm from entering the egg.
   b. When released, these enzymes digest away the jelly coat around the egg, and the acrosome extrudes a filament that attaches to a receptor on the vitelline envelope.
   c. A head of a sperm has a membrane-bounded acrosome filled with enzymes.
   d. Now the sperm nucleus enters and fuses with the egg nucleus, and the resulting zygote begins to divide.

2. Label this diagram of early development with the following terms:

Gastrula
endoderm
Blastula
ectoderm
blastopore
Morula
blastocoel (used twice)
archenteron

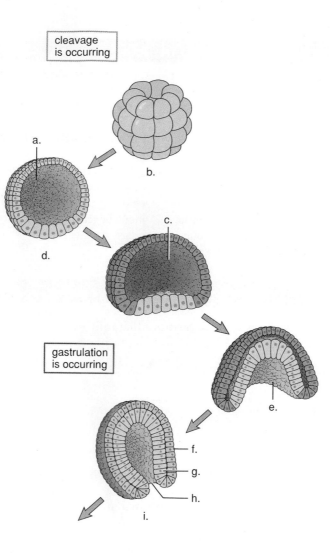

cleavage
is occurring

a.

b.

c.

d.

gastrulation
is occurring

e.

f.

g.

h.

i.

3. Indicate whether the following statements are true (T) or false (F):
   _____ a. Cell division during cleavage does not produce growth.
   _____ b. The blastula is a solid ball of cells.
   _____ c. The ectoderm and endoderm form after the mesoderm in the gastrula.
   _____ d. The germ layer theory states that the development of later structures can be related to germ layers.

4. Indicate the germ layer (ectoderm, endoderm, mesoderm) of the vertebrate gastrula stage that is the source of the following:

epidermis of the skin a._____

nervous tissue b._____

lining of the stomach c._____

muscles of the forelimb d._____

blood e._____

5. Complete these sentences by using the terms *lancelet, frog,* or *chick.* In the a._____ embryo, the cells have little yolk and cleavage is equal. In the b._____, the cells at the animal pole are smaller than those at the vegetal pole because those at the vegetal pole contain yolk. In the c._____, the cells with yolk cleave more slowly than those without yolk. Still, in both the d._____ and the e._____, the blastula is a hollow ball of cells. In the f._____, there is so much yolk that the embryo forms on top of the yolk and the blastocoel is created when the cells lift up from the yolk.

6. Indicate which of these describes formation of mesoderm and the coelom in the *lancelet, frog,* or *chick.*
    _____ a. invagination of cells along the edges of primitive streak followed by a splitting of the mesoderm.
    _____ b. migration of cells from the dorsal lip of the blastopore followed by a splitting of the mesoderm.
    _____ c. outpocketings of the primitive gut form two layers of mesoderm and the coelom.

Neurulation Produces the Nervous System (p. 917)

•   In vertebrates, the nervous system develops above the notochord after formation of a neural tube.

7. Label this diagram of a vertebrate embryo using the following terms:
    coelom
    ectoderm
    endoderm
    gut
    mesoderm
    neural tube
    notochord
    somite

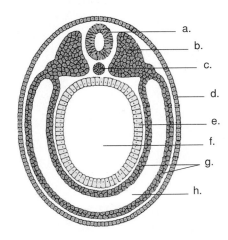

a.
b.
c.
d.
e.
f.
g.
h.

8. The diagram in question 7 shows the neural tube above the notochord. Explain the significance of this tissue relationship. _____

_____

- Cellular differentiation and morphogenesis are two processes that occur when specialized organs develop.
- Induction explains development of the nervous system and why development in general is an orderly process.
- Homeotic genes are involved in shaping the outward appearance of the developed animal.

9. Cellular differentiation begins with which developmental process? a._____. Hans Speman showed that a frog embryo needs a portion of the gray crescent in order to develop normally. Why might that be? b._____

10. Morphogenesis begins with which developmental process? a._____. Hans Speman showed that presumptive notochord tissue induces the formation of the nervous system. Relate these findings to the process of morphogenesis. b._____

_____

11. Homeotic genes are involved in pattern formation. In *Drosophilia* what happens when a homeotic mutation occurs? _____

_____

51.3 HUMANS ARE EMBRYOS AND THEN FETUSES (P. 922)

- Humans, like chicks, are dependent upon extraembryonic membranes that perform various services and contribute to development.
- During the embryonic period of human development, all systems appear.
- Humans are placental mammals; the placenta is a unique organ where exchange between fetal blood and mother's blood takes place.

12. Label this diagram of the extraembryonic membranes of the human embryo with the following terms:
       allantois
       amnion
       chorion
       embryo
       fetal portion of placenta
       maternal portion of placenta
       yolk sac

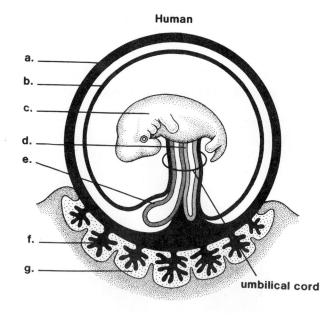

Human

a. _____
b. _____
c. _____
d. _____
e. _____
f. _____
g. _____

umbilical cord

13. Complete the following table:

Membrane	Chick Function	Human Function
chorion		
amnion		
allantois		
yolk sac		

14. To describe human embryonic development, complete the table with the number of the event that occurs at each time indicated.

    1 all internal organs formed; limbs and digits well formed; recognizable as human although still quite small

    2 fertilization; cell division begins

    3 limb buds begin; heart is beating; embryo has a tail

    4 implantation; embryo has tissues; first two extraembryonic membranes

    5 fingers and toes are present; cartilaginous skeleton

    6 nervous system begins; heart development begins

    7 head enlarges; sense organs prominent

Time	Events
a. first week	
b. second week	
c. third week	
d. fourth week	
e. fifth week	
f. sixth week	
g. two months	

Fetuses Look Human (p. 927)

- During fetal development, the fetus grows large enough to live on its own. Birth is a multistage process that includes delivery of the child and the extraembryonic membranes.

15. Indicate whether the following statements about fetal development (months 3–9) are true (T) or false (F):

    _____ a. It is possible to distinguish sex.

    _____ b. The notochord is replaced by the spinal column.

    _____ c. Limb buds are still present.

    _____ d. Fingernails and eyelashes appear.

16. What events are associated with the three stages of parturition?

first stage a._____

second stage b._____

third stage c._____

Review key terms by completing this crossword puzzle, using the following alphabetized list of terms:

allantois
amnion
blastula
chorion
cleavage
differentiation
gastrula
germ layer
induction
morphogenesis
morula
placenta
trophoblast
umbilical cord

Across

1 cord connecting the fetus to the placenta through which blood vessels pass (two words)

6 spherical mass of cells resulting from cleavage during animal development prior to the blastula stage

8 developmental layer of the body—that is, ectoderm, mesoderm, or endoderm (two words)

11 structure during the development of placental mammals that forms from the chorion and the uterine wall and allows the embryo and then the fetus to acquire nutrients and rid itself of wastes

13 cell division without cytoplasmic addition or enlargement; occurs during the first stage of animal development

Down

2 movement of early embryonic cells to establish body outline and form

3 ability of a chemical or a tissue to influence the development of another tissue

4 extraembryonic membrane for respiratory exchange in birds and reptiles; contributes to placenta formation in mammals

5 specialization of early embryonic cells with regard to structure and function

7 outer membrane surrounding the embryo in mammals; when thickened by a layer of mesoderm, it becomes the chorion, an extraembryonic membrane

8 stage of animal development during which the germ layers form—at least in part—by invagination

9 extraembryonic membrane that accumulates nitrogenous wastes in birds and reptiles and contributes to the formation of umbilical blood vessels in mammals

10 hollow, fluid-filled ball of cells occurring during animal development prior to gastrula formation

12 extraembryonic membrane of birds, reptiles, and mammals that forms an enclosing, fluid-filled sac

OBJECTIVE QUESTIONS

Do not refer to the text when taking this test.

_____ 1. The _____ develops first.
  a. morula
  b. blastula
  c. blastocoel
  d. gastrula

_____ 2. The _____ is a hollow ball.
  a. morula
  b. blastula
  c. gastrula
  d. Both *a* and *b* are correct.

_____ 3. The _____ contains germ layers.
  a. morula
  b. blastula
  c. gastrula
  d. All of these are correct.

_____ 4. The _____ undergoes cleavage but lacks a morula.
  a. lancelet
  b. frog
  c. chick
  d. Both *a* and *b* are correct.

_____ 5. The _____ has a notochord during development.
  a. lancelet
  b. frog
  c. human
  d. All of these are correct.

_____ 6. The nervous system develops from the
  a. ectoderm.
  b. mesoderm.
  c. endoderm.
  d. notochord.

_____ 7. Cellular differentiation is due to
  a. parceling out of cytoplasm.
  b. activation of particular genes.
  c. parceling out of genes.
  d. Both *a* and *c* are correct.
  e. Both *a* and *b* are correct.

_____ 8. What induces the development of the nervous system?
  a. endoderm
  b. presumptive notochord
  c. ectoderm
  d. presumptive neural tube

_____ 9. Homeodomain proteins
  a. occur in the nucleus.
  b. regulate transcription.
  c. regulate translation.
  d. Both *a* and *b* are correct.

For questions 10–14, match the extraembryonic membranes with the following descriptions:
  a. placenta
  b. umbilical blood vessels
  c. watery sac
  d. first site of red blood cell formation
  e. treelike extensions that penetrate the uterine lining

_____10. chorionic villi
_____11. chorion
_____12. amnion
_____13. allantois
_____14. yolk sac

_____15. The zygote begins to undergo cleavage in the
  a. cervix.
  b. ovary.
  c. oviduct.
  d. uterus.

_____16. Which of these is mismatched?
  a. cleavage—cell division
  b. morphogenesis—fertilization
  c. differentiation—specialization of cells
  d. growth—increase in size

_____17. The placenta
  a. brings blood to the developing fetus.
  b. allows exchanges of substances between the mother's blood and fetal blood.
  c. forms the umbilical cord.
  d. Both *a* and *b* are correct.
  e. All of these are correct.

_____18. When an embryo is clearly recognizable as a human being, it is called a
  a. developed embryo.
  b. fetus.
  c. newborn.
  d. blastocyst.

_____19. Which system is the first to be visually evident?
  a. nervous
  b. respiratory
  c. digestive
  d. skeletal

_____20. During which stage of parturition is the baby born?
  a. first
  b. second
  c. third

Answer in complete sentences.

21. Should the chemicals functioning during induction be considered hormones?

22. What is the significance of the homeobox?

Test Results: _____ Number right ÷ 22 = _____ × 100 = _____ %

EXPLORING THE INTERNET

Use the Internet to further explore topics in this chapter, such as heart development or embryo development. Go to the Mader Home Page (http://www.mhhe.com/sciencemath/biology/mader/) and click on *Biology,* 6th edition. Go to Chapter 51 and select a Web site of interest.

ANSWER KEY

STUDY EXERCISES

1. c, b, d, a   **2. a.** blastocoel **b.** Morula **c.** Blastula **d.** blastocoel **e.** archenteron **f.** ectoderm **g.** endoderm **h.** blastopore **i.** Gastrula   **3. a.** T **b.** F **c.** F **d.** T **4. a.** ectoderm **b.** ectoderm **c.** endoderm **d.** mesoderm **e.** mesoderm   **5. a.** lancelet **b.** frog **c.** frog **d.** lancelet **e.** frog **f.** chick   **6. a.** chick **b.** frog **c.** lancelet **7. a.** neural tube **b.** somite **c.** notochord **d.** ectoderm **e.** endoderm **f.** gut **g.** mesoderm **h.** coelom   **8.** The notochord induces the formation of the neural tube. See Figure 51.4, p. 917, in text.   **9. a.** cleavage **b.** The chemical molecules in the gray crescent may act as signals to turn certain genes on in certain cells.   **10. a.** migration of cells during gastrulation b. During morphogenesis, one tissue induces another in sequence and this explains why development is so orderly.   **11.** Body parts are misplaced. See Figure 51.8, p. 921, in text.   **12.** See Figure 51.9, p. 922, in text.

13.

Chick Function	Human Function
gas exchange	exchange with mother's blood
protection; prevention of desiccation and temperature changes	protection; prevention of temperature changes
collection of nitrogenous wastes	blood vessels become umbilical blood vessels
provision of nourishment	first site of blood cell formation

14. a. 2 **b.** 4 **c.** 6 **d.** 3 **e.** 7 **f.** 5 **g.** 1   **14. a.** T **b.** F **c.** F **d.** T   **15. a.** dilation of cervix **b.** The mother pushes as the baby moves down the birth canal. **c.** Afterbirth is expelled.

KeyWord CrossWord

¹U	²M	³B	I	L	⁴I	C	A	L		C	O	R	⁵D
	O	N			H								I
	R	D	⁶M	O	R	U	L	A					F
	P	U			I								F
	H	C			O							⁷T	E
	O	T			N		⁸G	E	R	M	L	⁹A	Y	E	R
	G	I					A		S	E		L	O
	E	O					S		N		L	P
	N	N					T		T		A	H
	E						R		I		N	O
	S						U		A		T	B
	I						L		T		O	L
	S						A		I		I	A
				¹⁰B					O		S	S
			¹¹P	L	A	C	E	N	T	¹²A		T
				A						M	
				S						N	
				T						I	
				U						O	
				L						N	
		¹³C	L	E	A	V	A	G	E		

Chapter Test

1. a 2. b 3. c 4. c 5. d 6. a 7. c 8. b 9. d
10. e 11. a 12. c 13. b 14. d 15. c 16. b
17. b 18. b 19. a 20. b 21. Traditionally, a hormone is considered to be a secretion of an endocrine gland that is carried in the bloodstream to a target organ. According to this definition, the chemicals that function during induction are not hormones. In recent years, some scientists have broadened the definition of a hormone to include all types of chemical messengers. Therefore, in the broadest sense these chemicals are hormones. 22. A particular sequence of DNA nucleotides, called the homeobox, occurs in homeotic genes in almost all eukaryotic organisms. This suggests that this sequence is important to development because it has been conserved for quite some time.

Across
- 1. UMBILICAL CORD
- 6. MORULA
- 8. GERM LAYER
- 11. PLACENTA
- 13. CLEAVAGE

Down
- 1. MORPHOGENESIS
- 3. INDUCTION
- 4. CHORION
- 5. DIFFERENTIATION
- 7. TROPHOBLAST
- 8. GASTRULA
- 9. ALLANTOIS
- 10. BLASTULA
- 12. AMNION